Scientific Growth

CALIFORNIA STUDIES IN THE HISTORY OF SCIENCE

J. L. HEILBRON, Editor

Scientific Growth

**Essays on the Social Organization
and Ethos of Science**

Joseph Ben-David

**Edited and with an Introduction by
Gad Freudenthal**

UNIVERSITY OF CALIFORNIA PRESS
Berkeley / Los Angeles / Oxford

The University of California Press gratefully ac-
knowledges the support of The Sidney M. Edelstein Center for the History and Philosophy of
Science, Technology and Medicine, The Hebrew
University of Jerusalem; The Israel Academy of
Sciences and Humanities; the Department of Sociology, The Hebrew University of Jerusalem; and
the Shaine Center for Research in Social Sciences, The Hebrew University of Jerusalem.

University of California Press
Berkeley and Los Angeles, California

University of California Press
Oxford, England

Library of Congress Cataloging-in-Publication
Data

Ben-David, Joseph.
   Scientific growth : essays on the social organi-
zation and ethos of science / Joseph Ben-David ;
edited and with an introduction by Gad
Freudenthal.
      p.   cm.
   Includes bibliographical references and index.
   ISBN 0-520-06925-0 (cloth)
   1. Science—Social aspects. 2. Social ethics. I.
Freudenthal, Gad. II. Title.
Q175.55.B44 1990
303.48'3—dc20   91-12304
                                                CIP

Printed in the United States of America
1 2 3 4 5 6 7 8 9

The paper used in this publication meets the minimum requirements of American National Standard
for Information Sciences—Permanence of Paper
for Printed Library Materials, ANSI Z39.48-1984 ∞

Permission to reprint essays will be found on page
569.

Contents

Preface

This volume brings together twenty-five of the late Professor Joseph Ben-David's papers in the sociology of science; these are followed by the draft of what was scheduled to become a monograph on the changing relationships of the ethos of science to different ideologies. Underlying the volume is a three-fold conviction: first, that Ben-David's work represents a major contribution of lasting importance to the sociology of science; second, that although Ben-David was widely known, the central theoretical insights of his work have not yet been adequately appreciated and received; and third, that given the present state of the sociology of science, Ben-David's outlook can—and indeed should—have a great fructifying influence on the future development of this discipline.

Two approaches predominate today in the sociology of science, and both of them have had only little interaction with Ben-David's work. There is one disciplinary trend that grew out of the works of R. K. Merton and D. de Solla Price and that is largely concerned with empirical, mostly quantitative studies of sociological features of contemporary science (e.g., the reward system, stratification, etc.). This approach is in general sympathy with Ben-David's views but can make little use of it inasmuch as the latter is largely historically oriented. A second approach, which made its appearance in the early 1970s and which is usually referred to as the "sociology of scientific knowledge," is indeed historical but adopts a perspective very different from Ben-David's. Whereas Ben-David and, for that matter, Merton were interested primarily in the institutional factors integrating the social system of science, this new approach sees greater significance in the study of local, usually extrascientific, social contexts in which knowledge is produced. The proponents of this stance rejected Ben-David's theoretical views as conflicting with their own, whence the neglect of Ben-David's work among these historically minded sociologists of science, too.

That Ben-David's historical approach to the sociology of science is complementary to the first-mentioned, synchronic trend is obvious. More controversial, but nonetheless true, is the statement that Ben-David's stance and that of the sociology of scientific knowledge are also complementary: far from being incompatible, each in fact reveals the limits of the other and steps in where it leaves off. Time seems ripe now for the sociology of science to take cognizance of this state of affairs and to move forward to the elaboration of a synthesis of these two diachronic approaches to the discipline. What is needed is a conceptual framework that will take into account both the local, context-dependent social factors operative in the production of science *and* the institutional integrating factors giving the cognitive and social systems of science their relative unity, coherence, and continuity. In this task, I believe, Ben-David's historical-comparative sociology of science will prove helpful, indeed indispensable. It is with a view to promoting this synthesis—toward which Ben-David himself already made some steps late in his life—that the present collection of Joseph Ben-David's essays has been produced.

The volume opens with a general introduction giving a summary account of certain stations in Ben-David's life and work. It is hoped that by situating Ben-David, the man and the sociologist, within the historical contexts in which he lived, a better understanding of some essential features of his thinking will be afforded. Then follow the essays (including the draft of the monograph on the ethos of science), distributed among seven parts: each part is preceded by a brief introduction giving some hints concerning the central ideas of the papers and their place within the entire corpus. This occasionally makes for some overlap with the general introduction, but it allows each part to stand independent of the rest of the volume.

The papers are reprinted essentially unaltered. The only modifications are: change of English spelling; elimination of misprints and some abbreviations; an occasional change of punctuation. The notes and references could not be checked or updated, nor made entirely uniform. An attempt has been made, however, to supply bibliographic data of papers and books which the original publication referred to as "forthcoming": these few additions are surrounded by square brackets.

The preparation of this collection of essays was possible thanks to the indefinite measure of freedom to pursue research that I enjoy at the Centre national de la recherche scientifique (C.N.R.S.) in Paris. It was facilitated through a fellowship at the Sidney M. Edelstein Center for the History and Philosophy of Science, Technology, and Medicine, The Hebrew University,

Jerusalem, during summer 1986 and through the hospitality of the Van Leer Jerusalem Institute. I am very grateful to all three institutions.

I am much indebted to John L. Heilbron of the University of California, Berkeley, for his good advice and efficient help in bringing this project to completion.

Preparing this volume allowed me to deepen my acquaintance with an esteemed teacher for whose person I have had great affection.

Paris/Jerusalem   G. F.
December 1986

General Introduction:

Joseph Ben-David, An Outline of His Life and Work[1]

Gad Freudenthal

Joseph Ben-David, then Gross, was born on August 19, 1920, in Györ, a small town in northwestern Hungary, halfway between Budapest and Vienna. The Grosses were an upper-middle-class, forward-looking yet strictly orthodox Jewish family: they had adopted modern dress and German and Hungarian as their languages but remained very observant. They were intellectually exceptionally open-minded and innovative printers and publishers. Ben-David's grandfather, in particular, was imbued with the German culture of his day. He went to Germany to learn his trade, and he was the first Hungarian publisher to produce a popular high-level series of scientific and literary books, modeled on the Ullmann Verlag in Berlin. His central place in the provincial Hungarian intellectual milieu also made him a semiofficial publisher for the members of the Benedictine order, whose center was the abbey at Pannonhalma near Györ.

The attachment to two distinct cultures—which were not, however, taken

---

1. The following outline is neither a biography of Joseph Ben-David nor a comprehensive study of his sociology of science. It does nothing more than give a description of certain stations of Ben-David's life, in relation to which it seeks to situate some of his major ideas and themes. In particular, no attempt is made to locate his work within the sociological tradition: this has been done by Ben-David himself; see [38] (= chap. 19, below) and [50]. (In the text and in the notes, numbers surrounded by square brackets refer to items in the bibliography, at the end of this volume.) The major source of biographical information on which I draw is a three-hour interview conducted with Professor Ben-David on December 26, 1985, by Mara Beller (The Hebrew University, Jerusalem) and Timothy Lenoir (now at Stanford University). I am grateful for the permission to use this interview, the transcription of which is deposited in the library of the Sidney M. Edelstein Center for the History and Philosophy of Science, Technology, and Medicine, The Hebrew University, Jerusalem, Israel. All quotations for which no reference is given are taken (occasionally with slight editing) from this interview.

to be irreconcilable—determined the quite unusual pattern of the young Ben-David's education. Between the ages of ten and fourteen, he was registered in the local Benedictine Gymnasium. In practice, however, he followed in parallel two courses of study. He spent most of the day in a *heder*, an elementary Jewish religious school, in which, of course, nothing secular was taught. During the few off-hours from the *heder*, he received at home private tuition of the subjects taught at the Gymnasium. Ben-David visited the Gymnasium regularly only during the last month of each school year, after which he had to pass examinations on the entire year's program. The subjects taught at the Gymnasium were both literary—languages (Latin, German, and either French or Greek), European literature, and history—and scientific, mathematics and classical physics on a fairly high level, with only a little natural science.

At the age of fourteen, the already independent-minded Ben-David interrupted his studies. Both the Jewish religious studies at the *heder* and the Latin-dominated studies at the Gymnasium seemed to him a waste of time when (it was 1934), feeling acutely threatened by Hitler's rise to power, he wished to study a practical craft on which he could live, especially when—as he already intended—he would immigrate to Palestine. During his last year at school, he had developed a strong interest in chemistry and therefore decided to undergo training as a dyer's apprentice in Budapest, in one of the textile factories of his wealthy uncles on his mother's side. He quickly became disappointed, however, for there was little intellectual challenge there. The next year or so he spent in a yeshiva (Talmudic high school), first at a very extremist, anti-Zionist Hassidic yeshiva and then at a German-type modern yeshiva. In parallel, he became an apprentice in his father's shop and passed the printer's apprentice examination. At the age of seventeen, finally, Ben-David decided to return to the Gymnasium: he completed the four-year course of studies within two years and passed the *Reifeprüfung* only slightly later than if he had followed the regular course of education.

It was 1939, and Ben-David had to wait for some two years before obtaining a certificate allowing him to immigrate to Palestine. During this time, he belonged to an informal circle of young Jewish intellectuals, "a group of really brilliant people," who seem to have had an important impact on his intellectual development. In particular, he met a young man by the name of Haïm (Hugo) Horn, who was to perish not long afterward on the Russian front in the Hungarian Jewish labor troops. At that time, Ben-David pondered studying either chemistry or history, and Horn—according to Ben-David, both an intellectual genius and an exceptional personality who influenced him strongly—told him that to become a historian, one should study sociology thoroughly. Although a very religious person, Horn induced Ben-David to study the writings of Marx. A couple of years later, in Jerusalem, Ben-David was to follow Horn's injunction and complement the study of history with that of sociology. It thus seems that the roots of Ben-David's historical sociology of science go back to the encounter with Horn.

Ben-David's years in Hungary had yet another, and crucial, shaping influence on his thinking. Europe of the 1920s and 1930s was a battlefield on which the political left and right confronted one another continuously and violently, leading to the crumbling of democracy. This is also true of Hungary, where the short-lived Béla Kun revolution of 1919 was followed by the rightist Horthy regime. During most of the Regency, social cleavage, unrest, political agitation, and violence ("white terror") remained endemic, with anti-Semitism running ever higher; in 1938, numerus clausus laws were promulgated. In Györ, not far from the Austrian border, the events in Germany were probably followed very closely, particularly by Jews. Ben-David, who lost a large part of his family in the Holocaust, hardly ever talked about this period of his life, but it stands to reason that it is his firsthand experience of the turbulent interwar period, together with its disastrous consequences, that invested him with a deep-seated lifelong repugnance toward any association of ideas with a self-confident preparedness to defend them through violence. The fact that he literally dreaded ideology as a set of ideas postulating that social thought is determined by interests and therefore not subject to nonviolent debate must be understood in this context. Indeed, Ben-David himself on one occasion wrote of the "indelible impression" that the consequences of totalitarian ideologies made "upon the overwhelming majority of the generation which reached adulthood in the 1930s and 1940s." [2] This explains why, throughout his life, Ben-David was so vehemently, indeed passionately, committed to the idea of science as a unique social institution (whose existence has all the odds against it!), where empirical and rational arguments, not physical force, carry the day. For Ben-David, casting doubt on the possibility of rational debate following the scientific method was not only an intellectual issue but also—and perhaps foremost—a moral and practical problem that "concerns . . . everyone for whom the resolution of social conflicts by rational rather than violent means is important," [3] a problem in which "emotional elements" [4] are involved. Whence also Ben-David's great concern for the universities, the privileged seat of free debate, where "the opportunity to study and discuss social and political issues in an atmosphere of dispassionate tolerance and objectivity is crucial. For if this opportunity is withheld at the university, there is little hope for tolerance outside, in politics or in the street." [5]

In 1941, Ben-David finally obtained his immigration certificate and, after a long overland journey through Yugoslavia, Greece, Turkey, Syria, and Lebanon, he arrived in Palestine. In the summer term of 1941, he was already a student at the Hebrew University in Jerusalem, where he initially intended to

2. [44], 470.   3. [45], 34.   4. [80], 64, n. 1.   5. [71], 90.

study chemistry. However, chemistry studies required that the student spend many hours in the laboratory, for which also an extra fee had to be paid. Since by that time Hungary was at war with Britain, making it impossible for Ben-David to receive support from his parents, he had to give up this plan and choose more literary subjects instead. It is perhaps not farfetched to think that when, some twenty years later, the sociologist Ben-David turned to the (social) study of the sciences, he was thereby in a way realizing the unfulfilled wish of his youth to study chemistry.

Ben-David's first stay at the Hebrew University lasted for one semester only. With the growing threat of Rommel's army in North Africa, the Hebrew University decided that the students should enlist in the British army. Ben-David at first did not. Following a decision from the orthodox youth movement to which he belonged, he again joined a yeshiva for a short while. But he then enlisted in a unit that was officially a part of the police but unofficially an army unit destined to stay behind the lines in case the Germans should occupy Palestine. At the end of 1944, he was released and went back to the university, where he took general history, Jewish history, and what was called "sociology of culture" as his subjects.

The influence Ben-David's studies had on his thinking is not limited to the contents of these studies only. One of Ben-David's first teachers was Isaac Baer (1889–1980), a major historian who specialized in the history of the Jews in medieval Christian Spain. Of him, Ben-David recounted the following anecdotal, yet significant, story:

> When I submitted my first seminar paper, which was in the second year of my studies, I took it to Baer, expecting that I would receive it back with some comments half a year later. It was about the constitution of Jewish communities and he asked me to use the Rabbinic Responsa literature. Now I spent all my days in the library (because it was heated). The next day I did as usual and, lo and behold, I saw old Baer coming in with my seminar paper in his hand. He went straight to the shelves where my Responsa were and I saw him consulting them one after the other, one after the other. After a day or two he called me and I received my paper back with detailed comments of the sort: "Why didn't you continue this quotation?" He treated my poor unpretentious paper as if it had been a paper submitted to a leading journal in the field. I was absolutely knocked out and I think that made me into a scholar somehow. I was so impressed and so touched by his devotion. . . . Baer (as well as other teachers) was really devoted to learning and took it very seriously.

This view of scholarly "seriousness," and the notion that learning is something one must devote oneself to (or else leave it to others), in fact, the view that science is a vocation, is indeed one of the basic convictions that informed and sustained Ben-David's work: not only did it characterize his own scholarly practice but, no less important, it grew into one of his central theoretical notions—that of the scientific ethos as defining the scientist's role. Ben-David's ethical view of science is thus somehow grounded also in his own personal experience at the small Hebrew University of the early 1940s.

As a second major subject, Ben-David took up a course called "Sociology of Culture" which was given by Martin Buber (1878–1965). This, Ben-David said, was a "a strange course" given by "an amazing person" and a "very impressive teacher," who, however, "did not have an inkling of an idea of what sociology was about."

> Professor Martin Buber was a theologian-philosopher, whose interest in the subject he taught was, as he himself admitted, marginal. His two courses, "The Sociology of Religion" and "The Sociology of Ethics," were comprehensive overviews of the history of sociological thought in Europe and they provided summaries of the major monographs about the religion, the customs and the law systems of ancient peoples and of tribal societies. All this was organized around his theological outlook. . . . Buber was a fascinating teacher and he made the sociology of culture into an interesting subject. Few could speak of religion, of ethics or of culture in general with his authority. But to those who had in mind to become sociologists by profession, he showed no way, not even an example. He himself was no sociologist, and he left no doubt about this.[6]

Nonetheless, Buber's course prompted Ben-David to undertake extensive reading in sociology, including the writings of Karl Marx (again) and of Emile Durkheim.

At that juncture, accidental social circumstances interfered which determined the subsequent course of Ben-David's life. Being economically entirely on his own, he had to make a living to study. For a time, he had a job as a sanitary worker ("my career at the university really started with cleaning the laboratories and lecture rooms of the first-year agriculture students"), but then he joined a student group (initiated by J. L. Magnes, then president of the Hebrew University), who settled in the Jewish quarter of the Old City of Jerusalem to do social work in the slum there. Ben-David himself became the secretary of the group and worked with juvenile delinquents. The expertise he eventually acquired in this domain earned him (it was 1947) the position of a youth probation officer. At the time, this was a very good job, which also allowed Ben-David to get married to Miriam Sternberg, who was to remain his lifelong companion. After a few months in this position, Ben-David, who had not yet entirely completed his master's degree but who had already received the Hebrew University's Bialik Prize in Jewish History (1946), was awarded a Colonial Welfare and Development Scholarship of the Government of Palestine, which took him to the London School of Economics for two years, 1947 to 1949.

6. [H-10], 16.

In London, Ben-David studied foremost under Edward Shils, with whom he was to remain in close contact throughout his life.

> For me the LSE was for a great part what I learned from Shils, because he really taught sociology there. The other teachers in sociology were either mainly social philosophers, like Morris Ginsberg, or social statisticians like David Glass. They were good people but of what, by that time, was understood as sociology in the United States they had only very vague ideas. The one who probably had some idea was Thomas Marshall, but he did not like to work hard and I don't know whether he ever gave a seminar. The person who really taught practically everything was Shils. Somehow the person around whom the dynamics of the graduate students crystallized was Shils, who really was much more alive than all the English people around. I usually did not attend lectures, because I learn much better from reading than from listening. But there were the seminars of Shils about everything, where you had to work like hell. Really, he expected you to do reading that I think no teacher anywhere could expect.

His two years at the London School of Economics as a graduate student gave Ben-David a good all-around training in sociology. Two subjects whose relevance for a student of social welfare was not immediately apparent were to prove to be particularly beneficial: sociological research methodology and statistics. The familiarity with quantitative methods largely determined the character of much of Ben-David's later work. He used quantitative methods extensively in his doctoral dissertation, and, more important, these methods went into and shaped his early and innovative studies of the factors influencing scientific productivity.

But beneath and beyond these purely intellectual influences, Ben-David's stay in Britain was an important experience that contributed much to shaping his outlook on modern society in general and on the role of modern science in society in particular. Until then, all societies with which Ben-David had first-hand acquaintance—interwar Europe and Palestine—were ridden with violent conflicts, ideological or national. Therefore, according to Ben-David's own account, when he first came to Britain, this was not merely his "first contact with a really advanced society" but, more fundamentally, a transition from "the fairly barbaric European or Palestinian societies to a really civilized society, where people lived in peace with each other." Indeed, Britain at that time appeared to Ben-David to be *the* model society, that is, the society that is the model to the rest of the world. Consequently, British society was to him a privileged object of observation and study, one whose understanding he took to be a prerequisite to the understanding of other societies. Indeed, Ben-David often expressed the view that a sociologist must have an immediate experience of the social systems he is studying, that analysis of already codified information is not sufficient. In point of fact, it seems that Ben-David's experience of the specificity of British society and institutions went into his analysis of the rise and institutionalization there in the seventeenth century of the scientistic movement. Thus, in *The Scientist's Role in Society,* Ben-David explains that the Baconian program on the empirical sciences was hailed as "the true prophecy" by important social circles for the following reason: "Both before and after the Commonwealth it had become increasingly difficult to maintain public consensus on anything of potential religious importance because of the numerous theological dissensions with political implications." In this context, Ben-David argues, the method of empirical science appeared as a way not only to innovation but, more important, also "to social peace, as it made possible agreement concerning research procedures to specific problems without requiring agreement on anything else." [7] This insight seems to echo the marked impression that contact with the "civilized" British way of conflict resolution made on the violence-abhorring young Ben-David. And it highlights again that to Ben-David, the social significance of science goes far beyond its practical or cognitive values. Rather, it is the only means through which a society can resolve conflicts peacefully, in a civilized manner.

In 1948, the Israeli War of Independence broke out. Ben-David enlisted immediately but was not requested to return home. He returned to Jerusalem in 1949 and became a research officer at the Ministry for Social Welfare. He took his M.A. in Jewish history, general history, and sociology of culture in 1952. His M.A. thesis ([H-1]), was entitled "The Emergence of a Modern Jewish Society in Early Nineteenth-Century Hungary," and it already reveals some of what were to become typical traits of Ben-David's sociological approach to the study of historical developments. The work begins with a *structural* analysis of Jewish society in eighteenth-century Hungary. Ben-David first examines the economic and organizational features of this society and then analyzes the structure of the various social roles and statuses within the community; he endeavors to identify the factors that, over a long period, maintained the individual's loyalty to the community, thereby producing the stability of Jewish Hungarian society. In a second move, Ben-David seeks to determine what undermined that stability from the 1820s onward. Arguing that the social cohesion of a society is maintained by elite strata that ensure internalization of social values by the individuals (either as religious or moral consciousness or through an aspiration to a social status), he claims that social stability depends on the unity of the (intellectual and economic) elite. Therefore, when a new strata with new ideas and ideals emerges which strives to reorganize society around its own ideas, the unity of the elite—and with it, the stability of the society—is in jeopardy. This, Ben-David holds, is precisely what happened in Hungarian Jewry in the middle of the nineteenth century, leading to its splitting up between those who joined the secular move-

7. [4] (= [9]), 73.

ment of the Enlightenment and those who, on the contrary, stuck still faster to traditional learning in the yeshiva. Not only, then, does Ben-David already draw here on the notions of "role" and "status" that were to be central in his later work but, more fundamentally, he seeks to explain sociologically historical processes: he does not content himself to account functionally-structurally for an existing social order but endeavors to understand also the factors involved in the transformation of that order.

Ben-David's stay at the Ministry of Social Welfare did not last for very long. After a year and a few reports, he realized that in the politicized ministry, it was not competence that counted foremost and that he had few prospects of advance. At that time Morris Ginsberg (1889–1970), his former teacher at the London School of Economics, was organizing a department of sociology in the Hebrew University. Ben-David obtained an assistanceship there in 1951. This move, we may note in passing, calls to mind a pattern Ben-David himself was to describe in his sociological analyses of scientific innovation: when a young, capable, and ambitious person finds that his initial career does not offer enough prospects of social mobility (within the scientific system and/or society at large), he will tend to leave that career for another that offers more challenging and rewarding perspectives. Occasionally, such a move results in what Ben-David called "role hybridization," and to some extent, this holds for Ben-David himself, for in the early 1960s, the former youth probation officer brought sociological theory to bear on questions of youth delinquency in Israel (see [H-5], [H-11]).

At the Department of Sociology, Ben-David set out doing straightforward sociological research. His first subject, on which he had collaborated with S. N. Eisenstadt even before going to London, was the sociology of youth movements. The subject was "in the air": "Eisenstadt and I," Ben-David said, "were really very much caught up with the feeling, prevailing at that time, that the spirit of the pioneering days was passing away. We thought that by studying the youth movements, we would gain a key to that." However, whereas Eisenstadt pursued this subject for a number of years, Ben-David dropped it after only four publications ([10], [H-2], [12], [26]). The reason for this can probably be gleaned between the lines of one of Ben-David's first papers in the sociology of science. Reflecting on the characteristics of science in a small country, Ben-David writes of the "debilitating effects" on scientific activity of a situation in which scientific judgment and personal matters become inextricably intermingled because "everyone knows everybody": "probably its most detrimental effect is that it makes cooperation and teamwork impossible. . . . Whenever two people, working on the same topic, are likely to be either in a hierarchical relationship, or in direct personal or institutional competition, cooperation is bound to be very difficult." [8] Eisenstadt was

___

8. [21], 14; see also [H-9], 14–16.

by that time already the chairman of the Department of Sociology, and this institutional setting, it seems, induced Ben-David to seek for himself a domain in which his peers would not be his colleagues next door: "only when one is alone with his subject-matter does one find the detachment and peace of mind necessary for concentration," he wrote in a rare, probably autobiographical phrase.[9]

Ben-David thus set out to find for himself a new domain of research. Inasmuch as this move, which felicitously was to lead him to the sociology of science, came in response to social circumstances, it is again reminiscent of the pattern that Ben-David described in his studies of scientific innovations resulting from role hybridizations: the insight into this pattern may thus owe something to repeated personal experience. In the present case, no role or idea hybridizations occurred, however. Rather, Ben-David's choice of his new subject, the sociology of professions, was motivated by a recent development within sociological theory.

> So at that time—it was 1951—appeared Talcott Parsons' book, *The Social System*. This was something of an event in sociology, because it was an entirely new kind of attempt to analyze total societies in a way which somehow related the macro- with the micro-structure. The most interesting chapter in my (and others') view was the tenth chapter on the medical profession. In reality it was probably 70% wrong, but it conceptualized the problem of the function and the status of the medical profession, especially in the United States, in a very original and striking way. So I decided I would do my thesis on professions in Israel.

The dissertation, whose supervisor was S. N. Eisenstadt and which earned Ben-David a Ph.D. in 1955, was entitled "The Social Structure of the Professions in Israel" ([H-3] = [1]). It consists essentially of an analysis of the teaching, medical, and legal professions in the Jewish society of Palestine and (after 1948) of Israel. The details of the analyses cannot, of course, be discussed here. But it is of interest to note that, to a large extent, the theoretical framework of this study is already the Weberian-Mertonian one that was to underly all of Ben-David's subsequent work in the sociology of science. In a paper summarizing his thesis, he wrote,

> The purpose of this paper is to analyze the relationship between the changes of the Jewish society in Israel (and formerly Palestine) . . . and the development of professional roles within it. . . . The theoretical background of this paper is the "Theory of Action" as developed by Parsons, Bales and Shils. . . . [A]ccording to this school of thought the development of occupational, professional, etc., roles is not merely a result of external factors, such as scientific and technological knowledge and the availability of investment capital or other circum-

9. Ibid.

stances usually regarded as essential, but also of social value-orientations which impinge on personal motivation.

The thesis was originally developed by Max Weber in his studies on the rise of Western capitalism and was successfully applied by R. K. Merton to the explanation of the development of natural science in 17th-century England. Their work shows that—at least in these two instances—economic and scientific developments were conditioned by the prior accordance of religious sanction to activity aimed at the exploitation of economic possibilities and understanding of the empirical world, i.e., it was the high evaluation of economic and scientific achievement that served as an impetus to the unimpeded development of these activities and brought about a redefinition of the roles of the capitalist and the natural scientist, and not—as generally assumed—the other way round, that appreciation followed success.[10]

Thus, the Weberian-Mertonian theoretical premises, in general, and, more specifically, the analysis of the evolution of roles in time within a changing society already directed Ben-David's inquiries and hypothesis formation at that stage. It is also these very premises that suggested to him the importance of a sociology of science, or rather of a sociology of the scientific role or profession. Although his dissertation deals with three professions, only one of which (medicine) is related to science, he writes,

What interests us most is the analysis of the place [in society] of science and of the scientific roles. There are very strong social forces which oppose the development of scientific research. It is erroneous to think that scientific development is a by-product of the solution of practical problems. Only when some incumbents of scientific roles are allowed to practice science for its own sake, can science reach high levels of abstraction and generalization and develop methodical research procedures. But the vested interests of all those with a stake in maintaining a social equilibrium run against science, for science requires the abandonment of various beliefs—e.g., magic—which have a function in preserving a system of social relations and orientations of the members of society. Therefore, unless the corresponding social roles are defined very clearly, there will always be a tendency toward traditionalism.[11]

From the dissertation of 1955 onward, then, through *The Scientist's Role in Society* (1971), and up to the late "Puritanism and Modern Science" (1985; chap. 16, below), this same theme, the dependence of science on an autonomous social role and the conditions for the establishment and maintaining of the latter, remained paramount in Ben-David's thinking.

During the following two or three years, Ben-David pursued the study of professions. He published a number of papers drawing on his dissertation ([11], [H-4], [15]) and, in 1956, made his debut in the international socio-

10. [11], 126–127.
11. [H-3], 18–19.

logical community with a paper on a related subject presented to the Third World Congress of Sociology in Amsterdam ([13]). At the congress, he became acquainted with a number of French sociologists—notably, Michel Crozier and Georges Friedmann—who subsequently invited him to lecture in Paris (see [14]).

The next important juncture of Ben-David's career was a year's stay at the Center for Advanced Study in the Behavioral Sciences at Stanford (1957–58), where he was invited on the recommendation of Talcott Parsons (who became aware of his dissertation through S. N. Eisenstadt). This stay was of great importance in at least two respects. To begin with, it was a further step in Ben-David's integration in the international sociological community, a fact that, as Ben-David himself pointed out, is always of crucial importance for a scientist working in a small country ([21], [H-9]). In particular, at the Center, Ben-David was in close contact with a number of sociologists, notably, Parsons and the young Ralf Dahrendorf. More important, however, seem to have been Ben-David's relations with two outstanding economists, George Stigler and Milton Friedman. Indeed, according to Ben-David's own account, his intellectual contacts with these economists were at least as important as those with the sociologists. Milton Friedman was of particular significance.

> Certainly, Milton Friedman was such an overwhelmingly influential personality that you just could not disregard him. You were either pro or con. My views are not very far from his on many subjects. Although he is much hated, I still think he is very nice and at the Center Friedman somehow took us [a group of people mainly from Chicago] under his wings.

Indeed, from Friedman, Ben-David adopted an idea that was to become an essential component of his theory of scientific growth—the notion of competition in a decentralized system as the most efficient motor of innovation and of the diffusion of innovations. "With Friedman, of course, competition is a very important idea and I certainly was influenced by him and by his idea of competition. There can be no question about it."

Like the period of study in Britain a decade earlier, the stay at Stanford was important also through the immediate experience of American society. The pivotal point is again democracy as a means of nonviolent resolution of conflicts. After the Second World War, Ben-David realized, the United States replaced Britain as the model society. This realization goes hand in hand with Ben-David's appraisal of, and relation to, the ideas of Parsons.

> When I came to the United States in 1957, I had a very poignant experience, and realized that the British were not up to date any longer. Now, Parsons was the person who formulated this in a conceptual way and described the great transformation which occurred after the Second World War, making the United

States the center of the world, something I felt as inconceivable even in 1949. Indeed, Parsons had what is to me the hallmark of a great sociologist: he had a vision of present-day society. He usually wrote and spoke only of American society and he was criticized for that. But this criticism is only partly justified: for just as you cannot write about the industrial revolution and industrial society in Europe without centering first on England (and then perhaps go on to Germany, France, etc.), so also you cannot study present-day democracy without concentrating first on the United States. Parsons realized that after the Second World War the United States has become the model society.

This view of American society, which derives at once from Ben-David's own experience and from Parsons's sociology, is of particular importance inasmuch as it contributed to Ben-David turning to the sociology of science.

In Parsons's scheme of things of what a modern society is, I think one of the central ideas—sometimes made explicit, sometimes only implied or not stated at all—is that modern society is a scientific society. It derives its legitimacy from science. Science is its source of revelation. And this is really what most people believe: that science is the most effective source of truth today. So this is Parsons's influence: I think essentially he pushed me—not personally, but intellectually—in the direction of sociology of science.

Ben-David's turn to the sociology of science, therefore, must not be viewed as a more or less accidental choice of an academic specialty. Rather, it derives from a comprehensive view of modern society and of sociological theory, a view that implied that the sociology of science was a strategic research site: moved by his experience and abhorrence of violent conflicts, Ben-David was committed to British, then American, democracy as a model society, a social order of which (as Parsons taught him) science was an essential element and therefore a privileged research object.

Ben-David became conscious of these basic underlying lines of force directing his thinking only very gradually, however. While at the Center for Advanced Study in the Behavioral Sciences, Ben-David's move toward the sociology of science—or, rather, medicine—appeared as a logical extension of his dissertation. Of the three professions he studied there, medicine, the most directly linked to science, was the most characteristically modern and therefore the one most directly related to the sociology of a modern society. But instead of studying it structurally and functionally in the context of contemporary society, Ben-David chose to adopt a historical perspective, not unlike the one he followed in his early study of the mutations in Hungarian Jewish society in the nineteenth century, and to examine the *transformation* of roles in the context of a changing social setting. This research yielded two papers that quickly became classics: "Roles and Innovations in Medicine" and "Scientific Productivity and Academic Organization in Nineteenth-Century Medicine," both published in 1960 ([17], [18]; chaps. 1 and 5, below). They offer models explaining, respectively, cognitive innovation within science as resulting from role differentiation and role hybridization and quantitative growth of scientific knowledge as depending on competition among universities in a decentralized academic system.

At this point, the "hard core" (in I. Lakatos's sense) of Ben-David's research program had crystallized: all the crucial theoretical elements of what was to become his distinctive sociology of science were already there and only needed unfolding through systematic application to historical material. In point of fact, one part of Ben-David's subsequent work is an autonomous consequential execution of that research program, whereas another part arose in reaction to external events—political, social, and intellectual—or in response to requests for reports. A number of distinct clusters are therefore discernible in Ben-David's work, so that when we now pursue the biographical sketch beyond 1960, this will take the form of a summary description of these clusters. At the same time, it will also be a description of the parts of the selection of essays reproduced below, for the two divisions largely coincide. It must be kept in mind that Ben-David's entire work, even on apparently distant and unrelated themes, is informed and sustained by a theoretically unified vision of science and of its institutions, so that the divisions according to topics is never neat. Every essay has some bearing—direct or indirect—on the underlying theory of science and therefore also on issues it does not address explicitly.

A first cluster is formed by the essays dealing with conditions of scientific growth: in these papers, the existence of modern science as a specific, institutionalized social system is taken for granted, and the attempt is made to determine the organizational factors *within* that system which influence the rate of growth of knowledge. These studies, which chronologically cover the period up to about 1972, are in direct continuity with the 1960 papers on productivity and innovation within medical science in that they use the same theoretical concepts, mainly those of role, role hybridization, and competition between universities in a decentralized academic system. It is this line of inquiry that led Ben-David to an intensive study of the history of higher education, which, he maintained, is a major factor accounting for the successive shifts in the location of the world's scientific center. Another important message of these studies is that science grows through differentiation, rather than through conflict and revolutions. This basic tenet, it may be noted in passing, determines one of a number of areas of disagreement between Ben-David and T. S. Kuhn, while (and this is how Ben-David himself thought of the matter) it is consistent with the view of scientific growth described by G. Holton.[12] These papers

12. G. Holton, "Scientific Research and Scholarship," *Daedalus* 91, 2 (1962): 362–399; cited by Ben-David in [4] = [9], 3, n. 6, and elsewhere.

form two groups, according to whether they put the emphasis on the individual scientist's role or on the university as the main variable explaining the growth of knowledge (see Parts I and II in this volume).

Ben-David's theoretical work on the institutional factors influencing scientific productivity quite obviously has practical implications for science policy. This applies particularly to the analysis of the factors that allowed the United States to replace Germany as the world scientific center ([22]; chap. 6, below). When, in the mid-1960s, the Paris-based Organization for Economic Cooperation and Development became concerned about the technological gap between Europe and the United States, Ben-David seemed to be the person well qualified to elaborate theoretically based recommendations for a European science policy. He was appointed Temporary Consultant at the Department of Scientific Affairs of the OECD (1966–1971), and it is in this capacity that he wrote the report, *Fundamental Research and the Universities* ([3]; an extract is reproduced as chap. 11, below). Presumably because, in his view, the best science policy is to have as little as possible of science policy—research thrives best when a competition in a decentralized academic system is allowed to operate a "natural selection" of institutions, persons, and ideas—Ben-David did not write much on this subject, the theme of Part III. A notable exception is his in-depth criticism of an OECD report that viewed favorably the central planning of scientific research ([57] = [67]; chap. 12, below).

At that point, Ben-David had acquired a considerable international reputation as a sociologist of science and of higher education. His scientific achievements were recognized (and "rewarded"), for example, through his nomination in 1966 as secretary and later (1974–1978) as president of the Research Committee on the Sociology of Science of the International Sociological Association. Similarly, Ben-David became the member of the editorial board of a number of scholarly journals: *Administrative Science Quarterly, American Journal of Sociology, Current Sociology, Minerva,* and *Sociology of Education.* It was natural, therefore, for the Carnegie Commission on Higher Education to turn to Ben-David with a request for two reports, one on the state of higher education in the United States and the other on higher education in Britain, France, Germany, and the United States in historical and comparative perspective.

Both reports pursue themes that were central to Ben-David's work before, but they do not simply carry this earlier line of research farther. In the meanwhile, the social and political context had changed considerably, and, writing in the early 1970s, Ben-David conceived his work as having practical significance, too. There was, first, the gradually growing feeling that since higher education was becoming ever more generalized, the university's functions must be redefined. But what appeared to Ben-David to be still more urgent was the recent strong politicization in American and European universities. Indeed, he had very little sympathy with the student movements that reached their peak in 1968. Both his past personal experience with ideologically in-spired movements and his theoretical perspective made him resent any sort of ideological commitment and violence, especially in the university. The poli-ticization of the students, which he did not foresee when he wrote on student politics of 1966 ([32]; chap. 10, below), was perceived by him as a threat not only to free scientific inquiry but, beyond it, to the freedom of thought and to democracy as well. Both reports were therefore written with practical con-cerns in mind, and in turn, they bring the theoretical insights they afford to bear on immediate issues of policymaking.

The first report, originally entitled *American Higher Education: Directions Old and New* (1972) ([5]; republished as [6]), provides a sociological analysis of the development of the American college and university system from 1860 onward. Its main concern is to redefine two fundamental functions of the uni-versity, taking into account the change of its place in society after about 1960, especially the great increase in the number of students: the relationship of teaching and research at the university and the role of the university in dis-pensing general education. But in two of its recommendations, the report bears the stamp of the time in that they concern phenomena that proved to be ephemeral—the politicization of the campus and the existence there of an "intellectual-Bohemian proletariat." The second report, five years later, took up higher education, now enlarging the scope to compare the effectiveness of different national systems of higher education in four major Western coun-tries, past or present scientific metropoles: *Centers of Learning: Britain, France, Germany, United States* ([7]). Its main, theoretical purpose was, as before, to reconceptualize the notion of the university, that is, to redefine the university's various functions and the relationships between them. But, in par-allel, there was again the deep concern about the autonomy of the university, which, Ben-David felt, was strongly threatened.

All the work considered so far concerns growth *within* science. Very quickly, however, Ben-David sought to extend his sociological theory to bear on, and explain, the very fact that in seventeenth-century Europe, modern sci-ence, as a distinctive social institution producing a specific kind of knowl-edge, came into existence in the first place. As has been seen, the question concerning the social conditions necessary for the emergence and continued existence of science had already been on Ben-David's mind in the early 1950s, when he wrote his dissertation. It seems to have been the much-noticed vol-ume, *Scientific Change* (1963), edited by A. C. Crombie, that redirected his attention to this basic problem. Ben-David wrote an extensive review article of this book ([24]; chap. 14, below), and this article, in fact, set in motion a research program that was to culminate in *The Scientist's Role in Society* ([4] = [9]). In Ben-David's view, the emergence of modern science is above all a social process, a process through which a specific type of social activity—namely, autonomous inquiry, unconstrained by prejudice or authority and characterized by the central place accorded to empirical evidence and by free and rational debate—became not only legitimate but even prestigious. Ben-David formulated his thesis using a new theoretical concept, that of the scientist's role, a generalization of the former concept of a specific scientific role. He argued that in mid-seventeenth-century England, the scientist's role was for the first time institutionalized as a distinct social role and that its existence was a conditio sine qua non for regular and continuous scientific research (see [29]). It is the changing fortunes of that role in different social contexts which account for the successive shifts of what he defined as scientific centers from England to France, from the latter to Germany, and finally to the United States (see [36], [39]), a theme that obviously connects with the earlier ones concerning scientific productivity and the systems of higher education.

Ben-David's account of the institutionalization of science in terms of the emergence of the scientist's role is obviously indebted to R. K. Merton's *Science, Technology and Society in Seventeenth-Century England* (1938),[13] which had also inspired Ben-David's dissertation. Therefore, the various kinds of criticism that were directed against Merton's thesis were no less pertinent to Ben-David's position. In a late work ([77]; chap. 16, below), Ben-David rejected this criticism. This is of interest to us here because by doing this, he not only reinforced his and Merton's theses but also shed interesting light on their reception. Ben-David showed that Merton in fact put forward two distinct claims that were not clearly distinguished. One is a social-psychological hypothesis asserting that Puritans had a particular propensity to engage in scientific work, whence their alleged relatively important share in the production of the new science. The second thesis, which Ben-David developed in his own work, contends that in mid-seventeenth-century England, there occurred a value shift that moved experimental science to the top of the intellectual hierarchy and that this shift of social values resulted from the Puritan revolution. As Ben-David points out, most of the discussion and criticism concentrated on the first hypothesis and remained irrelevant to the second, which, however, is confirmed by historical work on the rise of the Baconian movement during the 1640s. This analysis implicitly explains the relative neglect of Ben-David's work on the institutionalization of seventeenth-century science, specifically, the fact that Merton's Puritanism thesis drew much more attention than Ben-David's apparently very similar thesis. Indeed, concerning their respective elaborations of the value shift thesis, it can now be seen that Merton's and Ben-David's works in fact shared the same fate. The reason for the neglect of this thesis, the more fundamental of the two, Ben-David implies, is that only few scholars could appreciate it adequately. The first thesis was accessible to empirical testing by historians and historians of science who, therefore, became the main participants in the debate, which conse-

---

13. First published in 1938 as vol. 4, pt. 2, of *Osiris,* 360–632. Reprinted with a new introduction (New York: Harper and Row, 1970; also New Jersey: Humanities Press/Sussex: Harvester Press, 1978).

quently concentrated on that thesis; these historians, however, were uninterested in the distinctively sociological value shift thesis. As for sociologists, they were conspicuously absent from the entire debate (presumably because some did not believe at all that science was an autonomous institution, while the others often lacked historical interest and competence), but only they, from a perspective informed by Max Weber's theoretical sociology, could have adequately appreciated the significance and explanatory import of the value shift thesis.

The value shift thesis hinges on the tenet that science is a distinctive kind of social activity, conforming to specific values and norms: the thesis indeed explains the emergence of modern science in mid-seventeenth-century England as being due to a compatibility of these values and norms with those of the environing society. The complex of these values and norms is called by Ben-David, following Merton, the *scientific ethos,* and in fact it is precisely the scientific ethos that defines the scientific role. But does a single scientific ethos, an ethos, that is, shared by all scientists, in all disciplines and throughout all periods from the seventeenth century onward, really exist? Or is it an unwarranted theoretical abstraction?

During the 1960s, when Ben-David was elaborating his views of the emergence of modern science, he could confidently draw on the notion of the scientific ethos because in the Western world it was almost unanimously taken for granted. As Ben-David made clear in a paper devoted to this topic ([63]; chap. 23, below), casting doubt on the autonomy of scientific inquiry, namely, the stance that the scientific ethos is an ideological notion because in reality all science is (and/or should be) subservient to parochial interests (of the nation, the class, etc.), was historically associated with Nazism and fascism, later also with Marxism (particularly with Stalinism); conversely, commitment to the notion of science as an autonomous activity oriented by a distinctive scientific ethos (a view developed notably by Merton and M. Polanyi) was considered as a defense of democracy. From the late 1960s onward, attitudes toward science changed, however. The scientific ethos as a descriptive and normative notion came under attack.

The idea that underlying all scientific activity is a single scientific ethos had been implicitly called into question by Kuhn's notion of paradigm as developed in his *The Structure of Scientific Revolutions* (1962). But this implication of Kuhn's work remained almost unnoticed until, in 1972, Kuhn himself made it explicit in his review article of Ben-David's *The Scientist's Role in Society.*[14] Kuhn's views were radicalized during the 1970s by the so-called sociology of scientific knowledge, which quickly gained wide hearing. The substance of these multifaceted debates cannot be discussed here, where we need only note their impact on Ben-David's work. Thus, from the 1970s onward, a major pre-

14. T. S. Kuhn, "Scientific Growth: Reflections on Ben-David's 'Scientific Role,'" *Minerva* 10 (1972): 166–178.

occupation of Ben-David's work was to defend the view that both the notion of the scientific ethos and the notion of the single interconnected scientific community as developed mainly by Michael Polanyi (the two notions in fact mutually depend on one another) indeed cover social and historical realities. Ben-David, therefore, worked in three directions: he answered the arguments adduced against the notion of the scientific ethos; he reflected on the apparent differences in the application of the scientific ethos between the social sciences and natural science; and, most important, he sought to describe and explain sociologically the changing views over the scientific ethos.

Ben-David gave a forceful statement of the difference between his views and Kuhn's in a paper published in 1977 ([55]; chap. 15, below; see also [49]). He points out, notably, that the notion of paradigm led Kuhn to construe "role" as "the cognitive and technical contents of what the incumbent of the role knows and does," so that "when those contents change, the role changes." This obviously means that the notion of a single, fixed scientific role and of a scientific ethos shared by all scientists whatever their theoretical commitments—that is, the main explanandum of Ben-David's historical sociology of science—is spurious. In response, Ben-David stresses again the meaning and crucial importance of the institutionalization of the newborn science (whence the inclusion of this paper in Part IV): he argues that only the postulated institutionalization of science and of the scientific role can explain how, over long stretches of time, scientific activity continued in the absence of important scientific achievements capable of giving rise to "paradigms." And he goes on to show that cognitive upheavals in science did not lead to any institutional revolution of the social system of science. In sum, it seems warranted to postulate a single overarching scientific community and a single scientific role, although, to be sure, every real scientist also follows the norms of other roles, for example, those of his disciplinary paradigm.

Kuhn's rejection of the notions of scientific ethos and of scientific community was exacerbated by the proponents of the sociology of scientific knowledge. Whereas in Kuhn's scheme science is largely autonomous (even if its norms are supposed to vary with its cognitive contents), the new "strong program" advocated the application of Mannheimian and Durkheimian ideas to the study of science and consequently the view that the very contents of science depend on social factors. This program therefore implied that the production of scientific (just as any other) knowledge should be studied in its immediate, local, social context, the premise being that scientists (and other producers of knowledge) relate to their nonscientific environment no less (perhaps even more) than to their "peers," that local interests, not (only) institutionalized norms, should be taken into account. Obviously, this stance threatens to undermine the notion of science as a distinctive—and distinguished—social activity, characterized by appeal to empirical evidence and by rationality. For Ben-David, much more than an intellectual challenge was at stake here, and this explains why he devoted a great number of papers to issues raised by this new sociology of scientific knowledge (see Part VI). In fact, he reacted to this new development within the discipline on several levels. On the programmatical-theoretical plane, he emphatically rejected the relativistic stance of the new program in the sociology of science: on this crucial issue, he never wavered. In particular, he endeavored to defend the view that science is a social activity with specific norms and, as such, is demarcated from other social spheres (see, e.g., [83]; chap. 22, below, and [52]). But Ben-David quickly recognized that some of the historical case studies inspired by the "strong program" afforded important new insights. He therefore accepted the idea (which he had previously rejected) that the study of the local social contexts of the production of scientific knowledge was an integral and important part of what the sociology of science was about. Indeed, he construed his own (or, for that matter, Merton's) institutional approach to the sociology of science and the sociology of scientific knowledge as being complementary, rather than contradictory, perspectives.

In this context, the social sciences posed a particularly delicate problem. Ben-David's view seemed to imply that these sciences should not differ in any fundamental way from the natural sciences. Specifically, social scientists should constitute one scientific community (and not fall asunder into ideologically oriented schools of thought), and social scientific research must progress. But there are obviously some differences in these respects between the social and the natural sciences, and Ben-David attempted, first, to define them and, second, to explain them sociologically as arising precisely from an inadequate institutionalization of the social scientist's role: the observable differences between the social and the natural sciences thus, in fact, confirm, rather than contradict, Ben-David's views. The sociology of the social sciences is the explicit subject of the papers assembled in Part V, but concern with it can be discerned also in a number of articles in Part VI.

But for Ben-David, the rise of the sociology of scientific knowledge, palpably associated with a widespread change of attitude toward science, raised also a problem that was itself sociological. Indeed, since Ben-David shared Weber's and Merton's belief that science was contingent on cultural values, the question why, within certain quarters, science rapidly changed from a highly considered to a fiercely attacked social institution, was of great theoretical significance to him. Inasmuch as for Ben-David, science also was the archetypical nonviolent consensual discourse, this question also had a moral and existential dimension. Thus, on a first level of analysis, Ben-David sought to account for the radical change of perspective among those engaged in the social studies of science, specifically, for the emergence of the sociology of scientific knowledge in Britain. He does this by invoking various factors operative both within the academic system—for example, differences in the institutionalization of sociology in the United States and in Britain—and without it—for example, the rise of a younger generation with no firsthand experience of previous assaults on the autonomy of science (see [59], [83];

chaps. 20 and 22, below, respectively). Yet Ben-David was acutely aware that the developments within the sociology of science must be seen in the context of changing attitudes toward science in society at large. On a second level of analysis, he therefore sought to describe and analyze sociologically the swing from a widespread utopian confidence in science as offering privileged access to knowledge—scientism—to a distrust in, and criticism of, science—antiscientism. According to him, the recent tide of antiscientism has little to do with science itself but is an offshoot of a widespread disillusionment with the Western democratic liberal social order of which science has been an integral part (see [79]; chap. 25, below).

This can hardly be the whole story, however, for swings between scientism and antiscientism have occurred in European countries a number of times since the rise of modern science. Ben-David therefore sought a general explanation for this phenomenon. This subject remained his central preoccupation during his last three years: on his death (Jan. 12, 1986), he left a draft of what was intended to become a monograph on the ethos of science in a historical and comparative perspective (see below, Part VII).

From the early 1970s onward, Ben-David was recognized as a leading sociologist of science and of higher education. Consequently, he held a number of prestigious appointments: in 1976, he was a member of the Institute for Advanced Study in Princeton; in 1977, he was nominated Stella M. Rowley Professor of Education and Professor of Sociology at the University of Chicago and thus shared his time between Chicago and Jerusalem where, in 1980, he was appointed to the newly created George Wise Chair of Sociology at the Hebrew University. Ben-David was also awarded several important honors and distinctions: the Borden Prize of the American Council on Education (1972), the Israeli Rothschild Prize in Social Sciences (1982), the Bernal Award of the Society for Social Studies of Science (1985). In 1971, he was elected Foreign Honorary Member of the American Academy of Arts and Sciences and, shortly afterward (1973), Foreign Associate of the National Academy of Education of the United States. In 1981, he at last became a member of the Israel Academy of Sciences. To celebrate Ben-David's sixty-fifth birthday, an international symposium was held in Jerusalem in December 1985, barely a month before his death. The large international participation in this symposium testified to the high regard Ben-David's scholarly achievements have earned him.[15]

A word should now be said about how Ben David's ideas were received within the several disciplines to which they are relevant. A comprehensive and

15. Some of the papers given at his symposium, together with others, form a memorial volume for Professor Ben-David. It was published as a double issue of *Minerva*, vol. 25, no. 1–2, (Spring-Summer 1987).

balanced review would require a very extended and thorough research. This cannot be done here, and the following sparse and conjectural remarks necessarily reflect my own partial acquaintance with, and subjective view of, the relevant material.

Throughout his life, Ben-David was engaged in working out a unified sociological theory of scientific growth. It is this concern that led him to investigate numerous distinct developments in the history of science, of scientific institutions, and of higher education. Now, although all these investigations were inspired by Ben-David's theory of scientific growth, which they were also intended to test and, eventually, confirm, the resulting accounts could be received independently of it. Specifically, Ben-David's variegated case studies could be—and indeed were—read dissociated from the underlying sociological theory, by distinct, sociologically as well as historically minded audiences. We must therefore ask what Ben David's influence was within the two disciplines, the history of science and the sociology of science.

Ben David's work has had a strong fructifying impact on the (social) history of science. Several of his case studies were relevant to the concerns of historians specializing in the corresponding geographic regions and periods, and they often influenced subsequent research in the area. In fact, Ben-David provided historians with working hypotheses, directing their attention to aspects or variables they might otherwise have ignored. A case in point is, for instance, the debate engendered by Ben-David's thesis on the rise and subsequent decline of France as a scientific center ([39]): the great amount of new research produced during this debate doubtless owes its existence to Ben-David's challenging (some have felt, provocative) thesis.[16] Within the history of science, therefore, in line with this discipline's character, the impact of Ben-David's work was that of a discrete set of unconnected studies in the social history of science, each addressed to a distinct and limited group of specialists. More often than not, historians were uninterested in (and perhaps unaware of) the underlying theoretical vision binding together the studies on distant places and periods; they therefore examined each of Ben-David's claims against the relevant historical evidence and judged it on its own merits, without bothering much about the consequences of their findings for the global sociological theory. This, indeed, was not their, but the sociologists', business.

Within the sociology of science, however, Ben-David has remained a lone rider. To be sure, his notoriety was great, and his writings were widely read and taught; even those who did not adhere to his views recognized in his work the most genuinely sociological theory of science.[17] And yet Ben-David's real impact on the theory and on the orientation of the empirical research within

16. The last contribution to this debate is Mary Jo Nye, "Scientific Decline: Is Quantitative Evaluation Enough?" *Isis* 75 (1984): 697–708, where some of the earlier literature is mentioned.

17. Randall Collins, in his "Comment" following Ben-David's [80], 76–77.

the discipline seems to have remained slight. This impression is confirmed by Susan E. Cozzens's survey, which systematically studies the reception of Ben-David's and Collins's paper, "Social Factors in the Origins of a New Science: The case of Psychology" ([31]; chap. 2, below). Between 1966 and 1979, this important paper was cited only forty-seven times in the periodical literature.[18] This is surprising enough, but a qualitative analysis of the citations is still more significant. Cozzens examined thirty-eight of the citations and determined whether or not they refer to the paper's "main knowledge-claim," which she took to be the thesis concerning the emergence of psychology. Only *three* papers were found to do so, of which one alone evoked the paper's central theoretical and conceptual innovation, that is, the notion of role hybridization.[19] Again, another important "knowledge-claim" of the paper, namely, the general idea that ideas survive only if carried by appropriate social roles, is cited merely *five* times.[20] All the citations considered come from sociologists, so that we may conclude that in the thirteen years following this paper's publication in 1966, the sociological community has produced only *eight* references to its main theoretical ideas. Now "Social Factors in the Origins of a New Science" appeared in the highly prestigious and visible *American Sociological Review,* it is among Ben-David's best-known works and is certainly a paper of great theoretical importance for the sociology of science. The conclusion thus seems warranted that Ben-David's work has suffered from a relative neglect.

Indeed, Ben-David never had a following comparable, say, to Merton's, and, except for occasional collaboration with students or former students (notably, A. Zloczower, R. Collins, and S. Katz), scarcely anyone tried to work within the framework he set up. One obvious reason for this is that the kind of research required by Ben-David's "paradigm" was not congenial to most sociologists. Merton's and Price's theories gave rise to fairly flourishing enterprises of "normal science," conducted with traditional sociological research tools (study of stratification, citation analysis, etc.), but Ben-David's theory called for sociologically informed research on *historical* material, something most sociologists shunned.

Yet Ben-David's relative lack of influence also stems from other, far more important reasons that have to do with the general intellectual and social climate. *The Scientist's Role in Society,* Ben-David's most systematic opus, was published in 1971, the precise moment at which the sociology of science was

18. Susan E. Cozzens, "Comparing the Sciences: Citation Context Analysis of Papers from Neuropharmocology and the Sociology of Science," *Social Studies of Science* 15 (1985): 127–153, on p. 139 (deleting 6 self-citations).

19. Ibid., 142 and 152, n. 42.

20. Ibid., 144. Cozzens gives only percentages, but since 12 percent of the "empirical literature" (whose size is not specified) can be inferred to correspond to 3 citations (n. 42 and the text to it), the 20 percent of the same "empirical literature" should correspond to 5 citations. The "nonempirical" papers apparently did not refer to these two knowledge-claims (ibid., 145).

radically changing orientation. After 1968, often in sequel to the students' movement, a growing interest in studies of the place of science in society led to a rapid expansion of the discipline, which now appropriately labeled itself "social studies of science." From the early 1970s onward, therefore, most people working in the discipline were newcomers, many of whom were drawn to it through a morally motivated wish to reflect critically on the social functions of science. This post-1968 generation was often animated by a personal experience, very different from the one that had moved Ben-David or Merton. The latters' experience during the 1930s gave them an attachment to the ethos of science in which they saw an apotheosis of the liberal-democratic social order: this made the scientific ethos—its historical reality and moral desirability—into the central motif of their sociology of science. By contrast, the new generation's perception of science was connected above all with the Vietnam War. There, they felt, science manifested itself not through a democratic ethos but through its association with power, specifically, with highly destructive military technology. Further, according to Ben-David's own analysis ([79]; chap. 25, below), the Vietnam War gave rise to a general antinomian attitude toward the Western liberal-democratic social order of which science was a central symbol. The new generation of sociologists of science therefore rejected the traditional—to them, apologetic—view of science and considered the notion of the ethos of science as spurious, indeed as ideological. Similarly, as a heritage of the students' movement (and also because they were mostly not educated in departments of sociology), the post-1970 generation rejected the entire functionalist "paradigm" in sociology. Ben-David's central notion of "role" was therefore unacceptable to them, as was also his (as it appeared to them) positivist view of scientific method. Still less were the notion of "competition" and Ben-David's claims on its behalf, associated as they were with Milton Friedman's economic theories of a free capitalistic market, liable to draw sympathy to his approach.

After 1970, therefore, a new perception of the tasks of the sociology of science emerged, one very different from Ben-David's (or Merton's): the new generation applied conflict theory where Ben-David had sought to demonstrate the emergence of consensus; it revived the sociology of knowledge (the target of Ben-David's criticism already in his 1955 dissertation) and applied it to science, claiming that the very contents of scientific theories can be explained with reference to their local, extrascientific, social contexts. In short, something like a new "paradigm" emerged, to which most of those active in the field adhered. Work within this paradigm was naturally guided by its own ("strong") program, the characteristic consequence being that the entire "traditional" sociology of science was rejected *en bloc* and bypassed altogether. Ben-David's ideas were neither used nor even opposed and criticized; they were simply ignored. His sociological theory of scientific growth, in other words, was not rejected because thorough historical investigations had shown it to be inadequate—in fact, the historical research has had little feedback on the appraisal of the theory within sociology—but simply because after 1970, most of those engaged in the social studies of science regarded it as both irrelevant to their concerns and as ideological.[21]

This is most unfortunate. To be sure, the new approaches to the social study of science have come up with important new insights. In particular, they have drawn attention to the role of local social contexts in the production of scientific knowledge and have thereby counterbalanced the earlier all too abstract—and undoubtedly idealized—picture of science. But there can be little doubt that the picture of science they have provided is one-sided and partial. Most important, the new "paradigm" inexorably drifts toward relativism and is therefore incapable of accounting for the *integration* of scientific knowledge, that is, for the conspicuous fact that, as a result of the process of selection, some locally produced knowledge-claims end up by becoming parts of comprehensive, translocal frameworks about which, eventually, a general consensus is formed.[22] There is no escape, therefore, from the conclusion reached by Ben-David himself: *in fine,* the old and the new—the institutional and the contextualist—approaches are complementary. Indeed, it should be realized that Ben-David's early work in fact already provides something of a paradigm for such a sociology of scientific knowledge. For by showing that some theoretical disciplines resulted when social conditions induced certain actors (Pasteur, Freud) to an institutional move that resulted, first, in a role hybridization and then led to an idea hybridization—that is, to the *constitution of a new object of scientific research*—Ben-David accounted sociologically for the *contents* of science (while yet avoiding relativism).[23] Similarly, in his last years, Ben-David sought to promote a synthesis of the two approaches, to show, for instance, that in order to understand the emergence of physiology in nineteenth-century Germany, we have to take into account both the personal, extrascientific circumstances and motivations of the scientists involved *and* the institutional settings and constraints within which they operated ([80], reproduced as chap. 24, below, and [81]). Such a synthesis remains a desideratum, and the time now seems ripe for the sociology of science to engage in it. Indeed, during the last fifteen years or so, the erstwhile outsiders have become the mainstream: their research program has shown its

21. S. Cozzens (n. 18, above) takes her findings concerning the reception of Ben-David's and Collins's "Social Factors in the Origins of a New Science" to reflect general characteristics of social science, distinguishing it from natural science. My own interpretation would be that these findings also have much to do with the very particular predicament of Ben-David's work.

22. See Gad Freudenthal, "The Role of Shared Knowledge in Science: The Failure of the Constructivist Programme in the Sociology of Science," *Social Studies of Science* 14 (1984): 285–295.

23. See Gad Freudenthal, "Joseph Ben-David's Sociology of Knowledge," *Minerva* 25 (1987): 135–149; Gad Freudenthal and Ilana Löwy, "Ludwik Fleck's Roles in Society: A Case Study Using Joseph Ben-David's Paradigm for a Sociology of Knowledge," *Social Studies of Science* 18 (1988): 625–651.

merits by giving rise to many detailed and insightful investigations. This should give the proponents of this approach both enough self-confidence and enough empirical material to become aware also of the limitations and one-sidedness of their approach. At this juncture, Ben-David's legacy, his histori-cal-comparative method, more than any other approach to the sociology of science, will, I believe, prove helpful in any attempt to elaborate a comprehensive and balanced theory of scientific growth, one that will integrate local and institutional aspects, factors both external and internal to the social system of science. It is with confidence in this perspective and out of the wish to promote it that the present collection of Joseph Ben-David's major articles in the sociology of science has been produced.

Part I

Conditions of Scientific Growth

The Scientist's Role

Introduction

The four papers assembled in this part constitute the starting point and, largely, also the hard core of Ben-David's research program in the sociology of science. They introduce three of Ben-David's central theoretical notions— "role," "role-hybridization," and "competition"—that are drawn on to account both for cognitive innovation in science (notably, the emergence of new scientific disciplines) and for its quantitative growth.

The notion of role is crucial to Ben-David's entire sociology of science: nothing less than the notion of the "scientist's role in society" hinges on it. Yet in his papers in the sociology of science, he takes this concept for granted and explains neither its meaning in his usage nor the theoretical assumptions underlying it. He did this to some extent in the Appendix to "The Professional Role of the Physician in a Bureaucratized Medicine" (1958). Since the subject matter of this paper falls outside the scope of this volume, the Appendix alone is included here (as chap. 4).

For Ben-David, a role is what a person, a group, or an institute is institutionally expected to do as a unit of the various systems of society. These expectations constitute the *norms* defining the role. Associated with the role is a *reference group* from which issue expectations and which sanctions its members' conduct. A basic tenet of this analysis is that the reference group allocates *reward* in the form of *status* in the group and that the agent's *social motivation* to fulfill the role depends uniquely on the rewards received within the group, that is, not on rewards in any other, therefore "incidental," system. (Hence, as Ben-David shows in that paper, the physician's role conflict: he is expected to comply with two sets of conflicting norms—the scientific standards, on the one hand, and the norms of helping the suffering, on the other.)

This general tenet forestalls the idea that scientists act in accordance *only* with the "scientific norms" (or the scientific ethos) and do not respond to expectations or rewards coming from outside the scientific community.

In "Roles and Innovations in Medicine" (1960), his first, now classic, paper in the sociology of science, Ben-David uses this model to account for cognitive change in science. Its central question is, whence come innovations within the professions? For a professional is the incumbent of a well-defined role into which he was socialized through a long process of training; the professional's conduct is, moreover, continuously monitored by a professional reference group in accordance with strict norms. Prima facie, therefore, a professional has little incentive to innovate. In the sociology of professions, it was therefore argued that changes (at least revolutionary ones) indeed necessarily come from outsiders, and the paper examines this hypothesis. It argues that some basic medical innovations (bacteriology, psychoanalysis) were made when, following upon certain social conditions, new roles emerged as a result of *role hybridization*. Specifically, social circumstances induced Pasteur and Freud to turn from basic science to practice, applying in the latter domain methods of the former. Each of them thereby created not only a new scientific object and a corresponding discipline but also—and this is of equal importance—a new, hybridized, role, one conforming to norms of the two reference groups involved (basic scientists and medical practitioners). It is the social "anchoring" of the intellectual innovation—the fact that it was acceptable to one reference group although rejected by the other—that assured its survival. Ben-David has here discovered an important mechanism of the emergence of innovations in general and in science in particular. Let us note in passing that two years before the publication of T. S. Kuhn's *The Structure of Scientific Revolutions*, we have what was to become one of the subjects of disagreement between Ben-David and Kuhn: against Kuhn, Ben-David points out that some scientific innovations did not, and indeed (at least at the time) could not, arise through the internal dynamics of "normal science." Specifically, many, perhaps most, innovations in science, revolutionary ones included, do not involve conflict but rather differentiation, a branching off into a new direction. (See below, chaps. 14 and 15.)

Simultaneously with the above investigation that drew on the notion of the role of the individual scientist to account for qualitative scientific change Ben-David also examined the social system that created and defined these roles and careers. This is the academic, university system whose internal functioning Ben-David considered a crucially important factor in the sustained growth (or its absence) of certain disciplines in certain countries. These investigations, which deal with the impact of the university on quantitative aspects of scientific growth, are assembled in Part II.

"Social Factors in the Origins of a New Science: The Case of Psychology" (1966) again accounts for cognitive innovation in science, namely, for the emergence of psychology in nineteenth-century Germany. The account is given in terms of role hybridization: as a result of conditions prevailing in the competitive German university system (see Part II, below), career opportunities favored mobility from physiology to philosophy and thereby the application of the methods of natural science to the study of "mind." This paper goes beyond "Roles and Innovations in Medicine," however, in that it addresses a further question, which are the conditions necessary for a cognitive innovation to become the fountainhead of an enduring research tradition, that is, of a new scientific discipline? The answer is that unless ideas are "cultivated by people whose regular jobs are to cultivate them," these ideas remain ephemeral. To give rise to a research tradition, an idea must be institutionalized, that is, it must be associated with a corresponding social role. Specifically, to last, a "hybrid idea" must be sustained by a new, "hybrid," role. In a more general form, this tenet underlies the entire argument of *The Scientist's Role in Society*.

> The persistance of a social activity over long periods of time, regardless of changes in the actors, depends on the emergence of roles to carry on the activity and on the understanding and positive evaluation ("legitimation") of these roles by some social group. In the absence of such a publicly recognized role, there is little chance for the transmission and diffusion of the knowledge, skills, and motivation pertaining to a particular activity and for the crystallization of all this into a distinct tradition.[1]

"Socialization and Career Patterns as Determinants of Productivity of Medical Researchers" (1968) is an empirical case study testing Ben-David's theoretical framework. Its argument is that in view of the physician's role conflict (discussed in [15]), a physician must undergo a process of "resocialization" to become a basic scientific researcher who has internalized the norms of the scientific community. Indeed, the scientific productivity of a physician depends on whether, how, and when he has been socialized into the scientific community as his new reference group. Thus, inasmuch as the paper's findings are accounted for by using the notions of role, socialization, reference group, and institutionalization, it is a straightforward confirmation of Ben-David's theoretical ideas.

1. [4] (= [9]), 17.

Roles and Innovations in Medicine   1

Until approximately the middle of the last century the majority of men engaged in scientific research were not scientists in their main occupation. But contemporary research in most of the sciences has become a career, chosen like any other profession. This trend was first discernible in Germany in the second half of the last century, and it has further developed during this century, mainly in the United States and lately in Russia. In Britain and France the development was slower, but the same tendency is observable there.

The development of scientific research into a separate profession brought about a considerable acceleration in the process of discovery. Indeed, it has been one of the conditions which made it possible to turn science from an unpredictable process into a tool which can be applied to practical purposes.[1] But scientific advance has many facets: besides increased activity, measured by indexes such as discoveries, publications, or, in technology, patents, there are questions of the quality and the type of discovery.

In the latter respects, the results of professional science may not be unequivocally superior to those of amateur science. Doubts are raised by at least one plausible hypothesis often mentioned in the literature on technological in-

The first draft of this paper was written while the author was a fellow at the Center for Advanced Study in the Behavioral Sciences, Stanford, California. He wishes to express his thanks to Professors S. N. Eisenstadt, Jerusalem; M. Janowitz, Ann Arbor; E. A. Shils, Chicago; and Mr. A. Zloczower, Jerusalem, for their valuable comments, and to Mr. A. Howard, graduate student at Stanford University, for his assistance with the research.
1. The present author has summarized this in a forthcoming paper, "The Development of the Medical Sciences." [This volume, chap. 5.] About the emergence of applied science from professionalized pure science in chemistry, see D. S. L. Cardwell, *The Organisation of Science in England* (London, 1957), p. 184.

ventions: that "revolutionary" inventions are usually made by outsiders, that is, by men who are not engaged in the occupation which is affected by them and are, therefore, not bound by professional custom and tradition.[2] This proposition—if it has any substance—suggests interesting implications for the development of science. According to it, professionalization, which necessarily turns scientific research into a monopoly of insiders rather than—as it used to be until well into the nineteenth century—of inspired amateurs (i.e., outsiders), may ultimately endanger its revolutionary character.

Propositions formulated in such general terms are often of limited relevance. In addition, the professionalization of science is an inevitable corollary of its development, and there seems to be much empirical evidence that the process has not, in fact, diminished the revolutionary character of science. Indeed, one of the chief proponents of the proposition suggests that it may be increasingly less relevant under present-day conditions.[3] Yet there is a simple and straightforward logic behind the argument, and the historical material which supports it is intuitively convincing.

The difficulty with the application of the proposition seems to be the loose definition of the outsider as well as of revolutionary innovation (or invention, or discovery). Obviously, the meaning of outsider changes with increasing differentiation of roles. The distance between the respective roles of a farmer and a medicine man in a primitive society—in terms of the knowledge which is necessary to perform them, the socialization through which the individual reaches them, and the social context within which both roles are performed—is perhaps less than the distance between the experimental physiologist and the physician who uses the results of his work.[4] It is obvious, therefore, that any useful application of the proposition has to be based on a precise definition and analysis of roles. Similarly, the term "revolutionary" innovation has to be replaced by a more specific one. We must investigate, therefore, the relationship between the definitions of the roles of people engaged in research and in practice in a certain field and the kind of innovations produced there.

We propose to investigate the relationship in the field of medicine. In medicine it is relatively easy to find two distinct roles which are interrelated and mixed in various ways in various countries: the career scientists, especially in the basic medical sciences (whether trained in medicine or not), and the medical practitioners who receive considerable scientific training but are not engaged in research as an occupation. Until the middle of the last century the two roles were only rudimentarily differentiated. Science was not yet a career, and the majority of biologists, and quite a few scientists in other fields, too,

2. S. C. Gilfillan, *The Sociology of Invention* (Chicago, 1935), pp. 88–91.

3. W. Kaempfert, "A New Patent Office for a New Age," in J. E. Thornton, ed., *Science and the Social Order* (Washington, D.C., 1939), pp. 160–63.

4. As noted by Gilfillan, most outsiders mentioned in the literature of technical invention were, in fact, relative outsiders only, with various connections with the fields in which they eventually made their discoveries.

were practicing doctors or at least initially chose medicine as their career, only later, as a result of exceptional achievement, to become full-time scientists. In a few countries the undifferentiated pattern has survived until quite recently, at least in some fields of medicine.

The proposition of the role of the outsider can be applied to this development as follows: The range of practical problems which force themselves upon "practitioners" is, at any moment, infinitely varied. The range of scientific problems, on the other hand, is largely confined within the theoretical boundaries of the scientific disciplines. Specialized research personnel working in autonomous and affluent scientific organizations, which can determine their policies without paying attention to practical demands, may be, therefore, the most efficient agents in promoting rapid scientific growth in a period—but only in a period—when a good idea is at hand of how to explore a series of well-defined phenomena. In such periods there is great advantage in concentrating upon those phenomena rather than dispersing resources on problems which may be unsoluble by the existing methods.

But in the long run the returns in knowledge which can be gained from the increasingly precise investigation of a limited range of problems may be diminishing. Continuous productivity can follow then only from shifting the focus of attention to new problems and developing adequate methods of investigating them. Practice in such times is an invaluable guide in locating relevant problems—rather than finding illusory ones, which happened not infrequently in the history of academic thinking—and in adapting existing methods or devising new ones. Its problems are always real, and it usually possesses a tradition which is the result of a long collective process of trial and error and which may suggest the way toward new theory and new methods.

Similar arguments can be put forward in favor of training and keeping scientists interested in a broad variety of scientific and perhaps also humanistic disciplines, as against specialization in a relatively narrow field. However, the social conditions determining the relationship between research and practice are different from those determining the degree of specialization. In this paper, therefore, we shall restrict ourselves to the exploration of the first of these two problems, namely, the effects of medical practice on research.

First, we shall investigate the relationship between scientific and practical roles in countries where the differentiation of these roles has occurred on a considerable scale to see the extent of the opportunities for practitioner research and the kind of communication between those in the two roles. Then we shall analyze the reception of a type of innovation which proved fruitful in the long run but in which there was good reason a priori to expect initial lack of interest, even hostility, among professional scientists, because it implied a fundamentally different view of illness than that scientifically accepted and because the new view was at first established by standards scientifically not quite acceptable. If our reasoning is valid—that influences coming from practice direct research to significant problems not implied in the existing scientific theory and methodology—then the influence will certainly show in this type of innovation.

The old system whereby medical practitioners conducted their own research and created organizations which contributed to the advancement of science still existed in Germany in the sixties and seventies of the last century.[5] But it had begun to decline as early as the forties. The fast development of the medical sciences created a paradoxical situation, since, in the state of knowledge at the time, the only thing one could do with good conscience was research, the accepted cures of the practicing profession having been shown to lack scientific foundation. Thus a cleavage arose between those who regarded themselves as medical scientists and those who practiced medicine. The spirit prevailing among the former is reflected in the opinion of the director of a public hospital in 1845: "Just as our precursors were more concerned with the success of their cures, so are we more concerned with our inquiries. Our purpose, therefore, is a purely scientific one. Medicine is a science, not an art."[6]

In spite of the limited use of medical science, there soon came into being a profession of medical scientists who, within a short space of time, monopolized not only the medical faculties but, as a matter of fact, the public hospitals, too.[7] Thus practitioners gradually lost all access to facilities—laboratories and hospitals—necessary for research, while, owing to technical advance, facilities even for clinical research became increasingly elaborate.

This development had been paralleled by a decrease in the opportunity for meaningful communication between the two sectors of the profession. Around the middle of the century, when the monopolization of the academic and hospital facilities and positions by the scientists in the profession were already far advanced, the yearly meetings of the natural scientists and physicians—the *Naturforscherversammlungen*—still played an important role in German scientific life. Out of these assemblies arose the German medical association in the seventies, which was a much more narrowly professional affair, mainly of practitioners alone. Finally, at the turn of the century, there came into being a new association of medical practitioners, overwhelmingly absorbed in "unionist" activities designed to better the economic status of the profession.[8] The staffs of medical faculties and public hospitals were often not members of these associations at all.[9]

5. P. Diepgen, *Geschichte der Medizin* (Berlin, 1955), vol. 2, no. 1, pp. 213–14, and vol. 2, no. 2, pp. 282–83.

6. Quoted by Diepgen (ibid., vol. 2, no. 1, pp. 152–53).

7. Th. Billroth, *The Medical Sciences in the German Universities* (New York, 1924), p. 27; A. Flexner, *Medical Education in Europe* (New York, 1912), pp. 145–66.

8. W. Ewald, *Soziale Medizin* (Berlin, 1911), 2, pp. 403–08.

9. *Final Report of the Commission on Medical Education* (New York, 1932), p. 344.

The introduction of the new type of scientific medical training and research in the United States took place under rather different circumstances; much of the initiative came from the professional organization of the practitioners. The decisive steps toward the establishment of proper scientific facilities were taken around 1890 when it became apparent that medical research could greatly benefit therapy (i.e., after the great bacteriological discoveries), and the innovations were designed to benefit practice as well as research. The balanced development of the up-to-date facilities in the large American research hospitals differs from the development in Germany, where there may be excellent facilities, such as a laboratory in the field of special interest of a head of a department, but where the facilities for the treatment of most patients may be, as a rule, quite modest.[10] As a result, no type of important facilities came to be monopolized by the full-time scientific professionals. Some practitioners continue teaching part-time in medical schools, and, more important, an increasing number of them have access to first-class hospital and laboratory facilities.[11] Practitioners as well as full-time research personnel have remained members of the same professional organization which has played an active part in the academic and research policies of the medical schools as well as in defending the material interests of doctors. Organizational unity among all the sectors of the medical profession has often been accompanied by tension, but there is no doubt that the professional organization has provided an efficient means of communication between practitioners and scientists—in both directions.[12] Activities of the organization, such as the medical conventions, have preserved the kind of symbolic significance and spectacularity for the public as well as the profession as the *Naturforscherversammlungen* had in Germany around the middle of the last century.

A further reason why the American scientific system is more open to pressures coming from practitioners or even the public at large (though the public would not ordinarily take a stand in matters concerning science) is largely due to the scientific administrator, who is usually a man who had acquired an academic standing and then left it for full-time academic administration. Admin-

10. A. Flexner, *Medical Education: A Comparative Study* (New York, 1925), pp. 223–26; cf. Diepgen, op. cit., vol. 2, no. 2, p. 281.

11. This situation is the result of constant and often open conflict between various sectors of the profession rather than of generally accepted policies. The conflict has usually centered around full-time clinical appointments in teaching hospitals, which, had they become the general rule, might have created a situation similar to that in Germany (Flexner, *Medical Education*, p. 278; cf. M. A. Fishbein, *History of the American Medical Association* [Philadelphia, 1947], pp. 322–24; James H. Means, *Doctors, People and Government* [Boston, 1953]). On a case where the problem reached the courts, see "Hospital Hassle: Who's Exploiting Whom?" *Medical Economics* 33 (November 1956): 321–62. About the actual state of affairs, see the President's Commission on the Health Needs of the Nation, *Building America's Health* (Washington, D.C., 1951), 2, pp. 202–3.

12. R. H. Shryock, *American Medical Research: Past and Present* (New York, 1947), pp. 119–20, and the sources quoted in n. 14.

istrative tasks make it imperative for him to be practical, especially in the United States, where pressure groups are powerful. On the other hand, he possesses a sufficient understanding of the nature and requirements of research and identifies himself mainly with the scientific profession. This makes it possible, at least in principle, for him to be a link between research and practice.[13] (In Germany, in spite of individual exceptions, this role has not developed. Administration and scientific leadership were kept strictly apart. There were two separate roles, the *Kurator,* an administrator appointed by the state, and the *Rektor,* elected head of the faculty for a limited period of time.)[14]

The following further differences between the United States and the German systems are presumably a result of the described conditions:

In Germany academic personnel have used their academic titles (*Professor, Dozent,* etc.) rather than their medical designation (*Doktor*); in the United States the last-named has usually been preferred. In the training of student physicians, the German faculties defined their task as providing an introduction into the science of medicine; most practical knowledge was supposedly acquired in practice. On the other hand, American medical schools— even the most research oriented—undertake to teach the student how to practice, making considerable effort to approach eminently practical problems in a systematic fashion rather than to delimit science authoritatively from practice.[15]

Thus the definition of the roles of people engaged in medical research had undergone the following changes during the late nineteenth and early twentieth centuries. In Germany research and teaching became an entirely separate role from practice by the end of the nineteenth century. About the same time began the differentiation of research roles from practice in the United States and Britain, but in the latter the development had been limited to the basic medical sciences. This role differentiation led in Germany to the deprivation of the practitioners from all the facilities necessary for research and to a lowering of the status of the practitioners as compared with the scientists. None of these results followed the large-scale development of medical research roles in America. Finally, in Britain and even more in France, the early-nineteenth-century type practitioner-scientist had predominated until quite recently.

We have to see now whether scientists acting in these different roles displayed different attitudes to the innovations we are interested in, namely, where there is good reason to expect that interest in practice played an important role in the discovery. To repeat, the innovations involve a fundamentally

13. L. Wilson, *The Academic Man* (New York, 1942), pp. 84–93; A. Flexner, *I Remember* (New York, 1940); D. Fleming, *William Welch and the Rise of Modern Medicine* (Boston, 1954), pp. 129–32.

14. A. Flexner, *Universities: American, English, German* (New York, 1930), pp. 321–24.

15. Flexner, *Medical Education in Europe,* pp. 145–66; R. K. Merton, G. G. Reader, and P. L. Kendall (eds.), *The Student Physician* (Cambridge, Mass., 1957).

different view of the investigated phenomenon—illness—from the view scientifically accepted; they are fruitful in the long run but are established in a way not quite acceptable by the standards of scientific methodology. Perhaps one could distinguish these as "fundamental marginal innovations." Two instances of these aroused a long controversy, international in scope, so that the material relating to them is sufficient to show the alignment of various positions and differences in the nature of contributions: the beginnings of bacteriology and psychoanalysis.

A great deal of what was to constitute the bacteriological view of illness had been for a long time part and parcel of the medical tradition. The idea of contagion goes back to antiquity, and so does the practice of inoculation; even the idea of *contagium animatum* had been put forward in the seventeenth century.[16] But the great advances in pathological and physiological studies of illness, from the beginning of the century, lent no scientific foundation or support to the bacteriological view. The theoretical analysis of the requirements of bacteriological research by one of the leading anatomists of the age, Jacob Henle (1840), was regarded, as a recent historian of medicine put it, as a "rear-guard action" in defense of a traditional approach to illness which had no scientific future.[17] Nevertheless, for more than ten years before the decisive experiments of Koch finally settled the question whether or not illness can be caused by specific living agents transferred from one person to another, there was a growing interest in the problem. Striking clinical evidence had come much earlier in the work of Semmelweis, which, however, had been well-nigh forgotten. But interest in it was revived by the work of Lister and the laboratory experiments of Pasteur and other French scientists. Before the crucial experiments of Koch, however, they were open to other interpretations.[18]

At this time Germany was already leading in medical research. Indeed, the first important clinical discovery in the field of bacteriology was made in Austria, and the clarification of the methodological requirements for testing the new theory and some very pertinent research were done by German professors of medicine. Yet during all this time (roughly from the mid-forties to the mid-seventies of the last century) the majority of the academic profession in Germany stood aloof from bacteriology. They regarded it as a matter of minor importance and did their best to quench the enthusiasm of the practitioners for the discoveries of Lister—having succeeded previously in consigning the work of Semmelweis virtually to oblivion. With few exceptions (Cohn, Klebs) all incentive for research during the sixties and early seventies came from France and Britain, where science was much less professionalized, and

16. F. H. Garrison, *An Introduction to the History of Medicine* (Philadelphia, 1929), pp. 75, 117, 253.
17. G. Rosen, *A History of Public Health* (New York, 1958), pp. 297–99.
18. Diepgen, op. cit., vol. 2, no. 2, pp. 115–25.

from the German practitioners, by one of whom, indeed, the crucial experiment was made.[19]

It was no coincidence that practitioners were more interested in this line of research than scientists. The increasingly refined pathological studies proved most satisfactory in helping the latter to understand illness. The fact that they provided no means of curing illness might have been a sad conclusion for the more humane among the doctors but one which scientists bore—and spread—with heroic resignation worthy of a profession whose destiny was the *Entzauberung* of (removing the magic from) the world. Besides, they preferred the negative views of Liebig, Hoppe-Seyler, Virchow, and other outstanding representatives of established academic disciplines, as against a new kind of theory which threatened to revive the discredited ideas of vitalism. Practitioners, on the other hand, even though they had to submit intellectually to the scientific argument, could find little satisfaction in it. They turned eagerly, therefore, to the works of Pasteur and Lister and evinced more interest in them than in the scientifically more impeccable work of physiologists and pathologists. The crucial investigations of Koch, too, were connected with a practical problem: the causes of anthrax, which caused great damage in the district where he worked as medical officer. His experiments are considered classic examples of correct scientific method. Yet quite a few hypotheses crucial for the design of his experiments were derived not from the traditions of the scientific laboratories but from the everyday observations of the people about the climatic conditions under which the disease occurred.[20]

Problems of medical (and veterinarian and agricultural) practice thus had been important in the initiation of bacteriological research; originally, more interest was taken in it by practitioners than by professional scientists. Although only the early experiments of Koch took place entirely outside the academic framework (later he became the director of a research institute and a university professor), at least three of the most important discoveries took place under conditions marginally academic. Semmelweis was unable to establish his case by the accepted rules of the academic game and was rejected by the Austrian academic profession. Even discounting some of the legends attached to this tragic figure, it seems that he was greatly motivated by the wish to help, which was at considerable variance with the crude form of "therapeutic nihilism" prevalent at that time in Vienna, and that, in spite of his scientific capacity, he always had been "maladjusted" to the academic framework.[21]

19. Ibid., pp. 123–24; R. H. Shryock, *The Development of Modern Medicine* (New York, 1947), pp. 283–84.
20. R. Dubos, *Louis Pasteur: Franc-tireur de la science* (Paris, 1955), pp. 119–22, 245–46; Diepgen, op. cit., 2, pp. 115–25.
21. Garrison, op. cit., p. 436. Even as late as 1861 his book activated a new campaign against him in which Virchow participated (see A. Castiglioni, *A History of Medicine* [New York, 1947], p. 726).

As a chemist, Pasteur falls outside the framework of this discussion, but the importance that the solution of practical problems played in his discovery fits very well into this framework. For reasons connected with his career, he abruptly left his early work of great theoretical interest and abandoned his self-image of pure scientist for that of a helper of the human race through science. This led him to the investigation of the phenomena of fermentation and prevention of diseases out of which emerged his discoveries.[22] Lister worked in Britain, where there was no differentiation between academic medicine and medical practice. Villemin and Davaine also worked outside the academic framework. Among all the pioneers in bacteriology, only Klebs was a proper academic physician.[23] Yet, in spite of their marginal positions in relation to the circles of authoritative science, their work—and Koch's as well—grew out of the academic milieu. Semmelweis came from the Vienna clinical school; Pasteur's work is related to the Franco-German school of chemistry; Lister's work was a result of Pasteur's; and Koch's was the last link in a chain which started with Henle and included much important research as well as the clarification of methodological requirements. Finally, once the decisive beginnings were made, the further development of the discipline was most efficiently pursued by the academic machinery of Germany.

In assessing the contribution of practitioners to this field of inquiry, therefore, it seems that their importance in the early stage of bacteriological research was that they provided an alternative frame of reference (or "reference group") to the scientific one. For one whose career is the exploration of the question, "What can be known about illness?" the choice of bacteriology could not have seemed a very good risk at a time when it seemed almost impossible to investigate bacteriological problems in a methodologically satisfactory way. Besides, committing one's self to research in this field implied a conflict with the materialistic ideologies then prevailing in scientific circles.

All these considerations mattered very little if one chose as one's frame of reference medical practice rather than science. In this case the question decisive for the choice of subject was, "What can be done about illness?" and from this point of view bacteriological research looked more promising than either physiology or pathology. Besides, it must have been much easier for a practitioner, or for someone identifying himself with practitioners (in medicine, in industry, etc.), to disregard the professional ideologies of the scientists which would have prejudiced him against anything suspect as vitalism. Thus, while some of the important early discoveries were made by academic

22. Dubos, op. cit., pp. 16–17, 86–87, 362–89.
23. Garrison, op. cit., pp. 575–77, 580–81, 616. Many of Koch's early co-workers—Löffler, Gaffky, Hueppe, and Fischer—were former army surgeons, as was the French pioneer of bacteriology, Villemin (Garrison, op. cit., pp. 581–82, 616). The only academic group proper which supported the bacteriological approach was the botanist (Dubos, op. cit., pp. 119–22). They obviously had an interest in a theory which used something from their discipline in the explanation of phenomena previously attributed to chemical factors.

scientists, those who committed themselves most to the bacteriological hypotheses were mostly practitioner-scientists of the old type. The central innovator, Pasteur, it is true, was a professional academic scientist, but at a certain stage of his career he was compelled to use his scientific talent for the solution of practical problems. From this point on, he consciously adopted the new role of what might be called today "applied scientist," in which the criteria of relevance and success were different from those accepted in the academic profession. This explains, too, why the practitioners as a group accepted the new theories in opposition to the view of the academic profession.

All this tends to support the hypothesis that practice plays an important and systematic role in the orientation of research toward new problems. Psychoanalysis provides additional confirmatory evidence.

Before Freud started his investigations of the neuroses, he was a scholar engaged in the kind of medical research that was the usual preparation for an academic career in German and Austrian medicine.[24] The influences which turned his interests into new directions were his studies with French clinicians; later, after he had to renounce his academic plans, his association with a well-known Viennese *Hausarzt* (family practitioner), Breuer; and, finally, his own private practice.[25] There he encountered neuroses which were either unknown to or neglected by academic medicine. He approached these phenomena with the mental habits of a person trained in scientific research.

Like the great French clinicians early in the century, when he found the existing methods of treatment useless and the definitions of mental illness irrelevant to his cases, he started to make painstaking clinical observations, keeping his eyes open to things that were usually considered irrelevant and abandoning methods and theories (including, at the beginning, his own) when contradicted by evidence.[26] In this way, his attention was directed to phenomena which were all known to practicing doctors as part of the "art" or the etiquette of medicine but not systematically thought of as etiological in the causation and the therapy of illness. This is obvious in such key concepts of psychoanalytic therapy as transference and counter transference, which are descriptions of what goes on between doctor and patient in many kinds of treatment and not only in psychotherapy. And, as pointed out by Parsons, many elements of the medical etiquette have come to be used as technical tools of psychoanalysis.[27] Such things are the relationship of trust between doctor and patient (both ways), the handling of uncertainty, and the insistence

24. On Freud's early scientific career see E. Jones, *The Life and Work of Sigmund Freud* (London, 1955), vol. 1, chaps. 5–6, 10.

25. Ibid., chap. 6; S. Freud, *An Autobiographical Study* (London, 1935). The most perceptive summary of these influences is Philip Rieff, *Freud: The Mind of a Moralist* (New York, 1959).

26. Freud, op. cit., pp. 26–27, 58, 60–62, 109–10.

27. T. Parsons, *The Social System* (Glencoe, Ill., 1951), pp. 326–479.

on the autonomy of the patient and on his will to be cured. Even fee for service has been treated in psychoanalysis as a technical problem of therapy.[28]

This exposition may seem to emphasize unduly the method of psychoanalysis at the expense of its more controversial substantive hypotheses about sexual development. There was a great deal of nonscientific element in Freud's thinking and declarations about sex; like D. H. Lawrence in England, he regarded it as his mission to destroy all the mystery, shame, and guilt surrounding it. But such prophetic overtones were not unusual among nineteenth-century scientists, and—at least in the early writings of Freud—they are not difficult to separate from the scientific elements of his work.[29] The latter consisted of the systematic clinical description and analysis of neuroses and the search for a positive biological basis of these elusive mental phenomena. Even his emphasis on pregenital sexuality was, to a large extent, an attempt to apply the developmental concepts of embryology to the explanation of complex human behavior.[30]

If this interpretation of the beginnings of psychoanalysis is correct, it justifies quoting it as a parallel to bacteriology. Psychoanalysis, too, was a novel theory of illness containing, however, traditional elements of medical thinking and practice. As a theory it was even more suspect than bacteriology. Scientific opposition to the latter was largely to the reintroduction of elements reminiscent of vitalism while psychoanalytic concepts were frankly anthropomorphic and to some extent voluntaristic. To this extent it was justifiable to see it as something akin to prescientific medical thinking.

The methodological problems raised by psychoanalysis also looked hopeless (again, not unlike but even more than in the case of bacteriology). True, it was a striking application of rigorous clinical thinking to new phenomena; but by that time clinical methods were increasingly replaced, or supplemented by laboratory research, and no one envisaged the possibility of this kind of research in psychoanalysis, although, in the beginning at least, Freud was confident that eventually a physiological basis of his theories would be found.[31]

Few people would doubt nowadays that all these objections to psychoanalysis were correct. But the objections of Liebig and Virchow to Pasteur's work also proved to be correct in the long run. Yet in both instances scientific

28. Freud, op. cit., pp. 46, 48; S. Lorand and W. A. Console, "Therapeutic Results in Psychoanalytic Treatment without Fee" and "Discussion" of the article by W. C. M. Scott in *International Journal of Psychoanalysis* 38 (1956): 59–65.

29. Cf. E. H. Erikson, *Childhood and Society* (London, n.d.), pp. 58–59. It has been correctly emphasized by Rieff (op. cit.) that, even in his "prophetic" role, Freud tried to behave much more like a scientist than did Virchow or Pasteur. Freud always shunned dramatic effect and popular appeal. But, of course, this might have been due partly to his greater insecurity about his status as a scientist.

30. Apart from Freud's own writings, especially the earlier ones, see Erikson, op. cit., pp. 59–61; J. Bowlby, "The Child's Tie to His Mother," *International Journal of Psychoanalysis* 39 (1958): 1–24.

31. Jones, op. cit., chap. 2.

and practical progress was achieved for some time by less than perfect methodology.[32] On these grounds one feels justified in classifying psychoanalysis in the same category as bacteriology as a fundamental marginal innovation.

Let us now turn to the social structure of the process of innovation and of the reaction of academic circles to it. Important elements of the innovation came from academically less developed, more anarchic France, where there were no qualms about using the ill-understood but for many purposes useful method of hypnosis. Freud himself came from German academic medicine, but he had to renounce his academic career for practice. He was interested in research and had to abandon his scientific career because of a combination of lack of opportunity, inadequate means, and insufficient success, owing probably to a limited talent for exact research.[33] Going into practice was a comedown for him; besides, he was not attracted to the role of the healer ("Aus frühen Jahren ist mir nichts von einem Bedürfnis, leidenden Menschen zu helfen, bekannt. . . . Ich habe auch niemals 'Doktor' gespielt").[34] Having to become a practicing doctor, therefore, threatened his self-identity. He solved this problem by turning the searchlight of research on the neuroses specific to private practice and by making scientific techniques of various elements of the traditional healing role which repelled him.

There were, then, differences in the motivation of Freud, on the one hand, and the pioneers of bacteriology, especially Pasteur, on the other hand. Freud wanted to prove that he was a scientist, though engaged in practice; Pasteur wanted to prove that he, as a scientist, could make decisive contributions to the solution of practical problems. But the social situations out of which the innovations emerged were similar. In both cases there were phenomena which presented practical problems but were not promising in the mind of the person whose aim was to find out what could be known about illness; in both cases the innovation was the result of applying systematic scientific thinking to these phenomena as well as to the traditions existing about them among those accustomed to deal with them. Finally, in both cases those whose work to some extent led up to the innovation were people in the loosely defined role of practitioner-scientist, like the French clinicians, Lister, and perhaps Breuer, while the central figures who established the innovation were professional scientists, or at least were trained for such careers but were thrown into situations where they had to prove themselves through the solution of practical problems. Now they had to choose their problems according to the criterion of "something to be done" rather than the accepted scientific criteria of their times.

32. Shryock, *Modern Medicine*, p. 305; Dubos, op. cit., pp. 155–56.
33. Jones, op. cit., chaps. 5–6.
34. From S. Freud, "Nachwort zur Frage der Laienanalyse," *Gesammelte Schriften* (London, 1948), 14, p. 290.

This process whereby a person in Role A is set to achieve the aims of Role B can be described as "role hybridization." The innovation is the result of an attempt to apply the usual means in Role A to achieve the goals of Role B. Obviously, successful innovation is not the only possible outcome. The means of Role A may be irrelevant to the goals of Role B, or the relearning of Role B may be a more acceptable solution than the creating of a new combination out of the elements of the two roles. In our cases the means of the scientific role—exact observation and isolation of factors through experiment or clinical reasoning—were relevant to the practical goals to which they were applied, and the definition of the situation created a problem which could not be solved, or not satisfactorily, by learning the other role as it then existed. Pasteur was expected to prove himself through practical results as a scientist; Freud, of course, could have become a practitioner, but this would have meant an admission of defeat on his part. He was interested in science and not interested in practice; furthermore, in Austria and Germany at that time, when the status of the scientist was high, that of the practitioner relatively low, and the old role of practitioner-scientist almost extinct, to abandon the scientific career was also to lose status. Innovation, therefore, remained the only satisfactory solution.

In Austria and Germany the new theory—psychoanalysis—was not taken seriously by the academic circles and was not given any opportunity in the universities. Criticism of it was often hostile and coarse; it was censured as immoral because of its sexual theories, and the psychoanalysts were at times boycotted, especially by universities and public hospitals. Freud and his followers did their best to expose the narrow-minded prejudice, stupidity, and, in some cases, dishonesty of their most virulent opponents.[35] However, the opposition could not have been successful had psychoanalysis been recognized by at least part of the scientific public. The academic leadership of Germany did not consist of the people made ridiculous by the psychoanalysts, and, if the new theory was practically boycotted in German academic medicine, this happened with the consent of quite a few unprejudiced and brilliant people who were afraid of neither Jew (some were Jews themselves) nor, one presumes, sex. Their behavior was motivated by the fact that psychoanalysis was bad science and that their definition of science was a strictly professsional one. Working where there was an organizational cleavage between practice and scientific research, they took no interest in a theory which had only practical achievements and aesthetic appeal to commend it.

In consequence, psychoanalysis was driven in Vienna—and, indeed, everywhere in Austria and Germany—very nearly into the position of a medical sect officially denounced at scientific meetings, instead of having been ab-

35. Jones, op. cit., vol. 2, chap. 4; the official psychoanalytical view of the subject as stated by Freud was that opposition to psychoanalysis had emotional and not intellectual sources ("Die Widerstände gegen die Psychoanalyse," *Gesammelte Schriften* 14, p. 108).

sorbed, transformed, and utilized to any great extent in psychological and psychiatric research and practice.[36] At least this was the case until the 1920s. It is difficult to determine to what extent the exclusion of psychoanalysis from academic science for a period of about twenty years was due to its very grave shortcomings as a science or to the fact that by that time academic science, including academic medicine, had become a much more closed system than it was at the time of the controversy over bacteriology. But the latter explanation is supported by the reception of psychoanalysis in the United States. Objections and doubts existed in American circles not less than in Germany; there were, moreover, attempts to suppress the new theory by official denunciations at scientific congresses, as in Germany, but without success. The new theories received the attention of some practitioners as well as of professors of medicine and psychology.[37]

This can be attributed partly to the fact that, from the point of view of the organization and professionalization of science, the United States at the beginning of the twentieth century was in the same stage of development as was Germany in the 1850s and 1860s. The process had just started to gather momentum. However, if only the rudimentary stage of the organization and professionalization of science had been the cause of the different reception of psychoanalysis in the United States, one would expect opinion to be divided, as it was about bacteriology in Germany: support for the theory would have come from practitioners and opposition from academic scientists. But, as a matter of fact, the cleavage of opinions was never on these lines; much of the support came from academic circles. The scientific reference group in the United States was more open than in Germany, owing apparently to the institutional arrangements (as previously described), which provided a link between science and the groups interested in its application.[38]

This analysis of the beginnings of bacteriology and psychoanalysis lends general support to the proposition that contact with practice may be important in reorienting research toward the investigation of new and fruitful problems. The practitioner-scientists appear as forerunners, supporters, and disciples in the history of two innovations, bacteriology and psychoanalysis. The central figures in both were "role hybrids" who were led to the innovation by an

36. Jones, op. cit., pp. 107–25; Freud, *An Autobiographical Study*, pp. 87–101.

37. Jones, op. cit., pp. 111–16; Shryock, *American Medical Research: Past and Present*, pp. 225–33.

38. For evidence that the relative openness of the academic system to psychoanalysis and other marginal medical trends was maintained by precisely these institutional arrangements, see H. Cushing, *The Life of Sir William Osler* (Oxford, 1925), pp. 181, 221; Jones, op. cit., 2, p. 99; R. Sand, *The Advance to Social Medicine* (London, 1952), pp. 516–20, 545–49; Fleming, op. cit., pp. 140–41, 144–45, 161–73. About the attitude of the representative psychiatric circles to psychoanalysis, see G. Zilboorg and G. W. Henry, *A History of Medical Psychology* (New York, 1941), pp. 500–6; J. K. Hall, ed., *One Hundred Years of American Psychiatry* (New York, 1944), p. 305.

abrupt change from theoretical research to applied science. The practitioner-scientist, as well as the role hybrid, are each in a position to shift frames of reference relatively easily. But it can be assumed that those whose training and main role is that of the "scientist" will be more capable of generalizing, and more motivated to generalize, their findings and establishing themselves as innovators than the practitioner-scientists.[39]

This interpretation may be relevant to the eventual investigation of patterns of discovery resulting from shifts from one scientific discipline to the other. Scientific disciplines differ from one another in the degree of their theoretical closure and methodological precision. The phenomena most similar to role hybridization would be shifts from a theoretically and methodologically more advanced discipline to one less advanced. These must be distinguished from shifts between two disciplines of the same level and from less to more advanced disciplines.

As far as the organization of science is concerned, the seemingly paradoxical conclusion is that professionalization of research does not in itself decrease the chances of innovations by outsiders. As a matter of fact, theoretically, it increases the chances, since, the more differentiated a field, the greater the likelihood of role hybridization in it. In practice, however, the differentiation of research from practice and the professionalization of science may take place in such a way as to make it difficult for scientists to engage in marginal problems without endangering their status beyond the risk taken by every innovator. Where an academic system reacts to marginal innovations, as the German system did to early bacteriology and, even more, to psychoanalysis, there is great risk in investigating problems considered irrelevant by academic authorities. It will be, therefore, relatively difficult to shift frames of reference. This is, indeed, shown in the relatively unimportant share of German academicians in establishing bacteriology as a science and in the fact that psychoanalysis developed into a movement rather than a science in Austria and Germany.

If this analysis is correct, one would expect such "closed" academic systems as the German to lose efficiency because of their resistance to marginal innovations. This is, indeed, what happened to German academic medicine. On the other hand, this loss of efficiency may be temporary. Once the innovation is sufficiently established in another system, it may be taken up by the closed one and developed there rapidly, as, in fact, happened to German bacteriology.

At a later stage of the differentiation and professionalization of scientific roles mechanisms arose which mediated between the two types of activity and

39. On priority in innovation as an institutionalized feature of science, see R. K. Merton, "Priorities in Scientific Discovery: A Chapter in the Sociology of Science," *American Sociological Review* 22 (1957): 635–59. According to this, it can be assumed that professional scientists are more motivated than practitioner-scientists to innovation.

apparently broke down the barrier to communication found between practice and research in the last decades of the nineteenth century. The kind of professional structure which emerged in the United States made possible the differentiation of scientific roles, yet prevented a cleavage between the outlook of the academic and practicing sectors of the profession.

From this point of view medical "professionalism," which consciously aims at maintaining a balance between the development of medical sciences and practice, can be regarded as a sequel to the establishment of research as a separate institution during the nineteenth century. It is a social structure or, rather, one of the structures, since there are certainly more than one, which represents a phase of growing integration between science and practice following the differentiation of academic research in the medical field out of the context of amateur and practitioners' research during the last century. The spread of professionalization in an increasing number of disciplines suggests that the sequence of events observed in medicine may have its parallels in other fields.

Social Factors in the Origins of a New Science   2

The Case of Psychology*

The Problem

The growth of scientific disciplines, as of many other phenomena, can be represented by an S-shaped curve.[1] First there is a long period, going back to prehistory, during which there are various ups and downs but no continuous growth; this is followed by a spurt of accelerated growth; eventually the development slows down and approaches a ceiling.[2] This typical pattern is obtained whether one uses as the index of growth the numbers of publications, discoveries, or people doing research in the subject; the pattern corresponds well with the intuitive picture one obtains from the histories of the different sciences.

The process, as presented in the accounts of scientific development, can be presented schematically as follows. Ideas beget ideas until the time is ripe for a new and coherent system of thought and research to arise. Thenceforth the system possesses a life of its own. It is identified as a new field of science, is eventually given a name of its own (such as chemistry or psychology), and grows rapidly into maturity. This still leaves open the question of beginnings.

*With Randall Collins.

This paper is partly based on an M.A. thesis by Randall Collins (University of California, Berkeley, 1965). The authors are indebted to Professors David Krech and Harold Wilensky for their comments and suggestions and to the Comparative National Development Project of the Institute of International Studies of the University of California, Berkeley, for financial support.

1. Derek de Solla Price, *Little Science, Big Science* (New York: Colombia University Press, 1963), pp. 1–32; Gerald Holton, "Scientific Research and Scholarship: Notes Toward the Design of Proper Scales," *Daedalus* 91 (Spring 1962), pp. 362–99.

2. Although this may be followed by escalation into further growth, it is unnecessary for the purpose of the present paper to consider this possibility.

If the whole story consisted of ideas begetting ideas, then growth would have to start at an exponentially accelerating rate (to a point of saturation) right from the first relevant idea. Since this does not happen, it has to be assumed either that only a few ideas are capable of generating new ones—the rest simply being sterile—or that ideas are not self-generating and, even if potentially fertile, have to be carried from person to person and implanted in some special way in order to give rise to new generation.

Common sense indicates that both statements are true. Not all original ideas are fertile, and some potentially fertile ideas are lost or left unused because they are not communicated effectively. Nevertheless histories of science have concentrated on the first type of explanation. If an idea has no historical consequences, the historian of ideas will take it for granted that something must have been at fault with the idea. Conversely, when an idea with a seemingly not-so-brilliant beginning proves capable of further growth, he will assume that it must have had hidden qualities which ensured its success. Obviously he will find no difficulty after the fact in demonstrating the correctness of his hunches.

In this paper, we shall pursue the other tack. Instead of trying to show what inherent qualities made one idea fertile and another infertile, we shall ask how it happened that at a certain point in time the transmission and diffusion of ideas relating to a given field became strikingly increased in effectiveness. Instead of contemplating the internal structure of intellectual mutations,[3] we shall concentrate on the environmental mechanisms which determine the selection of mutations. Specifically, we postulate that: (1) the ideas necessary for the creation of a new discipline are usually available over a relatively prolonged period of time and in several places;[4] (2) only a few of these potential beginnings lead to further growth; (3) such growth occurs where and when persons become interested in the new idea, not only as intellectual content but also as a potential means of establishing a new intellectual identity and particularly a new occupational role; and (4) the conditions under which such interest arises can be identified and used as the basis for eventually building a predictive theory.

The Case of Psychology: The Take-off into Accelerated Growth

The earliest beginnings of psychology reach back into prehistory. Explanations of human thought and behavior are inherent in every language; with the

3. This is not to say that such contemplation is necessarily useless. Its potential utility depends on finding identifiable characteristics which predict what is and what is not a "fertile" idea.
4. This accords with the oft-noted phenomenon of multiple discoveries in science. Cf. Robert K. Merton, "Singletons and Multiples in Scientific Discovery: A Chapter in the Sociology of Science," *Proceedings of the American Philosophical Society* 105 (1961), pp. 471–86.

Table 1. Number of Publications in Experimental and Physiological Psychology, by Nationality and Decade, 1797–1896

	Nationality					
Decade	German	French	British	American	Other	Total
1797–1806	1	1	. .	. .	. .	2
1807–1816	2	1	. .	. .	. .	3
1817–1826	1	. .	3	. .	. .	4
1827–1836	4	3	2	. .	. .	9
1837–1846	11	4	2	. .	1	18
1847–1856	15	2	6	1	. .	24
1857–1866	16	8	7	. .	3	34
1867–1876	38	11	15	1	4	69
1877–1886	57	22	17	9	12	117
1887–1896	84	50	13	78	21	246

Source: J. Mark Baldwin (ed.), *Dictionary of Philosophy and Psychology* (New York: Macmillan, 1905), vol. 3, pt. 2, pp. 950–64.

rise of philosophies, more abstract and systematic formulations came into being. Finally, in the nineteenth century, the methods of natural science were applied to the subject. Using publications in experimental and physiological psychology as an index of the growth of modern scientific psychology, we find that the acceleration started about 1870 and that the period of rapid growth was reached about 1890 (table 1).[5]

The place where accelerated growth began can be ascertained from comparisons of the growth in different countries. The pattern is similar to that found in other nineteenth-century sciences. The main development occurs in Germany, to be continued in the twentieth century in the United States, with a much more modest growth in Britain. For a while France also seems to develop strongly, but production there declines soon after the initial spurt around the turn of the century (table 2). Moreover, French development seems to have been isolated from the mainstream; it has been quoted in major textbooks less than its relative share in production of publications would indicate (table 3).

These are the data to be explained. Since the conditions under which something new is created are not necessarily the same as the conditions under

5. These publications do not represent the total number of reports of experimental and physiological researches in psychology but rather review articles, books, and papers dealing with the theory and methodology of experimental and physiological psychology. Complete tables of research reports are not available for this period; however, this particular bibliography may be more useful for our purposes than they would have been. It represents a set of self-conscious summaries of scientific work in the field; therefore, it indicates the rise of interest in scientific psychology better than would a collection of researches which may not at the time have been considered relevant to psychology.

Table 2.   Annual Average Number of Publications in Psychology, by Language, 1896–1955

Years	German	English Total	English American	English British	French	Other	Total
1896–1900	765	749	....	...	709	271	2494
1901–1905	1119	747	....	...	700	215	2781
1906–1910	1508	941	....	...	578	158	3185
1911–1915	1356	1090	....	...	376	160	2982
1916–1920	386	1639	....	...	179	191	2395
1921–1925	1163	1850	....	...	326	315	3654
1926–1930	1955	2654	....	...	428	913	5950
1931–1935	1362	3371	....	...	468	975	6176
1936–1940	1160	....	3238	328	399	747	6330
1941–1945	216	....	3411	296	72	299	4462
1946–1950	203	....	4257	346	246	382	5663
1951–1955	459	....	5947	557	461	572	8385

Source: Samuel W. Fernberger, "Number of Psychological Publications in Different Languages," *American Journal of Psychology* 30 (1917), pp. 141–50; 37 (1926), pp. 578–81; 48 (1936), pp. 680–84; 59 (1946), pp. 284–90; 69 (1956), pp. 304–09.

[Note: A number of misprints in the original publication has been rectified on the basis of the source material; the last four lines do not add up because the total in the right column includes all English language publications, of which the publications by authors from the United States and the British Isles are only a part. Ed.]

Table 3.   Percent Distribution of References in Psychology Texts by Language

Text	Total	Language English	Language German	Language French	Language Other
Ladd, *Elements of Physiological Psychology*, 1887.	100.0 (420)	21.1	70.0	7.4	0.5
Ladd & Woodworth, 2nd edition, 1911.	100.0 (581)	45.6	47.0	5.2	2.2
Woodworth, *Experimental Psychology*, 1938.	100.0 (1735)	70.9	24.5	3.1	1.5
Woodworth & Schlosberg, 2nd edition, 1954.	100.0 (2359)	86.1	10.9	2.5	0.5

[Note: The first line carries a minor error which could not be rectified. Ed.]

which the innovation is effectively received somewhere else, we shall confine ourselves to the explanation of the take-off and leave the analysis of the diffusion of the new field for another discussion.

Procedure

Originally the subject matter of psychology was divided between speculative philosophy and physiology. Toward 1880, specialized psychological publications came to constitute the bulk of the work in the field, and philosophical psychology was widely disparaged by the "new psychologists."[6] The acceleration of production was associated with a growing consciousness among these men of the existence of a distinct field of psychology and of the need for distinguishing their work from traditional fields. It is usually assumed that the emergence of a new group devoting itself to a new specialty is an effect of intellectual growth. As knowledge in a field increases, no one is able to master all of it any more, and specialization is the necessary result. We shall try to show, however, that the new scientific identity may precede and indeed make possible the growth in scientific production. At least in the rise of the new psychology, social factors played an important role, independently of intellectual content.

The first step is to determine the persons who consciously identified themselves as practitioners of a new science investigating mental phenomena by means of empirical methods such as experimentation, systematic observation, and measurement (irrespective of whether they called themselves "psychologists" or "experimental philosophers"). Operationally, there are three conditions for the existence of such a new scientific identity: (1) the person must do empirical work in the subject matter of psychology; (2) he must not have some other clearly established scientific identity, such as physiologist; (3) he must be a part of an ongoing group of scientific psychologists, rather than an isolated individual.

Taking these points in order: (1) The first group to be excluded are speculative philosophers such as Descartes, Locke, Hartley, Herbart, and even Lotze as well as various "social philosophers." However much they may have theorized about the use of empirical methods, they are not classified as scientific psychologists if they did not actually use such methods. (2) Also excluded are those natural scientists, principally physiologists, whose experiments can be retrospectively included in psychology but whose identification was clearly with the natural sciences. Psychiatrists are also excluded: at the time in question, they belonged to a medical discipline which was quite inde-

6. Richard Müller-Freienfels, *Die Hauptrichtung der gegenwärtigen Psychologie* (Leipzig: Quelle & Meyer, 1929), pp. 3–6.

pendent of philosophy and thus of psychology. Moreover, their theories were rather self-consciously based on the views of nineteenth-century medical science.[7]

(3) Finally, we must make an operational distinction among three categories of persons: *forerunners, founders,* and *followers.* The first two are distinguished by whether or not they had students who became psychologists. An example of a forerunner would be the scientific dilettante—such as Francis Galton. These men did not consider themselves psychologists, nor were they so identified by their contemporaries. Generally they remained isolated from any specific discipline until historians of the science—which was created by other forces—offered them a posthumous home.

Those who were not themselves the students of psychologists but who trained their own disciples as psychologists are the *founders* of the new discipline of psychology. Their disciples are the *followers.* The latter two classes can be considered psychologists proper. What we have referred to as "discipleship"—the fact of having studied under a man, or having worked under him as a laboratory assistant—is, we believe, an adequate measure of the existence of a consciously self-perpetuating identity, a "movement" or discipline. The use of purely objective criteria in establishing such lines of descent has the disadvantage that we may misjudge the extent of actual influence and identification, but the overall picture should be accurate.

The names to be classified are taken from five histories of psychology, including ones written in each of the countries to be examined.[8] For Germany and the United States, all names between 1800 and 1910 were taken. Beyond the latter date, the numbers of psychologists in these countries become so great that the histories are necessarily selective; moveover, scientific psychology was well into its second and third generations in these countries by this point. For Britain and France, all names between 1800 and 1940 were taken, since the numbers of names involved were much smaller than for either Germany or the United States. Scientific psychology became established in Britain or France considerably later than in the other two countries.[9]

7. Gregory Zilboorg, *A History of Medical Psychology* (New York: Norton, 1941), pp. 400, 411–12, 434–435, 441. Breuer and Freud were developing a psychological psychiatry at the end of the nineteenth century, but there was no contact (except of the most negative kind) between Freudianism and German academic psychology for many decades thereafter.

8. Germany: Müller-Freienfels, op. cit.; France: Fernand-Lucien Mueller, *Historie de la psychologie* (Paris: Payot, 1960); Britain: John C. Flugel, *A Hundred Years of Psychology,* 2nd ed. (London: Duckworth, 1951); United States: Edwin G. Boring, *A History of Experimental Psychology,* 2nd ed. (New York: Appleton-Century-Crofts, 1950); Robert I. Watson, *The Great Psychologists* (Philadelphia: Lippincott, 1963). Russia has not been treated in this analysis. The number of its contributions to psychological literature until recent years has been very small; its great innovators, Sechenov, Pavlov, and Bekhterev, were all physiologists and would therefore have been excluded from the population of psychologists. They provide good examples of persons whose work could be integrated into scientific psychology only because subsequent developments elsewhere created such a discipline.

9. Information about biographies and careers has been drawn from the five histories of psychology cited above (especially Boring) and from Mollie D. Boring and Edwin G. Boring, "Mas-

Results

Figures 1-4 show the population of scientific psychologists for each country in the form of genealogical charts.[10] A great many names of physiologists and philosophers had to be excluded from the histories of German psychology, among them many of the most eminent men in those fields in the nineteenth century. In Germany our population includes 32 names, 5 of which have no predecessors on the chart (fig. 1). Two names do not appear in the figure. Gustav Fechner has all of the characteristics of an innovator save one: he gave rise to no personal school of followers, although, as will be seen, he influenced some of the founders. On balance, he was probably more of a forerunner than a founder, as one cannot say that his innovation of psychophysics would have been developed into a discipline of experimental psychology if an institutionally based movement had not been founded subsequently.[11] Karl Groos appears rather late to be an indigenous developer, having habilitated in 1889, nine years after Ebbinghaus, who was the last of the self-starters. In any case, he cannot be considered a founder, as he gave rise to no following. This brings us down to 5 men who can be regarded as the founders of scientific psychology in Germany: Wilhelm Wundt, Franz Brentano, G. E. Müller, Carl Stumpf, and Hermann Ebbinghaus.

In Britain, the biologists C. Lloyd Morgan and George Romanes were excluded, as well as the statistician Karl Pearson. Francis Galton, who instigated psychological testing in Britain but whose scientific interests extended from geographical exploration to chemistry, photography, and statistics and who left no school of psychologists to carry on is also omitted. This leaves 9 names in British psychology, virtually all of whom go back to the German inno-

---

ters and Pupils among American Psychologists," *American Journal of Psychology*, 61 (1948), pp. 527–34; Carl Murchison (ed.), *A History of Psychology in Autobiography*, vols. 1–4 (Worcester, Mass.: Clark University Press, 1930–1952); Carl Murchison (ed.), *Psychological Register*, vols. 2 and 3 (Worcester, Mass.: Clark University Press, 1929–1933); *Minerva: Jahrbuch der Gelehrten Welt* (Leipzig: 1892–). "Germany" is taken to include Austria and the German-speaking universities of Switzerland and Central Europe; "France" includes French-speaking Switzerland and Belgium.

10. Clearly, those charts do not represent the total population of such psychologists for this period, and men may appear to have no psychological followers only because they are not listed in the texts from which the names are drawn. Nevertheless, we feel justified in using this form of measurement of the rise of a discipline, because the visibility of the men who form such a movement is an important factor in its existence.

11. Fechner was a retired physicist who devoted many years to writing pantheistic, anti-materialistic philosophical works. His writings met with little success, due to the reaction against Idealism that had developed by the mid-nineteenth century. In 1850, he took up physiologist E. H. Weber's experiments on touch and muscle sense, in an attempt to establish mathematical laws of perception. This research, however, was an integral part of Fechner's pantheistic system; the laws of psychophysics were intended to give a demonstrable proof to his belief that mind and matter were aspects of the same thing, and he went on to propose an explanation of the entire physical world as composed of souls related to each other by material bodies. Cf. Robert I. Watson, *The Great Psychologists* (Philadelphia: Lippincott, 1963), p. 215, and E. G. Boring, "Fechner: Inadvertent Founder of Psychophysics," in E. G. Boring, *History, Psychology and Science: Selected Papers* (New York: Wiley, 1963), pp. 126–31.

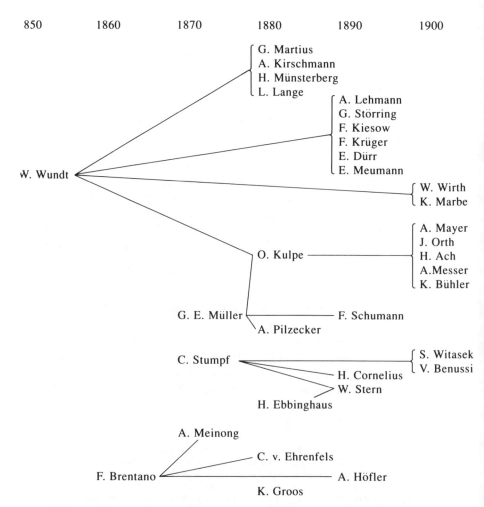

Fig. 1.   *Founders and Followers among German Experimental Psychologists, by Decade of Habilitation, 1850–1909*

vators, Wundt and Müller (fig. 2). The exceptions are G. H. Thomson who is not shown in the figure, who took his degree at Strassburg (a German university at the time) in 1906; and W. H. R. Rivers, who studied with Ewald Hering, a physiologist closely identified with the "new psychology" in Germany. But by the 1890s, one could hardly study in Germany without becoming aware of the new developments, and Rivers cannot be called an originator of experimental methods in the field of psychology.

In France, the names of numerous psychiatrists and some physiologists and biologists were excluded, leaving 10 names (fig. 3). Two men comprising the

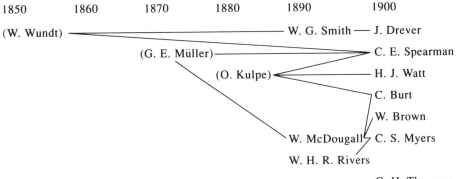

Fig. 2. *Founders and Followers among British Experimental Psychologists, by Decade of Highest Degree, 1850–1909*

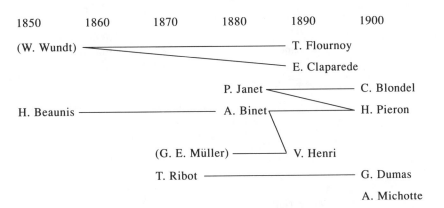

Fig. 3. *Founders and Followers among French Experimental Psychologists, by Decade of Highest Degree, 1850–1909*

Swiss school can be traced back to Wundt; one—Victor Henri—worked with Müller, although he had previously worked with Alfred Binet. The self-starters appear to be Théodule-Armand Ribot, Henri Beaunis, Pierre Janet. Ribot cannot be considered a major innovator, as he made his reputation by publicizing German psychology and was given the first chair of Experimental Psychology in France in 1889 as a result; he remained by and large a speculative philosopher. Beaunis was a physiologist who set up the first psychological laboratory in France in the same year; again, it is difficult to assign Beaunis a role as an independent innovator since a rash of laboratory foundings had already been going on in Germany and the United States for a decade. Janet was an M.D. who succeeded to Ribot's chair in 1902 at the Collège de France; he

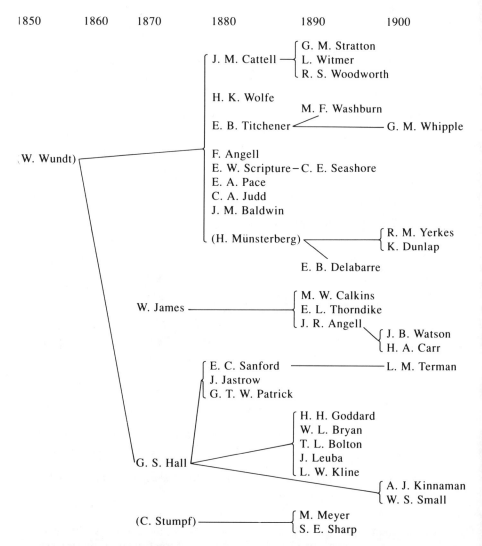

1850   1860   1870   1880   1890   1900

J. M. Cattell — G. M. Stratton / L. Witmer / R. S. Woodworth

H. K. Wolfe

E. B. Titchener — M. F. Washburn — G. M. Whipple

W. Wundt) — F. Angell / E. W. Scripture — C. E. Seashore / E. A. Pace / C. A. Judd / J. M. Baldwin

(H. Münsterberg) — R. M. Yerkes / K. Dunlap

E. B. Delabarre

W. James — M. W. Calkins / E. L. Thorndike / J. R. Angell — J. B. Watson / H. A. Carr

E. C. Sanford — L. M. Terman / J. Jastrow / G. T. W. Patrick

G. S. Hall — H. H. Goddard / W. L. Bryan / T. L. Bolton / J. Leuba / L. W. Kline — A. J. Kinnaman / W. S. Small

(C. Stumpf) — M. Meyer / S. E. Sharp

Fig. 4. *Founders and Followers among American Experimental Psychologists, by Decade of Highest Degree, 1850–1909*

was primarily a psychiatrist, however, and maintained a private practice throughout his career.

In France, then, there appear to be a number of figures without direct antecedents among the German psychologists. Some of them were obviously influenced by the Germans, others had ideas of their own. Had ideas been enough, the French school might have become an effective rival to the German school. But the French development differs from the German in that there was no continuity in France. Ribot and Beaunis each had but one important follower, and Janet had two. This relative lack of descent resulted from a lack of interest in creating new roles for the new ideas. As will be shown later, those working in the new field were content to remain philosophers, psychiatrists, or broad-gauged scientific intellectuals, often interested in finding a scientific solution to some practical problem, like Binet. They did not attempt, therefore, to create a coherent and systematic "paradigm" and to transmit it to the next generation.[12]

Finally, in the United States virtually all excluded figures were speculative philosophers, among them George T. Ladd and John Dewey. Very few American physiologists or other natural scientists appeared in the histories. The remaining 37 figures, presented in figure 4, were overwhelmingly influenced by the German innovators, particularly Wundt. Only one name lacks an antecedent: William James, who began as a physiologist and set up a small demonstration laboratory at Harvard in 1875 which he later claimed was the first psychological laboratory in the world. He became Professor of Philosophy at Harvard in 1885 and had his title changed to Professor of Psychology only in 1889. James is the closest America comes to an indigenous development in psychology, but his work was largely an exposition of European ideas and discoveries (he had visited Germany in 1869, while preparing to teach physiology); he himself became increasingly interested in philosophy during the time that experimental psychology was developing in America. (All of James's major philosophical works date from 1897, when his title was changed back to Professor of Philosophy.) The first generation of experimentalists were almost entirely students of Wundt, including G. Stanley Hall, who did not take his degree with Wundt. Hall in 1881 set up the first functioning psychological laboratory in the United States at Johns Hopkins after returning from a visit with the German psychologists, and the lines to succeeding generations can be

12. Cf. Thomas S. Kuhn, *The Structure of Scientific Revolutions* (Chicago: University of Chicago Press, 1962), for a discussion of how sciences are able to make cumulative advances because they are integrated around a particular "paradigm" or model of scientific reality, with its implied methodology and research directions. Of course, it can be argued that psychology even today still lacks overwhelming consensus around a central, reality-defining theory of the sort that Kuhn means by a "paradigm" and that the term should be used only in such fields as physics which do have such a theory. We have used the term here more broadly, to refer to the necessity of a new discipline to have at least minimal consensus on the boundaries of the subject matter upon which its practitioners will focus their attention and on an acceptable range of research methods.

clearly traced. Without any important contributions from American philosophers or natural scientists, experimental psychology suddenly sprang up in the United States, transplanted from Germany.

Germany, then, is where the crucial conditions for the innovation of scientific psychology are to be sought. Ideas which could have given rise to a cumulative tradition could be found outside of Germany. In fact, toward the end of the nineteenth century, France nearly rivaled Germany as a center for such ideas. But as shown in table 2, French production declined rapidly after a momentary peak around 1900, while German, American, and, to a much lesser extent, British work continued to grow. Figures 1-4 indicate that only in Germany had there developed an autonomous network for the regular transmission and reception of the new ideas. Subsequently the United States and later Britain linked up with this network, and the United States eventually became its center. France only partially linked up with it, and it did not develop a network of its own. In the absence of such a network, innovations remained isolated events; only the existence of networks could make them into a cumulative process.[13]

We shall not here follow the entire story of the creation of communication networks and their diffusion from country to country but shall confine ourselves to the original establishment of the German network. For this purpose, all the other countries will be treated as negative instances, with Germany as the sole positive case. The question to be answered is: Why did an effective network for the communication of these new ideas develop only in Germany?

Role-hybridization

The answer is that the conditions for the establishment of a new professional role variety, committed to the new field, existed only in Germany. Ideas which are not cultivated by people whose regular jobs are to cultivate them are like souls hovering in a mythological limbo before entering a body. They can light upon the dreams or the imagination of one person here and another one there, of someone who lives today or of someone else who will be born in a thousand years. If, however, ideas become the end-products of scientific roles, they can be likened to genes which are transmitted from generation to generation through a reliable and natural process; under normal conditions, they will not only survive but increase.

13. A further indication of the weakness of the French system is the relatively greater mortality of French psychological journals. Between 1850 and 1950, 70 percent of the psychological journals begun in France had ceased, as compared to 50 percent for the United States, 51 percent for Germany (before 1934, excluding the many stoppages during the Nazi era), and 21 percent for Britain. Cf. Robert S. Daniel and Chauncey M. Louttit, *Professional Problems in Psychology* (New York: Prentice-Hall, 1953), pp. 25, 358–74.

There are several ways in which new scientific role varieties arise. The present instance is a case of role-hybridization: the individual moving from one role to another, such as from one profession or academic field to another, may be placed at least momentarily in a position of role conflict.[14] This conflict can be resolved by giving up the attitudes and behaviors appropriate to the old role and adopting those of the new role; in this case, identification with the old reference group must be withdrawn. However, the individual may be unwilling to give up his identification with his old reference group, as it may carry higher status (intellectual as well as perhaps social) than his new group. In this case, he may attempt to resolve the conflict by innovating, that is, fitting the methods and techniques of the old role to the materials of the new one, with the deliberate purpose of creating a new role.

One example of a scientific role created by this process is psychoanalysis, which was created by a man who moved from the prestigious profession of scientific research to the relatively lower status occupation of German medical practice; Freud attempted to maintain his status by trying to raise medical practice into a form of scientific research and as a result created psychoanalysis. Similarly, Pasteur gave rise to bacteriology by maintaining his theoretical perspectives after moving into research on wine fermentation and elaborated his discovery into a new specialty.

Mobility of scholars from one field to another will occur when the chances of success (i.e., getting recognition, gaining a full chair at a relatively early age, making an outstanding contribution) in one discipline are poor, often as a result of overcrowding in a field in which the number of positions is stable. In such cases, many scholars will be likely to move into any related field in which the conditions of competition are better. In some cases, this will mean that they move into a field with a standing relatively lower than their original field.[15] This creates the conditions for role conflict. Of course, not everyone placed in such a position will choose to or be able to innovate a new role, nor

14. Joseph Ben-David, "Roles and Innovations in Medicine," *American Journal of Sociology*, 65 (1960), pp. 557–68 [this volume, chap. 1]. John T. Gullahorn and Jeanne E. Gullahorn, "Role Conflict and Its Resolution," *Sociological Quarterly*, 4 (1963), pp. 32–48, have distinguished between two kinds of role conflict: "status-produced role conflict," in which the occupant of a single status position is subjected to conflicting expectations by the different persons with whom he deals, and "contingent role conflict," in which the conflicts arise from the simultaneous occupancy of two statuses. Most of the discussions in the literature have dealt with the first variety, e.g., Robert K. Merton, "The Role-Set: Problems in Sociological Theory," *British Journal of Sociology*, 8 (1957), pp. 106–20; and Neal Gross, Ward S. Mason, and Alexander W. MacEachern, *Explorations in Role Analysis* (New York: Wiley & Sons, 1958). We are distinguishing a third kind of role conflict, resulting from mobility rather than from the "static" situations indicated above. See Peter M. Blau, "Social Mobility and Interpersonal Relations," *American Sociological Review*, 21 (1956), pp. 290–95. For a discussion of why scientists would tend to identify with a traditional discipline rather than with an emerging specialty of lower prestige, see Warren O. Hagstrom, *The Scientific Community* (New York: Basic Books, 1965), pp. 53, 209.

15. For the scholar or scientist, this is not simply a matter of social status or prestige but rather of the effectiveness or ability of the field to make progress as judged by its own intellectual

is it possible to predict exactly which individuals will do so. It is possible, however, to say that the chances of such a major innovation occurring in a discipline into which there is mobility from a higher-status discipline are considerably greater than in a discipline into which there is no such mobility, or which stands higher in status than the discipline from which mobility takes place. For example, if physiology has higher standing in an academic system than philosophy, but competitive conditions are better in the latter than in the former, one might expect a role-hybridization in which physiological methods will be applied to the material of philosophy (at their most adjacent point, psychology) in order to differentiate the innovator from the more traditional practitioners of the less-respected discipline. This would not be expected if philosophy's status were equal or higher, or if the competitive conditions in philosophy were equal or worse than those in physiology.

Moreover, since a major academic innovation has a chance of success only if it can attract a sizable following, it is usually not enough (except perhaps in cases of striking utility, such as bacteriology) that an individual innovator be placed in a situation of role conflict. The conditions have to be general so as to ensure a widespread response to the innovation. The motivation of the man who merely joins such a movement is quite similar to that of the man who begins it—moving into a discipline of lower standing than his old one, he is likely to welcome the opportunity to raise his status through adopting the innovation. Even more important, the existence of such relationships between disciplines may have a vicarious effect upon individuals within the system who do not personally move from the high-status discipline to the low-status discipline. For example, the younger men in the low-status field may attempt to upgrade themselves by borrowing the methods of a high-status field. The simplest way to upgrade themselves would be to move to the other field, but .they are restrained from doing this by the differences in competitive conditions. If they do not make the innovation themselves, they may be very receptive to an innovation by a migrating scientist. Even young scholars who have not yet chosen a field, knowing the relative prestige and conditions of competition in the several fields, will be attracted to the new hybridized role.

It is important to distinguish role-hybridization from what might be termed "idea-hybridization," the combination of ideas taken from different fields into a new intellectual synthesis. The latter does not attempt to bring about a new academic or professional role, nor does it generally give rise to a coherent and sustained movement with a permanent tradition.

Antecedents of modern psychology as far back as Descartes had discussed psychological functioning in a physiological perspective but without giving

---

standards. Cf. Hagstrom, op. cit., pp. 9–104, for a theoretical exposition of science as a form of social organization in which competition for recognition by the colleague group is a prime mechanism of control; see also pp. 208–20 for a general discussion of disciplinary differentiation.

rise to any movement to extend these ideas as other sciences were doing with their respective materials. Similar connections were made by the British associationists, from John Locke and David Hartley up to Alexander Bain, James Ward, and James Sully at the end of the nineteenth century, but without giving any indication that a continuous scientific tradition would ever result from these theories. In Germany, Herbart and Lotze certainly fall into this category, along with Fechner, who introduced experimental methods into philosophical psychology in the 1850s with his psychophysics, but who did not thereby create any movement to reform the role of the psychologist-philosopher. Galton in England, and in France such men as Ribot, Beaunis, and Binet, must be considered more "idea-hybrids" than "role-hybrids"; rather than creating a new role, they merely added another facet to the established role of the multipurpose intellectual such as had existed in these countries since the seventeenth century. Finally, William James in the United States would fall into the category of an "idea-hybrid," particularly since he finally decided on the traditional role of philosopher rather than the new role of scientific psychologist.

The Positive Case

In the German universities of the nineteenth century, physiology was a highly productive, expanding science. One of its greatest periods of productivity took place between 1850 and 1870, when most of the chairs of physiology were first split off from anatomy. Fifteen chairs were created between 1850 and 1864. After that date, the field rapidly reached a limit of approximately one chair per university in a system comprising 19 universities before 1870 and 20 after 1870.[16] Table 4 shows that physiology, with approximately half as many chairs as philosophy, added only two full chairs from 1873 to 1910, whereas philosophy, already the largest field in the universities, added eight. The number of Extraordinary Professors and Privatdozents in physiology grew much more rapidly during this period than in philosophy. But these were poorly paid and largely honorific positions; their number indicates something of the competitive pressures in these fields for the truly desirable positions, the full professorships. Advancement was particularly difficult in physiology, since most of its full chairs, having been created at about the same time, were filled with men of about the same age who held them for decades.[17] Table 5 shows that in the 1850s, the chances of becoming a full professor were

16. Awraham Zloczower, *Career Opportunities and the Growth of Scientific Discovery in Nineteenth-Century Germany with Special Reference to Physiology,* unpublished M.A. thesis, Department of Sociology, Hebrew University, 1960. [Now published by Arno Press, New York, 1981.]
17. Ibid.

Table 4.   Number of Academic Positions in Philosophy and Physiology in the German University System, 1864–1938

Field and Academic Position	1864	1873	1880	1890	1900	1910	1920	1931	1938
Philosophy									
Ordinary Professor	36	40	43	44	42	48	56	56	36
Extraordinary Professor	21	16	12	14	14	23	30	51	34
Dozents	23	20	18	19	25	43	45	32	21
Total number of university positions	81	79	75	81	85	117	140	163	117
Physiology									
Ordinary Professor	15	19	20	20	20	21	24	27	21
Extraordinary Professor	3	3	4	6	9	12	15	24	18
Dozents	9	1	2	7	20	27	22	23	15
Total number of university positions	27	23	27	33	49	61	66	80	67

Source: Christian von Ferber, *Die Entwicklung des Lehrkörpers der deutschen Universitäten und Hochschulen, 1864–1954*, vol. 3 in Helmuth Plessner (ed.), *Untersuchungen sur Lage der deutschen Hochschullehrer* (Göttingen: Van den Hoeck, 1953–1956), pp. 204, 207.

Note: In the German university system, the rank of Ordinary Professor is equivalent to Full Professor and Extraordinary Professor to Associate Professor. Dozents are private lecturers.

[Note: Some misprints have been rectified on the basis of the source material; the columns do not always add up because the total number of university positions in each discipline includes categories of teaching positions not shown in the table (professors emeritus, visiting lecturers, etc.). Ed.]

better for those habilitating in the medical sciences than in the philosophical disciplines. In the next decade, however, the situation was reversed and the relative competitive situation within the medical sciences steadily worsened through the rest of the century. Clearly, from about 1860 on, philosophy offered much more favorable competitive conditions that did physiology. The first condition for the occurrence of role-hybridization was thus present.

The second condition was provided by the trend of the prestige conflict that raged between philosophy and the natural sciences throughout the nineteenth century in Germany. Before 1830, the great systems of Idealism claimed for philosophy the position of a super-science, deriving by speculation all that might be painstakingly discovered by empirical methods. But these pretensions were shattered by the rapidly expanding natural sciences, led first by the chemists, then by the physiologists. Paulsen notes the contempt in which speculative philosophy came to be held after the rise of the sciences in the 1830s, a contempt which was receding only at the end of the century.[18] Her-

18. Friedrich Paulsen, *The German Universities and University Study* (New York: Longmans Green, 1906).

Table 5.   *Highest Rank Reached by Scholars in the German University System Who Habilitated in the Medical Faculty and Philosophical Faculty (Natural Sciences Excluded), 1850–1909*

Year and Faculty	Rank				Percent remaining dozents
	Ordinary Professors	Extra-ordinary Professors	Privat-dozents	Total	
1850–59					
Medicine	57	19	15	91	16.5
Philosophy	55	13	15	83	18.1
1860–69					
Medicine	72	44	37	153	24.2
Philosophy	68	24	22	114	19.3
1870–79					
Medicine	94	74	53	221	24.0
Philosophy	138	24	26	188	13.8
1880–89					
Medicine	89	59	64	212	30.2
Philosophy	118	25	36	179	20.1
1890–99					
Medicine	131	57	138	326	42.3
Philosophy	162	33	66	261	25.3
1900–09					
Medicine	184	48	249	481	51.8
Philosophy	142	25	75	242	31.0

Source: von Ferber, op. cit., p. 81.

[Note: One misprint has been rectified on the basis of the source material; the right column indicates the percentage of habilitations by "inofficial teaching staff" (notably dozents) in relation to the total number of habilitations. Ed.]

mann von Helmholtz, the physicist and physiologist, was the leading propagandist for the scientific attack on philosophical speculation; in his student days in 1845 in Berlin, he banded together with a group of young scientists (including Emil Du Bois-Reymond, Ernst Brücke, and Carl Ludwig), who swore to uphold the principle: "No other forces than common physical chemical ones are active in the organism." [19] By the 1860s, the scientists were near to extinguishing the academic reputation of philosophy and its "super-science" pretensions. [20]

Wundt began his career as a physiologist in 1857, at the height of the com-

19. Edwin G. Boring, op. cit., p. 708.
20. G. Stanley Hall, *Founders of Modern Psychology* (New York: Appleton, 1912), p. 138.

petition for the new chairs being created in physiology. He remained a Dozent for 17 years, however, and after being passed over for the chair of physiology at Heidelberg in 1871, made the transition to philosophy.[21] This transition was made in 1874 with the chair at the University of Zurich, which served as something of a "waiting-room" for appointments to one of the great universities in Germany proper. On the strength of his *Physiological Psychology* in that year, he won a first-class chair of philosophy at Leipzig in 1875.

Before Wundt began to take philosophy as a second reference group, he was doing the same kind of things that Helmholtz, Hering, F. C. Donders, and many other physiologists were doing—experimenting on the functions of the sense organs and the nervous system and occasionally pointing out that their work made speculative philosophy a superfluous anachronism. Wundt had once been an assistant to Helmholtz, the leader of the antiphilosophical movement; Wundt's move into philosophy must have been an acute identity crisis for him, which could be resolved only by innovating a new philosophical method.[22] Using Fechner's empirical methods of studying perception, Wundt proposed to build metaphysics on a solid basis, thus making philosophy a science.[23] To preserve his scientific status, he was forced not only to carry out a revolution in philosophy by replacing logical speculation with empirical research but also to widely advertise the fact that he was in a different kind of enterprise than the traditional philosophers.

Brentano, Stumpf, Müller, and Ebbinghaus were all philosophers who became interested in using empirical methods in their field. Apparently, they were aware of the onslaught physiology was making into the territory of philosophy; rather than accept its deteriorating position, they in effect "went over to the enemy." It is known that Stumpf met Fechner and E. H. Weber in his days as a Dozent;[24] Müller also corresponded with Fechner;[25] and Ebbinghaus apparently decided to reenter the academic world after accidentally encountering a copy of Fechner's *Elements*.[26] Brentano, although he makes reference to Helmholtz, Fechner, and Wundt in his first major work, *Psychology from an Empirical Standpoint* (1874), was considerably less influenced by them than were the others. He also remained the least experimental of this group of founders. Wundt is undoubtedly the central figure. He had the largest following, and he articulated the ideology of the "philosophical revolution" most clearly. The others, originally philosophers, put the position less strongly and had smaller personal followings. Yet they were role-hybrids to some extent, as clearly appears when one compares them with Fechner. The latter had the de-

21. Edwin G. Boring, op. cit., p. 319.
22. Helmholtz may well have seen it as a kind of treason; there are reports that it was Helmholtz's antagonism to his former assistant that blocked the appointment of the latter to Berlin in 1894. Cf. ibid., p. 389.
23. Hall, op. cit., pp. 323–326.   24. Edwin G. Boring, op. cit., p. 363.
25. Ibid., p. 374.   26. Ibid., p. 387.

cisive idea but was content to write about it and submit it to what Derek de Solla Price calls "the general archives of science." The philosophers, however, influenced by the example of Wundt, used it for the creation of a new role variety.

The Negative Cases

In France, there was no innovation of using experimental methods in philosophy. There was heavy competition in the French academic system for positions in all the natural sciences; the physiologists were fairly hard-pressed, having fewer than one chair per university even at the turn of the century (table 6). The number of available positions in philosophy was a little better. However, the relative situation was nothing like in Germany, where physiology had been filling up for several decades, whereas in France it was still expanding into all of the universities for the first time.

Besides, in France a central intellectual elite existed whose status was dependent on a diffuse evaluation of excellence rather than on regular university appointments and specialized attainment.[27] The lines of demarcation between disciplines were too amorphous to mean anything for a man like Binet, who could afford to dabble in law, entomology, psychiatry, experimental psychology, and educational testing. He could expect that some kind of facilities would be created for his particular needs and that his achievements would be recognized without the need for justifying them in the terms of a specific academic discipline.

Existing positions allowed a broad range of possible activities for their holders; Lucien Levy-Bruhl, the anthropologist, for example, held a chair of philosophy; Emile Durkheim, the sociologist, held a chair of education, and the few chairs of experimental psychology were likely to be turned over to men who were primarily psychiatrists such as Pierre Janet or Charles Blondel. The Collège de France, the most prestigious institution in France, rewarded unique individual accomplishments but did not provide much opportunity for those following an established career, nor did it allow the training of "disciples," since its positions were for research rather than teaching. Ribot, by proselytizing German psychology, could have a new chair in Experimental Psychology established for himself at the Collège de France, but this personal recognition probably prevented him from developing a school of followers. The purely individual basis of recognition is indicated by the fact that Henri Pieron could have a new chair created for himself at the Collège de France (in

27. Joseph Ben-David and Awraham Zloczower, "Universities and Academic Systems in Modern Societies," *European Journal of Sociology* 3 (1962), pp. 45–85 [this volume, chap. 6].

Table 6.   Number of Academic Positions in Philosophy and Physiology in the French University System, 1892–1923

| | Philosophy | | Physiology | | |
Year	Full chairs	Total	Full chairs	Total	Number of universities [a]
1892	17	27	10	17	15
1900	20	28	12	20	15
1910	22	30	14	27	15
1923	22	*	17	*	16

Source: *Minerva, Jahrbuch der Gelehrten Welt* 2 (1892), 10 (1900), 20 (1910), 27 (1923).
[a] Includes Collège de France.
*Figures on positions below the level of full professor are not available for 1923.

the Physiology of Sensation) because the Professor of Archaeology died without a suitably eminent successor.[28]

Unlike in the German system, disciplines were not differentiated sharply enough to create serious role conflicts among men with ideas. The elite comprised a single reference group of relatively nonspecialized intellectuals and "philosophers" in the old eighteenth-century tradition, and prestige adhered to the individual, not to the discipline. The French system, in short, was suited to picking up intellectual innovations by specific individuals but was not at all suited for giving rise to movements attempting to create a new discipline.

The same conditions which prevented the development of a reference group conflict in France existed to an even greater extent in Britain. The relative number of chairs in philosophy and physiology was similar to that in France (table 7). Both were about one per university, with chairs in philosophy in a slight lead over those in physiology but with the latter expanding. The necessity of gaining an academic position was even less important than in France. In the latter country, one eventually had to obtain some kind of official position. In England, even this was unnecessary.

Before 1832, there were only two universities in all England and four in Scotland, and they were little more than an upper-class intellectual backwater. Four provincial universities were founded throughout the remainder of the century and another half dozen in the first decade of the twentieth century. Under the threat of being left behind by these technologically minded, "lower-class" universities, Oxford and Cambridge began to take in the new

28. Henri Pieron, "Autobiography," in Carl Murchison (ed.), *A History of Psychology in Autobiography*, vol. 4 (Worcester, Mass.: Clark University Press, 1952).

Table 7.   Number of Academic Positions in Philosophy and Physiology in the British University System, 1892–1923

	Philosophy		Physiology		
Year	Full chairs	Total	Full chairs	Total	Number of universities
1892	13	15	9	20	10
1900	16	20	12	21	11
1910	19	38	14	29	16
1923	22	*	16	*	16

Source: *Minerva, Jahrbuch der Gelehrten Welt* 2 (1892), 10 (1900), 20 (1910), 27 (1923).
*Figures on positions below the level of full professor are not available for 1923.

sciences and in the process to recover intellectual as well as merely social preeminence.[29]

This process was still going on in the late nineteenth century; both philosophy and physiology were still centered to a considerable extent outside of the British universities.[30] From the point of view of the physiologist fighting for entrance into the conservative strongholds, the academic philosophy taught there must have seemed a somewhat outdated and unduly privileged field. But the mobility factor was missing; it was still possible to attain the highest prestige in philosophy or in physiology outside of the universities. This non-university tradition provided a safety valve which let off the pressure which might have led to the innovation of a new psychology.

In the United States as well, an indigenous innovation of experimental psychology failed to appear; however, a large and successful movement of followers of the German psychology did spring up in the 1880s, a full decade or two before such movements (on a smaller scale) appeared in France and Britain. Before this period, there had been a very large number of small colleges in the country.[31] In these colleges, psychology was a branch of philosophy of the eighteenth-century Scottish variety, with heavily religious overtones. It was taught by the college presidents, 90 percent of whom were clergymen.[32]

29. Walter H. G. Armytage, *Civic Universities* (London: Ernest Benn, 1955), pp. 178, 206.

30. Both Herbert Spencer and J. S. Mill, for example, held no academic positions. Physiological research was largely carried on by medical practitioners in the independent hospitals. Cf. Abraham Flexner, *Medical Education: A Comparative Study* (New York: Macmillan, 1925).

31. There were 182 colleges in 1861, averaging six faculty members each. Cf. Richard Hofstadter and Walter P. Metzger, *The Development of Academic Freedom in the United States* (New York: Columbia University Press, 1955), pp. 211, 233.

32. That is, the "faculty psychology" of Thomas Reid, Dugald Stewart, and Thomas Brown; for the role of the president, see Hofstadter and Metzger, op. cit., p. 297.

Philosophy occupied the same dominant position as in Germany in the early part of the century, but in other respects the colleges resembled the philosophical faculties (the lower, "undergraduate" section) of the German universities before von Humboldt's reforms in 1810. Learning was by rote, salaries were low, and there were no facilities for research. Teaching positions were merely sinecures for unsuccessful clergymen.[33] Under these conditions, there could be no movements to innovate new disciplines: there were no positions worth competing for, the institutions were too small for specialization, and research was not a function of the academic community at all. A vigorous movement in experimental psychology, clearly derivative of the German movements, grew up only after the foundings of the first graduate schools beginning in 1876.

Summary

The innovation of experimental psychology was brought about by the mechanism of role-hybridization. Excluding the independently originated practical traditions in Britain and France which only later became attached to the movement in experimental psychology, this innovation took place only in Germany. Three factors were required: (a) an academic rather than an amateur role for both philosophers and physiologists; (b) a better competitive situation in philosophy than in physiology, encouraging the mobility of men and methods into philosophy; (c) an academic standing of philosophy below that of physiology, requiring the physiologist to maintain his scientific standing by applying his empirical methods to the materials of philosophy.

Germany had all three factors. France had a measure of the first. All the persons involved eventually acquired full-time scientific appointments, but their careers had often started outside the academic framework, and their official positions were little standardized. The second factor was present to an insignificant degree, and the latter not at all, as prestige was attached to the individual and the formal honors he received rather than to the discipline. Britain was similar to France concerning the last two factors, and the first was present to an even more limited extent than in France, since the amateur pattern still prevailed widely among philosophers and physiologists. The United States before 1880 lacked even the rudiments of an academic system in which these factors could operate.

This explains why the take-off occurred in Germany. The reason France never linked up with the mainstream of the development while the United States, and eventually Britain, did, remains to be investigated.

33. Bernard Berelson, *Graduate Education in the United States* (New York: McGraw-Hill, 1960), p. 14.

Socialization and Career Patterns as Determinants of Productivity of Medical Researchers * 3

Introduction

Research has been part of the medical tradition since the days of Hippocrates. But the rapid accumulation of medical knowledge had only begun in the middle of the last century when research became a specialty in its own right. Still, the training of the medical doctor has remained the same for all types of specialty, and in its traditions and values it is still mainly clinically oriented. Medical schools have made very great efforts to raise their scientific standards in teaching as well as in research, yet they train first and foremost practitioners, although a significant proportion of students are expected to become researchers. Gradually, an elaborate system of socialization into the research role has been developed and grafted on the basic professional training. But even the trained researcher usually works in a hospital, the main job of which is to cure. Consequently, the occupational role of the clinical researcher contains both the elements of practice and of scientific work. These two components of the role are governed by different sets of norms and values and link the doctor to two different systems of professional communication. This results in an inner conflict within the role image of the clinical researcher and a considerable strain in the role pattern. Yet, this role pattern seems to be more efficient than the role patterns in other fields of applied science, in which production and research are separated. On the other hand, the socialization and role patterns in clinical research appear cumbersome and wasteful compared

*With Lydia Aran.
This research has been supported by a grant from the Ford Foundation. Paper presented at the Sixth World Congress of Sociology, Evian, September 4–11, 1966.

to basic sciences in which training, career, and organizational setting of work display continuity of norms and orientations.

The orientation to clinical aim is clearly reflected in the research on the socialization of the physician. So far this has been concerned mainly (a) with the problem of the transition of the student from the exact approach imparted in the study of basic science to the necessarily more flexible approach required in clinical practice;[1] and (b) with the inadequacies of the clinical preparation of the doctor in general.[2] The concern of this paper is the opposite question, namely, to determine to what extent the medical school is an adequate socializing agent and place of work for the medical researcher and to identify those components of the organization of medical work and training which make the development of a medical researcher and his productive work possible.

The study of clinical research in Israel is well suited for this purpose since its origins are recent enough to make possible the reconstruction of the process which led to the rise of clinical research and to distinguish the crucial steps in this process.[3]

More specifically, we shall attempt to show:

(a) that even where scientific training, interest, and facilities had been available for some time, sustained high-level research activity only developed when attainments in research were explicitly established as criteria for a distinct type of medical career;[4]

(b) that in order to become a researcher, the M.D. has to be retrained and that his productivity in research is a function of the timing and the contents of his resocialization. The shorter the period between graduation as an M.D. and postdoctoral training in research, the greater will be the increase in his research production following training; and furthermore the increase will be greater in those cases where the postdoctoral training takes place in a basic research unit than in the cases where it takes place in a clinical research setting;

(c) that an important aspect of the resocialization consists of linking the beginning researcher into a network of scientific communication, thus inducing him into an international scientific community and exempting him to some

1. Cf. R. C. Fox, "Training for Uncertainty," in R. K. Merton, G. G. Reader, and P. Kendall, *The Student Physician* (Cambridge: Harvard University Press, 1957), pp. 207–41; Howard S. Becker, e.a., *Boys in White, Student Culture in Medical School* (Chicago: University of Chicago Press, 1961).

2. S. W. Bloom, "The Sociology of Medical Education: Some Comments on the State of a Field," *The Milbank Memorial Fund Quarterly* 2 (April 1965); D. Caplovitz, *Student-Faculty Relation in Medical School: A Study of Professional Socialization*, Ph.D. dissertation, Columbia University, 1961.

3. For a general description of the field, see M. Prywes (ed.), *Medical and Biological Research in Israel* (Jerusalem: Hebrew University and Hadassah, 1960).

4. The importance of the conditions of the medical career for the development of research has been emphasized by A. Flexner, *Medical Education in Europe*, Carnegie Foundation for the Advancement of Teaching, Bulletin no. 6, 1912.

extent from the standards and norms of the professional community of local medical practitioners.

The first hypothesis refers to a specific historic event, the establishment of the first medical school in Israel in 1949, and it will be investigated by a comparison of the productivity of the medical researchers at two points of time. The other two hypotheses refer to the present state of medical research in Israel and will be investigated through comparisons of individual researchers at a single point of time.

Procedure and Sample

Our research included (a) a study of the historical development, structure, and organization of medical research in Israel based mainly on documentary sources; (b) personal interviews based on a standard questionnaire of open-ended questions about the socialization, career, present work, and professional contacts of the interviewee; and (c) a count and analysis of the publications of the subjects.

The sample consisted of all the researchers in internal medicine in Israel. This field was chosen because a relatively high proportion of its practitioners are engaged in research while at the same time it remains an eminently clinical specialty. It is therefore a suitable field for the study of the relationship between research on the one hand and clinical practice on the other.

The population was identified with the aid of the associate dean of the Hebrew University-Hadassah Medical School and of the heads of departments of hospitals who were asked to name internal medical specialists engaged in research in their own and other hospitals. The original list consisted of 50 persons. After the elimination of those persons who had not produced published work, who were not known or accepted as researchers beyond their own departments, or who had done most of their work before their immigration to Israel and/or before the period with which we are concerned, we arrived at a list of 32 specialists in internal medicine engaged in research, who had published research papers and were known to each other and mutually accepted as researchers.

The Effect of the Establishment of Research as a Major Component of the Medical Career

Before World War I, scarcity of physicians and lack of facilities and organization were responsible for the neglect of the scientific aspect of medicine.

Since the end of the war, Palestine has had a high ratio of doctors to population and since the late 1920s also an effective network of medical services. However, the research potential of the existing organization was not activated because of the dominance of interest in the social aspects of medical work. With enormous problems of public health, particularly endemic diseases and infant mortality, research was considered a luxury. Thus the innovating energy of *Hadassah*, the pioneer medical organization in Palestine, had been channeled into the search for new ways of supplying health services.

The necessary conditions for the emergence of medical research had been created gradually in the course of the 1930s and were definitely present in Palestine by 1940.[5]

(a) The immigration from Central Europe following the rise and expansion of Nazi power brought to Palestine a large number of well-trained physicians, quite a few of whom had excellent backgrounds in research.

(b) The Hadassah Hospital—the biggest and most advanced in the country—moved in 1939 to new, modern premises, planned and equipped by overseas experts for research as well as curative work and situated in close proximity to the university, which by then included science and biology departments expanded and reinforced by refugee scientists from Central Europe.

(c) An affiliation agreement was signed between the Hebrew University and the Hadassah Organization in 1939, according to which a prefaculty of medicine was established and preparations for the establishment of the medical school were started.

(d) Kupat Holim (The Sick Fund of the General Federation of Jewish Labor) had greatly expanded its services during the 1930s and had gradually taken over the provision of public curative services in the country. This left for the powerful Hadassah Medical Organization the task of developing medical research.

(e) The situation was ripe for the development of medical research also from the point of view of medical priorities. Social diseases no longer presented a challenge since patterns of preventive medicine and treatment had been evolved by then. There was also an ample supply of doctors and equipment and a reasonable number of hospital beds to take care of the treatment of patients.

The only important difference in the situation between the 1940s and 1950s was the establishment of the medical school. From 1939 until the opening of the medical school in 1949, medical research, though practiced by many of

5. For a survey of conditions in that period, cf. S. Adler, "The Medical Activities," in *The Hebrew University of Jerusalem, 1925—1950* (Jerusalem: Hebrew University, 1950), pp. 135–139; *The Hebrew University of Jerusalem, Its History and Development* (Jerusalem: The Hebrew University, 1948), pp. 69–82; Th. Grushka (ed.), *Health Services in Israel, 1948–1958* (Jerusalem: The Ministry of Health, 1959); *Reports of the Hadassah Medical Organization*, Jerusalem, 1940, 1941, 1945 (mimeo.).

the physicians working for Hadassah and by a few others throughout the country, and encouraged by the hospital authorities, did not become a career.[6] The absence of a medical faculty made it impossible to confer academic status on the researcher, and research achievement could not be recognized through a formal appointment. Thus, while scientific achievement was both possible and greatly honored as a culturally valuable activity, and because it contributed to the objectives of the hospital—the high standard of diagnosis and treatment and, to some extent, teaching—it contributed little to one's career. The legitimacy of research was derived from its importance for the institutional objectives.[7] It was not yet considered an activity to be supported for its own sake, as it was already at that time at the Hebrew University.[8] Thus, research emerged as an important function, but it had not yet become an essential part of any kind of medical role. The pattern was somewhat similar to that which had existed in the British and the American teaching hospitals early in this century.[9]

When the medical school was finally established and instruction started in 1949, the situation changed in favor of research in one respect only. The procedure of academic appointment introduced at the new school was the same as that prevailing at the Hebrew University, which before that time had consisted, except for a small school of agriculture, essentially of a faculty of arts and a faculty of sciences. According to this procedure publications were a necessary condition for academic appointment and promotion at the medical school. The various bodies considering these appointments and promotions applied the same criteria to candidates from all the faculties: first and foremost publications, and then, to a much lesser degree, teaching aptitude, personality, and professional standing.[10] Thus, almost overnight, research became a major component of a university hospital career.

Other conditions for research had improved very slowly and until the mid-

6. Whatever scientific work had been done in Hadassah or elsewhere in Palestine before was of the "patriotic science" or "prescientific" type (see *Hadassah Medical Organization*, op. cit., pp. 65–192). The tone for this type of "local" research, partly based on some mystic faith in "Hebrew Medicine" was set by the Second Aliyah doctors (see Editorial in *Ha-Refuah*, I, no. 6, (1924/25): 5–6). While in Hadassah reorientation toward scientific universalism took place in the 1940s, in some nonuniversity centers this local patriotic bias has survived until recent times.

7. See Haddassah Medical Organization, *Yearly Reports on Activities*, 1940–49. (Mimeo.) Also, unpublished correspondence with Hadassah Organization in the U.S. on Scholarship Program for Research Training, 1946, Archives of the Hadassah Medical Organization, Jerusalem.

8. *The Hebrew University of Jerusalem, Its History and Development*, op. cit.

9. A. Flexner, op. cit.

10. The university bodies considering appointments and promotions are: a Screening Committee appointed by the Standing Committee of the Senate of the University which performs a prima facie examination of the candidate's qualifications, the Professional Committee which considers his qualifications by eliciting opinions from foreign experts on the candidate's publications, and, finally, the Appointment Committee composed of representatives of the Executive Council of the Senate of the University (see *The Hebrew University of Jerusalem* [Jerusalem: Hebrew University, 1963], p. 32).

fifties they had actually been even worse than before 1949.[11] The modern buildings and equipment were lost during the Israel War of Independence of 1948–49, and both the university and the hospital were removed into ill-suited and poorly equipped temporary buildings. The real value of the salary of senior hospital staff was lower in the fifties than in the forties, so that practically all of them were compelled to complement their incomes by private practice.[12] The War, the establishment of the State, and the mass immigration of the years 1948–1951 had created an emergency situation and many of the university hospital physicians were called upon to organize and supervise national medical services and emergency services in transit camps and new immigrant settlements. A considerable proportion of Hadassah's budget and resources was diverted from the development of the university hospital and used for the establishment and running-in of new hospitals in the main immigrant absorption centers.[13] Thus we can assume that the only change that occurred in favor of research in the fifties as compared to the forties was the institutionalization of the role of the medical researcher.

To test our first hypothesis, that, other things being equal, productivity in research should increase following the acceptance of research as a major component of career, we compared the research output in 1941–1952 with that in 1953–1964. The year 1952 was used as the turning point for the purpose of our analysis on the assumption that it should have taken at least three years for the effect of the establishment of the medical school to manifest itself in the number and type of papers produced.

It can be seen from table 1 that not only did the productivity of the researchers in the university hospital double in the period after the establishment of the medical school but that the pattern of research work changed as well. Productivity in work classified as "scientific" grew sixfold, that is, three times as much as the total output per person.

It was the university hospital in Jerusalem that established a career in medical research. Other hospitals—those in the coastal plain—moved in the mid-fifties into the stage in which Hadassah University Hospital had been a dozen years earlier. From the point of view of physical conditions and work load, the conditions for research are still more inferior in these places than they used to be in Hadassah in the forties. From the point of view of social incentives for research, the situation is more favorable there now than it had been in Hadassah in the forties because doctors with research attainments can get aca-

11. For a survey of conditions in that period, see S. Adler, "The Medical Activities," op. cit.; *The Hebrew University, 1948*, Jerusalem, pp. 69–82; Th. Grushka, (ed.), op. cit. and "Reports of the Hadassah Medical Organization," Jerusalem, 1940, 1941, 1945, and 1950–1955 (mimeo.).

12. Cf. the report on the deliberations of the "Goori Committee" on salaries, in the Hebrew daily *Haaretz*, Dec. 18, 1955, p. 2.

13. See n. 11.

Table 1.   Comparison of Research Output Before and After 1953

Research output: Period	Total number of publica-tions	Output per person	Publications in foreign journals[a]			"Scientific"[b] publications			
			No.	Percent of total	Output per person	No.	Percent of total	Output per person	Number of re-searchers
1941–1952	199	17	105	53	9	26	12.5	2	12
1953–1964	1107	35	709	64	23	402	36	13	32
Increase (percent)	456	105	575	..	133	1450	..	550	170

[a] Number of publications in foreign journals is considered an index of quality in view of the fact that only papers refused by foreign journals or those considered inferior by the researchers themselves are submitted to local medical journals.

[b] Reporting on work designed to establish general principles; excluding case reports, surveys, descriptions of therapeutic procedures or specific clinical situations.

demic titles such as "clinical lecturer" or "clinical professor" and their departments may become recognized as training centers for interns.[14] Consequently, if our hypothesis is true, the productivity of the researchers in hospitals other than Hadassah during the period 1953–1964 should be lower than that of the Hadassah researchers during the same period.

Comparison of the research output in the two different settings during 1953–1964 is summed up in tables 2 and 3.

Tables 2 and 3 show that in the hospitals which were not directly affected by the establishment of a research career through the opening of the Hebrew University-Hadassah Medical School, the productivity of researchers and especially the proportion of "scientific" work remained much lower.

Table 3 also shows that while 66 percent of the Hadassah researchers had a median-and-above output of publications and 72 percent had a median-and-above output of "scientific" and foreign journals publications, only 27 percent of researchers outside Hadassah attained the median-and-above mark on any of the indices.

To avoid bias through possibly unequal distribution of talent between the Hadassah and non-Hadassah doctors, we tried to hold the overall prestige within the scientific community constant. The index of this prestige is the mean mark achieved by a researcher on a one-to-five scale in a mutual evalua-

14. A faculty of science including a department of human biology was opened at the Tel-Aviv University in 1962. A medical school was launched in 1964. Regular instruction at the medical school started in 1966–67, and it will probably change the situation with regard to the place of medical research in the Coastal Plain hospitals.

Table 2.   Comparison of Output per Person in Hadassah (Research Career Established) and Other Hospitals (Research Career Not Yet Established), 1953–1964[a]

Organization	Output per person	All publications	Publications in foreign journals	"Scientific" publications	Number of researchers
Hadassah	42	27	17	20
Other Hospitals	25	15	5	12
					32

[a] This comparison is heavily biased in favor of the non-Hadassah group: in contrast to Hadassah where all medical specialists were included in the sample, the non-Hadassah group represented in the sample consists only of the small minority of medical specialists engaged in research. Had we included all the medical specialists in the "Other Hospitals," too, the difference would have been much greater.

Table 3.   Publications by the Staffs of Hadassah and Other Hospitals, 1953–1964

Organization	N	All publications		Publications in foreign journals		"Scientific" publications	
		No. of researchers whose output was:		No. of researchers whose output was:		No. of researchers whose output was:	
		median and above	below median	median and above	below median	median and above	below median
Hadassah	18	12	6	13	5	13	5
Other Hospitals	11	3	8	3	8	3	8
Total	29[a]						

[a] Three researchers whose careers began after 1955 were not included in this table.

tion of all subjects in the sample. The High Prestige Group includes only those researchers whose mean mark was median (2.5) or above. The use of prestige rank as index of scientific talent is made on the assumption that the "overall prestige" is a function of (a) institutional affiliation; (b) the number and quality of publications; and (c) ability. Since (a) and (b) are in this case controlled, any bias due to them is accounted for. It can be assumed, therefore, that the less productive non-Hadassah groups are at least as equally talented as the Hadassah group.

Although the numbers are small, it can be seen from table 4 that research output is, above all, a function of institutional circumstances. As could be ex-

Table 4. Researchers by Productivity in Hadassah and Other Hospitals, 1953–1964, With Prestige in Scientific Community Held Constant

Organization	N	All publications		Publications in foreign journals		"Scientific" publications	
		No. of researchers with output per year: median and above (M = 2.9)	below median	No. of researchers with output per year: median and above (M = 1.6)	below median	No. of researchers with output per year: median and above (M = 1.1)	below median
High Prestige Group							
Hadassah	7	6	1	6	1	6	1
Other Hospitals	5	3	2	3	2	2	3
Low Prestige Group							
Hadassah	10	5	5	7	3	5	5
Other Hospitals	5	0	5	0	5	1	4
	27 [a]						

[a] Of the five researchers not included in this table, two have not had postdoctoral training so far, two are still abroad, and one just came back when the data were collected.

pected, more gifted investigators did better than their less gifted colleagues in every organization. But individuals of similar capacity stood a significantly higher chance of producing more and better research if they worked in an organizational setting where research was an important component of the career than otherwise.

The Effect of Resocialization on Productivity in Research

Following graduation from the medical school the young doctor enters a clinical department of a hospital and begins a five-year postgraduate training period for specialists during which, if he is in a university hospital, he is also expected to begin to work in research. He is given—at some time during the specialization period—one year's leave from routine clinical duties to devote himself entirely to research work, usually under the guidance of the head of his department. Usually after the completion of his training as a specialist (sometimes before), the young doctor is granted a scholarship for research work abroad, in most cases in the United States, which takes from one to two years. He then returns to his department in the hospital and resumes the combined role of a clinician and clinical investigator.[15]

In nonuniversity hospitals only some of the specializing young doctors go into research work. There is no provision for one year's laboratory work with freedom from ward duties, and no scholarships are provided by the hospital for research training abroad. Those doctors who do take some time off to learn research methods (usually a few months in the university hospital or the medical school laboratories) do this by some special nonroutine arrangement. If a scholarship for training abroad is obtained from a foreign medical center or research foundation, it is usually through the private initiative and effort of the aspiring researcher himself, sometimes with and sometimes without the help of the head of his department. Training abroad is not considered part of the doctor's career in the hospital, and, on his return, the hospital is under no formal obligation to accept him back in his former department or to ensure conditions for his continued research work in his field.

Only those doctors in our population who had undergone research training abroad showed identification with their research role. Those who had not yet been trained abroad showed lack of confidence in their image as researchers and, in most cases, considerable anxiety concerning their capacity to assume the scientific role. In most cases training abroad marks also the beginning of a continuous line of interest in a subject and/or a method of inquiry. The feeling that the training period abroad had been an "eye-opener" as to the true meaning of scientific investigation found expression in most interviews.

Most significantly perhaps, none of our respondents considered himself— as a researcher—a disciple of the local teachers with whom he had studied for the M.D. degree. The answer to a direct question, "Whom do you consider your teacher as far as research is concerned?" was an almost unanimous "No one" for local teachers. The exceptions were a few advanced researchers who had been working with some local basic scientists in the course of their early research work and who felt that these scientists had significantly affected their own capacity for research. All respondents listed without hesitation one or several of their former seniors abroad as those who had significantly influenced their development as scientists.

Much of the contact between medical students and scientists takes place at the early stages of medical training in classrooms and student laboratories. Under these circumstances this contact does not induce scientific attitudes in the student. Later on, the advanced students and the graduates are exposed to learning experience mainly in a clinical setting, and only those very few who deliberately choose to specialize in a nonclinical science department have the opportunity of exposure to direct influence by scientists.

15. The scholarship program was started by Hadassah Medical Organization in 1946. The one year's research training during clinical specialization became a routine arrangement only recently.

Thus, there is no continuity between the medical training and the research role. Our interview material shows that the clinical investigators themselves are acutely aware of the discontinuities between their training and clinical specialization, on the one hand, and their scientific role, on the other. They also feel that research training abroad is essential for their identity as medical scientists. The following statement by a young associate professor sums up the general feeling on the subject.

"The Medical School cannot make up its mind what it wants us to be. When we leave the School everyone is practically on his own as far as his further training in research is concerned. There are postgraduate training programs for general practitioners but none for those who remain in the university hospital and hope to become researchers. . . . If you get the right placement for your work abroad then there is your chance to find out what it is that you want to do and also how to go about it. You mix with people, some of whom you like to emulate. . . . The novelty, the scale and the diversity of your contacts help to create new perspectives. . . . You have free interaction with people some of whom are great teachers of medical science and some also great scientists."

All this led us to formulate the hypothesis that in order to become a researcher a medical doctor must be reoriented or "resocialized" in a framework different from the one in which he had been trained as a doctor and medical specialist.

To examine this hypothesis, we investigated the connection between this resocialization (postdoctoral research training abroad) and efficiency of research in terms of the volume and pattern of research output. More specifically, we took a sample of individuals who had been back from their postdoctoral work (usually a two-year training period in one of the important medical centers in the United States) for more than a year and studied their productivity before and after resocialization. The indices of change were (a) the difference between the mean output per year before and after postdoctoral training; (b) the difference between the proportion of papers published in foreign journals before and after the postdoctoral training; and (c) the difference between the proportion of papers classified as "scientific" before and after the postdoctoral training.[16]

Out of the 27 subjects who qualify for this comparison, increase in all three indices occurred in 18; increase in output-per-year occurred in 25; increase in proportion of papers published in foreign journals occurred in 21; and increase in the proportion of "scientific" papers occurred in 22. Of the 25 who showed increased output per year, it actually doubled or more in 20 cases.

It may be of interest to note here that the few researchers who were not

16. We chose publications as a criterion because of its immediate relevance to our question and its generally accepted utility for the purpose.

quite positive about the importance of their postdoctoral training abroad for their research efficiency show the same mean rate of increase on all the indices of productivity as the rest.

A comparison of the number of scientific papers produced by researchers who had not yet had their postdoctoral training abroad with that by their colleagues of equal seniority in the profession (number of years since graduation from Medical School) who had already undergone postdoctoral research training shows that the latter produced from two to six times as many papers as the former during the same time period and with other conditions (such as organizational setting) kept constant.

We further hypothesized that the resocialization process should be the more efficient, in terms of changed productivity pattern, the earlier after graduation from the medical school it takes place. We assumed that it should be easier for a young person to change his identity as a medical practitioner into a medical researcher than for an already well established practitioner.[17]

The subjects were divided into two groups. One consisted of younger people whose training and resocialization took place at a time when research had already become part of the career and who—as a result—went abroad for further training relatively soon after graduation (one to eight years). The second group consisted of those who retrained as researchers after a lapse of twelve or more years, a short time before or after the establishment of the medical school. Table 5 summarizes the findings on the effect of the timing of resocialization on consequent research productivity.

Table 5 shows that productivity in research increased more in the early than in the late resocialization group in spite of the fact that the early resocialization group had already had a higher rate of publication prior to resocialization than the late resocialization group.[18] The higher publication rate of the early resocialization group even before their resocialization makes the greater change that occurred in this group even more significant because the rate of growth tends to decrease after the initial period of fast growth of output.

The comparison of professional personalities represented in the early and the late resocialization groups shows that indeed the difference between them extends far beyond the mere difference in age and in the length of time separating their resocialization from previous exposure to learning experience. The late resocializer is as a rule a well-established clinician, in many cases an active and influential member of a professional association and a representative of the profession on public bodies and more often than not a successful private practitioner. In other words, he is firmly rooted in his community of

17. For similar considerations affecting creativity in general, see I. H. Page, "Age and Creativity," *Science* 3544 (Nov. 30, 1962): 647 ff.
18. The higher rate of publication prior to resocialization in the early resocialization group is, of course, the result of the fact that these doctors began their medical activities after the establishment of the medical school.

medical practitioners, has probably strongly internalized the norms of this community, and enjoys considerable social rewards attached to conforming behavior in his conventional role.

The early socializer, on the other hand, is usually in lower echelons of hospital hierarchy, has no private practice at all, and as a rule is not active or even involved in professional-organizational activities. His identity as a clinical practitioner is less firmly established, and since his social position is still in the making he is more open to change than his late resocializing counterpart.

Another, somewhat related hypothesis concerns the type of postdoctoral training. If the function of training is to make the doctor into a researcher, then the process should be more efficient if the training takes place in a basic rather than clinical research, since the clinical setting reinforces his old identity. A comparison of the productivity of those who received their training in basic research units with those trained in clinical research units supports this hypothesis (cf. table 6).

It can be seen that the productivity in research increased more among those researchers whose resocialization took place in basic research than among those whose resocialization was in clinical research units.[19]

These results are especially striking in view of the fact that prior to resocialization the clinical-research group had been the more productive. This eliminates the possibility that the choice of basic research unit as the place of training was the effect of prior excellence in research.

To avoid bias by the influence of different local conditions on research productivity upon return from postdoctoral training, a comparison between those trained in basic and those trained in clinical research has been made with the organizational setting upon return held constant. Controlling this factor has left the results unchanged.

Another factor to be controlled was ability, since it was suspected that it might be connected with the choice of a basic research unit as the place of postgraduate training. To eliminate this possible influence, change in productivity following resocialization was calculated for groups trained in basic and clinical research units, respectively, with the timing and the overall prestige within the scientific community held constant. Again the results remained unchanged.

The findings show that other conditions being equal, the decisive factor determining effectiveness of resocialization are contents and environment of the postdoctoral training program. The researchers who took their postdoctoral training in basic research units show twice as great an increase in output per year and in percentage of "scientific" papers as those whose resocializa-

19. On the importance of hybrid types of training, cf. J. Ben-David, "Roles and Innovations in Medicine," *American Journal of Sociology* 65 (May 1960): 557–68 [this volume, chap. 1] and Derek de Solla Price, *Science Since Babylon* (New Haven: Yale University Press, 1961), pp. 21–22.

Table 5. *Productivity Before and After Postdoctoral Training in the Early and the Late Resocialization Groups*

Time interval between M.D. and Postdoctoral training	Mean number of publications per person per year				Mean proportion of output published in foreign journals				Mean proportion of "scientific" out of total output				N
	before	after	increase	%	before	after	increase	%	before	after	increase	%	
8 years or less	2.0	5.2	3.2	160	51	78	27	54	22	63	41	250	16
12 years or more	1.5	2.7	1.2	92	47	60	13	27	12	25	13	108	11
													27 [a]

[a] Of the five researchers not included in this table, two have not had postdoctoral training so far, two are still abroad, and one just came back when the data were collected.

Table 6. *Productivity Before and After Postdoctoral Training in Basic and Clinical Research Groups, For Early Resocialization Group Only*

Type of postdoctoral training	Mean number of publications per person per year				Mean proportion of publications in foreign journals				Mean proportion of "scientific" publications				N
	before	after	increase	%	before	after	increase	%	before	after	increase	%	
Basic research	1.7	5.1	3.4	200	54	77	23	42	19	68	49	256	10
Clinical research	2.6	4.6	2.0	77	48	72	24	50	26	53	27	100	6
													16

tion took place in clinical research units, and this effect remains unchanged whatever other conditions conceivably influencing it are held constant.[20]

Change in Productivity Patterns Following Resocialization as Function of the Induction of the Medical Specialist into the International Scientific Community

The finding that postdoctoral training was most effective when taken in basic research environment, the observation that most researchers seemed to attach great importance to their continued contact with the scientists whom they had met during their resocialization period abroad, and the findings reported in the literature on the importance of informal social control by the scientific community for the productivity patterns and norms,[21] led us to formulate a hypothesis that the main function of the resocialization process consists in linking the young clinical researcher to the international community of scientists.

To investigate this hypothesis, the information on the volume and frequency of communication with researchers abroad following postdoctoral training has been analyzed. This communication includes correspondence, mutual visiting, regular exchange of manuscripts for criticism, and continued joint authorship. The population was divided into three groups by the intensity of communication. Those researchers who regularly used all the above-mentioned forms of communication with their colleagues abroad were classified as the High Intensity Group. Those whose contact with peers and seniors abroad was limited to a few or even one type of communication, but frequently and regularly used, were classified as Medium and those whose communication was sporadic and formal were listed as Low (see table 7).

This shows that change in productivity following resocialization is indeed a function of the intensity of communication of the researcher with other scientists, that is, of his induction into the scientific community. The reasons for the importance of linking the young researcher to the international community of scientists have been made clear by the interview material. To some extent they are connected with the small size of the country and of her scientific community.[22] The small number of medical scientists are split by advanced spe-

20. The single exception is a slightly greater increase in the percentage of papers published in foreign journals among the high prestige group trained in clinical units.
21. On the importance of the scientific community, cf. Thomas S. Kuhn, *The Structure of Scientific Revolutions* (Chicago: Chicago University Press, 1962); D. C. Pelz and F. M. Andrews, "Autonomy, Coordination and Stimulation, in Relation to Scientific Achievement," *Behavioral Science* 2 (March 1966): 89–97; W. O. Hagstrom, *The Scientific Community* (New York: Basic Books, Inc., 1965), pp. 49–52, and footnote on pp. 126–27.
22. On effect of size and attending conditions of working in a small country, see Renée C. Fox, "Medical Scientists in a Château," *Science* 3515 (May 11, 1962): 476–83; J. Ben-David,

Table 7.   The Relationship between Intensity of Communication with Colleagues
Abroad and the Productivity of Research

Intensity of post-resocialization communications [a]	Mean increase following resocialization in:			N
	Output per person per year	Proportion of publications in foreign journals	Proportion of "scientific" publications	
High	3.5	22	51	8
Medium	3	17	37	4
Low	0.6	16	6	3
Total				15

[a] Quantitative information on intensity of communication was available for these 15 researchers (all early-resocialization groups) only.

cialization. There has been so far a single medical school which left no opportunity for parallel work on similar problems by different teams of researchers. The resocialization in research invariably takes place abroad and disrupts continuity of interest and expertise between teachers and pupils, seniors and juniors. All this leads to an intense feeling of isolation, saliently evident in the interview material. Difficult living conditions and little leisure further impede informal communication. As a result, the scientific communication among the medical researchers in the country is limited to exchange of vital technical information and rarely involves exchange of ideas. Most of the respondents emphasized the importance of informal communication with scientists for the efficiency of their work and the frustration of isolation. Under these circumstances the induction into an international scientific community during postdoctoral research training abroad is particularly meaningful for their identity as scientists.

One can only speculate how these things work out in a large scientific center.[23] The international nature of the contacts may be much less important than in Israel, but the problem of scientific contacts outside the place of work is probably similarly important. With very few exceptions, the medical researcher works among practitioners interested in practical results more than in knowledge.[24] The medical researcher has to anchor himself into a community

"Scientific Endeavor in Israel and the United States," The American Behavioral Scientist, 6 (Dec. 1962): 12–16.
    23. The opportunities for a rapid rise of a widespread scientific community is illustrated by M. Finland, "The Training of the Physician, The Harvard Medical Units at the Boston City Hospital—a Perspective," New England Journal of Medicine 271 (Nov. 17, 1964): 1096–1100.
    24. For a discussion of a parallel situation in industry, see W. W. Kornhauser, Scientists in Industry: Conflict and Accommodation (Berkeley and Los Angeles: University of California Press, 1962).

outside his hospital in order to receive that kind of response to his work which is necessary to maintain his identity as a scientist.

Discussion and Conclusions

That making research an explicit criterion of certain types of a medical career was a necessary condition for the development of modern clinical research was recognized already by Flexner.[25] Our data on the transformation of medical research in Israel and, indeed, the transformation of the professional personality of several doctors as a result of a change in the career, have only supplied confirmation and filled in some details of this view.

The second set of findings, those on the importance and the effects of resocialization for research, show that the socialization of the clinical researcher follows quite a different path than that of researchers in the basic sciences. These latter are trained for research from the beginning of their graduate studies, while the clinical investigator has to be, so to speak, born twice professionally. He becomes first a practitioner and only after a few years' practice—in our case in a new environment—does he develop his identity as a scientist.

This type of training has not been the result of deliberate planning. It evolved from the necessity to retrain for research practitioners for whom research was to become part of their career. The development of the present pattern of training and career is somewhat reminiscent of the evolution of medical specialties. Like the latter, specialized training has been grafted on the basic training of the practitioner without altering the generality of basic training. There are, however, significant differences. The clinical skills have been, in contents and method, a direct continuation of the medical studies. They are acquired and practiced in the traditional medical organizations, and the specialists fit in without difficulty in the organic division of labor of medicine. Not so with medical research. As it has been shown here, optimally this is done in a nonclinical setting. This result was confirmed by the interview material—still to be published—about the communication networks of these researchers. In every case contacts with basic scientists (biochemists, biophysicists, etc.) were highly valued, and it is our impression that they were more highly valued than contacts with medical colleagues. It seems that the medical researcher is in many respects a person in permanent role conflict, because, on the one hand, his background and professional and organizational affiliation make him a clinician, while on the other hand, the principal paradigm for his work is provided by a basic discipline. Unlike the basic scientist, he is not a member of the scientific community of the basic disciplines but of the professional community of medical doctors and has to make special efforts

25. A. Flexner, op. cit.

to keep up his lines of communication with the scientific community, a thing which for the basic scientist comes without effort. Research, then, is a problematic medical specialty.[26]

It is difficult, however, to decide what practical conclusions should be drawn from this. Our material may be somewhat biased by the small size and the recency of the scientific development of the country where the study was conducted. In order to isolate the factor of size from that of specific historical conditions of the development of the role, it would be interesting to compare the relevant aspects of medical research and training in Israel with those in other small but historically different countries. In large scientific centers there may arise more continuous schemes of training, and sizable groups of clinical researchers in each field may be found to form scientific subcommunities of their own. It is nevertheless our feeling that essentially the problem of the hybrid nature of clinical research is general. There is in all cases an element of institutionally generated conflict through turning out practicing professionals and then putting them to work in research.[27]

The question is whether and to what extent this pattern should be made smoother and more continuous or whether the unplanned evolution of the role has as a matter of fact produced an efficient pattern which is well worth the extra cost in time, money, and effort involved in it as compared with the socialization pattern in basic research. It is possible that the disadvantages of discontinuity in training and of a relatively segregated system of professional and scientific communication are more than compensated for by the hybrid vigor generated by the ongoing process of creation of ever new linkages between different aspects of a developing practice, on the one hand, and of several developing scientific disciplines, on the other. Even if some of the hybrids may be incapable of reproduction, they may be still well worth having for their own lifetimes. Another possible advantage of the pattern may be in the reduction of the career risks for the applied researcher. The latter is always in danger of losing his contact with his scientific community since he investigates questions which are not shared by that community. In this case he may become altogether isolated with harmful consequences for his creativity. The apparently cumbersome pattern of socialization into medical research elimi-

26. Its only parallel among the clinical specialties is the psychiatrist who also has to reorient himself to a large extent to another professional and scientific community, that of psychologists and social scientists in general. Cf. Talcott Parsons, "Some Trends of Change in American Society: Their Bearing on Medical Education," in his *Structure and Process in Modern Societies* (Glencoe, Ill.: The Free Press, 1960), pp. 280–94, who treats this problem from a different angle.

27. One attempt to deal with this is suggested by E. A. Stead. His plan provides for heterogeneous experience in medical studies through a curriculum consisting of a two-year core and six-year elective courses program for individually planned heterogeneous careers. This university-type medical training should preserve the unity of scholarly attitude, not the unity of information. Cf. E. A. Stead, Jr., "The Evolution of the Medical Education," *Journal of Medical Education* 39, 1 (1963): 368.

nates this danger, since as a result the medical researcher can always fall back on his professional community. From this point of view, then, this role pattern, which seems so inefficient when compared with the patterns of basic research, may prove very efficient when compared with the attempts—none too successful—of creating efficient role and organizational patterns in other fields of applied research.

As it has been pointed out, our data on the relative efficiency of resocialization in a basic, as compared with clinical, setting do provide some support to the hybridization hypothesis. However, they concern only part of the problem which, we suggest, is well worth further inquiry.[28]

28. The considerably greater vitality of medical as opposed to applied research has been observed by C. P. Snow. The only parallel he finds to this is military research, and his explanation is that in both cases there is a clearer objective and higher social priority attached to its attainment than in other fields. Cf. C. P. Snow, *Science and Government* (London: Four Square Books, 1963), pp. 68–69. We are not sure about the greater clarity of objectives. As to social priorities, these affect scientists like anybody else and they are as good or better than others resisting them if they perceive them as incompatible with their professional priorities. The question, therefore, is how to make researchers accept these extra-scientific priorities. We think this happens in medicine by making the researchers first into doctors. In military science, however, it happens only under the exceptional stress of war, provided that the scientific community as a whole identifies with its objectives. In peacetime it is not easier to create first-rate military than other applied science. Both can be done only by exceptionally great investment and/or where the military objective happens to be of great intrinsic interest to science.

The Concepts of 4
"Role," "Status," and
"Reference Group"

A Theoretical Statement

Role, status, reference group, and a number of related concepts have been used and defined in recent sociological literature in a variety of ways. Therefore, one has to explain one's own usage. By role I mean what one or more persons (e.g., a group, organization, etc.) are institutionally expected to do as a unit of the various systems of society, and by status I understand the rewards they receive in virtue of being the incumbent of the role, insofar as these rewards have a more or less permanent effect on their hierarchic position vis-à-vis all the other units participating in the same system. Thus, role defines the functional, and status, the hierarchic, position of a unit in a social system. (It is implied that every unit has both a functional and a hierarchic position.)

It has been pointed out lately that many roles cannot be defined in terms of a single logically coherent set of expectations but that they rather involve relatedness to a variety of, not necessarily congruent, expectations. The same, of course, applies to the status aspect of the social unit. This position has been accepted in this paper but with an important qualification, namely, that the expectations directed toward a role are not infinitely variable but are determined by the institutional definition of the role in the most inclusive system to which it belongs. Thus, for example, in the present case of doctors, expectations of "service" and "science," although they involve quite different norms and may not always be in perfect harmony, are both part and parcel of the definition of the doctor's role. At the same time there may be expectations toward the incumbent of a role, which are, from the point of view of the in-

This appeared as an Appendix to paper [15] in the Bibliography. Only the references relevant to the discussion in the Appendix have been reprinted. Ed.

stitutional definition, incidental to the role as, for instance, the bureaucratic requirements in the case of some of our doctors.

This distinction is not merely theoretical. It implies that conflict between the institutionalized norms, if it occurs, will be internal, and the tendency will be to resolve it and to establish a balance. If, on the other hand, expectations that are not institutionalized parts of the role clash with those that are, this will be an external conflict and will not evoke any mechanisms of equilibration. It will result either in institutional change or in the elimination of the incidental expectations. Indeed, one of the criteria by which structural expectations can be distinguished from incidental ones might be whether the nonexistence of certain expectations toward a role will automatically evoke a tendency to establish such expectations. I suggest that it might help to avoid confusion if we called the first type of situation "intra-role," and the second "inter-role," conflict. Thus, if a doctor should feel in a certain kind of medical organization that devotion to the patients is not an important criterion of evaluation, he will perceive the situation as "wrong" from his professional point of view. But the existence or nonexistence of certain bureaucratic expectations will be perceived by most doctors (and by people in general) as unimportant from the professional point of view—although it may be regarded as of great importance for other reasons—as long as it does not interfere with medical practice.

My concept of reference group is intrinsically related to the concept of role. I use it to denote the system—obviously "group" is a mistaken word in almost any current definition of the concept—which serves as a frame of reference for self-evaluation in any aspect of a role. Since role has been defined by expectations issuing from the various systems of society, these will be the potential reference "groups" of a role (under conditions that have to be further specified). This of course implies that I distinguish between the structural reference groups—which are limited in number—and the incidental ones, whose number is theoretically unlimited.

The present definitions differ from most of the others that are current in introducing the concept of institutionalization in the definitions of role and reference group. While, on the one hand, this is no more than the application of some key concepts in the analysis of whole societies to role analysis, there are, on the other hand, some quite obvious objections to it. It can be argued that the concept of institutionalization does not fit roles in informal groups. However, (a) the so-called informal situations are all at least institutionally circumscribed, this being most apparent from the fact that what an informal situation is and what being informal means are quite different things in different societies; and (b) a minimum definition of institutionalization, such as "behavior commonly and (relatively) permanently accepted as obligatory for the unit of a social system," is applicable for any kind of situation.

With regard to reference groups, there is the question as to how our concepts relate to individual behavior, which has been so far the major focus of reference group research. In this respect I should only suggest that institutionalization has its personality counterpart in the concept of internalization, which in its turn may be the decisive factor in the choice of reference groups, wherever such choice is possible. This is obviously inadequate, but the problem cannot be dealt with exhaustively here. Of the numerous references about the subject, I should like to mention, Eisenstadt (2, 3); Merton (4, pp. 235–386); and Turner (9).

References

1. Ben-David, J. *The Social Structure of the Professions in Israel.* Unpublished Ph.D. dissertation, Hebrew University, Jerusalem, 1955.
2. Eisenstadt, S. N. "Studies in Reference Group Behavior. I. Reference Norms and the Social Structure," *Human Relations* 7 (1954): 191–216.
3. ————. "Reference Group Behavior and Social Integration: An Explorative Study," *American Sociological Review* 19 (1954): 175–85.
4. Merton, R. K. *Social Theory and Social Structure.* (Rev. Ed.) Glencoe, Ill.: The Free Press, 1957.
5. Merton, R. K., et al. *The Student Physician.* Cambridge: Harvard University Press, 1957.
6. Parsons, T. "The Professions and Social Structure," *Social Forces* 17 (1939): 457–67.
7. ————. *The Social System.* Glencoe, Ill.: The Free Press; London: Tavistock Publications, 1951.
8. ————. "Illness and the Role of the Physician: A Sociological Perspective," *American Journal of Orthopsychiatry* 21 (1951): 456–60.
9. Turner, R. H. "Role-Taking, Role Standpoint and Reference Group Behavior," *American Journal of Sociology* 61 (1956): 316–28.

Part II

Conditions of Scientific Growth

Academic Organization and the Profession
of Science

Introduction

The essays of Part I showed how scientific growth and change depend on social conditions through their influence on *individual* scientists acting in response to the incentives and constraints of their reference groups. Of crucial importance in this context is, to be sure, the university. Therefore, from the early 1960s onward, much of Ben-David's research has concentrated on the university as an organizational framework of scientific research. The essays assembled in this part have the university, its development, and its impact on research for their principal subject.

The first paper devoted to this topic, "Scientific Productivity and Academic Organization in Nineteenth-Century Medicine" (1960), examines the marked differences in the growth of nineteenth-century physiology in Germany and the United States, on the one hand, and France and Britain, on the other, and argues that the rise of physiology in the first two countries is due to the successful institutionalization there of the role of a professional scientist. This institutionalization of science as a professional career involved a transformation of the university, specifically, the creation of research laboratories. This transformation did not depend on the farsightedness of any decision makers or on the philosophical idea of the university. On the contrary, where the course of events was determined by centrally deciding wise men, physiology failed to be institutionalized. Its institutionalization was the outcome of a series of unplanned, uncoordinated, local, and stepwise decisions in a *decentralized* system whose elements—the universities—were in *competition*. The crucial importance of this new academic system lies in the fact that it largely shielded science from society at large, thereby allowing it to progress continuously, irrespective of whether or not its values were congruent with those of the prevailing social order. In this paper, then, Ben-David introduces for the first time (1) the university as an important variable of the analysis and (2) the idea that competition in a free (decentralized) market is the most efficient motor of the diffusion of cognitive and organizational innovations and hence of scientific growth. Some twenty-five years after having written this paper, Ben-David critically reflected on its merits and shortcomings, comparing it with more recent approaches to the study of the same events. See chapter 24, below, and "Comment" on a paper by T. Lenoir, [81] in the bibliography.

The next paper, "Universities and Academic Systems in Modern Societies" (1962; with A. Zloczower) is an immediate sequel to the last one, as well as to A. Zloczower's M.A. thesis.[1] Since Ben-David's research has shown that the modern German university played a crucial role in the progress of science and in its institutionalization as an autonomous activity, it was only natural to study its emergence. The impetus the German university gave to science is attributed to the workings of "blind forces": the operation of competition in a decentralized system, which brought about the rapid diffusion of innovations, mainly through role differentiation in an expanding market. In this context, Ben-David also gives an intriguing account of the emergence of the doctrine of *Wertfreiheit* (value neutrality) of scientific research: "It was the doctrine best suited to the maintenance of the delicate balance in a situation where free, nonutilitarian enquiry was supported and given high status by an absolutist state." This explanation, let us note in passing, squarely falls within the sociology of knowledge. And it seems implicitly to reject R. K. Merton's notion of a congruity between free scientific inquiry and democratic social order. Ben-David goes on to analyze the cases of Britain, in which a situation of competition in a free market did not obtain, and of the United States, where the diffusion of innovations in a competitive system conforms to the explanation of the German case. Thus, the main *explanans* in Ben-David's account of the universities is again competition in a decentralized academic system, a system whose operation results in the autonomy of science. The United States emerges here as the country whose system comes closest to realizing the optimal conditions for the furtherance of science. The paper closes with some unsparing observations on contemporary European universities, which Ben-David characterizes as "woefully out-of-date." This remark was to get more substance in the invited OECD report, *Fundamental Research and the Universities* (1968; cf. [3] in the bibliography).

The development of the modern university system in its relation to research is further retraced and analyzed in "Science and the University System" (1972). The paper shows how scientific research became professional in Ger-

1. Awraham Zloczower, *Career Opportunities and the Growth of Scientific Discovery in 19th-Century Germany, with Special Reference to Physiology* (M.A. thesis, The Hebrew University, Jerusalem, 1960; now published by Arno Press, New York, 1981).

many, an unintended development that was in fact inconsistent with the official doctrine of the unity of teaching and research. It goes on to show how, through a process of diffusion through imitation motivated by the German accomplishments in basic scientific research, professionalism in research was differently instituted in Britain, France, and the United States. The latter, the most decentralized and competitive of these systems, succeeded best in developing professionalism in research and in realizing a unity of teaching and research in graduate schools.

After World War II, the role of research became preponderant at the expense, Ben-David maintains, of other important functions of the university. The one-sided emphasis on the research function of the university emerges from this paper as the outcome not of considered decision making but as the combined result of the working of the competitive research system biased by the one-sided support of research by governments.

In "Academy, University, and Research Institute in the Nineteenth and Twentieth Centuries: A Study of Changing Functions and Structures" (1978), Ben-David sheds additional light on the functioning and historical evolution of different institutions involved in scientific research. He shows that, the decline of the French Academy of Sciences in the nineteenth century notwithstanding, scientific academies and societies maintained important functions in that age of growing scientific specialization, namely, the representation, indeed the institutional embodiment, of the unity of science. The idea that the totality of science is socially connected, let us remark in passing, is indeed crucial to Ben-David's sociology of science: it underlies his notion of the—unique—scientific role and, by implication, his rejection of T. S. Kuhn's view of science as consisting of distinct "paradigms." In the second part of the paper, Ben-David analyzes the role of research in the university and its relation to student training. Toward the end of the nineteenth century, science became both more expensive and more theoretical, and it was therefore thought that the classic principle of the unity of research and teaching must be given up. This led to the creation of research institutes, first for applied research and then for basic research. But even the latter did not really spread, for by creating the graduate school, the American university reestablished a successful framework in which research and teaching were united. This implies (although it is not explicitly stated here) that the university system, that is, the system uniting research and professional training, usually adapts itself to new needs of the society better than other institutions and is therefore the best institutional framework for basic scientific research.

The preceding studies showed how the German organizational innovation—making scientific research the subject of systematic training at the university—gradually diffused to most Western societies, and it was argued that the professionalization of research was a major factor in scientific growth. The subject of the following two papers is science as a profession, that is, an occupation characterized by certain specific features, notably by corporate self-regulation. "The Profession of Science and Its Powers" (1972) asks how science obtained the privileged status of a profession. It shows that in the seventeenth and eighteenth centuries, the scientific academies became the only bodies capable of evaluating scientific work, thus assuming the role of corporate bodies and ensuring the autonomy of science. In the nineteenth-century German university, science became a full-time paid occupation, and thus the university took over the function of regulating scientific work. In this function, the university, while giving professional training, also enjoyed "academic freedom," that is, independence of the lay users of science. After World War II, this self-regulation of the scientific community involved a further function, namely, the allocation of resources. The tendency of the scientific community to extend its professional autonomy and to control all circumstances pertaining to science, Ben-David warns, may prove damaging in the long run, for the scientific community has no special competence to pronounce judgments on the relative importance of different branches of knowledge.

Academic freedom is, in Ben-David's view, a kind of professional freedom: it is one of the institutional arrangements making of science a profession. Inasmuch as it involves self-regulation, it can be violated both from outside by lay users of knowledge and from within, when members of the academic profession misuse their power to establish one-sided authority over their peers. "A Comparative Study of Academic Freedom and Student Politics" (1966; with R. Collins) retraces various possible sources for conflict over academic freedom. It offers a fourfold typology of universities according to (1) whether they employ and train an elite or experts, and (2) whether there exist role models in society for their graduates. Where, as in Britain, universities train an elite and there exist role models in society (an elite civil service), there is a minimum of conflict, for universities are allowed great autonomy. This trust induces the universities to be very prudent in academic innovations, however. By contrast, where (as in nineteenth-century Russia or present-day Latin America) an educational system sets itself the aim of promoting social change (i.e., educating a new elite for nonexisting social roles), this will necessarily lead to conflict, for the existing elite will attempt to control the teaching activity. If the university professors do not corrupt themselves by joining the ruling class, they will tend to engage in politics, thus creating a situation in which academic freedom is jeopardized from within. Here nineteenth-century Germany is a particular case, where the successful institutionalization of academic freedom in an autocratic society was due to the decentralization of the university system. The university system in the United States is an expert system in which academic freedom is partly an organizational device in which the staff function as experts and partly a union-type arrangement for defending the staff's interests. The conflict over academic freedom in the expert system occurred in new fields (e.g., Darwinian biology, Keynsian economics), where no university-trained experts have yet reached dominant positions. An important difference between the expert and the elite system is that whereas the latter is highly restrictive and confers the privilege of academic freedom only on highly qualified institutions, the former tends to be less selective and to seek to encompass in its application also marginal domains, more prone to be sources of conflict.

The paper concludes in a similar mood: in both elite and expert systems, "the crucial role of students and intellectuals in ideological politics will probably pass." Ben-David and Collins allowed for the possibility that "where there is general political oppression, students and intellectuals may show greater sensitivity and display more activity for reforms," but they believed that this activity will not "be directed toward changes in the university." Needless to say, this prediction was blatantly refuted in the years following 1968. In the papers included in Part VI of this volume, Ben-David sought to account precisely for the fact that, as he interprets it, a general, politically motivated antinomian movement gave rise to an antiscientific movement, among whose principal demands was a university reform.

Scientific Productivity and Academic Organization in Nineteenth-Century Medicine

5

The purpose of this paper is to describe and explain differences as well as fluctuations in the productivity of the medical sciences in Germany, France, Britain, and the United States, from 1800 to about the time of World War I. Scientific productivity as defined here does not comprise any evaluation of the greatness or depth of various scientific ideas, or of the "efficiency" of scientific production as measured by some input-output ratio. It refers only to two gross quantities: the number of scientific discoveries (including scientifically important technical inventions) and the numbers of people making such discoveries. Provided that these numbers are not a fixed proportion of the general population or some other general quantity, they are a measure of the active interest in science existing in a society at a certain point of time.

The two suggested indexes of productivity—the numbers of discoveries and of discoverers—have not precisely the same meaning, and there are obvious objections to both. It can be argued that since scientific discoveries are disparate units of unequal significance, it is meaningless to count them.[1] The

A preliminary draft of this paper was written while the author was a fellow at the Center for Advanced Study in the Behavioral Sciences, Stanford, California. He is indebted to Harry Alpert, S. N. Eisenstadt, Jacob Katz, Morris Janowitz, Robert K. Merton, D. Patinkin, Dr. George G. Reader, and the late Dr. J. Seide for comments on the manuscript or discussion of its subject matter, and to A. Zloczower for his help with the research.

1. The method is applied and discussed by T. J. Rainoff, "Wave-like Fluctuations of Creative Productivity in the Development of West-European Physics in the Eighteenth and Nineteenth Centuries," *Isis* 12 (1929): 291–92. See also S. C. Gilfillan, *The Sociology of Invention* (Chicago: Follet, 1935), pp. 29–32; Joseph Schneider, "The Cultural Situation as a Condition for the Achievement of Fame," *American Sociological Review* 2 (1937): 480–91; Frank R. Cowell, *History, Civilization and Culture: An Introduction to the Historical and Social Philosophy of Pitirim*

first part of the claim is true but not the deduction from it. It has been shown time and again that "great" discoveries had been preceded by intensive activity manifested in numerous "small" discoveries, often leading to the simultaneous finding of the final solution by more than one person.[2] Similarly, one of the signs of a great discovery is that it leads to a greater number of smaller discoveries based on the newly discovered principle.[3] Therefore, viewing science as a flow of constant activity, great discoveries appear as waves built up gradually by the antlike work of predecessors, leading first to an upsurge of activity by followers and disciples and then diminishing into routine when the potentialities of the great idea have been (or seem to be) exhausted. Thus, there is no need to weight the individual discoveries. The weighing is done automatically by the clustering of discoveries around the significant event. This is not to deny that there are lone discoveries, neither expected beforehand nor understood after they are made. For the historian who sits in judgment of individual greatness and stupidity, these are important events that prove the absurdity of our method of counting. But if one's purpose is to gauge the extent to which various social systems induce people to scientific productivity, then the relatively negligible weight accorded to the lone discovery is a good index of the relative lack of inducement to engage in research in that society.

The use of the number of discoverers (not students or graduates) as an index of scientific activity can be justified by similar reasoning. Such men as Newton, Lavoisier, and Einstein did not spring up in scientific deserts but in environments of intensive scientific interest, and their work inspired disciples and followers. So we can expect a general correspondence between this index and the previous one. Yet, there are numerous problems involved in the use of this index. In principle, the same numbers of discoveries can be made by quite different numbers of people, so that there may be no relationship between the two counts. In fact, however, the variation is quite limited, because the accomplishment of even a single scientific discovery demands as a rule considerable investment of time and training: one can assume that discoveries will be made by persons with special characteristics ("discoverers") and not randomly either by them or others. Thus, we take this figure too as a good index of the social inducement to engage in research. No more than general correspondence between the two sets of data is expected, however, because, first, there may be variations due to institutional circumstances in the length of the creative period of discoverers and in the chances of "outsiders" for making

A. *Sorokin* (London: Black, 1952), pp. 90–106; and especially the methodological comments of Robert K. Merton, "Fluctuations in the Rate of Industrial Invention," *The Quarterly Journal of Economics* 59 (1935): 456.

2. Cf. William F. Ogburn, *Social Change* (New York: Huebsch, 1922), pp. 90–122; Bernhard J. Stern, *Society and Medical Progress* (Princeton: Princeton University Press, 1941), pp. 41–44.

3. Merton, op. cit., pp. 464–65.

discoveries; and, second, even if these things were constant, the shape of the two curves would still differ because each discovery is a single event counted only once, at the time of its occurrence, while discoverers must be counted over a period of time or at an arbitrarily fixed point of time (such as their age at the beginning of the professional career). For these reasons we expect this second index to correspond with the first only in registering relatively long-term and gross changes. But in such details as the exact time of the changes and short-term fluctuations, no correspondence between the two indexes can be expected.

A second problem requiring preliminary clarification is the definition of medical sciences. We have adopted the criteria of our sources, which include all discoveries that eventually became part of the medical tradition. Undoubtedly, this implies the inclusion of some nonmedical discoveries and discoverers; therefore, from the viewpoint of the history of scientific ideas, this may not be too meaningful a category. However, in a study of scientific activity one needs data reflecting activity in more or less homogeneous institutional frameworks, irrespective of whether they do or do not relate to a logically coherent system of ideas. On this score, medicine in the nineteenth century seems to be a good choice. Through most of the century it was closely interwoven with the natural sciences. It had been the first profession based on the study of natural sciences, and medical faculties were the first university departments to teach them. For many years the only large-scale and permanent organizations where research was systemically conducted were the teaching hospitals. Also, the art of the apothecary and the science of chemistry were often connected until the early nineteenth century. Thus, the sciences associated with medicine have formed a complex of scientific activity which has been related to well-defined social structures since the eighteenth century, whereas most of the basic sciences were the professional concern of only a few individuals in any country well into the second half of the nineteenth century. The medical sciences, therefore, appear to be well suited for discerning the effect of structural changes upon scientific creativity during the period under consideration.

The Questions to be Explained

Table 1 is based on a count of medical discoveries made in the countries here surveyed from 1800 to 1926, according to a "Chronology of Medicine and Public Hygiene." [4] The data reveal two different trends.

4. Published in F. H. Garrison, *An Introduction to the History of Medicine*, 4th ed. (Philadelphia and London: Saunders, 1929).

Table 1.   Number of Discoveries in the Medical Sciences by Nations, 1800–1926

Year	U.S.A.	England	France	Germany	Other	Unknown	Total
1800–09	2	8	9	5	2	1	27
1810–19	3	14	19	6	2	3	47
1820–29	1	12	26	12	5	1	57
1830–39	4	20	18	25	3	1	71
1840–49	6	14	13	28	7	—	68
1850–59	7	12	11	32	4	3	69
1860–69	5	5	10	33	7	2	62
1870–79	5	7	7	37	6	1	63
1880–89	18	12	19	74	19	5	147
1890–99	26	13	18	44	24	11	136
1900–09	28	18	13	61	20	8	148
1910–19	40	13	8	20	11	7	99
1920–26	27	3	3	7	2	2	44

Source: see n. 4.

First, between 1810 and 1819, a rise in the number of discoveries in France and Britain begins, followed in Germany in the next decade. By 1840, the rise has passed its peak in France and Britain and a decline sets in lasting until the 1870s. Second, an upsurge starts simultaneously in all these three nations and in the United States in 1880. These parallel movements reflect the story of the convergence of chemical, anatomical, physiological, and pathological discoveries in the first half of the nineteenth century and the spate of bacteriological and surgical innovations which followed the work of Pasteur, Lister, and Koch in the last quarter of the century. Both waves show only that certain fruitful ideas had been simultaneously, or nearly simultaneously, exploited in Western European countries beginning from the early nineteenth century and in the United States as well from the end of the century. Apart from indicating that scientific communication among these countries was well established by that time and that therefore the phenomena reflect the course of scientific ideas, they call for no sociological explanation. What needs to be explained is the conspicuous change in the relative shares of the countries during this period. French supremacy in the beginning of the century with Britain a close second gave way to an overwhelming preponderance of German discoveries through the second half of the last century. The American share was rapidly increasing from the 1880s and became the largest by 1910–1919. Since this was the time of World War I, comparison with the European countries may seem of doubtful validity; but the relative decline of the European countries started prior to the war and lasted well into the twenties, so that it should not be attributed

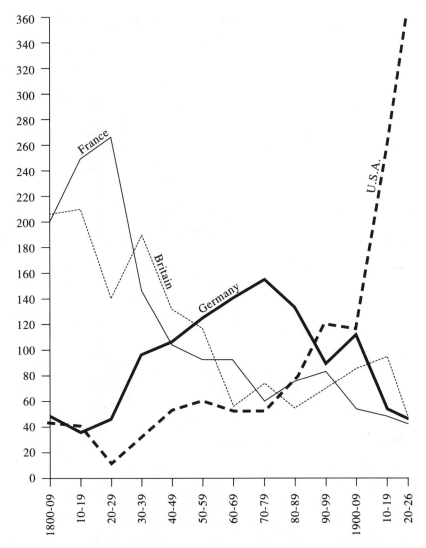

*Fig. 1.   Changes in the Relative Share of Medical Discoveries in Selected Countries,
1800–1926*

entirely to the war. Figure 1 shows the proportion of the total discoveries
made in each nation during each period as a proportion of the country's relative share over the whole period

$$\left(y = 100 \, \frac{\text{country's share in decade (\%)}}{\text{country's share over whole period (\%)}} \right).$$

Table 2.   Discoverers in the Medical Sciences at the Age of Entering Their Professions (Age 25) in Various Countries, 1800–1910

Year	U.S.A.	England	France	Germany	Other
1800	1	7	8	7	4
1805	1	8	5	8	2
1810	3	11	6	6	2
1815	2	12	12	7	3
1820	3	11	23	18	2
1825	2	17	15	18	6
1830	8	12	25	10	6
1835	11	13	26	29	7
1840	5	24	22	35	12
1845	5	14	13	33	5
1850	10	18	21	37	10
1855	15	16	20	49	27
1860	16	23	13	61	23
1865	25	15	36	71	26
1870	25	15	31	83	41
1875	40	31	23	84	46
1880	48	17	40	75	50
1885	52	16	34	97	52
1890	43	11	23	74	41
1895	47	9	27	78	29
1900	32	9	17	53	30
1905	28	4	4	34	25
1910	23	6	7	23	18

Source: Dorland's *Medical Dictionary* (20th ed.). See n. 5.

A significant aspect of this change of relative positions is that it is connected with an atypical growth in the curve of discoveries in the country which is gaining the largest share. Thus, the number of German discoveries continually increases through the middle of the nineteenth century in a period of decline in France and Britain. A similar deviation marks the change in the relative position of the United States at the beginning of the twentieth century.

A similar pattern marks the number of discoverers. Table 2 shows the "productivity" of the various countries in terms of scientists.[5] France and Britain, with the largest numbers at the beginning of the century, fall behind Germany starting about 1835. While the number of German scientists entering upon their careers increases regularly, with only one considerable drop until 1885–1890, there are fluctuations and a generally downward slope in

5. Based on W. A. Newman Dorland, *The American Illustrated Medical Dictionary*, 20th ed. (Philadelphia and London: Saunders, 1946).

France and England through the middle of the century. The American trend, like the German, shows much less fluctuation. Thus, with respect to major trends, the two indexes validate each other.[6]

Two questions emerge: What explains the change of scientific leadership from France to Germany to the United States? And what explains the "deviant" nature of the development in Germany during the middle and in the United States toward the end of the nineteenth century, as manifested in (1) the continuous rise in the number of discoveries during periods of relatively low creativity in the other countries, and (2) the relatively smaller fluctuations in the number of people embarking upon scientific careers in these two countries compared with the others?

Hypothesis:
The Organizational Factor

Neither the changes in scientific leadership nor the deviant nature of the German and American developments can be manifestations of differences in the scientific ideas in the various countries. This could be the case only if international communication had been deficient, so that new ideas in one country would have no effect upon the work of scientists in the others. This was by no means the case, as demonstrated by the parallel upward movements of the curves of discoveries in all the countries in periods of crucial scientific advance. Independently from this fact, whatever barriers to scientific communication had existed between France and Germany during the first decades of the nineteenth century had disappeared by the beginning of the fourth decade. By about the same time, the British too established contacts with Continental science, from which they had become isolated with decreasing splendor dur-

---

6. The pattern which emerges from these indexes parallels the qualitative descriptions of up-to-date histories of medicine and science. See, e.g., Arturo Castiglioni, *A History of Medicine* (New York: Knopf, 1947); Richard H. Shryock, *The Development of Modern Medicine* (New York: Knopf, 1947); H. T. Pledge, *Science Since 1500* (London: Philosophical Library, 1940). Rather than simply referring to such sources, I prefer to present the numerical indexes in detail for two reasons: (1) They contain some information not sufficiently emphasized—or even blurred—in those sources. Thus, the small amount of medical research in Britain is blurred in the qualitative descriptions by the dazzling brilliance of England's few scientist-intellectuals and by the glamour of the British medical profession. Also, the different patterns of growth of scientific personnel (discoverers) is a subject not sufficiently emphasized in the histories of medical science. (2) What is called here scientific productivity is only one aspect of the development of science; in terms of the interrelationships of scientific ideas, it is perhaps a peripheral one. Since traditionally the history of science is a history of ideas, even the few historians interested in such sociological phenomena as differences in the scientific development of various countries are not very explicit about the bases of their judgments, nor do they sufficiently differentiate between the various aspects of science as a social activity. It is important, therefore, to present explicitly the quantitative basis of the historians' judgment and clearly delimit the particular aspect of scientific activity dealt with here from others.

ing the eighteenth century, as did the Americas.[7] Therefore, nothing immanent to science as a body of ideas explains the observed differences and
changes. The explanation has to be sought in external circumstances.

Among the possible external causes there are some general and obvious
ones, such as population growth and the growth of national income. A few
unrefined attempts to assess the population factor suggested that this is not a
promising line of approach. The introduction of this factor does flatten out the
curves somewhat but does not eliminate the characteristic waves of development, and it hardly affects the changes in the relative position of the nations.[8]

Nor do differences in national or personal income seem to be relevant. The
indexes of national income in all the countries here surveyed show a fairly
gradual and constant rise through the whole period without such ups and
downs and such extensive changes in the relative positions of the countries as
indicated by our data. Moreover, the United States and Britain were the richest
of these countries, at least since the middle of the nineteenth century (and no
doubt earlier in the case of Britain). Yet, as to medical discoveries, these
countries were relatively backward during much of the period.[9] None of these
factors, therefore, seems to be directly and consistently related to the differences in the growth of discoveries in the various nations.

Thus, it is assumed that the conditions determining the differences are to be
sought in the *organization* of science. But this is a complex phenomenon: we
still must seek the particular organizational factor which reasonably answers
our questions. It is proposed to isolate this factor by comparing the main aspects of the organization of science in France and Germany during the first
half and the middle of the nineteenth century and those same aspects in Britain and the United States during the three decades preceding World War I.
This particular pairing is selected because France and Germany maintained a
publicly supported network of scientific instruction and research from the
early nineteenth century, while Britain and the United States did not begin to
develop their systems until the second half of the century. There were short-
lived experiments in Britain during the first half of the century, but these were
overshadowed by the archaic nature of the most important universities. If it is
possible to isolate a theoretically relevant condition common to the organization of science in Germany and the United States but absent in France and
Britain, that condition may reasonably be taken as the cause of the observed
differences.

7. Cf. Shryock, op. cit., pp. 193–96; Paul Diepgen, *Geschichte der Medizin* (Berlin:
Gruyter, 1955), vol. 2/1, pp. 204–07; Charles Newman, *The Evolution of Medical Education in
the Nineteenth Century* (London: Oxford University Press, 1957), pp. 265–69.

8. The sources used for population data were *La population française: Rapport du Haut comité consultatif de la population et de la famille* (Paris: Presses Universitaires de France, 1955),
p. 19; Michel Huber, Henri Bunle, et Fernand Boverat, *La population de la France* (Paris: Librairie Hachette, 1943), p. 19; W. S. and E. S. Woytinsky, *World Population and Production*
(New York: Twentieth Century Fund, 1953).

9. For national income data, see, e.g., Colin Clark, *The Conditions of Economic Progress*,
2nd ed. (London: Macmillan, 1951).

France and Germany

Three conditions are mentioned in the literature in explanation of German scientific superiority in the nineteenth century: (1) the relative excellence of laboratory and hospital facilities for research and the faster recognition of the importance of new fields of research, especially physiology; (2) the clear recognition of the aim of the university as a seat of original research and efficient organizational devices to achieve that aim, such as far-reaching academic self-government, the freedom of the teacher regarding the content of his courses, the freedom of the student in the choice of his courses and his teachers (including easy transfer from one university to another), the requirement of submitting theses based on research for attainment of academic degrees, and, above all, the institution of *Habilitation,* that is, the submission of a high-level scientific work based on original research as a precondition of academic appointment; (3) the existence of a large number of academic institutions which made possible the mobility of teachers and students and resulted in an atmosphere of scientific competition that did not exist elsewhere.[10] The superiority of the German scientific facilities from about the middle of the century is an undeniable fact. But instead of explaining the differences in creativity, it is itself a phenomenon that needs explanation.

The pioneering country in the establishment of modern scientific facilities was France. Founded in 1794, the École polytechnique had been the model academic organization in the natural sciences. Among other new features, it possessed the first academic research laboratories (in chemistry). The physiological laboratory at the Collège de France, where Magendie and Claude Bernard conducted their studies, was considered most inadequate by the middle of the nineteenth century. Yet it was there that modern experimental physiology began. The idea of studying illness as a natural phenomenon, not necessarily for the sake of cure, was first conceived in Paris, and the beginnings of systematic clinical research in medicine were made in the hospitals of that city.[11]

Until the 1830s, German medical research and natural science research in general was backward compared with the French and probably with the British, too. The famous network of modern German universities already existed from the time when, following tentative beginnings at Halle, Göttingen, and Jena, the University of Berlin was established in 1809.[12] But the universities,

10. Cf. Abraham Flexner, *Universities: American, English, German* (Oxford: Oxford University Press, 1930), pp. 317–27; Donald S. L. Cardwell, *The Organization of Science in England* (London: Heinemann, 1957), pp. 22–25; H. E. Guerlac, "Science and French National Strength," in E. M. Earle, ed., *Modern France* (Princeton: Princeton University Press, 1951), pp. 85–88.

11. Cf. Shryock, op. cit., pp. 70–71, 151–69; Newman, op. cit., p. 48; Guerlac, op. cit., pp. 81–105.

12. Cf. Flexner, op. cit., pp. 311–15; R. H. Samuel and R. Hinton Thomas, *Education and Society in Modern Germany* (London: Routledge & Kegan Paul, 1949), pp. 111–13; Jacob Barion, *Universitas und Universität* (Bonn: Rörscheid, 1954), pp. 14–20.

rather than promoting, retarded the development of empirical science. They regarded philosophy as the queen of sciences and usually disparaged empirical research. The biological sciences in particular were under the sway of *Naturphilosophie*, which stimulated much imaginative writing but little research.[13]

Only around 1830 did this atmosphere change under foreign influence. Liebig, who had studied in Paris, established in 1825 the first chemical laboratory at the small University of Giessen. A few years later, Johannes Mueller, the central figure of German physiology, abandoned his early attachment to *Naturphilosophie* and became converted to the empirical method by studying the works of the Swedish chemist, Berzelius. About the same time, the Vienna school of clinicians adopted the methods of investigation initiated by the Paris clinicians, and various learned journals began to propogate the new scientific approach in the medical sciences.[14]

Thus, the French showed at least as much understanding of the value and the needs of scientific research as the Germans. It should not be assumed that this understanding suddenly declined around the middle of the century. The influentials of French science at that time, such as Dumas, and later Pasteur, Claude Bernard, and Victor Duruy, were certainly not less enlightened and brilliant than their German counterparts. In fact, they may have been more sympathetic to the needs of scientific research than German academic policy-makers, since obscurantism was rather prevalent within both the faculties of the German universities and the governmental offices in charge of higher education.[15] The greater expansion of German scientific facilities and the more prompt recognition of new fields are therefore as much in need of explanation as the continuous growth in German discoveries.

The second condition—the presumably peculiar values and organization of the German university—is also a very doubtful explanation. The idea of academic freedom notwithstanding, atheists, Jews, and Socialists were often kept out of academic careers in Germany. Academic self-government was not necessarily enlightened: liberal scientists in the 1840s regarded it as an essentially retrograde arrangement. In fact, some of the most beneficial academic decisions—with relation to the growth of science—were taken by civil servants, most notably, Freidrich Althoff, who interfered with academic self-government. Even the *Habilitationsschriften* were often rather mediocre

13. Cf. Shryock, op. cit., pp. 192–201; Diepgen, op. cit., vol. 2/1, pp. 23–28.
14. Cf. Cardwell, op. cit., pp. 22–25; Shryock, op. cit., pp. 188, 195; Garrison, op. cit., pp. 451–52.
15. See Guerlac, op. cit., pp. 85–88, on France. On the relative backwardness of German academic administration, see Ervin H. Ackerknecht, *Rudolf Virchow: Doctor, Statesman, Anthropologist* (Madison: University of Wisconsin Press, 1953), pp. 130–40; Samuel and Thomas, op. cit., pp. 114–30; Max Weber, *Jugendbriefe* (Tübingen: Mohr, n.d.), pp. 151–52. In order to realize the amount of obscurantism and intolerance in German universities at the time, it is useful to read the otherwise shallow work of Richard Graf du Moulin Eckart, *Geschichte der deutschen Universitäten* (Stuttgart: Enke, 1929).

pieces of research, and there was nothing in the constitution of the universities efficiently to prevent mediocre professors from confirming inferior theses.[16] At the same time, the ideas as well as some of the arrangements said to be characteristic of the German universities also existed in France. Freedom of teaching already formed the core of the tradition at the Collège de France before the Revolution and was carried further than in the German universities. The ideals of pure research were formulated in French scientific ideology at least as clearly as in German, and they were practiced and encouraged in a great many ways.[17] There is no proof that the lack of the paraphernalia of academic self-government interfered with the research of French scientists more than in Germany. It is true that, compared with the *Habilitation,* the French *agrégation* and the system of open examinations seem to be inefficient ways of selecting people for academic careers. But there is little evidence that this irrelevant hurdle actually prevented potentially creative people from entering scientific careers. Moreover, there were other means, such as numerous prizes and public honors, which encouraged original research in France.[18]

Decentralization has been written about much less than the first two conditions, partly because it was an unintended circumstance and partly because its effect upon research is less immediately evident. The decentralization of the German academic system was the result of the political dismemberment of the German-speaking people. There were 19 independent universities in Germany proper, maintained by the princes of the numerous small states constituting Germany in the eighteenth and early nineteenth centuries, as well as German language universities in Switzerland, Austria (including the Czech provinces), and Dorpat in the Baltic Sea Provinces of Russia.[19] At the same time, the French boasted a unified academic system, most of it situated in Paris. Although some of the features of this centralization introduced by Napoleon were deplored, the central administration of science and academic institutions generally was considered to be desirable by French politicians of science.[20]

16. Cf. Flexner, op. cit., pp. 317–27; Samuel and Thomas, loc. cit.

17. See Claude Bernard, *Morceaux choisis,* dirigé et préfacé par Jean Rostand (Paris: Gallimard, 1938), pp. 16–18, for one of the most beautiful descriptions of the traditions of the freedom of teaching and research as it was practiced at the Collège de France. See also Ernest Lavissé, *Histoire de France* (Paris: Librairie Hachette, n.d.), vol. 9/1, p. 301, on the pioneering beginnings of the teaching of pure sciences in the same institution in the 1770s and 1780s.

18. For a good description of how the French system of examinations actually worked, see René Leriche, *Am Ende meines Lebens* (Bern and Stuttgart: Huber, 1957), pp. 53–55. Leriche, like others, attributes the lack of originality of French medicine to the examinations. But his own account shows that the problem was rather the lack of career opportunities for young medical scientists (ibid., p. 34).

19. With the addition of Strassburg in 1872, there were 20 universities in Germany. Cf. Christian v. Ferber, *Die Entwicklung des Lehrkörpers der deutschen Universitäten und Hochschulen 1864–1954,* vol. 3 of Helmuth Plessner, ed., *Untersuchungen zur Lage der deutschen Hochschullehrer* (Göttingen: Vandenhoeck & Ruprecht, 1956), pp. 37–38. The German-language universities of Switzerland were Zürich, Bern, and Basel and of Austria, Vienna, Prague, Graz, and Innsbruck.

20. Cf. Guerlac, op. cit., pp. 87–88.

Nevertheless, decentralization seems to have been the decisive factor in determining the differences in the scientific creativity of the two countries. It gave rise to academic competition, and competition forced upon the individual institutions decisions which would not have been made otherwise, or at least not made at that time. In all areas crucial to the development of the medical sciences, German policies turned out to be in the long run more farsighted and bold than French policies, although the first initiative was often taken by the French. What, then, was the actual competition and how did it influence the decisions about the crucial problems of academic policy?

The Crucial Decisions

Given the situation of the medical sciences (and perhaps of the sciences in general) at the beginning of the last century, the problem faced by the French and the German systems (and not confronted by Britain and the United States until later) was to find adequate criteria for the evaluation and support of science. The governments, and increasingly the people, too (especially in France), believed in the value and usefulness of science. Academies, universities, and other institutions were set up everywhere, or rejuvenated where they existed before, in order to promote research and to disseminate knowledge. One of the aims of these institutions was to enable a selected few scientists, who had already proved their greatness, to devote all of their time to financially supported scientific research. But it was not intended to create in these institutions academic careers which one entered as in any other profession. The large majority of the scientists had independent means or a lucrative profession (very often medical practice, even in sciences not connected with medicine) and pursued their scientific interest in their free time, often at a considerable personal cost. This idealistic pattern seemed to fit perfectly that sacred pursuit of truth which was science. Academic appointments therefore were regarded as honors rather than careers, and turning science into an occupation would have seemed something like a sacrilege.

A corollary, in this amateur stage of science, was the absence of specialization. The great names of the early nineteenth century were those of generalists who were creative in more than one field. And the new scientific disciplines developed from their work. While it was increasingly believed that the new disciplines required specialists, the fact that they were opened up by generalists seemed to indicate that specialization was not really necessary. Moreover, there persisted the reluctance to abandon the conception of general science which explains to the adept all the secrets of nature. Thus, there was considerable disinclination to substitute for the *savant* such narrow specialists as chemists, physiologists, and the like. And there was even more reluctance to redefine such a traditionally unified field as medicine into a number of subspecialties.

The second problem was the development of criteria for the support of research. Today it is still difficult, of course, to decide what constitutes adequate and sufficient support of research, but at least budgets can be drawn for determined purposes. At that time even this was impossible, since research was an unpredictable, erratic process, and important discoveries were made as often outside as inside the laboratories.

Finally, there was the question of training scientists. Until the second half and particularly the last quarter of the nineteenth century, science had few practical applications. Most of it was pure science benefiting no practice. Under these circumstances, to train every medical student, would-be chemist, and engineer in scientific research was about as justified as it would be today to teach every concertgoer advanced musical composition.[21]

These problems existed in both countries and were approached in France and Germany with the same concepts. Yet, to repeat, the long-term decisions made in France concerning all three problems were the opposite of those made in Germany.

Scientific careers and specialization

The creation of regular careers in science and the recognition of specialized disciplines were closely connected problems. Both may be illustrated with the case of physiology, the most decisive science for the development of medicine in the nineteenth century.

As a systematic discipline, physiology emerged at the beginning of that century. François Magendie, considered to be the founder of experimental physiology, was professor of medicine. He established the new specialty and could follow it undisturbed (though practically unsupported) at the Collège de France, because of the full degree of academic freedom prevailing in that institution. But his disciple, Claude Bernard, who became the most outstanding representative of the new field around the middle of the century, for many years had to use his private laboratory and private means to pursue his research. At last, against the opposition of those who regarded the new discipline as merely a branch of anatomy, a special chair was created for Bernard at the Sorbonne in 1854. Soon thereafter he also fell heir to Magendie's chair at the Collège de France and held both appointments until 1868; he then transferred his work to the Museum of Natural History, relinquishing the post at the Sorbonne to his disciple, Paul Bert.

The recognition of the discipline of physiology, however, did not create opportunities for purely scientific careers in the traditional field of medicine.

21. On the state of science in the early nineteenth century, see Pledge, op. cit., pp. 115–51. On scientists in the same period, see Elie Halévy, *History of England in 1815* (London: Pelican, 1938), vol. 2, pp. 187–200; René J. Dubos, *Louis Pasteur: Franc-tireur de la science* (Paris: Presses Universitaires de France, 1955), pp. 3–4; and Diepgen, op. cit., vol. 2/1, pp. 2–5, 66–69, 152–53.

In this connection, the only change was that after the retirement of the chair's incumbent a single successor would have to be found. This was not a prospect on the basis of which one could realistically take up research as a career. Therefore, potential scientists first had to build up a practice and engage in research as a part-time activity.[22]

Thus, the academic career changed very little in France through the nineteenth century. Appointments were made from an undifferentiated group of practitioners—amateur scientists—and usually at a fairly advanced age. Even academically successful persons did not become full-time scientists before they reached their forties or fifties, and since the chair to be vacated was not known they had to maintain as broad interests and activities as possible. But in the second half of the century, there was increasingly less chance for non-specialists to make important discoveries. French scientific productivity therefore declined even in fields pioneered by Frenchmen. Whenever a discipline reached the stage of development where its efficient pursuit required specialists, there was little chance that the French system would produce such scientists.[23]

Physiology as a science was received with more sympathy in Germany than in France, but its recognition as an academic specialty there also ran into difficulties. The man who did most for the introduction of the discipline to Germany, Johannes Mueller, was a generalist who taught, in addition to physiology, anatomy, ophthalmology, and surgery.[24] His eventual successor in Berlin, Du Bois-Reymond, had been refused one professorial chair after another because he was considered a mere specialist.[25] The early creation of a separate chair in physiology (for Purkinje in Breslau, 1839) had no general effect, and for some years physiology and anatomy continued to be taught by the same person in all other German universities. But pressure for the separation of the disciplines by the younger generation of scientists continued, and those with some bargaining power raised the demand when they were offered university chairs. Thus, when Carl Ludwig was offered a professorship at Zürich in 1849, he accepted it only on the condition that a separate teacher be appointed for anatomy;[26] thereafter, the recognition of the new discipline pro-

22. Cf. Bernard, op. cit., pp. 154–57, 263–85; J. M. D. Olmsted, *Claude Bernard: Physiologist* (New York: Harper, 1938), pp. 51–89. For the situation at the beginning of the twentieth century, see Edouard Rist, *25 Portraits de médicins français, 1900–1950* (Paris: Masson, 1955), pp. 29–40.

23. See Rist, op. cit., pp. 97–104, on the career of S. A. Sicard, who seems to have been a relatively lucky and successful scientist. When at the age of 51 he was appointed as professor he had to abandon his lifelong interest and research in neurology because the vacant chair was designated for internal pathology, and course preparation in the new field required a great effort.

24. Cf. K. E. Rothschuh, *Geschichte der Physiologie* (Berlin-Göttingen-Heidelberg: Springer, 1953), pp. 93, 112–18.

25. George Rosen and Beate Caspari-Rosen, *400 Years of a Doctor's Life* (New York: Schuman, 1947), pp. 248–50; Ernst Gagliardi, Hans Nabholz and Jean Strohl, *Die Universität Zürich und ihre Vorläufer 1833–1933* (Zürich: Erziehungsdirektion, 1938), pp. 548–49.

26. Ibid., pp. 539–48. Virchow, who was also offered the chair, refused to accept it on the ground that he wished a chair for pathological anatomy exclusively (without teaching responsi-

ceeded rapidly. No university could afford to neglect the new field, so that by 1864 there were already 15 full professors of physiology in Germany and several others in the wider system of German-language universities.[27] The separation of physiology from anatomy at this stage became the official policy of university administration. In some cases, where traditionally minded incumbents were reluctant to abandon one of the disciplines, the separation was forced upon them by administrative pressure.[28]

All of this led to a complete transformation of the scientific career in Germany. In spite of the strictures against narrowness and of the continuing lip service paid to the image of the scientist who works because of devotion, science became a specialized and regularized occupation. As we have seen, success, fame, or even sheer enterprise had a good chance for reward. Once a new and fruitful field was recognized in one university, strong pressures led other universities to follow suit, thereby creating more opportunities for those willing to work in the new field. Therefore, it was possible—and for the very able also worthwhile—to concentrate after graduation on one well-defined and promising field of research with the definite aim of a scientific career. Not only was it unnecessary first to build up a practice and to retain as general interest as possible but if one had taken such a course his academic prospects would have been negligible in competition with the full-time specialists. Thus, specialized science became a career, and the amateur general scientist disappeared in Germany.[29] This difference in career possibilities, not the distinction between *Habilitation* and *aggrégation,* explains the greater research orientation of German than of French science.

The same mechanisms which explain the development of scientific roles also explain the development of facilities for research and the introduction of scientific methods into the training of physicians. The creation of new facili-

---

bilities in either surgical anatomy or physiology). In Ludwig's time the nominal unity of physiology and anatomy was still maintained; the separate teacher in anatomy was only an extraordinary professor. But when Ludwig left Zürich in 1855 and the position was offered to Koelliker, the chairs were finally separated upon the latter's suggestion (although Koelliker himself refused the job). For similar instances of creating new specialties at the same university in order to attract or retain teachers, see ibid., pp. 562, 879.

27. Cf. von Ferber, op. cit., p. 204.

28. For example, Valentin in Bern, in 1865; see Bruno Kisch, *Forgotten Leaders in Modern Medicine* (Philadelphia: American Philosophical Society, 1954), pp. 174–75.

29. Max Weber, writing in 1918, regarded science as a most risky career; see his "Science as a Vocation," in H. H. Gerth and C. Wright Mills, *From Max Weber: Essays in Sociology* (London: Oxford University Press, 1947), pp. 132–34. But it should be realized that Weber was referring to a crisis situation in an already established discipline; the circumstances were much more hopeful in the middle of the nineteenth century. Of those who took their *Habilitation* between 1850 and 1859, 85 percent received full-time academic appointments, while for those who received their *Habilitation* between 1900 and 1909, only 62 percent received such posts. The corresponding proportions in medicine are 84 and 48 percent, respectively. (This does not necessarily mean a relatively greater decline of research opportunities in medicine, because there were good research opportunities outside the universities in public hospitals.) See von Ferber, op. cit., pp. 81–82, for the statistical data; and Adolf Struempell, *Aus dem Leben eines deutschen Klinikers* (Leipzig: Vogel, 1925), on the *Habilitation* as a preparation for a hospital career.

ties was part and parcel of the bargaining between universities and scientists. Facilities (laboratories, assistants, and so on) were offered to attract desirable candidates or to prevent scientists from moving elsewhere. The extension of facilities made possible, and to some extent made necessary, the training of a growing number of persons capable of doing research. Since not all such individuals could be given academic appointments in the basic medical sciences or otherwise, they used their research skills and interests to transform clinical medicine into an exact science. These processes and their results may be briefly illustrated.

Research facilities

As has been pointed out, the French were the first to establish modern institutions for scientific training and research. but the facilities and arrangements established in France about 1800, considered to be ideal for their time, were hardly extended or changed until World War I or later. The Pasteur Institute, established in 1888, was the first independent research institute of the world. Again, it remained the only one in its field in France at least until World War I.[30]

Thus, in France a new type of organization was apt to remain a single showpiece for 50 years, while in Germany such novelties became routine features of the organization of research in a much shorter time. By the 1840s, there were apparently more and better chemical laboratories in Germany than in France, and by the sixties, the contrast was extreme. At a time when it was an achievement for Pasteur to obtain any (and most inadequate) laboratory facilities, the Prussian government built new laboratories at Bonn and Berlin (the Bonn laboratory, for example, could accommodate more than 60 students) equipped with the most up-to-date facilities, and the older ones probably were also more adequate than anything that existed elsewhere. And there were good laboratories at other universities in Germany.[31]

There were similar differences between Germany and France in the development of facilities for medical research and of specialized research institutions. The New Vienna School of clinical research began in the thirties, and its facilities seem to have been modest even until midcentury. But there were gradual improvements in one place after another, and by the sixties, there evolved fairly uniform standards which made it possible to conduct clinical research with the aid of adequate laboratory facilities in a number of places.[32]

30. The ideal arrangements of French medical schools in 1798 are noted in Newman, op. cit., p. 48. Concerning the quite different picture presented by French academic medicine early in this century, see Abraham Flexner, *Medical Education in Europe* (New York: The Carnegie Foundation for the Advancement of Teaching, 1912), pp. 221–23; and Leriche, op. cit., p. 34. On the Pasteur Institute, see Guerlac, op. cit., p. 88.
31. Cf. Cardwell, op. cit., p. 80; and Dubos, op. cit., pp. 34, 78–79.
32. Cf. Diepgen, op. cit., vol. 2/1, pp. 207–09; on the situation in the 1860s, see Theodor Billroth, *The Medical Sciences in the German Universities* (New York: Macmillan, 1924), p. 27; and at the turn of the century, Flexner, op. cit., pp. 145–66.

Finally, the establishment of specialized research institutions became a matter of routine in Germany soon after the beginnings made in France. They became a tool regularly used by the universities' administrations, the governments, and local bodies to encourage and develop the work of famous scientists.[33]

Scientific training

The differences in the development of medical training were no less conspicuous. The fact that until about the 1880s all the great advances in the basic medical sciences contributed little to the cure of illness largely explains the persistent and overwhelming emphasis on the practical art of medicine rather than on its few scientific bases in the training of the student-physician. Indeed, apprenticeship and bedside demonstrations were the most important parts of medical training in France, England, and the United States.[34]

Only in Germany did the training of the doctor become a privilege of scientists. By the 1860s, even clinical chairs were given exclusively to people with attainment in research rather than to outstanding practitioners. And from the middle of the century, even public hospitals were increasingly staffed by doctors both interested and trained in research. Thus, much earlier than elsewhere (possibly prematurely), medicine in Germany became an applied science.[35] As a result, when the great opportunities for clinical research arose, following the discovery of the bacteriological causation of illness and the perfection of anesthesia and aseptic surgery, there were in Germany enough doctors trained in research to take full advantage of the opportunity and to transform public (even nonteaching) hospitals into veritable institutions of applied medical science.[36]

Decentralization and Competition

Thus, regarding all three crucial decisions—developing scientific facilities, creating scientific roles, and training larger numbers of research personnel than were justified by existing practical needs—the German system "behaved" with uncanny foresight. It has been shown that this foresight was

33. Cf. Flexner, op. cit., 1930, pp. 31–35.
34. Cf. Diepgen, op. cit., vol. 2/1, pp. 212–14; vol. 2/2, pp. 154–55, 286–88; Abraham Flexner, *Medical Education: A Comparative Study* (New York: Macmillan, 1925), pp. 211–12, 241, 248.
35. Diepgen, op. cit., vol. 2/1, pp. 152–53. See also Theodor Billroth, loc. cit.; Bernhard Naunyn, *Erinnerungen, Gedanken und Meinungen* (Munich: Bergmann, 1925), pp. 375–76.
36. There was a parallel development in chemistry. There, too, the availability of relatively large numbers of trained chemists afforded Germany the opportunity to build up within a short time a chemical industry based on applied science, after the discovery of the aniline dyes made the practical application of science a permanent possibility; cf. Cardwell, op. cit., pp. 134–37, 186–87.

not the result of greater individual wisdom. It was the result of competition due to the unintended decentralization of the German system.

"Competition" in this paper refers to the general condition underlying all the processes described above: it is a situation in which no single institution is able to lay down standards for the system of institutions within which people (in this case, students and teachers) are relatively free to move from one place to another. Under such circumstances, university administrators required neither exceptional boldness nor foresight for continually expanding facilities and training and for creating new scientific jobs. There was little if any need for fateful individual decisions. Improvements and innovations had to be made from time to time in order to attract famous men or keep them from leaving. In this way, laboratories and institutions were founded, assistantships provided, new disciplines recognized, and scientific jobs created. These innovations were repeated throughout the system because of pressure from scientists and students in general, irrespective of practical needs and of what a few scientific influentials thought.

If competition inevitably brought about the adoption of fruitful innovations in the universities, it also forced them to correct mistakes and to eliminate traditions which retarded scientific development. This process has been shown in the case of the separation of physiology from anatomy and the introduction of scientific criteria in clinical training in Germany.

Britain and the United States

The similarities, differences, and differential effects observed in the cases of France and Germany were, in essentials, repeated in the cases of Britain and the United States.

From the middle of the nineteenth century, British—and soon after, American—educators, scientists, and administrators displayed increasing interest in the organization of science in Germany. Scientists and intellectuals who visited Germany returned home enthusiastic about German academic life, and soon German university training became a standard preparation for scientific careers among British scientists.[37]

Consequently, British universities, though retaining certain traditions, introduced measures to bring themselves in line with German standards and practices. Oxford and Cambridge, which until the 1860s were training centers primarily for the rich and the clergy, began to emerge as institutions of empirical science and positive scholarship pursued in an atmosphere of academic freedom and autonomy. The newer University of London and the universities in the provinces imitated the German pattern even more closely and were imbued, from the beginning, with the spirit of empirical science.

37. Ibid., p. 50.

The rapid growth of the modern academic system also began in the United States in the 1860s. The Land Grant Act passed in 1862 and other circumstances brought about a large increase in the number of American colleges and universities between the sixties and the eighties.[38] In the present context, the most important events were the rise of the graduate schools in the seventies and in the following decade the establishment of Johns Hopkins Medical School which was directly influenced by the German example.[39] Eventually older institutions such as Harvard also abandoned certain traditions derived from pre-nineteenth-century England and adopted new methods in imitation of the German.[40]

In this development of a system of up-to-date institutions for medical research and training Britain had most of the advantages over the United States, similar to those possessed by France over Germany at the beginning of the century. The British began the adoption of the German patterns earlier, and they began from a higher level than did the Americans.[41] Nevertheless, while the effect of the academic reform on British science was slow and partial, in America it produced a conspicuous rise in scientific creativity.

That the social mechanisms at work in these cases were similar to those involved in our first pair of comparisons can be illustrated best by the organization of clinical research and the creation of clinical chairs. Attempts to copy the Germans by making hospital departments into virtual research establishments and filling the clinical chairs according to criteria of scientific achievement ran into serious opposition in both countries. They seemed like an infringement on the rights of the profession, whose members had run the teaching hospitals independently of the universities, and it also seemed to be endangering the charitable purpose of the hospitals. Therefore, when Oxford and Cambridge decided to overhaul their medical training programs along German lines, they confined themselves to the basic departments and sent their students to continue their clinical studies in the hospital medical schools of London. This division was a decision in favor of preserving the traditions of the professional fraternities attached to the various public hospitals and of the philanthropic bodies which governed these hospitals. Of course, it could also have been justified by the aim to keep apart pure research and professional practice.[42] However, a priori reasons for incorporating the teaching hos-

38. Ibid., p. 80.

39. Cf. Flexner, *Universities . . .*, op. cit., p. 73; and Abraham Flexner, *I Remember* (New York: Simon and Schuster, 1940), pp. 63–64.

40. Cf. Edward D. Churchill, *To Work in the Vineyards of Surgery: The Reminiscences of J. Collins Warren (1842–1927)* (Cambridge: Harvard University Press, 1958), pp. 193–97, 257–71.

41. Cf. Newman, op. cit., pp. 269, 276; Cardwell, op. cit., pp. 46–51, 80, 103–07, 110–14, 118–19, 134–37, and passim. Flexner, *Universities . . .*, op. cit., pp. 46–65; Richard H. Shryock, *American Medical Research: Past and Present* (New York: New York Academy of Medicine, 1947), pp. 106–08, 118–19.

42. Cf. "The First Hundred Years: Notes on the History of the Association," extracts from Ernest M. Little, "History of the Association," *British Medical Journal* 1 (1932): 672–76;

pitals in the universities and staffing them on the basis of attainments in research might have been advanced. As shown above, this was one of the
problems which could not at that time be decided on a priori logical grounds;
only future experience could indicate the effective choice.

The conditions for acquiring the needed experience existed in England,
since there were approximations of a proper university hospital and university
clinical departments in the London University College Medical School
(founded as early as 1836), and similar opportunities arose when the provincial universities were established.[43] Yet, instead of representing competing alternatives, none of these departments ventured farther than the model established by the Oxford-Cambridge-London triangle; that is, their clinical
departments were run by local practitioners as practical training centers rather
than being organized as university departments engaged in research and
staffed by persons selected on the basis of scientific eminence. This was quite
different from the situation in Germany, where, for example, the little University of Giessen successfully pioneered in establishing its chemical laboratory,
imitated later by universities of much greater prestige. It also differed from the
innovation of the Johns Hopkins Medical School, where a full-scale medical
faculty that included basic as well as clinical departments was established—
a pattern that was followed by other universities and led to a rapid transformation of American medicine reminiscent of the German, notwithstanding
the strength of a professional and philanthropic tradition similar to that of
Britain.[44]

All this shows unequivocally that the British system was not competitive.
Yet seemingly it was decentralized, since universities and public hospitals
were private institutions financed and governed in a variety of ways, as in the
United States. In fact, however, Britain also had a centralized system, though
centralized in a somewhat different way than that of the French. The provincial universities did not begin to confer degrees until 1880 (with the exception of Durham, established in 1831), and their status, as well as the status
of London University, never reached that of the two ancient universities.
The system was totally overshadowed by the Oxford-Cambridge duopoly,
which, in spite of differences in matters of religion and politics, represented
basically similar educational philosophies and academic policies.[45] The special position of these two institutions was maintained in large part by their

A. M. Carr-Saunders and P. A. Wilson, *The Professions* (Oxford: Clarendon Press, 1933), p. 87;
Flexner, *Medical Education* . . . , op. cit., p. 28; Newman, op. cit., pp. 49–50, 133 ff.

43. Cf. Flexner, *Universities* . . . , op. cit., pp. 242–44.

44. Cf. Donald H. Fleming, *William Welch and the Rise of Modern Medicine* (Boston: Little,
Brown, 1954), pp. 173 ff. On competition in American academic life in general, see Logan
Wilson, *The Academic Man* (London: Oxford University Press, 1942), pp. 154–74, 186–91,
195–214; and Theodore Caplow and Reece J. McGee, *The Academic Marketplace* (New York:
Basic Books, 1958).

45. Cf. Flexner, *Universities* . . . , op. cit., p. 249; Bruce Truscot, *Red Brick University*,
(Harmondsworth: Penguin Books, 1951), pp. 19–29. See also R. K. Kelsall, *Higher Civil Servants in Britain*, (London: Routledge & Kegan Paul, 1956), p. 137, on the preservation of the

unwritten exclusive right of educating the political, administrative, ecclesiastical, and professional elite of the nation. In the case of medicine, the two universities were, as we have seen, connected with the leading medical corporations of London, whose members traditionally received their preprofessional education in "Oxbridge." Thus, the centralization of academic life, which in France was the result of administrative design, was achieved in England through the subtler functions of a class system, in which academic institutions like people "were kept in their place" through internalized traditions and networks of semiformalized bonds among persons, groups, and independent organizations.

The United States, then, provides a case similar to the German, where competition within a decentralized system encouraged the establishment of specialized research roles and facilities. The usefulness and the necessity of such roles and facilities in the clinical field were not yet generally recognized at the turn of the twentieth century (in spite of the already existent German examples), and there was strong resistance against them in Britain as well as in the United States. At this time, like medical scientists (or natural scientists) in general, clinicians were still conceived as primarily practitioners and only secondarily as scientists. Thus, the problem of transforming the practitioner-amateur scientist role into a scientific career in the clinical field was similar to the earlier problem of the creation of scientific roles in general. At this stage as in the previous one, competition was the decisive factor in the emergence of the new career.

Conclusion

The continuous growth in the curves of German discoveries during the middle decades of the nineteenth century and in the American curves starting from the 1880s is thus attributed to the extent to which these societies exploited, through enterprise and organizational measures, the possibilities inherent in the state of science. They were quicker than France and Britain in the recognition of new disciplines, the creation of specialized scientific jobs and facilities for research, and the introduction of large-scale systematic training for research. They were also quicker to abandon traditional notions which had lost their usefulness. None of these conditions alone could have sustained scientific growth for a long period of time. It was no coincidence, however, that they went together, since a common underlying factor, competition, determined the crucial decisions concerning all of these conditions in the two decentralized systems. Successful scientists were rewarded with university chairs and facilities. Their success encouraged others to take up science and, incidentally, transformed the pursuit of science into a regular professional ca-

---

educational duopoly in another field; as late as 1950, 47.3 percent of British civil servants in the ranks of Assistant Secretary and above had attended Oxford or Cambridge.

reer; it created pressure for further expansion of facilities and training and exposed the inadequacies of out-of-date traditions.

This interpretation of the curve of scientific discoveries, according to which their growth was due to increased opportunities for entering research careers (and not, for example, to better selection of scientists), is also consistent with the differences between the countries shown in the second index based on the numbers of discoverers. As pointed out earlier, beginning in 1835 in Germany and in 1860 in the United States, the growth in the numbers of those entering upon scientific careers became continuous, while in France and Britain there were fluctuations over the whole period. Continuous growth represents a situation in which research becomes a regular career; fluctuations, a situation in which research to a large extent is a spontaneous activity engaged in by people as the spirit moves them.

In conclusion, some of the implications and problems raised by the existence of a positive relationship between scientific productivity and academic competition may be noted. According to the present explanation, this relationship is due to the impetus provided by competition for entering promising but undeveloped fields of research. This, however, suggests that the growth of discoveries in any field may be limited by the capacity for expansion of the institutional framework (jobs and facilities), a suggestion which seems to be worth further exploration.[46]

Another question concerns the *quality* of the impetus given to science by competition. The present hypothesis suggests that competition increases the gross amount of discoveries of all kinds through the thorough exploitation of potentially fruitful fields of research. It says nothing about the conditions conducive to the creation of fundamentally new ideas, and it is quite possible that the social conditions that stimulate basic innovations differ from those that facilitate the exploitation of fruitful ideas already discovered.[47]

Finally, nothing has been said about the conditions that maintain scientific competition. Political decentralization gave rise to competition in Germany, and political decentralization enhanced by private financing and administration of higher education led to competition in the United States. It is not argued, however, that competition is the only possible outcome of any state of decentralization, or that competition, once established, is self-maintaining. Decentralization may lead to collusion or mutual isolation as well as to competition; and competition may be replaced by either of these alternatives. Determination of the general conditions that ensure competition, therefore, is another problem which needs further study.

46. This is the subject matter of A. Zloczower, *Career Opportunities and Growth of Scientific Discovery in 19th-Century Germany with Special Reference to the Development of Physiology*, unpublished M.A. thesis, Hebrew University, Jerusalem, Israel, 1960. [Now published by Arno Press, New York, 1981.]

47. Cf. Joseph Ben-David, "Roles and Innovations in Medicine," *American Journal of Sociology* 65 (May 1960): 557–68 [this volume, chap. 1].

Universities and Academic Systems in Modern Societies*   6

Universities engage in teaching and research. They prepare students to become men of action in practical politics, the civil service, the practice of law, medicine, surgery, etc. Others studying at universities want to become scholars and scientists whose style of work is far removed from the on-the-spot decision making which is so important among the former category. The professions and disciplines taught and developed at universities require a great variety of manpower and organization of entirely different kinds. Universities nevertheless insist on comprising all of them, in the name of an idea stemming from a time when one person was really able to master all the arts and sciences. They, furthermore, attempt to perform all these complex tasks within the framework of corporate self-government reminiscent of medieval guilds. Indeed, there have been serious doubts about the efficiency of the university since the eighteenth century. Reformers of the "Enlightenment" advocated the abolition of the universities as useless remnants of past tradition and established in their stead specialized schools for the training of professional people and academies for the advancement of science and learning. This program was actually put into effect by the Revolution and the subsequent reorganization of higher education by Napoleon in France. The present-day organization of higher education in the Soviet Union still reflects the belief in the efficiency of specialized professional schools as well as specialized academic research institutions.

Even in countries where universities are the typical institutions of higher education and research there are constant doubts about the ways universities

*With Awzaham Zloczower.
The authors are indebted to Eric de Dampierre for his very useful suggestions and kind help in obtaining source material.

125

are actually going about their tasks.[1] Some accuse them of undue traditionalism and advocate the setting up of technological universities, training
for a much larger variety of practical callings than most universities (at least in
Europe) actually do. Others, on the other hand, accuse some of the universities (mainly in America) of having abandoned the true standards of science
and scholarship by the introduction of courses of study which are really vocational in their nature. Universities are often criticized for their inefficient
methods of teaching, resulting from the overwhelming interest of their staff in
research. At the same time it is deplored that some universities pay too much
attention to teaching, neglecting research which should be the principal task
of the university. There is general agreement that teaching and research should
be complementary rather than competing with each other, although it is well
known that the two functions are not always compatible. The ability for teaching does not always go together with the ability for doing research, and research requires a different organization than teaching.

There is, finally, the question of the "unity of science" which the university is supposed to represent. The more successful universities are in promoting research, the greater becomes the gap in communication between the various branches of learning. There has been a constant demand for bridging this
gap by means of some sort of general studies. The gap, however, does not
seem to have diminished. Increased specialization also seems to counteract
another cherished purpose of the university, namely, the formation of moral
character. It becomes more and more difficult to see how and which part of
university studies are suited for the accomplishment of this purpose. Finally,
there seem to be great inefficiencies in university self-government. The autonomy of the academic body is defended by all. But professors constantly com-
plain that their administrative duties encroach upon their time.

Yet, in spite of all these inconsistencies and contradictions, the university
has been a successful institution. Everywhere in the world universities have
expanded rapidly. New countries, which had not possessed universities before, regard the establishment of a university as one of their first priorities.
Universities have also been markedly successful in research. The overwhelm-

1. Most of the discussion about the subject has been influenced by Abraham Flexner, *Univer-*
sities: American, English, German (New York: Oxford University Press, 1930). For some of the
more recent discussion of the problems of universities, cf. Logan Wilson, *The Academic Man*
(New York: Oxford University Press, 1942); H. E. Guerlac, "Science and French National
Strength," in E. M. Earle, ed., *Modern France* (Princeton: Princeton University Press, 1951),
pp. 81–105; Helmuth Plessner, ed., *Untersuchungen zur Lage der deutschen Hochschullehrer*
(Göttingen: Vandenhœck and Ruprecht, 1953), 3 vols; Jacques Barzun, *Teacher in America* (New
York: Doubleday, 1954); Dael Wolfle, *America's Resources of Specialized Talent* (New York:
Harper, 1954); W. H. G. Armytage, *Civic Universities* (London: Ernest Benn, 1955); George F.
Kneller, *Higher Learning in Britain* (London: Cambridge University Press, 1955); Theodore
Caplow and Reece J. McGee, *The Academic Marketplace* (New York: Basic Books, 1958); David
Riesman, *Constraint and Variety in American Education* (New York: Doubleday, 1958); John J.
Corson, *Governance of Colleges and Universities* (New York: McGraw Hill, 1960); Hans Anger,
Probleme der deutschen Universität (Tübingen: Mohr, 1960).

ing majority of Nobel Prizes and other scientific distinctions have gone to university professors, and their output of scholarly work has not been less impressive.[2] Universities, therefore, present a baffling problem for the sociologist. They have apparently chronic and irremediable problems of internal organization, yet they manage to be in some important ways extremely efficient in accomplishing their tasks; and in spite of the constant flow of criticism directed against them, there is a general belief in their necessity even among their critics.

It is not the purpose of this essay to take a stand for or against this widespread belief in the idea of the university or to suggest a solution for its problems. We shall rather ask the question how and why universities became what they are today. Instead of trying to arrive at some concept about the essence or the idea of the university, we shall try to find out under what conditions universities assumed their great variety of functions and to what extent have they been able to cope with them.

German Universities and the Idea of the Modern University

For about a hundred years, between the early nineteenth century and the advent of Nazism, German universities served as model academic institutions. The education of an American or British scientist was not considered complete until he had spent some time in Germany, studying with one of the renowned professors, far more of whom had won acclaim and scientific distinction than the scientists of any other country.[3] The still prevalent conception or "idea" of the university, as well as the definition of the professor's role, originated in Germany during the nineteenth century. It was, furthermore, in the German universities, more than anywhere else, that the main fields of scientific enquiry developed into "disciplines" possessing specialized methodologies and systematically determined contents.[4] Students who wanted to know what a discipline really was had to read German textbooks, and those who wanted to keep abreast of scientific research had to read German journals.

The outside world, which became aware of the excellence of German achievements, connected these achievements with the internal structure and organization of the German universities. It came to be widely believed that what a university should be and how a university should be run was discovered in Germany. The discovery was—and still is—often attributed to the ideas of

2. Cf. Bernard Barber, *Science and the Social Order* (Glencoe: The Free Press, 1952), pp. 139–69.
3. Cf. D. S. L. Cardwell, *The Organization of Science in England* (London: Heinemann, 1957).
4. Cf. F. Paulsen, *The German Universities* (New York: Longmans Green, 1906), p. 56; Plessner, op. cit., vol. 1., pp. 23–24.

German philosophers from Kant to Hegel who conceived of the university as a
seat of original secular learning pursued as an end in itself and who imparted
to it supreme dignity.[5] During the nineteenth century reforms were introduced
following the German example in Britain, France, and the U.S., leading invariably to a rising standard of scientific work and a growing volume of production.[6] This confirmed the belief that the peculiar ideas and arrangements of
German universities accounted for their excellence.

We shall attempt to show that these ideas and arrangements were not the
cause but rather the result of the circumstances which had historically shaped
the German university; that it was not the idea of the university which explains
the success of the German university system, nor the diffusion of this idea
abroad which explains the impetus to science in those countries introducing
organizational reforms under its impact. In order to do this, we shall have to
examine the circumstances which determined the strength as well as the weaknesses of the German university system.

The pioneering period of the German universities, marked by the rapid development of the different academic fields and their differentiation into systematic and specific disciplines lasted until about the end of the nineteenth
century. By about 1860, the original four faculties of theology, philosophy,
law, and medicine, comprising just about all higher knowledge existing at the
beginning of the century, had been transformed beyond all recognition. A host
of new disciplines had found their place within the loose frame of the faculties, none of which—with the exception of theology—seems to have been
averse to incorporating new fields. Commencing with the third quarter of the
century this process of expansion and differentiation slowed down. Neither
the emerging social sciences nor the various fields of engineering attained
proper academic status at the universities. The latter was banished to the *Tech-
nische Hochschulen,* which only over the strenuous opposition of the universities attained the right of conferring the title "doctor."[7] The universities not
only began to offer increasing resistance to the introduction of new sciences
which had mushroomed outside their walls but they also placed often insur-

5. The main protagonist of this idea was Flexner, op. cit., p. 326; cf. also Paul Farmer,
"Nineteenth-Century Ideas of the University," in Margaret Clapp, ed., *The Modern University*
(Ithaca: Cornell University Press, 1950), pp. 16–17.
6. Cf. about England Élie Halévy, *History of the English People,* Epilogue: 1895–1905.
Book 2 (London: Penguin Books, 1939), p. 24; about France, Guerlac, op. cit., and about the
U.S.A., Abraham Flexner, *I Remember* (New York: Simon and Schuster, 1940), pp. 63–64.
About the fluctuations of scientific productivity in different countries, cf. T. J. Rainoff, "Wave-
like Fluctuations in Creative Productivity in the Development of West European Physics in the
Eighteenth and Nineteenth centuries," *Isis* 12 (1922): 287–319; and Joseph Ben-David, "Scientific Productivity and Academic Organization in Nineteenth Century Medicine," *American Sociological Review* 25 (1960): 828–43. [This volume, chap. 5.]
7. Cardwell, op. cit., pp. 184–85; Flexner, *Universities,* op. cit., pp. 331–32. There were,
however, some who were sympathetic to the introduction of engineering studies at universities,
cf. Paulsen, op. cit., pp. 112–13.

mountable obstacles on the path of disciplines which had begun to develop organically within the established disciplines. Where previously it had been relatively easy to carve out new disciplines from the broad fields and gain recognition through the establishment of separate chairs for them, new specialties were increasingly condemned to permanent subordinate status under the pretext of being too narrow or shallow, and, therefore, *"nicht ordinierbar."* The division of labor which arose in the *Instituten* (research laboratories usually attached to a university chair but not properly integrated within the university) raced far ahead of the increasingly out-of-date academic division of labor. The unity of teaching and research broke down when the academic scientist was forced to specialize in the *Institut* in research that threatened to isolate him from the main discipline which he had to teach if he wanted to become a full professor. The usual rule that each discipline was represented by only one professor contributed much in the previous decades to the establishment of new chairs, because the expansion of the academic staff could take place only in this manner. After the development of the institutes, however, the same rule became a veritable strangling noose: research could be conducted only in the *Institut,* but only one person, the director, could be professor.[8]

Thus, gradually a fence was drawn around the existing academic fields, excluding an increasing part of scientific and scholarly enquiry from the universities. Originally the university was meant to embrace all intellectual enquiry.[9] It absorbed all existing disciplines, theoretical and practical. Even its philosophical founding fathers, like Fichte, Schleiermacher, and Schelling, were as much publicists as "academic" philosophers. In the middle of the century the university became more strictly academic, but it created new disciplines and enlarged its scope, so that practically all the important scientific activity of that time originated at the university. Toward the end of the century both processes of extending the scope of the university came to a standstill.

This growing resistance to differentiation within, and to intellectual (or practical) influence from without, was accompanied by inflexibility of the organizational structure. The professorial role, and the career pattern *Privatdozent-Professor,* so well suited to the needs of research and teaching at the beginning and in the middle of the nineteenth century, when techniques and organization of research were simple, became unable to carry any more the whole burden of research and teaching. *Privatdozentur* in particular became an anomaly in fields where the most necessary research facilities were open

8. Christian v. Ferber, *Die Entwicklung des Lehrkörpers der deutschen Hochschulen 1864–1954,* vol. 3 of Plessner, op. cit., pp. 67–71; for particular cases, cf., e.g., F. v. Müller, *Lebenserinnerungen* (München, 1953), pp. 150–51; H. Friedenwald, "A *Chronique Scandaleuse* in the Vienna School," in Emmanuel Berghoff, *Festschrift zum 80. Geburtstag Max Neuburgers* (Wien, 1948).

9. Cf. René König, *Vom Wesen der deutschen Universität* (Berlin: Verlag Die Runde, 1935), pp. 134 sqq.

only to assistants in the *Institut*, so that a *Privatdozent* without a position in an *Institut* had no oppportunity for doing scientific work. The main career line became, therefore, the assistantship. Yet the constitution of the university and its official structure of roles had hardly taken note of the change. Officially, even today the institutes are only appendages facilitating the professor's research.[10] Even if in some cases this arrangement works well (depending on the personality of the professors and the nature of the discipline), it shows extreme traditionalism and ritualistic clinging to organizational forms which no longer reflect the changed functions of the university.

The explanation of this contradiction between the innovative vitality of the early years of the German university and its subsequent rigidity lies mainly in two circumstances:[11] the fact that the German cultural area, extending over the major part of Central Europe, has always exceeded the limits of any German state and the position of the university in Germany's class system.[12] Due to the first factor, there did not arise in Germany central national universities, like Paris in France, or Oxford-Cambridge in England. The university system was decentralized and competitive. Universities tried to outdo each other or, at any rate, had to keep pace with each other. As a result innovations were introduced in Germany more easily and accepted more widely than elsewhere. The second factor, namely, the position of the university in the class system, accounts for the inflexibility of its organizational structure which became manifest late in the nineteenth century. As it will be shown later, the status and the freedom of the university, seemingly so well established and secure, were as a matter of fact precarious, engendering fear of and resistance to any organizational change.

This interpretation of the developments is not in accordance with the usually accepted view which relates the rise of the German universities to the reforms introduced early in the century under the influence of the then current philosophical ideas, especially the establishment of the University of Berlin. We have to see, therefore, what was the share of ideas, and of competition and class structure, in the process. Indeed, Berlin was the first university in which the philosophical faculty (including arts and sciences) obtained a status formally equivalent, but in influence superior, to the old faculties of law, medicine, and theology. There is no doubt that the granting of academic status to the new arts and sciences was a decisive step and that philosophers had a great part in this innovation. There was a growing class of intellectuals in Germany

10. Plessner, op. cit., vol. 1., pp. 37–49, 192, 223; v. Ferber, op. cit., pp. 87–88; Flexner, *Universities*, op. cit., p. 332.
11. This *Erstarrung* of the German university was observed by Troeltsch; cf. Richard H. Samuel and R. Hinton Thomas, *Education and Society in Modern Germany* (London: Routledge and Kegan Paul, 1949), p. 123.
12. The importance of these circumstances in the development of scientific research has been treated in Joseph Ben-David, op. cit., and in "Roles and Innovations in Medicine," *American Journal of Sociology* 65 (1960): 557–68. [This volume, chap. 1.]

toward the end of the eighteenth century who would not enter any more into the clergy as people like them had done before and who interested themselves in the broad field of learning and methodical thinking which was called at that time philosophy. They were seeking social recognition and economic security, but these were unattainable for them under the existing circumstances: the bourgeoisie was relatively poor and backward, most of the aristocracy had no tradition of education, and the minority who had such interests preferred French to German education. The only career open to young German intellectuals was a university appointment which, in the philosophical faculty, carried little prestige and did not allow real freedom of thought and speech, since universities were subject to the double control of the state and the church.[13] Partly as a result of this control, universities were also intellectually poor institutions. They were harshly criticized, as French universities had been prior to the Revolution, and there was a tendency among enlightened circles to replace them with specialized professional schools. As a matter of fact, quite a few universities were closed down and some professional schools were established during this period.[14]

The Napoleonic wars gave a new chance to the philosopher-intellectuals as well as to the universities. Their advocacy of German instead of French culture, unheeded before, became now the popular ideology affecting even the French-educated upper class. There was a feeling that the real strength of the nation was in the realm of spirit and culture. Indeed, after their subjugation by Napoleon, Germans had little else left to fight with but spiritual strength. This seemed all the more so because political and military defeat coincided with an unprecedented flowering of German philosophy and literature. Philosophers now became national figures, and education was given high priority. Under these circumstances, the philosophical faculty was given its full university status.[15] Since at the same time, and for the same reasons, secondary education was also reformed (through the introduction of the *Abitur*), the new faculty had plenty of students preparing for teaching in the *Gymnasium*.[16]

Undoubtedly, these reforms, which grew up in response to this constellation of circumstances, gave an important impetus to academic work, especially in philosophy and the humanities, the subjects most in fashion at that time in Germany. But only this initial impetus can be attributed to the philosophical ideas attending the birth of this new type of university. All the upsurge of the various *Fachwissenschaften*, especially of the natural sciences,

13. About the situation of German intellectuals at the end of the 18th century, cf. Henri Brunschwig, *La crise de l'État prussien à la fin du XVIIIe siècle et la genèse de la mentalité romantique* (Paris: Presses Universitaires, 1947), pp. 161–86.

14. König, op. cit., pp. 20ff., 49–53; Paulsen, op. cit., p. 443. The closing down of some of the universities was connected with French occupation.

15. Alongside a number of other reforms designed to create a popular identification with the state, cf. Koppel S. Pinson, *Modern Germany* (New York: Macmillan 1955), pp. 33–49.

16. Paulsen, op. cit., p. 63.

occurred not as a result but rather in spite of these ideas. The intentions of the founders and the ideologists of Berlin University would only have made it into a unique showpiece radiating light to all corners of Germany and attracting students and scholars to the somewhat provincial Prussian capital.[17] The decisive thing, however, in the transformation of higher education and research in Germany was the fact that exactly the opposite happened. Berlin never became a unique center but rather the archaic little universities which had been hovering for decades on the verge of dissolution became transformed within a short period of time into institutions modeled on the example of Berlin. In addition, a number of new universities were founded.[18] This quite unintended success was the result of the decentralization of the German academic life. The universities, competing with each other, had to follow the successful example established in one university.

Instead of asserting, therefore, that philosophy created the new German university, we propose that the German university system provided the basis for the great development of philosophy as a systematic discipline. But contrary to the intention of the philosophers, the university system made philosophy into just one of the academic disciplines and added to it a great many new ones. The competitive system worked according to a logic of its own. The establishment of new universities, the raising of the status of the philosophical faculties, and the firm establishment of the new type of philosophy in them created a widespread demand for philosophers in a system comprising more than twenty universities. The student of "philosophy" in Berlin who habilitated himself could take his choice: Bonn, Greifswald, Königsberg, Göttingen, Iena were all in the market for the bright young scholar, offering professorships in the new philosophical faculties of the reorganized university system. By 1840, the philosophical faculty—fifty years previously a mere preparatory part of the theological faculty—was by far the largest in its number of teachers comprising nearly half of all the professors, *extraordinarii* and *Privatdozenten* (270 out of 633; 124 out of 253; and 142 out of 326, resp.). In addition, there was a demand for the philosophically trained person in the theological, legal, and even the medical faculties which, in the latter case, prevented the development of the empirical approach for quite a while.[19]

During the first twenty to thirty years after the reform of the universities, the general intellectual approach which hardly distinguished between philosophy, history, literature, and even natural sciences was broken down into specialized disciplines: history, linguistics, philology, etc. All these were closely connected with the ideological bias of German philosophy which identified

17. Fichte certainly thought of one central university; cf. König, op. cit., p. 82.
18. Bonn 1818; München 1826; Zürich 1833.
19. About the predominance of *Naturphilosophie* in medicine, cf. Richard H. Shryock, *The Development of Modern Medicine* (New York: Knopf, 1947), pp. 192–201, and Paul Diepgen, *Geschichte der Medizin* (Berlin: Gruyter, 1955), vol. 2-1, pp. 23–28.

culture mainly with the humanities.[20] But the breaking down of "philosophy" into specialized disciplines was in itself a departure from the ideological bias, and it occurred as the result of a simple mechanism: whenever the demand for professors in a certain field was saturated, there was a tendency among the more enterprising students to enter new fields regarded until then as mere subspecialties of an established discipline and to develop the specialty into a new discipline. Thus, when the humanities were saturated around 1830–1840, there occurred a shift of interest toward empirical natural sciences, and the interest in speculative philosophy at the universities abated.

This process has been traced in the development of physiology.[21] Lectures in the subject were held already during the first decades of the nineteenth century at German universities, but work was sporadic and haphazard. In 1828, physiology as an experimental discipline was represented in only six German universities by seven lecturers.[22] It was a sideline of anatomy which was beginning to separate from surgery, staking out the entire field of theoretical medicine as its domain. This process took place during the thirties and forties, and by the end of that period anatomy had become the main discipline of scientific medicine, the nucleus from which medicine was turned into a natural science. This new anatomy was taught at almost all German universities in connection with physiology. Competence in physiology, rather than in surgery, became a necessary qualification for attaining the chairs for anatomy. It was, however, not always possible to implement this requirement. Vacant chairs for anatomy could be staffed with scholars familiar with and competent in both fields, but what was one to do with the anatomists of the old school whose privilege to teach anatomy could not be revoked, who yet would not, and could not, teach the new subject? To establish separate chairs for physiology was easier than the creation of a second chair, part of whose function would be to duplicate work entrusted already to the incumbent of a recognized discipline.[23] The forties and fifties were thus periods when specialization in physiology was encouraged and scientific activity in this sphere stimulated. Scholars who hoped for calls to chairs in anatomy were encouraged to focus their research on physiological problems, since most universities still hoped to entrust the teaching of both physiology and anatomy to a single professor, while here and there separate chairs for physiology had already established the complete independence of the new discipline. The prospect of separate chairs for physiology stimulated those

20. Cf. Paulsen, op. cit., pp. 55–63.
21. Awraham Zloczower, *Career Opportunities and the Growth of Scientific Discovery in 19th-Century Germany, with Special Reference to Physiology*, M.A. thesis, Hebrew University, Jerusalem, 1960 (unpublished). [Now published by Arno Press, New York, 1981.]
22. K. E. Rothschuh, *Geschiche der Physiologie* (Berlin: Springer, 1953), p. 93.
23. Bruno Kisch, *Forgotten Leaders in Modern Medicine* (Philadelphia: American Philosophical Society, 1954), p. 174. On the refusal of physiologists to accept chairs obliging them to teach anatomy as well, cf. E. Gagliardi et al., *Die Universität Zürich 1833–1933 und ihre Vorläufer* (Zürich: Erziehungsdirektion, 1938), pp. 539–48.

scientists with special aptitude to devote themselves entirely to the new discipline. Their concentrated work partly, no doubt (in response to the prospect of rapid advancement), soon disqualified the nonspecialists from effective competition, and universities had to grant the demand of physiologists for the establishment of separate chairs.[24] The separation of physiology from anatomy, which had been a temporary "emergency solution" to cope with obstacles to the modification of the role of "anatomists," thus became inevitable. This separation was implemented during the fifties and sixties of the nineteenth century. When in 1858 Johannes Müller died, and his chair was split into one for anatomy and one for physiology, this was not a pioneer innovation but the rectification of an anachronism. Although the final separation in Giessen did not take place until 1891, the process of separation had been accomplished at almost all universities by 1870.[25]

Between 1855 and 1874, twenty-six scientists were given their first appointment to chairs of physiology (sometimes still combined with anatomy). Ten of these were appointed between 1855–59 alone. But therewith the discipline reached the limit of its expansion in the German university system (the number of chairs for physiology in German universities—excluding Austria and Switzerland—had reached 15 by 1864, 19 in 1873, and remained at 20 in 1880, 1890, and 1900).[26] Between 1875 and 1894, only nine scholars received appointments to chairs in physiology, stepping into chairs vacated by their incumbents.

That aspiration to a professorship in physiology during the seventies and eighties was all but hopeless is shown by the tenure of chairs at various univesities throughout that period by first-generation physiologists, the generation which had in a cohortlike manner conquered the chairs which the university system was capable of providing. Du Bois-Reymond monopolized the chair in Berlin from 1858–96; Brücke reigned in Vienna for four decades, 1849–90; Eckhard held the chair in Giessen from 1855–91. Karl Ludwig, after more than fifteen years in the Josefinum in Vienna, Zürich, and Marburg, managed to put in a further thirty (fruitful) years in Leipzig between 1865–95; Karl Vierordt remained in Tübingen from 1855 until his death in 1884; Göttingen, Breslau, Bonn, and Munich were held during 1860–1905, 1859–97, 1859–1910, and 1863–1908 by Meissner, Heidenhain, Pflüger, and Voit, respectively, while Ecker and Rollett kept the chairs in Freiburg, 1850–87 and Graz, 1863–1903 out of circulation. Large and small universities alike had not a single vacancy in physiology for decades, and no prospect of such an occurrence was in sight during the seventies and eighties.[27] The result was that research in physiology lost momentum. A count of discoveries relevant to physiology in Germany shows that 321 such discoveries were made during the twenty years period of rapid expansion between 1855–1874

24. Zloczower, op. cit.   25. Rothschuh, op. cit., p. 108.
26. v. Ferber, op. cit., pp. 204–205.   27. Zloczower, op. cit.

compared with 232 during the subsequent (and 168 during the preceding) twenty years.[28] Scientific idealism notwithstanding, young scholars sought greener pastures. The number of *Privatdozenten* and extraordinary professors, which had been 12 in 1864, declined to 4 in 1873, 6 in 1880, and rose again only in 1890 to 13. There were better ways of becoming a professor than through the study of physiology: hygiene, for instance, had only one chair in 1873 and grew to 19 by 1900. Psychiatry grew from one chair to 16 and ophthalmology from 6 to 21 during the same period, while pathology, which had only 7 chairs in 1864, had reached 18 by 1880.[29] The enthusiasm for physiology cooled considerably.

This was the characteristic manner in which the German universities operated *as a system*, determining the life cycles of academic disciplines. It was the decentralized nature of the system and the competition among the individual units which brought about the rapid diffusion of innovations and not the internal structure of each unit, or the dominant philosophy of education. More than twenty first-rate full-time research positions in any one discipline was a huge market for early and mid-nineteenth-century conditions, and an emerging discipline could attract considerable talent competing for those positions.

The same twenty positions, however, fell dismally short of the requirements of sustained scientific research under modern conditions. But the internal structure of the individual universities, bolstered by the idea of the university, allowed the perpetuation of this archaic arrangement in the face of changing conditions and obstructed the growth of research roles capable of meeting the demands of modern science. The structural limitations of the German university remained latent so long as role-differentiation permitted the continued expansion of the academic profession, but once the *Institut* blocked this path toward professorial chairs, the inadequacy of the structure became manifest.

The reason why at that stage the structure of the university was not modified lies, as pointed out, in the class structure of Germany. In order to understand the way this affected the universities, we have to go back again to the origins. Prussia's rulers, even when, heeding the propaganda of intellectuals, they established the University of Berlin, were no intellectuals themselves. For them the professional training of lawyers, civil servants, doctors, and teachers was the main function of higher education. By inclination they would have preferred the Napoleonic type of separate professional schools and indeed had established such schools themselves earlier. They were converted to the idea of the university, since, as shown above, under the circumstances philosophy served the political interests of the nation and because this was also a reasonable decision from the point of view of their absolutistic principles. By

28. Tabulated from K. E. Rothschuh, *Entwicklungsgeschichte physiologischer Probleme in Tabellenform* (München and Berlin, 1952).
29. v. Ferber, loc. cit.

granting corporate freedom to the universities, they not only showed themselves as enlightened rulers, sympathetic to the intellectual mood of the time, but also vindicated the principle of legitimacy; the corporate rights of the university had been, after all, a medieval tradition destroyed by the French Revolution.[30]

As a result, the newly founded University of Berlin, as well as the other universities following its example, have never been the institutions of which the philosophers had dreamed. The freedoms effectively granted to them were limited, and the functions assigned to them were much more practical and trivial than desired.

First of all, the influence of the state was always decisive, even where not visible. One of the simple ways through which state interference worked was the existence of government examinations for various professional titles. Formally, these examinations did not infringe the freedom of the universities to confer their own degrees, or establish their own courses of study. Since, however, the overwhelming majority of the students learned for practical purposes, the curricula were greatly influenced by the wishes of the government. The influence was all the stronger, since the establishment of new chairs also depended on the government.[31]

The curricula and in consequence the chairs and the faculties were, therefore, so constituted that the university was overwhelmingly a professional school. The freedom of the academic staff could only manifest itself within the framework established by the interest of the state. It manifested itself in the emphasis on basic subjects rather than practical training and on theory rather than knowledge. This was the case even in the faculties of medicine and law, not to speak of the humanities and natural sciences.[32] In these latter, the fact that the overwhelming majority of students prepared for secondary school teaching was only recognized in the usual combinations of disciplines studied but not at all in the contents of the teaching. This aimed only at imparting the systematic knowledge of the disciplines but took no account of teaching methodology, educational psychology, etc., all of great importance to the future teacher.

Academic freedom furthermore manifested itself in the criteria used for appointments or promotions. Achievements in original research were considered—at least in principle—the most important criteria, even in such supposedly practical fields as, for example, clinical medicine, and the expert judgment of the academic staff, supposedly the most competent to judge people according to this criterion, was always one of the important bases of appointments (made actually by the state).[33]

30. Paulsen, op. cit., p. 51.
31. Samuel and Thomas, op. cit., pp. 114–15.
32. Cf. Diepgen, op. cit., vol. 2-1, pp. 152–53; Theodor Billroth, *The Medical Sciences in the German Universities* (New York: Macmillan, 1924), p. 27.
33. Paulsen, op. cit., pp. 83–86.

These circumstances then determined what was studied at the university and how it was studied. The philosophical or, later, the systematically scientific aspects were emphasized in courses, the contents of which were determined largely by professional requirements. And the dual role of the professor, officially paid for teaching a subject to would-be professionals but actually appointed for outstanding research (not necessarily central to his subject of teaching), arose as a result of similar compromise. The idea of the university, according to which both arrangements were considered as the best ways of promoting university study as well as research, was but an ideological justification of this practical compromise. Like all ideologies, it was used in defense of a constantly threatened position. Universities had to be on their guard, lest by being used openly for practical purposes—for which they were used as a matter of fact under the guises and compromises here described— they lose their precarious freedom of engaging in pure research. Hence the resistance to the dilution of the charismatic role of the professor chosen from the ranks of free *Privatdozenten* by fully institutionalizing the new research and training roles growing up in the institutes. These latter looked "dangerously" like mere bureaucratic-technical careers. For similar reasons the granting of academic standing to technology and new practical subjects was usually opposed. In brief, the freedom and the prestige of the German universities seemed to be safest when the university was kept isolated from the different classes and practical activities of society; it pursued, therefore, a policy aimed at the preservation of an esoteric and sacred image of itself.

Another important limitation of academic freedom was the fact that university professors were civil servants and considered it a privilege to be part of this important corps. They were, therefore, expected to be loyal to the state, which under absolutist rule implied a great deal. As long as one genuinely agreed with the purposes of the rulers, this problem was not apparent. There was, therefore, a semblance of real freedom at the universities during the nationalist struggle and shortly thereafter, when, on the one hand, intellectuals often identified with Prussian politics, and, on the other hand, state-power was not very efficient. But after the middle of the century, when social problems and imperialism became the main political issues and the state increasingly efficient and powerful, the potential restraints on freedom became felt. Identification with the politics of the state often meant fanatical nationalism and obscurantism, a famous example of which was Treitschke, while opposition to it might have provoked interference by the state, as it happened in the case of Social Democrats seeking academic appointments.[34]

Thus, again, freedom had to be sought within these given limits. It was clear that under the prevailing conditions the introduction of actualities, whether in the form of philosophical publicism or in the form of politically

34. Samuel and Thomas, op. cit., pp. 116–18; Paulsen, op. cit., pp. 105, 246–47; C. D. Darlington, "Freedom and Responsibility in Academic Life," *Bulletin of the Atomic Scientists* 13 (1957): 131–34.

relevant social science, would not have led to detached discussion and the emergence of objective criteria but to the flooding of universities by anti-democratic demagogues and the suppression of the limited amount of liberalism which existed in them. Thoughtful liberals, such as Max Weber, for example, chose, therefore, the doctrine of *Wertfreiheit* of scientific enquiry.[35] Declaring value judgments to be incompatible with true scientific enquiry and academic teaching seemed the most efficient way of ensuring freedom of discussion at the university. It was a morally respectable and logically justifiable principle which could be defended without recourse to the actual situation. But it was the actual situation which made this approach more or less the accepted doctrine of the university. It was the doctrine best suited to the maintenance of the delicate balance in a situation where free, nonutilitarian enquiry was supported and given high status by an absolutist state; and where free-thinking intellectuals taught students usually sharing the autocratic views of the rulers of the state and preparing for government careers as civil servants, judges, prosecutors, and teachers.[36]

This doctrine of *Wertfreiheit,* most clearly formulated by Weber after the First World War, had been as a matter of fact an important guiding principle of academic thinking and action in the second half of the nineteenth century, that is, as soon as the possible conflict between academic freedom and absolutism became acute.[37] It explains the extreme caution and wariness toward intellectual influences coming from outside the universities, especially if these influences had some ideological implications.[38]

The observed inflexibilities of the German university were, therefore, the results of its precarious position in the German class structure. Intellectual enquiry in Germany did not thrive as part and parcel of the way of life of a "middle class" of well-to-do people, whose position was based not on privilege but on achievement in various fields. It started thriving as a hothouse flower mainly on the whimsical support of a few members of the ruling class and desperately attempted to establish wider roots in society. The universities created under the—from the point of view of the intellectuals—particularly favorable conditions of the struggle against Napoleon were the only secure institutionalized framework for free intellectual activity in the country. The status and the privileges of the universities were granted to them by the military-aristocratic ruling class and were not achieved as part of the growth of

35. Max Weber, "Science as a Vocation," in H. H. Gerth and C. Wright Mills, *From Max Weber: Essays in Sociology* (New York: Oxford University Press, 1947), pp. 129 sqq.; cf. Samuel and Thomas, op. cit., pp. 121–23.

36. Ibid., pp. 116–21, 128, about the delicate balance of the status of the *Gelehrtenstand* and the spirit prevailing among students.

37. Ibid., p. 118, about the reaction in the spirit of *Wertfreiheit* of the first Congress of German Historians in 1893 to the imperial decree of 1889, directing education to the task of combating revolutionary political doctrines.

38. E.g., the social sciences; about their limited development, only somewhat modified after the First World War, cf. Flexner, *Universities,* op. cit., pp. 328, 332–33.

free human enterprise. It was, therefore, a precarious status based on a compromise whereby the rulers regarded the universities and their personnel as means for the training of certain types of professionals but allowed them to do this in their own way and use their position for the pursuit of pure scholarship and science (which the rulers did not understand but were usually willing to respect). The universities had to be, therefore, constantly on the defensive, lest by becoming suspected of subversion, they lose the elite position which ensured their freedom.

The idea of the German university evolved as a result of these conditions. It stressed the pursuit of pure science and scholarship as the principal function of the university, divided learning into disciplines with specialized methodologies, extolled *Wertfreiheit* in scholarly teaching and writing, was wary of applied subjects, as well as nonacademic influence (including nonacademic intellectual influence), and refused to grant institutional recognition to any teaching or research roles besides those of the *Privatdozent* and Professor. As it has been shown here, these ideas were not originally conceived as a means to an end. They were rather the description made into an ideology of the tactics actually employed by the universities in their struggle for maintaining their freedom and privileges.

It is true that the German universities had been highly successful in the development of the so-called pure scientific and scholarly fields. This success, however, was not due to any deliberate design or purpose on their part (according to the original idea there should have been a single German university devoted mainly to speculations in idealist philosophy) but to the unintended mechanism of competition which exploited rapidly all the possibilities for intellectual development open to the universities. That this development was largely limited to the basic fields was the result of the factors here described, as were the other aspects of growing inflexibility; the slowing down of the differentiation of existing disciplines into their unfolding specialties as well as the ossification of university organization refusing to take proper notice of the transformation of scientific work.

The English Universities: Higher Education for the "Classes"

If Germany was the first country to develop a system of modern universities, England was the first major country to be influenced by it. From the 1830s to World War I, German universities were held up as a challenge, and/or a model to the English ones, and all the numerous new foundations and reforms of higher education and research were influenced by the German example.[39] Nevertheless, there never developed in England a German type of

39. Cardwell, op. cit.

university. What emerged was something rather baffling to observers accustomed to use the German "idea of the university" as a yardstick for measuring academic accomplishment.

They admired English universities for the quality of their graduates; criticized them for their mediocre performance in many fields and their seeming indifference toward the active promotion of research; and were mystified by the nevertheless brilliant work of some English scientists.

This lack of success of the English universities in matching the German—or more recently the American—ones in the systematic development of research as well as their success as institutions of higher training and education has been the result of the social conditions of their growth. The same conditions used in the explanation of the German case, namely, the extent of centralization and the relationship of the universities to the different classes of society, seem to have been also the main determinants of university development in England. But the English university system has been centralized to a much greater extent than the German, while the class structure of England was much more open than that of Germany.

The influence of these two factors has been apparent from the very beginning. The emergence of modern German universities can be closely linked to the foundation of the University of Berlin, an action of the Prussian government marking the adoption of a policy of higher education which—due to competition—had to be followed all over Germany. There is no such single event marking the beginnings of the modern English university. As the product of an open class system, its origins were in a variety of institutions created by various groups of people pursuing different interests.

The core of the English university system has always been Oxford and Cambridge. Until the middle of the last century they had educated the sons of the nobility and future clergymen.[40] They were educational institutions of the elite. Their scholarly standards were low, according to some even extremely low, but scholarship or science was irrelevant for the majority of elite positions. The few students who subsequently became physicians, surgeons, or lawyers could comfortably learn their professions as apprentices in their respective professional corporations, and all the erudition required by a clergyman could be acquired by private study. Intimate knowledge of the ways of the gentry was certainly more important for the ecclesiastical career than theological sophistication.

While Oxford and Cambridge served the gentry and the clergy, a new type of intellectual, interested in science and secular philosophy, grew up in the cities. Under their influence, and with the support of a liberal upper middle class, there arose different institutions, such as the Royal Institution, mechan-

40. Cf. C. Arnold Anderson and Miriam Schnaper, *School and Society in England: Social Background of Oxford and Cambridge Students* (Washington: Public Affairs Press, 1952).

ics institutes, philosophical societies, colleges, etc., providing some facilities for research and a platform for the dissemination of modern science. University College, London, was the first university to emerge from these various popular efforts. It was meant to be a utilitarian institution designed for the acquisition of knowledge useful in practical life (about half of the students prepared for medicine).[41] This utilitarian tendency was enhanced in the University of London, chartered in 1836, which became an examining body, granting recognized degrees to students of an increasing variety of London colleges, provincial and colonial institutions, and later even to students preparing for the examination privately. This arrangement had incidentally introduced a great deal of uniformity to a great variety of provincial institutions.[42]

The modern English university arose, therefore, out of two traditions: aristocratic elite education designed to mold the character and impart a peculiar way of life, on the one hand, and utilitarian training and teaching for professional and industrial middle class careers, on the other hand. Universities were not—as in Germany—preserves of privileged intellectuals, isolated from the various classes of society, granted the monopoly of teaching for middle-class careers, and enjoying the freedom of doing, as a matter of fact, a great many other things (especially research). They were educational institutions providing training for the diffuse positions of the elite or for specific middle-class careers, in both instances for a practical purpose.

Until the middle of the nineteenth century the two kinds of universities existed side by side without the one affecting the other. The reform of Oxford and Cambridge after 1850 was not the result of these universities attempting to change their function of elite education but of apprehensions about the loss of their elite function. The new scientific and professional class acquired an increasingly important position in society and exercised a growing influence on the conduct of public affairs. Some of them were rising into the elite, others became the "new clerisy" replacing the influence of the clergy on the minds of men as writers, philosophers, advisers, experts, and last but not least, teachers.[43] Had Oxford and Cambridge not accepted the new learning, then inevitably they would have lost their central place in the so-called Establishment.

The reforms starting about 1850, with the establishment of degrees with a serious intellectual content in the arts as well as the sciences, and culminating in the establishment of up-to-date research laboratories in the 1870s, turned Oxford and Cambridge into something deceptively like German universities, or, more correctly, like the ideal which its ideologists would have liked the German university to be. They were teaching academies where a creative intellectual elite informally taught the cream of the youth. Students did not

41. Armytage, op. cit., pp. 173–74.
42. Ibid., p. 216; Cardwell, op. cit., pp. 36–37, 72.
43. Armytage, op. cit., pp. 178, 206.

study for some particular bread and butter profession but in order to become a creative elite themselves in the arts and the sciences, or in politics and the service of the state. The subjects taught at the university and the contents of the majority of its degrees were not determined by the needs of some professional practice but by the internal logic of scholarship and science. The arts and sciences were really the core of the studies, and there were few professional degrees conferred by the universities. They taught law as part of the humanities, claiming no university monopoly of training lawyers, and taught the basic medical sciences, leaving clinical training to the hospital medical schools. In addition these were extremely wealthy and prestigeful institutions which paid their teachers relatively better and conferred on them higher status than German universities ever did.[44] For these reasons they could easily attract the best teachers as well as the best students.

Seemingly there existed, therefore, in Oxford and Cambridge after 1870 all the conditions for their becoming the most important centers of scientific and scholarly research in the world. As a matter of fact, however, they have remained, as they had been before their reform, mainly undergraduate institutions. In some fields they have attained high distinction but by no means in all. Even in fields where most outstanding work was done, research was often hampered and limited because of the lack of facilities which poorer universities than Oxford or Cambridge did not find impossible to procure.[45] Neither the adoption of modern ideas of scientific and scholarly excellence nor the availability of exceptional resources of talent and wealth have been enough to turn the two leading English universities into research centers comparable to the German universities of the past, or the American ones at present.

The fact that this did not happen was due to lack of competition. Research—apart from very limited fields—had not been a much sought after commodity until the Second World War. It was highly respected and, if successful, sometimes even paid for, like poetry. But sustained demand for research in all fields of science and scholarship could only develop where a competitive system of universities created a special market for it. The question then is: why did not such a market arise in England in spite of the existence of a relatively large number of universities? In order to answer this question we have to turn again to the development of provincial universities (including London).

All through the nineteenth century these institutions had been in flux, and it was not clear which way they would develop. There were suggestions of developing them into institutes of technology following the model of the *Eidgenössisches Polytechnikum* in Zürich and similar German institutions. At

44. Flexner, *Universities,* op. cit., pp. 300–01.
45. Ibid., pp. 280–87; Darlington, op. cit. (for the description of the state of experimental physics in Oxford at the end of the last century. The present authors do not agree with Darlington's interpretation).

the turn of the century there were suggestions of following American models by turning the new universities into "community service stations." [46] This latter idea indeed left its mark on the provincial universities of Britain, each of which (with the exception of Durham which as a church foundation does not properly belong to this category) established subjects of study in commerce, technology, or agriculture peculiarly adapted to the needs of the region.

Thus, all through the nineteenth century it seemed that there would emerge in England universities of a different type than Oxford and Cambridge, challenging the leadership of these two universities and changing the character of British higher education and research. It seemed that these universities would develop into advanced and pioneering institutions of professional training and applied research.

This, however, happened to only a very limited extent. The pioneering diversity of these institutions has been increasingly reduced. From the beginning of this century, when the provincial universities were given their charters, they have grown increasingly like each other concerning the types of study pursued in them and the way these studies are pursued.[47] The great variety of degree courses offered by the different universities including such things as commerce, household, social sciences, journalism, fine arts, public administration, etc., do not prove the contrary, since the large majority of the graduates in all universities studied the traditional arts and science courses or medicine and engineering. The innovations made in provincial universities were not adopted elsewhere. They remained isolated and tended to become little different from more traditional and generally accepted courses.[48]

The process seemed to have worked somewhat like this. The two ancient universities possessing superior privileges and incomparably larger means had usually the best teachers and the best students. As a result subjects adopted at these two universities after their reform automatically attracted relatively more first-rate minds than those taught only at a provincial university. Thus, in these subjects there arose an impressive group of graduates whose prestige was enhanced by their Oxford and Cambridge background. They were readily given chairs at the provincial universities where they became the most prestigeful and influential members of the staff.[49] The difference in quality—real or imagined—between graduates of Oxford and Cambridge and those of other universities has been so great that vacancies in subjects not existing at the two

46. Armytage, op. cit., 224–25.
47. The typical pattern of the development of the provincial universities was: "Foundation, through the generosity of one or more private benefactors, of a college designed to teach chiefly scientific and technical subjects to the people of a great industrial town; the expansion of this into a university college by the addition of 'faculties' in the humane subjects and a department for the training of teachers and, finally, the securing of a Royal Charter." H. C. Dent, *British Education* (London, 1949), p. 28.
48. Cf. Kneller, op. cit., pp. 96–99.
49. Flexner, op. cit., p. 256; Armytage, op. cit., p. 231.

ancient universities were preferably filled by their own graduates trained in related fields, rather than graduates of other universities possessing specialized training. This of course did not add to the prestige of these "provincial" subjects, so that there was little interest to introduce them elsewhere and a great deal of interest to turn them as much as possible into something respectably, though humbly, like a related, higher-prestige discipline. One outstanding person at Oxford or Cambridge might have been enough to create a "school" in a certain field strongly represented in the next generation at all British universities whereas the chances of the same thing happening to a subject with one outstanding representative elsewhere were much less (except if he so impressed the two leading universities that one of his students was invited to them). The strong development of physiology, physics, economics, and social anthropology, compared with the much slower development of clinical medicine, many branches of psychology, sociology, business administration, education, etc., illustrate the working of this mechanism.[50]

The English university system has, therefore, never become competitive. Universities, like so much else in that society, arranged themselves in a relatively neat hierarchy. Authority in academic matters has been centrally wielded by groups of people, most of whom were related one way or another to the two ancient universities. There has been no incentive for academic innovations: the two leading universities did not need it, and the rest had limited chances of competing with them through the introduction of novelties. The way to academic prestige has been through imitation of the accepted disciplines, of the "solidly established standards" and the habits of thinking of the most prestigeful universities rather than through innovation and experimentation.

This explains the way the English system has worked. The universities, unlike those in Germany or, as will be seen later, in America, did not create new disciplines, or professions, and did not develop research systematically. At the same time, however, they were much more open to outside influences than were the German universities. Both parts of the system served certain classes of the society: Oxford and Cambridge the elite, and the provincial universities the middle classes. They have responded with relative flexibility to demands arising in these classes. Thus, the two old universities introduced, in addition to arts, empirical science and a limited amount of professional studies, while provincial universities admitted a much greater variety of professional subjects. Research was also introduced as a result of specific outside

50. Cf. e.g., Flexner's (approving) remarks about the difference between the Department of Commerce at Birmingham University and American business schools, ibid., pp. 257–58. About the influence of Oxford and Cambridge, cf. also, E. A. Shils, "The Intellectuals, I: Great Britain," *Encounter*, April 1955; A. H. Halsey, "British Universities and Intellectual Life," *Universities Quarterly* 12 (1958): 141–52.

demands (e.g., in agriculture), or as a requirement of teaching certain subjects, mainly experimental natural sciences, at a university level. This is why its development has seemed haphazard; it followed the emergence of this variety of demands, rather than its own internal logic.

The hierarchic structure of the system of universities has also in the end somewhat reduced its flexibility to satisfy outside demands. The case of engineering illustrates this point. English universities introduced engineering studies to their curricula quite early, overcoming with relative ease the qualms about the academic respectability of this subject which were so evident in Germany. But having admitted them, they never developed them to a very large extent. The field, peripheral in Oxford and Cambridge, remained somehow peripheral in the system as a whole. Institutions like Imperial College, or some of the provincial universities, originally established mainly as technological universities, became isolated parts of the system. The bulk of technological education was relegated to technical colleges lacking university status, and applied research in technology developed—so far as it did— largely in specialized government establishments.[51] Only quite recently have Colleges of Advanced Technology been established.

It is interesting to compare this development with that of higher technological education in Germany. Universities there were less flexible than in England. They did not admit engineering into the universities and were opposed to the granting of full academic status to them. Only through direct intervention of the government were these institutions granted academic standing. But then they became veritable technological universities. Inflexibility broken down by direct government intervention in academic affairs produced better results than flexibility limited by the working of an academic hierarchy.

This flexibility, limited by lack of competitiveness, also explains the development of academic roles in England. English universities managed to institutionalize a greater variety of roles than the German ones. Concrete—even sustained—achievements in research, such as publications and discoveries, are not the only criteria for university appointments and promotions. In mathematics and the natural sciences where there are few acceptable criteria apart from outstanding achievement in research, the definition of the professor's role is not much different from that which developed in Germany. But in the humanities, social sciences, and the professions, intellectual excellence may be manifested in other ways than research. Essayists, writers, brilliant public speakers, and administrators have found their way to universities to a greater extent than in Germany. The differentiation between teaching and research careers is manifested to some extent in differently defined positions, such as

51. Cf. Sir Eric Ashby, *Technology and the Academies* (London: Macmillan, 1959); George Louis Payne, *Britain's Scientific and Technological Manpower* (Stanford: Stanford University Press, 1960), pp. 172–73.

tutors, senior lecturers, etc., on the one hand, and readers, on the other, though usually the differences are not formalized.

This relatively greater willingness to face the fact that universities perform a variety of functions on a variety of levels has prevented the development of such rigidly hierarchical relationships as developed in German institutes. The question of some specializations being broad or profound enough, or of some new discipline academic enough, did not have to be decided in each case as a matter of principle. Permanent university appointments in the lower ranks could be made relatively easily, and a more complex division of labor could arise without much difficulty.

But the amount of flexibility in the adaptation of the academic roles to the changing functions of the university has also been limited—like the introduction of new disciplines—by the lack of innovativeness of the system. The different criteria for appointment are not clearly differentiated. Rather a more generally—at times one feels rather subjectively—defined excellence seems to be accepted as the principal criterion, with research achievements, teaching ability, and all the rest as subsidiary criteria. Such a loose conception of excellence allows a fair amount of leeway for all kinds of practical considerations, since excellence can manifest itself in different ways. Besides, it makes possible to consider from time to time new kinds of excellence without entanglement in ideological arguments. This approach has produced in English university departments a greater diversity of intellectual orientations, and skills, than in the German ones.[52] But as long as the criteria are not made explicit, and the different functions of teaching, training, research, and education more consciously considered, the results are bound to remain partial and unpredictable.

In this case, too, the hierarchic structure of the universities seems to have limited their adaptability to their varied functions. Loosely defined excellence is well suited to the needs of institutions designed to educate a national leadership with relatively diffuse functions, such as higher civil servants, politicians, and heads of large corporations. But through the peculiar working of this hierarchic system the criterion has seeped down, preventing the emergence of a clear differentiation of roles and functions in the whole system.

The American University: The Large-Scale Academic Enterprise

The transformation of the modern university into a system serving a variety of purposes and adjusting itself to the needs of different classes of society be-

52. The authoritarian homogeneity of German departments was, however, mitigated somewhat, though insufficiently, by the custom of students transferring from one university to another, in order to have an opportunity for study under different teachers; cf. Flexner, *Universities*, op. cit., p. 326; Plessner, op. cit., p. 196.

gan, as we have seen, in England. The transformation, however, was limited and with the passing of time lost momentum, due to the centralized hierarchic system of universities which turned the middle-class provincial universities into intellectual colonies of Oxford and Cambridge. The potentialities of the English beginnings were only realized in the United States. American universities grew out of the British tradition, and American class structure was even more open than the British: there was constant interchange and movement between the classes, and, in addition, there was no central hierarchy regulating these movements. The mobility of individuals, classes, and universities did not have to assume, therefore, the form of a gradual approach to the central model but took place through competition, each unit exploiting its relative advantages.

During the first half of the nineteenth century the American academic scene was very similar to that of Britain. On the one hand, there were the colleges, similar in their organization and scope of studies to the English or the Scottish universities, but their numbers were much greater, and none of them possessed a relative standing similar to Oxford and Cambridge. These were at that time institutions of modest intellectual caliber, usually of religious character. On the other hand, there was a bewildering variety of professional schools in medicine, law, and technology. There existed also numerous societies and colleges which advocated the cause of science but did very little about it. The reasons for this backwardness were the same as those which retarded academic development in England: scientific knowledge and research had few practical uses, and America was an even more utilitarian and pragmatic society than England. There were groups and individuals interested in science and scholarship as a hobby and quite a few who believed in its ultimate usefulness: but a great deal of conviction was needed to believe that one would go further by extending the frontiers of knowledge than by pushing back the frontier in the West.[53]

The transformation starting about 1860 was due to similar circumstances as in Britain, namely, increasing conviction of the practical usefulness of science and higher education, on the one hand, and the growth of scientific interest among a few rich and/or influential people, on the other. As in England, the first, utilitarian influence led to the establishment of vocationally oriented institutions, such as the M.I.T., the land-grant colleges, state universities, etc., while the second led to the reform of Harvard and other older institutions and the establishment of Johns Hopkins University aimed at fostering pure scholarship and science. In the United States, therefore, as in England, the introduction of modern science and up-to-date specialized scholarship into existing

53. Cf. Richard Hofstadter and C. DeWitt Hardy, *The Development and Scope of Higher Education in the United States* (New York: Columbia University Press, 1952), p. 21; Richard J. Storr, *The Beginnings of Graduate Education in America* (Chicago: University of Chicago Press, 1953), pp. 1–6, 24, 52, 63, 79–80, 102, 107; Richard H. Shryock, *Medicine and Society in America 1660–1860* (New York: New York University Press, 1960), pp. 138–43.

universities, as well as the foundation of new types of colleges and universities, followed rather than created the emergence of social demand for such activity. Both were in these respects "open" educational systems, readily influenced by pressures arising at the same time in various classes of society.[54]

Here, however, the parallel ends. As indicated above, the United States has never possessed a representative university situated in the capital or near to it, with the intellectual elite of the country residing in the vicinity. This created the conditions necessary for competition, such as existed in Germany during most of the nineteenth century but not in Britain. The old established universities could not, therefore, be content in the United States to stay out of the race for innovation, and even less could they inhibit by their example and the all-pervasive influence of their alumni the innovations made in the newer universities. They were rather compelled to follow suit and to engage in innovations themselves, trying to preserve their preeminence through executing those innovations better than the others or through different innovations of their own.

Thus, when Gilman, the president of the newly founded university of Johns Hopkins, refused to follow the example of Harvard and established a research university such as did not exist anywhere, Harvard and eventually all the important universities had to follow suit. A similar mechanism brought about the growth and diffusion of the practical professional training developed in the land grant colleges.[55] As a result old colleges developed graduate departments and professional schools, technological institutes and state colleges introduced humanistic studies and social sciences, and all types of schools— though not all individual schools—developed research in a variety of basic and applied fields.

Thus have arisen the very large American universities within which there is a clear differentiation of functions. Undergraduate teaching is separated from the research-oriented graduate school, and in addition there are professional schools and often research institutions of one kind or another.

Another result of competition in this equalitarian system is the tendency toward specialization. In spite of the constant addition of functions, universities may decide to do without certain departments or faculties altogether and concentrate their resources in fields where they have the greatest chances of success. A good university may exist without a medical school or may deliberately neglect some of its basic science or humanities departments; some tend to concentrate on their graduate schools, other on undergraduate teaching. These are of course things which occur in England as well. But (a) some of the differentiations hardly exist there at all (e.g., undergraduate/graduate schools); and (b) the smaller universities specializing in certain selected fields never at-

54. Donald H. Fleming, *William Welch and the Rise of Modern Medicine* (Boston: Little Brown, 1954), pp. 173 sqq., Hofstadter and Hardy, op. cit., pp. 26–28, 38, 60 sq.; Abraham Flexner, *Daniel Coit Gilman* (New York: Harcourt, Brace and Company, 1946), pp. 38 sq.

55. Flexner, ibid., 108; Richard Hofstadter and Walter P. Metzger, *The Development of Academic Freedom in the United States* (New York: Columbia University Press, 1955), pp. 378–83.

tain real excellence through specialization. In the United States there are specialized undergraduate colleges of very high prestige and first-rate law and medical schools in mediocre universities; and small generally unimportant institutions may attain fame in a short time through concentrating on one or two subjects. This possibility of establishing the high standing of a university through developing a field neglected by others has introduced into American universities departments of creative writing, dramatic arts, music, etc., that is, cultural traditions—and such less "cultural" ones as football and sports—which remained in Europe largely outside the universities.

Thus, in spite of the unprecedented comprehensiveness of the large American university, there does not exist in America the conception that a university has to consist of so many faculties and that each faculty has to contain a certain well-defined series of departments as a minimum. A number of relatively large universities would be considered by European standards as only part institutions. The conception of the university has obviously changed: it does not pretend to refer to some assumed organic whole of all humanistic and scientific knowledge. The fact that the different faculties and professional schools have entirely different requirements is more clearly faced than in Europe. The question, therefore, of which faculties and schools should exist in a given university is not considered as a matter of principle but rather as one of expediency.

The same applies to the internal structure of the faculties. Here too the fiction that a faculty consists of professors, that is, individuals rather than departments, has disappeared. The units within the faculty are departments which are not a one-man show but an institution deliberately designed to provide an efficient and well-rounded unit where experts in the different specialties complement each other. This is an entirely different organization from the German institute which exists to foster the research of its head and where the representatives of other specialties than that of the head of the institute are invariably in a subordinate position. In an American department there may be, and in a good one there always are, several professors of equal rank, there is often a strong spirit of colleagueship, and the division of labor is functional rather than hierarchic.[56]

This provides a basis for teamwork and graduate training such as exists nowhere in Europe. Even in England where, as we have seen, there arose more differentiated departments than in Germany, the "chairs" are severely limited and there are many invidious distinctions of status and power which prevent the development of an atmosphere of independence and self-confidence necessary for genuine cooperation.[57] It has to be repeated that the development of the departments into such self-contained and efficient units has been the

56. Logan Wilson, op. cit., pp. 53–93; Caplow and McGee, op. cit.
57. Cf. J. M. Ziman, "The American Scientist," *New Statesman* 62, no. 1591 (1961): 300–02.

result of competition. The distribution between universities of Ph.D. degrees in different subjects shows that only a relatively small number of institutions confer such degrees at all and that the list of universities conferring Ph.D. degrees in each subject is constantly changing.[58] This shows that only efficient departments can compete at this level, so that universities have to concentrate constantly on building up their individual departments (and, as shown, quite often to make their choice among them). The existence of a growing number of industrial and governmental research units in a great many fields only enhances this tendency toward building up the departmental organization.

This variety of schools and departments each with its specialized function is reflected in the differentiation of academic roles which goes much further even than that existing in England. There are specialized academic educators and administrators, academic researchers who are hardly teaching at all, as well as advanced practitioners of professions and arts.

This peculiar working of the system explains the often stated fact that the research function evolved in German universities and grafted onto both the English and the American ones took much better hold on the latter than on the former. But it is a mistake to assume simply that American universities took over and developed what they learned from Germany. Research in America has developed in the departments which, as we have seen, are quite different organizations from German university institutes. It has thus become a regular university operation which, at times, may be of equal or superior importance to teaching. Universities, furthermore, fostered applied research of a kind which never developed in Germany.[59] One cannot, therefore, attribute these developments to beneficial European influence. They were rather the result of the same inherent characteristics of the American system which brought forth the much less admired proliferation of professional schools. This has been a system which placed a premium on innovations and has been open to a great variety of social pressures. It adopted and developed, therefore, an ever-increasing variety of functions in reseach, as well as professional and other types of education. Innovation became a pervasive tendency of the American university system, as in the similarly competitive German one during the nineteenth century, but in contrast to the German case, this innovativeness has not been limited to pure nonutilitarian science and scholarship but has been extended to applied and professional fields too.

Comparing the three systems so far surveyed it can be said that while German universities were bent upon creating new science, and English universities intended to teach it to those using it (provided that they proved themselves "respectable" enough for higher education), American universities

58. Cf. Office of Scientific Personnel, *The Baccalaureate Origins of the Science Doctorates Awarded in the United States* (Washington: National Academy of Sciences/National Research Council, Publication no. 382, 1955), p. 19.
59. Hofstadter and Metzger, op. cit., pp. 380–83.

have tried not only to teach and create new science but also new applications and professions catering for the elite as well as the masses. Thus, universities assumed an important function in the growing professionalization of occupational life and in making research an increasingly permanent aspect of business, industry, and administration.

For better or worse, the American university system, with its constantly expanding and heterogeneous functions, is now the most influential system of higher education and research. Most of the discussions about higher education and of the changes introduced in it since the end of the Second World War all over the world have been the result of American influence. This influence spreads partly through the increasing international contacts of academic workers which converge nowadays on America as they used to converge in the past on Germany and partly through the emergence of new demands among development-minded government administrators, industrialists, and businessmen for American-type professional training.

France and the USSR: A Note

Before summarizing our conclusions in detail a few remarks have to be made about the French and Soviet systems of higher education. Neither of these fits precisely into the tradition here dealt with. They too have their universities, but specialized institutions for higher education and research play a more important role in these countries than in Germany, Britain, or the United States.

France is the only country which did as a matter of fact abolish universities as institutions combining within one structure several faculties engaged in teaching as well as research.[60] She was without such institutions for about a century (1793–1896). Like all radical reforms in the organization of higher learning and research treated in this paper, the abolition of the universities in France ushered in a period of great scientific productivity. The first decades of the nineteenth century mark the high tide of French predominance in the natural sciences. The French organization of higher education and research, as developed after the Revolution and under Napoleon, was perhaps the most farsighted, taking account of all the needs and uses of higher education and scientific research as far as these could be perceived at that time. There was a clear differentiation of functions between the "university" faculties (which were in fact separate professional schools) and other institutions of higher

60. About the development of the French academic system, cf. *Œuvres de Monsieur Victor Cousin* (Paris: Pagnerre, 1850), 5ᵉ série "Instruction publique," vols. 1 and 2; Stephen d'Irsay, *Histoire des universités françaises et étrangères* (Paris: Auguste Picard, 1935), vol. 2; Guerlac, op. cit.; Abraham Flexner, *Medical Education in Europe* (New York: The Carnegie Foundation for the Advancement of Teaching, 1912), pp. 221–23.

education such as the École polytechnique, the École normale supérieure, etc., on the one hand, and organizations designed as centers for original research and intellectual endeavor on the highest levels, such as the Collège de France, the Muséum national d'histoire naturelle, the École pratique des hautes études, and even to some extent the "Institut," on the other. This system has been extensively criticized and blamed for the decline of French science. It appears that this criticism was not entirely justified, since the decline set in only about 40 years after the reforms (around 1840) and was due to the centralization of the system rather than its organizational features usually criticized.[61] As a result of this criticism a series of reforms were undertaken, culminating in the reestablishment of the universities in 1896. But even after this reform the peculiar characteristics of the French academic system have remained. The "Grandes Écoles" and other specialized institutions have not changed their structure. In addition, some of the provincial universities did not have all the customary university faculties and remained in fact specialized professional schools. The Academy has also retained some of its importance as the dispenser of high intellectual prestige, and the separation of research from teaching has been preserved to a considerable degree. The research facilities of the universities are limited, but there exist separate organizations with considerable funds, most notably the Centre national de la recherche scientifique designed to promote research. However, unlike most research foundations in Western Europe and America which mainly allocate grants for research carried out at universities, the C.N.R.S. provides regular employment in its own premises for research workers, the most senior ones of whom are usually also employed by universities.[62]

The separation of functions between universities, specialized professional schools, and separate research institutions is even more pronounced in the USSR than in France.[63] The fact that the organization and financing of research in the Soviet Union is done mainly by the Academy and not by a separate organization like the C.N.R.S. does not alter the essential similarity. There is also a parallel beween the allocation of universities: in France there has to be a university in each territorial "académie" though some of these, as mentioned before, do not possess all the faculties. In the USSR, there is a university in every republic, and similarly, not all of them possess all the usual faculties. Finally, in both countries high academic prestige lies in membership

61. Cf. Ben-David, op. cit., *American Sociological Review* [this volume, chap. 5] Cousin, op. cit., 1, p. 44.

62. About the present-day organization, cf. J. B. Piobetta, *Les institutions universitaires en France* (Paris: Presses universitaires, 1951); Étienne Gilson, "La maison à l'envers," *Le Monde*, March 21, 1947; "Avons-nous des universités?" ibid., June 17, 1947.

63. For descriptions of the Soviet academic system, cf. Nicholas DeWitt, *Soviet Professional Manpower* (Washington: National Science Foundation, 1955); Alexander G. Korol, *Soviet Education for Science and Technology* (New York: John Wiley, 1957); Vyacheslav Yelyutin, *Higher Education in the U.S.S.R.* (New York: International Arts and Sciences Press, 1959).

of the Academy or Academies and *not* in university appointments (with this qualification that, in France, professorship at the Collège de France is the appointment which commands the most prestige of all).

The main difference between the academic organization of the two countries is the extensive development of specialized professional schools in the Soviet Union. The pioneering specialized schools in France, such as the Polytechnique, the École normale, the Conservatoire national des arts et métiers, and so forth, have all remained unique institutions, guarding their traditions rather than trying to expand and innovate. Those among them which were elite institutions (e.g., the École polytechnique and the École normale) even managed to eliminate altogether the specialized professional aspects of their early days and became general educational institutions for the technological/managerial elite of the civil service, on the one hand, and the professorial elite of the lycées and—as a matter of fact—of the universities as well, on the other hand. In the Soviet Union specialized education for the professions has become the most widespread form of higher education. It has developed in practical directions, often reminiscent of higher professional education in the United States.[64]

This has been a relatively decentralized branch of the Soviet system of higher education, since the various schools are financed by different ministries, both at the national and local level, with a good deal of overlapping. Engineers, for instance, are trained in a variety of schools, some under the aegis of particular industries, others belonging to various branches of the armed forces, and still others financed directly by the Ministry of Education.

It appears that there is a parallel between the development of French and Soviet systems of higher education and research, on the one hand, and that of the English and American systems, on the other. All four seem to have been relatively flexible systems which adapt themselves to the carrying out of a great diversity of functions: in France and the USSR through division of labor between different types of organizations, and in England and America through division of labor within the universities. This division of labor remained rudimentary in France and England but developed very highly in the Soviet Union and America. Thus, the formal organization of the French academic system is like that of the Soviet Union, but its functioning and evolution is similar to that of England; while the Soviet Union resembles the United States in this latter respect.

France and the USSR eliminated the hold of aristocratic and corporate traditions on their government and intellectual life through revolutions. This led

64. The growth of professional education in the USSR has, however, been limited largely to technological, medical, and pedagogical fields. Education in the broader sense, management, social work, and other human relations fields have been much less developed, perhaps because of the schooling in these spheres received by professional Communists in various courses organized by the party.

to the conscious use of higher education for the training of highly skilled personnel necessary for the efficient performance of certain functions of the state (civil service, secondary school teaching, law, medicine, and later engineering) without regard to academic tradition. This was the educational program of enlightened absolutism initiated in both places before the Revolution but put into full effect by the autocratic regimes following the revolutions which were unhampered by respect for traditions and established rights.

The function of higher education was conceived in both countries as training for practical purposes and teaching in the right spirit. In addition there was in both countries "enlightened" recognition of the importance of research, for which purpose separate institutions were established. These were conceived in both places as restricted elite institutions. Thus, there was created in both countries an academic system conceived as a whole, purposively adapted to a variety of purposes, and considered as an integral part of the machinery of the state. The formal organization of these systems, then, is the result of the working of an open class system where—as in England and America—academic structure is open to provide for the needs of different classes of society. But while in the first two countries those needs have been communicated to the universities by groups and organizations directly representing the interested elements of the population (though in England this is now increasingly less the case), in France and the USSR they were communicated to it through the government.

The second parallel, concerning the extent of the division of academic labor, is particularly clear in the cases of England and France. In both countries there is great centralization of academic life, in France even more than in England. The most important academic institutions being all concentrated in Paris, differentiation of functions between them becomes to a large extent illusory. The same intellectual and scientific circles—and very often the same individuals—hold the chairs at the universities, are in control of research at the C.N.R.S., and later in life are elected to the vacant chairs of the Collège de France and the various Academies of the Institut. Thus, in spite of the existence in France, like in Britain, of considerable outside pressure from the educated middle classes and the government to diversify the framework of higher education as well as research, in the end all are assimilated to the conservative traditions of Paris academic circles who, having no competition, can easily afford to remain conservative. The limited development of specialized institutions and the unsystematic development of research (in spite of very rationally conceived plans) is, therefore, the result of similar factors as in England: the whole academic system has constantly adjusted itself to the tastes and traditions of an intellectual "establishment" concentrated in a few elite institutions, monopolizing influence, and colonizing provincial universities.[65]

65. Cousin, op. cit., 2, pp. 400–70; Gilbert Gadoffre, "Facultés ou instituts," *Le Monde,* April 17, 1947.

The situation in the Soviet Union, so far as the present authors can judge from secondary sources available to them, is still in flux. The much greater dimensions of the country and the determined efforts of the government at diversification and decentralization of the academic framework might well serve to check the tendencies inherent in hierarchic centralization. It is certain that there does exist in the Soviet Union a problem of overlapping positions, as a result of which a relatively small number of individuals, located in Moscow, have a decisive influence over a vast field of research. Government-sponsored decentralization does not necessarily assure the sensitivity of these central agencies to innovations at the periphery.[66] This is a situation very similar to England and France.

Thus, the Soviet system of higher education and research, in spite of its spectacular achievements, has structural features impeding organizational innovations and their diffusion. Its successes, though on a much more vast scale, may be comparable to those which occurred in France during the decades following the reforms of the Revolution and Napoleon, those in England following the university reform, in the United States after the Civil War, and in Germany after the introduction of empirical science into her universities. A great deal of academic deadwood was cleared away and a new, imaginative, and broad framework was created, providing unprecedented new opportunities for a relatively large number of scientists and scholars. Such a situation must bring about an upsurge of scientific creation. The question, however, is whether the new system which thus emerged will be able to differentiate and expand further out of its own initiative or whether there is no such built-in dynamism in the system, so that changes will have to be forced upon it from the outside, as usually happens in England and France.

Conclusion

Universities only a hundred years ago were exclusive academies of scholars pursuing privately their learned interests and instructing a small number of highly selected students who prepared to enter the civil service or one of the traditional professions, and in exceptional cases became scholars themselves. Today universities educate—in some countries—as much as a fourth to a third of all the young people in the appropriate age groups and conduct research of vital importance for the survival or destruction of human society.

This change of functions has been to a large extent the result of the work of the universities, though not everywhere and not at every time were universities equally active in creating new functions for themselves. As shown in

66. For tendencies of centralization and conservatism, cf. Eric Ashby, *Scientist in Russia* (Harmondsworth: Penguin Books, 1947), pp. 19–23; for recent attempts at decentralization, cf. Korol, op. cit., pp. 145–52.

this paper their eagerness to recognize and develop innovations into new disciplines depended on the existence of a decentralized competitive market for academic achievements; while their willingness to try and develop bits and pieces of practical insight and professional tradition into systematic theory depended on their direct, or government-mediated, relationship to the different classes of society.

For reasons connected with their social structure the large countries of Western and Central Europe—England, France, and Germany—have not kept pace with this evolution of the functions of higher education and research. They adhered to a conception of the university of a hundred years ago. This conception stems from an age when science had few practical uses, its fields seemed clearly mapped out, and significant research could be conducted in private libraries and laboratories. Today there seems to be no end to the potential uses of systematic research and knowledge; research in every field has become a cooperative enterprise where the lone worker becomes an increasingly rare phenomenon; specialization is so complex that most of the disciplines which about a hundred years ago still seemed narrow specializations are nowadays considered too broad fields for any one person to comprehend; and few people would dare to predict any more what will be the legitimate scope of science tomorrow. The European conception of the university is, therefore, woefully out-of-date. Incomparably more differentiated organization is needed to carry out all the greatly increased and increasingly varied functions of higher education and research.

Such complex academic organization has arisen in the United States and in the Soviet Union. In spite of the vast difference in the formal organization of their higher education and research, both countries have developed clearly differentiated functions of pure as well as applied research and purely scientific and scholarly education alongside highly practical professional training. And both countries managed to create a much greater variety of higher educational and research institutions—whether called universities or not—and, correspondingly, to institutionalize a greater variety of academic roles than the European countries.

European systems of higher education have, as a result, found themselves under pressure from a variety of sources urging them to adopt American academic forms and practices (the influence of the Soviet example is perhaps more felt in America than in Europe). These have resulted in considerable expansion of university education and research facilities and, to a more limited extent, in the establishment of new types of institutions (such as the establishment of technological universities in Britain). These reforms and the expansion which they involve will probably be beneficial to scientific work as such things always are. If, however, the present analysis is correct, the long-term success of university reform in Europe will be dependent on the establishment of much less hierarchic and much more decentralized systems of higher education and research than those existing in England and France and a much less authoritarian and much more flexible university structure than that existing in Germany.

This involves, besides concrete changes of organization, an important modification of the thinking about universities. It is feared that by consciously adapting to new functions, academic systems may neglect the one function which, so far, no other organization has managed to foster efficiently: free research, unhampered by any practical consideration, aiming only at original and scientifically significant discovery. There is no doubt that in this respect American and Soviet work often fell below acceptable standards. The criticism leveled against their providing room for courses of doubtful academic standards, or research of no significance, may be justified but not the conclusion drawn from it that these failures prove the correctness of the European approach, where academic institutions safeguard their standards by strict adherence to established academic forms placing the preservation of established standards before innovation and emphasizing the exclusive esoteric nature of scientific work. Such a conclusion is based on the same kind of fallacy which at the time of the industrial revolution led people to believe in the superiority of the old handicraft system over the new industries since the latter produced at times rather shoddy goods. It is simply not true that the expansion of scientific work lowered standards. The elite group of pure scientists working freely on their own problems has not disappeared in America and the Soviet Union but has rather developed much beyond whatever exists in Europe. The exodus of European scientists and scholars to the United States has not only been motivated by higher income but often by better conditions for and greater freedom of research.[67] It is clear, therefore, that the irreverent uses made of higher education and research have not estranged science from its immanent standards and values. They have presented to it such dangers, but academic institutions are in a position to safeguard their own ideas where they form a huge and powerful system vitally involved in the affairs of society. There is, however, very little which is worth safeguarding where excessive fear of lowering established standards has led academic institutions to prefer the function of the critic to that of the active initiator of scientific and professional advance.*

67. Cf. the interesting accounts of André Weil, "Science française," in *La nouvelle revue française* 3 (1955): 97–109; Ziman, op. cit., and for a French testimony about conditions at the beginning of the century, René Leriche, *Am Ende meines Lebens* (Bern/Stuttgart: Huber, 1957), p. 34.

Science and the University System   7

Introduction

The purpose of this paper is to disentangle the various aspects of the function and organization of scientific research in the systems of higher education of Britain, France, Germany, and the United States by tracing their development from the beginning of the nineteenth century to the present day. Until the 1930s, these four major systems of higher education served as models for the rest of the world. By that time the Soviet system of higher education and research started to develop its unique features, but its importance was still limited.[1] This was also the case with Japan, which began to develop into an independent scientific center only during the 1960s. Therefore, these two countries will not be treated systematically in this paper.

Complex institutional arrangements, such as the place of research in an educational setting, develop over time and space in an unpredictable fashion. Arrangements based on ideas and intentions, formed under given conditions, are altered as a result of experience, changes in the conditions, and the emergence of new ideas and intentions. The language in which the original ideas had been formulated might nevertheless be retained. This is usually the case, since changes in institutional arrangements occur piecemeal, at different times and in different places. Those who make these changes have practical and specific interests, and they rarely have the time and motivation to think about the broader and more long-range implications. In fact, it may be in their interest to divert attention from these implications.

1. J. D. Bernal, *The Social Functions of Science* (London: George Routledge, 1939), p. 194 (for a comparison of the Anglo-American, French, etc., "circles").

With time, the discrepancy between the professed aims and the reality becomes disturbing, since it results in misunderstandings and reduces the effectiveness of language as a convenient map or guide for action. It is one of the tasks of the sociologist to compare the language in which institutional arrangements are formulated with their actual functioning and thus help to overcome these difficulties. The present paper is intended as a contribution to this end.

Historical Development

Until the end of the eighteenth century, universities were engaged in the education of the professional, administrative, and in some cases, the political elites. University teachers were usually learned men, and quite a few of them engaged in what would today be called scholarly research in such fields as law, philosophy, theology, classical languages, literature, and science. Natural sciences did not form an important part of the curricula of the universities, except, to some extent, in the medical faculty. Since few branches of science were relevant to medical practice in those days, only on occasion did professors of the medical faculty engage in scientific research, and even those who did, did not consider this as part of their formal duties, or "role"; nor did they, or anyone else, consider the universities as institutions of research. The only institutions which supported science in the eighteenth century (there were no institutions of organized research) were the academies.[2]

The combination, or as it was called, the "unity of teaching and research" in a single role—that of the university professor—and in a single institution—the university—emerged only at the beginning of the nineteenth century. In the University of Berlin, founded in 1809, and soon thereafter in the other German language universities, the unity of these two functions became a doctrine. "Unity" implied that the two functions were organically connected so that separating them would be contrary to the "immanent nature" of research and teaching.[3] From the middle of the nineteenth century this idea has been the most important theme in university reforms and in the establishment of new systems of higher education the world over. However, as the contents, methods, and functions of both teaching and research changed, the practices associated with the general idea of the unity of teaching and research have altered too. Looking back, it is possible to distinguish four different aspects of these changes.

2. On the state of the universities in the eighteenth century, see Adam Smith, *The Wealth of Nations*, bk. 5, chap. 1, art. 2; see also René König, *Vom Wesen der deutschen Universität* (Berlin: Die Runde, 1935), pp. 17–27; see also Nicolas Hans, *New Trends in Education in the Eighteenth Century* (London: Routledge & Kegan Paul, 1951), pp. 41–54.
3. F. Schnabel, *Deutsche Geschichte im neunzehnten Jahrhundert*, vol. 2 (Freiburg im Breisgau: Herder, 1965), pp. 201–08.

These aspects are: (1) the personnel aspect; (2) the contents aspect; (3) the method aspect; and (4) the organizational aspect.

(1) *The personnel aspect,* that is, have academic teachers to be qualified and productive researchers? One of the most important decisions taken at the establishment of the new type of German university was that contribution to research was to be the principal qualification for an academic appointment. This led to a steep rise in the status of university professors. From then on, in Germany, the criterion of their appointment was to be the same as that of the members of official academies. Until then the status of the professors in the faculties of philosophy was about the same as the status of teachers in the upper grades of the better academic high schools today. Only professors of law, medicine, and theology enjoyed higher status due to the prestige of these professions. Afterward, university professors in Germany became an elite, irrespective of what they taught.[4]

This upgrading of status could not have worked without a corresponding upgrading of the faculty of philosophy (the equivalent of the American faculty of arts and sciences). Until the early nineteenth-century reforms, philosophy was a preparatory faculty of nonspecialized studies (like the American college of liberal arts). The higher faculties were those of law, medicine, and theology (which were kinds of graduate schools). After the reforms, all faculties became formally equal. In effect, however, the university became dominated by the philosophy faculty, which had the largest number of professors and, as a rule, the most outstanding researchers.[5]

This was important for the German intellectuals, since, owing to the social and economic backwardness and the political absolutism of the German-speaking countries—relative to Britain and France—the opportunities for the intellectuals for social betterment were limited. They needed official positions and the salaries that went with them in order to maintain an upper-middle-class way of life; they needed even more the formal recognition of their position by the government, since only a high position in the hierarchy of offices could ensure a high social status.[6] Such considerations did not apply to Britain, where intellectuals usually came from wealthy families, where there were numerous and varied opportunities for advancement for those who were not so well-off, and where formal office had little to do with social status.[7]

In France, the situation was more complex. Official position was probably more important than in Britain as a source of income as well as of prestige. However, there were many positions open to intellectuals in general, and to

4. H. Brunschwig, *La crise de l'Etat prussien à la fin du XVIII⁰ siècle et la genèse de la mentalité romantique* (Paris: Presses Universitaires de France, 1947), pp. 161–86.

5. J. Ben-David and A. Zloczower, "Universities and Academic Systems in Modern Societies," *European Journal of Sociology* 3 (1962): 52–54. [This volume, chap. 6.]

6. H. Brunschwig, loc. cit.

7. N. G. Annan, "The Intellectual Aristocracy," in J. Plumb (ed.), *Studies in Social History* (London: Longmans Green, 1955), pp. 241–87.

successful researchers in particular, in the educational administration and in a relatively large number of scientific and higher educational institutions outside the universities—such as the Musée d'histoire naturelle, the Collège de France, and so forth. Some were connected with teaching duties, but these were usually negligible. Thus, researchers had no particular interest in monopolizing university chairs.[8]

In the United States, until the second half of the nineteenth century, an intellectual class existed only on the East Coast. They were mostly people with independent means and a social position similar to that of the corresponding class in Britain. College presidents and some professors were an important part of this class. Elsewhere in the United States, pioneering conditions existed until the second half of the nineteenth century. The representatives of culture were clergymen, college presidents, and some professional people. The colleges here played an important role in the creation of a cultural atmosphere. There was a great gap between the status of the college president who was often a leading figure in the community and that of the college teacher who was not considered to be a professional. Compared to the presidents and the professional class, college teachers felt deprived of their proper status.[9] There existed, therefore, a potential here to follow the German pattern of upgrading the college teacher through promoting him from the status of "teacher" to that of "researcher." But in general there was little interest in research in the United States. Besides in the eastern states, intellectuals had no need to improve their status. In the Midwest and elsewhere, where some of them might have been interested in such an improvement, the German pattern was too aristocratic and elitist.

As a result of these status differences, the German role type of professor-researcher had, in the beginning, little appeal in Britain, France, and the United States. Some university teachers were outstanding researchers in all those countries. But teaching at a university was not considered as the most suitable occupation for a researcher, nor was it required of all university teachers that they be researchers. The German pattern began to be imitated only in the second half of the nineteenth century when new types of research practices and new ways of training researchers emerged in Germany. Through their impetus, Germany surged ahead in science, so that scientists elsewhere felt that they had to adopt the German methods in order to prevent the decline of science in their countries.

(2) *The Contents Aspect.* Here the German conception of the unity of teaching and research was radical: the academic teacher was free to lecture on whatever subject he wanted, and the employer—that is, the State, or the cli-

8. J. Ben-David, *The Scientist's Role in Society: A Comparative Study* (Englewood Cliffs, N.J.: Prentice-Hall, 1971), pp. 96–97.
9. Richard Hofstadter and Walter Metzger, *The Development of Academic Freedom in the United States* (New York: Columbia University Press, 1955), pp. 124, 229–32.

ents—namely, the students, could not interfere with the contents of his teaching in any manner. Teaching was supposed to be as free and as spontaneous as research.[10]

In actual fact, both the state and the student had considerable influence on what was taught. The approval of the establishment of new chairs and the final selection of the teachers were made by the governments. Furthermore, they determined the contents of the state examinations qualifying for professional practice. At the same time, students were free to choose their courses and to transfer credits freely from one university to another, and the teachers, in addition to their salaries (or, in the case of the Privatdozent, instead of salary), were paid a course attendance fee by each student registering for a course. Since the majority of the students (including those on the philosophy faculty— who prepared for high school teaching) intended to become professionals, and therefore had to take state examinations, it was predictable that contents which were deemed necessary by the authorities would be taught quite willingly by most professors. Simultaneously, however, many specialized subjects were taught in fields which did not prepare the students for any professional career (except that of the academic teacher-researcher). Only the contents of these courses—attended by a negligible fraction of the students—were determined exclusively by the research interests of those who taught them.

It was this aspect of the unity of teaching and research which had the least effect outside Germany. The idea that the individual professor should be allowed complete freedom in the determination of the contents and the nature of his courses was not accepted in any of the other countries surveyed here. The university authorities in Britain, France, and the United States eventually agreed to delegate the function of determining the curriculum to collegial bodies elected by the teachers, but everywhere there was some official control of *what* was taught (though not of *how* it was taught). Complete individual freedom of the teachers, controlled only by the choices of the students preparing for examinations, was not considered as a sufficient safeguard of the adequacy of teaching.

(3) *The Method Aspect.* Those who conceived of the new university in early nineteenth-century Prussia did not envisage research laboratories, nor probably even seminars. Research for them was a private act of creation of which only the results would be shared with others. Their conception of the methodological unity of teaching and research was not of a scholar doing research with the aid of, together with, or supervising the work of someone else but of the teacher-researcher whose lectures were based on original thought and firsthand inquiry.[11] The best results of this approach were the brilliant lecture courses of some of the outstanding professors. The texts based on these

10. Friedrich Paulsen, *The German University: Its Character and Historical Development* (New York: Macmillan, 1895), pp. 85–86.
11. F. Schnabel, loc. cit.

courses have been much admired as monuments of scholarship, but the method itself has never been universally approved either as a particularly successful way of instruction or as the best way of presenting the fruits of research.

For the majority of foreign observers, the most impressive aspects of the unity of teaching and research were the seminar and laboratory methods of teaching. These required the student to try his hand at research and provided an opportunity for the teacher to share with the students not only the results but also the methods and techniques of his enquiry. These methods of instruction developed by stages and not as a result of a preconceived design. The seminars were originally established for the purpose of providing intensive, pedagogically oriented training to those intending to become schoolteachers (hence also the name "seminar").

Laboratory instruction, which emerged first in chemistry, aimed similarly to provide technical know-how, especially for future chemists. Practical professional training, rather than scientific research, was the original intention in both cases.[12] The development of these modest beginnings into research workshops was the result of "accidental" innovation by outstanding teacher-researchers (such as Liebig in chemistry) and the rapid spread of this innovation in the university system.

This innovation and its diffusion transformed the modern German university in a manner not envisaged by its founders. The successful seminars and laboratories produced relatively large numbers of trained researchers, who had all the advantages of the "professional" over those who became researchers in the old-fashioned, semi-amateur ways. This new breed of researcher mastered the techniques of research and knew how to produce concrete results efficiently, while those who did not have such training had to grope their way on their own toward some kind of scientific competence.

As a result these "professional" researchers had a better chance of appointment to university chairs than the others. Of course, in the beginning there were few chairs, especially in the experimental sciences. The founders of the new German university did not think highly of experimental science—which they considered as a kind of technology. They emphasized philosophy, the humanities, and mathematics.

But here too an unintended transformation of the system occurred. "Professional" experimental science produced the most impressive research results among the academic fields and therefore gained prestige, relative to other fields, in the decentralized and competitive German system, in spite of the antiexperimental ideology pervading it. New specializations were given academic recognition through the establishment of new chairs in chemistry,

12. F. Paulsen, *Geschichte des gelehrten Unterrichts* (Leipzig: Veit, 1885), pp. 586–89.

philosophy, and later, in experimental physics and even experimental psychology.[13]

This most influential development in the combination of teaching and research was in actual fact inconsistent with the original idea of the unity of teaching and research. That idea conceived of *all* teaching as based on research, irrespective of the purpose of the studies. Research here was identical with original and systematic thought, and it was intended that all university students should be taught by original and systematic thinkers. Professionalism of any kind was discouraged and belittled. It was thought that training in any techniques, including those of research, could and should be acquired privately and informally.[14] Professionalism in research was, therefore, a fact but not an admitted principle.

These formal philosophical considerations were of little importance for the foreign observers of the system. Compared to anything else they knew, the German universities were ideal places for training in advanced research. Mature researchers in Britain, France, and elsewhere envied the productivity of their German colleagues—the result of working together with groups of students in well-appointed laboratories. They realized that there was a more stimulating environment for research in Germany than elsewhere.[15]

By the 1890s, aspiring researchers from the entire Western world went to Germany in order to obtain advanced training. Some German professors—like Liebig in chemistry, Ludwig in physiology, and Wundt in experimental psychology—raised virtually entire generations of researchers in Europe and America.[16]

The concern of all the foreign observers was not education but scientific research, and a German university was, for them, the most suitable place to do it. They advocated the professionalization of research and admired and imitated the method of laboratory and seminar instruction as forms of research training and organization. Thus, the professionalization of research, an unintended development in Germany, was the very aim of the imitators of the German arrangements. British and French scientists, intent on transplanting the arrangements of the German universities to their respective countries, were

13. F. Schnabel, op. cit., pp. 219–20, and also vol. 5, pp. 203–76; also R. Stephen Turner, "The Growth of Professional Research in Prussia, 1818–1848," *Historical Studies in the Physical Sciences* 3 (1971): 137–82.

14. A. Flexner, loc. cit.; also Turner, op. cit.

15. R. B. Perry, *The Thought and Character of William James*, vol. 1 (Boston: Little, Brown, 1935), pp. 249–83; S. Reznick, "The European Education of an American Chemist and Its Influence in Nineteenth-Century America: Eben Norton Horsford," *Technology and Culture* (July 1970): 366–88. D. Fleming, *William H. Welch and the Rise of Modern Medicine* (Boston: Little, Brown, 1954), pp. 32–54, 100–05.

16. J. Ben-David and R. Collins, "Social Factors in the Origin of a New Science: The Case of Psychology," *American Sociological Review* 31, no. 4 (1966): 451–65. [This volume, chap. 2.]

interested in catching up with German science. Being concerned with research alone and not with education, they were much more willing to face the organizational implications of the emergence of professional science than their German counterparts.

(4) *The Organizational Aspect.* The professionalization and formalization of training for research presented a serious dilemma for those who adhered to the unity of teaching and research as a general principle of all instruction at university level. If participation in research was to be a preparation for professional research work, then those who did not intend to become researchers would not need to participate in research. Such a differentiation would have given rise to two kinds of teaching at the universities: one where there was unity of teaching and research and another where there was little or no unity. This would have implied the abandonment of "unity" as a general principle. This step was not taken in Germany. Instead, laboratory and seminar work was required from everyone, justified by the plausible argument that one could not expect to learn about science without a taste of its very substance, namely, research.

Since, however, there is a great difference between research which is undertaken for getting the taste of it and that which is done in earnest for the purpose of making a discovery, there occurred, as a matter of fact, a division between the two types of research at the universities. The former came to be performed more and more perfunctorily, while the latter moved out of the formal curriculum of the university into the so-called institutes. These were research organizations attached to a chair (usually for the lifetime of the professor) but financed from a separately allocated grant (that is, not from the regular university budget). In these institutes, serious research took place, organized as the professor thought fit, and here researchers were trained.[17]

This development shows that with the emergence of professional science, the original conception of the unity of teaching and research became untenable. There was now a level of research which could not be integrated with teaching. Probably for reasons of status and power, German professors preferred to maintain the fiction that all "real" teaching took place at the university, that all "real" research took place within the minds of individuals, and that the bureaucratically organized institutes were merely organizational aids to the private research of the professor. This fiction justified the absolutism of the professor in his research institute and the function of the university as a guild of the professional estate engaged only in the protection of the rights and privileges of its members and in safeguarding the standards of the university. This was deemed preferable to turning the university into an organization for professorial work. This resistance to organizational change was not a satisfac-

17. A. Flexner, *Universities: American, English, German* (London: Oxford University Press, 1968), pp. 42–45, 287, 314–15.

tory solution and caused a great deal of dissatisfaction among junior scientists. It was probably one of the causes of the eventual loss of German scientific superiority.[18]

Other countries approached the organizational problems of professional science in a more instrumental way. They tried to tackle separately three aspects of the problem: how to train professional researchers; to what extent and how to reinforce research orientation in university instruction in general; and how to organize and support professional research.

In each of the other three countries dealt with here, new measures were introduced for training researchers. The arrangements of the German university institutes served as the model everywhere, but nowhere was it followed slavishly.

In Britain there emerged university departments which officially combined the functions of teaching with those of a research institute. These innovations were, however, restricted to a few departments of experimental science and to students preparing for honors degrees.[19] In France the École pratique des hautes études was established in 1868, as a kind of graduate school. The plan was to pool the research talent and resources available in the Paris area and use them for organizing seminars and laboratories where advanced students would be trained for research.[20] In Britain, as well as in France, such researcher-oriented studies constituted a small fraction of the total activity of higher educational institutions. The bulk of the latter were conceived essentially as teaching institutions designed for the instructional needs of the professional and political elites. The idea that research-oriented teaching might be suitable for this category of students was not generally accepted. Neither of these two countries was prepared to diverge significantly from their established traditions in higher education. Universities have been considered as principally teaching institutions in both of them.

However, there has been a growing emphasis on the scientific qualifications of those to be appointed to university chairs, particularly in the natural and exact sciences.

The most important developments, however, took place in the United States. The U.S. graduate school, which emerged in the 1870s, was an attempt to build a complete, formal program of specialized training for professional research, culminating in the Ph.D. Furthermore, graduate professional schools of medicine, agriculture, engineering, business, etc., combined professional training with applied research. Perhaps owing to the absence of any local traditions in research, the American graduate schools followed German precedents more closely than either the British or the French.

18. J. Ben-David, op. cit., pp. 133–38.
19. D. S. L., Cardwell, *The Organization of Science in England* (London: Heinemann, 1957), p. 95.
20. J. Ben-David, op. cit., p. 103.

But the American university as a whole did not follow the overall German pattern. The American graduate school took the German research institute only as a starting point. Rather than being the private domain of a professor who was tied to the university only through his chair, the graduate department became an integral and public part of the university, and all its scientific personnel held regular university appointments. It provided formal rather than informal training, and it conferred regular degrees.[21]

The conditions for the development of this type of school in the United States were optimal. The professionalization of research and of academic teaching (which was, at the graduate level, training for research) was an important status interest of American college teachers, who, as we have seen, had been traditionally regarded as subprofessionals. In Germany, it will be recalled, professionalization would have meant a loss of status for university professors; and in Britain and France they had the status of higher professionals from the outset.

Furthermore, the U.S. system was even more decentralized and competitive than the German one. Since research is inherently a productive and innovative process, the chances were that a competitive system would more fully exploit its potential than a centralized or hierarchic system. University presidents and chairmen of departments often acted like entrepreneurs investing in research talents and facilities, in hopes of getting a return in the form of publications, fame, donations, and desirable students.

As a result, the trend toward the development of professional scientific research, and increasingly research-based training for some of the practical professions which had been initiated at the German universities, continued to develop in the United States more than elsewhere. The sociological phenomenon which arose in Germany, of "schools" of students working with a great teacher, developed in the United States into more differentiated types of teamwork. There were "schools" as in Germany but also pairs or groups of peers, working together for a more or less prolonged period of time, usually with students who were not personally subordinate to any single teacher. Thus, interdisciplinary teams and institutes of research emerged in the professional schools.

This was the fruit of entrepreneurship, which resulted in its turn in the expansion of the use of research and researchers. Since these institutes were situated at universities, they trained students who had some practical know-how in research, which could be used more or less directly by industrial firms, in agriculture, or in business administration.

It has to be emphasized, however, that all this development toward a much closer integration of research and teaching was, with few exceptions, confined to the graduate schools, which constituted a small fraction of the total opera-

21. Ibid., pp. 139–47.

tion of the universities. The bulk of the students were undergraduates, and their studies had usually little research content.

Thus, until the late 1930s, nowhere outside Germany was the unity of teaching and research accepted as a principle governing all higher education. Only in Germany, and the countries following the German pattern, was there in principle a complete integration of teaching and research. In fact, as has been shown, there existed a division there, too, on somewhat similar lines as in the United States—since serious research was located in the institutes, whereas the research content in undergraduate studies was as a rule extremely shallow. Only with respect to academic appointments and promotions was there a complete unity of teaching and research in these countries, since appointments and promotions were based overwhelmingly on success in research.

The Postwar Years

Since the Second World War, and especially since the mid-fifties, the place of science at the universities has greatly changed. The wartime mobilization of scientists in the United States, Britain, and Canada opened up new vistas for the application of science for technological purposes. The experience of collaboration among groups of scientists and of organizational leadership and know-how among American academic scientists who were willing to cooperate with outsiders from the military and industry were among the most important conditions of this success.

To the reputation created by the wartime achievements of American science was added, in the years following the war, the recognition that the American universities, or more precisely, the graduate schools of the twenty-or-so best American universities, were by far the best places in the world for both doing and for being trained in research. Mature researchers and research students from all parts of the world now flocked to the United States as immigrants, visiting scholars, or advanced students, just as they used to go to Germany prior to 1933.[22]

The success of the graduate schools was not confined to the worldwide scientific community. Science rose in prestige dramatically in the general society as well. From the mid-fifties up until 1967, there had been a seemingly insatiable demand for scientists in general, and research scientists in particular,

22. The large inflow to the United States of scientists and engineers began in the late 1950s and reached a peak in 1967. See B. Thomas, "Modern Migration," in Walter Adams (ed.), *The Brain Drain* (New York: Macmillan, 1968), p. 44. In 1958, 4,032 engineers and 1,108 scientists immigrated to the United States; in 1959, 3,950 engineers and 1,094 scientists; in 1960, 3,354 engineers and 924 scientists; in 1963, 4,014 engineers and 1,397 scientists; in 1964, 3,725 engineers and 1,503 scientists; in 1966, 4,920 engineers and 1,570 scientists; and in 1967, 8,822 engineers and 1,795 scientists. See, OECD Committee for Scientific and Technical Personnel, *The International Movement of Scientists and Engineers*, pt. 1 (Paris: OECD, 1970), p. 101.

in the American economy, and the prestige of scientific occupations rose between 1947 and 1963 from modest levels to very near the top of the occupational prestige scale.[23]

These developments led to a growing emphasis on research orientation at all the levels of higher education in the United States, in practically all types of schools. A Ph.D. degree and publications became increasingly required from the teachers at colleges of quite modest academic quality, and more and more students came to regard the first degree as a preparation for graduate school, rather than as a terminal degree.[24]

With some delay, these developments affected all the university systems of the world. Just as in the middle of the nineteenth century, scientists and scientific policymakers everywhere in the world realized that the German universities had initiated a new phase, so their successors a hundred years later were conscious that a new stage in the organization of research had been reached in the United States. There followed a spate of university reforms, or at least proposals for reform, all over the world. Their principal objective was to strengthen graduate training at the universities and to foster organized team and interdisciplinary research at the universities. Some recommendations aimed to restructure the undergraduate curriculum so that it should serve as a general preparation for either a well-informed choice of graduate specialization or for equally well-informed consumership of intellectual products and research services.[25] The production and consumption of original scientific and scholarly creations, rather than education for social and political leadership, or preparation for professional practice, became the central theme of higher education.

These developments have probably greatly improved the quality of higher education everywhere; nonetheless, this improvement in quality was not well balanced. Some of the traditional (and still relevant) functions of higher education—e.g., leadership and professional training—were neglected, while scientific research and creativity were emphasized to an unrealistic extent. The governments were mainly interested in supporting research, which they regarded as a potential source of technological and military innovation. Even in a country like the United States, where many of the leading universities

---

23. Robert W. Hodge, Paul M. Siegel, Peter H. Rossi, "Occupational Prestige in the United States, 1925–63," in R. Bendix and S. M. Lipset (eds.), *Class, Status and Power.* 2d ed. (New York: Free Press, 1966), p. 324.

24. James A. Davis, *Undergraduate Career Decision* (Chicago: Aldine, 1965), p. 201. According to this report, only 24 percent of a representative sample of American college students in 1961 did not have intentions to go to graduate school.

25. For Great Britain, see H. J. Perkin, *New Universities in the United Kingdom* (Paris: OECD, 1969), pp. 58–60, 115–38, 163–70; for France, see C. Gringnon and J. C. Passeron, *French Experience Before 1968* (Paris: OECD, 1970), pp. 50–51, 99, 104–05, 131–33; for Germany, see E. Böning and K. Roeloffs, *Three German Universities* (Paris: OECD, 1970), pp. 34, 60–63, 68–69, 143.

were private institutions dependent for their income mainly on students' fees, endowments, donations, and other kinds of community support, the support of the central government—given mainly for research—increased to such an extent that the leading universities became dependent for 20 to 50 percent of their budgets on central governmental support.[26] Hence the other functions of the university could not compete with research. No doubt the idea of the unity of teaching and research helped to rationalize and justify this monopolization of all the university activities by research: there was always a way to prove that all research somehow benefited teaching.

Of course, there is much truth in this, since research, which leads to new discovery, provides new content and new inspiration for teaching. However, in practice, the question never is whether, in principle, teaching benefits from research but how much a given course of teaching benefits from a given project of research. Thus, the general arguments about the unity of teaching and research were irrelevant to the situation which arose in the early 1960s. The emphasis on research and creativity in higher education grew concomitantly to the percentage of the relevant age group attending higher educational institutions—attendance having more than doubled between 1950 and 1965 in the majority of industrially advanced countries.[27] In other words, the emphasis on research and creativity grew in direct proportion to the entrance into the universities of less and less talented and less and less intellectually motivated students and teachers.[28] Furthermore, as the number of students rose to levels exceeding 10 percent of the age group, their prospects of engaging in high-level professional and managerial work were bound to diminish even in industrially advanced countries. A reconsideration of the one-sided emphasis on research at all university-level instruction seems, therefore, inevitable.

Conclusion

The original conception of the unity of teaching and research envisioned a small and highly selected group of teachers lecturing to a student audience on topics related to the research of these teachers. It was assumed that teaching by original researchers, even if it did not provide full coverage of a field, would be more inspiring for able and advanced students than more systematic teaching by merely competent instructors.

26. Clark Kerr, *The Uses of the University* (Cambridge: Harvard University Press, 1964), p. 55.

27. *The Development of Higher Education, 1950–1967* (Paris: OECD, The Education Committee, 1970), p. 67.

28. Martin Trow, "The Expansion and Transformation of Higher Education." [*Advancement of Science* (Great Britain) 27, no. 134 (June 1971): 357–63, as well as in *International Review of Education* 18 (1972): 61–84.]

By the middle of the nineteenth century the idea of the unity of teaching and research became associated with laboratory and seminar work. Originally, it appears, participation in these activities was voluntary and thus limited to students genuinely interested in research. Later, laboratory and seminar work became compulsory for all students and came to be regarded as the ideal way of combining research with teaching. For the run-of-the-mill student, this innovation had little appeal. In fact, there was a great difference between the routine laboratory exercises of the ordinary undergraduate and the advanced work done in the institutes by the few students who had a scientific bent. Eventually, in the American graduate schools which emerged during the last three decades of the nineteenth century this distinction became formalized. Training in research techniques and carrying out research became the main content of graduate instruction, while in other parts of the curriculum a modest amount of research done by the student might or might not be used as a didactic device.

By the end of the nineteenth century, all advanced national systems of higher education trained at least some of their students as researchers. On the other hand, there was no university system where all teaching was based on research and where all students were supposed to engage in more than token research. But university systems differed in the extent to which they emphasized the one or the other type of instruction and in the method employed by them for determining the role of research. These two differences were probably interrelated. In the United States, as in Germany, the trend has been to further the growth of research in the universities as much as possible. In neither case was this policy deliberately followed; rather, it was the result of the competitive, entrepreneurial nature of both systems. Research being a dynamic and expanding resource, competitive systems pressed its uses to the very limits that the system could bear.

At the other extreme was and still is France, which is now joined by the USSR. In these two countries higher education serves a variety of teaching functions, and research is integrated with teaching only in the rather small part of the system specifically designed to train researchers. In both of these countries higher education as well as research have been centrally planned and financed activities, and their share is decided by deliberation, not by market forces.

In between these two extremes is Britain, and probably Japan, where universities have much freedom to determine the extent to which they want to emphasize research at different levels and in different kinds of instruction. But these university systems are much less competitive and much more traditionally hierarchic than either the German or the American systems. Hence, custom and conservatism have set much narrower limits to the expansiveness of research entrepreneurs at these university systems than in the German or in the American ones.

In a very general way, the idea of the unity of teaching and research has furthered the development of the emphasis on research in the competitive university systems. They treat science as an inexhaustible resource, an endless frontier. Therefore, more and more fields of research were considered relevant for more and more fields of study. It could be envisaged, therefore, that at some future time all teaching would be integrated with and/or based on ongoing research.

As has been shown, however, there has been a fundamental difference in all systems between the integration of teaching and research in the training of future researchers and advanced professionals, on the one hand, and the degree of integration customary in other frameworks or courses. The general principle of the unity of teaching and research has not helped to understand the nature of these differences. In fact, it served as a means to obscure them and to distract attention from the real problem which is the determining of the relationship between research and teaching. Owing to the very nature of research as a constantly changing activity, the determinants cannot be established in advance for a definite period of time. The question then is, what mechanisms should be employed for the determination and review of the relationship between these two functions? As we have seen, the periodic redefinition of this relationship has been accomplished, until recently, by competition between universities where such competition has existed. Other countries have usually followed the lead of these entrepreneurial systems, and the competitive mechanisms have helped to extend the integration of research and teaching. It is true that at times this was done at the expense of the educational functions of the university. However, such imbalance has been caused not by the competitive mechanism itself but rather through one-sided support of research by various governments which has hindered competition. Therefore, it seems that a competitive system of some sort would continue to be the best means of determining the relationship between teaching and research. Since no one can foresee what the progress of science and its applications will be, only the hindsight provided by a competitive system can accomplish the task of ongoing revision of the relationship. However, some means of protecting the competitive system against being thwarted by special academic and other interest groups is needed.

Academy, University, and Research Institute in the Nineteenth and Twentieth Centuries

8

A Study of Changing Functions
and Structures

There is a tendency to view institutional change as an organic process. Institutions—according to this approach—have a life cycle. They arise in response to new challenges and opportunities, have a period of efflorescence during which they perform their functions successfully, then they develop internal rigidities, and when new challenges and opportunities arise, they are incapable of dealing with them. They enter a period of crisis and become a hindrance to development. At this point, they are ripe for destruction in order to clear the place for new emerging institutions adapted to the new conditions.[1]

This cyclical view of history has also influenced the history of institutions. In order to investigate the fit between this approach and the way institutions actually develop, I shall review two cases: the alleged decline of the academies at the end of the eighteenth century and their alleged replacement with institutions of higher education; and the difficulties encountered by university research—often referred to as "crisis"—at the end of the nineteenth century which prompted the establishment of specialized, nonteaching, research institutes.[2]

1. The origin of this view is in various philosophies of history; see Frank E. Manuel, *Shapes of Philosophical History* (Stanford: Stanford University Press, 1965), pp. 2–6, 123–24, 154–57.

2. See Roger Hahn, *The Anatomy of a Scientific Institution: The Paris Academy of Sciences 1666–1803* (Berkeley and Los Angeles: University of California Press, 1971), pp. 284–85, 301, 312. Lothar Burchardt, *Wissenschaftspolitik im Wilhelminischen Deutschland* (Göttingen: Vandenhoeck und Ruprecht, 1975), pp. 1–24.

Academies, Scientific
Societies, and Universities

The Paris Academy of Sciences abolished under Jacobine rule in 1793 was resurrected as the first class of the *Institut* in 1795. But according to Roger Hahn, it has never regained its erstwhile importance, since it did not serve any longer either as an important center for the formation and exchange of ideas or as a source of authoritative publication. To these failures—which he believes were due to increasing scientific specialization—he attributes the eventual decline of the Academy. In his view the whole venture of reestablishing the Academy was a mistake. The institution was not needed any more by science or scientists. "Considered as the nerve center of science, the Academy now passed through its full life cycle, from birth to fossilization." [3]

However, while there is no doubt that the importance of the Paris Academy declined in the nineteenth century, compared to its importance in the twentieth century, the decline of academies was not general, as Hahn's explanation would have us expect. The nineteenth century witnessed the reformation of the Royal Society of London, following a century of torpor, and the foundation of new academies in many parts of the world, among them the National Academy of Sciences. [4] The establishment of the Nobel Prizes in 1901 lent unprecedented importance to the Swedish Academy of Sciences.

These academies continued to perform the same functions as their seventeenth- and eighteenth-century predecessors. They published their transactions (some of which retained considerable importance), distributed honors and prizes, and played an important and active role as advisers to governments and representatives of science to the public.

In fact, also, the decline of the Paris Academy was not instantaneous. In the first years following its reestablishment, the Academy continued to play an important role in the scientific and educational life of France. In the late 1790s, the Academy appeared as a most important institution, perhaps more important than ever. In 1798, it pioneered the first international congress in science, that on weights and measures, [5] thus giving rise to a type of scientific institution that has played a crucial role in the development of science since then.

The impression that one cannot speak of a decline of the academies in the nineteenth century becomes even stronger if one does not restrict oneself to organizations actually called academies but considers the entire category of

3. Hahn, op. cit., p. 312.
4. Dorothy Stimson, *Scientists and Amateurs: A History of the Royal Society* (New York: Henry Schuman, 1948), pp. 205–17; A. Hunter Dupree, *Science in the Federal Government* (A History of Policies and Activities to 1940) (Cambridge: Belknap Press/Harvard University Press, 1957), pp. 135–48.
5. Hahn, op. cit., p. 309.

scientific societies devoted to the advancement of science in general (and not to any specialized discipline). Then, of course, the nineteenth century becomes the century par excellence of the foundation and rise of such societies. Beginning with the Swiss *Allgemeine Schweizerische Gesellschaft für die gesamten Naturwissenschaften* (1815) that inspired the foundation of the world-famous *Gesellschaft der deutschen Naturforscher und Ärzte* (GDNÄ) (1822), there followed other similar associations, the best known of which were the British and the American Associations for the Advancement of Science (BAAS and AAAS).[6]

Initially, the most important activity of these societies was the organization of scientific congresses. The yearly meetings of the GNDÄ and BAAS were important events attracting the attention of scientists from other countries also, and congresses soon took their place alongside periodical publications as one of the principal means of scientific communication, recognition, and publicity.

Although nowadays meetings are also organized by ad hoc groups, universities, foundations, and so on, scientific societies have continued to play a crucial role in the initiation and regular maintenance of congresses. They are also important publishers of scientific periodicals, as the academies have been for more than three centuries. It is true that the overwhelming majority of these societies are specialized today. But specialization—which started about the middle of the nineteenth century—has not eliminated the general nonspecialized societies.[7] And nonspecialized publications, such as *Nature* and *Science,* have retained their importance until today.

This shows that the new societies performed functions similar to those of the academies. The difference between the two types of organization was political. The academies represented an elite sponsored by kings and princes (and retain their ties to governments to this very day). The associations admitted democratically everyone active in the field and were self-governing bodies, independent from the rulers and the nobility.

Thus, specialization and the emergence of institutions of scientific research and teaching have not led to the decline of academies and general scientific societies. If anything, it increased their importance and led to the establishment of new ones.

The decline of the standing of the Paris Academy was probably due to two reasons. First of all, beginning with Napoleon, French governments centralized all educational power in their own hands and exempted the erstwhile functions of the Academy as the initiator of all official schemes for the support

---

6. Frank R. Pfetsch, *Zur Entwicklung der Wissenschaftspolitik in Deutschland* (Berlin: Duncker und Humblot, 1974), pp. 252–58.
7. Ibid., pp. 215–17, 258–92.

of science and the administrator of many. As Hahn shows, the Academy was made into a public relations department for cultural affairs by Napoleon. Prior to his rule, it performed the same vital functions as the Royal Society of London (if anything, it was more enterprising and influential than the Royal Society).[8] Second, the decline of French science in general during the nineteenth century also reduced the standing of the Paris Academy.

The reason for the relative lack of importance of general scientific societies in France was also probably due to the general discouragement of spontaneous social organizations by the all-pervasive patronage of government bureaucracy and the highly centralized, hierarchic structure of the entire system of higher education and research. This relative weakness of voluntary social organizations is characteristic of French society in general and not only of French science.

Thus, it can be concluded that the nineteenth century was not a period of decline but one of rise of academies and scientific societies. Parallel to the rise of the scientific university, there emerged a complex and hierarchic institutional structure for the furtherance of science outside the universities. At the top of the hierarchy were the academies followed by national associations for the advancement of science, both branching out into disciplinary sections and subsocieties. Academies, as well as scientific societies, engaged in publications, especially periodical publications, and the organization of congresses.

Specialized associations complemented the functions of the more general ones, particularly in facilitating scientific communication and in the allocation of scientific recognition and the public representation of the relevant branch of science. The academies and associations did not compete with the universities. These latter performed a new function, namely, teaching and training in research through practical apprenticeship under the supervision of a competent researcher, that had not been performed by any institution previously.

The survival of general scientific societies, in the age of specialized science pursued at universities, has not been a mere coincidence. Universities could not have effectively replaced academies and similar institutions in the allocation of scientific recognition and the public representation of science.

The universities produced disciplinary science through research and diffused it through teaching. The "chairs" and the departments in each field were in many ways like competing units of production. Therefore, the universities could not represent science as a whole. The disciplinary concerns and often one-sided involvement of professors in intradisciplinary debates also made the universities unsatisfactory institutions for the authoritative evaluation of scientific contributions. Of course, they were engaged in the evaluation process through citation and recommendation of literature and appointments and promotion of personnel. But they could never monopolize this function,

8. Hahn, op. cit., pp. 304–08.

and much of it continued to remain in the hands of specialized and general scientific societies.

Although the evaluations of individual contributions increasingly required specialized knowledge, general societies and academies still retained their function of checking tendencies of disciplinary sectarianism and dogmatism and recognizing new fields.[9] This function is worth stressing, since it is often overlooked or belittled by practicing scientists who tend to view science *exclusively* as a set of highly specialized pursuits.

Universities and Research Institutes

The German universities reached their peak of fame and success during the seventies and eighties of the nineteenth century, about a hundred years after the Paris Academy of Sciences had reached its peak. At this point, they began experiencing difficulties. Since these difficulties were not accompanied by political upheaval, there was no ideologically legitimized hatred of universities, and universities were not closed down or abolished. But there was a belief that university research combined with teaching students for nonresearch degrees, conducted in informal groups of a teacher and his students, was ill-adapted to the needs of up-to-date research. It was thought that many branches of science became too specialized to be combined with teaching undergraduates and that some research required formal organization and full-time work that were inconsistent with the functions and traditions of the universities.[10]

Some observers believed that the university would not be able to cope with the new situation and that it was a declining institution. Others—of a more pragmatic bent—refrained from generalizations and prediction and simply proceeded to propagate and establish new types of institutions in every instance when they felt that the university was inadequate to perform up-to-date work in a given field.

Finally, in 1911, the Kaiser Wilhelm (now Max Planck) Institute was founded, as an institution meant to do research in the basic sciences in general.[11] Although this was not officially conceived of as something to replace university research, it was an unambiguous recognition of the obsolescence of university research in central branches of science.

9. For further elaboration of these points, see Joseph Ben-David, "Organization, Social Control, and Cognitive Change in Science," in Joseph Ben-David and Terry N. Clark (eds.), *Culture and its Creators* (Chicago: University of Chicago Press, 1977), pp. 244–65. [This volume, chap. 15.]

10. Frank R. Pfetsch, "Scientific Organization and Science Policy in Imperial Germany 1871–1914: The Foundation of the Imperial Institute of Physics and Technology," *Minerva* 7, no. 4 (October 1970): 557–80, esp. p. 568.

11. On the foundation of the Institute, see Burchardt, op. cit.

As we know today, the new foundation has not replaced universities, at least not thus far. But the problem of whether universities or research institutes are the best places to conduct research is still unsettled. In applied science—which includes basic science in fields in which there is an expectation of eventual application—there are research institutes in practically every country. In other fields of basic research, there is in most countries competition between universities and institutes, whereas in some, among them the United States, this kind of research is overwhelmingly a university function.

Universities seem to be able to hold their own even in this age of very big science. Thus, the share in the university expenditures on basic research of the Federally Funded Research and Development Centers administered by the universities has declined since the early sixties, and the share of the universities in the total national expenditure on basic research increased from 37 percent in 1960 to about 55 percent in 1974.[12]

Thus, the institutional decline thesis does not fit this case either. There has been no decline or fossilization of the university as a center of research (although this might have occurred in the universities of some countries), but there were developments in the relationship between research and study which required institutional changes that cannot be understood by recourse to the organicistic analogy.

Until the 1880s, university research had been performed as a by-product of training students for careers in high school teaching, medicine, pharmacy, law, theology, and a few other professions. This was possible because of the state of the art in science and scholarship, on the one hand, and the state of the professions, on the other. For example, classical philology was the basic discipline for practically all the humanistic studies pursued at the universities. It was the principal tool in the study of ancient and medieval history or literature, served as the paradigm for the study of linguistics and literature in general, and was considered as highly relevant for theology, law, and to some extent even medicine. This having been the case, it was reasonable to make the study of classical languages the centerpiece of high school education.

Thus, there was a broad overlap between the needs of students in the arts faculties, the majority of whom prepared for a career in high school teaching, and the research of the professors. Of course, the interests of the professors were more specialized and deeper than those of the students, so that the latter were in a way overtrained for their careers, but they were not mistrained. What they studied was to be directly useful for their future teaching at

12. U.S. National Science Board, National Science Foundation, *Science Indicators* 1974 (Washington, D.C.: U.S. Government Printing Office, 1976), pp. 50, 186, table 3-2, showing that basic research expenditures at Federally Funded Research and Development Centers administered by universities declined (in constant 1967 dollars) from a peak of 265 in 1968 to 201 million in 1974, while the expenditure of universities on basic research declined only from 1,586 to 1,486 million dollars.

schools, and their research experience only enhanced their competence and devotion to their subjects of teaching.[13]

There was a similar situation in the natural sciences. Until well into the 1830s, chemical and physiological research could still be pursued in simple— usually private—laboratories, and the facilities and courses required to train a pharmacist or a medical doctor were not different from those used by research workers. In these fields, like in the humanities, there was a considerable overlap between the interests of a well-trained practioner (such as a pharmacist or a physician) and those of a professional researcher.[14]

The situation changed in the last two decades of the nineteenth century. In the humanities, the study of languages, literatures, and histories began to include all the variety of cultures. This opened up a new vista of cultural variation, the interpretation of which led to the rise of new, more theoretical subjects, like anthropology, sociology, political science, and theoretical linguistics.

There were similar developments in the natural sciences. With physics leading the way, specializations became increasingly numerous and theory more and more abstract. Here the problem was even more serious than in the humanities and the new social sciences. Not only did disciplinary research and specialization outgrow the needs of training for the professions but it also required increasingly complex instruments, large facilities, and bureaucratic organization to run those facilities which were expensive as well as alien to the academic environment and tradition. This means that concomitant to the increase of the cost of research there was a decline in its usefulness for the training of students—a serious problem from the point of view of the university.

Those concerned with the future of research—especially in the expensive natural sciences—saw the creation of research institutes as the only way to maintain further scientific growth. But research unconnected with teaching had to be justified in some socially meaningful terms. Initially, the new type of research institutes (founded in the 1880s), such as the Physikalisch-Technische Reichsanstalt (Berlin, 1887) or the Pasteur Institute in Paris (1888), engaged in research with obvious, or seemingly obvious, practical applications. The former served as the model for the American Bureau of Standards and similar institutions elsewhere, and the latter for institutions of hygiene founded in several countries.

But the same problem of insufficient connection between the contents and direction of research and the interest of the clients which emerged at the uni-

13. Friedrich Paulsen, *Geschichte des gelehrten Unterrichts auf den deutschen Schulen und Universitäten vom Ausgang des Mittelalters bis zur Gegenwart*, vol. 2 (Berlin and Leipzig: Walter de Gruyter, 1921), pp. 263–78.

14. Bernard Gustin, "The Emergence of the German Chemical Profession," Ph.D. dissertation, University of Chicago, Department of Sociology, 1975.

versities arose even faster in the applied research institutes. In physics, the discrepancy was obvious from the very beginning, and observers noted and complained about the fact that so much of the research done at the Reichsanstalt did not actually serve practical purposes.[15] In the institutes of hygiene the situation was better. There scientific discovery and practical usefulness went hand in hand. But this period did not last long, ten to twenty years at the utmost.

Because of the temporary nature of overlaps between the intrinsic developments in science and practical interests, the history of applied research institutes is replete with the decline of once glorious or promising institutions. There is no escaping the fact that the solution of practical problems does not usually stimulate or require intellectually significant research and that much intellectually significant research is not readily applicable to any practical purpose. Institutes of applied research have been beset by the dilemma of either disregarding their official mission and engaging in scientifically important work in a broadly defined field of potential applications, but without worrying about actual application,[16] or doing what was required by their clients at the cost of becoming intellectually sterile.

This disappointment with both the university and the applied research institute led to the establishment of basic research institutes. If research could not be harmonized either with teaching or practical applications, then—it seemed—the only thing to do was to set up institutions purely for the basic research. However, as has been pointed out, the basic research institutes turned out to be less of a success than expected. They spread slowly, and they did not replace the universities as the sites of most advanced research. The reason was that the universities—first in the United States and since the 1950s also elsewhere—were capable of reforming themselves in a way that had not been envisaged at the end of the nineteenth century in Germany.

The crucial development was the creation of the American graduate school beginning in the 1870s. In these, research could be effectively relinked to teaching, although not to the teaching of professional people in general but to that of professional research workers.

In Europe, this step was not taken until the 1950s and then too only hesitatingly, because in spite of every indication that research required systematic professional training, it was still assumed that training in advanced research techniques and other skills and habits needed for research was best acquired through personal apprenticeship and trial and error. The idea was that one learned to become a researcher, as one learned to become a writer, a painter, or a composer.

In contrast, in American graduate schools, the task of training researchers

15. Pfetsch, "Scientific Organization," p. 576.
16. This has been the policy of the British Research Councils.

was approached as a task comparable to the training of physicians or engineers, namely, putting the student through an organized program of practical training in which he could learn to exercise all the various skills needed for his work under supervised conditions. Since there were no research facilities in which students could be trained outside the university—like there were hospitals or firms suited to the training of medical or engineering students—the appropriate facilities had to be established in the university. Graduate faculties had to be large and composed of people representing all the major branches of a field so as to be able to provide complete well-rounded training. It had to be organized like a research institute designed also for training students, rather than as a teaching institute for undergraduates in which teachers and their assistants also engaged in research.[17]

After the event, it is not difficult to understand why the graduate schools proved more successful than pure research institutes. Pure research is the production of new knowledge for the satisfaction of intellectual curiosity. Such knowledge would have no social function, and would probably cease to be produced, without the existence of a public capable of developing such curiosity. In a democratic society, such a public can only be created and maintained if research is accompanied by teaching.[18]

Thus, the problem was not to find some kind of institution that could serve the needs of pure research, since pure research cannot survive very long without close links to teaching. The real problem was how to create a teaching framework that could utilize the new increasingly specialized advanced research. The solution to this problem was the graduate school, not the pure research institute.

Conclusion

This analysis has shown that thinking in terms of the organicistic metaphor of declining and dying institutions to be replaced by new ones led to serious misperceptions and misinterpretations. The institutional crises were interpreted as signs of decline and of the need for new institutions, and vital functions performed by the old institutions thus condemned to death were ignored.

Apart from this negative conclusion that is similarly illustrated by both cases, there are also some positive ones. These cannot be stated as simply as the negative conclusion, since the two cases are different in many ways.

At the end of the eighteenth century, there emerged a new function of science, namely, the possible use of sciences as school disciplines. This function

17. Joseph Ben-David, *Trends in American Higher Education* (Chicago: University of Chicago Press, 1974).
18. In the eighteenth century, science had a public without any connection between research and teaching due to the support of science by absolutist rulers and wealthy aristocrats.

had never been performed before—either by academies or by other institutions. At the end of the nineteenth century, there was no new function. Large-scale basic research was not qualitatively different from existing university research, but only required greater resources, and was difficult to fit into the guildlike structure of the university and to be integrated with the teaching of undergraduates.

The common feature of the two situations was that both indicated the need for institutional innovation or reform and that—as has been seen above—the successful way of dealing with the problem was university reform, a solution that did not seem obvious, or even feasible, for those who perceived the needs for the first time.

Their reaction was to leave existing structures intact and devise a new institution specifically designed to fill the gap left by the existing ones. In both cases, this was the path taken by the scientifically leading countries, namely, by France at the end of the eighteenth century and by Germany about a hundred years later. French scientists in the eighteenth century recommended that specialized schools, such as the Polytechnique or the École de santé, be set up for the teaching of science to potential users; and German scientists around 1900 recommended that specialized research institutes be set up to complement the universities that began faltering in their research efforts.

The other possibility, namely, to try to reform and use the existing universities for the performance of the new function, was not considered feasible, since universities were seen as unfit for the pursuit of experimental work or, at the later period, as unfit for large-scale highly specialized work.

This course of the reform of the university—rather than its replacement—was eventually adopted in Germany at the beginning, and in the United States at the end, of the nineteenth century as a result of difficulties in making the recommended changes and of compromises forced on the scientists.

The reason for this paradoxical outcome was that France, in the first period, and Germany, in the second one, were the leading countries in world science. Senior scientists in these countries were, by and large, satisfied with the support of science and justly so, because—in spite of the difficulties—they were still far better off than scientists in other countries. Therefore, it was reasonable for them to think in terms of filling in specific gaps. They did not realize that there was no such thing as filling gaps without altering the system. This was realized only much later.

Scientists in early-nineteenth-century Germany and late-nineteenth-century United States had much more limited resources and influence. Although they would have preferred to imitate the advanced French and German models, respectively, actually they had to find accommodation within an existing institution, namely, the university. This unwanted compromise turned into their advantage, since having succeeded to transform the universities according to their purposes, they acquired a base for the advancement of research and the training of research workers such as did not exist elsewhere.

The narrowly conceived teaching or research institutes created promptly in the scientific centers lacked the resources needed for advance. Pure teaching institutes did not intellectually rejuvenate themselves through research, and pure research institutes did not transplant and rejuvenate themselves through the constant flow of new trainees. Their viability depended on the institutions they came to complement originally. But because these parent institutions were not reformed, they could not maintain their own viability, not to mention the viability of their complementary institutions.

The pattern of private research often aided by governmental support (in a variety of ways) that was characteristic of early-nineteenth-century France could not keep up with the regular research work of German universities of the midcentury. And in this century, the increasingly problem-ridden chair system of German universities with its professorial research institutes (now being modified) fell behind the collectively organized system of American graduate schools. Thus, there was institutional rise and decline in certain countries, not due to quasi-biological causes but to specific constellations of interests and resources.

The Profession of Science and Its Powers 9

Today scientific research as an occupation is a "profession," like medicine, law, and engineering. There are considerable differences among these occupations, but certain common features justify their inclusion in a single category. These features are: (1) a higher educational qualification as a prerequisite to entry into the occupation; (2) the privilege of monopoly in the performance of certain functions (such as treating patients, signing blueprints for construction projects); (3) a measure of control of admission into the occupation, as a means of maintaining its standards and status; and (4) the formal or informal authority of a professional body over the conduct of its members, a resistance against lay interference in the affairs of the profession, and regulation of competition among members of the profession.[1]

While other occupations possess some of these features, they are considered as legitimate only among professions. Thus, for example, the regulation of competition among physicians is enforced by law; all kinds of rights in this respect are granted to local medical associations. The same actions, however, are considered illegitimate or actually criminal if performed by businessmen and are viewed as economically pernicious extortion if they are enforced by trade unions.

The final component of this distinctive constellation of features of the pro-

---

1. The most exhaustive and systematic description of the development of the professions and professionalism is still A. M. Carr-Saunders and P. A. Wilson, *The Professions* (Oxford: Clarendon Press, 1933). This book deals only with Great Britain, but the present conception of the professions and of the professional ethos developed mainly in that country and the United States. See also W. J. Reader, *Professional Men: The Rise of the Professional Classes in Nineteenth-Century England* (New York: Basic Books, Inc., 1966), and Wilbert E. Moore, *The Professions: Roles and Rules* (New York: Russell Sage Foundation, 1970).

fessional occupations is: (5) a limitation on the contractual obligations of the professional toward his client or employer. The patient cannot order a certain kind of treatment from his doctor; university teachers enjoy academic freedom to teach the way they want and to some extent what they want.

These features are not equally present in all the professional occupations. The educational qualification, the privilege of monopoly, and the discretionary freedom are probably present in all of them. Control of the right to practice and corporate self-regulation are also widespread. There are, however, large differences in the exercise of these functions among various professions within the same country and within the same profession in different countries.

The possession of these features is itself a corporate privilege. In other occupations this kind of privilege was abolished in most European countries between the seventeenth and nineteenth centuries. This is not to say that all occupational privileges were effectively abolished or that there are equal occupational opportunities for everyone in the regime which succeeded that of corporate privilege. Monopolies and cartels have been established by industrialists and merchants of the most diverse kinds; bureaucracies and trade unions have restricted the free market for labor. But none of these is a corporate privilege in the medieval sense, since, at least in principle, control over the exercise of the privilege is vested in bodies which are not part of the occupational group. Monopolies are granted and supervised by governments, bureaucracies are controlled by nonbureaucratic bodies, such as entrepreneurs and parliaments, and trade unions exercise their privileges through bargaining and strikes. Only in the professions is the right to control the exercise of the privilege vested in the profession itself. The question of why this special privilege was granted to the professions and not to other occupations has been asked before, but the explanations given were valid only with regard to the classical learned professions of medicine and law. Here I propose to deal with the occupational activity of scientific research as a profession.[2]

Corporate Organizations: Academies

Autonomous corporate scientific bodies became centers of scientific activity in the seventeenth century, at a time when science was practiced by unpaid amateurs and when this corporate autonomy had no economic importance. The original models were the Italian academies, but the most im-

2. Because of the great conspicuousness of academic scientists, and the sharp distinction between academic and nonacademic scientists in some countries (which is discussed in this paper), the profession of scientific research in general received little systematic attention. An outstanding exception is Edward Shils, "The Profession of Science," *The Advancement of Science* (June 1968): 469–79.

portant were the Royal Society of London and the Paris Academy of Sciences. They became important when the development of the practice of science into a coherent, acknowledged intellectual activity engendered formally established institutions for communication and competent assessment of scientific works; hitherto, informal correspondence between individuals and the conventional publication of treatises had sufficed. Another factor in the emergence of the corporate institutions of scientists was the need to legitimate the new type of activity within the existing social order; otherwise scientific activity might have been regarded as subversive of traditional, particularly religious, institutions.[3]

Subversion of traditional beliefs is an inherent potentiality of science, as it is of any activity the aim of which is original discovery or expression. The very emergence of modern science could be interpreted as a denial of the traditional view of the universe and thus it had far-reaching implications for religion. It was moreover a process the end of which could not be foreseen. The early "statesmen of science" saw that it would be necessary to protect scientific activity against attacks by the custodians of the traditional views of the cosmos and that corporate bodies enjoying the auspices of governmental authority were therefore in order.

The patrons and protectors of science believed that the dangers could be contained; they were confident that the scientific method was a means of distinguishing truth from error in a way which would not be destructive. Unlike the verbal arguments of speculative philosophers which culminated in unresolvable dissension and conflict, the rigorous logic of mathematical proofs and experimental tests led to results which sooner or later were bound to command universal assent. The granting of intellectual autonomy to science was, therefore, not considered as especially dangerous since the freedom of science to subvert tradition, it was believed, was not, if appropriately brought into the framework of institutions, inconsistent with the maintenance of social responsibility and order. In fact the scientific method was seen as the most effective way to establish such order, more powerful than any speculative philosophical tradition or theological doctrine. Therefore, science was granted the freedom of "cognitive subversion," because the scientific method was seen as a self-regulating mechanism, which, through its internal discipline, was capable of delimiting the spread of the subversion which it brought in its train and preventing the abuse of intellectual freedom.

The scientific method was not a divine revelation; it was a creation of man. Only if used by competent persons in an appropriate manner could the scientific method decide between the true and false. In the hands of the incompe-

3. The present view on the social conditions of the rise of modern science in the seventeenth century is elaborated in Joseph Ben-David, *The Scientist's Role in Society: A Comparative Study* (Englewood Cliffs, N.J.: Prentice-Hall, 1971), pp. 45–74.

tent, or the dishonest, the method was useless and even dangerous. If the administration of science lay in incompetent hands, mankind would be exposed to the dangers of "false prophecy" which subverts tradition for diabolical purposes or at least for ulterior motives. It was regarded as necessary, therefore, that some kind of social body be established for the competent assessment of scientific works, to define and maintain the boundary between valid scientific findings on the one side and error and nonscience on the other. Not the scientific method alone but its proper use by competent persons was regarded as a guarantee of an effective self-regulation.

Such a social mechanism was required not only for the protection of the lay public from quacks and intellectual counterfeiters but also for the protection and just reward of scientists. Since the public, even if it wanted and valued science in general, was usually uninterested in, and incapable of appreciating, particular contributions to its advancement, scientists would have been deprived of the appreciation and stimulus emanating from the like-minded and qualified. Hence the desire for a special body the judgments of which were scientifically competent and at the same time accepted and honored by the general public.[4]

These functions were performed by the academies, which, in order to perform them effectively, had to have some official standing. They also had to be completely autonomous; otherwise they could not truthfully represent the objective scientific view as established by the self-regulating methods of experiment and mathematical proof.

The Regulation of Subversion

The substantive frontiers of science have never been stable and cannot be established a priori. The scientific method has been only a procedure for criticism and testing, not for discovery. Discovery could not be as formally codified as the canons of criticism and the criteria of testing. Hence the degree of risk allowed in the search for the scientific understanding of fields not previously explored in a scientific manner has been a major problem in the institutionalization and organization of science. Some societies have been ready to assume a considerable risk in laying themselves open to the unforeseeable outcome of the efforts of discovery. Others have been much less so.

The first course was taken in England. Or, to be more precise, the increased appreciation of science in seventeenth-century England was part and

---

4. The analysis of the importance of an institutional framework in the proper assessment of scientific works is mainly the achievement of Robert K. Merton, "Priorities in Scientific Discovery," *American Sociological Review* 22 (December 1954): 635–59; see also Harriet Zuckerman and Robert K. Merton, "Patterns of Evaluation in Science: Institutionalisation, Structure and Functions of the Referee System," *Minerva* 9, 1 (January 1971): 66–100.

parcel of the process of change which, between 1640 and 1689, turned England from a traditional, religious society into a pluralistic, democratic one. Science served during this time as the symbol of modern, "advancing" knowledge, as contrasted with knowledge attested by the authority of tradition.[5]

Therefore, except for a brief period under the Restoration, the *institutional* demarcation of science from nonscience was not a major issue.[6] Strenuous efforts had been made by scientifically more or less competent intellectuals to use the scientific approach as a model for the solution of political, economic, moral, and technological problems. The fact that many of these attempts were quasi-scientific was not perceived as presenting a grave danger either to the integrity of science or to the order of society, perhaps because religious and political homogeneity had already been destroyed and a quite wide range of diversity had come to be tolerated. Hence, the extension of the scientific approach to these socially sensitive concerns did not arouse much apprehension. There had already been so much conflict that these "scientific" inquiries were accepted because they held out the possibility of softening and diminishing conflict. The self-regulatory mechanisms of science did not seem very far removed from the self-regulating market, the self-regulating polity of checks and balances, and the toleration of religious and political heterodoxy. Openness to criticism and innovation were characteristic of the latter, and the same sympathies were extended to scientific arrangements.[7]

In France, on the other hand, science was less in harmony with the prevailing trends of religious and political thought. It could be protected only if it were insulated, and this was accomplished by the establishment of an authoritative, governmentally sponsored academy charged with maintaining a strict boundary between science and nonscience. Discoveries were regarded as legitimate. They could be freely published when they occurred in the

5. The role of science in the transformation of the traditional religious culture of Europe into a modern one is treated in R. F. Jones, *Ancients and Moderns: A Study of the Rise of the Scientific Movement in Seventeenth-Century England* (St. Louis: Washington University Press, 2d ed., 1961), and Richard S. Westfall, *Science and Religion in Seventeenth-Century England* (New Haven: Yale University Press, 1958). For some important qualifications of Jones's views, see Allen G. Debus, *Science and Education in the Seventeenth Century* (London: MacDonald, and New York: Elsevier, 1970), pp. 1–64, and P. M. Rattansi, "The Social Interpretation of Science in the Seventeenth Century," in P. Mathias (ed.), *Science and Society, 1600–1900* (Cambridge: Cambridge University Press, 1972), pp. 1–32.

6. This is not to say that demarcation itself was not a problem. It was and has always been. But there is a difference between demarcation taking place as an ongoing debate and an officially established line of demarcation.

7. For the emergence of the idea of the self-regulation of the economic system and its relationship to the new scientific method, see William Letwin, *The Origins of Scientific Economies* (Garden City, N.Y.: Anchor Books, Doubleday & Co., 1965), pp. 187–92, 205–20. The systematic generalization of this idea to political self-regulation (*laissez-faire*) occurred later, but for this too the basis was laid in the seventeenth century in the tendency to view moral laws as laws of nature.

proper domain of science, but they were subject to censorship when they appeared to fall in the sphere of nonscience.

The Royal Society of London, in contrast, took upon itself the function of representing science to the public and of rewarding scientific discovery; it was less concerned with the function of the institutional demarcation of science from nonscience. The Royal Society was never granted the power to regulate the work of scientists or to determine, in an officially binding way, who was a scientist and who was not, what was science or was not. Its authority rested purely on the excellence of the accomplishment of its members and the freely granted acknowledgment of scientists all over Europe that judgments rendered by fellows of the Royal Society were scientifically valid.

The Paris Academy of Sciences had a considerable degree of actual control—as distinct from influence—over scientific publications and the granting of letters-patent to inventors. Membership in it was not merely a public recognition of excellence but also a source of income, power, and legally guaranteed privileges.[8]

So the Academy of Sciences came to be perceived as a political body charged with the regulation of science, rather than the representative body of the self-regulating scientific community. This regulating function—unlike the representative one—could not be effectively performed by a small elite over a long period of time. With the growth and diversification of scientific endeavor, however, the need to subject every discovery—and even every invention—to the authoritative decision of a small body of scientists became increasingly cumbersome, stifling, and inefficient. In consequence, the supremacy of the Paris Academy was short-lived, while the Royal Society has managed to maintain its standing for more than three centuries. The latter never claimed to be a body apart from and in control of the scientific community. It played an important role in the self-regulation of the scientific community, but it never claimed any sovereignty over the regulation. It had no coercive power to add strength to its regulation. The demarcation of science from nonscience, as well as the evaluation of excellence, was left to some degree to the scientific community in general.

Until the end of the eighteenth century the organizational needs of science were satisfied by corporate bodies—that is, the academies—of the scientific elite which were guided by the currents of opinion in the scientific community. The variations between the functions of these corporate bodies in differ-

8. For the similarities in, and the differences between, the structure and the functions of the Royal Society in London and the Paris Academy of Sciences, see Harcourt Brown, *Scientific Organizations in 17th-Century France (1620–1680)* (Baltimore: Williams and Wilkins, 1934); Dorothy Stimson, *Scientists and Amateurs* (London: Sigma Books, 1949); and Roger Hahn, *The Anatomy of a Scientific Institution: The Paris Academy of Sciences, 1666–1803* (Berkeley, Los Angeles, London: University of California Press, 1971). The comparisons made between the two institutions by the critics of the Paris Academy during the French Revolution are of particular interest. See Hahn, op. cit., pp. 181–82.

ent countries depended on the extent of general freedom of speech and dissent in religion, politics, etc. Where there was no such freedom, the demarcation of science from nonscience was a matter of great practical importance. It lent to science an invidiously attractive status and also protected its standards from being diluted by amateurish work. But with the growth in the numbers of scientists and of scientific works—partly as a result of the high status of science—the position of the academies became anomalous in the eyes of some scientists themselves. At that point, these powerful academies became a hindrance to the free growth of science. Their formal privileges became unjustifiable, anachronistic class privileges in the eyes of those scientists who did not possess them. But it was only the control of science by privileged central academies which was resisted. The existence of independent scientific societies continued to be regarded as a suitable framework for the self-regulation of the scientific community.

Charismatic Inspiration
Versus Institutionalization

Scientific research gradually became a salaried occupation in the course of the nineteenth century. There then arose problems of providing careers, organizing the work, and allocating the resources and rewards of scientific work. Once scientists began to be paid for their work, amateurs had little chance to compete. The mechanisms allocating payment became in practice the mechanisms by which science was demarcated from nonscience. This eliminated the ambiguity previously prevailing in the demarcation of scientific activity. The establishment of an institutionally defined boundary line between science and nonscience was a threat to the charismatic character of science.

Scientific achievement at the highest level was viewed as the work of genius. Genius was the result of inspiration or possession by the spirit which drives its carrier, the one possessed, to reach into and discern the center of existence. Like prophecy, great scientific discovery was perceived as being performed by extraordinary spirits, driven by a profound inner force. Priestly functions could be institutionalized, training for the priesthood could be institutionalized, but prophecy could not be, either in its preparation or its performance. A similar conception prevailed concerning great scientific discovery, and only great discovery counted.

This conception was an obstacle to institutionalization. When resources and rewards were preempted by scientists who made a career of scientific work, genius which lacked formal qualifications was handicapped. It was particularly difficult to establish a salary scale for the creative activity of genius. Who could decide how much to pay per month, or year, for work with unknown, and from the point of view of the employer, perhaps undesirable results?

These were some of the reasons why scientists, as well as their patrons and supporters, were extremely reluctant to see scientific research become a full-time occupation for which aspirants qualified through formal training and the acquisition of degrees and in which they then engaged continuously for the rest of their working life.

The first stage in the development of scientific research into a salaried profession occurred in France between the 1780s and the early decades of the nineteenth century.[9] It consisted of the establishment of a relatively large number of higher educational institutions for the training of physicians, engineers, and secondary school teachers and for the provision of advanced lectures for the general public. In the educational philosophy which prevailed in these institutions, the scientific subjects were accorded a prominent place. It was argued that a sound training in science was a necessary foundation of professional practice in engineering and medicine, as well as of a good education in general.

These institutions had to employ scientists as teachers, and thus teaching became the main source of livelihood for the majority of scientists. But this did not lead to the professionalization of research. The new educational institutions did not train their pupils to conduct research, and their teachers were not employed with the understanding that they themselves would do research. Scientists received salaries on the grounds of their scientific knowledge, but they were not paid to do research. Entry into a scientific role was still not institutionalized; becoming a scientist was still a kind of charismatic process. The aspirant scientist studied where and what he thought fit and worked as an apprentice in someone's laboratory. There was no formal termination of the period of training and no definite point of entry into a "scientific career." The

9. The growth of opportunities for the employment of scientists in France is described in Maurice Crosland, *The Society of Arceuil: A View of French Science at the Time of Napoleon I* (London: Heinemann, 1967), and in Maurice Crosland (ed.), *Science in France in the Revolutionary Era Described by Thomas Bugge* (Cambridge and London: MIT Press, 1969). Professor Crosland considers this increase in opportunities for employment as the beginning of professional science (see his Letter to the Editor, *Minerva* 8, 3 (July 1970): 453–54) on the ground that these opportunities made possible a greater continuity of research than had been the case previously. But this was only a first step toward professionalization. In fact, the social structure of the scientific career in France did not become professional until the second half of the nineteenth century. There was no place like Paris to learn science, and scientists could easily find appointments and income in Paris which could sustain them and enable them to do research incidentally. But there was no institutional arrangement for the training of scientists, nor were there any careers designed or provided for those who wished to concentrate on research continuously and exclusively. Paris was the world center of science, attracting aspiring scientists from everywhere in Europe, as it had been a center for art and literature. It was an important stage on the path toward science as a profession, but the actual emergence of professional science took place elsewhere. By the time professionalization occurred, Paris had ceased to be the center. See Joseph Ben-David, "The Rise and Decline of France as a Scientific Centre," *Minerva* 8, 2 (April 1970): 160–79.

scientists were those who were at a certain point "recognized" as being scientists.

The same conception of what was involved in being a scientist prevailed everywhere in the West, including Germany. But in the organization of higher educational institutions, there was an important difference between France and Germany. The German universities assumed the function of the "recognition" of the scientist; and they reserved their teaching positions for recognized scientists and scholars. While in France recognition had no rules and no definite site but occurred in a spontaneous and unspecified manner,[10] in Germany recognition was an official certification by the university. It took place in accordance with certain rules. Furthermore, while recognized scientists in both countries could obtain their livelihood as teachers in higher and secondary education (and, in France, in other capacities as well), in Germany a university professor was also, by definition, a recognized scientist. This was not the case in France. In Germany, professors were appointed on the basis of their scientific qualifications and accomplishments. To do research was at least as much a part of their official duties as teaching. Thus there arose in Germany a full-time occupational role, that of the university professor, whose professional duties explicitly included research. That was what he was paid to do. It was not something which he did in his spare time alongside teaching, providing medical services or acting as custodian of a museum or botanical garden.[11]

All this did not yet mean that research had come to be considered a regular occupation. There were still safeguards explicitly designed to preserve the charismatic quality of science. Lectures, seminars, examinations, and other prescribed tasks were not sufficient conditions of entry into academic positions, which were the only recognized and paid positions in research until the end of the nineteenth century. The would-be academic scientist still had to do his work on his own and submit it for a recognition only after its completion.

10. There was, of course, official recognition through prizes, and election to the Institut, but these rewards came much later than the informal recognition of the scientist by his peers and the instructed public.

11. The steeply hierarchical character of academic science and its demarcation from non-academic professional science are described in Friedrich Paulsen, *Die deutschen Universitäten und das Universitätsstudium* (Hildesheim: Georg Olm, 1966) (first published in 1902); Max Weber, "Science as a Profession," in H. H. Gerth and C. Wright Mills (eds.), *From Max Weber: Essays in Sociology* (London: Kegan Paul, Trubner & Co. Ltd., 1947), pp. 129–56 (first published in 1919); Alexander Busch, *Die Geschichte des Privatdozenten* (Stuttgart: F. Enke, 1959); Alexander Busch, "The Vicissitudes of the *Privatdozent:* Breakdown and Adaptation in the Recruitment of the German University Teacher," *Minerva* 1, 3 (Spring 1963): 319–41; A. Zloczower, *Career Opportunities and the Growth of Scientific Discovery in 19th-Century Germany* (Jerusalem: Hebrew University, Eliezer Kaplan School of Economics and Social Sciences, 1966 [now published by Arno Press, New York, 1981]); Eric Ashby, "The Future of the Nineteenth-Century Idea of a University," *Minerva* 6, 1 (Autumn 1967): 3–17; Joseph Ben-David, op. cit. (1971), pp. 108–38; and R. Stephen Turner, "The Growth of Professorial Research in Prussia, 1818–1848: Causes and Context," *Historical Studies in the Physical Sciences* 3 (1971): 132–82.

The acceptance of the *Habilitationsschrift* and the conferral of the *venia legendi*—the right to teach in a university—were acts of recognition given for original (and, therefore, unpredictable) accomplishment; they were not the recognition of the successful completion of a prescribed course of training for professional activity. The right to lecture at the university was a right of the recognized scientist. The recipient of the *venia legendi* became a *Privatdozent;* he received no salary, only the fees of the students who attended his lectures. Although he was expected to do research, no provision was made for it and he received no payment for doing it.

The *Privatdozenten* were to constitute a stratum of unsalaried, free-lance, albeit qualified scientists. Only a few of them could expect to be appointed as professors with regular salaries. And although professors were appointed on the basis of their research and were expected to do research as well as teach, *Privatdozenten* had to do their research privately. Just as they were free to decide how to teach and what to teach, so they could decide on what research to do and how to do it; they were not provided with laboratories in which to do it, although they were provided with teaching and seminar rooms.

The universities were, therefore, conceived as teaching academies and conferred upon their members the privileges of corporate freedom similar to those of the academies. The term "academic freedom" was coined for these universities to emphasize that these were not educational institutions in the ordinary sense but centers of research and of teaching based on original inquiry.

For a variety of reasons these arrangements did not work as intended, and research became a regular occupation, in spite of the intentions of preventing such a development. Those who decided to vie for recognition through the submission of a *Habilitationsschrift* did so in the hope of ultimately becoming university professors. And since there were numerous universities, it was not unreasonable for the *Privatdozent* to calculate his chances for appointment. These varied a great deal at different times and in different fields.

The possibility of a career in research, even if it was accessible only to a tiny fraction of the students, led to the provision of seminars and laboratory instruction where students were actually trained in research. In the laboratory sciences, where several students and assistants could work on experiments based on the ideas of a single person, there emerged by the end of the nineteenth century bureaucratically organized research institutes. As a result of this evolution the universities produced considerable numbers of more or less competent research workers capable of doing more or less original work, just as they produced physicians, lawyers, etc. In the course of time the *Habilitation* became increasingly a formal qualification for which one worked in a programmatic way. The title of *Privatdozent* had become a professional degree, like a second and higher doctorate, and ceased to be a testimonial of charismatic recognition. Scientific work, like other highly skilled work, became an occupation in which there was a wide range of talents and achievements. It ceased to be regarded as something which could be done only by charismatic geniuses. The assumption that scientific discovery was a charismatic action became openly self-contradictory. On the one side, it treated the research of the professional stratum as charismatic and therefore not subject to institutional organization while, at the same time, students were being trained to do research. The anomaly was not aggravated because the charismatic quality of scientific activity was disappearing; on the contrary, it had never been so evident. Never were more great discoveries made by great scientific personalities. There were no dissenters about the importance of the recognition of the great discoveries and discoverers in science, or about the inevitability of very unequal distributions of scientific genius. The anomaly which many intelligent observers began to sense consisted in the fact that not all the great discoverers were professors, while scientific influence and financial resources for research were monopolized by the professors, that is, the ordinary or full professors.

Although the anomaly was widely acknowledged, the remedy of abolishing excessive academic privilege seemed to be worse than the illness. Without some distinction, such as existed between professors and other research workers, there could not be a clear-cut institutional demarcation between true innovative science and routine research. The abolition of such demarcation was considered as threatening in nineteenth- and even twentieth-century Germany, as under the *ancien régime* in France. In addition to the status-consciousness of a hierarchical society, there was also genuine concern about the need to preserve the arrangements required by the charismatic character of scientific discovery, which might be threatened by the abolition of the line of demarcation between profoundly original contributions to science and the more routine achievements of institutionally trained professionals who were no more than competent.

The problems which had appeared in late eighteenth-century France thus reappeared in late nineteenth-century Germany. The academic freedom of the universities, originally designed as a safeguard of the freedom of all qualified scientists and students and a condition of the maintenance of the non-bureaucratic, charismatic character of science, became a source of bureaucratic power and invidious distinction. For *Privatdozenten* and assistants who saw themselves as persons on the lower rung of the ladder of the academic career and saw the powers of the *Ordinarien* as obstacles to their upward movement, the salaries, the research institutes, and the self-governing rights of the professors were constant reminders of their servitude and subordination. Even if they shared the view of scientific discovery as a product of charismatic inspiration, they could not but regard the existing distribution of facilities and rewards as handicaps to their own charismatic potentialities.

The Progress of Institutionalization: Training for Research

Misgivings about the professionalization of science were not confined to Germany. Nevertheless, certain features of research were professionalized in the United States and to some extent, in Great Britain as well. The Ph.D. course in the United States became a program for training persons for scientific careers.[12] The qualification entitled a person to full membership in specialized professional associations. The possession of a Ph.D. carried with it a set of expectations in the employment market. The employer of a Ph.D. took it for granted that such a person would conduct research and would have to be granted considerable autonomy in his work. It was also taken for granted that research, even if useful to the employer, could properly be evaluated only by other scientists and that the research worker would be interested in their recognition and not only in the income received from his employer.

The universities did not lose their special importance in the "recognition" of who was a scientist. The procedures of selecting incumbents for professorial chairs at the leading universities have carried the connotation of reward for exceptional achievement. The freedom of the academic teacher in his teaching and research, bolstered by permanent tenure, was the model for research workers who were engaged in scientific activity outside academic institutions. But still the difference between academic research and other kinds of research, and between the full professor and those at the lower grades, ceased to be an unbridged disjunction. There was no charismatic status automatically attached to a salaried position, whatever its rank. Some professorships were usually filled by persons of exceptional gifts, but a professorship in the United States became little more than the best-remunerated stage of a normal career.

In England the situation has been essentially similar.[13] There the Ph.D. has even now not attained the importance which it acquired in the United States, but there, too, there emerged a conception of professional qualification in science and of membership in a professional community. All scientific positions

12. For the development of the Ph.D. degree and some of the accompanying doubts, see Laurence R. Veysey, *The Emergence of the American University* (Chicago and London: University of Chicago Press, 1965), pp. 149–79, 313–14, 418–23. Professor Veysey thinks that the missionary zeal of the pioneers who established the Ph.D. program was partially in contradiction to the professional character of the doctoral training. But pioneers of other professions have shown similar missionary zeal, and this seems to be a characteristic of the founders of professions generally.

13. About the circumstances and the motives of the introduction of training in science in England, see D. S. L. Cardwell, *The Organization of Science in England in the Nineteenth Century* (London: Heinemann, 1957). Although it does not deal directly with this subject, an impression of the professional career and of the relatively unified professional character of English science can be gained from Eric Hutchinson, "Scientists as an Inferior Class: The Early Years of the DSIR," *Minerva* 8, 3 (July 1970): 396–411.

were open, in principle, to all qualified scientists (i.e., those possessing an honors degree), and no salaried positions were institutionally demarcated for the monopoly of scientifically charismatic individuals.

This acceptance of professionalism has not led to the abolition of the demarcation between science and nonscience. This was maintained by a system of scientific recognition and reward operating through such processes as the refereeing of publications, election to honorific bodies like the Royal Society, appointments to posts in the universities with the most eminent departments, and informal professional opinion. In the absence of the institutional abyss which separated the German professor from his inferiors and which was intended to protect genuine science from spurious science, the institutions in Great Britain, such as the various scientific associations, academies, societies, councils, and journals, which administered this system of allocation of appointments and honors on behalf of the scientific community and its various branches, assumed great importance. They performed the function of maintaining the conditions in which the charismatic element in scientific discovery could operate without obstruction at a time when research was becoming extensively institutionalized.

The "professional" character of scientific work was the result of the interaction between the processes and representative organizations of the scientific community and the conduct of research as a lifelong, remunerated, and graduated career. Leadership in each field was the outcome of scientific opinion. It was to a large extent concentrated at the leading universities; it set standards of training, qualification, and achievement for the profession. The scientific community regulated scientific work independently of the lay users of science and the lay employers of scientists; it did not, however, do so exclusively, since users and employers also exerted some influence. Still, the influence of the scientific community was extremely powerful. Unlike that of the users and employers, which varies from place to place and from time to time, the influence of the scientific community is consistent and persistent. Furthermore, users and employers exert their influence on the trained scientist, while the scientific community forms the scientist through his training and through continued pressure of its standards and expectations. These are determined by academic scientists who, enjoying "academic freedom," are subject only to the self-regulation of the scientific community.

Changes in the Loci
of Self-Government

This arrangement, which gave a larger place in the allocation of resources to the mechanisms of the market than had been characteristic of science before it became so pertinent to technology, was not adequate to the charismatic element in science, that is, to the need for original research. To the academic visitor from Europe, the American university of the first decade of this century was a bureaucratic teaching institution, with no safe provision for research.[14] But this opinion took no account of the likelihood that those market conditions would be increasingly influenced in favor of science by the spread of scientific professionalism. Initially, scientific research in the United States received little support, and that came mainly from private sources, that is, from the leading private universities which were eager to promote research and from individual philanthropists and private foundations which helped them to do so. A consequence of this private support for research was a gradual improvement of the standards, first, of the academic profession, and then of those professions which had an increasingly scientific basis. This rise in standards furthered the demand for original research, which in turn lent more power to professionalism; the reciprocal influences continued to the benefit of the quality of scientific work.

As a result, the professional autonomy of science in the United States has grown constantly. In the beginning its main results were the constant strengthening of academic freedom, in particular, and of professional autonomy, in general. University professors obtained more or less complete freedom to decide what and how to teach and investigate in their respective fields and less than complete, but still considerable, freedom to determine the time spent on research. Scientific associations, including medical, technological, etc., associations with large proportions of their members engaged in professional practice, followed suit by raising standards of training, increasing the emphasis on research in the course of training, and instituting sabbatical arrangements, refresher courses, etc., for keeping their members abreast of ongoing research. All this has had a considerable effect on the allocation of resources for research. As a result of increased demand, financial resources increased, although the actual allocation of funds took place through the market.

This structure considerably mitigated the invidiousness of the distinction between scientists of different ranks. The demarcation between original and routine research became less definite and more realistic than the sharply defined separation. It also demonstrated the rigidity and injustice of the identification of scientific charisma with the incumbents of certain positions.

The demarcation of the sphere of "true," that is, fundamental and original, science from that of doubtful, routine, or applied scientific work took various forms in various countries once science became a salaried occupation. The mode of demarcation was embodied in the organization of scientific work and the structure of the scientific career. The main alternatives were two: one, an

14. For an account of the American university as given by a very penetrating European observer, see Max Weber, op. cit., pp. 129–33.

official institutionalized demarcation between the two types of science by setting apart certain positions, such as the professorship, and certain rights, such as academic freedom, for the first type ("true science"), thus creating an institutionalized distinction between classes of scientists. The other alternative was to consider all professional (i.e., formally qualified) scientists as possessing the standing of citizens in the scientific community, leaving the separation of "true" from other science to the institutions of assessment in the scientific community and treating academic freedom as a variant of professional autonomy. Both these arrangements rested on the assumption that the scientific community was capable of and in need of effective self-regulation and that some kind of corporate autonomy was required as a framework for this self-regulation. They differed from each other in that in the former arrangement the universities were the corporate bodies, dominating the machinery of self-government of the scientific community, and in the latter case scientific societies and associations exercised a larger share of the power, in partnership with the universities. Both systems distinguished original research and fundamental discovery from other types of scientific work and rewarded them accordingly, but in the system in which the universities had an almost monopolistic voice, the distinction was much more radical and the hierarchical ranking much steeper. In the system in which the power was shared between universities and the scientific and professional societies, the hierarchy was not disjunctive and the strata were not mutually exclusive.

The self-regulation of the wider professional scientific community has important limits. With the exception of organized medicine, which has had a monopoly of a vital service in the United States since the 1920s, so that the medical community could virtually determine the raising of its standards, and thereby, the scale of financial support for medical research, other fields in the United States and Western Europe still depended much more directly on the "general public" and the market mechanisms for the financial support of their endeavors to raise their intellectual standards through increased research.

Changing Powers of the Self-Government of Science

This situation changed after the Second World War as a result of the more ample availability of governmental funds for research. Of course, the magnitude of these funds is ultimately determined by government. But in this decision, and even more in the decision of how to spend these funds, governments have relied on the representatives of the scientific community. Thus the scientific community assumed a new function. Previously it had allocated scientific recognition and thereby established the leaders of the different fields of science. Now it also took upon itself responsibilities for the direct allocation of funds for research and claimed the right to an important voice in the determination of the total sums spent on research. The question is to what extent the institutional arrangements and traditions of the scientific community have been capable of discharging these new functions satisfactorily.[15]

The justification for charging the scientific community with these functions of allocation has been that there are many problems of the allocation of funds with which only scientists can deal. Only they can determine what is and what is not a problem worthy of investigation, and only they can assess the results.

This argument is particularly relevant to the allocation of funds within a given field. But considerable differences exist between fields. Allocation by the scientific community itself has been most effective in experimental science, where it was originally conceived. There, the complete freedom of the individual investigator has usually been consistent with the tradition of responsibility to the criteria by which achievement is evaluated; there is much consensus about these criteria which are fairly unambiguous. Arbitrariness and eccentricity are thus controllable in this sphere. Experimental scientists are professionally the most rigorous of all the members of the intellectual community. There is, furthermore, in comparison with other intellectual endeavors, much consensus among experimental scientists concerning the goals of research. They agree more about what are the worthwhile and fruitful questions to investigate, and their work is usually much more closely articulated with that of their colleagues than in other fields. This consensus about important and fruitful problems is to a large extent the result of the constitutive constraints of experimental work.

The possibilities of such work are limited by available instruments and processes. Powerful new instruments such as the particle accelerator and the electronic microscope, and processes such as chromatography, offered new opportunities which could be exploited for work on a given range of problems. Every new invention of this kind will, therefore, attract many able scientists to work on the problems which these techniques render open to fruitful study. Experimental work is, furthermore, a laborious and expensive process where every experimenter is limited to a few problems. Without reliance on the work of others, no single worker in the field can get very far. This encourages cooperation and division of labor.

Hence, in these fields there will be no better mechanisms for the allocation

15. The changes which have occurred in the role and influence of the scientists since the Second World War have been described and analyzed in Robert Gilpin and Christopher Wright (eds.), *Scientists and National Policy Making* (New York and London: Columbia University Press, 1964); Don K. Price, *The Scientific Estate* (Cambridge: The Belknap Press of the Harvard University Press, 1965); Daniel S. Greenberg, *The Politics of American Science* (Harmondsworth, Middlesex: Penguin Books, 1969); and Harold Orlans (ed.), *Science Policy and the University* (Washington, D.C.: Brookings Institution, 1968).

of resources than the processes whereby the scientific community allocates recognition and prestige. It would be ineffective and wasteful to rely on the judgment of any body other than the scientific community.[16]

Internal Limits to the
Powers of Self-Government

Even in experimental fields, however, the working of the scientific community will be perfect only as long as there are worthwhile discoveries to evaluate, assimilate, and develop. However, there is no procedure or institutional arrangement to ensure that there will always be new discoveries, since, although there are methods for testing discoveries, there is none for making them. Scientific communities can arrive at a theoretical impasse which makes advance impossible. Or, at any rate, the state of a scientific field may be such that only modest advances can be made, and no amount of investment can accelerate progress. In such situations the sense of being part of an advancing front is lost and is replaced by behavior on a basis of individual trial and error. This cannot provide the basis of consensual judgments about priority in research. Hence, self-regulation will become less effective even within an experimental field.

In nonexperimental fields, the effectiveness of allocation by the mechanisms of self-government is more doubtful. Even in mathematics, where the criteria of validity and excellence are firmly established, there is the problem of deciding what is important. Even where this produces valid and theoretically important results, there is always a danger of a field of research falling apart into a large number of disconnected investigations. Not subject to the limitations of natural events and experimental tools which impose a commonly accepted range of worthwhile inquiries among empirical scientists, the community of mathematicians cannot ensure the coherence of its activities. The self-regulation of the scientific community can break down, not just as a

16. The view of the "scientific community" as a body which evolves its own policies emerged in the 1940s and the 1950s: see Michael Polanyi, *The Logic of Liberty* (London: Routledge and Kegan Paul, 1951), pp. 53–57, and Edward Shils, "Scientific Community: Thoughts After Hamburg," *Bulletin of the Atomic Scientists* 10 (May 1954): 151–55 (reprinted in Edward Shils, *The Intellectuals and the Powers: Selected Papers*, vol. 1 (Chicago and London: University of Chicago Press, 1972), pp. 204–12). The sociology of this community has been explored by Gerald Holton, "Scientific Research and Scholarship," *Daedalus* 91 (Spring 1962): 362–99; Thomas S. Kuhn, *The Structure of Scientific Revolutions* (Chicago: University of Chicago Press, 1962); Derek J. de Solla Price, *Little Science, Big Science* (New York: Columbia University Press, 1963); Warren H. Hagstrom, *The Scientific Community* (New York: Basic Books, Inc., 1965); Norman Storer, *The Social System of Science* (New York: Holt, Rinehart and Winston, 1966); and Diana Crane, *Invisible Colleges: Diffusion of Knowledge in Scientific Communities* (Chicago and London: University of Chicago Press, 1972).

result of the exhaustion of ideas but as a result of the absence of criteria for the comparison of achievements.

In principle there is no solution to these problems. The self-regulating mechanism of science cannot ensure the continued production of new ideas, nor, in the absence of such criteria of relevance which exist only in the empirical sciences, can it establish a consensus about goals which are worthy of exploration. It is true that so far there has always been a way out. Mathematics has from time to time been revitalized by turning to "applied" problems (that is, to the solution of theoretical problems arising out of empirical science). Moreover, the exhaustion of theory has never occurred in all the fields of science at one and the same time. The blocking of the advance of science in one field has not prevented it from advancing at the same time in other fields and from eventually removing the obstacles by outflanking them.

This, however, does not mean that self-regulation is adequate to resolve all the possible difficulties of the scientific community. First of all, there is no assurance that what occurred in the past will also happen in the future. Underlying the progress of science has been the belief in the inexhaustibility of nature and in the unending amplitude of the stock of interesting problems. If the assumption of inexhaustible possibilities is true (which, of course, no one can know), the belief in the value of the unending search, or the determination to pursue it, might become attenuated. It is not known what may cause them to come to an end. Their persistence appears to depend on the continuing occurrence of conspicuous discoveries which prove the continued charismatic power of the scientific enterprise; it depends too on a belief that the discoveries of science are useful and meaningful to the nonscientist as well as to the scientist. Both conditions might be endangered by exclusive reliance on self-regulation by the professional scientific communities. The possibility that such a community might encourage the continuation of routine research beyond the exhaustion of ideas and/or talent could shake the belief in the charismatic powers of science. The tendency of the scientific community to overreach itself is inherent in the tendency to force professional standards higher and higher. The unbridled extension of the professional autonomy of scientists, without regard to the social uses of the results, might well lead to a surfeit of scientific information of doubtful importance and a resultant loss of sense of relevance.

Another limitation on the power of the self-regulation of the professional scientific community is to be seen in its difficulties in making rational decisions about the shift of resources from one field to another. The outflanking of the obstacles which made possible the continued growth of science was the result of spontaneous shifts of interests among scientists. When scientific research was inexpensive and was done more or less singlehandedly, the shifts could occur by trial and error and by the selection of the more successful trials by alert young scientists and later by alert academic administrators. These solvent responses to the pioneers' way out of the impasse in the center of the scientific community occur at its periphery. Young scientists who have not yet "arrived," students, and administrators are all at the periphery of the self-governing community of science.

Nowadays research usually requires large funds, and the administration of research funds is either in the hands of or is greatly influenced by the representatives of the various scientific communities. The shifting of funds is difficult to accomplish when it comes to transfers from well-established to less well-established fields which are not represented in the honorific and decision-making bodies of science. Certainly the assessments made within the different sectors of the scientific community are not what is needed, since effective communication and valid assessment exist only within given fields. There is nothing comparable over a wide range of different specialized fields. A biologist is a poor judge of achievements in physics and vice versa. It is, therefore, meaningless to say that the allocation of funds for different fields should take place according to the relative importance attached to them by the scientific community, because there is no body of knowledge and opinion within the wider scientific community for making comparisons between fields. And the more professionalized the different scientific communities are, the more difficult it is to arrive at decisions entailing comparisons of separate fields of research.[17]

Most scientific work is supported because of the expectation of social benefits, such as improved health, higher productivity, etc. Research related to health, agriculture, and manufacturing industry is much more heavily supported than research which has no such apparent relationship to social welfare, economic progress, or military effectiveness.

The rationale of support for this type of research is not unambiguously established because thus far it has been impossible to measure whether the returns to the investor from applied research have been as great as some alternative uses of his capital. Nevertheless the support continues, because the plausibility of the belief that on a global scale and in the long run mankind has derived material and not only cognitive or cultural benefits from research. Because of the indeterminateness of the relationship between investment in research and the return from the investment, attempts to fix the magnitude of expenditures on research, on the bases of recommendations by the scientific

17. The problems of establishing criteria and mechanisms for the allocation of funds for research have been dealt with in Don K. Price, op. cit.; The National Academy of Sciences, *Basic Research and National Goals: A Report to the Committee on Science and Astronautics, U.S. House of Representatives* (Washington, D.C.: U.S. Government Printing Office, 1965); Alvin M. Weinberg, *Reflections on Big Science* (Cambridge and London: MIT Press, 1967); Edward Shils, op. cit. (1968); and Harry G. Johnson, "Some Economic Aspects of Science," *Minerva* 10, 1 (January 1972): 10–18. See also Edward Shils (ed.), *Criteria for Scientific Development: Public Policy and National Goals* (Cambridge and London: MIT Press, 1968), especially the essays by Alvin M. Weinberg, Stephen Toulmin, and Simon Rottenberg.

community, to the effect that all qualified research workers or all promising research projects should be supported, can only discredit the belief in the usefulness of science. In the most fortunate outcome, such recommendations culminate in potentially useful discoveries. But this is not enough. A potentially useful discovery, to become actually useful, must meet such requirements as practical exploitability and a high position in the prevailing scale of social priorities. Neither of these can be established by the self-regulating mechanisms of the scientific community.

Successes and Failures
of Self-Regulation

I can now undertake to answer the question I asked at the beginning of this paper—the question why scientists have been accorded the privilege of corporate autonomy. The original purpose of this autonomy was not to confer economic privilege, since in the seventeenth and eighteenth centuries scientific activity was not a paid occupation. Nor was it an attempt to gain corporate powers for scientists to make legally binding decisions in their field of intellectual interests, since scientists believed, with considerable justification, that the validity of scientific finding could be established without recourse to any other than intellectual authority. The scientific community saw itself as a self-regulating group which could combine intellectual freedom with responsibility, discipline, and consensus.

Corporate privileges were required to safeguard science from political and religious interference, and some corporate organization was needed to represent science to lay society and to serve as a framework for the communication, assessment, and rewarding of scientific achievement. Corporate privileges could of course be abused for selfish purposes. This happened in societies where corporate privilege created an institutional boundary separating the scientific elite from the rank-and-file scientists.

Present-day scientific professionalism has eliminated many of the invidious aspects of institutional distinction between the elite and the rank and file of science and probably enhanced the effectiveness of the processes of communication and assessment in the scientific community as a whole. This professionalized system of science has furnished a suitable set of institutions for scientific self-regulation. The evidence for this is that its incorporation into itself of a considerable measure of equality and democracy did not prevent, but rather encouraged, the exercise of the charismatic powers of scientific creativity and the vesting of leadership of the scientific community in the hands of those possessing these charismatic powers.

Scientific professionalism has also been an effective means of securing funds for research. But with the rise of governmental support of science on a large scale, scientific professionalism has perhaps become too successful for its continued health. The success of the claim of the profession for autonomy in the distribution of the funds for research and for influence in decisions regarding the total amount has placed in the hands of the profession powers such as it never possessed before. Instead of depending on the appreciation and goodwill of university presidents, students, philanthropic industrialists, and other potential beneficiaries of science, the power has passed to the representatives of the scientific community. They now possess great power in the allocation of very large sums for research to universities, in influencing the assignment of research contracts to industrial enterprises, and in offering stipends and employment to graduate students and other scientists.

By and large, this power has probably been exercised wisely. In many phases of the allocation of funds (especially in the distribution of funds within intellectually thriving fields), the self-regulating activities of the scientific community have resulted in effective guidance. In dealing, however, with stagnating fields, or with the task of shifting resources from one field to another, this guidance has proved much less effective. Had the scientific community possessed fewer powers of decision over its own affairs, it might perhaps have fared better when the slowdown of investment in science occurred.

It is clear that the self-regulating arrangements of the scientific community cannot offer guidance for decisions regarding the total outlay of funds for science. Even if there were perfect public knowledge about the inherent potentialities of each scientific field for the discovery of new and useful knowledge under the conditions prevailing in a society at a given time, so that there were no risk of waste in any investment, this would still not be enough. The final decision could only be taken on the basis of a judgment of the value of new knowledge and of the different applications of scientific knowledge as compared to other alternative social ends. Such a decision far exceeds the jurisdiction and competence of the self-regulatory mechanisms of the scientific community. The attempt of the scientific community to monopolize social decisions about science might, therefore, in the end be as self-defeating as the attempts of the priesthoods of great religions to control the course of religious sensibility and religious beliefs.

The professional ethos of science has generated an aspiration to control all the conditions thought necessary for the continued growth of science; latterly it has been compelled to yield to a more differentiated attitude which distinguishes between various sets of such conditions. Complete, or almost complete, professional autonomy has now been restricted to the allocation of funds for different projects within particular fields of basic research and to the ways of spending the research funds. In other decisions the representatives of the scientific community can only act as expert consultants, as spokesmen for science as a value, and as a legitimate professional interest.

Thus, in the determination of the total expenditures on basic research by

governmental or other agencies, the function which only scientists can perform is the estimation of the upper limits of the funds which can be expended
on research without undue risk of waste (in view of the state of the art and the
availability of scientific manpower) and the lowest limit needed to maintain a
given scientific capacity. Beyond this scientists can only plead and contend for
maximal expenditure between these two points.

The scientific community should not try to act as the allocator of funds
between different fields. As has been shown by Dr. Alvin Weinberg,[18] purely
scientific considerations do not offer all the criteria needed for a rational
choice between alternative fields. Since, moreover, active scientists are committed to specific fields, they are unlikely to possess a detached view of the
whole field of science and the objectivity needed for such a choice. Historical
precedents indicate that university presidents, other academic administrators,
and the professional aspirations of students have played a very important role
in this respect. Control of the allocation of funds between fields by central
consultative bodies representing the community of scientists engaged in research might well deprive university administrators and, to some extent also,
students of influence in scientific choice.[19]

Finally, the scientific community has to beware of the tendency to lay down
directions for mission-oriented science. Of course, the propagation of the
view that science can be of sevice in the solution of practical problems has
always been an important part of the rhetoric of scientists. In a general way,
the argument is true and reasonable. It is also legitimate for scientists to suggest possible applications of scientific discoveries.

The role which the scientific community can play in the application of science is quite different from its role in basic science.[20] In the latter, the scientific community has all the competence (and *only* the scientific community has
the competence) to assess the results of research. Furthermore, within a given
field (especially in advancing fields), the leading members of any particular
scientific community are most likely to be in a better position than anyone else
to make informed estimates about the scientific potentialities of persons and
projects.

When, however, it comes to the application of science, the scientific community is not more capable than others of judging the practical results of the
research properly or guessing the practical potentialities of initiators and
projects. It is occasionally less capable of doing so. A Watt, an Edison, or

    18. Alvin M. Weinberg, op. cit., pp. 65–84.
    19. For the role of academic administrators and students, especially in competitive academic
systems where there is variety and choice, see R. Stephen Turner, op. cit., A. Zloczower, op.
cit., and Joseph Ben-David, *American Higher Education: Directions Old and New* (New York:
McGraw-Hill, 1971), pp. 25–47, 87–109.
    20. I deliberately avoid using the term "applied research" because its definition is
ambiguous.

even a Siemens probably would not have passed the scrutiny of a representative scientific body. And even a Pasteur, who might personally have passed the scrutiny, would probably not have succeeded in getting his projects accepted.

Of course, there are also contrary examples, such as the manufacture of the atomic bomb, computers, electronics, and some fields of chemistry, where scientists were the ones who foresaw some of the practical results. But even in these fields scientific imagination and knowledge were not enough. Only in combination with technological inventiveness, organizational talent, economic enterprise, and financial competence did the results attain practical value.

In view of all this it may be concluded that scientists and the scientific community can only participate in the still inadequately understood processes of using scientific research for the solution of practical problems. Claims for the exclusiveness of their expertise, for an exclusively professional control over the allocation of funds and the execution of projects with such ends in view might bring short-run benefits for science. They are unlikely to serve the long-range objective of making research an increasingly more useful tool for man.

A Comparative Study of 10
Academic Freedom
and Student Politics*

Difficulties concerning academic freedom are usually considered as interference in the teaching and research functions of a university, to be resolved by recourse to formal authority or brute force.[1] The most blatant of such interferences occur in the purges of universities that follow the ascent to power of autocratic regimes. But this is only a single aspect of a broad attack on freedom of all kinds and rarely a specifically academic issue. Why certain regimes are opposed to freedom may be a sociological question, but it will not teach us anything about the sociology of universities or intellectual life in general.

We propose, therefore, to treat academic freedom as a set of institutional arrangements designed to facilitate teaching and research on the most advanced level. It is the same kind of thing as the freedom or autonomy of doctors, lawyers, or other professionals; it is one of the necessary conditions of the efficient and effective performance of a job which requires specialized knowledge, ability, intellectual integrity, and, preferably, creativity.

This, of course, is not the only approach to academic freedom, nor even the most important one. Like all freedom, that of academic teachers, researchers, and students is first of all a moral question. That aspect, however, requires a discussion of basic principles and ultimate goals. Here, we shall

*With Randall Collins.
We are indebted for comments on the first draft of the manuscript to Professors Reinhard Bendix, S. M. Lipset, Talcott Parsons, Gerald Platt, and Norman Storer. The research was supported by the Comparative Student Project of the Institute of International Studies of the University of California, Berkeley.
    1. On academic freedom, cf. R. Hofstadter and W. Metzger, *The Development of Academic Freedom in the United States* (New York: Columbia University Press, 1955); Robert MacIver, *Academic Freedom in Our Time* (New York: Columbia University Press, 1955); *Law and Contemporary Problems*, Special Issue: *Academic Freedom* 28 (Summer 1963).

restrict ourselves to the discussion of means-ends relationships: given the goals of teaching and research, what are the means of attaining them, and what are the conditions facilitating or impeding their attainment. Besides, defining academic freedom as one kind of professional freedom makes it possible to include under the heading not only authoritarian interference from the outside but also abuses and misuses of the arrangements by the academic community itself.

It makes little difference whether academic freedom is violated by a ruler refusing to appoint persons to university positions who belong to the political opposition or whether self-governing academic cliques refuse to appoint people whose scholarly views they do not like. In fact, the latter may be more harmful to intellectual advance, since it is more likely to be aimed at the suppression of specific intellectual arguments, or even truths, than the former. Finally, this perspective makes it possible to compare specific arrangements of academic freedom both as the result of different conditions and as causes of distinct consequences.

Let us first define the institutional arrangements of professional freedom in general:

1) Monopoly rights over the performance of certain functions, namely, teaching and granting recognized university degrees (as treating patients is a monopoly of doctors or pleading before the courts is a monopoly of lawyers).

2) Maintenance of its standards of talent, erudition, and as a result, of its status, by control of admission into the profession.

3) Authority of the professional community (organized for the purpose) over the ethical conduct of its members, thus avoiding lay interference by convincing the public that the profession itself protects the public interest; and the regulation of competition among members so as to maintain their economic security and not to compromise their professional judgment under the pressure of material circumstances.

4) Strict limitation of the contractual obligation of the professional toward his client or employer, to the performance of only those services which are approved by the profession, and to their performance in a manner approved by it. A doctor cannot be charged with malpractice for not doing what the patient asks him to do, as long as what he does is in accordance with the standards of practice. Similarly, an academic can choose to teach, study, or write whatever he thinks is relevant to his subject matter and to do it in whatever manner he wants, as long as he remains within the accepted framework of the standards of his specialty.[2]

2. For definitions of professionalism in general (not only of professional freedom), cf. A. M. Carr-Saunders and P. A. Wilson, *The Professions* (Oxford: Clarendon Press, 1933), Bernard Barber, "Some Problems in the Sociology of Professions," *Daedalus* (Fall 1963): 669–88. Joseph Ben-David, "Professions in the Class System of Present-Day Societies," *Current Sociology* 12

Table 1. Professions by Presence or Absence of Principal Characteristics of Professional Freedom

	Characteristics of Freedom			
Professions	*1*	*2*	*3*	*4*
Academics	+	+	+	+
Doctors and Lawyers	+	+ −	+	+
Engineers	+ −	+ −	−	−

If professions were to be ordered on a scale according to how fully they realize these conditions, academics would come out on the top (table 1). They are the only profession which, at least in principle, possesses all the characteristics of professional freedom. All the rest, including doctors and lawyers, have to share the control of admission into their profession with the academics, or sometimes surrender it to them entirely.

Infringements of academic freedom by outside interference can be seen as violations of various of these professional norms. Interference with the content of teaching infringes on the monopoly rights of academics over the teaching function; political criteria for appointment or promotion violate the profession's control over admissions to its own ranks and its disciplinary authority over the ethical conduct of its own members; attempts to ban or dictate research or publication violate the autonomy of the profession's limited contractual obligation to those who employ it.

On the other side, there is a completely parallel set of abuses, or failures of the members of the academic profession themselves to live up to these norms. The monopoly rights over teaching and the control of admission into the academic profession may be used not to keep up standards but to keep out competition or new ideas; disciplinary authority may be used not to uphold legitimate professional standards but to enforce extraneous political, class, or racial criteria; contractual autonomy (and such safeguards as tenure) may be used not merely to do what work one is interested in but to do slipshod work, political propaganda, or nothing at all.

The norms, then, can be violated on both sides, from within and without the profession. Academic freedom depends, therefore, on the balance between factors within the academic community and those outside of it. As will be seen, abuses on one side tend to lead to abuses on the other, with a resulting decline in the force of the norms themselves.

(1963/64): chap. 1; Harold L. Wilensky, "The Professionalization of Everyone?" *American Journal of Sociology* 70 (September 1964): 137–58.

In the following pages we shall first describe and trace back to their origins the main types of conflict which usually accompany the realization of these norms. Later, we shall examine national differences in the conflicts about academic freedom and their solutions and relate them to the different uses made of the university in different types of societies.

Conflicts Concerning Academic Freedom

Academic freedom became a controversial issue as soon as there emerged a full-time academic profession attached to independent university corporations during the Middle Ages. The most usual type of conflict was the clash between "town" and "gown." The gathering of several thousand young men in cities with a fighting population of perhaps an equal size gave rise to a great many disputes and often to violence. To increase their mutual protection and power, the scholars sought to incorporate themselves as a *universitas* (at the time, a term applied to any guild), basing their claims for corporate privileges and exemption from the public jurisdiction on both the general rights of corporations and on the traditional rights of the individual scholar in Roman and Canon law.[3]

Furthermore, the universities became politically very important, also due to their size and privileges. The University of Paris played a decisive role in the conciliatory movement that ended the Great Schism, and the universities were a natural center for the different religious movements preceding and during the Reformation.[4] In them were concentrated the experts, as well as much of the intelligent and active public concerned with these religiopolitical issues.

This concern, on the one hand, had led to the decline of their intellectual importance, since those interested in true scholarship and science could not find the necessary tolerance among colleagues engaged in bitter doctrinal fights; while on the other hand, it provoked political interference with their liberties.[5] These two things mutually reinforced each other: the moving of the intellectual elite from the universities reduced the legitimacy of their claim for rights, while political interference induced more scholars to seek other places

3. Pearl Kibre, *Scholarly Privileges in the Middle Ages* (Cambridge: Medieval Academy of America, 1962), pp. 20–21; Hastings Rashdall, *The Universities of Europe in the Middle Ages*, ed. by F. M. Powicke and A. B. Emden (Oxford: Clarendon Press, 1936), vol. 1, p. 164.

4. Rashdall, op. cit., vol. 1, pp. 540–84; Friedrich Paulsen, *The German Universities: Their Character and Historical Development* (New York: Macmillan, 1895).

5. Rashdall, op. cit., vol. 1, pp. 541–43, 580; Mark H. Curtis, *Oxford and Cambridge in Transition, 1558–1642* (Oxford: Clarendon Press, 1959), pp. 278–80; G. F. Kneller, *Higher Learning in Britain* (London: Cambridge University Press, 1955), p. 18; Paulsen, op. cit., p. 545.

of work for themselves. As a result, starting from the fifteenth century and lasting until the nineteenth, the stature as well as the freedom of the universities was greatly reduced.

This change, however, does not imply the elimination of either the academic role or of academic freedom. What occurred was simply that the universities, or to be more precise, their arts faculties, came to be regarded increasingly as secondary schools are today. Creative intellectuals were not usually expected to work there. Instead they were accorded greater freedom and new privileges in the academies founded all over Europe.[6] Besides, some faculties of arts, and all the advanced faculties of law, medicine, and theology, had maintained their autonomy and status. Thus even in these ages which are usually considered the *nadir* of academic freedom—roughly between 1400 and 1800—the continuity of the autonomy of the academic role and community had not ceased (and was in fact extended to new fields of learning); its seat was merely transferred from one institution to another, and distinctions were made—not so dissimilar to those existing today—between teachers of undergraduates and those of graduates. To some extent, therefore, it was merely a change in the definition of the groups to which the freedom was extended and not a change in the principle of the freedom itself.[7]

This development had been connected with the emergence of a problem concerning the limits on the contents of academic freedom. This may seem a more basic matter involving not only the freedom of the profession but the philosophical principle of freedom itself. In fact it can—and has—been argued that the ancient and medieval autonomy of the learned was not academic freedom in the modern sense, since the scholar was free to teach and write only within the framework of an accepted doctrine and was always liable to charges of heresy and subversion. Even if he had felt subjectively free, having been in agreement with the basic tenets of the existing religious and social order, he was not objectively so, since he could not go beyond those limits.[8]

This view is true, yet the usefulness of identifying academic freedom with freedom in general is questionable. There is a whole world of difference between the medieval and the modern conceptions of freedom of thought, speech, and political activity. But academic freedom is a much more limited affair than the freedom of the ordinary citizen in a liberal country. It is conferred on only a few, at the end of a prolonged period of instruction and—whether one likes the word or not—indoctrination, on the basis of extensive and intensive evidence that the person is fit and properly prepared for the academic role in the judgment of the established authorities in his chosen field. In

6. M. Ornstein, *The Role of Scientific Societies in the Seventeenth Century* (Chicago: University of Chicago Press, 1938), pp. 73–197, 257–63.
7. This statement refers only to the freedom of the full-fledged academics. The change had affected the freedom of students for whom there were no alternative institutions.
8. Hofstadter and Metzger, op. cit., p. 16.

fact, even his choice of a field is limited by whatever the established authorities consider as worth choosing from, and the difficulties of getting new fields recognized are well known. Once admitted to the professional fraternity, he still has to play the game according to the accepted rules (which may well be stupid and restrictive), and innovations of a revolutionary kind may embroil him with his fraternity, even if they are scientific by accepted standards. Objective academic freedom is therefore a myth, since there are always some people who authoritatively define what its limits are. The stupidity of Aristotelian professors of philosophy opposing Galileo's discovery has been matched by the stupidity of modern natural scientists in the mid-nineteenth century who opposed Semmelweis and Pasteur and was of precisely the same kind.[9] They were also similar in their staunch adherence to "academic freedom."

It can still be observed that this is a different kind of problem than opposition to some teaching on the basis of extraneous religious or political criteria. The disputes between the Aristotelians and the new philosophers of the seventeenth century, or those concerning the bacterial causation of illness, one may say, were controversies; while the interdiction of the Church on the teaching of Galileo was a suppression of intellectual freedom, since instead of arguments, force was used. This is true and is precisely the reason why the action of the Catholic church was considered scandalous at that time even by many a good Catholic.[10] But the problem involved was not the enunciation of a new principle of academic freedom but rather the extension of this freedom to new fields—physics and astronomy—which had not been regarded previously as separate fields justifying the recognition of the autonomy of those specializing in them. The difficulty in making distinctions between external and internal criteria becomes clear concerning an earlier controversy, that about Averroism, and other philosophical doctrines. The interference of Bishop Tempier in this controversy in 1277 condemning the view that matter is eternal (and denying thereby creation from nothing by God), the belief in the unity of the "active intellect" which casts a doubt on the survival of the individual soul, and astrological determinism leading to a negation of free will was regarded by the academic community as a violation of its freedom. Yet by the criteria of our present-day knowledge, Tempier was in many ways right, and even by the criteria of his own times, he was perhaps not more bound doctrinally than the masters of the university.[11] Thus, while his attempt to use his authority was an

9. J. Ben-David, "Roles and Innovations in Medicine," *American Journal of Sociology* 65 (May 1960): 557–68. [This volume, chap. 1.]
10. Giorgio di Santillana, *The Crime of Galileo* (Chicago: University of Chicago Press, 1963), pp. 344–47.
11. Pierre Duhem, *Le système du monde*, Tome VI (Paris: Hermann, 1954), pp. 20–29; Jacques Le Goff, *Les intellectuels au moyen âge* (Paris: Seuil, 1957), pp. 123–27; Guy Beaujouan, "Motives and Opportunities for Science in the Medieval Universities," in A. C. Crombie (ed.), *Scientific Change* (London: Heinemann, 1963), pp. 224–31.

interference with academic freedom—and was so regarded by the academics—his invocation of the authority of the Bible against Aristotle and other philosophers cannot be considered as a recourse to external criteria. The Bible and religious doctrine were considered scientifically relevant truths and admissible evidence at that time. It should not be forgotten that even today there are very different standards of admissible evidence in different fields.

Thus, instead of defining the difference between academic freedom in the Middle Ages and the present day as a difference in the idea of freedom, asserting that the Middle Ages had a bound and the modern times an unbound view of that freedom, we suggest that academic, like all professional freedom, is linked to certain topics and methods but that the range of topics and methods in which this professional freedom is applicable has been gradually extended. The advantage of this approach—which is, in a way, a choice between two alternative languages—is that it makes possible a wider range of comparisons and, more important, enables us to include in the discussion of academic freedom the question of how the fields where this freedom applies are defined. As will be seen, this is a crucial question. There is a whole series of conflicts about academic freedom which are closely related to certain fields. The absence of such conflicts in some academic systems may, therefore, simply be a result of their exclusion from the academic world, a worse curtailment of professional freedom than any attempts at influence.

The origins of still another kind of problem concerning academic freedom are even more recent, being the result of the combination of large-scale research with large-scale teaching. Most types of creative intellectuals today work in universities maintained by public or private philanthropic funds primarily for the purpose of teaching and training. The autonomy of the academic person has to be accommodated, therefore, with the needs of the students as well as the purposes of the supporters. In a free society in which all these groups are permitted to fight for their own interests, as they conceive them, there is a great likelihood of conflicts. Many of these would simply not exist if teachers and students made their own arrangements, if research were a matter of private enterprise, and some would be avoided if research were, as a rule, separated from teaching. This is not to say that these alternatives would be preferable to the present state of affairs, only that as things are today, the maintenance of academic freedom presents a complex problem of the relationships between groups and categories of people and difficult matters of organization.

These, then, are the principal issues, inherent in the relationship of the university and society, which give rise to conflicts about academic freedom: the potential involvement of the university in political conflict as a participant or interest group; the definition of the group to which academic freedom should be extended and the determination of the limits of the professional competence of the university within which academic freedom should prevail; and, finally, the division of authority and powers between donors, administrators, faculty, and students. We shall now examine international differences in the development and solution of these conflicts.

Academic Freedom in the Principal Types of Modern University

The political problem presented by the size, physical strength, and wealth of the university corporation to the medieval city had—as it has been shown—disappeared in the fifteenth century with the emergence of centralized states. Within these the universities had become a politically negligible quantity. They had become purely educational institutions, where young people, dependent on their parents and politically inactive, had spent three or four years preparing for a career. Starting from the nineteenth century this situation changed again. Universities in some countries became concentrations of politically conscious intellectuals playing very important roles as ideologists and organizers of political movements. Unlike in the Middle Ages, however, the university as an organization did not play a role in the struggle for power on its own behalf; only its students and/or its teachers joined as individuals, or organized groups, broadly based social movements and political parties.[12] Lately with the tremendous growth in size of university enrollments, and the rising age of full-time students for many of whom the university and its attached institutions provide a long-term—if not lifetime—career, the situation may change again in a direction similar to the Middle Ages. The universities' population may become again a politically conscious group, fighting for causes of its own and not merely acting as elites representing the causes of others. For the time being, however, these are only possibilities about which one can only speculate. To the extent that we are concerned with conditions which have actually existed either in the recent past or in the present, the political involvement of the universities has been a secondary phenomenon, depending on the relationship of its members—faculty and/or students—to the leading groups in society. This in its turn has been—as will be shown—to a large extent a function of the definition of the educational aims and the governance of the universities, or, in other words, of the difficulty of finding a satisfactory definition of the fields and the levels within which academic freedom should prevail and the allocation of authority to decide in these matters.

Concerning the definition of fields, the questions which pose themselves

12. For a recent survey of student politics containing references to nineteenth-century material as well, cf. Seymour Martin Lipset, "University Students and Politics in Underdeveloped Countries," *Comparative Education Review* 10, no. 2 (1966): 132–62.

daily are: whether certain subject matters should be considered as science or scholarship or rather as ideology or politics; or whether certain other subjects should be considered as properly academic—thus conferring upon their teachers and students academic privileges and titles—or whether they are merely vocational studies, in which case the issue of academic freedom does not pertain to either. If a kind of study is declared in advance as nonacademic, teachers need not be autonomous in planning their research and teaching; students need not have a choice between different courses and will not receive academic degrees. These two questions are quite closely related. As has been noted, by defining certain subjects, e.g., social sciences, as not sufficiently scientific, one can eliminate a great source of potential friction between faculty and whoever are the "owners" of the university, without any formal violation of academic freedom. Similarly, by separating a great deal of professional education from the university, one can restrict the numbers of students and academics so drastically as to make their freedom quite unimportant, or to make their scrutiny and selection very easy. Both measures can be taken in a way which is perfectly consistent with the principle of academic freedom. If certain studies are not sufficiently *wertfrei,* or if they are directed to the acquisition of a specific practical technology, it means that they are bound to ulterior, nonintellectual ends, and, therefore, it is neither justified nor useful to treat them the same way as the unbiased and nonutilitarian pursuit of knowledge is treated. Controls and restrictions on teachers and students can be justified in ideological and technological instruction even if rejected in "pure" science and scholarship.

The criterion usually employed to decide whether there is or is not an infringement of freedom in such cases is whether the decision to exclude or include new fields is taken by the academic body. This, however, is a poor criterion. Academics, like everyone else, are not too anxious to share scarce resources or power and honor with others, and they may be the hardest to convince that a new specialty should be given full recognition.

Closely related to this issue is the problem of admission to practice. What distinguishes freedom from privilege is that in the former people have equal chances to attain scarce ends and there is no doubt that those are allocated according to relevant criteria. As Max Weber has shown, it did not take much to destroy this sense of equality and equity in Germany, one of the systems known as an ideal case of academic freedom.[13] Another example of such a change—less well known today—occurred within the French Academy prior to the Revolution.[14] The *Académie des sciences* had been at the height of its success in terms of integrity and autonomy. One of the ways this elite institution had succeeded in strengthening its autonomy versus the king and his min-

13. Max Weber, "Science as a Vocation," in H. H. Gertz and C. W. Mills (eds.), *From Max Weber: Essays in Sociology* (New York: Oxford University Press, 1958), pp. 129–56.

14. Joseph Fayet, *La révolution française et la science* (Paris: Marcel Rivière, 1960), pp. 17–21.

isters was by making standards of admission so strict and unequivocally scientific as to make appointments on any but purely scientific grounds so glaring an abuse that they would not even be attempted. This implied putting all the burden of the proof on those considered for cooptation and the rejection of all the cases in which there was the slightest doubt. This, as in the later case of Germany, was enough (a) to create an invidiously great social distance between people whose attainments were only slightly different in quality; and (b) since even the best men are not infallible, nor is the quality of intellectual creation of people over time constant—some decline and others improve— there were a few cases of mistakes. The bitterness and recrimination aroused by these were compounded by the high status and restrictiveness of the institution. Thus, the very safeguards of freedom—an autonomous body of impeccably qualified people controlling admission by recourse to impeccable standards—may create a sense of injustice and authoritarianism. This will be a particularly great danger in scholarly and philosophical fields in which the ranking of excellence is more equivocal than in the exact sciences.

These are issues which, though rarely identified as problems of academic freedom, lie in fact nearer to its heart than many spectacular cases which have little to do with specifically academic matters. Their neglect is partly the result of the tendency to be concerned with the infringements of existing privileges but to leave unnoticed the cases where privileges have never been granted. Partly, however, it is the result of semantics—academic freedom is defined as a right of recognized scholars, working in academically recognized fields; those not appointed to an academic position, even though equally qualified, do not appear under the same heading. These semantics have concealed a great many problems of restraint and authoritarianism in science and scholarship in some places but have highlighted them elsewhere. Thus, authoritarian supervision of teaching in German or French high schools; the illegitimate exercise of authority by "experts" over fields in which they were not expert— anatomists over physiology, philosophers over psychology, strict direction of research in university research institutes—have not usually been considered infringements of academic freedom,[15] but restrictions on nineteenth-century American college professors, engaged in less creative work and often less qualified, were so considered.

This problem is compounded by organization. Due to their very complexity, academic research and teaching need large investments, planning, and organization. In response there arose a university which—in this respect like private or governmental bureaucracies—is owned by others rather than those who work in it or who are the main direct users of its services. There is a potentially vicious circle here; the more the scope of academic activities expands—and freedom of research and teaching is supposed to expand them—

15. J. Ben-David and A. Zloczower, "Universities and Academic Systems in Modern Societies," *European Journal of Sociology* 3 (1963): 45–85. [This volume, chap. 6.]

the more frequently financial and administrative decisions have to be taken and therefore the greater the likelihood of clash between governing bodies and academics.

Students are affected by these developments in several ways. Where academic freedom is safeguarded by restrictive policies concerning admission of new fields and new men to the universities, the main sufferers will be the students, or at least some of them. Because of the narrowness of academic study they may be prevented from learning what they want, or even what is up to date, and they may feel blocked in their aspirations by lack of opportunity. On the other hand, where development is rapid, they may be caught up in the conflicts and uncertainties accompanying change. Furthermore, the extension of research at universities may place them in a somewhat similar position to patients in advanced research hospitals. On the one hand, they enjoy the services of creative researchers, often of unique accomplishment; on the other, they have to pay for this privilege by scant attention paid to some of their needs which do not require original solutions. The greater, therefore, the freedom of the teachers, the greater the need for freedom of the students. There have to be safeguards concerning practicability of the requirements—which may impose a limitation on the discretion of the teacher—and students have to have some freedom in the organization of their studies and choice of courses and institutions to protect themselves against the inevitable vagaries of a system which at best is a compromise between the requirement of research and teaching and is altogether very loosely coordinated.

Among the dramatis personae of academic freedom, the students will be treated as a group which reacts to, rather than acts independently in, the situation. The problem around which the different solutions of university government have so far crystallized is then defined as a search for an optimal division of labor between academics, considered as free professionals, on the one hand, and governing bodies and administrations who are financially responsible for the university, on the other, in a situation which necessitates frequent decisions about the proper fields and levels of academic study and research. The solutions arrived at determine the way students can fit themselves in the university and eventually in society. If this turns out to be unsatisfactory, students may be led to political action which—in its turn—may affect academic freedom in various ways.

The usual aim is an administration without any coercion and with a great measure of active participation of those administered. An essential requirement for this is mutual trust. This is presumably established on the basis of the same considerations we generally use in making individual decisions. Where the risks are unknown or great, general trustworthiness becomes decisive; where the risks are small—either because of the triviality of the affair or because the odds are known to be low, personal acquaintance will be less important.

Translated to the problem of academic freedom, these considerations manifested themselves partly in attempts at the restriction of the acadmic privileges to a very small number of people, amounting to the definition of the academics as an elite rather than a profession, and partly in attempts at the restriction of the functions of academic institutions to fields in which patterns and outcomes of training and research are known well enough to regard the risks as negligible. Different academic systems have chosen different ways to minimize their risks. Some have preferred to create a restricted elite, failing to take advantage of extending the uses of the university. Others, starting out somewhat later, tried to exploit fully the potentials of the university. Since this made the establishment of personal trust such as can exist among small circles of people rather difficult, they have tried to reduce their risks by specifying as far as possible procedures and results. Whether the one or the other course is taken, trust is more easily established in situations which are reasonably well known to both parties. Such is the case where people and roles of the same kind as the universities are expected to produce have existed for a long time and where the intellectual activities engaged in by the university are continuous with activities engaged in outside the university. On the other hand, misunderstanding is likely to arise in the absence of concrete models so that agreement has to be based on abstract principles. Besides, the absence of role models in society makes it difficult to adjust the supply of graduates to the demand for their services. As the exact size and nature of this latter are unknown, the expectations concerning the rewards for university studies will be unrealistic, and frustration will be inevitable. The tensions resulting therefrom may seriously jeopardize academic freedom.[16]

We shall therefore expect different kinds of conflicts about academic freedom and different kinds of outcomes in four types of university systems (see table 2).

Theoretically, an eightfold classification would be required, since there may be systems where professors are considered as an elite but not necessarily the students, and vice versa. Since, however, in practice the two tend to go together, it is preferable not to complicate the scheme. It must be made clear that the dichotomization of the components is arbitrary. All university systems, as well as the majority of the individual universities, try to turn out an elite and at the same time train experts who are not necessarily destined to become an elite. These are only differences of emphasis which form a continuum. A scale of reasonable validity can be established by simply taking the ratio of students to population. These ranged in 1958 from 185 per 10,000 of general population in the United States to 19 per 10,000 in Britain and less than that in most of the Latin American and Middle Eastern countries. Conti-

16. Ben-David, "Professions in the Class System of Present-Day Societies," op. cit., pp. 273–75.
17. Ibid., p. 263.

Table 2.   Types of University Systems by Aim and the Availability of Models

	Model	
Aim	Available	Unavailable
to employ and train { elite	Type I	Type II
expert	Type III	Type IV

nental Europe is much nearer in this respect to the lower than to the upper end. These differences have been, with few exceptions, stable since the beginning of this century.[17] These variations reflect differences of purpose: the European systems had started out and were meant to be first and foremost elite intellectual institutions, providing positions for the leaders in scholarly and scientific fields. At the same time they were responsible for the training of an intellectual and political elite, as well as some of the higher professions which, to some extent, share in the elite status. Leading lawyers, physicians, and clergymen have been traditionally part of the central elite of European countries, while the rank and file, alongside of teachers in the European *gymnasia* and *lycées,* have had a respected place among local notables. To perform this function, it was not necessary to have large numbers of teachers or students. These people were not expected to make very important direct contributions to the economy; they were only supposed to contribute to it indirectly by creating new knowledge and providing excellent leadership for the country. Restriction of admission, as long as it was done according to impeccable standards, was considered an advantage; it safeguarded quality.

In those countries, on the other hand, in which the ratios are high—the prototype of which has been the United States—the system as a whole has been designed to train experts and to extend research into fields which, partly perhaps because they had not been considered worth specialized attention, promised to yield useful results quickly. This is not to say that the elite function of education was lost sight of. The universities do train the elite in these systems, too. Besides, expertise and research which produce new knowledge are a kind of leadership. The difference between these and the previously discussed elite systems is that the expert systems do not regard it as a debasement of the university to train also people for positions which are not elite roles.

The difference is not limited to the range of fields taught at universities but extends also to the way they are taught. The elite type of university, even when it requires high technical standards from its staff, does not care much about the technical training of the students. This, it assumes, will be acquired by trial and error, or through in-practice training and not necessarily in the university. It suspects professional schools—the ideal solution is that of English medical schools, in which the university medical schools concentrate on the basic fields, whereas clinical training is provided in teaching hospitals possessing considerable autonomy and only loosely tied to the university.[18] Ideally, this type of university is an academy, the staff of which also does a limited amount of teaching but has practically no responsibility for training.

The prototype of the expert university, on the other hand, is the professional school. Even if it teaches pure science or humanities, it endeavors to impart to the student the actual tools for his research. Thus, the most original innovation of the American universities has been the graduate school which is an extension of the techniques of training in professional schools to all the arts and sciences.

The distinction between countries in which models are available and those in which they are not is also a matter of a continuum. In most countries there are fairly clear-cut models of physicians or engineers, and in few is it clear what the model is for a young man studying for an arts degree. The situation also changes through time: where there is no model today there may be one tomorrow. At the same time, a distinction can be made between systems in which the university trains and educates for roles which are well known and accepted in the society and systems which are created by a traditional, or at any rate uneducated, elite for the purpose of eventually reforming themselves or increasing their efficiency through training new and better qualified people of a kind that do not exist yet in the country.

In England, France, the United States, and probably some other countries, modern higher education developed in the nineteenth century, shortly after the changes in occupational system and the rise of an educated class. The universities of Oxford, Cambridge, or Paris, at least since the sixteenth century, have not had the privilege of intellectual leadership. For a long time, in fact, they were followers rather than leaders. In both countries during the eighteenth century, and in England during the nineteenth as well, many of the most outstanding scholars, intellectuals, and scientists did not hold academic positions. The change was instigated partly by this nonacademic intelligentsia, who were civil servants, politicians, professionals, or—especially in England—simply wealthy people often of noble descent.[19] The kind of people

18. "Elite" as opposed to "expert" is a distinction between diffuseness and specificity. The academic in the elite systems has to be an expert, too, but that is not a sufficient condition. His expertise itself is judged according to criteria of diffuseness. Such questions typically asked as, "Is his specialization broad enough, or important enough?"; "Is he not merely a good technician?" imply (a) that the academic person has to cover a broader segment of fields than those who are merely "experts"; and (b) that he must possess qualities of leadership which are not easily defined, only intuitively distinguishable when compared with those who do not possess those qualities.

19. D. S. L. Cardwell, *The Organization of Science in England* (London: Heinemann, 1957), pp. 46–51.

who should form the academic elite as well as the nature of the products were not in question. There was consensus between those who taught at the universities and those who decided about the fate of university budgets as civil servants, donors, or politicians. They all belonged to the same class and spoke the same language. Similarly, there had been a long nonuniversity tradition in higher education, scholarship, science, and technology in the United States before the country seriously embarked on the reform of its higher education. Although this has been true for the northeastern part of the country, elsewhere the situation has often been one of the "nonmodel": governments and/or philanthropists of pioneering and educationally backward states setting up institutions to bring their own areas up to the standards of the East.[20]

The best-known examples of nonmodel systems are Austria, Prussia, and Russia in the eighteenth century, and the latter also in the nineteenth century (or the reformed system of the USSR in the twentieth). In all of these cases the universities were established by a minority of educated rulers and officials with the purpose of creating a new educated elite of the Western type, not to replace landed aristocracy as the mainstay of the respective regimes but to educate the latter and selectively introduce into it able people of nonaristocratic origin. Apparently, similar conditions prevailed in Japan and China at the end of the nineteenth and early twentieth centuries, when their modern systems of higher education were established, as well as in the eastern and southern European, Latin American, Asian, and African countries at various times in the nineteenth and twentieth centuries. Obviously, there is a great deal of variation here concerning the efficiency and determination of those in power to carry through their attempts at modernization and thus change a situation of "nonmodel" into one in which the model becomes available. Still the two categories are clearly enough distinguishable.[21]

Clearly, these types present separate and distinct problems for the maintenance of academic freedom. We shall try to explore these by taking each type in turn. We shall not give a detailed account and classification of the existing academic systems but seek to present models of the working of those which seem to be most representative of each type.

Type I: Elite Systems with Accepted Models

There is a nearly perfect example of this type in the English academic system. Germany, the Scandinavian countries, and France presumably also be-

20. Hofstadter and Metzger, op. cit., pp. 413–14.
21. It should be possible to define them in quantitative terms by relating the numbers and kinds of students at the early stages of modern university growth to the numbers of trained and qualified people in the ruling elites or in the country in general.

long to this type, but the workings of these, especially that of France, are much more complex. We shall, therefore, describe the model mainly with reference to England.

The governing of this type of system is effectively shared between the academics who have complete autonomy in running their own affairs and the government which has effective means of letting its views be known and seriously considered without openly interfering with the universities. This is so because there are no basic differences between the two sides involved. The exchange of opinion between the higher civil servants and the leadership of the universities takes place either through a formally constituted body (like the University Grants Commission in Britain or the Chancellor of the Universities in Sweden) or informally since the people know each other quite well. The civil servants are of similar education and background as the university professors, so that there are no barriers to communication between them.

One of the important effects of this situation is that the civil servants form an effective buffer between politics and the universities.[22] Certain parties may have opinions about the necessity of making the universities more representative, or they may want to look into the finances of the universities. In these cases some solution is worked out informally which then makes the execution of the policies acceptable to the academics as well as to the politicians.

Thus, even though there may be a good deal of public discussion and criticism of the universities, there is no attempt to interfere with their autonomy. It is taken for granted that, whatever changes may prove to be desirable or necessary, they will be carried out autonomously by the universities. The consensus necessary for such a degree of trust is the result of keeping the academic system exclusive, small, and so highly selected as to command universal or near-universal respect. Conservatism is the price paid for this: academic innovations, whether in education or research, have to be relegated to peripheral parts of the system, since the elite cannot take chances without endangering its status. An example of this in England has been the great hesitancy of Oxford and Cambridge (particularly the former) in making provision for the social sciences: economics was introduced only in the 1920s and then without adequate library facilities or sufficient staff; psychology achieved its first chairs in 1931 and 1947 at Cambridge and Oxford, respectively; sociology was introduced only in 1961 and still does not have a chair at either institution. There have been similar lacks in medical science, particularly in the integration of basic and clinical research.[23]

At first sight this delay does not seem too inefficient. It is logical to develop

22. Don K. Price, *Government and Science* (New York: New York University Press, 1954), p. 122; Lord Chorley, "Academic Freedom in the United Kingdom," *Law and Contemporary Problems* 28 (Summer 1963): 647–71.

23. A. Flexner, *Universities: American, English, German* (New York: Oxford University Press, 1930), pp. 289–96; E. G. Boring, *A History of Experimental Psychology.* 2d ed. (New York: Appleton-Century-Crofts, 1950), p. 494; Howard Becker, *Social Thought from Lore to Science.* 3d ed. (New York: Dover Books, 1961), vol. 3, p. XCVIII.

new things by trying them out on a small scale in a peripheral setting and then decide on the basis of experience whether to pursue or drop the matter. The trouble is that this kind of wisdom only occurs retrospectively in the pages of official histories. For a new field to succeed, those who believe in it have to be given a chance to fight for it with as good resources as they can possibly muster and to vie for as good students as they are capable of attracting. By being shunted to a third-rate university, or to some kind of more gilded academic ghetto where there is no chance of getting disciples or support for research, the novelty is doomed to failure.

This, however, is beside the point here. The purpose of this paper is not to investigate the innovative capability of different systems but to study academic freedom. From this point of view, the important thing is that the situation is not perceived as an unjust limitation of the opportunities by a privileged clique but as a fair, if not perfect, system. The possibilities for this lie in the efficiency of selection and allocation. Limitations and restrictions are perceived as just, if their rationale is reasonable and their administration equitable. As long as the elite does reasonably well what it is supposed to do, people have a good grasp of what the criteria of admission into the elite are, and the elite does not make life too difficult for the rest, there will be a feeling of justice. This is assured by the existence of what we have called a "model." That is, when academic systems have been shaped by successful people in their own image. The image is well reflected throughout the educational system, and children from a very early age are made aware of it and learn what their chances are. Expectations are geared to reality, and there are no (or insignificantly few) aspirants for academic careers, especially for top positions who will have to be frustrated. Since, therefore, much of the envy is taken out of competition—or disposed with at an early age before the personality is formed in its final shape—there is no vindictiveness on the part of the elite and no aggression on the part of those professionals and intellectuals who are not academics.[24] To the extent that some of the latter feel that the definition of the academic fields and roles should be broadened, they will be listened to and often given a chance "to prove" themselves. They will rarely succeed, although they will be treated fairly enough to end up blaming only themselves.[25]

Another way of bringing the educational system in accord with available social models has been the conscious attempt to make the composition of the academic elite representative of all the important political and social groups. Universities may make (and have made) efforts to find a person of working class origin for a position or to have a Communist or two on their staff. Such

24. Glen H. Elder, Jr., "Life Opportunity and Personality: Some Consequences of Stratified Secondary Education in Britain," *Sociology of Education* 38 (Spring 1965): 173–202. In addition, we are indebted to Professors Max Gluckman and Hilde Himmelweit for information about different enquiries showing the decisive effect of the ranking system within and between schools on the self-perception and level of aspiration of students in England.

25. Cf. Michael Young, *The Rise of Meritocracy: 1870–2033* (London: Thames and Hudson, 1958), for a semiliterary presentation of this atmosphere and its imagined consequences.

steps, if taken before the emergence of a frustrated group of alienated anti-establishment intellectuals, lend to this type of system an air of generosity and limitless tolerance and freedom. In fact, however, when combined with the selective, elite-oriented, process of education, this policy has the effect of giving the system maximum stability and of enhancing to the limit its conservative tendencies. Since selection is thorough and efficient, and consensus about important things great, the likelihood of individual dissent having any disrupting effect on the system is negligible. The effectiveness of scientific policymaking by a small group which knows itself to be the best in a certain field in the country, and is recognized by the relevant others as such, will not be affected by one of its members publicly advocating communism or free love. The same member, when it comes to professional policymaking, may be the "soundest" or even the most conservative of all. And, if members of the group, possibly including even the dissenter, have been known for a great many years to the civil servants who advise the minister (or, perhaps, to the minister himself, too), then no one will come to suspect them of being politically or morally unsound and therefore not to be supported by public money. Paradoxically, the tolerance probably also reduces the dissenter's effectiveness as a propagator for his subversive nonacademic interests. Having been admitted to the establishment and not being victimized by it for his views and activities, his activities only confirm the fairness of the system. The rebel himself will usually feel so and his revolutionary fervor will be blunted.[26] But even if he does not feel this, his public will. A brilliant scientist and scholar victimized for his views in his academic career makes a very good agitator. As a martyr he is a living indictment of the system. But the same person, treated fairly, is living propaganda for the status quo.

Such a system is in near perfect balance, with a minimum of conflict and a maximum feeling of freedom. Compared with more enterprising systems, it may seem too restrictive both in its expansion of scope and its selection of personnel. But for those within it, it provides a stable, fair, and predictable system. Lack of innovativeness is counterbalanced by flexibility and openness for suggestions of reform and innovation coming from outside the society, or—in principle—even from within.

The French system, operating in a much more impersonal way, achieves similar results. There is an elaborate system of selection and allocation which produces a somewhat similar elite as in England, but instead of reducing conflict and effective dissent through group consensus, the same end is achieved there, though probably accompanied by qualitatively different emotions, through careful isolation and delimitation of spheres of influence.[27]

26. On the general point of the cooptation of dissenters by controlling elites, cf. Philip Selznick, "Foundations of the Theory of Organizations," *American Sociological Review* 13 (February 1948): 25–35.

27. Michel Crozier, *The Bureaucratic Phenomenon* (Chicago: University of Chicago Press, 1964), pp. 238–44.

Type II: Elite Systems without Models in Society

While Type I tends toward a more or less stable balance, this second type is the most likely to be out of balance. This is implied in its very purpose, since it is founded in order to foster social change. Simply because these systems were all instigated by more advanced examples, they were initially built so as to create conflict. Historically, the line of educational reform leading to social conflict (and often culminating in revolution) can be traced back as far as the seventeenth century. The enlightened circles of France propagandizing for the establishment of the Academy of Sciences and Baconian educational ideas, and supported by "modernizing" civil servants like Richelieu or Colbert, had English models before their eyes. The movement which arose as a result eventually played an important role in the overthrow of the old regime. The reforms of Austrian and German higher education in the end of the eighteenth and early nineteenth century were first an imitation and then a reaction to French models; Russian higher education, established mainly in the nineteenth century, took its model mainly from Germany; the even newer systems of higher education in Latin America, Asia, and Africa have usually followed one of those three models.

The common characteristic of all these imitations has been that they are not mere adoptions of innovations in education and research made elsewhere but deliberate attempts at facilitating a change in the character and/or composition of the ruling elite, and/or the creation of entirely new secondary elites, by means of the educational reform. This distinguishes the present type from such cases as the adoption of certain features of the German academic system in the nineteenth century by English, French, and American universities. In these earlier cases the "models" for educated administrators, politicians, professionals, or even scientists and scholars had existed prior to the adoption of the foreign pattern. The innovation was a means of producing more and better of the same kinds of people as already existed in society. This, of course, might have led eventually to unexpected political problems. But the replacement of existing elites with a new one, or the introduction of a new stratum in society, is bound to lead to direct conflict. No existing elite will put up gracefully with an open attempt to transform and replace it, and even less will young men reared as future elite according to models of more advanced societies admit to the authority of a traditional ruling class. One can postulate, therefore, that at some point attempts will be made by the authorities to regulate the university and tell professors what to teach and what not to teach and what in general should be the model they present to their students. It is nearly inevitable that under such circumstances students, and at least some of the teachers, will become politically rebellious.

Since, therefore, this is a system which by definition starts from imbalance, no single case can be regarded as representative of it. Some systems never attain balance, so that the universities become permanent centers of intellectual and political conflict over a long period of time; others manage to establish some kind of a balance which may be more or less precarious depending on conditions to be specified. We shall, therefore, attempt first to describe a model of chronic disequilibrium, based mainly on the nineteenth-century Russian and twentieth-century Latin American cases, and then referring to the well-known case of Germany in the nineteenth and early twentieth century, we shall treat an example of a temporarily successful establishment of balance.

One of the distinguishing features of these systems, compared with the previous type, is the high degree of formalization of the rights and privileges of the academic person and the academic corporation. In principle these may appear as not too different from the arrangements of the first type—both are designed to ensure the autonomy of the profession—but in the first type of system there are few or no laws to define these rights, so that in principle it would probably be quite easy for any government which so desired to impair them without any change in the legal situation. The necessity of spelling out the rights in the nonmodel systems is the result of lack of communication and mutual trust between the academics and the rulers. Almost immediately after the establishment of the new University of Berlin in 1809, which was to serve as a model of academic freedom, there arose conflicts in Berlin and elsewhere about a variety of issues concerning the freedom of teachers to participate in opposition politics, present religiously heterodox views, and a variety of major and minor issues concerning freedom of publication, academic self-government, and honors. Such difficulties were, however, prevented wherever the minister of education was a cultivated person with good connections to the academic world. Since, however, the majority of the politicians and higher civil servants at that time were not people who valued intellectual achievements nearly as much as they valued noble birth or political and military excellence, the autonomy of the profession was constantly in danger and, therefore, required formal safeguards.[28] In countries like nineteenth-century Russia, or Latin America today, where military dictatorship is always an imminent possibility, these needs have been even greater.[29]

How effective are such formal safeguards in preserving or—since there are often countries where civil freedom is very limited—creating academic freedom? Of course, no safeguards help against a government which wants and

28. Franz Schnabel, *Deutsche Geschichte im Neunzehnten Jahrhundert* (Freiburg: Herder, 1934), vol. 3, pp. 140–41; Frederic Lilge, *The Abuse of Learning* (New York: Macmillan, 1948), pp. 20–23, 30–34; Richard Graf du Moulin Eckart, *Geschichte der deutschen Universitäten* (Stuttgart: Enke, 1929), p. 350.

29. This is not to say that they actually obtained such safeguards. In Russia they never have. In Latin America, on the other hand, they did. Cf. Luigi Einandi, "University Autonomy and Academic Freedom in Latin America," *Law and Contemporary Problems, Special Issue: Academic Freedom* 28 (Summer 1963): 636–46.

has the power to disregard them. But, as has been noted, most governments most of the time do not want to tamper with the universities and the academic profession. Formal safeguards, therefore, have some value since violating them will be regarded as a breach of legitimacy which governments can ill afford. The problem, however, is to what extent the formal safeguards, even if more or less honored by the government, will ensure that the autonomous academic community will use its power to promote an ever-growing freedom of inquiry. The assumption that by granting to the academic community visibly high status and responsibility, the norms of scholarship and science will prevail is based on some kind of concept of noblesse oblige. Unfortunately, what is true of other cases of privileged nobility is true of the academic case as well, namely, that the rule has been abuse of privilege. Only under circumstances where the privilege was rather limited have such groups lived up to their obligations out of their own free will. The conditions of "nonmodel" societies, however, are usually such that the privileged academic community will be corrupted sooner or later.

Even minor matters of chicanery and honor will have their effect. Where lack of personal power means subjection to arbitrary authority, and lack of special honors means dishonor, university professors will fight for these and, since they fulfill an important function and are able people, will sooner or later succeed. They will become part of, or at least friendly with, a corrupt ruling group, which inevitably involves a measure of corruption. Such corruption which replaces academic standards with nepotism and subordinates scholarship to politics had been widespread in nineteenth-century Russia and is said to be even worse in many Latin American countries today.[30] The tragic thing is that many who do not want to be corrupted by the rulers, and oppose the falsification of the purpose of the university through turning it into one of the fortresses of personal privilege, often end up by similarly falsifying these objectives by using their privileged position as a lever for opposition politics. Morally their stand may be impeccable. There is an excellent argument for giving priority to the larger interests of defending freedom and justice over academic duties. But the line between a temporary situation of emergency in which the professor and the student, as well as the doctor, the lawyer, the merchant, and the worker, must leave their places of work and study to man the barricades and fight for justice and a situation in which one has to go on working and to use one's spare time for discharging one's political and civic duties has to be clearly drawn. If everyone else works, but professors (and/or students) supported by public funds and special facilities and immunities conferred upon them to pursue their studies use those facilities and immunities for political activity, they may come dangerously near to abusing their privileges.

30. Frank Bowles, *Access to Higher Education*, vol. 1 (Paris: UNESCO and the International Association of Universities, 1963), pp. 147–52; Rudolph P. Atcon, "The Latin American University," *Die deutsche Universitätszeitung* 17 (February 1962): 9–48.

There are situations in which this is justified. But one should not include those under academic freedom; these rather involve a deliberate abandonment of the professional concerns of the academic in order to engage in something much more important than any professional obligation. This seems to have been the case in many individual instances in a great many places. But where—as it seems to be the case in some of the Latin American (and southern European) countries—professors have come to regard their positions conferring on them high status, public visibility, immunities, and income (or access to income) as sinecures provided by the State to engage in politics, then whatever the worth of those politics, they are abusing academic freedom. Not only because freedom and facilities meant to be used for the advancement of knowledge are thus diverted to other ends but because almost inevitably such actions will be justified by an ideology which identifies intellectual activity with activist politics and thus opposes or even suppresses free and unbiased enquiry in all ideologically sensitive fields. What starts out as (and in individual cases may continue to be) a justified subordination of intellectual freedom to the cause of freedom in general may then turn into a threat to the principle of freedom of inquiry.

Even more serious problems arise because of the difficulty in controlling the students. Since models are nonexistent, criteria of student selection cannot be too efficient. Besides, since the society is backward relative to the educational model it adopts, it will tend to lack a similar range of alternatives as the model for useful and respectable nonelite professional jobs for those who cannot make the elite. Finally, even those who are suitable in every respect to enter the elite will usually find that they are admitted by the ruling class only with very specialized qualifications and on sufferance and then only to positions of secondary importance. It is almost inevitable, therefore, that many are admitted to universities and their aspirations raised without any hope of realizing them. Even those who, due to exceptional ability and/or the fact that they come from upper-class families, should expect elite status will also encounter difficulties for a number of reasons. Almost inevitably, the system will be fairly inefficient, since the country will usually lack enough people of sufficient qualification to teach at a university, and even those qualified will lack experience and know-how to run such an institution. Worse yet, where the faculty has been corrupted, the able students will become very cynical; where the faculty is honest, students will learn to despise even more that kind of authority to which they are expected to subordinate themselves when leaving the university; and when the faculty is partly corrupted and partly honest they may conclude that the whole existing adult society makes no sense. In any case they are likely to be in a situation of the type Durkheim called *anomie*, where norms of conduct are unreliable and do not lead to their expected ends. Thus, the students become alienated from the very ruling class which had created the university. The honeymoon period with enlightened absolutist rulers is followed by absolute disillusionment on both sides.

This general pattern, which has a great many variations, is most clearly discernible in Russia in the nineteenth century and in present-day Latin America. The sequence of events in Russia was somewhat like this. The modern university started out as an institution to which Messianic hopes for social betterment were attached. After a very short time, however, the hopes went sour. Instead of preparing themselves for entering the slots in society which they were intended to enter, the students grew impatient with both society and the slots and organized themselves for (or at least threatened) subversion. This was followed by government attempts to restrict entrance into universities and to control what happened in them. This action caused even more dissatisfaction. The restrictions were perceived as injustices by those who were now prevented from entry, and their sense of injustice was incensed by the corrupt and erratic way admission was administered. Those who were admitted became alienated nonetheless, since they were made to suffer from the usually stupid attempts at controlling the instruction, speech, writing, and thought. Eventually the futility and injustice of the restrictive measures were recognized, and a new liberal era began, starting a new cycle of the vicious circle. This is in a schematic way what happened in Russian higher education starting from early in the nineteenth century with the reforms of 1804 and lasting until the first World War. The cycles were: first, a liberalization under Alexander I with the reforms of 1804, followed by a reaction after the Napoleonic War of 1812, and culminating in the Decembrist Revolt of 1825. The restriction of admissions to an ever-smaller elite and the tightening of controls over the teachings and the curriculum followed in the reign of Nicholas I, 1825–1855. Alexander II brought a new period of liberal reform, approximately during the years 1856–1866, but conflicts led to spasmodic repressions throughout the remainder of the reign, ending with the assassination of the tsar in 1881; Alexander III instituted a severe reaction until 1894, but student strikes and other forms of defiance continued; reforms were attempted in 1901 but without quelling the tide of disturbances. Revolution broke out in 1905, and liberal and reactionary policies fluctuated rapidly thereafter until the Revolution of 1917 ended forever the tsarist educational experiments.[31]

As a result, student culture became overwhelmingly politicized, and students came to regard academic freedom as equivalent to freedom of speech and agitation. The intellectual atmosphere which resulted from this was one of doctrinaire adherence to ideologies and the spread of ideological intolerance.[32] If all this did not completely exhaust Russian intellectual creativity, it was probably due to proximity to Western Europe. The best Russian intellectuals, irrespective of their field of activity, had studied in France and Ger-

31. Nicholas Hans, *History of Russian Educational Policy* (London: P. S. King, 1931); Hans-Eberhard Müller, "State, Society and Education: The Russian Case in the Nineteenth Century," unpublished M.A. thesis, Department of Sociology, University of California, Berkeley, 1966.
32. Richard Pipes (ed.), *The Russian Intelligentsia* (New York: Columbia University Press, 1961), p. 10.

many, or Switzerland, published in German and French, and/or were exposed to publications coming from those countries. This counteracted the tendencies for intellectual corruption and complete politicization inherent in the internal conditions.

The parallel between nineteenth-century Russia and present-day Latin America is particularly interesting, since this latter area has had some revolutions. As a result, individuals and groups from the alienated intelligentsia have found their way to supreme power. Due to the existence of many independent states in the area, there has been no period of time since the second half of the nineteenth century, without the existence in some of the countries of relatively liberal regimes respecting the independence and autonomy of the universities.

What, however, these countries have in common with pre-World War I Russia has been their social structures. These latter have been left virtually unaffected by political change: there is everywhere a very narrow and conservative stratum of extremely rich and conservative landowners; an overwhelmingly large and abjectly poor and backward peasantry and urban *lumpenproletariat;* and in between, a small, economically insecure mobile and relatively educated middle class.

Since the universities have been modeled on elitist European examples—Spanish traditions going back to the Middle Ages and the universities of Continental Europe—they imbue the students with aspirations for leadership. But in these economically backward and unstable countries the only way to obtain positions of economic security and honor (for those who were not born into such position) is through political power or patronage. Therefore, even though the proportion of university trained people in positions of responsibility is among the highest in the world, this remains an extreme nonmodel situation nevertheless. The professionals in high positions are there not as a result of their training but of political success or connections. There are no models in society of the kind of elite roles for which the universities are supposedly training their students—creative scientists and scholars, high-grade professionals, or broadly educated intellectuals with a keen sense for practical affairs whose services are rewarded because of their superior intellectual training and abilities.

The very high degree of legally safeguarded freedom (which is actually observed in some of the countries) is used deliberately and consciously to secure for those connected with the university fargoing privileges to engage in politics. Furthermore, this freedom is often used to prevent improvements of academic standards, or to suppress the expression of views unpalatable to an important political faction, or simply to victimize certain individuals.

This case is particularly important since unlike the Russian failure which could be attributed to the insufficiency of the safeguards of academic freedom and to constant interference by bumbling autocratic governments, the failure of the Latin American university must be blamed on the actions of relatively autonomous scholars and students. If nevertheless the results have been similar or worse than those in Russia, they have to be attributed to the dynamics of elite nonmodel systems.[33]

In contrast to these failures of elite nonmodel systems, Germany, or rather the system of German-language universities, in the nineteenth century is considered a great success. Here autonomy was used wisely and responsibly. The universities had not been deflected from the pursuit of the highest standards of science and scholarship for a period of more than one hundred years. The people appointed were generally of a high caliber, the quality of the lectures, seminars, and research was among the best in the world, the graduates were well trained, and the German universities attracted many of the best students from all over the world. Much of this success has been attributed to the specific arrangement of academic freedom prevailing in the German universities.[34]

We should like to suggest, however, that those formal arrangements were not a sufficient condition for the scientific success of the universities. An abuse of these freedoms in a manner similar to Latin America (or their suppression similar to Russia or under Peron, in Argentina) was only prevented by a set of circumstances which had nothing to do with these formalities.

We shall trace now the way the system had worked. The first effect of the new freedom of the Prussian universities was indeed an attempt to politicize them, on the one hand, as in present-day Latin America, and to regulate them authoritatively, as in Russia, on the other. One of the first and most famous manifestations of the newly won freedom of the academic profession and of the students was the Wartburgfest in 1817—a festival arranged by the student organizations to commemorate the Jubilee of the Reformation. One of its features was the burning of books which were not in accordance with the taste of one of the principal ideologists of the "youth" movement, Professor Massmann. Several other professors were active in fomenting extremist nationalist

33. Gabriel del Mazo, *La reforma universitaria (1918–1940)* (La Plata: Edicion del Centro Estudiantes de Ingeniera, 1941), 3 vols; and his *Estudiantes y gobierno universitario*, 2d ed. (Buenos Aires: Elateneo, 1956), Roberto MacLean y Estenos, *La crisis universitaria en Hispano-America* (Mexico, D.F.: Universidad Nacional, 1956), pp. 51–56, 73–75; Focion Febres Cordero, *Reforma universitaria* (Caracas: Universidad Central de Venezuela, 1960), pp. 65–68; Arthur P. Whitaker, *The United States and Argentina* (Cambridge: Harvard University Press, 1954), pp. 67–74, 152–53; Frank Bonilla, "The Student Federation of Chile: 50 Years of Political Activity," *Journal of Inter-American Studies* 2 (July 1960): 311–34; Kalman H. Silvert, *The Conflict Society: Reaction and Revolution in Latin America* (New Orleans: Hauser, 1961), pp. 162–82, and his "The University Student" in John J. Johnson (ed.), *Continuity and Change in Latin America* (Stanford: Stanford University Press, 1964), pp. 206–26. On the general setting of the problem, cf. S. M. Lipset, "Values, Education and Entrepreneurship in Latin America," in S. M. Lipset and Aldo Solari (eds.), *Elites in Latin America* (New York: Oxford University Press, 1967).

34. Friedrich Paulsen, *The German University: Its Character and Historical Development* (New York: Macmillan, 1895), pp. 85–86; Flexner, op. cit., 1930, pp. 317–20.

movements among the students, and their agitation led among other things to the murder of the Austrian playwright Kotzebue and to several anti-Semitic outbursts.[35]

The authorities started reacting to this by restricting entrance to the universities so as to prevent the admission of students from popular backgrounds who might be insecure and potentially subversive. There were also attempts to discipline academic teachers with an ineptness similar to the tsarist government.[36] But the worst, nevertheless, did not follow. In addition to the fact that the German ruling class contained a much greater minority of enlightened and educated people than its Russian counterpart, German universities had the advantage of decentralization. Whenever one of the governments decided to interfere highhandedly with a university, the academic elite of that university usually had the choice of resigning and finding a haven in another state which happened to have a more enlightened ruler at that time or just taking an opportunity of the occasion, so as to benefit its own university. As a last resort there was also democratic Switzerland with its German-language universities. Moreover, reactionary measures against the universities were never general, so that the system developed by the initiative taken first in one place, and then in another. This decentralization could have such a favorable effect, of course, only because of the unevenness of the situation; the lack of "models," of sympathetic, educated men in society, was not completely general throughout German society; thus, it was less in a position of "nonmodel" than Russia or Latin America.[37]

The outcome was a strengthening of genuine research and learning, since this was in the long run the most useful strategy from the point of view of the profession. Playing autonomous politics, as in Latin America, was not tolerated anywhere in the area and would not have been feasible anyway due to the greater differentiation of society. Becoming martyrs for freedom in general, as in Russia, was not necessary. There was a third and respectable possibility of practicing professional freedom efficiently. Although in the beginning the inefficiencies of a "nonmodel" situation caused considerable damage, competitive pluralism prevented complete bankruptcy and brought about rapid improvement.

35. Du Moulin Eckart, op. cit., p. 222; Carl Brinkmann, *Der Nationalismus und die deutschen Universitäten im Zeitalter der deutschen Erhebung*, in *Sitzungsberichte d. Heidelberger Akademie d. Wissenschaften*, Philosophisch-historische Klasse (1931/32) 3. Abhandlung (Heidelberg: Carl Winter, 1932). Cf. especially pp. 72–78 for parallels with late-nineteenth-century Russia and p. 72 for social background—insecure, downwardly mobile parents—of alienated students.

36. After the number of students in Prussia had increased from 3,311 (or 29.3/100.000 of population) to 15,751 (52.5/100.000) between 1820–1830, measures were taken to restrict entrance. The figures for the following decades were 1841: 11,593; 1851: 12,314; 1861: 13,248 (34.0/100.000; 34.2/100.000; 33.8/100.000). These figures and the description of the measures are based on Volker Eisele, "Democratization in German Higher Education" (unpublished seminar paper, Dept. of Sociology, University of California, Berkeley, 1965).

37. Schnabel, loc. cit.

The balance which emerged and the conditions under which it eventually broke down between the two World Wars precisely reflect these various forces. The political freedom of the academic profession as well as of the students was limited. It was assumed that the academic teacher as a civil servant had to have political and ideological convictions acceptable to the rulers. Even though the majority of the academic profession opposed the *Lex Arons,* passed by the Prussian legislature in 1898, requesting positive identification with the government, they would have preferred Arons to resign his position as a *Privatdozent* in physics, believing that activity in the Social-Democratic party was inconsistent with the "civil service" position of a member of a university.[38] Political prejudice and extremism of the kind acceptable to the ruling class (extreme chauvinism, incitement to war, anti-Semitism) were, on the other hand, quite frequent among university professors. It went without saying that Jews were discriminated against in appointments and that the appointment of Catholics and Protestants was often influenced by considerations of religious politics. Liberal academics did not accept these things. But apart from being active in liberal politics outside the university, as some of them were, the only thing they could do about it within the university was to try to keep the institution on as high a level, and as far above and away from topics which might open it to contact with the outside world, as possible. They opposed everything that might have implied value judgments or technological application, arguing that those were matters to be discussed and taught elsewhere. In principle, of course, this attitude is impeccable, and everyone would accept Paulsen's statement that "Ein gebundener Unterricht ist kein wissenschaftlicher" (a restricted education is not a scientific one), and it probably was the best way to reduce attempts at controlling the university or corrupting the integrity of the staff. But it should be clear that it was a compromise and not a clear and simple criterion of what is academic and therefore what should be free. This is evident from the actual decisions made. Theology was an acceptable discipline, but sociology was usually not; medicine and law were traditional subjects, but engineering or business administration were kept outside the universities. The principle, therefore, cannot be taken too seriously. It was an adjustment to a precarious situation. Academic freedom could be maintained only in limited subjects which were old and venerable so that they became part of the unquestioning routine and in those which either because of their highly abstract nature or, at times, because of their complete remoteness from any practical application or social implications were absolutely certain not to produce any friction.[39]

Thus, academic freedom, as it actually existed, was a Janus-faced institution, and none of its faces represented that ideal of beauty which had been so

38. Friedrich Paulsen, *The German Universities and University Study* (New York: Longmans Green, 1906), pp. 228–31.
39. Ben-David and Zloczower, op. cit.

often attributed to it. On the one hand, academics shared the honors, emoluments, and privileges of the ruling classes in an authoritarian society, and only a negligible minority felt any pangs of conscience. To the extent that violations were "localized," the majority tolerated abuse and corruption, such as enumerated (right wing bias, etc.), and often actively participated in them. On the other hand, they were good enough professionals not to want the system to be totally corrupted into one of the domains of ascribed privilege reflecting the exercise of bureaucratic power. In this concern they agreed with the liberal minority. Building up the university into a kind of holy shrine and establishing impressive rituals to symbolize the elevated status of the place and the profession were acceptable to all. They added even more status to those who were corruptible, and they could be used by the honest academics as weapons against corruption.

Thus, the successful institutionalization of academic freedom in this elite nonmodel setting has to be attributed to the effective decentralization of the system. The academic profession was able to maintain a decent measure of autonomy and freedom in a relatively authoritarian society, because it had been able to opt out easily from oppression. The establishment of German unity did not change this situation, because (a) it did not include the Austrian lands and Switzerland, and (b) because by that time the German system, which had started out as "international" in the German-language area, had already become the center of a new cosmopolitan world of universities. German universities had trained most of the academic elite of Eastern and the rest of Central Europe, much of that of England and the United States, and practically all the new academic elite of Japan. Thus, the German university professor had a role of international significance and influence which no German government could attack without hurting its own international standing.

This outcome was a more or less satisfactory solution only for those who had been admitted into the academic profession. The majority of the students, however, had to find their way within German society and face its general authoritarianism. From their point of view the privileges of the established academics, strictly restricted to a few lucky incumbents of positions and a limited number of recognized academic fields, appeared as arbitrary intellectual authoritarianism. They reacted to this situation by the creation of a variety of what might be described as intellectual sects. Marxism with its tendency to build up a whole intellectual establishment parallel to the universities, psychoanalysis with only slightly more modest aims at intellectual self-sufficiency, and a variety of less well developed instances, such as that of Nietzsche and his followers, were all, at least in part, expressions of discontent and alienation by scholars and intellectuals who felt that they had been driven out into the wilderness by the academic establishment.[40] There are obviously limits to

40. For the invidious atmosphere concerning university honors, cf. Samuel and Thomas, op. cit., pp. 116–17. The ideologies of the period are described in Karl Löwith, *Von Hegel bis Nietzsche* (Zürich-New York: Europa Verlag, 1941); for some of the sociological aspects of the

who can and cannot be absorbed in an academic (or any other) establishment which exist everywhere. But it makes all the difference whether these limits are perceived as legitimate means to the purpose of the university or whether they are seen as illegitimate monopolization of scarce opportunities and honors for intellectual work. In Germany there was a widespread feeling of this latter kind, resulting from the defensive conservativeness of the academic profession, wary of moving out of time-tested precedents into intellectual fields which might have involved them in conflict with the ruling elite or undermine the justification of their high privileges and immunity from control.

The intellectual movements which arose in this situation were often connected with extremist politics of the left or the right. The question is how these onsets of student-intellectual unrest resembling those in Russia and Latin America were prevented from politicizing the university to the extent of seriously interfering with the quality of studies, as it happened in those countries. This was achieved by (a) emphasizing reasonably high and honest academic standards; in this respect there was much less room for feelings of cynicism and normlessness than in Russia, or in Latin America; (b) the "non-model" situation was mitigated by numerous exceptions: for the intellectual elite of the students there existed at different times reasonably good prospects for suitable careers at the universities, secondary schools, and professions; and for those coming from the upper and upper-middle class—who formed a considerable part of the student body—there were good and intellectually quite acceptable careers in the civil service or the military. The potential alliance of these student elites with the insecure and subversive part of the student body was further prevented by the existence of exclusive student organizations which kept these higher-class students apart from the others and placed them in a separate environment within the university which closely resembled in its social structure, if not necessarily in human values, the English and French elite institutions.[41] Thus finding themselves in a framework of interlocking elites, including part of the faculty and important sectors of the ruling class, the elite student culture was politically innocuous. This pattern explains why the crises of the system occurred in the beginning, before these new elite frameworks were consolidated. After World War I when, as the combined result of attempts at democratization and inflation, these frameworks broke down, the way was opened to extremists skillfully using the dubious symbols of valor and virility of the old upper classes to unite their descendants with many of the hopeless mass of students from the lower middle classes in a movement promising to make them all into an elite, not at the expense of the lower classes but of so-called lower races.[42]

The success of the German universities cannot, therefore, be attributed to

psychoanalytic movement, cf. J. Ben-David, op. cit., *American Journal of Sociology.* [This volume, chap. 1.]

41. Paulsen, op. cit., 1895, pp. 189–94; Samuel and Thomas, op. cit., pp. 120–21.

42. W. Kornhauser, *The Politics of Mass Society* (New York: Free Press, 1959), pp. 187–92.

the institutions of academic freedom and the freedom of students. Similar institutions elsewhere did not prevent deterioration; there was a considerable measure of political and ideological corruption in German universities, too. As in Latin America, the decentralization of the system enhanced the formal autonomy of the universities. Unlike Latin America, however, the decentralized system was much more pluralistic, with some parts of it very near and all parts of it closer to the model end of the continuum than either Latin America or Russia. Because of the much greater mobility of staff and students, the German system was also much more competitive than the other two systems dealt with here. Thus, academics had not only rights and privileges but also an opportunity to prove the value of real excellence.

In this context a word should be said about the formal freedoms of the students, which have not been dealt with yet. These consisted in an agreement to transfer enrollment credits from one university to another and to reduce the formal requirements for attending classes and passing intermediate examinations to a minimum.[43] Interestingly, these freedoms have not been imitated elsewhere and have rarely been mentioned as a desirable model. Indeed, they are of a quite different kind than those of the academic body. They are not privileges of a traditional, corporate kind but freedoms in the liberal-democratic sense. They have probably contributed a very great deal to the competitive nature of the system, serving as a check on the professors—if students did not like the way a part of their subject was taught at one institution they could go elsewhere; and they must have increased satisfaction by allowing the students to find the most congenial place for themselves by trial and error. Finally, they served to correct some of the shortcomings of the elite system. As said, such a system makes no point of training the student. The university staff is small. The most important thing is that they should be excellent. No particular care is taken that every aspect of the field should be covered and even less that the actual techniques of research should be taught. This, of course, greatly enhances the insecurity of the student in a "non-model" system, since he cannot safely look forward to a place of work or professional practice with traditions of technical excellence and socialization of the novice. By allowing the students to move from one place to another, they could make up for some of these deficiencies. Thus, while the structure of the individual university definitely places this system in the elite category, the working of the system as a whole pushes it along some way toward the "expert" end of the continuum.

The validity of this explanation can be tested by reference to more recent parallels. The most interesting of these is Japan. Its academic system had been in many ways the best and most successful imitation of the German system. The possibility and value of granting complete academic freedom to a highly

43. Paulsen, op. cit., 1895, pp. 187–88, 201.

selected intellectual elite of international standing was clearly recognized by the leaders of educational reform, though they were aware of the problems which might result from this for the maintenance of the stability of an otherwise authoritarian system. Great care was taken, therefore, to isolate the university system, to justify and legitimate the isolation by true adherence to high standards, and to ensure the loyalty of the graduates to the system by linking them through informal cliques to the elite (reminiscent of the function of German student corporations). Having linked its universities from the outset into the most advanced international academic network and possessing a considerable educated and honest administrative class as well as a potential middle class—like Germany—Japan had avoided in the beginning the instabilities attending the Russian and the Latin American systems. Yet after World War I a class of unemployable and increasingly radicalized intellectuals emerged as in Germany, which was open to ideologies of national superiority like their German counterparts.[44]

A parallel to Latin American developments may emerge soon in Africa. Prior to independence there had arisen in most places a conflict between the colonial ruling class and the embryonic native educated class possessing English or French education, spearheading more or less broadly based nationalist movements. With the attainment of independence these educated groups found themselves in a situation where they had easy access to power and great potential influence on educational policies. Individuals, or as in the case of the Mobutu administration in Congo, groups, attained actual power. But despite their progressive intentions, they have not been able to change the class structure. Apart from those having very great wealth, politics remains the main avenue to comfort and security. Those who are in the educational system have retained a completely and usually unrealistically elitist view of education. The expectations of the students concerning their futures as educated members of their societies are so unrealistic, in view of the actual opportunities which those societies can offer, that they are bound to become hopelessly frustrated. The relative success of some of the local universities in actually living up to the British or French ideal of a university and maintaining ivory towers of almost European academic standards, and more than European standards of living in splendid isolation from their environments, is apt to lead within a generation or two to a situation resembling Latin America.[45] The existence of culturally coherent, but politically decentralized, areas (particularly in English-speaking Africa), and extreme economic backwardness coupled with

44. Michio Nagai, "The University and the Intellectual," *Japan Quarterly* (Autumn 1964): 46–52; Herbert Passin, "Japan," in James S. Coleman (ed.), *Education and Political Development* (Princeton: Princeton University Press, 1965), pp. 272–312.

45. Cf. James S. Coleman (ed.), op. cit., articles by Coleman, pp. 35–50; Francis X. Sutton, pp. 51–74; Michel Debeauvais, pp. 7–91; Ayo Ogunsheye, pp. 123–143; Coleman, pp. 353–71; Anthony H. M. Kirk-Greene, pp. 372–407; Dwaine Marwick, pp. 463–97.

unstable, revolutionary politics, is closely parallel to the situation prevailing in Latin America. On the other hand, both the English- and the French-language African universities are closely attached to effective, high-standard European academic systems, which has not been the case in Latin America. This is a circumstance favoring the maintenance of international academic standards and preventing such far-reaching politicization of the university as occurs in Latin America. If other things remain unchanged, the situation may then develop somewhat in the same direction as in India, where a few institutions and individuals oriented toward the outside world struggle for high standards amidst a flood of academic pettiness, decadence, and politicization.[46]

There is finally the possibility that these elite systems will turn into expert systems. This had actually occurred in the more or less recent past in the USSR and in Japan. In both cases the transition took place under extraordinary conditions; revolution in Russia and defeat followed by foreign occupation in Japan. Otherwise the transition from an elite to an expert system of universities is very difficult, since it is inevitably opposed by the only experts available. These are necessarily the products of an elite system, and they will perceive the transition to an expert system as a threat to their status as well as to their values.

This resistance notwithstanding, it is possible that the Russian and Japanese examples will eventually be followed. This may occur not because of the immanent instability of the elitist system in developing societies—this could just as well become chronic as in Latin America—but because the internationally most influential system—the American one—is an expert system, as are the two others next in size and potential influence, those of the USSR and Japan. Since the African systems are linked to international networks, they may reorient themselves—especially the English-language ones—to the U.S. pattern.

Types III and IV: Expert Systems

Whereas in the elite systems the model and nonmodel types are poles apart, the distance between these two in the expert systems is not so great. The reason is that where the role definition of the academic is that of an expert, the differences between various fields and institutions within the system become relatively more important than in the elite type. Professors of engineering will always tend to be different kinds of persons than their counterparts in modern English poetry. But in the elite type, they will have more contact and more identification with each other and less with engineers, on the one hand, and

46. Cf. Edward A. Shils, *The Intellectual Between Tradition and Modernity: The Indian Situation* (The Hague: Mouton, 1961), and his "Towards a Modern Intellectual Community in the New States," in Coleman (ed.), op. cit., pp. 498–518.

poets, on the other, who are not academics than in the expert system. As a result, in expert systems, a situation of model may prevail in one field (e.g., medicine) and of nonmodel in another (e.g., mathematics). Transition from a nonmodel to a model state will, as a result, be easier. In elite systems such transition implies a change in the ruling elite, in practice often amounting to revolutionary upheaval. In the expert system this may be a more gradual process, such as the decision to hire certain kinds of new experts by government or business. We shall therefore treat these two types together, especially since the information on academic freedom in Type IV, the major representative of which is the USSR, is not sufficient or easily comparable with that existing for other systems. It is hoped, nevertheless, that the few comparisons which can be made at this point will make further research on the subject better focused and more useful.

Taking the U.S. academic system as an example of the expert type of university may seem misleading, since the American undergraduate school is anything but a school for experts. The word coined by Clark Kerr for the largest and most representative units of the system, the "multiversity," seems to be a much more fitting description of this combination of liberal education, training of experts, and large-scale research.[47] The very fact, however, that many of the individual units, as well as the system as a whole, try to do all of these things defines the role of the academic teacher as a specialized expert. The variety of the tasks and the size itself prevents the development of an esprit de corps such as is possible within communities of some 100 professors each regarded as the outstanding man in his field, comprising for all intents and purposes the university corporation. Furthermore, the variety of tasks also provides a variety of facilities for the full realization of one's scientific and scholarly capacity and for the advancement of one's career. An able chemist, political scientist, or what not, will probably work either simultaneously or at different stages of his career both as the member of a department and of the staff of a research institute and will be engaged at one time or another primarily in undergraduate teaching, in the training of graduates, or in full-time research, and in administration. The opportunity for such changes and variation is a very great advantage for the professional person, since it makes it possible for him to try out and develop his capacity under a variety of conditions and thus make the best use of them. The effect of this is that the career and the role pattern is defined more in terms of professional expertise than of academic elite position.[48] From the point of view of the teachers, therefore, this type of academic system consists of organizations employing experts and

47. Clark Kerr, *The Uses of the University* (Cambridge: Harvard University Press, 1964).

48. The mobility from university to university characteristic of German academics could not achieve quite the same effect, because of the formalized distinction between the academic and nonacademic careers (the former requiring Habilitation) and the very limited opportunities in the former career.

designed to create optimal conditions for the utilization of their knowledge and skills for a wide and expanding variety of teaching and research tasks, provided that these do not fall below the level commensurate with their qualifications and do not limit the unfolding of the creative potential. This is not to say that there are no elite academic institutions in the United States. Their elite position, however, is due to the ability and willingness of each of their departments to compete with all other similar departments in the country and only to a much smaller extent to the personal relationship of the members of the university to members of a generalized elite, or to the inherited fame and symbolical importance of the institution.

This type of university becomes a workplace. Professors in America have "offices"—elsewhere "rooms"; and in America they work in them regularly, whereas elsewhere they may only visit them. Whatever the function is—teaching undergraduates, training graduates in research, or doing research—there is an expectation that the academic will do a finished job. Even in the liberal arts college, the part of the university system which has a diffuse educational aim, the outline of each course, the requirements and the testing of achievements are much more clearly defined than in the European systems. At the graduate level and in research the aim is to turn out finished products, and at all levels there is a conscious attempt to measure quality and quantity of production.

All this necessitates much higher levels of professional staff employment as related to the number of students and much greater coordination of different kinds and levels of skill than in the elite systems. Such tasks need full-time administrative experts, so that the functions of academic self-government become necessarily much more restricted and partial than in the elite systems. It is quite inconceivable that this "multiversity" should be governed by temporarily elected representatives and assemblies of the faculty or that curricula and examinations be handled in quite the same informal way as in Europe. Even in Europe—with the growth in size and functions of the university—the informal system becomes increasingly inefficient. If it were adopted by American universities, they would probably not become freer but simply more chaotic. The university in the United States is not and never has been a corporation of teachers (and/or students). Self-government there is partly an administrative device for organizing the work of individual departments and using the faculty as staff experts on committees and partly a union type of activity defending the interests of the faculty against the administration by bargaining for agreed-upon principles of hiring, firing, promotions, tenure and conditions of work, and participation through representatives in all these processes. The professional freedom thus obtained may be much greater than any which a truly self-governing institution can confer. No one will be so tolerant of individual differences or helpful in catering to a variety of individual tastes as an efficient university administration which knows that the standing of the university depends on its ability to attract and keep the most sought after experts in the world. On the other hand, the power of the administration to make life difficult for academics where and when their bargaining position is weak is considerable. The only way to fend off such an eventuality is by good, legally enforceable contracts and union-type protection.

This explains the different and more endemic nature of conflicts concerning academic freedom in the American and—potentially—the Soviet systems from those in the European elite systems.

Let us take the clashes which have actually occurred. These were basically centered around three issues: the theory of evolution, anti-monopoly and Keynesian economics, and questions of loyalty in times of war. Surprisingly, although there were famous controversies about the teaching of evolution in secondary schools, problems of academic freedom in the American universities in regard to this issue were quite mild. The most famous case was the demand of President Noah Porter of Yale to William Graham Sumner in 1879 that he withdraw the use of Spencer's *Study of Sociology* in his classes. The question here, however, was not the teaching of biological evolution but its extension to the field of social philosophy. Thus, the controversy centered around a new area which lacked the precedents and the clear methodological criteria of the natural sciences. The outcome was something of a draw: the Corporation of Yale University refused to accept Sumner's resignation, due to his powerful support among the faculty; on the other hand, Sumner withdrew the text on the grounds that the publicity had impaired its usefulness.[49] In the long run, the principle of academic freedom was extended to this area as well, and Sumner's stand contributed to its victory.

There were two main periods of attacks on economics and economists at the American universities. The first came in the "Progressive Era" of the 1890s and 1900s. Among these cases were the dismissal of Henry Carter Adams from Cornell in the 1880s for having delivered a pro-labor speech; of J. Allen Smith, political scientist, from Marietta College, in 1897 for "anti-monopoly teaching"; of Edward W. Bemis, Chicago economist, in 1895 for holding antimonopoly views; and of Edward A. Ross, economics professor at Stanford in 1903 and John S. Bassett, history professor at Trinity (later renamed Duke) in 1903.[50] There were other cases, including the trial of the famous economist Richard T. Ely at Wisconsin in 1894 for believing in "strikes and boycotts," justifying and encouraging the one while practicing the other.[51] However, Ely won his case and retained his position, and the principle of academic freedom was upheld.

Thus, not all of the cases were lost, nor was it unequivocal that some of the

49. Hofstadter and Metzger, op. cit., pp. 335–38.
50. Ibid., pp. 491–51.
51. Ibid., p. 426.

cases may not have concerned personality conflicts and personal antagonisms as well as issues of principle. All of these, it should be noted, involved professors of economics or of social science, who took public positions on political issues. In other words, the conflict took place in relatively uncertain fields which lacked the secure position of the natural sciences; moreover, it was not merely a question of the political views of professors but of professors who might lay claim to a special expertise in politics because of their academic positions. Similarly, the attacks on Keynesian economists during the New Deal era of the 1930s and the period of the 1940s were directed toward academic specialists whose views might be given special weight in public policy and furthermore who held a relatively new point of view within their field. But this time, although there was considerable noise, there was little concrete 'action; the only major case known of economists resigning under pressure of such attacks took place at the University of Illinois, when Dean Bowen of the College of Commerce and Business Administration resigned in a general controversy about the appointment of new professors, along with the Chairman of the Department of Economics, Everett Hagen, and seven other economists.[52]

Finally, there is the issue of the loyalty of academic personnel which takes place in every wartime period. The charge of pro-Germanism led to a number of dismissals from American universities in 1917 and 1918 but led as a direct result to the rapid expansion of the A.A.U.P. in its efforts to protect academic freedom.[53] There were similar attempted purges during World War II and the Korean War. But in all of these cases, the attacks on academics were not specifically an issue of academic freedom but comprised part of general attacks on freedom in the society. Even in these cases, the same general principle applies: physicists were less likely to be harassed by the McCarthy-type probes than were Chinese experts (or State Department officials); the greatest attacks were always delivered on those fields with the greatest consequences for policy and which were most vulnerable due to the lack of a clear criterion of purely scholarly evaluation.[54]

The places where conflicts are most likely to occur have generally been in the less prominent universities; with the exception of Pennsylvania, Yale, and Smith, none of the major private or state universities were censured by the A.A.U.P. from its founding in 1915 to 1953. Otherwise, those censured included approximately random proportions of universities and colleges of every size, geographical location, and form of control.[55]

This shows that in no case has there been a general clash about principles of academic freedom in the society as a whole. The clashes occurred in new fields or in fields which were put to a new type of use. These new enterprises

52. Robert MacIver, op. cit., 1955, pp. 132–34.
53. Hofstadter and Metzger, op. cit., pp. 495–505.
54. Price, op. cit., pp. 109–10.
55. Hofstadter and Metzger, op. cit., p. 493.

were suggested either by the outside community or by the scholars and scientists. Hence, they could not count on having experts in the area in crucial civil service or other elite positions to serve as an effective buffer between the academics and politics. When a new kind of enterprise crops up, such a class of people in the new field simply cannot exist yet. They may be produced within a generation or two: until then the two sides to the enterprise may very well collide. In Europe this type of conflict was prevented by (a) a much greater apprehensiveness and caution in introducing such potentially "dangerous" fields as economics and social sciences into the universities; (b) the fact that where introduced, they were defined in a sufficiently abstract way as to make the drawing of practical conclusions out of place (after all academics were defined as intellectuals who should keep away from practice), whereas in the United States the academic is constantly challenged to do something practical; and (c) universities being elite institutions controlled by a central elite, and appointments being few, so that "unsuitable" persons are usually screened out in advance, especially in new and risky fields, or are put into positions where—as shown above—they constitute a harmless minority of one.

The second kind of factor contributing to conflict in the expert sysem is that the line between what is and what is not a university cannot easily be drawn, since the burden of the proof is on those who want to exclude something from it. They would have to prove why research and training in a new field cannot produce desirable results, or why giving freedoms usually given to creative people would harm the level of teaching of a faculty which had never attempted to create very much. Thus, there is a constant extension of academic freedom to categories of institutions which in elite systems would never be considered as academic institutions. Where the burden of the proof is on those who want to be admitted to the academic rank, and the question typically posed is whether the new field or the school lives up to the highest standards, exclusion is the legitimate procedure in case of doubt. The German universities resisted the granting of academic status to institutes of technology (they were granted this status by the government in spite of the universities), and much of the engineering and professional training in England has taken place in schools or in apprenticeship programs which were not considered academic at all.[56] The "expert" universities, therefore, are under pressure to expand and enter into risky marginal fields and thus are more in danger of getting into situations of "nonmodel," where either some of the research activities and/or the character of the expanding teaching and student body is such that it impresses the legislatures and/or the public as going beyond the accepted aim and character of the university.

The background of the conflicts between politicians and universities about military secrecy and diplomatic interests is of the same kind. These conflicts

56. A. Flexner, op. cit., pp. 330–31.

did not lead to attack on academic freedom in Europe because there this type of work has not been performed in the universities (whether the work concerns the manufacture of the hydrogen bomb or the policy toward China) but in properly constituted, centrally controlled civil service establishments. Thus, the taking of chances was to a large extent prevented in advance, and such problems as still arose could be dealt with as a civil service rather than an academic affair. In the United States, universities and other independent academic institutions have been charged with these tasks and have in fact suggested most of them. Some of these tasks involved the creation of new types of specialists, others, the use of old ones in tasks with which there had been no previous experience and in numbers which created a scarcity. To organize matters so as to ensure in advance proper control and communication between the experts and the politicians through an elite capable of serving as mediators—and to repeat this on the different local levels of a decentralized system—would have greatly retarded or entirely prevented developments. This is not to justify the stupidity and cruelty of the attacks on scholars and scientists. On the other hand, academic freedom cannot be used to prevent the legislature or the donor from making up their own minds even at the risk of committing a mistake. Such situations, even given the best intentions and maximum wisdom, involve legitimate conflict, controversy, and trial and error which may represent an interference with academic freedom. But it is a moot question whether a situation in which the academic has the opportunity to pioneer new fields, at the risk of getting involved in undignified conflict, means more or less freedom than where he is prevented from such conflicts by being confined to a closely guarded ivory tower.

Some of the interference with academic freedom in the USSR—though not the barbaric methods which were applied to resolve the issue—arose under comparable conditions. The Lysenko controversy was originally the result of dissatisfaction with the failure of geneticists to find a way to eliminate a potato disease which was of very great importance for the economy. Support given for applied research was—justifiably—used for the solution of basic problems, and the researchers were accused of dishonesty and of deliberate sabotage of the economy. The accusations were supported by a disgruntled old-fashioned member of the profession, in a field of study which had undergone revolutionary change shortly before the events.[57] In every respect the situation is comparable to what happened at the University of Illinois concerning Keynesian economics. Both cases were scandalous, and the Russian case was a much more cruel scandal than the United States one. But controversies of this kind are inevitable. Had the result been temporary rescinding of funds, it

57. David Joravsky, "The Lysenko Affair," *Scientific American* 204 (November 1962): 41–49.

would have been part of the risk that enterprising research, like all other enterprise, always has to take.

As all these instances show, the typical problem of freedom in the expert university is limited at one time to a certain selected field, is connected with a specific topic or method in that field (statistical genetics, antitrust theories, Keynesian economics, Chinese specialists in political science, etc.), and arises as a result of an academic innovation or of drastic changes in the economy or politics involving the applications of those specific studies. Thus, even though there may be political conflicts, they are too specific to become ideological ones. They do not involve the principle of free enquiry, or even the basic organization of the university. The attacks are on selected members of the faculty, or on selected departments, or research institutes, concerning issues which are in some doubt, and the greater the doubt, the more likely there will be conflicts. They may result in the victimization of certain people or the reduction of funds for some kinds of research or both. The danger resulting from this for the academic profession as a whole and the advancement of science in general is that it tends to introduce an element of incalculable and unpredictable risk in the work of the scientist, thus making the profession unattractive and suppressing, both as a result of short-term fear and long-term selection, creative pioneering.

The typical means of fighting this danger has been through defensive legal measures of collective agreements and contracts about tenure. An important role in the promotion of academic freedom in the United States has been played by the A.A.U.P., which is, in everything but its name, a kind of trade union. It has not been engaged in salary negotiations, but it has brought pressure on universities to raise salaries; it has no collective contract, but it tries to enforce common patterns of contracts safeguarding the professional autonomy of the academic profession.[58]

The working of the market is probably an even more important safeguard. Where academics are an elite, they are treated like a luxury, and their professional freedom is a privilege. Where they are widely used, they are a necessity and command a price. Attacks on them making the profession riskier are bound to be counteracted by raising the pay and status—and in consequence the autonomy—of the scientists. It is quite likely that in the not even so long run American scientists in general have benefited economically from the McCarthy attack and those at the University of California in particular from the loyalty oath controversy. (This may also explain the extremely high pay and extraordinary privileges of scientists in the USSR, relative to the rest of the populace.)

The conflict in the expert-type university between those supporting the uni-

---

58. Hofstadter and Metzger, op. cit., pp. 468–506.

versity and the professionals working in it is therefore of the same type as that occurring in governmental or industrial organizations which employ scientists. Although the fact that the principal product of the universities is what the scientists do, so that their interests are more likely to be given priority over other interests, their specific output is often supposed to be useful for practical purposes and, therefore, to some extent subject to outside scrutiny and criticism. Professional autonomy has therefore to be constantly redefined. Twenty, thirty, or fifty years ago the claims of the economists for professional autonomy were challenged, partly because the subject was less developed and partly because the outsiders who had to form an opinion about it received conflicting guidance about it. Today such conflicts about economics in America are inconceivable, since professionally trained economists abound in business and government, thus creating a model and serving as effective mediators between academics and politicians. A similar change has probably taken place in Soviet genetics during the last ten years and is not unlikely to take place in the near future in Soviet economics.

The basic problem of students and nonacademic intellectuals in the elite systems, namely, that they face an authoritative elite—in intellectual and other spheres—which may block their advancement and restrict the scope of their enterprise, does not exist in the expert systems. Since the intellectual situation is not defined in terms of a unidimensional hierarchy, it is unlikely to generate a sense of oppression such as may arise where an official body of intellectuals controls and restricts opportunities for other intellectuals. It is unlikely, therefore, that any discontent arising in such a situation will be formulated in terms of generalized ideologies.

Discontent which may arise will tend to center about problems of instruction and other conditions prevailing at the university, or about the share of the students, a growing and distinct social group, in political power. The specificity of the training may turn into pedantry of a not very inspiring kind. This is a distinct possibility and quite widespread in the lower-grade American and Soviet institutions. Since, however, this will be serious only in the weaker institutions, it will not affect the totality of students. Besides, these are technical matters which can be dealt with locally and in an open competitive system and are unlikely to reach very serious proportions. There may be an acceptance of a great deal of regulation in this system without being justifiably considered as a violation of the freedom of the student.

One would not expect in these systems the existence of widespread resentment or even of a significant politically conscious student movement. Student dissatisfaction with the relative deprivation of undergraduate teaching would generally manifest itself in such things as riotous behavior, which are problems of discipline but not of academic freedom. Of course, where there is general political oppression students and intellectuals may show greater sensitivity and display more activity for reform than others irrespective of the type of university, but these will not be generated by conditions prevailing at the university, nor will they be directed toward changes in the university.

Conclusion

Academic freedom is, on the one hand, a professional role pattern implying that those engaged in higher learning and creative research use their personal discretion and initiative to determine their work subject only to standards accepted by their own profession. In this sense academic freedom is a widespread phenomenon, known in all literate societies. On the other hand, the term refers to the organization of specialized institutions engaged in teaching and research in an expanding range of fields. Organization implies certain constraints in exchange for gains in efficiency. And an expanding range involves a procedure for the granting of facilities for new kinds of work and new types of people. The method originally adopted to administer the organizational facilities and make the decisions consistent with the autonomy of the professional pattern was a guildlike corporation. It has been shown that in the best case this created conservatism and some inefficiency in the expansion of the uses of learning and research, and in the worst cases it resulted in abuse or misuse of privilege.

It seems, therefore, that development toward some kind of an expert system is inevitable. The loss of freedom involved in this is deceptive: it is like the loss of "freedom" of the guilds which was inefficient privilege enjoyed at the expense of others. The means appropriate to protect the freedom of the role pattern in the new system are not corporate (i.e., faculty) government but contracts, some kind of unionization to resist organized pressure, and the opportunities and responsibilities of a market.

With the rise of this type of university, the crucial role of students and intellectuals in ideological politics will probably pass. Emerging student politics are likely to be concerned with the redefinition of the rights and duties of a student body which is greater in relative size, older in age, and spending more of its life at universities than previous generations of students and which both studies and, increasingly works, at universities which perform more productive work. Of course, with the growth of the proportion of students among the voting age population, their political influence is bound to grow. But again, this is not likely to result in a particular brand of ideological student politics but in the kind of pressure that other well-defined and able social groups exert on politics.

Part III

Questions of Policy

The Planning of Science and the Utilization
of Scientific Knowledge in Practice

Introduction

The papers assembled in Parts I and II elaborate an encompassing theoretical view of the functioning of science. This view of science has quite definite implications for questions concerning matters of policy, and the following three papers explore some of them.

"Scientific Research and Economic Growth" is a chapter from a report written in 1968 at the invitation of the OECD (see [3] in the Bibliography). This report described the scientific gap between the United States and Western Europe and sought to explain it by reference to the institutional frameworks in which research is done in these countries. It argues that the strength of U.S. science is due to the emergence there of what Ben-David calls here an "entrepreneurial system" of higher education and research. This view implies that, as a matter of policy, science must largely be left to develop autonomously, according to the state of knowledge in each field. But this view seems to be inconsistent with one of the rationales usually invoked to justify the ever-growing expenditure on science, namely, that science can be directed to socially useful purposes. Here Ben-David rejects the argument and, on the basis of a sociological analysis of the communities involved (the scientific and the technological), argues that the application of fundamental research can be neither planned nor systematic. Rather "practical uses of science should be conceived as the results of chance interactions between fundamental discoveries, on the one hand, and practical interests, on the other, which can occur in an infinite variety of ways." The two following papers take up the two aspects of the problems raised here: the possibility of planning science and the social mechanism required for successfully applying fundamental knowledge to practical purposes.

The question whether science can and should be planned has been debated since the 1930s. A three-volume OECD report published between 1972 and 1974 provided Ben-David with an opportunity to discuss the issue from his own perspective. "The Central Planning of Science" (1977) concludes that "permanent and comprehensive planning of science and technology is a futile, and in the long run, harmful method. This is not only a summary of the evidence; it is also what one would expect on the basis of theoretical considerations." Ben-David analyzes the American and European postwar experience in planning science and argues that its apparent successes are due not to the fact of planning but rather to exceptionally favorable research opportunities. His general conclusion is "that the main condition of scientific and technical innovation is the existence of a variety of effective institutions, such as universities, research institutes, and business firms using advanced technology, which are free to go their way and make their own decisions, capable, and motivated presumably by competition to recruit the best possible scientists and provide them with means, the incentives, and the atmosphere needed for creative work." The really important problem is, therefore, "how to reconcile the role of government as the preponderant source of financial support with the existence of autonomous and enterprising scientific institutions."

The notion that science is—and should be—an autonomous enterprise poses the question of how some fundamental knowledge is, after all, transferred to those who apply it to practical purposes (medical practitioners, technologists, etc.). In addition, the sociologist of science is expected to say whether this process of knowledge transfer can be ameliorated. These questions are addressed in "Scientific Societies, Professional Organizations, and the Creation and Dissemination of Practical Knowledge" (1982). The theoretical argument of the first part of the paper is founded on the notion of the scientist's role: a scientist who turns to practical problems will usually cut himself off from his disciplinary scientific community and thus cease to be a basic scientist. This implies that trying to induce fundamental scientists to work on practical problems will harm science without, in the long run, being beneficial to practice. However, it would seem that the social role of people working solely on the solution of a specific problem cannot be viable, for there is no continuity in research on such problems. Nonetheless, the examination of two case studies suggests a type of professional association in which practitioners and scientists can cooperate: where the necessary conditions for its existence obtain, such an association can be extremely efficient in the creation and dissemination of practical, scientifically grounded knowledge.

Scientific Research and Economic Growth 11

Before proceeding to recommendations, it is desirable to explore some-what further the relationship between fundamental research and its practical uses. As has been shown, countries which are unable to turn science to practical uses will not be able to finance fundamental research on an up-to-date level, however much they appreciate science for its own sake. Of course, they can give up science, but then it is unlikely that they will be able to maintain a viable national culture. They must, therefore, do their best to exploit science for economic purposes. But this may be very difficult, since trying to make science more useful for practice in the commonsense way, by preferring research projects with obvious practical applications, will be self-defeating.

The solution which has been indicated by the survey of European and United States developments is scientific enterpreneurship. This means regarding science as a resource to be developed according to its immanent potentialities and to be marketed as widely and as imaginatively as possible.

Here an attempt will be made to work out the rationale of the entrepreneurial approach. First it will be shown that investigations of the relationship between scientific research and technological growth are consistent with the view that there is no direct relationship between specific kinds of fundamental research and the eventual application of the findings in practice and that success in exploiting science for practical purposes does not, therefore, result from the guidance of fundamental research by practical considerations but from constant entrepreneurial activity aimed at bringing to the attention of potential users whatever may be relevant for them in science, and vice versa. Subsequently it will be shown that the entrepreneurial approach is also the one indicated by the social structure which evolved in scientific and technological work.

The relationship between scientific research and technological growth has been viewed in two ways. Everyone agrees that science may benefit technology; but according to one view, such benefits are a matter of random chance, and expenditure on research is therefore considered as consumption and not as investment. The other, currently more favored, view regards the existence of a systematic relationship between scientific and technological growth as proved, and expenditure on science is therefore considered an investment. It will be suggested here that the existence or absence of a systematic positive relationship between scientific and technological growth is not something given and inherent in the nature of the case but a state determined by entrepreneurial activity and certain other conditions still to be identified.

The assumption of the economic importance of research derives from calculations which show that if one wants to account for the output of different national economies in terms of all the known inputs from the traditional factors of production, there still remains a large unaccounted for residue.[1] It is assumed that this represents the contribution from the growth of useful knowledge. This knowledge, however, may consist of technological or organizational improvements, or the quality and extent of education. There is a whole host of examples bearing out this contention. The industrial revolution in England, or the rapid industrial development of Belgium and the United States in the last century and of Japan in this century, had not been preceded by any noticeable upsurge in scientific research, fundamental or applied. Japanese industry has done very well, in spite of the adverse balance of Japan's trade in technological know-how. A recent study of patents in the United States by J. Schmookler has produced very strong and systematic evidence that technological innovation in four important industries, railroads, agriculture, petroleum refining, and paper making, occurred in response to economic demand and *not* as a spin-off of fundamental research.[2]

Even in technologies which are directly and undoubtedly derived from scientific research, the practical exploitation of the results does not necessarily take place in the same country where the fundamental work was performed. A good example is provided by the applications of nuclear energy. This outstanding science-based technology of recent times derives directly from fundamental research in physics conducted between about 1900 and 1940, mainly in Western Europe. The practical applications of this research, however, took place to a much larger extent in the United States and in the USSR. Of the Western European countries which played an important role in the fundamental work, only Britain then proceeded to do important applied work.

1. Cf. E. F. Denison, "Measuring the Contribution of Education (and the Residual) to Economic Growth," in *Study Group in the Economics of Education. The Residual Factor and Economic Growth* (Paris: OECD, 1964), pp. 13–100.
2. Jacob Schmookler, *Invention and Economic Growth* (Cambridge: Harvard University Press, 1966), esp. pp. 165–78.

All this does not contradict the econometric conclusions about the residual factor in economic growth or the long-range importance of scientific research and dissemination of scientific knowledge in economic growth. It does, however, suggest that at least until recently there has been a very poor relationship between the place and the time of the production of basic scientific ideas, on the one hand, and the reaping of technological and economic benefits from it, on the other. In fact, one possible way of interpreting the evidence would be that, from the point of view of the expectation of economic returns, fundamental research is a bad and unjustifiable investment for any given country since the possibility that its results can be turned into useful technological applications is unpredictable, and it is particularly difficult to predict whether the applications will benefit the economy of the same country or those of its competitors. (Had international trade been as free as scientific communication is, this would, of course, not matter.)

From such an interpretation it would follow that, provided economic gain were the only consideration, the best policy for each country would be to reduce its expenditure on basic research to the minimum necessary for the training of people capable of "parasitizing" the results of research done elsewhere. In practice this would imply considerable expenditure on scientific education at the secondary and higher level, with just enough overhead for research to maintain the efficiency of the latter.

There is, therefore, no reason to assume the existence of a generally positive relationship between fundamental research and industrial growth. It seems, however, that there *has* been such a direct relationship in some countries, such as in Germany during the second half of the nineteenth century before the effects of the rigidity of its science organization had become felt and in the United States today.[3] The findings of Schmookler, as well as the impression from the historical cases, show that these cases have not been due to the effective guidance of fundamental work by criteria of applicability but have been the result of effective entrepreneurship (and, presumably, such related conditions as the size of the market).

The Sociological Aspect

We shall turn now to the sociological aspect of the problem and try to show that the entrepreneurial approach is also more consistent with the way research is actually performed and turned to practical uses than the common-

---

3. For Germany's research in industry, cf. D. S. L. Cardwell, "The Development of Scientific Research in Modern Universities: A Comparative Study of Motives and Opportunities," in A. C. Crombie (ed.), *Scientific Change* (London: Heinemann, 1963), pp. 675–76, and L. F. Haber, *The Chemical Industry During the Nineteenth Century* (Oxford: Clarendon Press, 1958), pp. 128–36.

sense approach. At least so far, scientists have found it more congenial to be guided by the logically inherent problems and methodologically determined potentialities of a "paradigm" common to a group of scientists (a scientific community) than by considerations of practical use. They have become stale and sterile when subjected in their work to extraneous considerations over a prolonged period of time. They worry about the solution of logical problems, and their scale of priorities is, and has to be (if science is to be good), determined by the intrinsic intellectual qualities of the problem and not by its practical usefulness.[4] This is not true of technologists, for whom practical efficiency matters, and who for that reason often have the same aims as businessmen. There is, in fact, an uninterrupted social continuity between technologists, on the one hand, and businessmen, on the other, as both tend to merge into management.

Accordingly, scientists in a given field usually have reliable estimates of the quality and prospects of the work done in their respective fields but are not particularly well informed about the prospects of technological applications of the work in their field and are not concerned with its economic potentialities. The converse is true of technologists and businessmen. It is unlikely, therefore, that the actual relationship between fundamental science and its eventual applications in productive technology should be of the kind that one tends to imagine on the basis of logical reconstructions after the event. These reconstructions, biased by the language habit which speaks of "application," make the technological invention appear as if "implied" in the fundamental discovery. Once the latter is made, it is only a matter of correct "application" to exploit these "implications" for practical purposes.

In fact, nothing is "implied" in a discovery beyond the questions answered by it and those to which it is related by the traditions and mental habits of the people who are its prime consumers. The circle or "community" of these "prime consumers" is very limited. According to the estimates of Price the scientific community in any field does not contain more than a few hundred active members all over the world (this in addition to such passive users of science as students, teachers, professionals, and occasional amateurs). The reason for this is that it is impossible to follow the work of a more extended group. Hence, efficiency requires the isolation and the limitation of the span of attention of scientific communities from each other.[5]

It would be even more senseless to try and link these small scientific communities to what can be called a "technological community." Very rarely is such a community directly and overwhelmingly linked to a field of enquiry practiced by a scientific community. Engineers, physicians, or other profes-

4. Cf. W. O. Hagstrom, *The Scientific Community* (New York: Free Press of Glencoe, 1962), pp. 9–58.

5. On the size and dynamics of the "invisible colleges," cf. D. J. de Solla Price, *Little Science, Big Science* (New York: Columbia University Press, 1963), pp. 62–91.

sionals making use of science for practical purposes have a range of problems, theories, methods, and techniques which consist of (a) the use of scientific elements in ways peculiar to that community; (b) traditions which are based only on experience; and (c) business practices concerning the marketing and the use of their products and services.[6]

The separation of the scientific from the technological and business communities explains the absence of direct links between fundamental and applied research. Of course it can, and has been, argued that this separation is not an optimal state of affairs and that by redrawing the boundaries of these communities, a better background would be created for the practical exploitation of research.

Furthermore, it can be pointed out, with a great deal of justification, that the difficulty of establishing a link between fundamental and applied work is not symmetrical. The link from economic and technological problems to fundamental research is more predictable than from fundamental research to economically useful technological innovation. As the range of science is much more limited than that of productive technology, it is easier to see which branch of science is relevant for the solution of any technological problem. Of course, from the point of view of any given branch of science, the problem may be trivial in the context of existing paradigms. Still, a technologist in search of a solution to a basic problem will more easily find the proper address where to obtain either the answer or the definitive denial of the answer than the basic scientist in search of a profitable application of his ideas.

The question, however, is not whether it is possible to redraw here and there the boundaries between some given scientific and technological communities or where to turn for consultation. There have been, and there probably will be in the future, cases of instant match between science and technology. But the restriction of research to such rare instances of immediate technological relevance would slow down the growth of scientific knowledge and make research extremely inefficient. Obvious leads to discoveries which might revolutionize broad fields of knowledge would be passed over for minor technological solutions, because there would be no professional scientists to pursue leads of merely theoretical significance. In the long run this would also be economically inefficient. Important theoretical advances usually have great indirect practical potentialities which can be exploited if there are entrepreneurs bringing them to the attention of technologists and others who may be concerned. But technological solutions, even if they have great potentialities for generalization, will hardly reach that stage in the absence of professional scientists whose job is to theorize and generalize.

6. For an analysis of the isolation of the community of medical researchers from that of medical practitioners, cf. L. Aran and J. Ben-David, "Socialization and Career Patterns as Determinants of Productivity of Medical Researchers," *Journal of Health and Human Behavior* 9, no. 1 (1968): 3–15. [This volume, chap. 3.]

With the exception of countries which are content to "parasitize" the results of fundamental research performed elsewhere,[7] the optimal way to increase the uses of science is, therefore, not to select projects according to their supposed promise of applicability but to increase the motivation and the opportunities to find uses for science and to find practical problems which can stimulate research. The relationship between fundamental and applied research should not be visualized as a series of separate links between certain fundamental discoveries and their "applications." Rather, practical uses of science should be conceived as the result of chance interactions between fundamental discoveries, on the one hand, and practical interests, on the other, which can occur in an infinite variety of ways. The purpose of policy should, therefore, be to influence the likelihood of these chance occurrences by increasing the density of both kinds of activities and the velocity of the circulation of ideas and problems from both areas of activity in spaces which ensure interaction. Increasing the density is a matter of investment, velocity is the result of entrepreneurship, and creating the properly enclosed spaces is a task for organization.

These, by the way, are not only the means for a utilitarian but also for an idealistic science policy interested first and foremost in the augmentation of scientific knowledge for its own sake. Such a science policy would still have to find the resources to finance research and thus it would have to take an interest in the practical uses of science. It makes, therefore, little difference whether economic considerations or scientific knowledge is considered as the more important social value: both scales of preference indicate the same practical policies.

7. Which can be to some extent afforded by countries from which migration of scientists and intellectuals is barred either by force or great national differences.

The Central Planning **12** of Science

The question whether science could or should be planned and directed by governments was the subject of a famous debate which took place in Britain during the 1930s. The arguments put forward at that time by J. D. Bernal in favor of planning and M. Polanyi in favor of the freedom of the scientific community were classic statements of the two points of view.[1]

However, as it usually happens in the social sciences, events overtake and outrun theory, and then theory is forgotten and has to be rediscovered again at a latter stage when the need for it arises. This is what happened also in the present case: the success of wartime and postwar research and development projects, and the subsequent generous support of research by the governments of all the industrially advanced countries, seemed to have shelved the debate until the late sixties. Governments accepted responsibility for research, and this worked reasonably well, so there was no question whether research should be planned and supported, only how this should be done.

Today there is a new despondency about science. Advanced technologies, like atomic energy plants, or new fields of biological research, like recombinant DNA research, are considered by many people as dark threats to society. There is much doubt and criticism about governmental support of research and actual cuts in support. Questions about what governments should do about science, which used to be raised in the thirties, are being raised again. It is therefore useful to investigate what has been learned or can be learned on

This paper was first printed in *Minerva* in 1977. I am deeply indebted to Professor Edward Shils, the editor, for his comments and suggestions on the first draft of the paper.

1. See J. D. Bernal, *The Social Function of Science* (London: Routledge and Kegan Paul, 1939); and Michael Polanyi, *The Logic of Liberty* (London: Routledge and Kegan Paul, 1951).

the subject from the postwar experience and how these new lessons relate to the classic debate between Bernal and Polanyi on the feasibility and desirability of planning.

An excellent opportunity to do this has been provided a few years ago in an OECD publication entitled *The Research System.*[2]

This work—begun in 1970 and completed in 1974—was originally undertaken as a follow-up to the Third Ministerial Meeting on Science of the OECD countries in March 1968. One of the conclusions of that meeting was that

> the development of fundamental research, particularly in Europe, encounters various difficulties. Outstanding among the difficulties which were indicated were the inflexibility of funding procedures, dispersion of effort, the difficulty of integrating research in interdisciplinary and borderline fields within traditional university structures, the lack of an established research policy on the part of institutions of higher education, obstacles to the mobility of scientists both within and between countries, and the lack of reliable statistical data as a basis for planning.

This conclusion was supported by a number of studies, showing that scientific research in Europe and Japan was backward compared to that in the United States and suggesting that this backwardness had economically harmful consequences.[3] There was also much concern at that time with the migration of scientists to the United States—the so-called brain drain—and the countries affected by it tended to view this migration as a threat to their economic resources, somewhat like a negative balance of payments.[4]

The purpose of the present study was to find out what were the causes of the relative lack of innovation and enterprise in European and Japanese uni-

---

2. See *The Research System: Comparative Survey of the Organization and Financing of Fundamental Research:* vol. 1: *France, Germany, United Kingdom,* by G. Caty, G. Drilhon, G. Ferné, and S. Wald under the direction of J.-J. Salomon (Paris: OECD, 1972), 258 pp.; vol. 2: *Belgium, Netherlands, Sweden, Switzerland,* by G. Caty, G. Drilhon, R. Enoch, G. Ferné, M. Flory, and S. Wald under the direction of J.-J. Salomon (Paris: OECD, 1973), 195 pp.; vol. 3: *Canada, United States, General Conclusions,* by G. Caty, G. Drilhon, G. Ferné, N. Kaplan, and S. Wald under the direction of J.-J. Salomon (Paris: OECD, 1974), 226 pp.

3. See Edward F. Denison, *The Sources of Economic Growth in the United States and the Alternatives Before Us,* Supplementary Paper no. 13 (New York: Committee for Economic Development, 1962); C. Freeman and A. Young, *The Research and Development Effort in Western Europe, North America and the Soviet Union; An Experimental International Comparison of Research Expenditures and Manpower in 1962* (Paris: OECD, 1965); Organisation for Economic Cooperation and Development, *The Technological Gap between OECD Member Countries* (Paris: OECD, 1968); and *Gaps in Technology,* prepared by participants to the Third Ministerial Meeting on Science (Paris: OECD, 1968).

4. See Harry G. Johnson, "The Economics of the 'Brain Drain': The Canadian Case," *Minerva* 3, 3 (Spring 1965): 299–311; Charles V. Kidd, "The Economics of the 'Brain Drain,'" *Minerva* 4, 1 (Autumn 1965): 105–07; Harry G. Johnson, "The Economics of the 'Brain Drain,'" *Minerva* 4, 2 (Winter 1966): 273–74; Brinley Thomas, "The International Circulation of Human Capital," *Minerva* 5, 4 (Summer 1967): 479–506; Walter Adams (ed.), *The Brain Drain* (New York: Macmillan, 1968).

versities and research organizations compared with the American ones. The emphasis was to be on fundamental research which was perceived as the main determinant also of the quality of applied research. But the authors considered that all types of research constituted a system and decided to study them all. Starting with the three major countries of Western Europe—France, Germany, and the United Kingdom—they planned to analyze the "systems" of most of the smaller Western European countries—Belgium, the Netherlands, Norway, Sweden, and Switzerland—and finally those of Canada, Japan, and the United States. Apart from the omission of Japan, all the other countries were included in the study as planned. The first and second volumes, which are devoted to the European countries, deal in different chapters with the organization and financing of research in the academic, governmental, and industrial sector, and the second volume also contains a chapter, "The Place of the Foundations in the Research System." Each chapter contains an excellent description and discussion of the arrangements in these different sectors in all the countries dealt with in the volume. This procedure leads to an emphasis on the characteristics common to the similar sectors in all these national systems, but there is little integration of the information on the different sectors in each country into a picture of the national "research system" of each country. Those interested in the general working of the "research system" of, say, France or Switzerland, will have to piece together this information for themselves from the different chapters and will probably have to have recourse also to other literature, especially the useful series of *Reviews of National Science Policy* also published by the OECD.

At the end of the second volume there is an attempt to compare the effectiveness of the different national systems. The impression of the authors is that—among all the European countries—the Netherlands, Switzerland, and Sweden did best in research, as well as its industrial applications. This is an interesting conclusion, since—unlike all the other European governments—the governments of these countries did little to stimulate research during the 1950s and the 1960s. They contented themselves with supporting universities and—if interested in particular items, such as military equipment in Sweden—to contracting with industry for the necessary research. With some exceptions in the field of nuclear research, these countries had no large governmental laboratories for big science and technology projects or—with few exceptions—institutions for complementing fundamental research at the universities. Among the most important institutions have been the main engineering schools which have maintained their excellence and nurtured close relations with industrial research for generations.

This is not to say that everything was found to be satisfactory in these three countries. According to *The Research System,* the universities are in many cases extremely conservative, opposed to research which does not fit into the traditional disciplines, and altogether lacking in initiative and enterprise.

And, their governmental research institutes in agriculture and other traditional fields are often dated and ineffective. But much of the potential harm from the ineffectiveness of the universities is undone by the openness of these systems to foreign research, particularly to their close links through exchange of teachers, research workers, and students with the United States.

Notwithstanding these conclusions, the authors do not recommend the continuation of the noninterventionist policies of the governments of these small countries. They believe that in many fields permanent research teams and facilities of the kind which only specialized institutes can offer are needed and that universities (including institutes of technology) primarily concerned with teaching and professional training neglect important lines of research—especially in physics—which are expensive and accessible to only a few advanced research workers. They insist that research can no longer be allowed to concentrate on specific intellectual or technological problems but rather has "to meet all the aspirations of society." For all these reasons—the authors conclude—"the scientific laissez-faire of past years seems to be doomed." Considering what they say about the Netherlands, Sweden, and Switzerland, this is a somewhat surprising conclusion. But, as will be seen, this is not actually a conclusion of the first two volumes but rather an introduction to the third.

In this last volume—dealing with Canada and the United States—there is a drastic change in the perspective of the inquiry. Instead of asking how to support research effectively, the question here is why it should be supported at all.

The shift of emphasis is no coincidence. The American organization of research has been a system in a different sense than those of the European countries. As has been pointed out, during the 1950s and 1960s research policy in every country of the world was deeply influenced by American developments. The United States possessed a set of thriving universities and industrial, governmental, and research laboratories which were in advance of similar institutions anywhere else in the world. American scientists were also in advance of their colleagues elsewhere—with the partial exception of Britain—in practically all the branches of science. And this advanced American science was linked at that time to the most successful industry and agriculture, the strongest military forces, and the most dynamic democratic government in the world. It trained the scientists and technologists necessary to run the system; some of the most conspicuous military and industrial products were based on relatively new scientific discoveries; and there was a lively exchange of ideas between scientists and others concerning policies of science and the uses of science. Economists were deeply involved in the conduct of government, scientists in the planning of weapons systems, the development of an entirely new electronics industry, and the exploration of space. It seemed that the United States was well on its way to realizing the utopia of an enlightened democracy in which science, policy, and education were harmoniously linked in order to produce a progressively wealthy and free society.

Given this impression, it was "natural" to perceive the situation in the United States as a system possessing a goal and inner logic of its own and to hold it up as a model for the other countries. The world of science—or perhaps the world of national societies as a whole—was perceived as consisting of one system which worked reasonably well and other systems which worked less well.[5] This defined the task of international organizations, such as many United Nations agencies, international scientific societies, and above all the OECD, as an endeavor to help the other systems to catch up with the model— American—system. As long as the American model worked well, and there were no competing models of equal attraction, the OECD followed the American model. This provided the Organization with a clear goal toward which to work; there was a large degree of consensus concerning this goal within the Organization and among the civil servants of the member countries, and the problem was how to devise ways and means to attain this goal. The workers of the OECD were mainly Europeans, attached to their own cultures, and more often than not critical and suspicious of some features of American life. But as far as science and technology were concerned, they considered the United States as highly successful in the attainment of the particular goals which they shared, such as continuous technological and economic growth, and the furtherance of scientific inquiry and universal educational opportunity. Therefore, they accepted the United States as a model or touchstone for scientific and technological development in the world.

But in 1968 the American system ceased to expand and even took a slight downward turn. The violent agitation in the universities against the continuation of the Vietnam war and the hostility against the science and technology associated with it were dramatic outbursts, and in the beginning it was not realized by observers that it was part of a wider and longer-lasting current of distrust toward science and technology. By 1973 it became evident that the situation of science and technology had changed. It was realized that the almost continuous economic growth involving very powerful technology in the Western countries since the Second World War depended on a precipitously rising energy consumption and that the long-term supply of energy was not ensured. Even apart from that, Western economies which had behaved so effectively since the end of the war began to become unpredictable and difficult to manage. And the agitation about the Vietnam war was not simply about a campaign started by mistake and poorly conducted, it was an accompaniment and prelude to a real crisis in the unity and the political resolve of the Western democracies.

There was to different degrees in various parts of the intellectual and political leadership of the Western countries a concomitant loss of confidence in the social and economic utility of science in general and of basic science in particular. As the authors point out, there occurred a "change of attitude in the

5. See J.-J. Servan-Schreiber, *The American Challenge* (New York: Atheneum, 1968).

OECD countries towards science and technology" and not only a "simple change of perspective of the authors" (III, p. 167). Many began to blame science and technology as the sources of nuclear threat and air and water pollution; there were fears of worse dangers to come from the manipulation of genetic material; and an impression that advanced technologies were based on the use of exhaustible sources of energy. The authors of the book are right; the OECD changed as opinion changed, and as before, it expressed its views with a trenchancy which ran beyond the more general body of opinion.

When the book on the United States—which had set the direction and the standard for science policies everywhere—came to be written, and the goals of those earlier policies were scrutinized, they were no longer appreciated. The affairs of science were in disarray, and many persons were in search of new goals and new policies in the United States, too. This change in a way destroyed the basis of the two first volumes. If it were not sure that it was worthwhile to master the new science-based technologies, to try to develop new ones, and to advance basic science in general, then the effectiveness of the organizations and procedures designed to promote science in different countries was no longer the most important question of science policy. This is how the emphasis in this volume shifted from the earlier question of how to support science to that of why it should be supported. The idea that the growth of science was a desirable goal in itself was rejected. The support of science had to be guided by social considerations, and the question was how to distinguish between different kinds of research according to some criterion of the social interest.

This change of mind and the attendant recommendations are—from a practical point of view—the most important part of the book, since they reflect the current views of science policy experts in the OECD countries. The reconsiderations contain sharp criticism of the policies of the 1960s, because of their failure to foresee and forestall the present difficulties, although it must be said that the OECD also failed to foresee and forestall them. Governments of the large countries concentrated their main efforts at that time on a race for the exploitation of certain scientific-technological opportunities, which appealed on grounds of military utility and national prestige, especially on large nuclear and space projects, and in Europe on the development of computers. This proved a narrow and unhealthy program for science, not only because these programs were bound to be rapidly fulfilled but also because of the skepticism about the very utility of such large scientific-technological schemes. Many persons are now much more cautious about apparently attractive technological opportunities and are inclined to ask searching questions about their possibly harmful effects.

But the authors are equally disappointed with the results of the support for basic science, which the different governments supported as a generalized resource out of which new inventions would arise. The accelerated growth of graduate schools and research projects in the United States and elsewhere did not have the expected effect of stimulating greater technological and economic growth but has led to increased expenditures on higher education and graduate unemployment. And in continental Europe—the authors say—all the innovations and dynamism of the past decades have not been able to eliminate what they allege to be the rigidities and inefficiences of the universities and the datedness of the older governmental research laboratories. In particular, universities are accused of failing to support "interdisciplinary research," which the authors consider as an essential characteristic of most socially useful research. In fact—they argue—American universities are not significantly better in this respect than their European counterparts. Thus, the support of a broad range of free basic research has produced a growth of disciplines but not socially useful results.

Therefore—the book concludes—the time has come for comprehensive technological planning and the establishment of long-term science policies designed to support these technological plans. These could—in the authors' view—prevent dangerous fluctuations in the support of science, establish socially useful and acceptable priorities for research and development, and effectively reform institutions which are incapable of adapting themselves to changing needs. The agencies charged with these widely ranging tasks of planning and coordination would have to combine policymakers and scientists, the former willing to "accept the fact that their decision can be challenged by research" and the latter ready "to abandon the comfortable ideology of the neutrality of science."[6]

The criticism of the policies of the 1960s is exaggerated and not always fair. It is too global a condemnation of the past, forgetting the very real achievements in discoveries and the extension of scientific education; it is too preoccupied with the failure to foresee the future which no one could foresee, including the authors of *The Research System* and the staff of the OECD. The authors attribute all the difficulties of science today to the failures of the science policies of the past, whereas many of these difficulties are the result of political and economic conditions which have little to do with the policies of science.

Nevertheless, the criticism contains some valid elements which I will try to formulate in my own terms.

There was in the 1960s an almost magical belief in the potentialities of research as an inexhaustible and unfailing source of discovery with econom-

6. The neutrality to be abandoned is not what Max Weber and others had in mind when speaking of the ethically neutral character of science. What they meant was that the validity of scientific findings was independent of the personal motivations of the discoverers and the judges of the discovery. Scientific neutrality has never implied that the choice of problems to be investigated is not influenced by criteria external to science. What the authors object to is the principle of academic freedom which is a different matter from the evaluative neutrality of science.

ically useful applications. This belief served as the basis for the adoption by governments of policies to foster a quantitative growth of research; all Western governments and many countries outside the West pursued such policies within the limits of their resources. There were attempts at measuring costs and the productivity of science, and since the latter could not be measured adequately, there was a tendency to rely on measures of expenditure and to speak and think about the support of science in terms of the percentage of the gross national product spent on research and development. In contrast with this preoccupation with expenditure on research, little attention was paid to the question of how the funds were used by the research institutions and their staffs. The tendency to disregard this question was reinforced by the reluctance of scientists to submit their work to formal supervision or to render formal accounts of it. This opposition is justified, since formal supervision or accounting could only lead—and in many cases has actually led—to the routine production of meaningless reports which benefit no one except those paid to produce them, to read them, and to file them. This resistance to formal supervision usually does not imply any wish to abuse scientific freedom, since the informal controls of the scientific community exercised through refereeing and criticism are powerful means of control. But those mechanisms are designed only to discriminate between works of different quality in given fields. They can only determine whether research is performed according to the standards of assessing achievement accepted in a discipline and how any one piece of research compares with other research performed in the same field. These mechanisms cannot determine the degree of triviality at which research should not be supported at all. When faced with this question, scientists can only be expected to act as any other group, which finds reasons to justify the demand for their services. They recommend support for scientifically marginal cases by anticipating some actual—or potential—uses of the data, by pointing out the usefulness of the research as a training exercise, and similar arguments. This is a perfectly legitimate way to act, as long as it is done in an adversarial situation in which others, representing other ends, other fields of science, and other public and private interests, can argue for alternative uses of the funds. Hence, only the allocation of funds within a given field can be a responsibility of its corresponding scientific community.

But the total allocation for a field has to be a matter of negotiation between those representing the field and members of other scientific communities and of the representatives of the public in the legislative and executive branches of government or of the management of business enterprise.

Scientists, like others, will do their best to gain monopolistic advantages in this negotiating process. In the 1960s they were in a good position to obtain such advantages, because of the belief in the magical potentialities of science. Using this opportunity they managed to convince a public eager to believe them that not only the internal division of funds but also their total size were a matter which could be decided through the informal working of the scientific community. The goal they arrived at was that every qualified scientist who could contribute to the advancement of a field, however modestly, should be supported. This goal was actually attained for a certain period of time in the biological sciences in the United States.[7]

It has not been conclusively shown that this monopoly was actually harmful. The support of utmost possible expansion, which was the result of the monopolistic advantages of science in the 1960s, may be the right policy when there are unexploited opportunities in a field and when there is an interest in their rapid exploitation. But it is a policy fraught with dangers. There is in research, as in everything else, a point of diminishing returns beyond which additional effort does not produce anything useful. If support continues beyond this point, this will be a diversion of funds from worthier objectives. Sooner or later this will be recognized within and outside the relevant scientific community and result in deterioration of morale, cynicism among scientists, and loss of faith in the field or in science in general within the general public.

There is some evidence that such a situation of public support for science beyond the point of diminishing returns was reached in several fields of science in the 1960s. There was certainly such a feeling among scientists.[8] If this was really the case—and the matter needs further investigation—then there is some substance to the argument that the disappointment with science, the sudden contraction of support for it, the subsequent drop in the morale of the scientific community after 1968, and the difficulties of adjustment to the straitened circumstances experienced by scientific institutions in the 1970s were to some extent rooted in the policies of the previous decade and that at least some of these results might have been avoidable. As has been pointed out, the OECD itself did not foresee the present situation, and its attitude of censure toward the policies of the earlier period would be more acceptable if it acknowledged how difficult it is to have foresight. Nevertheless, I find myself in partial agreement with the critical part of the conclusions.

It seems to me, however, that the recommendations of the authors to remedy the errors of the past by the comprehensive planning of technology and science do not follow either from the shortsightedness of the policies of the 1960s or from the evidence presented in these volumes; nor is there any other evidence to support its proposed remedies for past errors. The critical and polemical tone of the conclusions of *The Research System* suggests that the recommendations imply a drastic reversal of the policies of the 1960s. Actually, they are to a large extent a projection of certain lines of thought and policy

---

7. See Harold Orlans (ed.), *Science Policy and the University* (Washington, D.C.: The Brookings Institution, 1968), p. 144.
8. See Alvin M. Weinberg, *Reflections on Big Science* (Cambridge: MIT Press, 1968), p. 157.

which were current for several decades and which were to a large extent responsible for the mistakes of the 1960s. Since the 1940s, many scientists in
many countries have done everything they could to induce governments to accept responsibility for the support of research. Some governments, such as
those of Great Britain, Canada, France, and the United States, went a long
way toward actually accepting such responsibility. Except in France and Canada, this responsibility was not meant to involve planning. Indeed, if planning
means a central authority deciding on the establishment of every research
unit, position, and project according to a detailed blueprint for the whole
country, then there has been virtually no planning in the United States and
little planning in Great Britain. But the authors, perfectly aware of the shortcomings of Soviet and even French types of planning, do not have this sort of
thing in mind. By planning they do not mean bureaucratic centralization but
the establishment of national goals and schedules of priority and the coordination of efforts toward the attainment of those goals. They are much more cautious about the means through which this is to be carried out and are aware of
the dangers of excessive centralization and the importance of leaving sufficient autonomy to those who actually do the research. By the definition of
planning preferred by the authors of *The Research System*, the experiences of
Great Britain, Canada, France, and the United States have all in fact been instances of what is recommended in this book. Although the United States has
not had a minister of science—an office highly recommended by the OECD—
it was actually the pioneer in thinking about and planning of research in national terms and in the concerting of effort toward the successful attainment of
those goals.

The classic statement of this mode of thought—which is the essence of
what the authors now recommend—is Dr. Vannevar Bush's *Science: The Endless Frontier*. This official publication was written in response to a letter from
President Roosevelt of 17 November 1944; part of it is worth quoting:

> The information, the techniques, and the research experience developed by the
> Office of Scientific Research and Development and by the thousands of scien-
> tists in the universities and in private industry, should be used in the days of
> peace ahead for the improvement of the national health, the creation of new en-
> terprises bringing new jobs, and the betterment of the national standard of liv-
> ing. (p. vii)

Dr. Bush's report was a program which outlined the role of government in
the coordination and support of research on problems of national importance[9]

9. See Vannevar Bush, *Science: The Endless Frontier* (Washington, D.C.: U.S. Government
Printing Office, 1945). For a description of the relationship between government and science
since the Second World War, see also Don K. Price, *Government and Science* (New York: New
York University Press, 1954).

and in "promoting the creation of scientific knowledge and the development of scientific talent in [American] youth." [10] Dr. Bush's recommendations were by and large carried out. Between the end of the Second World War and the early 1950s, there was created in the United States a set of coordinating bodies and agencies in science with a clearer conception of scientific and technological goals to be attained than had ever existed before. The fact that this did not lead to the centralization of research is only evidence of the degree of sophistication of persons like Dr. Bush and his successors, not of any lack of a comprehensive view, determination, and skill. The American planning of science of the 1940s and the 1950s managed to obtain the enthusiastic cooperation of the entire scientific community, to encourage individual initiative, and to carry out its goals through developing existing and widely dispersed scientific capacities. This advantage accrued from the fact that the planners in this case were outstanding scientists who had a realistic understanding of the potentialities of various branches of science at that time and whose security of status and income enabled them to serve their country without being dependent on the government. As a result they could better conceive the feasible and worthwhile goals of scientific activity and think in a detached manner of the best ways of attaining the goals within the limits of the available means. They knew at first hand the tremendous theoretical potentialities of high energy research in physics, were better acquainted than anyone else with the actual and potential practical uses of atomic energy, and, as a result of the mobilization of scientists, including social scientists, during the war, they were aware of the existence of vast opportunities in practically every branch of science. As leading scientists themselves—or personal friends and acquaintances of those scientists—and experienced administrators, they did not think about scientific planning and development in the abstract but about concrete and feasible research, to be carried out by persons they knew in particular settings. The organizational "blueprints" and the arrangements for financial and other support were all conceived as means to carrying out these different kinds of research, the substance of which were well understood by the planners.

This was in sharp contrast with French and Soviet precedents in the planning of science, in both of which the motive of ensuring the power and of serving very generally conceived goals of bureaucracies and governments led to the establishment of the centralized bureaucratic organization of science. [11] It seems that the American experience of the late 1940s and early 1950s has

10. V. Bush, op. cit., p. 25.
11. This is not entirely true of French science policy in the late revolutionary and early Napoleonic period (between 1794 and 1803), which had many of the elements of the postwar American developments. The new institutions and projects reflected the ideas of the best scientists of France who represented the scientific consensus rather than general bureaucratic and political interests. See Roger Hahn, *The Anatomy of a Scientific Institution: The Paris Academy of*

been—so far—the closest approximation to comprehensive technological-scientific planning in history and that this fact has been overlooked only because this took place without the imposition on science of a centralized bureaucratic administration. Centralized bureaucracy has been for such a long time associated with the idea of planning that many do not distinguish between these two very distinct things.[12]

Having made this distinction between planning as a setting of goals to be autonomously pursued and centralized bureaucratic planning, it becomes evident that British and French planning since the Second World War was in an important respect more rudimentary than American planning. The governments of these countries followed the American model in adopting responsibility for the coordination of activities for the attainment of some very generally defined goals and for the advancement of scientific knowledge and higher education. But whereas in the United States there was in 1945 a comprehensive vision of development of science, followed closely by legislation and the establishment of a complete framework of governmental agencies (National Institutes of Health, Atomic Energy Commission, National Science Foundation), advisory bodies, offices, and institutional arrangements for awarding grants and contracts, in Britain and in France there were much less comprehensive schemes. As far as the goals were concerned, these were the same as in the United States, namely, the development of advanced technology in atomic energy, computers, high energy research, and later space research, and a general strengthening of the support for basic science. In Great Britain and France, there has been no general scheme for the reorganization of research as there was in Canada and the United States. This came about to a large extent from the fact that, unlike Canada and the United States, those two countries had had a long history of governmental support of research. Because of reliance on traditional arrangements, organizational innovations in Great Britain and France occurred in a more sporadic and uncoordinated manner than they did in Canada and the United States: many of them were responses to the American example. Thus, what appears as more comprehensive planning in Great Britain and France than in the United States was in fact not so much planning as it was centralized administration, and Canada had both. There is little doubt that for about 20 years, the American experience was in everybody's view—including that of the OECD—a great success. American scientific organization began to falter in the late 1960s, and it has not regained its stride since then. The reasons for this change of fortunes are crucial to understanding the problem of comprehensive science planning.

Sciences, 1666–1803 (Berkeley, Los Angeles, London: University of California Press, 1971), pp. 281–312.

12. As a matter of fact, the authors of *The Research System* go some way, but not far enough, in making this distinction.

The planning of science in the United States succeeded because it was the exploitation of a unique historical opportunity. The opportunity was not created by the planners but was the result of past scientific discoveries, the wartime mobilization of scientists, and a concatenation of political and economic circumstances following from victory and the wealth and size of the United States. The planners succeeded because they perceived the opportunity and were technically competent to devise or discern the means appropriate to the situation. However, and this has to be emphasized, they did not foresee or create the opportunities, and they could not have foreseen or created them.

Once the historical opportunity was exhausted—as it probably was by the early 1960s—the system which had worked so well since the end of the war ceased to work satisfactorily. Geared to the exploitation of specific opportunities, it began to fumble when the opportunities ran out. There began a frantic search for new scientific and technological opportunities. The space project served for a while as a lonely and somewhat disappointing substitute for the variety of projects—atomic energy, accelerators, computers, electronics—of the preceding two decades. There were ill-fated attempts, like Project Mohole, and scientist-administrators in charge of fundamental research tried to stimulate new scientific growth by sponsoring research and conferences on "creativity," establishing "centers of excellence," and trying to discern areas in which "breakthroughs" might be expected. All this was of no avail. It was the disappointment with the inability of the American system to produce new and convincing objectives for scientific development and to prevent a recession in research and higher education which is expressed in the critical tone of *The Research System* and in its resolution to search for new objectives for scientific growth.

The authors of *The Research System* are well aware of these facts. But instead of interpreting the developments as evidence of the inability of central planners to come up with new goals for science and technology, they explain the failure of planning by arguing that there was no real science policy in the 1960s, since policy "merely boiled down in the end to distributing a growing volume of resources." However, this was the situation only in the mid-1960s when—as I have pointed out—the opportunities perceived at the end of the war were exhausted. If planning for the attainment of specific goals or for the development of well-chosen areas—as had been the case in the 1950s—was replaced by the pursuit of purely quantitative growth, this was because the different planning bodies were unable to produce any new goals, or even to suggest a credible plan for the reordering of priorities. Many persons warned that it would be impossible to sustain the existing rate of growth. Since, however, they did not offer alternatives, policymakers preferred to base their decisions on the expectation that further investment in scientific effort would produce some spectacular breakthroughs and thus justify the investments retrospectively.

Therefore, I cannot accept the argument that the science policies of the past did not amount to much. It is difficult to accept this argument for the United States, since there has been highly informed thinking and discussion of those policies in that country and since the existing organs of science, like the President's Science Advisory Committee, the heads of governmental science agencies, and representative bodies of scientists like the National Research Council, had sufficient capacity to initiate policies. In addition there have been the cases of Canada and France which have practiced formal and permanent planning. The case of Canada is particularly important, since that country pioneered or followed many of the arrangements recommended by the OECD, such as the establishment of a post of a minister of state for science without departmental responsibilities in charge of the coordination of the scientific activities of the government, and of broadly representative central and regional committees for the planning and development of science. Neither Canada nor France has been able to formulate new, feasible national objectives for research and development and to prevent the recession in the demand for research. Their problems in this respect are not smaller—they are probably greater—than those of the United States.[13]

The correct interpretation of the experiments in comprehensive planning of science since the end of the Second World War is that they were a temporary success, attributable to the wartime experience in large research and development projects, the exceptional opportunities which existed in science and technology at that time, and the exceptional circumstances prevailing in the victorious countries. Once these opportunities were exhausted, all the institutions for the planning and promotion of science were unable to define new objectives and to plan for their attainment. The idea that the experience of the Second World War and the ensuing two decades, in which the scientific community was mobilized to work toward the attainment of a few consensually agreed national goals in research, can be perpetuated into permanent planning of science is a utopia based on the misreading of history.[14]

This interpretation fits not only the case of the United States but also those of the other countries surveyed in *The Research System*. Britain and Canada had participated actively in the scientific war effort, as did a few French scientists who escaped from France to join the allies. This created in all the victorious countries a mood of scientific elation and optimism similar to that in the United States. They perceived the same scientific and technological oppor-

13. See speech by Dr. Alexander King mentioning the Canadian experience in OECD, "Seminar on the Research System," The Hague: 3 and 4 June 1975; Paris: 31 December 1975, mimeographed.

14. Thus, the Marxian ideal of an economy in which "social labor power" is totally organized for the purpose of doing such work as is needed by society—unperverted by the anarchic play of private interests—has also been realized in a relatively satisfactory manner only under wartime conditions. See A. D. Lindsay, *Karl Marx's Capital: An Introductory Essay* (London: University Press, 1925).

tunities, and their scientific communities were eager to take advantage of them. Their success was considerable. The position of Great Britain in basic science throughout the first 20 years after 1945 was excellent, and that of Canada was impressive. Both of these countries had great success in mastering the new advanced technologies. France—the scientific institutions of which deteriorated during the war—also advanced rapidly. However, their size and economic resources were not equal to those of the United States, and as a result their attempt to compete with American industry in the economic utilization of the new technologies was on the whole a failure. The strain imposed by the effort to pursue the objectives pursued by the United States was altogether too great, and there were therefore early disappointments and failures, especially in the field of atomic energy and space research.

It is quite likely that in the long run these countries would have done better without any comprehensive planning of science. At least, this can be inferred from the fact that the scientific and technological performance of the Netherlands, Sweden, and Switzerland has been—in the estimate of *The Research System*—the most satisfactory among the countries surveyed and that West Germany—the government of which did not try to compete with the great powers in atomic and space research and left the development of advanced technology to a large extent to private industry—has done in the long run as well as, if not better than, Great Britain and France in these fields. The governments of West Germany and the three small countries were content to aid science and technology from time to time but did not adopt general responsibilities for their development. As a result their research was guided by the experiences of those actually engaged in research and development and were not committed to long-term goals of uncertain outcome but only to such as they could successfully attain.

Permanent and comprehensive planning of science and technology is a futile, and in the long run, harmful method. This is not only a summary of the evidence but it is also what one would expect on the basis of theoretical considerations. Science and technology are interrelated, but they are essentially different things, and their mutual relationships vary depending on historical circumstances.[15] Furthermore, there is no single and undifferentiated science and no single and undifferentiated technology; they both take many forms. Any one body responsible for the planning and guidance of both over a long period of time is undertaking an impossible task. Discovery, invention, and development are highly specialized activities, success in which depends on a constellation of personal characteristics, facilities, resources, social atmosphere, and organization. The optimal conditions are not the same in different fields, and they change from time to time even within a field, alongside

15. Of course, if the purpose is to come abreast of an existing state of technology or scientific knowledge, a much more streamlined structure might do equally well or better.

changes in the state of the scientific art and the wider social and cultural conditions. From this it follows that the main condition of scientific and technological innovation is the existence of a variety of effective institutions, such as universities, research institutes, and business firms using advanced technology, which are free to go their own way and make their own decisions, capable, and motivated presumably by competition to recruit the best possible scientists and provide them with the means, the incentives, and the atmosphere needed for creative work. Within and between these institutions, there have to be optimal conditions for the exercise by the individual of free scientific choice and discretion. Such conditions will further innovations when the opportunities for innovation and the persons capable of making them exist. But neither these nor any other conditions can guarantee a steady flow of discoveries and invention or that the scientific discoveries will lead to socially and economically useful innovations.

Accordingly, the role of government in science and development should be different from and much more limited than is proposed by the authors of *The Research System*. Governments can be very large "customers" of science, and they can stimulate or carry out projects of their own, in any or all fields. As such, they have to act with the same degree and kind of prudence as any "customer" of scientific research. They have to know what they want and ascertain that the price is right. Their problem in this respect is that they are such large "customers" that they can easily obtain monopolistic power over one or several fields of science and create a potentially dangerous dependence of those fields on governmental demand. This might have happened in the physical sciences. During the Second World War and until the 1960s, the demand for research in physics and to some extent chemistry were for a long time devoted to a succession of military and other governmentally set tasks, so that when these came to an end, a crisis in these fields was inevitable. Such excessive concentration on specific governmentally set tasks can be ascertained and perhaps forestalled.

In addition to such specific demand, governments also influence science and technology indirectly through their economies and directly through their higher educational and science policies. These two modes of influence are not distinguished in the conclusions of *The Research System*, probably because of a long tradition of assuming that most research and higher educational policies serve both economic and cultural goals. In principle, however, this confusion is entirely unjustified.[16] Anything needed by a given sector of industry is best known by that industry and should be decided upon by it—irrespective of whether the economy is a socialistic one or is directed by private enterprise. A comparison of the research laboratories of large industrial firms, such as CIBA, Bell Telephone, or Imperial Chemicals, with most state agricultural

16. A. Weinberg, op. cit., pp. 85–100.

research stations or governmental laboratories designed to serve entire industries—such as those of the former DSIR in England—are convincing examples of the superiority of the dispersal of responsibility.

Finally, central and state governments have overwhelmingly accepted the financial responsibility today for higher education and for research not directly related to industrial needs. It is most unlikely that research not directly related to particular industrial needs will be supported by private patronage. If such research is to be carried on on a large scale, then it must be supported by governments. As governments accept that responsibility, they will have to decide how much to spend on different types of research of this kind, and they will have to make sure that the funds are not misused. But here, too, it is unrealistic to assume that any central body will be capable of planning for the entire field of science. The kind of research done at universities and in specialized research institutions and its success depends on the internal conditions and immediate environment of these institutions and the way they compete and cooperate with each other. The experience and the intuition required to support work in the different fields of science exist only in these institutions. They can determine best which are the directions and fields unlikely to yield new results and which are the ones worth the expenditure of money, time, and talent. Of course, their estimates are far from certain, but as long as each of these institutions is autonomous enough to make, and pay for, its own mistakes, and benefit from its own good judgment, the system will probably fare well.

The main problem of science policy—not to be confused with general economic and welfare policies—today is how to support research from governmental funds and yet to ensure the vigor, initiative, and independence of scientific institutions.

This alone may not be enough to deal with the problem of misuse of funds, and the determination of the total sums to be provided for science as a whole, or what proportions are to be assigned to the different fields of science. These are not new problems; they have only become intractable because of the utopian attempts of central governments to promote science as a whole. By breaking down the task of the government and limiting it, these problems will become easier to handle, as they were in many cases in the past.

These conclusions are in some respects diametrically opposed to those of *The Research System*. The main disagreement between us is, however, about the role of the government in science policy; about the content of science policy there is less disagreement between us. *The Research System* concludes that the difficulties of the present are the result of insufficient planning and intervention by central governments in the past. Therefore, they recommend more intervention and suggest that governments should assume "wide responsibilities for coordinating and animating the scientific and technical effort" in accordance with social needs and priorities established by them and that they should balance the growth of science in order to prevent cycles of overexpansion and recession such as in recent years. In contrast, my interpretation of the postwar experience is that present problems are the result of too much central initiative and intervention and that the major task ahead is how to decentralize decision making through reinvigorating the autonomy of scientific and economic institutions. I think that the attempt to chart the course of science and society by central government is impossible. However, it is just that governments should use research for the solution of particular problems, but they can do this as customers of particular research projects dealing with particular problems. The coordination of the work in each field within the country is also a worthwhile aim but an impossible task to perform from any central position. However, some systems have been fairly well coordinated without central guidance, by entrusting decisions to those who actually do the work and leaving to them to evolve their own ways of cooperation and division of labor. Similarly, the prevention of cycles is an important objective, but probably the main contribution which governments can make to it is to be more circumspect in the use of their monopolistic power over science. It was, after all, governments which encouraged and made possible the overexpansion of the two decades which followed the Second World War.

The root of these considerable differences of view between the authors of *The Research System* and myself is—I believe—related to the conceptual framework in which the authors and perhaps the majority of the students of the field think about science policy. As has been pointed out, that framework was established in the 1930s and 1940s in the debate between J. D. Bernal and Michael Polanyi. In this debate Bernal represented the Marxist view of central national planning of science which asserted that such planning was being carried out in the Soviet Union, while Polanyi recommended reliance in the field of pure science on the informal mechanisms of the scientific community. Since then Bernal's views have become almost an orthodoxy in science policy, while Polanyi's ideas have been widely accepted in the philosophical, historical, and sociological research on scientific development. The conclusions of this book are also presented in terms of the controversy between Bernal and Polanyi in the sense that central planning and guidance are juxtaposed to laissez-faire.[17]

But my analysis of the experience of the past three decades shows that these terms no longer provide an adequate framework to the analysis of the present problems. Things have developed far beyond the point at which the debate took place, and we have to ask different questions today than were asked in the 1930s. Bernal foresaw correctly the vast intervention of govern-

---

17. This in spite of the fact that the limited relevance of this debate is pointed out in the "General Introduction"; see *The Research System: Comparative Survey of the Organization and Financing of the Fundamental Research*, vol. 1, p. 12.

ment in research, and much of what he recommended as far as the scale and intentions of governmental activity in science are concerned is today a reality in all the advanced countries. But his idea that science could be centrally planned as part of a system of comprehensive social planning has proved to be wholly mistaken. A large number of attempts to plan science have been made since then; their success has been limited to the planning of specific projects only. Polanyi's ideas about self-regulation are a good description of what is going on in different scientific fields. He also correctly foresaw the difficulties of central planning in science. But as a guide to governmental policy his writings are valid only as cautions against policies which might extinguish the necessary self-regulatory mechanisms of the scientific community. This is of crucial importance, but scientists can act as a self-regulating community only if the scientific institutions in which the community is set enable them to act as a community; scientific institutions are dependent on government, which may easily deprive them of the means and freedom necessary to act as a scientific community, with all the benefits and safeguards which the scientific community affords. Polanyi's principles are silent on all this and on how large the total sum spent on research should be and how it should be distributed over the major fields.

No good will result from adhering to the belief that the alternatives of science policy are central planning by government and laissez-faire. The questions are how to distinguish between the role of the government as a customer of specific scientific services and as a general patron of science and how to reconcile the role of government as the preponderant source of financial support with the existence of autonomous and enterprising scientific institutions. These—and not the utopian planning of the development of science by governmental agencies—are the tasks required of science policy today.

Scientific Societies, Professional Organizations, and the Creation and Dissemination of Practical Knowledge* 13

The purpose of this paper is to explain why scientific societies, such as academies or disciplinary organizations, which have been so successful in the encouragement, evaluation, and dissemination of basic and pure research, could not repeat their success in the field of applied knowledge and to suggest that there exist in the applied fields other kinds of organizations which are capable of performing those functions.

The main reason for the relative lack of success of scientific societies in the applied field has probably been that the interests which unite their members are the advancement of disciplinary knowledge and the solicitation of support for science. Practical problems of production appear as petty and trivial concerns in such societies. While, for example, a new theoretical presentation for plant-soil-water relationships or the structure of a new penicillinlike molecule will be of general interest to almost all of the participants of a scientific conference, questions such as what is the optimal amount of irrigation to be given to a specific crop at a certain place, in different parts of the year, or what are the conditions for the optimal yield of a fermentation process in a given plant, are bound to interest few people in a group of soil scientists, or organic chemists.

Therefore, the intellectual atmosphere of these societies will favor the kind of research which subsumes particular phenomena under general principles and theories, rather than investigations into the application of such principles and theories to the solution of specific problems of a practical nature. Because of this limited interest of the scientific societies in practical knowledge, the creation and dissemination of such knowledge in agriculture and the manufacturing industries takes place typically in other frameworks:

*With Shaul Katz.

(1) In many cases, especially in small-scale industry and agriculture, practical knowledge is being created in the traditional manner, as part of the production process, through intuition and trial and error by workers and technicians.

(2) In other cases special research and/or information services are organized for a branch of production, usually with the aid of government agencies. Such organizations are most widespread in agriculture (experimental stations and extension services) but are quite frequent also in manufacturing industries such as the British Boot, Shoe and Allied Trades Research Association founded in 1919 or the British East Iron Research Association founded in 1921.

(3) Finally, more and more large firms establish their own research and development departments.

To begin with the traditional trial and error process, its main shortcoming is that it is unable to cope with the growth of specialized knowledge. This phenomenon can be illustrated by examples from agriculture. The number of "items of knowledge" in the manuals of strawberry growers in Israel grew from about 40 to about 300 items during the 1960s. Such growth has been both the consequence and the precondition for the introduction of plastic tunnels to the strawberry branch in Israel.[1] A similar phenomenon has followed the introduction of cotton growing in Israel during the 1950s. During this period, and during the 1960s, the number of items of knowledge grew by a factor of 3—from about 300 to more than 1,000 items.[2] Behind this quantitative growth of knowledge there is a story of qualitative change, involving a veritable revolution in the basic concepts of farming. Thus, in the traditional gardening technology, strawberry growing (which is one of our examples) involved a series of operations determined by the natural life cycle of the plant. Their purpose was to aid nature in producing somewhat more effectively what it would have produced anyway. The time of harvesting, for example, was determined by the natural ripening of the fruit; the grower just picked every day whatever was ripe. Furthermore, because traditional farming was essentially a complement of natural processes, it consisted of the performance of a number of distinct operations and application of certain substances, such as fertilizers. There was no need to speculate a great deal about the interrelatedness and mutual repercussions of the different inventions, because these had limited effect on the life cycle, determined by nature. It was a kind of work which required patience, power of observation, but little abstract knowledge

1. Shaul Katz, "The Growth and Turnover of Knowledge in an Agricultural Crop: The Case of the Strawberry" (Hebrew), mimeographed (Jerusalem: Department of Sociology, Hebrew University of Jerusalem, 1971).
    "Item of knowledge" is defined in this paper as any specification of distinct activity, or instrument, or installation, or material which the grower may employ by the instruction booklet of the Israel Agricultural Extension Service, in the course of growing a certain crop.
2. Shaul Katz, "Cotton in Israel" (Hebrew), mimeographed (Jerusalem: Department of Sociology, Hebrew University of Jerusalem, 1975).

and calculation. In contrast, modern farming requires an entirely different orientation to time and a firm grasp of rather abstract relationships. In our case of strawberry growing in Israel, the fruit *has to be ripe* for harvesting just a few days before Christmas in order to reach the European markets during, or slightly before, the holidays. From this market-determined harvesting time there is a "counting back" to set up a precise schedule of operations, with the aim of getting the fruit to market exactly at the desired dates. This requires a thorough, more or less scientific understanding of the growth process as a system of interrelated processes, controlled to a considerable extent by man. This knowledge has to be precise and finely tuned, since relatively minor differences in the timing of certain interventions, or quantities of added substances, may have far-reaching consequences. The work of the farmer becomes increasingly like that of the engineer.

In the absence of such finely tuned knowledge, adapted to special local circumstances, the application of advanced science-based technologies may be difficult and may not be worthwhile. We suspect that the resistance of some traditional producers to new technologies may be based on the correct intuitive assessment by the producers that this knowledge is not in the form in which they can apply it without undue risk. Their suspicion that only some components of the whole complex of the technology have been adapted to local conditions of production and consumption may be frequently justified.[3]

The other two alternatives, namely, research associations and in-house research departments, are also not sufficiently effective. These arrangements are based on the use of researchers and research methods for the creation of applied knowledge. However, in both of these arrangements there is a division of labor and physical separation between researcher and producer and in some cases also between producer, researcher, and mediator such as the agricultural extension worker. In research associations and extension services there is also institutional separation between the incumbents of the different roles participating in the process.

This gives rise to several difficulties. Researchers and producers do not think and speak in the same terms and find it difficult to communicate with each other. Furthermore, there is frequently a divergence of interests between

---

3. A good example of this kind is a case of rejection of improved wheat seed in India. According to the farmers, the rejection was explained as follows: "The grain is indeed big—so big and tough that the women cannot grind it well in the old stone flour mills. Dough made from the new flour is difficult to knead and hard to bake into good bread. The new bread, which is all a poor farmer would have to eat, does not taste like the good old bread: it is flat and uninteresting (the explanation being in part, of course, that it does not contain that potpourri of barley, pease, gram and mustard seeds that 'wheat' contained in the old days). Next, look at the cows and bullocks! They do not like to eat the straw of the new wheat; they will die of hunger if we grow it. The straw is worthless, too, for thatching roofs. It does not even make a good fire to warm our hands in winter." McKim Marriott, "Technological Change in Overdeveloped Rural Areas," in *Economic Development and Cultural Change* I (December 1952): 261–72. Quoted by Gunnar Myrdal, *Asian Drama* (New York: The Twentieth Century Fund, 1968), vol. 2, p. 1292.

researchers and producers; the researchers are supposed to serve the producers, but to the extent that the researchers actually adapt their work to the requirements of the producer, they, the researchers, will run the risk of cutting themselves off from their scientific colleagues because concentration on the solution of the practical problems of one agricultural or industrial unit means, in most cases, the neglect of more fundamental problems likely to interest other researchers. This will result in loss of professional skills and reputation.

This loss is not being compensated for by the acquisition of new kinds of skills and conferral of rewards from the producers for effective practical work because, once a problem is solved, there is no way of telling whether it will have anything to do with the next one to be solved, so that knowledge gained in the solution of one problem may not be transferable to the solution of the next one. In other words, it is very difficult to create specialized research roles for the solution of the variety of complex and highly specified problems attending modern industrial or agricultural production.

The situation may be better in some research and development departments of industrial firms. Those may provide a reasonable balance between highly specific applied work and work on longer-range problems of more general application. Thus, it may be possible to serve practical needs and still maintain one's professional skills and standing. However, the knowledge produced by such departments usually remains a trade secret. Of course, such secrets can be disseminated through licensing, but this is not the same kind of dissemination which is facilitated by scientific societies in basic science. This latter knowledge becomes public and available to everyone who wants to use it. Thus, every piece of published, or publicly discussed, knowledge becomes immediately part of an ongoing process of communication and new discovery and may be transferred from one context to another. But an item of knowledge sold under license to another company does not make this knowledge public, does not become part and parcel of an ongoing process of communication, and cannot be transferred, except by special arrangement, to a new context.

If this interpretation is correct, then it is evident that the absence of societies devoted especially to the creation and dissemination of practical knowledge is detrimental to the growth and diffusion of such knowledge. This is not to say that the diffusion of modern technology has not been sufficiently rapid. But one has to make a distinction between the diffusion of easily operated tools and goods, or "turnkey" technologies, and the diffusion of advanced technological knowledge which has brought about the invention of all these.

This is why the diffusion of technologies has been much more effective than that of technological knowledge. Technologies, even some very advanced ones, are being diffused in a uniform way and within a relatively short time throughout the world. But their operation in many cases requires expatriates, since the diffusion of technological knowledge has been slow, ineffective, and spotty. Very few developing countries have succeeded to raise relatively large groups of technologically sophisticated practitioners such as farmers, workers, and other small-scale producers who are capable not only of using technologies but also of adapting them to their needs and occasionally inventing some new ones. In other words, the question we are dealing with is: how is it possible to create in the field of practical technological knowledge including agriculture some kind of organizational analogs to the scientific communities the rise of which has been fostered to a large extent by scientific societies.

Of course, it can be argued that practical technological knowledge is by its very nature unfit to serve as the basis for the formation of societies. Technologists, it is said, are doers and not talkers or writers, and besides they are frequently competing with each other as owners or employees of profit-making enterprises. All this is probably true to some extent, but still, in some cases of highly practical fields, there emerged groups which performed effectively the functions of stimulating research and disseminating knowledge. It remains to be seen what these societies were and under what conditions they emerged.

The most widespread types of society for the advancement of practical knowledge are the professional associations of service industries such as those of the various medical specialties, educators, or clinical psychologists. They all are actively concerned with the advancement of scientific knowledge in their fields, encourage their members to engage in research, run scientific publications, organize conferences, and tend to cooperate with associations in the same and neighboring fields on an international scale. It seems that their success in the encouragement of research and diffusion of knowledge can be attributed to several circumstances. First of all, there is in these fields no rigid division of labor between researchers and practitioners but a considerable overlap between the two functions. This is possible because of the prolonged, and to a large extent, common scientific training received by all members of the professions. As a result associations include the entire profession, from those engaged in relatively basic work to those finding solutions for highly practical problems or engaging in practice alone. Furthermore, researchers and practitioners in these fields collaborate with each other in a way which is not only practically but also intellectually important to both groups. This is particularly evident in medicine. Most of the important medical discoveries today are probably made by more or less full-time researchers. In this sense the practitioner is dependent on the researcher. But there is also a reverse dependence because the final test of medical innovation has to be done in the field by practitioners.

Finally, although the members are frequently private practitioners, the professional associations have generated incentives of honor and fame, which lead also to increased income, and sanctions of ostracism by colleagues in order to motivate members to innovate, ensure the prompt publication of new knowledge, and avoid secrecy among members. This also explains why such associations have not proliferated in goods-producing industries. In those industries practitioners have no common professional background; there is a tradition of competition and trade secrets; and, as has been pointed out, the cooperation between researchers and producers is impeded by diverging interests.

Nonetheless, we found two cases of associations which, for a long period of time, functioned in a way very similar to those of associations of professionals in combining researchers and practitioners and encouraging effective collaboration between them in the creation and diffusion of open knowledge. One of these cases is ironmaking in Sweden during the eighteenth and early nineteenth centuries; the other is farming in Israel today.

The Case of Ironmaking in Sweden[4]

During the eighteenth century, iron became the dominant industrial product in Sweden. There were a large number of ironworks producing pig iron and reworking it by forge and hammer into bar iron. The iron became a major component of Swedish exports, as well as a basis for further industrial processing activities. In 1747, an organization called Jernkontoret (the executive body of the Ironmasters' Association) was founded, with the objective to further innovation. Its considerable funds came from fees imposed by the State on all Swedish iron export. With the encouragement and under the supervision of export officials of the Board of Mining, these funds were allocated mainly for experimentation with improvements in iron technology. In the course of the eighteenth century, the Ironmasters' Association promoted research and development by prizes for manuscripts or grants to cover printing expenses and by loans and other financial support for practical experiments. Many owners of ironworks had ideas of how to improve iron production, especially the handling processes. Members of the Ironmasters' Association who wanted to do experiments applied to the Association for support. This unusual phenomenon of dissemination of new knowledge and support of the research of member firms by an industrial association may be understood by reference to the market conditions in which these firms operated. The Swedish iron producers (somewhat like Japanese firms today) did not compete with each other on the protected internal market but acted as a collective—supported and guided by the State—on the competitive international market.[5]

This arrangement changed toward the end of the nineteenth century, when

4. This description is based on Rolf Torstendahl, "Industrial Research and Researchers in Sweden 1880–1940," *Social Science Information* 19, 3 (1980): 641–61.

5. Because of this international competition there was some concern that the knowledge disseminated by the Association would fall into the hands of foreign competitors; ibid., p. 643.

the small firms were amalgamated into large ones. These no longer cooperated with each other but kept their innovations as trade secrets to themselves.

However, we are here interested in the early stage when, for a period of more than a century, the Ironmasters' Association, in cooperation with the State Mining Board,[6] acted in many respects as an academy or an association of a learned profession supporting research from public funds and disseminating new knowledge through publications. This, as will be shown below, was very similar to the situation prevailing in Israeli agriculture today.

The Case of Israeli Agriculture[7]

Farming in Israel is divided into a private and a collectivistic sector. The former is similar to that found elsewhere; the latter consists of communal and cooperative villages, *kibbutzim* and *moshavim*[8] organized within the Israel General Federation of Labour. While the farmer in the private sector is, like most of the farmers in the world, simultaneously cultivator, entrepreneur, and tradesman, who has to finance his operation and market his products, his counterpart in the collectivistic sector is to some extent released from most of these nonagricultural tasks. Especially in the communal villages (*kibbutzim*), financing and marketing are taken care of by other officials than those who manage the different branches of agricultural production.

Furthermore, whereas the private farmer, especially the small one, tends to be a generalist who may have some cattle, as well as grow some vegetables and fruit trees, the managers of *kibbutz* farming tend to be specialists in a single branch of agriculture and therefore have more opportunities for advanced learning and professionalization than their colleagues in the private sector. As a result they have become quasi-professional people, with many of them keenly interested in the scientific and technological aspects of their particular branch, alert to innovation and in some cases, developing new ideas themselves.

The bifurcation of agriculture into a private and collectivistic sector also gave rise to a bifurcation in farmers' associations. Those of the private sector are primarily engaged in activities designed to defend and promote the economic interests of farmers, such as obtaining credit on favorable terms, government subsidies, protection from competitive imports, etc. Those of the collectivistic sector are much more like the above-mentioned professional as-

6. The Board of Mining had been established by the State already in the middle of the seventeenth century. Its officials supported the Jernkontoret from its beginning; ibid., p. 642.

7. Shaul Katz and Joseph Ben-David, "Scientific Research and Agricultural Innovation in Israel," *Minerva* 13, no. 2 (Summer 1975): 152–82.

8. Joseph Ben-David, "The Kibbutz and the Moshav," in J. Ben-David (ed.), *Agricultural Planning and Village Community in Israel* (Paris: Unesco, 1964), pp. 45–57.

sociations in the service sector. There are some dozen and a half such organizations with memberships ranging from about twenty to several hundred. These organizations not only initiate research like industrial associations but like service associations, they organize professional conferences and publish professional newspapers which inform members about inventions and innovations, both local and foreign. At conferences, growers, extension workers, and researchers report their ideas and suggestions about potential improvements and their experiences with their latest inventions. All these are discussed publicly, and as a consequence, participants obtain a good grasp of what is new and feasible in the field.

A second structure which has encouraged the furtherance of the creation of new practical knowledge in Israeli agriculture are the so-called branch committees. There are about 30 such committees. Most of them act as public bodies under the auspices of the Ministry of Agriculture which appoints their members. These are research and extension workers, prominent farmers, and representatives of agricultural organizations, chosen for their professional accomplishments. In addition to the regular committees, there are several ad hoc committees. The branch committees have dealt with five types of activity: (1) Collection of knowledge relevant to a given crop. Sources of such knowledge are the accumulated experience acquired by growers, extension workers, and research workers and the information collected from various local and foreign sources. (2) Discussion of new knowledge derived from research, whether such research has been done by researchers, extension workers, or growers cooperating with research workers. Following discussions and specific experiments, the branch committees promulgate practical recommendations for the farmers. (3) Identification of crop problems; specification of the knowledge which is needed for the solution of these problems; and initiation of relevant research. The committees are also active in the organization of observations and experiments which require the cooperation of extension workers and agriculturalists. (4) The branch committees take responsibility for the allocation of research for these and other relevant research. The allocation of research funds is one of their most important activities, and they act in this respect very much like the study groups and other committees of—for example—the American National Science Foundation or the National Institute of Health. The kind of research of development work undertaken under the auspices of these organizations can be illustrated by the following cases: selection of cotton varieties for better germination; optimal timing of thinning by synthetic hormones; assessment of irrigation efficiency of various sprinklers; and eradication methods of the Mosaic Cucumber virus on eggplants. Although the committee may support both basic and applied research, the emphasis is on the promotion of applied research of a kind likely to produce results for immediate adoption in the field. (5) Discussion of other professional and organizational policies relevant to the development of the branch.

In spite of their orientation to research and the dissemination of new knowledge, the committees are not swayed by disciplinary leadership. The chairman of the committee may be a university professor or a government research worker, but only in those cases when their work proved to be of practical importance to a given branch. Otherwise, the chairman will be a farmer, or an extension worker, but in every case a person with an outstanding record of practical attainments in the field.

The conditions of the emergence of these organizations in Israel have many similarities to those encountered in the Swedish case. These are the relative absence of competition between farmers of either the private or the collectivistic sector (due, in this case, to the largely cooperative organization of marketing); the central support and planning of agriculture as a national resource and guidance of agriculture by professionally trained civil servants; and the relatively good educational background of many of the farmers and their willingness to learn.

Thus, in Israeli agriculture, there are two kinds of producers' organizations for the furtherance and dissemination of new practical knowledge which can be compared to scientific and professional organizations. Growers' organizations act like professional or disciplinary societies, and branch committees do work similar to that of study committees of research-funding agencies.

As in the Swedish iron industry, these agricultural organizations serve as an interface between production and research.

Conclusion

Scientific societies have played a very important role in the stimulation and dissemination of basic scientific knowledge and the establishment and upholding of scientific standards on a national and international scale. This has been of tremendous importance for development because scientific knowledge is a necessary and central part of all higher technological education. However, this knowledge is not always sufficient for the modernization of agricultural and manufacturing production and has to be complemented by applied research and development.

The insufficiency of basic or even systematic applied research for practical purposes and the difficulty of transferring and spreading an advanced scientific and technological approach from top scientific institutions and societies to much broader groups of practitioners and producers in various fields has often led to pressures on scientific institutions and societies to abandon their traditional concern with basic or systematic applied science and to engage in the advancement of knowledge of a more practical kind. These pressures can only harm advanced scientific work without doing any good to production. Appropriate applied research and development work, with good prospects of being adopted, can be carried out only by those who have experience of their own industrial or agricultural work. This practical knowledge has to be production or practice, by people who have a knowledge of both practice and research, and at facilities which are part of the productive organization. However, it is difficult to foster such activity from the outside. Problems have to be defined in terms of practical production processes. And in order that research and development work closely linked to practice should add up to more than isolated and ephemeral attempts, those engaged in this work have to become part of an association of like-minded people with whom they can communicate, whom they can inspire, and who can inspire them. This paper has been concerned with the conditions of the emergence of such associations.

It has been seen that they emerged in the professions, manufacturing, and agriculture, provided that (1) practitioners and producers in a given branch are well educated and technologically competent; (2) they do not compete with each other on a local market but cooperate with each other in marketing and in furthering exports; and (3) there is active cooperation with professionally trained civil servants intent on advancing the technological level of the industry. The latter condition seems to be absent in the professional service industries, but as a matter of fact, those too benefit from government protection through licensure and the creation of institutions (hospitals, schools, welfare bureaus) which employ qualified professionals.

It appears that this kind of organization fulfilled a unique function in the establishment, nurturance, and dissemination of technological traditions capable of bridging the gap between researchers and practitioners or producers. In both of the cases presented here, it led to the emergence of a widespread and highly skilled and sophisticated class of producers (ironworkers and farmers). Furthermore, in the Israeli case, this occurred in a population consisting of people from a great variety of traditional and modern cultural backgrounds, some of whom had no agricultural tradition to speak of, and others of whom had a background of traditional peasant farming, which was judged by many people as hopelessly backward and incapable of development as recently as twenty years ago.

Part IV

The Ethos of Science

The Emergence and Institutionalization of Modern Science

Introduction

In 1963, *Scientific Change,* edited by A. C. Crombie, appeared. This, it seems, induced Ben-David to broaden the scope of his inquiries. Instead of studying only growth *within* science, Ben-David now turned to the question of why science as a social institution emerged in Europe and nowhere else. Ben-David first addressed this question in "Scientific Growth: A Sociological View" (1964), emphasizing that the history of ideas approach (to which *Scientific Change* was largely limited) cannot explain how science—"an esoteric, impractical, and potentially dangerous activity"—became institutionalized, that is, recognized as a legitimate, indeed prestigious, social activity. The answer given to this question here differs in emphasis from the one it was to receive in *The Scientist's Role in Society* (1971). In the 1964 paper, Ben-David attributes the institutionalization of science to the emergence within the medieval university of the role of a secular scholar, a scholar, that is, in search of truth for its own sake and engaged in judging and criticizing the ideas of his peers. The scientist's role, in other words, has its roots in the medieval university, inasmuch as that institution constituted a reference group monitoring the pursuit of disinterested truth. This role did not emerge in other advanced cultures, where the role of the intellectual was fused with roles associated with power. Ben-David makes clear that this interpretation is consistent with the fact that seventeenth-century science emerged largely outside the universities and that it found its way into the university only during the nineteenth century: his point is that it was the institutionalized social role of the scholar engaged in the search of knowledge which allowed the role of the scientist to be differentiated out of it.

In the second part of "Scientific Growth," Ben-David takes issue with

T. S. Kuhn's account of scientific change, arguing that in many instances (notably, outside the "deductive" sciences), novelty depends not on the internal evolution of science (namely, on the "exhaustion" of a paradigm) but on organizational mechanisms leading up to differentiation through hybridizations of disciplines and of social roles (see chaps. 1 and 2, above). Further, to explain the acceptance of a new idea (the institutionalization of a new paradigm), one has to take into account organizational features of scientific institutions. Thus, in the case of nineteenth-century physiology, the new paradigm became victorious in Germany owing to the German decentralized competitive system constituted of many universities (see chap. 5).

This line of investigation was pursued in a number of papers and eventually culminated in *The Scientist's Role in Society*. The argument of this book is entirely in the tradition of Max Weber's sociology. Robert K. Merton approvingly quotes Weber's statement that "the belief in the value of science is not derived from nature but is a product of definite cultures," [1] and in his own work he further developed this insight. Merton's central claim—in Ben-David's formulation—is that "the emergence of modern science requires a basic change in the general social outlook in which rational understanding and mastery of the environment and human affairs replace tradition as the supreme criterion of conduct." [2] More precisely, Merton "showed that the growth of science was not merely a function of knowledge, talent and money but also of motivations, values and norms of behavior and that these latter could originate from, and be reinforced by, sources outside of science (such as religion)." [3] In *The Scientist's Role in Society*, Ben-David argued along similar lines that in seventeenth-century England a new social role—that of the scientist— emerged and became institutionalized. This role is characterized by the specific norms and values making up the scientific ethos, and the conduct of its incumbents is monitored by the scientific community as a reference group. According to this view, the institutionalization of science is epitomized in the foundation of the Royal Society.

Ben-David's theory was criticized by T. S. Kuhn who, in line with the views he developed in *The Structure of Scientific Revolutions*, construed "science" as consisting of a multitude of traditions whose life history begins with the emergence of the corresponding paradigm: on this view, obviously, it is misguided to speak of "*the* scientific role" construed as "single and unified," and (once Newton is disregarded) seventeenth-century English science and the foundation of the Royal Society have no privileged role in the history of science.[4] In "Organization, Social Control, and Cognitive Change in Science"

---

1. R. K. Merton, *The Sociology of Science* (Chicago and London: University of Chicago Press, 1973), p. 254.
2. [38], p. 13 (reprinted below as chap. 19, p. 419).
3. [45].
4. T. S. Kuhn, "Scientific Growth: Reflections on Ben-David's 'Scientific Role,'" *Minerva* 10, 1 (1972): 166–78.

(1977), Ben-David answers this criticism. He argues that *the* scientific revolution (which stretches from Copernicus to the foundation of the Royal Society) is not to be put on a par with "scientific revolutions" that occur *within* science: the latter transform the cognitive contents of science but do not impinge on its institutional structure. By contrast, the scientific revolution of the sixteenth and seventeenth centuries was not only a cognitive upheaval but also— and foremost—an institutional transformation, for it resulted in the "establishment of science as an intellectual activity to be controlled only by its own norms." In a word, seventeenth-century English science is the cradle of the scientific ethos and of the scientist's role in society, a role that, cognitive changes within science notwithstanding, has persisted ever since.

The scientific ethos and its continuity since its inception are dealt with in a number of papers in which Ben-David defends his views against the proponents of a relativist sociology of scientific knowledge (see below, Part VI). The sociological analysis of the emergence of this ethos is the subject of only one further paper: "Puritanism and Modern Science: A Study in the Continuity and Coherence of Sociological Research" (1985). In it, Ben-David analyzes the celebrated Merton thesis of 1938, showing that it, in fact, consists of two independent parts: one, which in Ben-David's view is of lesser import, affirms that Protestants had a greater propensity to science; the other, more consequential thesis is that Protestantism was conducive to the emergence of the scientific ethos and the scientific role, that is, to the institutionalization of science. Only this hypothesis, Ben-David maintains against its internalist critics, "can explain the continuity and seriousness of scientific endeavor, even in fields in which advancement was slow and unimpressive." Ben-David analyzes the research pertaining to these two theses and shows that it has been largely irrelevant to the former and that it has confirmed the latter.

Scientific Growth 14
A Sociological View

The development of science is often viewed as a process where the intellectual heroes of mankind speak to each other above the heads of nations and down the generations.

The publication of the papers presented and of the ensuing comments and discussions at the Symposium on the History of Science at the University of Oxford in July 1961 is an important step toward the establishment of a more realistic approach.[1] Its main importance lies in the fact that in it a group of illustrious scholars have posed some of the problems of scientific growth in a sociological way. Dr. Crombie, who was the moving spirit of the symposium, put the following questions, among others, to the participants:

> Who were the people taking part in scientific activity? What were their numbers, education, social position, means of livelihood, personal motives, and opportunities, means of communication, institutions? What critical audience was there to be convinced by, use, transmit, develop, revise or reject their conclusions? What social pressures were there within the scientific community itself to affect the consensus of opinion in favour of the old or of the new? . . . How have scientific changes been located in the context of general ideals and intellectual motives, and to what extent have extra-scientific beliefs given theories their power to convince? . . . What value has been put on scientific activity by society at large, by the needs of industry, commerce, war, medicine, and the arts, by governmental and private investment, by religion, by different states and social systems? To what external social, economic, and political pressures

---

1. A. C. Crombie (ed.), *Scientific Change: Historical Studies in the Intellectual, Social, and Technical Conditions for Scientific Discovery and Technical Invention, from Antiquity to the Present* (London: Heinemann, 1963), pp. xii + 896. Page numbers in square brackets in the text always refer to this book. In the footnotes, it will be referred to as *Scientific Change*.

have science, technology and medicine been exposed? Are money and opportunity all that is needed to create scientific and technical progress in modern
society? (p. 10)

Dr. Crombie set other questions—not less interesting—about the history
of ideas and techniques and the relationship between them. Naturally, the majority of participants who were historians of science preferred these latter
questions. The minority who addressed themselves to the sociological questions included experts on many different periods of science and technology;
their papers are contributions to the sociological explanation of the unique occurrence of modern science in seventeenth-century Europe and of the process
whereby science has become a highly organized, rapidly growing and economically important activity since the nineteenth century.

For a sociologist whose problems center on the growth of science, the symposium represents a valuable starting point for the discussion of some basic
questions in the sociology of scientific growth. In the first part of my analysis,
I shall first summarize the views presented at the symposium about the factors
facilitating the emergence of modern science and the development of large-
scale scientific organization in Europe. Using this as my point of departure, I
shall then put forward a different and, I hope, more systematic explanation of
these events.

In the second part, I shall present my own sociological interpretation of
scientific innovation, building on Professor Kuhn's paper.[2]

The Emergence of Modern Science

The questions relevant to this topic which were discussed at the symposium
were: why did science in the modern sense not develop in ancient Greece, or
medieval China; what facilitated the rapid technological development in medieval Europe; what were the opportunities and incentives for scientific work at
medieval universities; and, finally, under what conditions did organized research develop in the European universities during the nineteenth century?

The social relations of Greek science were presented by Dr. Ludwig Edelstein.[3] For the Greeks, science was "one form of the human quest for *eudae-
monia*," so that the motives for engaging in it were religious and aesthetic.

---

2. Thomas S. Kuhn, "The Function of Dogma in Scientific Research," *Scientific Change*,
pp. 347–69. Also his *The Structure of Scientific Revolutions* (Chicago and London: University of
Chicago Press, 1962).

In a subsequent paper I hope to explore the implications of these ideas for the problems involved in the transplantation of scientific institutions from the few societies in which they developed to the majority where they did not.

3. "Motives and Incentives for Science in Antiquity," *Scientific Change*, pp. 15–41. See
also Ludwig Edelstein, "Recent Trends in the Interpretation of Ancient Science," *Journal of the
History of Ideas* 13, 3 (October 1952): 573–604.

While other branches of philosophy were practically useful, both for the individual to whom they taught wisdom and for society for which they helped clarify the basic issues of political life, scientists were regarded as philosophers interested in a particularly esoteric and impractical branch of knowledge. One could change oneself and one's society by following the precepts of philosophers, but the possibility of changing nature did not enter the Greek mind. The reason why it did not was, according to Dr. Edelstein, religious. Unlike the Jews, and following them the Christians and Moslems, the Greeks did not think that their gods created the world out of nothing. Therefore, they did not aim either to change or influence physical nature but were content to understand it. The social structure of scientific activity supported this conception of science. Scientists built their individual systems without reference to those of others and established rival schools which, like so many religious sects, did not communicate with each other.

There were signs of change in the unified Roman Empire. Academies were founded, and something like a unified scientific activity began to emerge. The failure of this process to develop further seems to have been due to cultural and social factors. Greek science, neither in its content nor in its personnel, ever became markedly differentiated from philosophy and religion. There were some approximations to such a differentiation among the great geometers, but all the other sciences were permeated by a great many religious beliefs, and much of the philosophical thought of those who did science was actually hostile to empirical science. With the advent of Christianity this hostility was further reinforced by the church.[4] It would have needed either very striking inventions of great practical value or a strongly established body of professional scientists uninvolved in philosophy and religion to preserve the continuity of science after the rise of Christianity. Since, in fact, the various intellectual roles were little differentiated from each other and science was an enterprise of no practical importance in which only very few participated, it is no surprise that the grandiose religious "discoveries" of Christianity with their vast practical implications dwarfed the small and little understood games of a few scientists.

Medieval Chinese science was the second instance of scientific development up to a level where an advance to modern science should have been intellectually possible. Some of the reasons why this did not happen were, according to Dr. Joseph Needham,[5] religious, similar to those used in the explanation of the limitations of Greek science. In China

---

4. S. Sambursky, "Conceptual Developments and Modes of Explanation in Later Greek Scientific Thought," and the commentary by G. E. M. de Ste. Croix, *Scientific Change*, pp. 67–78, 79–87. For an attempt to link the development of Greek science to the evolution of the *Polis*, see the commentary by J. P. Vernant, ibid., pp. 102–07.

5. "Poverties and Triumphs of the Chinese Scientific Tradition," ibid., pp. 117–53. His monumental work on Chinese science is too well known to need a specific reference.

the available ideas of a Supreme Being, though certainly present from the earliest times, became depersonalised so soon, and so severely lacked the idea of creativity, that they prevented the development of the conception of laws ordained from the beginning by a celestial law-giver for non-human nature. Hence the conclusion did not follow that other lesser rational beings could decipher or reformulate the laws of a great rational Super-Being if they used the methods of observation, experiment, hypothesis and mathematical reasoning. (p. 136)

Finally, the same line of interpretation appears in Dr. White's explanations of technological progress in the Middle Ages.[6] The popular worship of saints in Europe "smashed animism and provided the cornerstone for the naturalistic (but not necessarily irreligious) view of the world which is essential to a highly developed technology" (p. 283). Among the theologically more sophisticated classes, the active attitude to nature was determined by other religious elements, such as the high evaluation of labor expressed first in Jewish Talmudic sources, which later became an integral part of Christian monastic religiosity and worldly activism emphasized in Augustinian theology and the Christian idea of equality (which, according to White, served as an incentive to reduce physical hardship in labor).

In addition to these religious beliefs, both Needham and White, as well as some of the discussants of their papers, also adduced certain features of social structure.[7] They pointed out the greater openness and flexibility of European as opposed to Asian society. In China the monopoly of the mandarin-landholding class had never been seriously challenged by an urban merchant class. The latter were able to amass fortunes, but their position always remained marginal and semilegitimate. Whenever it was deemed useful, their fortunes were confiscated. A mandarin career had always remained, therefore, the exclusive aim of the gifted person.

M. Guy Beaujouan's "Motives and Opportunities for Science in the Medieval Universities" (pp. 219–236), an excellent description of the place of science in medieval academic thinking, as well as of the variety of limited yet distinct opportunities and encouragement offered to academic scientists, makes clear that as much, or even more, scientific work took place outside the universities, especially at royal and princely courts. What is contained there, as well as in the comments and discussion following the papers by R. W. Southern and A. C. Crombie (pp. 301–06, 316–24), is an interesting parallel to Dr. Needham's description of medieval science in China. Medieval European and Chinese science were far from negligible; both made more progress

6. L. White, Jr., "What accelerated Technological Progress in the Western Middle Ages?" ibid., pp. 272–91. See also his *Medieval Technology and Social Change* (Oxford: Clarendon Press, 1962).

7. See the commentary of Wong Chu Ming and the discussion by S. E. Toulmin and J. Needham, *Scientific Change*, pp. 166–67, 169–70, 171–77.

than has usually been assumed, but, in both cultures, science was either merely technology with little systematic theory or subservient to theological and philosophical views of the world.

The question still remains as to why the revolutionary transition to modern science took place in Europe and not in China. The question could have been asked in connection with M. Beaujouan's paper, but it was not, perhaps because the author accepted the *Fragestellung* of a historian of ideas. Medieval science can be legitimately studied as part and parcel of the general intellectual atmosphere determined by scholastic philosophy; different conclusions will be obtained if it is viewed from the point of view of the development of a given scientific field through the ages. In the latter case, the relevant elements of the same things are taken out of their contemporary context and placed in a different framework. As a result of this bias toward intellectual history, as I shall show later, an essential link in the explanation of the emergence of modern science in Europe was left out of the discussions.

The emergence of modern science in the seventeenth century is the emergence of a pattern which combines continuity with rapid innovation. The views put forward at the symposium do not adequately explain this phenomenon both because they emphasize conditions which had also existed elsewhere, in constellations not much different from those prevailing in Europe, and because they failed to come to grips with the basic question of how it occurred that a specific group of people—and not just an occasional odd individual—came to regard the scientific investigation of nature as a major source of truth about the world and that they were not only allowed to do so but also, to some extent, rewarded for it. The importance of this way of formulating the problem cannot be sufficiently emphasized, since nothing seems more "natural" today than the support of science, whereas even 50 years ago there were probably few people who regarded science as the most important source of knowledge about the world, or even as the most important source of technological discovery.

The institutionalization of an esoteric, impractical, and potentially dangerous activity is only conceivable under conditions in which intellectual activity in general has been previously accepted and embodied in publicly recognized institutions enjoying far-reaching autonomy. Within this institutional context, in which finding out and codifying the truth for its own sake became a specialized activity, the results of which are used and judged by other specialized intellectuals, it was inevitable that there would emerge competing schools of thought seeking the truth in different ways and devising increasingly effective means of proving it. The possibility of developing specialized intellectual tastes attractive to only a few is incomparably greater where there is lively intellectual competition in a framework of relative freedom from religious or other interference than in places where the intellectual is constantly obliged to prove his usefulness for a lay public (which, from the point of view of science, includes of course the theologians).

The Role of the Universities

One major factor which distinguished Europe from other areas was the development of a relatively autonomous intellectual class. Universities as corporations of scholars, many of whom engaged in secular intellectual pursuits, were a unique feature of medieval urban civilization in Europe, just as the whole corporate structure of city life was a unique European occurrence. Not only business but scholarship too became vocations in their own rights. This has nothing to do with the social status of the individual scholar which was high in Asian civilizations, such as China, Japan, India, the Islamic countries, and among Jews. But in all these societies the scholar or intellectual also was something else, usually a political or religious figure—a mandarin or a priest—or, in individual cases, a charismatic personality who was honored and supported as a unique phenomenon and did not earn his living as a member of an established intellectual occupation. The development of scholarship in Europe into a secular occupation in its own right was the result of the great corporate movement of the Middle Ages. This made it possible for groups of scholars as well as merchants and artisans to obtain a degree of autonomy in developing their diverse crafts, vocations, and ways of life unimaginable elsewhere.[8] It is probably true, therefore, that the greater flexibility due to the greater differentiation of European society was the main social factor contributing to the exceptional growth of science there, but it was the emergence of a specialized intellectual class which mattered, not that of a specialized business class.

It may appear paradoxical to regard the universities as a necessary adjunct to the emergence of modern science since the new science was in contradiction to what was taught at the universities; the new organizations for science, the academies, represented a secession of the scientists from the universities. As it has been shown by A. R. Hall, the scientific revolution was made by people who, with few exceptions, had been trained at universities and many of whom, including Galileo and Newton, taught at them. It is true that they acquired their scientific knowledge from a variety of sources of which university studies were usually a relatively unimportant part. But colleges in the sixteenth century, such as the Collège royal (Collège de France) in Paris and Gresham College in London, are the background for the informal meetings

8. About the autonomy and organization of medieval universities, see Hastings Rashdall, *The Universities of Europe in the Middle Ages*, A New Edition edited by F. M. Powicke and A. B. Emden (Oxford: Oxford University Press, 1936), vol. 1, pp. 1–24, 43–73. The sociological necessity of an autonomous group of professionals for the institutionalization of science was pointed out by Talcott Parsons, *The Social System* (Glencoe, Ill.: Free Press, 1951), pp. 335–45.

and privately arranged courses from which later the academies of scientists emerged.[9]

Most important of all, the universities had become during the Middle Ages centers for the formation of intellectual continuity and consensus, on the one hand, and dissent and revolution, on the other. Their pedagogical functions created continuity and required consensus, and due to this requirement, divergences of opinion became matters of public debate, leading to constant revisions of the intellectual tradition and at times to fundamental revolutionary changes. These revolutionary changes occurring within the framework of the universities created the opportunity, set the precedent, and served as models for the scientific revolution of the seventeenth century. It was the universities and the culture to which they gave rise which produced the elements which later became parts of the new science, eliminated others which could have proved harmful for it, made it possible to differentiate philosophical thought from the matrix of theology, and confronted with each other different schools of theological and philosophical thought, thus opening the way for ever new doubts and new resolutions.[10] Subservience to nothing but the logical and aesthetic potentialities of things was one of the necessary conditions of the unhindered growth of science.

The differentiation and enhancement of status of the secular scholar was also a product of the university system which prepared the way for the scientific revolution. Although universities became relatively autonomous institutions, and scholar-scientists had specialized intellectual roles already in the twelfth century, their status relative to that of the priest, from which the new role was only barely differentiated, was low. The esteem for their wisdom, in comparison with the dogmas of religion and the philosophy associated with prevailing religious thought, was no higher. The church's retention of some measure of control over the university provided a lasting incentive for revolutions aimed at establishing the secular scholar's equality of status with and the independence from theology.[11] The scientific revolution was only a reproduction of this earlier pattern; now the new scientists claimed equality with the already established philosophers.

This series of revolutions which created an expanding and more distinctive intellectual community was the necessary condition for the rise of science which was unique to Europe. No other areas of relatively advanced culture

9. A. R. Hall, "The Scholar and the Craftsman in the Scientific Revolution," in Marshall Clagett (ed.), *Critial Problems in the History of Science*, Proceedings of the Institute for the History of Science at the University of Wisconsin, September 1–11, 1957 (Madison: University of Wisconsin Press, 1959), pp. 3–23; Irene Parker, *Dissenting Academies in England* (Cambridge: Cambridge University Press, 1914), pp. 17–42.

10. A. C. Crombie, "The Significance of Medieval Discussions of Scientific Method to the Scientific Revolution," in Marshall Clagett (ed.), *Critical Problems in the History of Science*, op. cit., pp. 79–101.

11. Jacques Le Goff, *Les intellectuels au moyen âge* (Paris: Seuil, 1957), pp. 40–43, 74–76, 104–29.

experienced anything like it. The differentiation of natural science as a field of inquiry and as an intellectual identity separate from philosophy was the institutional event, predetermined by the structure of the universities, which brought about the acceleration of scientific growth. This differentiation could not have occurred earlier than in the sixteenth century. Originally the sciences were a subordinate part of the liberal arts. This subordination of science to scholastic philosophy was a consequence not of the direct pressure of the Church but rather of the intellectual slightness of natural science compared with the enormous complexity and difficulty of scholastic theology and philosophy. This state of affairs is clearly illustrated by the preference in the medical faculties for philosophy and ancient authorities even where they enjoyed complete independence from the control of the theologians (Bologna, Padua—cf. M. Guy Beaujouan's paper, p. 233). Scholastic theology and philosophy were thought to be intellectual disciplines worthy of the hospitality of the university, but science was not.

Other changes which weakened the prestige of scholastic learning in fields of central importance had to occur, therefore, before a "revolution" which established an institutionally indpendent science was possible. Thus, a revolution in theology—such as occurred in the Reformation—and in "philosophy"—such as occurred in the humanistic movement—were preconditions for the occurrence of the scientific revolution. While neither of these actually led to science, they effectively destroyed the rule of traditional authority in intellectual life. The humanists discovered a tradition intellectually and aesthetically so superior to that of the schoolmen that the latter were rendered ridiculous. The Reformation, though it only intended to replace a corrupt theology with a pure one, put an end to the claim of theology to be the queen of sciences by subjecting religious dogma to the scrutiny of scholarly inquiry, instead of using the dogma as a criterion for the evaluation of the correctness of scholarly or scientific ideas.

Thus, by the end of the sixteenth century, scholarship was sufficiently in disarray to make it possible, for a minority of intellectuals, to turn the hierarchy of disciplines upside down, raising—at least in their own eyes—empirical natural science from the least to the most important source of knowledge. The new academies which mark the revolution in science came into being, however, only in the seventeenth century, and the most famous ones, like the Royal Society and the French Academy, only in the second half of the century.

The Failure of the Seventeenth-Century University

Why did the new science, which came into being during the seventeenth century, remain outside the universities? The medieval universities had been established for the purpose of educating theologians, lawyers, and doctors in such a way that their studies should be well founded in logic, dialectic, and philosophy. They were different from professional schools in about the same way as contemporary university medical schools are different from the hospital schools which existed in the nineteenth century in England and the United States. Like the contemporary university medical schools, the professional training offered by the medieval universities gave, in varying degrees, practical and fundamental intellectual training to the students and the opportunity for their teachers to cultivate fundamental intellectual disciplines. The state of the arts and sciences during the Middle Ages was such that the university performed all these functions in theology and probably law and only the last function in medicine. Thus, it became the seat of all learning in spite of the limited purposes of professional education. During the fifteenth century, however, as a result of the growing differentiation of intellectual activities within the university, the rise of architecture and painting into something like rigorous aesthetic-intellectual disciplines outside of the university and the rediscovery of ancient learning which was external to the universities, theology, law and medicine ceased to represent the whole of science and scholarship.[12] The pattern of university studies took a new form. Some of the revolutionalized fields, such as theology and law—the revolution of which, due to the erection by Grotius and his followers of a secular system of laws, independent of theological presuppositions, took place in the seventeenth century simultaneously with the revolution in science—remained within the university. Others, such as humanistic scholarship, found their way back to it by stages.[13] Architecture, painting, music, creative writing, the new publicistic philosophy, and science remained outside. The attitude toward science during the seventeenth and eighteenth centuries was similar to the attitude of the majority of contemporary universities and public opinion in general toward the creative arts: irrespective of their appreciation of these activities, they do not usually consider the establishment of degree courses in them since it is assumed that these are activities in which continuity of production is not necessary for the society, nor do they believe that systematic training in these fields can importantly contribute to the quality of their products. There is no sign that this state of affairs was considered very anomalous by the scientists themselves. They were, of course, critical of the universities, but they made no effort to become incorporated into them.

Besides regarding the sciences as charismatic activities rather than as intellectual disciplines, universities justified their conservatism by the belief that

12. About the importance of architecture and painting as disciplines, see Giorgio de Santillana, "The Role of Art in the Scientific Renaissance," in M. Clagett (ed.), *Critical Problems in the History of Science*, op. cit., pp. 33–65, and John Herman Randall, Jr., *The School of Padua and the Emergence of Modern Science* (Padua: Editrice Antenore, 1961), pp. 129–38.
13. About the new humanities at the universities, see A. R. Hall, in M. Clagett (ed.), *Critical Problems in the History of Science*, op cit., 9–10, and J. H. Randall, Jr., op. cit. About the eighteenth century, Stephen d'Irsay, *Histoire des universités françaises et étrangères* (Paris: Auguste Picard, 1935), vol. 2, pp. 122–27.

the only real disciplines, the only systematic bodies of generally accepted knowledge, were classics, philosophy, and, perhaps, mathematics; science was regarded as irrelevant to any of the professions for which they were responsible and of little practical value for anything else. With the passing of time and the growth of scientific knowledge and nonacademic philosophical erudition, the state of the universities indeed became anomalous, but they were seldom willing to reform themselves. As a result, they not only taught things that were dated but they also taught them badly and were often corrupt. But even in the second half of the eighteenth century it was their low standards, not their backwardness in science, which made them the butt of criticism.[14]

The social structure of the scientific community in the seventeenth and eighteenth centuries was already clearly distinguished from the other sectors of the intellectual communities. Scientists, even though many of them were not exclusively scientists, had a recognized role, or perhaps one should say "identity." They were now regarded as being quite different from philosophers and theologians; the overlapping of these activities in the same persons did not obscure the distinctive image or role of the scientist.

Yet the scientific community was still very sparsely settled, its institutional system was meager, and its intellectual territory extremely limited. The academies were engaged in the public exchange of scientific information, the evaluation of scientific work through its public approval or disapproval or, in rare instances, material support of research. In mechanics, mathematics, and astronomy there were fairly clear criteria to distinguish between real scientists, dilettantes, and cranks. (In the sixteenth century, this had been not so easy.) In other fields the emergence of such effective communities had to wait until the end of the eighteenth or even the nineteenth century.

The sciences which reached maturity in the seventeenth century were all based on advanced mathematics which few people were able to understand; this helped their practitioners to differentiate themselves from other intellectuals. For this and other reasons, the activities of the individual scientists and the academies were public only in the sense that there were no attempts at concealment and mystification. The actual interest of the public in science and the importance attached to it were extremely limited. Science, after all, had hardly any important uses (outside navigation), and it was much too difficult to become a popular pastime.

14. See, e.g., Adam Smith, *The Wealth of Nations*, bk. 5, chap. 1, pt. 2, article 2d. The themes of the attack on the universities in Germany were similar. They were criticized for their stress on book learning and lack of contact with nature. They were also criticized for their emphasis on memorization. What was mainly advocated, however, was not experimental science but observation of nature, sports, learning to do things, and moral education. See René König, *Vom Wesen der deutschen Universität* (Berlin: Verlag Die Runde, 1935), pp. 17–27. For a new more positive evaluation of the eighteenth-century universities, N. Hans, *New Trends in Education in the Eighteenth Century* (London: Routledge and Kegan Paul, 1951), pp. 41–54.

As a result, there was no demand for the extension of scientific education or for the public support of research. The scientific community had no institutional mechanisms for regeneration. It neither taught nor trained people for research. It was dependent for its continued existence on the operation of the very same universities which its members despised and on the accidents by which original minds picked up their education independently of existing schools.[15] Even though many universities alienated their abler students and caused them to rebel against the scholastic tradition, this was not an adequate basis for the emergence of a continuous line of scientists carrying on an elaborate tradition of research.

Mathematics was the only field where succession was more or less continuous; there, the universities had played a more advanced role than in the other sciences.[16] Natural science—like music, painting, sculpture, and literature—carried some institutional rewards as an activity worth cultivating for its own sake and was provided with scattered and intermittent public facilities for the exhibition of its achievements and for the maintenance of its personnel. Great talent, once recognized, was often nurtured and supported. Little effort was expended in finding it or in ensuring the continuity of scientific education and research work.

In certain respects the rigorous training according to authoritatively promulgated models, which is characteristic of contemporary scientific instruction, is closer to the system which prevailed in the Middle Ages than it is to the science of the seventeenth and eighteenth centuries. There were no comprehensive textbooks or departments; there were no research institutes—except observatories and botanical gardens—devoted to a well-defined field. Disciplines existed only through the sense of affinity of loosely connected inquirers devoting themselves to related problems.

Organized Science and the Renewal of the Universities

The events and considerations which led the sciences back to the universities had initially nothing to do with science. The new institutions, such as the École polytechnique and other scientific establishments of revolutionary

15. The education provided by Jesuit colleges, on the one hand, and Protestant "academies," on the other, do not alter this picture. They were more efficient than the traditional grammar schools and—to the extent that they provided higher education—the universities, but even the academies in England paid little attention to science and none to research. They were modern in teaching literature, philosophy, languages, geography, and history for the needs of the educated trading classes. They were no pioneers in science or even professional training. See I. Parker, op. cit., pp. 103–23, 135–36. Also N. Hans, op. cit., p. 35, concerning the relatively low percentage of graduates of dissenting academies among eighteenth-century scientists.

16. Jacob and John Bernoulli were professors of mathematics at Basle, Maclaurin taught at Aberdeen and Edinburgh. Lagrange and Euler were typical international court scientists, but Eu-

France and, somewhat later, the new type of German universities were in the first instance the creations of politically interested groups of intellectuals. Their protagonists were mainly philosophers, supported by politicians some of whom were intellectuals and who were also interested in the training of professional people for the service of the state. What worried those intellectuals was not the state of science, about which there was no reason to worry (at least in France), but the scandalous intellectual backwardness of the universities by which, moreover, they had often been personally frustrated. University appointments had been closed to them, at least beyond the lower ranks, and they were in a variety of ways subject to the control, authoritative criticism, or, at times, censorship of the universities or the church authorities with which the universities were associated.[17] The criticism of the universities was made from a philosophical rather than a scientific standpoint. In revolutionary France prior to the fall of Robespierre, the main philosophical trend was essentially antiscientific—a kind of early Lysenkoism. It propagated an amateur science closely related to the practical arts and regarded biology—which was then in a prescientific state—rather than physics as the model science; it considered pure sciences, especially mathematics, as antisocial and aristocratic and therefore something to be suppressed. After Thermidor, professional science came again into its own; but the public support which it received was due to an ideology which sought for "a consistent philosophy . . . to unify sciences through a common conception of the nature of scientific explanation, and in so doing to link them, both institutionally and philosophically, to the realization of the idea of progress."[18]

The École polytechnique and the École normale were essentially new kinds of academies where the pick of a nation's scientists associated with each other and with the most brilliant of the oncoming generation. Their goal was the realization of a philosophical idea; in the course of this pursuit they also provided—like medieval universities—a good professional education. These institutions inaugurated a new stage in the teaching of science but not in the organization of research. This latter reverted in France to eighteenth-century patterns of private laboratories and academies as the centers of scientific

---

ler only started on his travels which took him to St. Petersburg and Berlin after he failed to obtain the appointment to a vacant professorship at Basle. H. W. Turnbull, *The Great Mathematicians* (London: Methuen, 1962), pp. 107–21.

17. The relationship of the intellectuals to the universities at the end of the eighteenth century in Germany is clearly described and analyzed by Henri Brunschwig, *La Crise de l'Etat prussien à la fin du XVIIIᵉ siècle et la genèse de la mentalité romantique* (Paris: Presses Universitaires, 1947), pp. 161–86. In France, where the intellectual life was more varied than in Germany, universities were not so much in the center of intellectual concern. They were attacked as part of the whole system of oppressive institutions; see Alexis de Tocqueville, *L'ancien régime et la révolution*, bk. 3, chaps. 1 and 2, and Stephen d'Irsay, op. cit., vol. 2, pp. 129–43.

18. Charles C. Gillispie, "Science in the French Revolution," reprinted in B. Barber and W. Hirsch (eds.), *The Sociology of Science* (New York: The Free Press of Glencoe, 1962), p. 95. For a more detailed treatment of the subject, see his *The Edge of Objectivity: An Essay in the History of Scientific Ideas* (Princeton: Princeton University Press, 1960), pp. 151–201.

exchange; there were no facilities for the regular training of students in research.[19]

The ideas which gave rise to the new type of German university were no less utopian and not only unscientific but often antiscientific. Some of the most influential German thinkers intended the new University of Berlin to be a super-academy. Unlike their French colleagues, who regarded the natural sciences as the queen of sciences and hoped to unify knowledge through the interaction of people from various disciplines, the German philosophers believed that they had already accomplished the unification of all that was worthy of being known. The atmosphere and practice of the reformed German university were actually antiscientific, with the philosophy of nature often passing for natural science. Indeed, until the 1830s Germany lagged behind France scientifically and—with the exception of mathematics—even behind England.[20]

Thus, at the beginning of the nineteenth century there was nowhere in Europe any widespread desire—even among intellectuals—for the organization of scientific research in general. This was especially true of the renascent universities. There was some demand for technological education and, especially in France, for the use of science as a major vehicle for a humanistic education. The emergence in Germany of a network of university laboratories after 1825 could therefore only be the result of unintended social evolution. It was a result of the existence of a great number of universities and the rivalry of their famous teachers and students for ascendancy within a large German-speaking area. The German universities of the middle decades of the nineteenth century were an almost autonomous subsystem of German society developing according to its own internal laws without being required to perform any important economic function. Because of the political and economic backwardness of the area (relative to Western Europe) and a consequent shortage of attractive alternatives, there was a large supply of able students and aspirants for academic careers. Under these conditions there was no need for science to be socially useful, or—in the long run—even to be approved by the prevailing philosophies. The academic outlook was expanding under the pressure of the rigorous competition of the universities, filled with talented men. They were forced to "discover" the empirical sciences, once the humanities ceased to provide excitement and the limits of philosophical speculation were recognized.[21] Science was assimilated into the university system; the actual organi-

19. Cf. Stephen d'Irsay, op. cit., vol. 2, pp. 290–97, and H. E. Guerlac, "Science and French National Strength," in E. M. Earle (ed.), *Modern France* (Princeton: Princeton University Press, 1951), pp. 8–105.

20. See my "Scientific Productivity and Academic Organization in Nineteenth-Century Medicine," *American Sociological Review* 25, 6 (December 1960): 828–43. [This volume, chap. 5.]

21. About the rise of the natural sciences in German universities, see Richard H. Shryock, *The Development of Modern Medicine* (New York: Knopf, 1947), pp. 188–201; Joseph Ben-David and Awraham Zloczower, "Universities and Academic Systems in Modern Societies," *Eu-*

zation of the work was determined by the requirements of the university degree course and the interests of the scientists themselves. The facts that the scientists now wanted laboratories for their students and that the universities wanted scientists were more or less sufficient for the required state support to be provided for this purpose, as it had been provided for other university purposes in the past.

But by about 1860, science, which had been supported because it was an essential part of the university system to which the public authorities were committed, started to have practical functions. Its uses in chemistry, medicine, and, later, electricity became obvious and increasingly significant. As a result the academic system of research was not only preserved in Germany but also copied by Britain, the United States, and France. Thus, before the turn of the nineteenth century the isolation of scientific research from teaching—they had been separated since the seventeenth century—began to come to an end everywhere.[22]

The Two Types of Scientific Structure

I should like now to summarize the main differences between the structure of scientific activity in the seventeenth and eighteenth centuries and that of the nineteenth century. During the earlier period: (a) the scientific movement moved in the wake of more embracing theological-philosophical movements. The latter were ascientific or even antiscientific in content; they used science—at times falsely understood—as part and parcel of their philosophical program or else unintentionally aroused widespread interest in science simply because of the skepticism to which their own unredeemed utopian claims gave rise. (b) The growth of interest in science was attended by the foundation of new types of scientific organizations rather than by the revitalization of existing institutions which were bitterly criticized. This was a feature common to the seventeenth-century academies, the new scientific institutions in revolutionary France, the movement which led to the foundation of the University of

ropean Journal of Sociology 3 (1962): 45–84 [this volume, chap. 6]; Franz Schnabel, Deutsche Geschichte im Neunzehnten Jahrhundert, vol. 3, Die Erfahrungswissenschaften und Technik (Freiburg: Herder Verlag, 1934). pt. 3, "Die Naturwissenschaften," pp. 163–238. The revolt in philosophy was represented by Marx and Kierkegaard; see Karl Löwith, Von Hegel bis Nietzsche (Zurich: Europa, 1941), pp. 124–39, 148–54.

22. About the adoption of the German pattern elsewhere, Abraham Flexner, I Remember (New York: Simon and Schuster, 1940); Edward D. Churchill (ed.), To Work in the Vineyards of Surgery: The Reminiscences of J. Collins Warren (1842–1927) (Cambridge: Harvard University Press, 1958), pp. 193–97, 257–71; D. S. L. Cardwell, The Organization of Science in England (London: Heinemann, 1957), pp. 46–51, and passim; W. H. G. Armytage, Civic Universities (London: Benn, 1955), pp. 173–78; H. E. Guerlac, op. cit.; J. Ben-David and A. Zloczower, op. cit.

Berlin in the early nineteenth century, and, to a large extent, also the various English institutions and societies for the advancement of sciences launched at about the same time. (c) The life cycles of the new organizations of science resembled those of religious sects. They burst into life with great élan amid considerable enthusiasm on the part of groups of individuals rallying around a few charismatic leaders. They settled down into routine soon thereafter, once the force of the intellectual revolutions which inspired them had subsided. As a result, the development of science during these two centuries consisted of a very small amount of continuous scientific activity, inconspicuously scattered all over Europe, at the courts of princes, at some universities (in Scotland, Holland, Switzerland, and Sweden), at academies and private homes, and two major eruptions of scientific creativity. These were instigated by general religious and philosophical movements at the beginning and the end of the period, and they called forth discoveries and new scientific organizations in Italy, England, France, and, finally, Germany. (d) Many of these scientific institutions had no—or only unimportant—teaching functions; while in those—like the French revolutionary and the German institutions during the first two decades of the nineteenth century—which did have such functions, there was no proper integration of the teaching and research functions despite the fact that in some circles, the principle of such integration was already accepted.

The conditions under which the organization of science developed since the nineteenth century have been quite different. (a) The crucial changes consisted in the transformation or reconstruction of existing institutions rather than in the creation of new types. (b) Neither the transformation of science which occurred at the German universities through the introduction and expansion of laboratory training and specialized instruction in a growing number of fields nor the subsequent emergence of industrial research were accompanied by any general intellectual revolution. Even where there was agitation for the introduction of the German model, such as in England, the United States, and France, this was done by scientists and confined to the problems of empirical science. It was not part of any broader intellectual movement. (c) While the revolutionary scientific organizations of the seventeenth to early nineteenth centuries were unable to maintain their initial impetus, those founded since the middle of the nineteenth century unsupported by broader intellectual changes have been capable of sustained growth. (d) Teaching, training, and research have come to be regarded as inherently interconnected. Instruction was now given in highly specialized fields regardless of their practical application.

The transition from the revolutionary-charismatic system to the institutional system occurred as a result of the convergence of two factors. First, the large and competitive German academic system proved unexpectedly prolific in scientific research, particularly in empirical laboratory research. In a way this great productivity was all the more impressive since it was not a result of the appearance of an unusually great number of extraordinary talents. It was a product of organization, and it proved to scientists in other countries that research, through proper training and organization, could lead to determinate results. Second, the attainability of desired scientific results through the organization of research and training coincided with a new and deep awareness that the results of research could be useful.[23] This convergence which occurred around 1860 set the pattern which is now regarded as normal.

Scientific Organization and Scientific Policy

The preference shown by scientists all over the world for the German patterns of research and training and the undeniable acceleration of scientific growth in basic as well as applied fields which followed their adoption does not prove that this system was in every respect superior to the older scientific institutional systems still prevailing in France and England. Perhaps only certain of the features of the German system contributed to its impressive achievements. The crucial problem for those concerned with scientific policy today is the relationship between particular scientific institutional systems or components thereof and particular kinds of scientific production such as basically new ideas, discoveries based on existing ideas, contributions to industry, medicine, and other practical fields.

No one has yet attempted to study this question systematically, but the theory of scientific revolutions which Professor Thomas Kuhn presented first in a

23. The application of the discovery that science could be useful defended another feature of the German university system in its period of unpractical autonomy. Dr. Cardwell, in his paper "The Development of Scientific Research in Modern Universities: A Comparative Study of Motives and Opportunity" (*Scientific Change*, pp. 661–77), showed that the training of research chemists in the German universities preceded and provided the basis for the development of the German chemical industry. Although the first discovery of aniline dyes in 1856 by W. H. Perkin was made in England, the British chemical industry could not keep pace with the German because there were not enough research chemists in England to cater to the needs of the industry. In Germany, on the other hand, there were, since the universities produced chemists in advance of industrial demand as a by-product of an academic organization which was driven by an internal momentum.

Dr. Cardwell attributes the greater output of research workers in the German universities to the emphasis on creativity and originality in their philosophy and to the belief that their creativity could be expressed through systematic and disciplined research as well as to the competition between them due to the large number of universities. Professor Shryock in his comment (pp. 728–31) discards competition as a potentially important factor but accepts the importance of academic tradition. He stresses the relationship between universities and industry, pointing out that the greater interest of German industry in research was due to the fact that it started developing about the time when research became potentially useful for industry and that research was the only field where Germany had comparative advantages over the established industries and technological tradition of England and the greater natural resources of the United States.

preliminary way at the symposium and then published in book form is a useful starting point for arriving at an answer.[24]

According to his view, there are two main types of scientific discovery and a single social structure adapted to the furtherance of both. "Normal science," that is, science as practiced by the overwhelming majority of scientists most of the time, is essentially a "mopping up" or "puzzle solving" operation. Scientists of each discipline believe that they know what the "world"— or rather that part of it which is in their focus of attention—is like, what sorts of units it is composed of, and the ways, methods, and tools with which it can be investigated. They work according to a "paradigm" based on previous research, the results of which they accept more or less unquestioningly; their aim is to find answers to the still outstanding questions with the aid of the same paradigm.

The austere and self-denying picture of the scientist who does not take anything for granted but sets up rigorous experiments to reexamine the basic tenets of his own science is merely a myth. By this standard there could be no science at all, since there are—and have been—negative experiments to falsify every theory so far invented. Normally, however, scientists do not regard the negative results as reason for the rejection of the theory but rather as puzzles to be solved within the same theoretical framework. They are trained to choose problems which can be predictably solved, and there are strong negative sanctions against preoccupation with basic problems for which there is no solution in sight.

Only when "puzzles" accumulate and do not yield to repeated attempts at solution do scientists start perceiving these puzzles as "anomalies" which arouse their doubts about the correctness of the theory. Then "normal science" gives way to a period of "crisis." In such periods, scientists almost behave as the intellectual heroes they are supposed to be, posing questions of basic and all-embracing theoretical significance. Even in these periods they do not declare their discipline bankrupt but prefer to carry on their work in spite of growing frustration within the existing theoretical framework. Only when an apparently better theory is discovered is the bankruptcy of the old theory openly declared, thus starting a "scientific revolution." At first, only a minority of, usually, younger scientists accepts the new theory, transferring its allegiance to the innovator. A "revolutionary" struggle ensues, ending usually with the total victory of the revolution and a new phase of normal science.

It is obvious that the principal characteristics of present-day scientific organizations are in perfect accordance with the requirements of Professor Kuhn's "normal science." These organizations—indeed, the social system of science as a whole—form a loose federation of departments organized around disci-

24. See fn. 2 above. Cf. in this connection, Michael Polanyi, *Personal Knowledge* (London: Routledge and Kegan Paul, 1958).

plines which are sufficiently similar everywhere to be in worldwide communication with each other. The student, at least starting with his postgraduate years, grows up in such a "discipline." If he becomes a research worker, he will probably go on working in a department similar to the one in which he had been trained whether he is in a university or in an industrial laboratory. This closed environment is well suited for the creation of a community working in accordance with a "paradigm."

This organization might not be equally well suited for the furtherance of "revolutionary" innovation. This necessitates a loosening of the rules of normal scientific activity. It requires the questioning of premises which had been unquestioned before; the consideration of theories and hypotheses which contain enough obscure points to make them inadmissible for "normal science"; attention to practical proofs and events which, due to the ambiguity of their theoretical significance, are normally regarded as irrelevant to science; or unorthodox combinations of theories and techniques which violate accepted standards of methodology and expertise. Leniency toward such deviations seems to increase among scientists at times when a paradigm ceases to provide further fruitful results. But when precisely a paradigm is exhausted is a far from unequivocal question in the majority of sciences. The matter is made more difficult by the fact that the logic of organizations, including academic ones, is such that they concern themselves more with their own continuity than with the possible exhaustion of their inherited subject matter or problems.

Thus, while present-day university organization seems to fit the requirements of normal science very well, there is hardly anything like that fit with respect to revolutionary innovations. All the detailed examples of scientific revolutions quoted in Mr. Kuhn's book, with the exception of two—the electromagnetic theory of Maxwell and Einstein's relativity theory—are about events which took place within the framework of the old revolutionary-charismatic period of science (Copernicus, Kepler, Newton, Lavoisier, Franklin, Dalton). Besides, all of them took place either in theoretical physics or in fields just emerging from the preparadigmatic into their paradigmatic stage. This suggests that the feedback mechanisms involved in the exhaustion of paradigms and the generation of new ones might be quite efficient in overcoming organizational resistance in such deductive fields as mathematics and theoretical physics, where there might be little disagreement about the nature of puzzles and their number and duration at any time. But by the same token, it suggests that basic ("revolutionary") changes in other fields require further organizational mechanisms which are still to be identified.

It seems that for the identification of these mechanisms a different classification of discoveries than the one used by Professor Kuhn is needed, and I suggest one based on the sources from which the elements constituting a new discovery are taken. The ideas, techniques, and data on which a discovery is based may all come from one discipline (or paradigm), or they might come from several disciplines. They might result from the application of the principles of a scientific discipline (or several disciplines) to the solution of a practical problem, or, vice versa, the preoccupation with a practical problem may lead to the discovery of new scientific principles. This classification cuts across that of Professor Kuhn, since any of these types of discovery may logically constitute the solution of a known puzzle or result in the overthrow of an existing paradigm.

The advantage of this classification is that it makes it possible to distinguish among the various organizational factors those which may be relevant to different types of discovery. Let us take an innovation of the first type, that is, the source of which is in a given discipline. To the extent that such an innovation is of the ordinary puzzle-solving variety, the modern academic systems will probably be adequate. But, if it involves a basic change of the accepted traditions of an existing discipline ("paradigm overthrow"), it will inevitably meet resistance. The conditions under which such resistances were overcome have been studied in the development of physiology in France and Germany during the last century. In both places great resistance was offered to the new approach by the anatomists who regarded it as a minor branch of their own discipline. In France, this resistance was successful (until the German example convinced the authorities of the anomaly of their position), but in Germany, the new discipline was recognized by the establishment of new chairs for young adherents of the new field who had sufficient bargaining power in their dealings with peripheral universities. The organizational condition making possible the victory (or, at least, the early victory) of the revolution was the existence of a decentralized competitive system of many universities. Without competition the organization of the discipline in departments engaged in normal science would have been—as it actually was in France—a retarding factor.

The inefficiency of departmental organization—which is, as shown, the main characteristic of "normal science"—is also evident concerning innovations through the fusion of elements of several disciplines. The precondition of this is specialization within several fields, but in practice this is usually made quite difficult even though lip service is paid to the idea. It is, of course, usually possible for a student to attend lectures and seminars outside his own department, but the advanced student has always to be identified with a single department. The host department will usually be reluctant to invest much effort in his training, or may even be hostile and suspicious to one who does something which seems to approach amateurism. The most serious problem, however, is that research facilities are monopolized by departments so that taking the first steps in a borderline field by young people—who are the most likely to take it—may be quite difficult. Such difficulties greatly retarded the development of physiological chemistry in Germany in spite of the natural advantages of that country for research in this field, having possessed the most advanced institutions in physiological as well as chemical research.[25]

The likelihood of innovations based on applications of principles to practical problems depends first and foremost on the availability of a supply of scientists trained in research which is in excess of the existing demand for research workers. These people will be the most likely to look for opportunities of research in some unconventional framework or field. Dr. Cardwell's comparison of the development of applied chemical research in Germany—where there was such an excess supply—and in England—where there was not—is an excellent example of such a case. Even though this kind of research is usually "normal science," the actual organization of training, which is so efficient in producing research workers for this kind of work in universities, is a barrier to its extension to industry. The student becomes overidentified with the kind of framework, problems, and rewards common in a university department and is reluctant to venture into a new environment, except when forced to do so by lack of employment elsewhere. A different method, occasionally found in the United States, is to place students in industrial jobs before they are fully trained at the universities and to train them for research on the job. This may be one of the advantages of the American type of semiprofessional B.S. degree.[26]

Innovations due to the intrusion of practice into science are facilitated by the openness and diversity of the scientific system. The German system had been particularly resistant to such intrusions, since, due to the relative authoritarian and hierarchical nature of the society, academic institutions developed defenses against any external influences. It was because of this resistance that

25. Zloczower has shown that the rise of the *Institute* (departments) at the German universities toward the end of the last century created a great deal of interdepartmental jealousy. As a result it was very difficult for a junior member of a department to enter a borderline field of research, since this was interpreted by the other department as an attempt to invade its territory. It was possible to leave one department in order to obtain employment in another, but since the assumption of the heads of the departments was that people coming from other specialties should play a subsidiary role within their department, such a move entailed considerable career risks. See his *Career Opportunities and the Growth of Scientific Discovery in Nineteenth-Century Germany with Special Reference to Physiology*, unpublished M.A. thesis, written in the Department of Sociology, Hebrew University, Jersulaem, Israel, 1960. [Now published by Arno Press, New York, 1981.]

26. For the problems of adjustment of scientists to industrial research, see S. Marcson, *The Scientist in American Industry: Some Organizational Determinants in Manpower Utilization* (Princeton: Princeton University Press, 1960); William Kornhauser, with the assistance of Warren O. Hagstrom, *Scientists in Industry: Conflict and Accommodation* (Berkeley and Los Angeles: University of California Press, 1962); William Kornhauser, "Strains and Accommodations in Industrial Research Organisations in the United States," *Minerva* 1, 1 (Autumn 1962): 30–42. For the significance of different levels of training, see G. L. Payne, *Britain's Scientific and Technological Manpower* (Stanford: Stanford University Press, 1960).

bacteriology developed in Germany only as a result of direct state interference and psychoanalysis—which in America has enriched experimental psychology—was forced in Austria and Germany into becoming a healing sect.[27]

Professor Kuhn's scheme of analysis seems to presuppose a considerable measure of consensus throughout much of the scientific community concerning any particular paradigm. The overthrow of paradigms has, therefore, to be socially embodied in a series of revolutionary events. But in our vast and minutely specialized scientific system where research is pursued on so many levels, it is very difficult to correlate clearly any particular scientific subcommunity with any particular paradigm. Every field is so differentiated into subspecialties and there are so many people working in between several fields that the impact of even the most revolutionary innovation is likely to be experienced throughout a wide field with very diverse concepts. It will constitute a question of yes or no for very few persons; for many, a more or less partial modification of the theories and methods which they use will be called for. Fewer revolutionary innovations will probably be totally rejected as premature. Somewhere, some group is likely to be able to use it. Innovations which would be considered by a consensual scientific community as "premature revolutions" and, therefore, rejected could be quite useful and not revolutionary for some specialized scientific subcommunity which does not share wholly in the paradigm-consensus. Elements of a paradigm rejected by one scientific subcommunity may be picked up by another one whose paradigm is consistent with the discarded elements. As a result, charges of paradigms may lose their violent all-or-none character. Like the pursuit of normal science, basic scientific change may become a regular function taking place by stages.[28] The dramatic progress which in the earlier history of science was

27. See my "Roles and Innovations in Medicine," *American Journal of Sociology* 65, 6 (May 1960): 557–68 [this volume, chap. 1]. For a case where a revolutionary discovery was suppressed as a combined result of the lack of academic standing of its discoverer and the resistance of the system to "fusions," see Bernard Barber, "Resistance by Scientists to Scientific Discovery," *Science* 1 (September 1961): 569–602.

28. The history of statistics provides an example of what I have in mind. The theory of probability which was due to be a central element in Maxwell's statistical mechanics had a long and scientifically somewhat peripheral history before becoming a constitutive element in a minor revolution in physics. The fact that there was some kind of social science which supplied material for it had kept it alive and ensured its development for about 60 years. The obverse had happened in Russia lately, where statistics had been suppressed as a "wrong" social science for a considerable period but had been kept alive by physics. Even though in this latter case the problem was not prematurely, it still illustrates the difficulty of identifying a particular discovery, or series of discoveries, with any particular scientific community and that something which may be considered "revolutionary" for scientific—or even ideological—reasons, and, therefore, to be suppressed as long as the situation becomes ripe, in one context, or by one scientific community, may be used and developed in the meantime in a different context or by an adjacent scientific community. See C. C. Gillispie's symposium paper, "Intellectual Factors in the Background of Analysis by Probabilities," *Scientific Change*, pp. 431–53, and Leopold Labedz, "How Free is Soviet Science? Technology under Totalitarianism," in B. Barber and W. Hirsch (eds.), op. cit.,

probably made through scientific revolutions might henceforward become a part of routine science. This epochal change in the structure of scientific progress might turn out to be a product of the change of the scientific community into a confederation of overlapping scientific subcommunities.

---

pp. 129–41. As a matter of fact, Kuhn is aware of this overlap between scientific communities. He does not, however, draw from it the conclusion that it may basically alter the social structure of scientific revolution to the extent, perhaps, that one cannot speak any more of revolutions in the strict sense. Instead, he regards this circumstance as a factor which makes revolutions possible; see T. S. Kuhn, *The Structure of Scientific Revolutions,* op. cit., pp. 49–51. But, perhaps, the difference between his interpretation and mine is only a matter of degree.

Organization, Social Control, and Cognitive Change in Science **15**

Sociologists of science have studied mainly the behavior of scientists, both as performers of a social role which implies certain values and norms and as members of a profession. They have had little to say about the relationship between social conditions and the cognitive contents of science. Methodologically and theoretically, the sociology of science has been closer to the sociology of professions and organizations than to the sociology of knowledge.

This state of affairs has been found disappointing by many, and they have criticized it as a shortcoming which should be corrected. Others have rejected this criticism, doubting that an important and systematic relationship exists between social structure and the substantive contents of science.[1]

Most of this debate has been conducted on an exhortatory and programmatic level where debates can never be resolved. The problem is not whether there is a relationship at all between the contents and the social conditions of science, since the existence of some relationships has never been denied, but what kind of relationship there is and what importance it has for the growth of science or for various aspects of social life that one might be interested in exploring.

"Social conditions" is obviously a mixed category, which includes everything from the relationship between nations to the organization and social atmosphere of a single laboratory. In this paper I shall deal with the effects of a

I am deeply indebted to Robert Merton for his comments on an earlier draft of this paper, to Stephen Toulmin for discussions of some of its themes, and to the Ford Foundation for its support of my research.

1. For a summary of this controversy, see Diana Crane, *Invisible Colleges* (Chicago: University of Chicago Press, 1972), pp. 8–11.

limited range of such conditions, namely, the effects of the way scientific research and teaching are organized and of the way scientific contributions are recognized and evaluated. These effects will be explored through the review of two historical turning points in science, namely, the emergence of modern science in the seventeenth century and the emergence of modern scientific disciplines at the end of the eighteenth and early nineteenth centuries.

The Significance of the
Seventeenth-Century Academies
of Science

The first case which I propose to consider is the often debated question of what conditions gave rise to modern science. Starting with Robert K. Merton, sociologists of science have considered the events leading to the establishment of the Royal Society of London as the most important step in the transition from medieval and Renaissance to modern science.[2] This importance has been called into question by Thomas Kuhn in a review article.[3] He argues that the sociologists' concentration on England as the place where modern science chiefly emerged is a mistake, since British supremacy in science at the end of the seventeenth century was due exclusively to Newton. Had Newton not been an Englishman, Britain would not have been considered the leading scientific power in the seventeenth century, and no one would have paid any attention to the social conditions prevailing in that country as "the main clues to the rise of modern science."

He then goes on to argue that intellectually Newton was not representative of English science. He belonged rather to the Continental tradition stemming from the abstract mathematical approach of Greek science, which was relatively independent of observation and experiment. The English tradition in the seventeenth and eighteenth centuries was nonmathematical, paid little attention to the Greek and medieval tradition, and depended mainly on instruments, observations, and experiments. This second tradition had little effect on "scientific theory or conceptual structure" until the middle of the eighteenth century. Only at the end of that century were the tools of the Continental mathematical tradition applied to the products of the English empirical movement, and only then did the modern scientific role, which combines mathematical thinking with experimental skill, emerge.

I shall not try to discuss the debatable proposition that Newton belonged wholly to the Continental tradition. But there appear to have been good rea-

2. Robert K. Merton, *Science, Technology, and Society in Seventeenth-Century England* (New York: Howard Fertie, 1970).
3. Thomas S. Kuhn, "Scientific Growth: Reflections on Ben-David's 'Scientific Role,'" *Minerva* 10 (January 1972): 166–78, on pp. 173–74.

sons for concentrating on British social conditions in order to discover "the main clues to the rise of modern science"—clues quite independent of Newton. In the seventeenth century there existed, all over Europe, a scientific movement which strove for recognition as a new kind of philosophic endeavor. For this movement the foundation of the Royal Society was an event of supreme importance. It was the first decisive victory in the fight for public recognition of science as an autonomous intellectual inquiry, free from the control of theology or philosophic doctrine. In France, members of this movement recommended the imitation of the new English institution; scientists everywhere had used it as a center of correspondence and recognition before anyone knew of Newton.[4] Thus the establishment of the Royal Society in 1660 (when Newton was eighteen) was an important event in the history of science quite apart from the glory bestowed on it by Newton's membership more than a decade later (1671).

But of course the question is not whether the foundation of the Royal Society was regarded as an important event by contemporaries but whether we can regard it as the beginning of the scientist's role in the modern sense.

Kuhn's definition of this role is based on scientific "tradition." He includes in this term a variety of things, but its crucial aspect seems to be the general (metaphysical) view of nature underlying scientific craftsmanship. Therefore, Kuhn dates the beginning of the modern scientific role from the time when the rise of a mathematical theory which could be effectively applied to the products of empirical observation and experiment pushed into the background the differences between the preconceived notions of scientists steeped in different philosophic traditions. "Role" is conceived of here as the cognitive and technical contents of what the incumbent of the role knows and does. When those contents change, the role changes.

On the other hand, sociologists who have investigated the beginnings of the scientific role have been interested in the normative, or moral, aspect of the scientist's behavior. For them, the question was not how scientists actually worked but how scientists demarcated themselves from other intellectuals, by what norms they wanted to judge one another's work, and how they wanted to be perceived and judged by the larger society. The scientists of the seventeenth (or the eighteenth) century did not invent the importance of either observation or mathematics or even the independence of these from religion and

4. See Thomas Sprat, *The History of the Royal Society of London for the Improving of Natural Knowledge* (London, 1667). Sprat speaks of the Royal Society as the "general *Banck* and Freeport of the world [in the new learning]" (p. 64); about England as the "Head of a *Philosophical League,* above all other countries in Europe" (p. 113); and about French recognition of England as the country which has "*Real Philosophy*" (p. 126). For a discussion showing that the existence of a "Philosophical League" and the recognition of English leadership following the foundation of the Royal Society were not merely an expression of patriotic bias on Sprat's part, see Harcourt Brown, *Scientific Organizations in Seventeenth-Century France (1620–1680)* (Baltimore: Williams & Wilkins, 1934), pp. 15–60.

philosophic doctrine. Many ancient and medieval scholars were well aware of all this and acted—within limits—accordingly.

The innovation of the seventeenth century was the insistence that the kind of inquiry that could be judged by empirical and mathematical criteria should be made the contents of a separate intellectual role and that there should be a separate institutional structure for the evaluation of those who performed this role. The extent to which there existed a consistent view of the world and a well-established tradition of intellectual craftsmanship to make the establishment of a separate role and separate institutions for this kind of inquiry worthwhile and feasible was a question about which there were serious doubts at the time.[5] It can be argued that the belief in the superiority of the empirical-mathematical method was a utopian faith throughout the seventeenth century and in much of the eighteenth. Before Newton it could claim little evidence in its favor, and afterwards it had to rely on a small number of cases (Newton, Huygens, etc.) for a very long time. But the faith arose, and was maintained in the absence of crucial evidence, as a result of the overwhelming problems which beset intellectual life. The theological and philosophic disputes of the time created an impasse where no debate could be resolved. There was an urgent need for a reliable method for adjudicating intellectual disputes and evaluating intellectual merit. This need prompted the members of the Oxford experimental philosophy club and subsequently the members of the Royal Society to regard their experimental and mathematical interests and methods as patently superior to those of the contemporary guilds and groups of theologians, philosophers, physicians, and lawyers. They possessed a method which made for uncoerced consensus and therefore promised cumulative growth of knowledge, at least in the field of natural philosophy. They did so at the price of abandoning the philosophic search for all-encompassing knowledge. But that search seemed to have led nowhere; moreover, there was a growing expectation, arising from Baconian philosophy, that the search for comprehensive knowledge, now to be abandoned by the individual, would be retrieved in the long run by the cumulative work of generations. Against this background the price to be paid did not seem excessive.[6] Thus the new role of the scientist as a philosopher applying mathematical and empirical, preferably experimental, methods to the study of nature arose in the seventeenth century, although in actual fact there were very few people who could combine the mathematical with the experimental method.

The situation which prevailed in late-seventeenth- and early-eighteenth-century natural science can be compared to that which exists today in much of social science. The success of social science is still not convincing enough to

5. The criticisms of and doubts about the Royal Society are summarized in R. F. Jones, *Ancients and Moderns: A Study of the Rise of the Scientific Movement in Seventeenth-Century England*, 2d ed. (Berkeley and Los Angeles: University of California Press, 1965), pp. 237–72.
6. Sprat, *History of the Royal Society*, pp. 22–58.

justify in all eyes the separation of the role of the social scientist from that of the ideologist, the journalist, or the practical man reflecting on his experience. It is often pointed out that some of the latter have shown a better grasp of the workings of society than the social scientists have. Or it is demonstrated that this or that social scientist has actually engaged in ideology and that, in fact, the criteria according to which he defines himself as a scientist, rather than as an ideologist committed to a political program, are far from unequivocal. Moreover, every now and then theories arise, such as Marxism or psychoanalysis, which manage to mix scientific rationality and self-fulfilling prophecy (the parallel to magic in relation to natural science) in such ingenious ways that the demarcation between social science and ideology becomes temporarily blurred. Yet people can still be identified as social scientists by their belief in the possibility of the eventual success of a science of society; by their insistence on judging one another's work on the basis of such criteria as empirical evidence, statistical inference, and logical reasoning; and by the fact that, though they constantly become involved with ideologies, they eventually are prodded, by interacting with other scientists, into extricating themselves from such involvements.[7] Thus, in spite of the diversity of the intellectual traditions of social science, a community of social scientists exists, held together by a common belief in the possibility of an objectively testable knowledge of society, by a common value that the attainment of such knowledge is socially desirable, and by a common morality (which is often transgressed but never with good conscience) of submission to being judged by the norms of the currently defined methods of scientific work. Similarly, natural scientists in the seventeenth and eighteenth centuries defined themselves as different from the general philosophers, theologians, and magicians, from whom—according to the contents of their work—they were barely separable, and from craftsmen and empirical practitioners, whose skills and insights were often superior to those of the scientists.[8]

The Impact of Scientific Academies on Eighteenth-Century Science

It has to be seen now how this—intellectually perhaps premature—institutionalization of science influenced its development. The purpose of the new

7. One of the most interesting documents showing a sociologist's attempt to make a basically Marxist position amenable to judgment by the accepted criteria of the scientific community is Karl Mannheim's *Ideology and Utopia* (New York: Harcourt, Brace, 1936), pp. 155–64. For a discussion of the relationship between science and ideology, see Edward Shils, *The Intellectuals and the Powers, and Other Essays* (Chicago: University of Chicago Press, 1972), pp. 37–38.

8. For discussions of the ambiguous relationship between science and these other modes of thought and the difficulty of demarcating one from the other, see Alan Debus, *Science and Education in the Seventeenth Century: The Webster-Ward Debate* (London and New York: Mac-

roles and organizations was, as I have pointed out, to establish and maintain the norm that scientific truth must be based on strict (preferably mathematical) logic and be supported by empirical evidence. According to the scientistic utopian belief, research, once this approach was adopted, would lead from one discovery to another, and science would be sustained by its sheer intellectual momentum and the utility of its discoveries.[9] With the appearance of the great discoveries of Newton, it appeared for a while that the utopian program would be fulfilled. But these great events were followed by disappointment. There were few discoveries and continued intellectual confusion. The hope that science would lead to a continuous orderly advance of consensual knowledge and that its distinctness as an experimental-mathematical enterprise would be preserved was far from assured. In order to maintain science as a distinct consensual enterprise—which was its main attraction—there was needed a social mechanism to promptly and justly decide which discoveries, however small, were acceptable by the standards of science and which were not. Since the belief in science was based on the assumption that experimental and mathematical methods were superior to other types of thought, only the existence of such a mechanism could ensure that science would be judged on its own merits; namely, that it would be given credit for its own achievements and would not be charged with the failures of quacks and other nonscientists.

But such a mechanism was needed for the maintenance of consensus not only at a time when science was particularly threatened by lack of significant advances and lack of theoretical consensus. The problem of judgment and recognition had to be taken care of by social means even at the best times of science. Although the methods of experiment and mathematical proof are in a way self-administering, in practice scientists, more than workers in other intellectual fields, require an institutional system of reward allocation. Scientists, like philosophers and scholars, must publish their findings in order to fulfill any social function. Furthermore, only through publication and recognition of authorship can they establish rights to their own intellectual property. In general philosophy and humanistic scholarship, things are relatively easy. Philosophers and scholars can appeal to a wide public, and they need not fear that their competitors will anticipate them or steal their creations. In these fields, style is so much part of the message that plagiarism requires actual copying and can easily betray itself.

Not so in science. Because of the technical nature of the contributions,

Donald and American Elsevier, 1970), pp. 1–57; P. M. Rattansi, "The Social Interpretation of Science in the Seventeenth Century," in Peter Mathias (ed.), *Science and Society* (Cambridge: At the University Press, 1972), pp. 1–32.

9. Margery Purver, *The Royal Society: Concept and Creation* (Cambridge: MIT Press, 1967), pp. 60–71, 77, 80–81; Roger Hahn, *Anatomy of a Scientific Institution: The Paris Academy of Sciences, 1666–1804* (Berkeley and Los Angeles: University of California Press, 1971), pp. 11–12, 24–36; Keith Michael Baker, *Condorcet: From Natural Philosophy to Social Mathematics* (Chicago: University of Chicago Press, 1975), p. 93.

evaluation of scientific work cannot be solicited from the general public (and, if solicited, it would be irrelevant and of little value). Therefore, only one's own colleagues can serve as a proper audience and as a legitimate source of recognition. This makes plagiarism a very likely possibility. Scientific results, because they are specific and are independent of writing style, are easy to steal. Moreover, because of the frequency of genuinely independent simultaneous discovery, it is difficult to detect plagiarism or, in the case of genuine multiple discovery, to assign property rights.

Therefore, problems of recognition, evaluation, and adjudication of priorities were major issues for the newly established scientific community, as they are even today, when that community is much better established.[10] As a result, the evaluation of contributions became the major function of the official academies. Originally they were designed as institutions for cooperation in research, and in the case of the Paris Academy of Sciences, even for cooperative research. But the state of the art, in which experiments could be performed in a workshop far simpler than a modern kitchen, called for little cooperation in research; and after a period of trial and error, the academies, especially the Paris Academy of Sciences, became in practice organizations for the public and official recognition of the contributions of individual scientists.[11]

There is ample evidence that in the practice of the academies "the scientific method" served as a set of procedural norms of judgment. Because of the diversity and immaturity of scientific theory, the debates of the day turned frequently on questions which were not and could not be empirically investigated. Here are a few among many examples:

> Mariotte, Frenicle, Buot, Claude Perrault, and Huygens could not agree upon the nature of gravitation. DuVerney and Perrault failed to interpret similar anatomical evidence on the function of the ear in the same fashion. Du Clos' explanation of the increase of weight in calcination and his treatment of the process of coagulation did not bring about any consensus either. To decide by a majority vote which position was correct was absurd, for all the scientists firmly believed that truth was determined by nature and not by the will of men. In practice, the most that the company could assert as being true was that portion of evidence about which there was no disagreement.
>
> Generally, it was the undigested observation of some phenomenon that was thereby considered as true "positively." For the rest, the greatest service the Academy could perform was to publish the opinion of each of its members, no matter how many contradictions might appear.
>
> The better part of wisdom, if the Academy was to have a long and useful

10. Robert K. Merton, "Priorities in Scientific Discovery: A Chapter in the Sociology of Science," *American Sociological Review* 22 (1957): 645–59; Warren O. Hagstrom, *The Scientific Community* (New York: Basic Books, 1965), pp. 69–104.

11. Hahn, *Anatomy of a Scientific Institution*, pp. 22–23, 26–34.

existence, was to resist the temptation to judge where judgment was premature. Fontenelle, who grasped the realities of the life of the Academy better than any of his contemporaries, became an eloquent spokesman for this philosophical position. While discussing academic disagreements over the circulation of sap in plants, he remarked that "The academy was the natural judge between these two views. But since a large part of wisdom consists in making no judgment, it declared that the subject was not yet sufficiently clear. It is necessary to wait until there is a fairly large number of experiments and facts before extracting a generalization. There is a common tendency to rush to formulate general principles, and the mind runs toward systems. But we must not always trust in the merit of this order." [12]

This account shows how significant for the development of science was the emergence of the new role and the new institutional structure, devoted to the cultivation of norms of scientific evaluation on the basis of experiment and mathematics. Even though the research practices of individual scientists did not always fit the norms, since they rushed "to formulate general principles" prematurely, the evaluation of their work by the official representatives of the scientific community, the Academy, was based on strict observance of these norms. The norms were necessary to maintain the moral cohesion and the motivation of the scientific community. They enabled the community to exist and to function over a long period of time, even in the absence of outstanding achievements and a unified tradition. Without these institutionally enforced norms the unity of the scientific enterprise might have been in jeopardy.

This was the importance of the social structures which arose in the seventeenth century for the cognitive development of science in the following century. The social control exercised by the academies of science ensured the maintenance of the unity of the scientific endeavor. It discouraged doctrinal approaches which threatened scientific consensus, and it treated with hostility doctrines, such as Mesmerism, which seemed to be inconsistent with good experimental procedure. On the other hand, it rewarded contributions based on experimentally testable knowledge. This had a selective influence on the development of science, and it probably created a predisposition for the favorable reception of the new mathematical-experimental tradition, which seemed to have succeeded in creating theories in which all concepts were linked to empirical observations. This was, of course, an indirect influence on the cognitive development of science. Yet it was a crucial one, since without it the scientific effort might easily have lost its purpose and direction.

12. Ibid., pp. 32–33. Hahn uses the apposite term "phenomenological positivism" to describe this policy. For a similar policy, adopted earlier by the Royal Society, see Sprat, *History of the Royal Society,* pp. 106–09. But there this method was part of the original design of the Society. See also Stephen G. Brush, "The Royal Society's First Rejection of the Kinetic Theory of Gases (1821): John Herapath versus Humphrey Davy," *Notes and Records of the Royal Society of London* 18 (December 1963): 161–80, for an example of a recourse to the principles of scientific method as a judicial-moral argument in a case in which substantive scientific opinion was divided.

The importance of the institutions created in the seventeenth century in maintaining the unity and purpose of science explains why sociologists of science have been more interested in the changes which occurred in science in the seventeenth century than in those that occurred in the eighteenth. These seventeenth-century changes, such as the programmatic creation of the new social role of the natural philosopher, and of the new organization of the scientific academy, were easily discernible social events. These were not trivial things from the point of view of the growth of science, in spite of the apparent lack of success of the new organizations in creating the kind of science and the kind of scientists that the founders of the scientific movement envisioned. Their importance lies in the fact that they influenced the volume and the location of research and, indirectly, by withholding recognition from the metaphysical elements of theories, its cognitive direction as well.

The Sociologists' Neglect of the Eighteenth-Century Revolution in Science

One can also understand why sociologists neglected the changes in science which occurred in the late eighteenth and early nineteenth centuries. Ostensibly, the emergence of new physical and chemical theories, which succeeded in combining experiment with mathematics, had no effect on the social structure of science. In contrast to the seventeenth-century British scientists, who at every point emphasized the difference between themselves and their philosophic predecessors, the scientific innovators of the eighteenth century claimed only to have carried to new heights the enterprise which had begun in the seventeenth century. They were quite content to be not revolutionaries but worthy heirs of their predecessors.

Nor did they initiate new organizations, as had their predecessors more than a hundred years before. They were pleased to take their place in the academies and other institutions which had been emerging throughout the seventeenth and eighteenth centuries, and all they wanted was to extend the influence of these institutions to increasingly wider circles of society. The revolutionary changes in French scientific institutions at the end of the eighteenth and the beginning of the nineteenth centuries resulted more from the political than from the scientific changes of the period.[13] Thus one can speak of the rise of a new kind of role in the seventeenth century but not of one at the end of the eighteenth or at the beginning of the nineteenth century. The cognitive change

13. See Hahn, *Anatomy of a Scientific Institution*, pp. 278–85, for the background of the French reforms of higher education after 1794; and see René König, *Vom Wesen der deutschen Universität* (Darmstadt: Wissenschaftliche Buchgesellschaft, 1970), pp. 27–40, for the antecedents of the establishment of the University of Berlin and the reform of higher education in Prussia during the first decade of the nineteenth century.

in science which occurred in the latter centuries gave rise to some organizational developments but not to changes in the institutional definition of either science or the scientist's role.

From a sociological point of view, the situation was the reverse of that in the seventeenth century. Then groups of scientists, supported by other believers in the utopian potentiality of science, chose an organization which they (wrongly) believed could actually generate and then propagate the kind of science they dreamed of. However, that science did not exist, and so the new organizations could not create it. This became clear very soon, when, though the institutional conditions were present, the discoveries did not follow as predicted. In contrast, at the end of the eighteenth century, the science capable of rapid development was there, but the motivation to create new organizations for training researchers and to exploit the opportunities inherent in the state of science was relatively weak. The innovations in scientific training and education made in 1795–98, such as the attempt to make the École polytechnique into an advanced scientific school, to make science an important part of the upper-secondary education, and to introduce research into the new schools of medicine, were initiated by scientists and scientistic intellectuals. But it was the latter rather than the former who were really interested in education. The scientists themselves maintained, throughout the revolutionary period, a relatively high degree of consensus and tried to support one another and to preserve the Academy of Sciences. Therefore, when Napoleon—who loathed intellectuals but liked scientists—suppressed the educational reforms favoring science, he encountered little opposition to this among scientists. The scientists were quite satisfied with the resurrected old Academy as the first class of the Institute, with increased support for their personal work, and with the extension of opportunities for the employment of scientists in some of the specialized institutions of higher education or in noneducational capacities; they did not worry too much about science education in general or about the organization of research in particular.[14] All this would seem to indicate that the emergence of new physical and chemical theories at the end of the eighteenth century had neither direct social causes nor direct social effects. The discoveries changed science but did not change the social definition of the role of the scientist.

The Effect of the Eighteenth-Century Scientific Revolution on the Uses and Organization of Science

However, the discoveries were connected—indirectly—with social conditions at both ends of the causal chain. Even the discoveries of Lavoisier and

14. Hahn, *Anatomy of a Scientific Institution*, pp. 245–46, 288–312.

Laplace were perhaps not entirely unrelated to the social control over science exercised by the Paris Academy of Sciences. As I have pointed out above, the insistence of that academy on upholding the ideal of perfect overlap between (preferably mathematical) theory and (preferably experimental) empirical evidence prepared the ground for the triumphant acceptance of these discoveries and probably enhanced their immediate effect.

There was also a reverse effect of the new theories on the organization of science. In order to understand this effect, we have to see what the social significance of the new discoveries was and what kind of social opportunities they created. From the point of view of the scientistic utopia of the seventeenth and eighteenth centuries, Lavoisier and Laplace were a kind of fulfillment. The entire eighteenth century awaited the reappearance of a scientific hero to carry on the work of Newton, and these two seemed to answer the expectation. Of course, like Newton, Lavoisier and Laplace failed to realize exactly the Baconian utopia foreseen by the founders of the scientistic movement in the seventeenth century. No method emerged for teaching mediocre minds how to be creative, nor did science contribute to technology except in a marginal way. Still, the results bore a respectably close resemblance to what was originally envisioned, since scientists made some well-advertised contributions to technology, and there were now theories and methods capable of generating relatively long-term programs of significant research. With the emergence of such programs, science became organizable.

The most immediate social opportunities inherent in this development were educational. Possessing a body of consensual and theoretically organized knowledge, science, especially physics, could be used as an educational discipline. Teachers of science could now claim as much authority for their knowledge as teachers of Latin or Greek grammar had always claimed for theirs. They could also claim authority to direct the research of disciples who wanted to become scientists, since the fruitful directions of research could be derived from existing authoritative knowledge, and those who mastered the field could discern and determine those directions. Therefore, research could be organized as a school where a master directed his student apprentices in carrying out a program of research conceived by him.

These opportunities, inherent in the new kind of scientific theory, were immediately recognized in France, where most of the major advances had taken place. However, as I have pointed out, except for the few transitional years between the Terror and the Empire, no need was felt in France to take advantage of these opportunities. That they were recognized is shown by the educational reforms of the mid-1790s and by the creation of the Society of Arcueil, but no significant group in society had sufficient motivation to exploit them.[15]

15. The Society of Arcueil (1807–1822) was a group of physicists and chemists, led by Berthollet and Laplace, who shared common interests and worked on related problems. See Maurice Crosland, *The Society of Arcueil* (Cambridge: Harvard University Press, 1967),

People were satisfied with classical education, and scientists who had no reason to be dissatisfied with either their scientific or their social attainments did not pay too much attention to missed educational opportunities.

The situation was somewhat different in Germany. Not that the attitudes toward science were more favorable there than in France. They were in fact much less favorable. But the attitude toward intellectuals and education was different. While Napoleon despised the philosophers and their educational schemes, the civil servants of defeated Prussia sought alliance with their philosophers. This led to the foundation of the University of Berlin in 1810 as a new type of institution, where teachers were expected to be creative scholars. The intention was to make the University of Berlin the center of all German intellectual life. Its actual effect was to induce the other German states to reform their universities as well. The existence of more than twenty German-language universities competing with one another for scholarly fame gave rise to a veritable market for scholars. As a result, the universities, which were originally designed only for producing future professionals—namely, high-school teachers, doctors, lawyers, and theologians—became to some extent training institutions in research.[16] This research impetus got its start in the humanities, especially in the classical languages, which were the most important teaching subjects for high-school (*Gymnasium*) teachers. Intensive special courses, "seminars," given to these future teachers for the purpose of increasing their proficiency in their field of teaching, became in fact schools of research when led by great scholars.[17] In the same manner, teaching laboratories in chemistry (established mainly for the training of pharmacists) and physiology (created for training doctors) were turned into research laboratories where a few of the abler students conducted original research under the guidance of a professor.[18]

This development of laboratory research at the universities occurred by default, since, as we have pointed out, experimental sciences were regarded as subjects barely worthy of the universities. Once it occurred, however, the opportunities for exploiting the potentialities inherent in the emerging scientific disciplines through research organized in schools became apparent. The competition between the universities of the different German states impelled the states to support the experimental fields which showed striking achievements, regardless of the educational philosophies held by the bulk of the academic profession or by the administrators and the rulers upon whom the universities

pp. 232–428; Robert Fox, "Scientific Enterprise and the Patronage of Science in France, 1800–1870," *Minerva* 11 (1973): 442–73.

16. Joseph Ben-David and Awraham Zloczower, "Universities and Academic Systems in Modern Society," *European Journal of Sociology* 3 (1962): 45–84. [This volume, chap. 6.]

17. Friedrich Paulsen, *Geschichte des gelehrten Unterrichts auf den deutschen Schulen und Universitäten*, 2 vols. (Leipzig: Von Veit, 1892), 2:269–74.

18. For the importance of the training of pharmacists, see Bernard Gustin, "The Chemical Profession in Germany, 1790–1867" (Ph.D. dissertation, University of Chicago, 1975).

depended. Starting about 1825, with the foundation of Liebig's laboratory at Giessen, the German universities became in less than two decades the undisputed centers of world science, surpassing in their scientific productivity both France and Britain.

The Social Functions of Nineteenth-Century Science

These developments changed the social functions of science radically. Intellectually, eighteenth-century science represented mainly the spirit of free and critical inquiry, subject only to logic and empirical evidence. Now, in the nineteenth century, it symbolized the triumph of comprehensive theoretical systems. The new physical and chemical theories had an air of perfection, or near perfection, about them. They could be interpreted as the beginning of an era of a logically complete system of experimental philosophy in the physical sciences. The task of the future appeared as a matter of filling in details and of extending the system to the biological and the social sciences. According to this view, the model of all science was classical physics.[19] Any inquiry which did not live up to this model or was not visibly advancing toward it, either because of insufficient overlap between observation and theory or because of imperfections of either theory or method, was suspect and considered inferior.

The change was even more dramatic in the educational functions of science. As noted above, there was little education and virtually no systematic training in science during the eighteenth century. What influence the scientific approach had on education was mainly limited to casting doubt on the value of the content and method of the prevailing education. In the nineteenth century, by contrast, the advanced study of science became one of the principal realizations of the new university ideal of integration of research and training. Training for research had many similarities to indoctrination. The student was brought up in a tradition of theories, methods, and exemplary cases of discoveries codified in textbooks, considered as constituting a coherent and closed system. He was assigned research topics which arose out of that tradition, and he was supposed to treat his research problems as "puzzles" to be solved by the theories and methods available within that tradition; in this way, he would contribute to its further perfection.[20]

This gave rise to another radical departure from the eighteenth-century

---

19. For the emergence of such a view, resulting from the spectacular advances in classical mechanics during the second half of the eighteenth century, see L. Pearce Williams, *The Origins of Field Theory* (New York: Random House, 1966), pp. 30–31. See also E. J. Dijksterhuis, *The Mechanization of the World Picture* (London: Oxford University Press, 1969), pp. 499–501.

20. This is still the prevailing tradition in science teaching; see Thomas S. Kuhn, *The Structure of Scientific Revolutions* (Chicago: University of Chicago Press, 1962), pp. 10–22.

situation, when scientific achievements could bring honor but seldom income to the scientist. Now, in the nineteenth century, his achievements often conferred on him more or less well-paying teaching positions and, especially in Germany, monopolistic powers over productive research resources.[21] This created a vested interest in blurring the distinction between the procedural rules of science and the actual research traditions of a particular group within science. Since these particular traditions were thought to be adhering strictly to the procedural rules, there seemed to be no need for a superior authority, situated outside the research group or school, to judge whether the achievements of its members lived up to the standards of science. This tendency to identify a discipline with a research school had particularly insidious results in Germany, where the teaching laboratory and the university institute were the principal resources available for research and could be obtained only through the recognition of a specialty as a discipline and the establishment of a separate chair for it. The result was an eagerness on the part of certain schools to monopolize disciplines, as well as an effort to turn research schools into recognized independent disciplines.

This development introduced a bias into scientific thinking. Discoveries which did not fit into one of the existing disciplines or did not promise to become "systematic" teaching disciplines (that is, relatively comprehensive and logically well structured) were either relegated to an inferior category of "narrow" specialties (the administrative corollary of which was that a person in such a field could not be made into a full professor—he was not *ordinierbar* [*Ordinarius* = full professor]) or were actually attacked and ridiculed. Many examples of such attitudes can be cited, such as the total rejection of Semmelweis's excellent work on the causes and prevention of puerperal fever; the nonrecognition of the discoveries of Mendel; and the hurdles placed in the way of bacteriologists, physiological chemists, and physical chemists, which made it very difficult for them to become established at the universities.[22]

21. For the monopolization of research resources by heads of institutions, see Awraham Zloczower, "Konjunktur in der Forschung," in F. Pfetsch and A. Zloczower, *Innovation und Widerstände in der Wissenschaft* (Düsseldorf: Bertelsmann, 1973).
22. For the case of Semmelweis, see Bernard J. Stern, "Resistance to Medical Change," in his *Historical Sociology* (New York: Citadel Press, 1959), pp. 363–65. On Mendel, see Hugo Iltis, *Life of Mendel* (London: Allen & Unwin, 1932), pp. 191–204. On biochemistry, see Robert Kohlen, "The Background to Edward Büchner's Discovery of Cell-Free Fermentation," *Journal of the History of Biology* 4 (1971): 57–58; Awraham Zloczower, "Konjunktur in der Forschung," on the difficulties that bacteriology as a discipline encountered at German universities; and James Richard Bartholomew, "The Acculturation of Science in Japan: Kitasato Shibasaburo and the Japanese Bacteriological Community, 1885–1920" (Ph.D. dissertation, Stanford University, 1971), pp. 170–71. [The essential substance of this thesis has been published in J. R. Bartholomew, "Japanese Culture and the Problem of Modern Science," in E. Mendelsohn and A. Thackray (eds.), *Science and Values* (New York: Humanities Press, 1974), pp. 109–155, and idem, "Science, Bureaucracy, and Freedom in Meiji and Taisho Japan," in Tetsuo Najita and J. Victor Koschmann (eds.), *Conflict in Modern Japanese History: The Neglected Tradition* (Princeton: Princeton University Press, 1982), pp. 295–341.]

Even people like Otto Hahn and Lisa Meitner, whose excellence and the importance of whose work were beyond doubt and dispute, had difficulty in overcoming the hurdles of disciplinary boundaries which were so conspicuous a feature of the German universities.[23]

Disciplinary Dogmatism, Monopoly, and Social Control in Nineteenth-Century Science

This disciplinary exclusiveness and rigidity became a hallmark of science education and training for research. Thanks to institutional differences, the actual policies toward innovations were more liberal in some countries than in Germany; this was especially true in the United States. However, the philosophy of disciplinary science had spread all over the world, and it dominated, in particular, the teaching of science.[24]

At first sight this disciplinary dogmatism of nineteenth-century science appears to constitute a change in the norms of scientific judgment. In the seventeenth and eighteenth centuries the academies evaluated scientific contributions according to formal criteria of mathematical and empirical inquiry which were relatively unbiased toward different theories. With the emergence of the new disciplines this general model gave way to specific disciplinary models containing more or less elaborate theories and unstated metaphysical assumptions about the nature of matter, light, electricity, living organisms, and so on. This development seems to have introduced into scientific judgment a bias which had not been there before. The disciplinary models now seemed to dominate scientific thought; there appeared to be no visible control over them by a central supradisciplinary authority, such as had been exercised by the Paris Academy of Sciences in the eighteenth century.

That this is only part of the picture will, however, become obvious if, instead of concentrating on the rejection of discoveries which did not fit the preconceptions of one or another particular scientific discipline, we ask the question: In how many cases did rejection result in the actual suppression of the innovations? It seems that this occurred very rarely. The two most well-known cases are those of Semmelweis and Mendel, whose innovations, rejected by scientific authorities, were forgotten and so had to be rediscovered. Only in the case of Semmelweis was there actual suppression, in the sense that the rejection of his discovery was unsuccessfully contested.[25] Mendel did not accept the erroneous opinion of the leading scientific authority, but he did not

23. For the hurdles against cooperation between the chemist Otto Hahn and the physicist Lisa Meitner, see Otto Hahn, *Scientific Autobiography* (New York: Scribner's, 1966), pp. 50–72.

24. Kuhn, *The Structure of Scientific Revolutions*, pp. 10–22.

25. On Semmelweis and Mendel, see n. 22, above.

fight it, either. Nägeli was probably prejudiced by his disciplinary orthodoxy against Mendel—who was a nonphysiologist—and so did not trouble to understand Mendel properly. But Mendel, who was somewhat of an amateur, was quite happy to follow the suggestions of Nägeli and turn to other investigations rather than follow up his own insights, especially since his further experiments (with hawkweeds) did not conform to his theory. Therefore, this was hardly a case of suppression.

As a matter of fact, what is surprising in the sociology of nineteenth-century science is not the prevalence of local attempts at suppression but the fact that they so rarely succeeded and that at no point was there any doubt among those with different prejudices that the contest of views could be resolved by accepted scientific procedures and that consensus would eventually be reestablished. No school managed to establish a monopoly over even a single discipline in science. When Laplacean physics ruled in France, there were physicists elsewhere, like Faraday and Oersted, who followed lines of inquiry not indicated by the French tradition. Again, the sway of a narrowly conceived theory of cellular pathology in Germany could not prevent the rise of bacteriology in France and eventually also in Germany. Some of the most important discoveries of the age, such as the evolutionary theory of Darwin, arose entirely outside any discplinary framework or research tradition. Finally, by the end of the century, discoveries which did not fit into any existing discipline, such as those in physiological chemistry, biochemistry, and physical chemistry, became increasingly numerous. They were all received with skepticism and they were often fought over, but with few exceptions their importance was recognized and prejudice was overcome with no significant delay. Intellectually, the "market" for scientific ideas worked reasonably well—much better than most other social institutions. This is not to say that productive resources, such as laboratories, institutes, and research funds, were placed immediately at the disposal of recognized innovations. That allocation depended also on other conditions: positively, on such conditions as the existence of an outside, nonscientific market for the innovation (e.g., bacteriology) and the availability of resources still unassigned to other purposes (a condition which, at the end of the nineteenth century, was much more characteristic of the new, still rapidly developing systems of the United States and Japan than it was of Europe);[26] or, negatively, on the fact that the direction of research institutes was monopolized by those who occupied chairs (a condition which, as we have seen, characterized German science).

Furthermore, while disciplinary monopolies undoubtedly retarded the granting of autonomy and adequate resources to new fields, they do not seem to have oppressed the innovative spirit. Thus most of the new fields originated in Germany and Austria, where the disciplinary monopolies were the strong-

26. Bartholomew, "The Acculturation of Science in Japan," pp. 185–91.

est. Scientists from these countries were among the pioneers, or were the pioneers, of the theory that disease is caused by infection, of Mendelian genetics, of biochemistry, and of physical chemistry, although all these innovations were discriminated against, fought over, and in one case actually suppressed by the academic authorities. It should be noted, too, that the rise of the neo-Newtonian research school of Laplace was accompanied by the acceptance of the un-Newtonian wave theory of light by Arago, one of Laplace's outstanding disciples.[27] It appears that the disciplinary organization of teaching and research not only did not discourage innovation but perhaps was actually conducive to it. The necessity to make rational sense of an entire field and to map out its borders not only focused attention on certain problems but also must have exposed the logically weak points and limitations of the existing tradition. To adventurous minds this could be a challenge and a way of lifting themselves above the existing tradition. In addition, mastery of the tradition saved the student from useless efforts to rediscover things that had already been discovered. This made it possible for him to choose the unsolved problems, which presented a real challenge. Thus what may well have been blinkers for the mediocre served probably as eye-openers for students with original minds.

It appears, therefore, that a distinction must be made between the effects of disciplinary traditions and the effects of disciplinary monopoly. Indoctrination in the former does not seem to have diminished dissent and independence of thought. In fact, it may have produced more originality and independence. But disciplinary monopolies were detrimental to the development and diffusion of innovations. Unchecked, such monopolies could have led to the long-term deterioration of science (they probably did have this effect in Germany). The reason that this did not happen was that, in spite of appearance, the social control of science through the recognition, publication, and rewarding of contributions, established and institutionalized in the academies of the seventeenth and eighteenth centuries, was never entirely transferred to the organizations of teaching and research. The academies continued to exist. While the Paris Academy of Sciences and the Berlin Academy lost some of their importance, the Royal Society of London regained much of its central standing in world science. Eventually the establishment of the Nobel Prizes in 1901 created a new institution of worldwide allocation of rewards for science as a whole. Even more important were the new disciplinary and interdisciplinary journals and scientific societies which began to appear at the end of the eighteenth century and the national and international scientific conferences.[28]

27. Crosland, *The Society of Arcueil*, pp. 126, 427, 458–59.
28. For the rise of journals, see D. McKie, "The Scientific Periodical from 1665 to 1798," in A. Ferguson (ed.), *Natural Philosophy through the Eighteenth Century and Allied Topics* (commemoration number to mark the sesquicentennial of the founding of the *Philosophical Magazine*) (London: Taylor & Francis, 1948), p. 127.

Some of the latter, such as the International Chemical Conference of Karls-ruhe in 1860 or the Solvay Conference in physics in Brussels in 1911, settled questions of central importance in their fields.[29]

Hence, what happened, in the transition from the eighteenth to the nine-teenth century, was that the organization of science became both more differ-entiated and more decentralized. The new functions of organizing research and of training for research were taken up by university-based research schools, while the control functions were shared by the academies, scientific journals, societies, and conferences. Because of the consolidation of national scientific communities and the absence of a central worldwide elite, located in one place, international conferences, such as the two just mentioned, occa-sionally assumed the function of making authoritative decisions and formulat-ing new consensus in almost exactly the way this had been done in the eigh-teenth century. But these were exceptions. In general, the formal judicial procedure of the academies was replaced by the impersonal working of mar-ketlike mechanisms based on all these various organizations. The individual scientist who happened to be rejected by a disciplinary authority had several courts of appeal. He could submit his paper to several journals, present it as a book to the general scientific community, as Darwin did, or demonstrate it by impressive, highly visible experiments, as did Pasteur and Koch. These ap-peals were all made to organizations and publics which were separate from organizations of teaching and research and were often interdisciplinary in scope and international in their membership. These organizations and publics were relatively free of bias, and they applied the same universalistic norms of judgment as the eighteenth-century academies had. Prejudices and theories going beyond the evidence were disregarded, and well-supported empirical findings of significance were usually recognized even if they did not fit into any of the established fields or even if their theoretical underpinning was less than what was usually required within the established disciplinary traditions.[30]

Conclusion: Science as an
Intellectual and Moral Endeavor

This story stops about the end of the nineteenth century. Much has changed since then in science as well as in its organization, but some of the generaliza-tions that can be made on the basis of this material, about the social structures

29. See Armin Hermann, *The Genesis of Quantum Theory* (Cambridge: MIT Press, 1971), pp. 139–43, on the Solvay Conference.

30. A conspicuous case of appeal to a larger public has been described by Brush in "The Royal Society's First Rejection of the Kinetic Theory of Gases." John Herapath actually took his debate with the Royal Society to the columns of the London *Times*. This brought him some recog-nition and sympathy; however, his somewhat faulty exposition of the kinetic theory did not arouse much interest.

and mechanisms involved in and influencing scientific change, are still valid today.

One of these generalizations concerns the continuity or discontinuity of both the scientific role and the institutions of science. The cognitive contents of science have undergone great changes since the seventeenth century. Several of these changes were of fundamental significance, or, as some prefer to say, they were "revolutionary." But none of the so-called revolutions was accompanied by anything like the social and philosophical movement of the sixteenth and seventeenth centuries. There were no philosophical sects, no semi-conspiratorial international networks, no prolonged battles against the central institutions of learning, and no relentless campaigning for recognition of the institutional independence of a new philosophy like the one that accompanied the scientific revolution which began with the publication of Copernicus's work and ended with the foundation of the Royal Society in London. The institutional aim of that revolution—namely, the establishment of science as a distinct intellectual activity, to be controlled only by its own norms—was accomplished in the seventeenth century. After that, fundamentally significant ("revolutionary") discoveries could be made with no further institutional revolution.

The second conclusion concerns the kind of influence exercised by social structure—in this case the influence on the cognitive contents of science exercised by two kinds of mechanisms: those by which scientific research is evaluated and recognized, on the one hand, and, on the other, those by which scientific research is organized and supported. As we have seen, both kinds had a selective influence, recognizing or supporting some kinds of research and denying recognition to others. Of particular interest here is the effect of research organizations. As we have noted, these constituted potential monopolies which interfered with the development of certain innovations. However, further consideration has to be given to the way this interference occurred. One possibility would have been the kind of effect emphasized by most sociologists of knowledge, who postulate that the emergence of distinct schools of thought ("paradigms," etc.), particularly if reinforced by vested interests, tends to prejudice, shape, and limit human thought, making it resistant to innovations. The other kind of influence would have been simple and straightforward monopolistic practice to ensure the interests of a particular group in research resources and appointments.

Although it is impossible to say that the former effect was absent, there is no evidence that it was stronger than what one would expect on the ground of commonsense knowledge about the limited flexibility of the human mind and its dependence on the tradition it has acquired. In any event, the effect was neither universal nor, probably, unambiguous. Innovations and discoveries which broke through the boundaries of existing paradigms continued to be made in the nineteenth-century setting of strict disciplinary traditions bolstered by monopolistic or oligopolistic teaching and research organizations, and they were probably made with as great a frequency as ever or anywhere (or, perhaps, with even greater frequency). Moreover, they were made in the absence of internal crises within the tradition. There was no crisis in physics to prompt Arago to formulate his wave theory, nor was there one in biology to stimulate Pasteur to revolutionize important parts of the field.

Therefore, even though many people probably identified with the scientific tradition in which they were brought up, in the same way that people identify with their religion, there is no evidence that this presented a problem for science. Most people are not innovators in either science or religion, and the few who are original thinkers do not seem to be hindered by having been brought up within a given tradition. In fact, such upbringing is probably an important source of their innovativeness. The difference between science and religion is not that the one is innovative while the other is traditional. Both can be either. The differences reside in the fact that in science there are better criteria than in religion to distinguish the valid from the misleading innovations and, above all, in the fact that social control in science has been inimical to monopoly, whereas in religion its main function has been to strengthen monopoly.

The main condition which prevented the monopolization of science by any one scientific doctrine has been the separation of the social-control mechanisms for recognizing and evaluating research from the organizations for research and teaching in science. The reasons for this separation lie in the fact that, as has been shown in this paper, modern science has never been content to be either a pastime of private individuals in pursuit of esoteric knowledge or the handmaiden of technology. Since the very inception of the scientific movement in the seventeenth century, scientists have claimed universal recognition and authority for science as the manifestation of a superior type of public knowledge. They have maintained this claim successfully—in spite of the esoteric nature of science, which makes it accessible to only small numbers of experts in each field—because of the existence of institutional mechanisms which have maintained the unity of the scientific endeavor and have vouched for its integrity by authoritative control of what should be admitted into science and what should be rejected from it. This is essentially a judicial function. It is not enough that it be done competently; it must also be done publicly, according to norms and criteria which can be understood by everybody (including those unable to appreciate the substance of scientific contributions).[31]

Scientists who perform this function are like judges in a court. They must be careful and circumspect and must insist on impersonal rules of procedure which cannot be challenged. This is not to say that they always live up to these

31. The importance of the public nature of scientific knowledge has been stressed by John Ziman, *Public Knowledge: An Essay Concerning the Social Dimension of Science* (London: Cambridge University Press, 1968); see also Baker, *Condorcet*, p. 78.

requirements; but, if they do not, they are likely to be found out, to be exposed and criticized for the exercise of bias. Therefore, on this level there is a tendency to adhere to strictly universalistic rules of procedure and to eliminate from influence any extraneous interests or personal and philosophic prejudices. Of course, what is regarded as universally acceptable procedure will not be independent from the views prevailing in different scientific fields. But as far as evaluation of contributions is concerned, it is difficult, as we have seen, to reject something as nonscientific except on universally accepted grounds. This liberal tendency is reinforced by the fact that the allocation of scientific recognition is usually a supranational and, at least to some extent, a supradisciplinary process; the effect of any particular bias is thus minimized.

These judicial decisions are very different from the decisions which research workers have to make. The latter have to guess what is a live and promising question to be solved and what is likely to be a dead end. These questions cannot be decided on the basis of the strictly universalistic norms adopted in the evaluation of finished research. The difference is like that between judging well-processed evidence, presented in court, and deciding which of several clues to follow in a criminal investigation. Based on insufficient knowledge, the decision cannot be perfectly universalistic. Even the best hunch, as long as it is unsupported by evidence, cannot be judged by "preestablished impersonal criteria." One can also not expect at this stage either "disinterestedness" or "skepticism" on the part of the investigator. To the contrary, he is expected to be committed to and involved with his ideas; otherwise he would be unwilling to risk his time, effort, and occasionally also his money on the exploration of a mere hunch. This involvement and lack of objectivity are not contrary to the norms of scientific evaluation; for those norms apply only to the evaluation of results to be made public, while hunches are private and are not intended, and usually are not even allowed, to be published.

Recently several authors have interpreted this relatively normless behavior as a contradiction of the established sociological view which considers science an institution regulated by norms. They consider the normative variability of scientists' behavior with respect to their own research an indication that this behavior may be determined by value commitments and group involvements rather than by the logic of inquiry or the norms of scientific conduct. Whether this is a fruitful hypothesis for investigation remains to be seen.[32] But certainly there is no contradiction between this relatively normless behavior and the institutional view of science. As I have shown, social control in science is a function analytically and empirically distinct from research. The effectiveness of the social control, as well as its distinctiveness, is proba-

32. I. Mitroff, "Norms and Counternorms in a Select Group of the Apollo Moon Scientists," *American Sociological Review* 39 (1974): 575–96. See also S. G. Brush, "Should the History of Science Be Rated 'X'?" *Science* 183 (March 22, 1974): 1164–72.

bly one of the main conditions which make it possible for the individual investigator to use his imagination and intuition freely. Because he will eventually be judged by fairly strict and impartial norms, he can be allowed practically as much individual freedom as he wishes.

This is another way of saying that science, as science has been understood for the past 300 years, is a social endeavor and that scientists, in addition to being physicists, chemists, or economists, are also members of a moral community. As Edward Shils has pointed out, one of the characteristics of this community is that in principle it subjects "every single element in the [scientific] tradition . . . to critical appraisal." [33] The institutions and processes concerned with this appraisal have been an important part of the history of science. They have a logic and a structure of their own that interact with but are not determined by the cognitive contents of science and the organizations of research.

33. "The Scientific Community: Thoughts after Hamburg," in Edward Shils, *The Intellectuals and the Powers, and Other Essays*, p. 209 (this essay was originally published in the May 1954 issue of the *Bulletin of the Atomic Scientists*).

Puritanism and Modern Science 16

A Study in the Continuity and Coherence of Sociological Research

The apparently unending debate on Robert K. Merton's theory that Puritanism played a positive role in the emergence of modern science in the seventeenth century could easily be used as an example of the inconclusiveness of social research. Here is a relatively straightforward issue, intensively investigated for more than forty years, that has still not produced consensual conclusions. It appears that virtually all of the views that could be held by informed scholars at the time when Merton did his pathbreaking investigation can still be held today, all the research done since then notwithstanding. Some scholars hold that Puritanism was an important factor, or even a crucially important one, in the emergence of modern science, while others are very skeptical about the relationship. Merton, commenting on the literature between the first publication of his monograph, *Science, Technology and Society in Seventeenth-Century England,* in 1938 and the time of its reissue in 1970, does so in a cautious mood: "Even now, I am led to subscribe to the subdued concluding sentence of this aged but perhaps not yet obsolete essay" which

After completion of this paper, three publications appeared which are directly related to its subject matter: Gary A. Abraham, 1983, "Misunderstanding the Merton Thesis: A Boundary Dispute Between History and Sociology," *Isis* 74:368–87; Robert K. Merton, 1984, "The Latest Word: The Case of Pietism and Science," *American Journal of Sociology* 89:1091–1121; and Barbara J. Shapiro, 1983, *Probability and Certainty in Seventeenth-Century England: A Study of the Relationship between Natural Science, Religion, History, Law and Literature* (Princeton, N. J.: Princeton University Press). Merton's paper contains important clarifications about the relationship between Pietism and science, the existence of which is disputed in one of the papers referred to in this essay (Becker 1984).

The research underlying this essay was supported by the Spencer Foundation. I am indebted to James Wolf of the Department of Sociology of the University of Chicago for his help with the research.

The worst errors in the original publication of the paper have been corrected on the basis of the typescript. Ed.

reads: "On the basis of the foregoing study, it may not be too much to conclude that the cultural soil of seventeenth-century England was peculiarly fertile for the growth and spread of science" (1970:xxix, 238).

However, a sense of futility is unjustified. Research has produced new knowledge and clarified the theoretical issues. If the answer to the problem raised by Merton is still not a simple "yes" or "no," this is because research has discovered new aspects and new complexities involved in the relationship between Puritanism and science, so that today we speak no longer of the same question but of several interrelated questions that grew out of the original one. The way in which this advance has taken place and emerging new knowledge has been incorporated into sociological and historical scholarship has been quite different from, and perhaps less efficient than, the process by which new discoveries are incorporated into the natural sciences. The purpose of this essay is to show how this advance has taken place and of what it consisted.

The Merton Thesis

Merton investigated the whole web of social influence and relations impinging on science in seventeenth-century England. He found that interest in science, as evidenced by the number of biographies with predominantly scientific concerns in the British Dictionary of National Biography (DNB), rose conspicuously about the middle of the seventeenth century. In attempting to account for this rise of interest in science, which was documented by other evidence as well, Merton found that it was spurred by both ideological and economic conditions (though we will not deal with economic conditions here).

Puritanism, which was the dominant ideology of the time, contained elements that were supportive of science. Although Puritan theology was not more tolerant of freedom of thought and did not endorse scientific enquiry more than any other contemporary theology, the interpretation of this theology by some Puritan preachers and intellectuals—what Weber, and in his footsteps, Merton, called the Puritan "ethos" or "ethic"—did frequently contain such endorsement.

> The Puritan complex of a scarcely disguised utilitarianism; of intramundane interests; methodical, unremitting action; thoroughgoing empiricism; of the right and even the duty of *libre examen*; of anti-traditionalism—all this was congenial to the same values in science (Merton 1970 [1938]:136).

Due to this far-reaching congruence between the religious and the scientific world views, explanations of nature by systematic observation and experiment could be and were conceived by some scientists influenced by the Puritan spirit as the best method to understand the ways of God, arrive at true knowledge in the religious sense, and engage in good works likely to benefit mankind. In principle, these objectives could have occurred, and perhaps did occur here and there, among scientists belonging to other Christian denominations. But theological dogma and clerical authority, in places where the Puritan spirit was not influential, were much more inflexible and suppressed any such leanings.

Puritanism, as Merton carefully points out, did not create modern science and could not have created it. Modern science was created by scientists belonging to all the Christian denominations, who built upon knowledge created by Greeks, Arabs, Jews, Indians, and others. However, the Puritan ethos, by lifting science to a new level of significance, constituted an additional spur and lent a religious significance to scientific inquiry. Such an impetus was absent in other denominations and in countries not under the sway of Puritanism (Merton 1970: 86–87, 94–95, 102).

This Puritan influence, according to Merton, explains the shift in the officially endorsed scale of intellectual and cultural values, raising science to the pinnacle of intellectual pursuits, and arousing relatively widespread interest in science in English society as a whole, beginning in the revolutionary period.[1] Merton then provides further evidence, a "test of a hypothesis" about the "Puritan spur to science," by establishing the role played by scientists of Puritan background in the scientific movements and societies of seventeenth-century England and France, and the relative salience of scientific interests among Puritans (in Germany, among Pietists) and Protestants in general in other countries, continuing into the eighteenth and nineteenth centuries. Merton considered these associations to be important for his theory because they provided evidence that the affinity between science and Puritanism reflected not mere rhetoric but a deeply felt sentiment influencing actual behavior (Merton 1970: 110–111). Besides, having derived this further hypothesis, which pertained to the strengthened and lasting personal predisposition among Puritans to engage in science, from the original more comprehensive theory of the cultural affinity between the Puritan and scientific world views in seventeenth-century England, confirmation of the second hypothesis, concerning the Puritan predisposition to engage in science, helped reconfirm the original one.

This "test of hypothesis" turned out to be a source of misunderstanding and misinterpretation because it led many readers to believe that the greater propensity of Puritans to study science and take it up as a vocation was the only thing that the book was about. The background of this hypothesis, namely, the careful analysis of the shift of values in English society as a whole under the impact of a confluence between the Puritan ethos and the spirit of science, was obscured, or actually lost from sight. It was not generally realized that there were two phenomena to be explained. One was the shift of

---

1. This is not to say that it monopolized the pinnacle. Science still has to contest with theology and older types of scholarship, but it will do so on equal terms.

values that moved experimental philosophers to the top of the intellectual hierarchy and established scientific research as an official public concern in England in the wake of the rise of Puritanism and the English Revolution.[2] The other was the greater propensity of Puritans, relative to members of other denominations, to engage in science.

No careful reader of Merton's monography can fail to see that the main contribution of the book is an extremely rich description of the shift in cultural values (contained mainly in chap. 4 and 5, entitled "Puritanism and Cultural Values" and "Motive Forces of the New Science," respectively) and its macrosocial effects. But some readers missed the point because the "crucial experiment" focused attention on individual propensities rather than on macrosocial effects.

The Debate on Puritanism
and Scientific Practice

The result of this misconception was that most of the debate following Merton's publication centered on evidence concerning the propensity of Puritans to engage in science rather than on the influence of the Puritan spirit on the institutionalization of science.

This was an unfortunate outcome, given that the chapter entitled "Puritanism, Pietism and Science: Testing an Hypothesis" is the one easiest to attack in the whole monograph. It adds little to what was said on the situation in seventeenth-century England in the previous chapters. In fact, the only addition is an attempt to show the Puritan influence on a considerable fraction of the active scientists among the early members of the Royal Society. Insofar as many of these active scientists were not formally Puritans, and since the Puritan influence on them is discussed only briefly, the three and a half pages on the subject (not counting the two preceding chapters) are not very convincing. The rest of the chapter is based mainly on secondary sources, some of which are open to criticism and/or interpretation different from that of Merton (Becker, 1984). Thus, while there is plenty of information in this chapter in support of the existence of an affinity on the behavioral level between some varieties of Protestantism and science, as manifested in the greater predisposition to engage in science among Protestants compared to members of other denominations, this information is impressive only when it is considered as consistent with the confluence of the Puritan ethos and the ethos of science. Then the various bits and pieces of information obtained from the work of

---

2. As will be shown later on, the very definition of "experimental philosopher," which encompasses the same kinds of specialists following the same professional ethic and accepting in a rudimentary way ideas about research similar to those of scientists today, was also an innovation requiring explanation.

other scholars in "Puritanism, Pietism and Science" all seem to fall into place and become significant. But if this chapter is taken as the essence of all the arguments and evidence contained in the book (that is, as a testing of the entire hypothesis or all the hypotheses), as many readers did, then the case becomes easily assailable.

Furthermore, Merton refrained from trying to establish any direction of causation between Puritanism and science and was content with simply showing the existence of a relationship. This allowed for an interpretation according to which the relationship lost most of its significance. One could see the harmony between religion and science observed by Merton as merely smoothing the basically antagonistic relationship between the two. Such an interpretation would be consistent with the general rise of interest in science in the seventeenth century, as well as with the continuing Puritan predisposition toward science, but it would reduce the significance of Puritanism to no more than a facilitating condition of peripheral importance in the explanation of the origins of modern science.

Finally, by using evidence in the chapter entitled "Puritanism, Pietism and Science," which concerns Protestants whose Puritan leanings are not established, the importance of Puritanism as a particular variety of Protestantism tends to lose significance.

These kinds of interpretations were actually made in Westfall's *Science and Religion in Seventeenth-Century England* (1958),[3] the theme of which was very close to that of Merton's work and which reexamined in greater detail much of his evidence. Westfall confirms the existence of a connection between Puritanism, or rather Protestantism, and science (Westfall 1958:7). But in contrast to Merton, who focuses on the confluence of religious and scientific values and motivations, Westfall sees this unique situation as a halfway station between Deism and secular Enlightenment. Although his description does full justice to the perceived harmony of science and religion in the eyes of the seventeenth-century virtuosi, to whom "the heavens did declare the glory of God" (Westfall 1958:48), his final conclusion is that

> the skepticism of the Enlightenment was already present in embryo among them. To be sure their piety kept it in check, but they were unable to fully banish it. What else can explain the countless dissertations on natural religion, each proving conclusively that the fundamentals of Christianity are rationally sound? They wrote to refute atheism, but where were the atheists? The virtuosi nourished the atheists within their own minds. Atheism was the vague feeling of uncertainty which their studies had raised, not uncertainty of their own convictions so much as uncertainty of the ultimate conclusions that might be hidden in the principles of natural science (Westfall 1958:219).

3. Prior to this work there were no major attempts to verify or further develop Merton's thesis. The papers and books dealing with the subject until 1957 were surveyed and commented on by Merton (1957:595–606).

Westfall evidently understood Merton as suggesting simply the existence of a more favorable atmosphere for science among the Puritans than among members of other denominations. The possibility that the kind of religious-scientific ethos represented by the Puritan ethic made a qualitative difference in this development, and that it constituted a necessary condition of the institutionalization of science, was lost from sight.[4] Puritanism was seen as no more than an additional spur to the growth of science.

Indeed, this was the conclusion apparently reached by historians who tried to verify Merton's work by further research. It was formulated by Hall in 1963 (see also Rabb 1962). Hall is not clear whether Merton is concerned with the explanation of a necessary condition of the origins of modern science or only with the congeniality between Puritanism and science. He rejects the first possibility as historically untrue, since there are too many instances of Catholics and scientists in Catholic countries participating in the process. Having rejected this, he finds that the mere congeniality between Puritanism and science is not a very significant hypothesis. Clearly, Hall did not properly appreciate the argument about the need to provide legitimacy to a shift of social values; like Westfall he saw in Merton's work only evidence of some kind of vaguely defined connection between Puritanism and science.

Hall then proceeded to draw conclusions about the limitations of sociology of science in general, arguing that as an inquiry concerned with the external conditions of scientific work rather than its contents, sociology cannot come to grips with what really matters in science, namely, the emergence of new ideas. For him the rise of modern science was a revolution in scientific knowledge, not revolution in scientific practice and spirit (Hall 1962, 1963).

Thus, as far as historical literature is concerned, until the mid-1960s it seemed that the subject would be closed with some rather vague confirmation of Merton's findings but little understanding of its theoretical intentions and significance. In fact, the opposite outcome has occurred: interest in the Merton thesis reached its peak in the late 1960s and 1970s, probably due to the work of Hill (1965; see also Hunter 1981:113). Rather than attempting to summarize this literature, I shall refer only to a small part of it to illustrate the fate of Merton's thesis in this period.[5]

Certain historians (Hill 1965; Webster 1975) are essentially in accord with

4. Some of Merton's formulations contributed to the failure to grasp these conclusions (see Merton 1970:xxvii–xxix, 115, 238) suggesting a much more vague, more tentative, and less significant connection between science and religion than either the text of the main chapters dealing with the connection (Merton 1970:55–111) or the later explicit claims that the monograph was an explanation of the institutionalization of science and that either Puritanism or other "functionally equivalent ideological movements" were required "to provide the emerging science with widely acknowledged claims to legitimacy" (Merton 1970:xvii–xix). In the original edition of the monograph, Merton did not make such unequivocal statements about his theoretical intentions.

5. An important part of this literature is assembled in Webster (1974).

Merton's approach. They define Puritanism broadly and include within it members of different denominations who were exposed to and influenced by the ethic described by Merton and promulgated by some Puritan preachers (e.g., George Hakewill, John Preston, and others), who attributed religious significance to effort, industry, a sense of purpose, an appeal to individual conscience, rationality, knowledge, and progress. Their work elaborates and confirms Merton's argument that the emergence of a new religious spirit was sympathetic to science.

This revival of interest in Merton's hypothesis gave rise to a sizable literature critical of Merton, as well as of the historians who adopted his theory. This criticism hinges partly on the definition of Puritanism (Shapiro 1969). Others point out that the ethos attributed to Puritanism was shared by many non-Puritan Protestants (Mulligan 1973, 1980) and even by Catholics (Henry 1982); they have further noted that, on the other hand, the views of leading Puritan divines were frequently antiscientific and very distrustful of free thought (Morgan 1979; Mulligan 1980). With the exception of Mulligan (1973, 1975), while they do not deny the existence of a distinct religious ethos sympathetic to science, they refuse to derive it from Puritanism.

It seems that most of these criticisms proceed from the difficulty of identifying who was a Puritan at the time when this word was variably used either to describe a dominant social ideology accepted by a majority of politically and religiously conscious and active people or a few small fundamentalist or radical groups. Had Merton, Hill, and Webster settled on "Protestantism" instead of "Puritanism," they would have been spared much of this criticism.[6]

In any event, this criticism affects only the hypothesis of a long-lasting Puritan propensity to attach great value to science and to engage in scientific studies and research. There is nothing inconsistent between these findings and the hypothesis linking the value shift, which moved experimental philosophy to a place at the peak of the intellectual hierarchy, to the Puritan Revolution. This hypothesis is supported by evidence from Jones (1965), Hill (1965), and Webster (1975) that Baconism became a central element of the religious-scientific ideology in the 1640s and that this was brought about mainly by individuals and groups with definitely Puritan affiliations or sympathies. This justifies the conclusion that the religious-scientific ideology that emerged under Puritan influence did, indeed, provide a substantial part of the "socially and culturally patterned support" required "for a not yet institutionalized science" (Merton 1970:xviii).

---

6. This is essentially the view of Hooykaas (1972). The cases of Catholic natural philosophers surveyed by Henry (1982) could be regarded as exceptions that reinforce rather than weaken the hypothesis. At the time when the religious-scientific ideology became the dominant *Zeitgeist*, it was to be expected that some Catholics would try to accommodate their views to it, in spite of its Puritan-Protestant background.

The Debate on Puritanism
and the Scientific World View

Another part of the literature stimulated by the Merton thesis deals with the relationship between religious-political ideology and the rise of the mechanistic world view and the corpuscularian approach to physical phenomena. This relationship, explaining the adoption of scientific ideas, is, according to Hall (1962), the only kind of phenomenon worthy of the historian's attention. Merton touched upon this question but not in any detail. Recent literature has produced a great deal of new insight.

Debus (1970), Purver (1967), and Webster (1975) have shown that the conception of science among radical Puritans was rather different from that eventually adopted by the Oxford Experimental Philosophy Club and the Royal society. Early "Puritan science" was open to a variety of natural philosophies, such as Hermeticism and Paracelsianism, and it envisaged a utopian scientific enterprise, which, by providing an easily acquired method of empirical inquiry, would allow the participation of practically everyone in this intellectual endeavor and lead to a very rapid expansion of knowledge and its application. The science eventually adopted by the Royal Society, and subsequently in academies elsewhere, was based on a mechanical philosophy of nature, strictly controlled experiment, and rigorous mathematics.[7] These methods can be acquired only by an intellectual elite; they promise not instant utopia but gradual, piecemeal advance.

It has been suggested (Jacob and Jacob 1980) that the differences between the definitions of science and of the scientific philosophies adopted by these two groups reflected differences in their ideological preferences. In the early years of the revolution, radical Puritan views predominated among those recommending the public support of science, who ultimately adopted a utopian version of the Baconian philosophy. Later, in the 1650s, there was a revulsion to radical utopianism. Nonradical reformers, like Boyle, Petty, and others, disassociated themselves from the radicals and opted for cautious reformist politics and theological views more correctly described as latitudinarian Anglicanism and Puritanism. Parallel with this, the majority adopted a mechanistic, corpuscular scientific philosophy, rejecting alchemy, magic, and similar doctrines. According to Jacob and Jacob, this change in the scientific philosophy was made for primarily religious-political reasons. This is a debatable proposition. However, there is no doubt that the new view of science (such as that of the radicals) was explicitly, and in an elaborate way, used in support of the religious and political views of those who adopted it. This has provided for

7. However, there was no single scientific orthodoxy among the members of the Royal Society or Restoration scientists in general (Skinner 1969; Hunter 1981:16–21), and the demarcation between science and magic remained fluid to the end of the seventeenth century (Webster 1982).

a revised and more differentiated view of the relationship between Puritanism and scientific world view than that suggested by Merton and Westfall, but it is one that confirms the basic theory that scientific inquiry was seen as an undertaking with direct religious significance.

Thus, the sociological analysis of the relationship between science and religion is carried an important step further, such that a relationship is established not only between religion and scientific practice and the institutionalization of science but also between religion and specific scientific philosophies.

Conceptual Development

Sociologists only occasionally and at long intervals participated in this research and debate. Some of them reexamined the statistical basis of Merton's "test of hypothesis" and debated who was and who was not Puritan (Thorner 1952; Feuer 1963). Others accepted and used Merton's work without doing further research on the subject (Barber 1952; Parsons 1963). With the rise of interest in the sociology of science during the 1960s, some sociologists began to take an interest in the institutional part of Merton's work (Ben-David 1965; King 1971). Although written from different, at times even opposing, sociological points of view, the studies by these sociologists nevertheless converged in correcting some of the misinterpretations of Merton's theory. King was sympathetic to Hall's criticism, as noted earlier, but he still explicated Merton's rationale in a manner different from Hall. Merton's thesis, according to King, is plausible

> if we can agree that the scientific revolution was essentially a revolution in behavior or in practice. . . . Then we can treat the problem of discovering the "cultural roots" of modern science, as Merton does, as one of explaining the emergence of a new mode of work, or a new social discipline. If we started from this assumption, it is quite easy to accept that Puritanism might have created the scientific worker and reconciled him to the discipline of the laboratory much as Methodism is supposed to have formed the industrial worker and reconciled him to the discipline of the factory (1971:13).

This statement, of course, does not precisely reflect Merton's conception of the experimental philosophers of the seventeenth century, but it correctly identifies the kinds of institutional phenomena—a new mode of work, discipline (he should have added "new social role and status")—whose emergence can be explained by Merton's theory.

However, King is interested not in social institutions but in some kind of sociology of scientific knowledge. He maintains that the institutional point of view cannot be accepted by historians of science because for them the scientific revolution was, as previously mentioned, a "revolution in theory and explanation," not in practice; therefore, he does not follow up on his own suggestion about the creation of the scientific role.

In my own work (see Ben-David 1965, 1971, 1977), I have attempted to do the kind of institutional analysis that King was uninterested in doing, namely, to make explicit the centrality of the "role of the scientist" ("the scientific worker" of King) in the emergence of modern science and to reexamine, among other things, this part of Merton's theory in a comparative framework. I have found that the vision of the independent role (that is, independent from religious censorship and domination by metaphysical and epistemological doctrines) of the experimental philosopher emerged gradually, in several places in Europe and not only among Puritans. But the breakthrough to official recognition and legitimation of this social role, as manifested in the establishment of the Royal Society and the elevation of experimental philosophy and its practitioners to the top of the intellectual hierarchy, occurred in England. In that country the revolution and the subsequent religious turmoil effectively undermined central religious and intellectual authority, while at the same time the spread of individualistic forms of Puritanism created unprecedented opportunities to formulate bold and serious religious justification for the recognition of the autonomy of the scientific role and of scientific institutions.

These interpretations explicitly shifted the emphasis in Merton's theory from the social psychology of the Puritan propensity to do scientific work and from the acceptance of a mechanical world view to the historical events of institutionalization, namely, the establishment of scientific academies and the recognition of the new role and ethos of the experimental philosopher. Whether Puritanism was an added motivation to engage in science or not (it probably was), there were plenty of non-Puritans who also had such motivation. The problem of seventeenth-century science was religious suspicion and inferiority of intellectual status. Those in charge of safeguarding religion and enforcing theological authority were unanimously opposed to the freedom of scientific inquiry and publication, irrespective of denomination (Morgan 1979; Mulligan 1980; Hunter 1981: 162–175). Further, the official intellectual elite ruling the universities and academies, the churches, and the courts were humanistic scholars, scholastic or other kinds of speculative philosophers, theologians, and lawyers. Only a few of these had any serious interest in natural philosophy, and even fewer in experimental philosophy. The idea of granting experimental philosophy equal status with their own disciplines appeared preposterous to the large majority of them. The problem of science was how to break through these barriers of religious suspicion, oppression, and intellectual marginality (Jones 1965; Hunter 1981: 136–61). In this process, the English Revolution was of crucial importance, since it prompted the unique fusion of Baconian scientism with Puritan religious ideologies, thus creating a basis of legitimacy for the institutionalization of science.

The disjunction of the institutional-historical part of the Merton thesis from the social-psychological one, which is not made explicit in Merton's work,[8] and the substitution of intersocietal (England versus other societies) for interpersonal (Puritan background with other backgrounds) comparisons eliminates some of the main sources of confusion about the Merton theory and the criticism of it and is consistent with the results of the historical research surveyed here. However, it does not eliminate the objection raised by Hall and King to Merton's work—namely, that the origins of modern science were an intellectual event and that research into the origins of modern science must therefore center on intellectual changes rather than institutional ones. A somewhat similar objection was raised by Kuhn (1972), who suggested that the search for the ideological and institutional background of the emergence of modern science in seventeenth-century England was completely misplaced, since paradigms characteristic of modern science, which combined exact theories with specific experiments, emerged only at about the end of the eighteenth and early nineteenth centuries in France (and not in seventeenth-century England).

Kuhn's contention regarding the late beginnings of modern scientific paradigms prompted further clarification of the significance of the shift in cultural values that culminated in the recognition of the status and autonomy of experimental philosophy as an intellectual endeavor and in the institutionalization of science, both manifested in the establishment of the Royal Society of London. The significance of these events did not consist of the provision of motivation or inspiration to any particular discovery (although this might have occurred on occasion); rather, it consisted of the establishment of a permanent and authoritative framework for holding together the entire variegated spectrum of scientific endeavor and for keeping it on its course to the advancement of knowledge through rational investigation checked by observation and experiment. This was accomplished through the encouragement of publication and of public discussion, evaluation, and the rewarding of attainment in all the fields of science. These functions were probably crucial in securing a belief in the progressiveness of modern science and its institutional support, even over long periods in which no significant advances were made. Kuhn's assertion that modern science emerged only about 1800 is debatable as far as science as a whole is concerned, but it is quite plausible if restricted to chemistry and biology. Intellectually these became modern fields only in the late eighteenth or early nineteenth century. However, their practitioners had already adopted the modern program in the seventeenth century, and they stuck to it in spite of a prolonged lack of success (Ben-David 1977). The implication is that the belief in, and institutionalization of, science was dependent not on impres-

8. Nor is it made explicit in Max Weber's work on capitalism.

sive discoveries but on the ethos resulting from the fusion of religious and Baconian ideologies, as suggested by Merton, Hill, and Webster.

Despite all the differences between science and religion, one can compare the independence of the belief in science from continuing discoveries to the independence of religious belief from the continuing occurrence of miracles. Therefore, even if the sociological theories initiated by Merton had not contributed significantly to an understanding of the discoveries that marked the beginning of modern science, the contribution of those theories would still not be trivial. Only these theories can explain the continuity and seriousness of scientific endeavor, even in fields in which advancement was slow and unimpressive.

This interpretation of the origins of Western science is also supported by new comparative evidence. Following Joseph Needham, Sivin has recently observed that the main difference between traditional Chinese and premodern Western scientific traditions is not in the kinds and extent of knowledge. One can find in both cultures traditions of inquiry into specific fields; but the attempt to subsume all this under a common heading and a common system of institutions was made eventually only in the Western tradition (Sivin 1982, 1983).

Sivin considers this difference to be grounds for refraining from comparisons between the development of Chinese and Western science. But if we compare the state of Western science before its institutionalization in the seventeenth century to that of Chinese science in the same period, we find that the difference between them was much less than Sivin assumed, in viewing the two from the vantage point of today. It is true that the West inherited from Greece a vision of a unified all-embracing philosophy, but that vision included little of what is encompassed by the word *science* today or *experimental philosophy* as it was used in the seventeenth century. Chemistry, much of biology, observational astronomy, most parts of physics, and even historiography were practiced by people pursuing different callings, in ways unrelated to academic philosophy, which consisted mainly of logic, metaphysics, and moral philosophy. Besides, the Greek and medieval traditions never managed to create much of a unified enterprise, since they were unable to reconcile warring schools and doctrines. Only when those traditions were replaced by a new vision combining the Jewish belief in a single law-giving creator of the universe (Manuel 1974, pp. 66, 87), the Baconian idea that this universe could be explored through direct observation and experiment, and the Puritan utopias of the English revolutionary period, which reconciled all Christian denominations (and perhaps all religions) through the employment of the Baconian strategy of arriving at the truth revealed directly in the works of God, did the scientific endeavor in the West obtain an ideology. Very soon thereafter, moreover, it became an institutional unity, an enterprise different from its medieval European, Arabic, Chinese, or Indian antecedents. In fact one may suggest that the emergence of the ideology and the institutionalization of a unified enterprise of experimental philosophy ("science") pursuing a common aim of advancing scientific knowledge (rather than distant professional practices) is one of the most important distinguishing marks of modern science.

Conclusion

The research surveyed in this essay confirms the broad outlines of the picture presented by Merton in 1938 but modifies and refines it in many details. The ideas that eventually resulted in the recognition of experimental philosophy, and empirical inquiry in general, as a distinct and autonomous branch of inquiry of great social importance arose in many places during the sixteenth and early seventeenth centuries, predominantly, but not exclusively, among Protestant groups. Which of these should properly be called "Puritan" is a debatable but unimportant question.

The important point is that until the Puritan Revolution of 1640 the individuals and groups who adopted these ideas had little public influence. They were shunned by the official leadership of all the Christian denominations, including Puritans, as people with potentially subversive ideas (Morgan 1979; Mulligan 1980). The revolution changed all this, not necessarily by changing the minds of leading clergymen but by providing much more scope and freedom for small "dissenting" groups to propagandize their views and organize themselves around utopian schemes, including a focus on Baconian philosophy and science. The demarcation of science changed in the course of the events (Debus 1970; Rattansi 1963, 1972; Webster 1982), as did the sectarian loyalties of the leaders of the scientific movement (Shapiro 1969; Webster 1975; Jacob and Jacob 1980). But there is little doubt that without some kind of "Revolution of Saints," which placed the reform of religion in the center of the social agenda while at the same time throwing open to everybody the discussion about the basis of true faith and the true road to salvation, the "value shift" conferring religious significance to science would most likely not have occurred.

Concerning the exploration of the other hypothesis in the Merton monograph—namely, that of the alleged relationship between Puritanism and a personal propensity to engage in science—advance has been much less impressive. As has been pointed out, Merton did not insist upon a specifically Puritan propensity, insofar as some of his data are about Protestants in general. When the personal propensity to engage in science is attributed to "Protestants" rather than just to "Puritans," recent findings generally support Merton's views. However, these findings throw no light on why and how this relationship came into being and was maintained over a long period of time. These questions are as open today as they were in the 1930s.

I should like to suggest that the two phenomena—the institutionalization of science under Puritan influence and the Protestant propensity for practicing science—may have altogether different explanations. The most likely explanation of the lasting Protestant propensity toward science is probably their strong tradition and high valuation of education. Originally limited mainly to religious studies (and frequently suspicious of science and secular studies altogether), this tradition was easily extended to secular fields as soon as clerical control was relaxed. Modern, and particularly scientific-mathematical, fields were preferred, partly because Protestants in general and Dissenters in particular had much less attachment to the scholastic or humanistic traditions of learning than did the Catholics and therefore chose more "practical subjects" (after all, humanistic and scholastic learning was of the greatest practical use to the matter of advancement in the church hierarchy). Perhaps they preferred science also because it provided a greater scope to intellectual virtuosity, which is a matter of considerable importance in traditions placing a high value on educational attainment.[9]

A corollary to this disjunction between the "value-shift-institutionalization" and the social-psychological "Puritan propensity" hypothesis is a clearer definition of the variables and their relationship. Originally all the variables, such as "value shift," "institutionalization," and growing numbers of DNB biographees engaged in science, were considered as indexes of rising interest in science and increased motivation to practice it—all basically social-psychological phenomena. On the other hand, what is seen as the crucial phenomenon to be explained today is the rise of a new scientific role ("experimental philosopher") and new institutions (the Royal Society and other academies), which lent unity and common meaning to the hitherto separate activities of people engaged in different professions and branches of science. These are clearly institutional phenomena, which go beyond and are to a large extent independent from changing interests in science and from the motivations to practice it.

It is also possible today to see in clearer outline the religious-ideological variable of Merton. For him this is an affinity between Puritan and scientific ethos. His actual description shows more than "affinity"—namely, an actual fusion of religious and scientific elements into a new ideology. This view is confirmed and enlarged upon in more recent literature, which examines reli-

9. This hypothesis would also be consistent with the success in science of the Indian Brahmins, the Japanese, and the Jews, all of whom possess longstanding and strong traditions of learning but who have never produced anything similar to the religious-scientific ideology of seventeenth-century England.

gious issues in the light of scientific philosophies, those philosophies used in political and religious argument, and to some extent, those selected for and adjusted to such use. This is the first appearance of a scientistic ideology in which "science," at this time still in complete harmony with true religious belief, becomes a symbol of and guide to truth and the improvement of human fate.

I do not here imply that this was ideological science. Scientists used the scientific-religious ideology then as now to further the case of scientific research (in the virtue of which they usually believed, as they still do), but they were aware that research had to be kept free from ideology. The Royal Society, like other academies, symbolized and represented science in general but was careful to ensure the freedom of members to pursue research in the absence of ideological or religious prejudice. Indeed, this freedom was necessary for their ideological mission. Without the capability to reconcile diversity and freedom of inquiry with a unity of purpose and meaning, they could scarcely have served as a symbol of the way to truth and social welfare transcending differences in religion and politics.

Finally, a further theoretically important advance (though one not directly related to the Puritan-science thesis) occurred in the way that sociology of scientific knowledge has been introduced in this literature. Merton and most other sociologists shied away from attempts at social explanations of scientific contents because the attempts of Durkheim and Mannheim to establish a sociology of knowledge were failures (Merton 1973; Ben-David 1971). This failure derived from the fact that they had directed their efforts at the establishment of a relativistic sociology-based epistemology. The attempts reviewed here leave epistemology alone and concentrate on the question of what kind of political and religious uses were made of scientific theories, such as the corpuscularian view of physical nature, and how political-religious arguments were used in support of scientific theories (M. C. Jacob 1976; J. R. Jacob 1977).[10] This is not a relationship of correspondence between social structures and systems of thought, but a functional relationship between the two. The purpose of this kind of sociology of knowledge is not to explore the social origins of knowledge, but to place a system of thought (science or any other system) in the social context of a historical period.

It is hoped that these observations substantiate the assertion made in the beginning of this essay that an advance has taken place in the investigation of the relationship between Puritanism and science. They also show that advance has been halting, discontinuous, and marred by ineffective communication and poor conceptualization. It seems that, on the whole, research was done in

10. This is a sociology of knowledge consistent with the recommendations of King (1971) but not those of Bloor (1976), who attempts to revive the sociological epistemology of Durkheim and Mannheim.

a much less effective way than in the natural sciences. Whether this has been due to intrinsic differences between the fields, or to differences in the conditions, organization, and mores of research between them, remains to be explored.

References

Barber, B. 1952. *Science and the Social Order* (New York: Free Press).

Becker, G. 1984. "Pietism and Science: A Critique of Robert K. Merton's Hypothesis." *American Journal of Sociology* 89: 1065–90.

Ben-David, J. 1965. "The Scientific Role: The Conditions of Its Establishment in Europe." *Minerva* 4: 15–54.

———. 1971. *The Scientist's Role in Society: A Comparative Study* (Englewood Cliffs, N.J.: Prentice-Hall).

———. 1977. "Organization, Social Control and Cognitive Change in Science." In J. Ben-David and T. N. Clark, eds., *Culture and Its Creators: Essays in Honor of Edward Shils* (Chicago: University of Chicago Press), pp. 244–65. [This volume, chap. 15.]

Bloor, David. 1976. *Knowledge and Social Imagery* (London: Routledge and Kegan Paul).

Debus, A. G. 1970. *Science and Education in the Seventeenth Century: The Webster-Ward Debate* (London: MacDonald).

Feuer, L. 1963. *The Scientific Intellectual: The Psychological and Sociological Origins of Modern Science* (New York: Basic Books).

Hall, R. A. 1962. "The Scholar and the Craftsman in the Scientific Revolution." In Marshall Clagett, ed., *Critical Problems in the History of Science* (Madison: University of Wisconsin Press), pp. 3–23.

———. 1963. "Merton Revisited: Science and Society in the Seventeenth Century." *History of Science* 2: 1–16.

Henry, J. 1982. "Catholicism and Natural Philosophy in the Interregnum." *British Journal of the History of Science* 15 (3): 51, 211–39.

Hill, Christopher. 1965. *The Intellectual Origins of the English Revolution* (Oxford: Clarendon Press).

———. 1972. *The World Turned Upside Down* (London: Temple Smith).

Hooykaas, R. 1972. *Religion and the Rise of Modern Science* (Edinburgh: Scottish Academic Press).

Hunter, M. 1981. *Science and Society in Restoration England* (Cambridge: Cambridge University Press).

Jacob, J. R. 1977. *Robert Boyle and the English Revolution* (New York: Burt Franklin).

Jacob, J. R., and M. C. Jacob. 1980. "The Anglican Origins of Modern Science: The Metaphysical Foundation of the Whig Constitution." *Isis* 71: 251–67.

Jacob, M. C. 1976. *The Newtonians and the English Revolution* (Ithaca: Cornell University Press).

Jones, R. F. 1965. *Ancients and Moderns* (Berkeley and Los Angeles: University of California Press).

King, M. D. 1971. "Reason, Tradition and the Progressiveness of Science." *History and Theory* 10:3–32.

Kuhn, T. 1972. "Scientific Growth: Reflections on Ben-David's Scientific Role." *Minerva* 10:166–78.

Manuel, F. 1974. *The Religion of Isaac Newton* (Oxford: Clarendon Press).

Merton, R. K. 1957. *Social Theory and Social Structure*, Rev. and enlarged ed. (Glencoe, Ill.: Free Press).

———. (1938). 1970. *Science, Technology and Society in Seventeenth-Century England* (New York: Fertig).

———. (1938) 1973. "Science and the Social Order." In his *The Sociology of Science* (Chicago: University of Chicago Press), pp. 254–66.

———. (1945) 1973. "Paradigm for the Sociology of Knowledge." In his *The Sociology of Science* (Chicago: University of Chicago Press), pp. 7–40.

Morgan, J. 1979. "Puritanism and Science: Reinterpretation." *Historical Journal* 22:535–60.

Mulligan, L. 1973. "Civil War Politics, Religion and the Royal Society." *Past and Present* 59:92–116.

———. 1975. Rejoinder. *Past and Present* 66:139–42.

———. 1980. "Puritans and English Science: A Critique of Webster." *Isis* 71: 456–69.

Parsons, T. 1963. "Christianity and Modern Industrial Society." In E. A. Tiryakian, ed., *Sociological Theory, Values, and Sociocultural Change: Essays in Honor of Pitirim Sorokin* (New York: Free Press), pp. 33–70.

Purver, M. 1967. *The Royal Society: Concept and Creation* (London: Routledge and Kegan Paul).

Rabb, R. T. K. 1962. "Puritanism and the Rise of Experimental Science in England." *Cahiers d'histoire mondiale* 7:46–67.

Rattansi, P. M. 1963. "Paracelsus and the Puritan Revolution." *Ambix* 11:24–32.

———. 1972. "The Social Interpretation of Science in the Seventeenth Century." In P. Mathias, ed., *Science and Society 1600–1900* (Cambridge: Cambridge University Press), pp. 1–32.

Shapiro, B. J. 1969. *John Wilkins 1614–1672: An Intellectual Biography* (Berkeley and Los Angeles: University of California Press).

Sivin, N. 1982. "Why the Scientific Revolution Did Not Take Place in China—or Didn't It?" *Chinese Society* 5:45–66.

———. 1983. "Chinesische Wissenschaft. Ein Vergleich der Ansätze von Max Weber und Joseph Needham." In W. Schluchter, ed., *Max Webers Studie über Konfuzianismus und Taoismus: Interpretation und Kritik* (Frankfurt am Main: Suhrkamp), pp. 342–62.

Skinner, Quentin. 1969. "Thomas Hobbes and the Nature of the Early Royal Society." *Historical Journal* 12:217–39.

Thorner, I. 1952. "Ascetic Protestantism and the Development of Science and Technology." *American Journal of Sociology* 58:25–33.

Webster, Charles, ed. 1974. *The Intellectual Revolution of the Seventeenth Century* (London: Routledge and Kegan Paul).

————. 1975. *The Great Instauration: Science, Medicine and Reform, 1626–60* (London: Duckworth).

————. 1982. *From Paracelsus to Newton: Magic and the Making of Modern Science* (Cambridge: Cambridge University Press).

Westfall, R. S. 1958. *Science and Religion in Seventeenth-Century England* (New Haven: Yale University Press).

Part V

The Ethos of Science

The Social Scientist's Role in Society

Introduction

The two papers assembled in this Part are essentially concerned with a single theme: the social scientist's role in society. The fundamental idea is that in social science, no less than in natural science, scientists are—and should be—engaged in a disinterested pursuit of truth, monitored by their peers as the only reference group. This implies that theorists who address themselves to, and seek reward from, other (lay) reference groups infringe the norms of science. As a consequence, their theories may not be scientific. In line with his general theoretical outlook, Ben-David argues that to ensure the pursuit of unbiased social scientific research, social science must be adequately institutionalized.

"Innovations and Their Recognition in Social Science" (1975) asks, why is social science sensitive to changing moods and fashions in the lay public? The crux of Ben-David's answer is that the role of the social scientist has not been separated from other roles: many social scientists seek reward not from their peers on scientific criteria but from the lay public. In other words, the demarcation of social science from other social enterprises has not been sufficiently institutionalized. This is particularly perceptible in the acceptance by social scientists of transformational theories that are rejected in natural science. This argument is pursued further in "The Ethical Responsibility of Social Scientists: A Historical Survey and Comment" (1979; not included here), where Ben-David argues that the social scientist who invents or subscribes to a transformational theory exchanges the role of a scientist for that of a prophet: instead of contenting himself with interpreting the world in accordance with scientific criteria, he endeavors to change it. Comtean positivism and Marxism (as also psychoanalysis) are for Ben-David instances of secular religions, and the paper is largely devoted to a sociological analysis of their emergence in France.[1] In early-nineteenth-century France, social science was deinstitutionalized, so that social scientists were in need of cognitive legitimation and of alternative reference groups outside science as sources of social reward. They were thus induced to create comprehensive systems (systems were at that period the mark of an advanced natural science) and to create political movements as a surrogate scientific community. These "social scientific religions" necessarily developed into dogmatic systems and had a detrimental influence on the development of social thought. (The same subject is addressed also in [82].)

The second paper included in this Part, "Sociology and Its Uses" (1980), tackles the same problem again but from a different angle. The issue now is the danger for science when "pure" (or "basic") scientific research is not neatly distinguished from policy research. As long as research is done and judged according to the scientific norms, Ben-David claims, it will, at least in the long run, be value neutral. A real risk of systematic bias arises, however, in cases in which an entire community is engaged in policy research. In these cases, as a study suggests, results that are at variance with theoretically induced expectations may not have an immediate correcting impact on theoretical thinking. This implies that to function adequately and in accordance with the norm of "organized skepticism," the scientific enterprise must be kept apart from other concerns: to be a scientist, one has to assume the scientist's role only, which must not be fused with any other social role.

The issues addressed in these papers—whether in the social sciences ideology-free, disinterested research is possible and whether progress can be discerned in them—were of obvious importance to Ben-David. This explains why even in papers essentially devoted to criticism of adverse views, he often went out of his way to argue that the very debate in which he was engaged has in fact produced progress, thus confirming his views of the nature of the scientific enterprise and of the scientific ethos (see, e.g., chaps. 16, 20, 21, and 25).

1. This part of the paper is an elaboration of "The Structure and Function of Nineteenth-Century Social Science" [58].

I

The difference between the social and the natural sciences has often been discussed in philosophical terms. It is usually asked whether the social sciences can ever aim at the same kind (if not the same degree) of objective validity as the natural sciences.[1] Even those who believe that this is, in principle, possible, admit that for the time being social science is far from having attained this ideal. Social sciences are plagued by discontinuities in research and doctrinal debates.[2] These debates frequently raise doubts about the very possibility of discovering valid knowledge about social behavior through research. The obvious explanation of this state of affairs is that the social sciences have not yet developed a mature tradition of theory and investigation. They are in a state like the one in which chemistry, biology, and part of physics used to be in the eighteenth century, when doctrinal debates proliferated in those fields, too.[3]

However, it is precisely this parallel with the natural sciences which raises doubts about the sufficiency of this explanation. It is true that there were doctrinal debates in eighteenth-century natural science (and, to a lesser degree,

1. See E. Nagel, *The Structure of Science* (New York, 1961), pp. 447–546; and A. Kaplan, *The Conduct of Inquiry: Methodology for Behavioral Science* (San Francisco, 1964).

2. See Robert K. Merton, "Social Conflict Over Styles of Sociological Work," in his *The Sociology of Science: Theoretical and Empirical Investigations* (Chicago, 1973), pp. 47–69; Rolf Klima, "Theoretical Pluralism, Methodological Dissension and the Role of the Sociologist: The West German Case," *Social Science Information* 11, no. 3/4 (June/August 1972): 69–101; and Raymond Boudon, "The Sociology Crisis," ibid., pp. 109–39.

3. See Thomas S. Kuhn, *The Structure of Scientific Revolutions*, 2d ed. (Chicago, 1970), pp. 15–17.

also in subsequent centuries), but those doctrines were effectively neutralized by the insistence of the academies, in particular, the Paris Academy of Sciences, which was the most influential of all, on a clear distinction between verifiable discovery and doubtful dogma.[4] Thus, continuity of research and unity of purpose were much better preserved in eighteenth-century natural science than in the social sciences today. Above all, there were no serious attacks from within the ranks of scientists on the validity of science, as there were in the social sciences in the 1920s and the 1930s and as there are again today.[5]

Therefore, it seems that in addition to the relative poverty of the intellectual traditions of social science, there must be further reasons for this state of affairs. The proposition to be investigated in this article is that the discontinuities and the doctrinal fights in the social sciences are not due to anything inherent in their logic or stage of development but to the uses made of them by a variety of publics and to the resulting intrusion of nonscientific criteria into the evaluation of contributions to social science. To the extent that these criteria are clearly incompatible with science, they are rejected by the majority of social scientists. But it will be shown that even this majority is willing to recognize as scientific some innovations which contain both scientific and nonscientific elements and that the evaluation of these marginal instances has been a major condition of the weak resistance offered by social scientists to the intrusion of extraneous criteria into their field.

II

For natural scientists there are only two kinds of publics or audiences: their colleagues in basic research and technological clients such as industrial firms or farmers. Scientific peers are interested in original discovery and sound methodology. Clients are interested in contributions which can be used for a specific purpose. They need data, such as weather forecasts; or a specific kind of product, like the transistor; or a technique, such as a new way to smelt iron. In all these cases the contribution has to be empirically testable by specific

4. See Roger Hahn, *The Anatomy of a Scientific Institution: The Paris Academy of Sciences, 1666–1803* (Berkeley, 1971).

5. There is no systematic study of the rise of these views in the 1920s, but there are many documentary descriptions; see, for example, Hans Peter Bleuel, *Deutschlands Bekenner: Professoren zwischen Kaiserreich und Diktatur* (Bern, 1968), pp. 184–85, 203, 210–14, 222. For the present situation, see Rolf Klima's excellent description of the rise of antiresearch views in recent German sociology (Klima, supra n. 2, pp. 78–79, 93–94, 104, n. 18). On both occasions, there were sociologists who accepted and justified the attacks on the validity of social science and tried to use them as a basis for revolutionizing social thought and for the establishment of new schools of sociology. See Karl Mannheim, *Ideology and Utopia* (New York, 1936), pp. 5, 46, 187; Alvin W. Gouldner, *The Coming Crisis of Western Sociology* (New York, 1970). At least so far, none of these attempts has had any significant effect on sociological research.

criteria, such as a prediction specified in a hypothesis, or a marketable product, or a service which measurably increases efficiency.

Social scientists also have these two publics, but in addition, they have a third one, too. Potentially, every person can take a direct interest in contributions made by social scientists. Actually, of course, only a few people read their writings or anything else. But even these few are very many compared to those who interest themselves in the natural sciences. Journalists, higher civil servants, and politicians, although they tend to be skeptical about social science, are usually alert to new ideas originating in it.[6] Young people, immigrants, people who rise or fall socially, or any other groups which find themselves in a state of social disorientation are all receptive to information and interpretations provided by social scientists.

Finally, the social sciences are potentially very influential educational subjects. Moral education, which was based in the past on religious traditions, is often based nowadays on social studies. This is done explicitly in high schools and implicitly in college and is probably a source of frustration and conflict in graduate school, where many young people whose real vocation would be to become preachers and priests are expected to become scholars and scientists.

Serving the lay public by writing on matters of current interest is one of the legitimate functions of social scientists. The existence of such potentially widespread interest is considered to be an enviable characteristic of social science. It has been one of the contentions of scientists that the knowledge produced by their search for truth is also socially useful, but only in the social sciences does substantive research frequently arouse public interest. Natural scientists have made great efforts to create such a public by popularizing science and by emphasizing its social and economic implications, but their efforts have not had much success. Therefore, in order to convince the public of the social importance of science they have to rely mainly on the few instances in which scientific discoveries led directly to applications and on the belief that in the long run most scientific discoveries have such applications.

However, there is a crucial difference between the rare occasions when a scientific discovery also proves useful in a technological context and the frequent uses made of the findings of social science in debates on public affairs. As has been pointed out, in the former case the use of the discovery requires that the findings should have a high degree of validity, since research which contains mistakes is unlikely to be of much use to technology. But there is no such overlap between the criteria of scientific validity and those of usefulness

6. Cf. the oft-quoted remark of Keynes: "the ideas of economists and political philosophers, both when they are right and when they are wrong, are more powerful than is commonly understood. Indeed the world is ruled by little else . . . Soon or late, it is ideas, not vested interests, which are dangerous for good or evil." J. M. Keynes. *The General Theory of Employment, Interest and Money* (London, 1942), pp. 383–84.

in public debate. Validity may be of secondary importance from the point of view of the rhetorical uses made of the findings of social scientists. Thus, the fact that the racial theories of Gobineau and others were scientifically wrong did not make them less "useful" for the purposes of Nazi propaganda. Nor are present-day adherents of different economic and political theories deterred from using them in their rhetorics by the scientific refutation of all or part of these theories.

The distortion of scientific criteria by this "third public" which uses social science without being interested in its validity does not consist only of choosing the rhetorically effective but scientifically wrong theory. Distortions can occur also by conferring publicity on work which has little theoretical importance, such as the Kinsey Report.

Finally, service of this third public is probably one of the main reasons for the discontinuities in social research. The interests of this public have obviously a great influence on the choice of research topics. For example, in the period of 1964–1971 every self-respecting sociologist investigated university students' protest movements.[7] This work had many interesting results, which it would have been worthwhile to follow up. But when student activism subsided, the general public lost interest in student affairs, and this whole line of research was discontinued.

These last two discrepancies between the judgment of the scientific and that of the nonscientific users of discoveries also exist when science is used for technological (as distinct from rhetorical or recreational) purposes. Relatively trivial discoveries may be of greater use to industry than scientifically much more important ones. But scientists have always been aware of this and have been careful and successful in not mixing up the two kinds of criteria, by withholding scientific recognition for technological contributions.[8] Therefore, the problem is not the existence of a plurality of publics possessing their varieties of intellectually legitimate and illegitimate interests in science or the willingness of some social scientists to serve these publics (a service which is not inconsistent with the highest quality of scholarship as manifested by such examples as Raymond Aron, Milton Friedman, Paul Samuelson, and Edward Shils). The question is why so many social scientists—some of them obscure writers addressing exclusively their own professional community—are willing and occasionally eager to move from one subject to another according to the shifts in public interest and, above all, why they frequently adopt political criteria in the evaluation of each other's work.

7. For a survey of part of this work, see Philip G. Altbach, *Student Politics and Higher Education in the United States: A Select Bibliography* (Cambridge, Mass., 1968); and idem., *A Select Bibliography on Students, Politics and Higher Education,* rev. ed. (Cambridge, Mass., 1970).
    8. See Stuart S. Blume and Ruth Sinclair, "Chemists in British Universities: A Study of the Reward System of Science," *American Sociological Review* 38, no. 1 (February 1973): 126–38.

Part of the explanation may lie in the fact that because of the widespread rhetorical use of social science, it is much more difficult for social than for natural scientists to defend themselves against the intrusion of external criteria in the reward system of their field. Journalistic and political users of social science have direct access to the contributions of social scientists, make their own choices among the contributions, and create widespread nonscientific recognition for some of them. These choices and evaluations then become part of the general culture which is shared by social scientists and the general public. This is not the case with contributions in the natural sciences, since there the general public is incompetent to choose and judge for itself and has to rely on scientific popularizers or on technological experts.

This may be a reasonable hypothesis, but it is not a completely satisfactory one. It assumes that social scientists are unintentionally influenced by the intellectual judgment of various lay publics, but this is not how scientists usually behave. As has been pointed out, scientists, including social scientists, are careful to distinguish between work which is an original contribution to knowledge and that which merely has technological utility. But above all, much of social science is concerned with the criticism and the correction of popularly accepted notions on moral, political, economic, and cultural matters. Therefore, it is unlikely that social scientists should accept unwittingly the judgment of lay publics concerning their own work. Lay interest can probably explain the discontinuity in the choices of subject matters for research. In this respect social scientists quite often act as part of the general public by rushing in their studies from one topical issue to another, partly because they feel morally obliged to contribute as scientists to the solution of social problems and partly because of the intangible and tangible rewards of catering to fashion. But the adoption of nonscientific criteria of judgments concerning their own work cannot be attributed to the wish to serve the public as scientists, since this would require the opposite course—namely, the refusal to accept nonscientific criteria and an attempt at educating the public. The adoption of such extraneous criteria is the result of conscious decision which has to be explained as such.

III

In order to see how such decisions, so evidently inconsistent with the purpose and the logic of scientific inquiry, are legitimated, we have to explore the contexts in which they are taken. Typically this occurs in connection with the discussion and the evaluation of metaphysical ideas implicit in scientific re-

---

It is my impression that social scientists also distinguish between original ideas and practical applications.

search. In the natural sciences such ideas are rarely discussed and are never recognized as contributions, except indirectly, through the recognition of substantive discoveries associated with them. For instance, Oersted's discovery of the identity of electrical and magnetic phenomena may well have been influenced by the metaphysical idea of the unity of all the forces of nature, but only Oersted's substantive work, and not Schelling's speculations, has been recognized as an important discovery.[9] Only in rare cases when a metaphysical idea is directly linked to a specific concept, such as gravitation, does the former become a part of the scientific tradition.

It seems that such direct links are more frequent in the social than in the natural sciences. Marx's "labor," Bentham's "utility," Edgeworth's "units" or "atoms of pleasure," Durkheim's "anomie," and Weber's "charisma" are all metaphysical ideas which have been directly related to important substantive investigations and have been incorporated into the tradition of social science as contributions.

This, in itself, is not different in principle from the practice of the natural sciences. The difference between the traditions emerges when empirical research or logical analysis reaches the stage where it becomes possible to separate what can be unequivocally and operationally defined and investigated from the metaphysical elements contained in the original intuition. At that point present-day practice in the social sciences is sharply divided.

In some cases the practice is similar to that which prevails in the natural sciences. This is the approach of Joan Robinson's *Economic Philosophy*.[10] She traces the development of the guiding ideas in the history of economic thought since the eighteenth century and discloses the "ideological" and metaphysical character of such basic concepts as "value," "utility," and "development." She defines an ideological proposition as one which "if treated in a logical manner, either dissolves into a completely meaningless noise or turns out to be a circular argument." A metaphysical proposition, according to her, is one "that . . . is not capable of being tested" (pp. 2–3). But the purpose of her exercise is not to demonstrate that scientific thought in the social sciences is impossible. A concept such as utility may be metaphysical in its origin, but marginal analysis is still a powerful tool of economic analysis. Accounts of national income, productivity, savings, and so on, may be biased by unstated assumptions rooted in nationalist and laissez-faire ideologies. They put a

9. Indeed, to the extent that Oersted and others actually wanted to derive hypotheses directly from those metaphysics, they were unsuccessful. See Barry Gower, "Speculation in Physics: The History and Practice of Naturphilosophie," *Studies in the History and Philosophy of Science* 3, no. 4 (1973): 301–56.

10. See Joan Robinson, *Economic Philosophy* (Chicago, 1963), pp. 2–4, 14, 24–25, 147–48. See also George J. Stigler, "The Development of Utility Theory," in his *Essays in the History of Economics* (Chicago, 1965), pp. 66–155. Although not explicitly dealing with metaphysics and ideology, his essay too detects nonscientific bias in the development of economic theory and treats it much as Robinson does.

value on things that are sold at a price and undervalue things that are not (such as clean air and water). But national accounts are still very useful for monitoring changes in productivity or for comparing rates of saving in different countries, in order to obtain some standards of what is possible (p. 128). The purpose of the exposure of bias is to improve the accounts by the inclusion of values which are not measured at the present by money. This approach recognizes that what is considered scientific knowledge at any time may contain metaphysical elements and that those elements may reflect personal or group bias ("ideology"). But it believes that criticism and research are capable of overcoming this bias and can create objective knowledge which is separable (can be "demarcated") from metaphysics and bias.

However, there is also another approach which uses the disclosure of metaphysics and of bias in the social science tradition as evidence that, in principle, social science is not different from speculative moral, political, and religious philosophy and ideology.[11] This conclusion is then used to justify the application of political criteria to the evaluation of scientific work and to downgrade the importance of repeatable procedures in empirical research or of empirical research altogether.[12]

The difference between these approaches is not logical but strategic. They agree that the social science tradition contains metaphysical and ideological elements, and they agree that those elements can be disclosed. The question is what to do with the disclosure. This is a question about the future which cannot be answered scientifically. The different reactions to this question are essentially choices between two faiths and two loyalties. Those who believe in the future of science and who wish to maintain their professional identity as scientists will use the disclosure for the mapping out of new research strategies (such as including new kinds of values in the national accounts) in order to reduce bias and increase the objectivity of the tradition. Those who do not believe in or care much about science and who are willing to exchange their scientific vocation for that of the political ideologist will prefer to use the disclosure for the justification of abolishing the demarcation line between science and ideology and of using the former as a political instrument.

Therefore, the intrusion of political criteria into social science is the result

11. See the sources cited supra n. 5, esp. Klima, pp. 87–88 and 106, n. 32.
12. See, for example, T. R. Young, "The Politics of Sociology," *American Sociologist* 6, no. 4 (November 1971): 276–81, which contains reasonable suggestions about the use of provocation and emotional reaction in social research. The validity of the suggestion has nothing to do with politics, and its usefulness relative to other techniques can be explored empirically. Yet the author insists on presenting his ideas as part of a political viewpoint, contrasting it with the accepted procedures which he identifies with opposing political views. This deliberately turns science into politics and eliminates the possibility of testing the proposition. See also the manifesto of a group of radical economists in *American Economic Review,* May 1970, p. 487, quoted in Harry G. Johnson, "Economics and the Radical Challenge: The Hard Social Science and the Soft Social Reality," in *Culture and Its Creators: Essays in Honor of Edward A. Shils,* ed. J. Ben-David and T. N. Clark (Chicago: University of Chicago Press, 1977).

of the deliberate use of social science as a substitute for moral and religious philosophy, an endeavor which is shared by some social scientists and a considerable fraction of the public.[13] Next to a lasting core of social scientists aiming to increase the objectivity of the field, there have been in practically every period a number of people—some of them competent social scientists—who have turned against the scientific enterprise, preferring to use social science as the basis for the formation of ideological sects.[14]

IV

Since these are evidently two different purposes, it is difficult to understand why there has been no institutionalization of the split between these two groups. Why have social scientists failed to follow in this respect the practices of natural scientists, who have steadfastly refused to admit any religious, moral, or mystical elements in scientific judgment for three centuries?

An indication of the rationale for this reluctance to demarcate scientific from quasi-religious and political innovations can be found, among others, in a recent article about "major advances" in social science by Deutsch, Platt, and Senghaas.[15] Their list of advances includes, among others, the contributions of Freud, Jung, Adler, Lenin, Gandhi, and Mao Tse-tung. One of these, Lenin, even shares with Derek de Solla Price and Herbert Simon the distinction of being the discoverer of two innovations—in his case, the "theory of one-party organization and revolution" and the "Soviet-type of one-party state." Only one of the critics of Deutsch, Platt, and Senghaas objected to the inclusion of some of these innovations in this list of major advances in social science on the ground that they were only applications of previously discovered principles.[16] Although the fame of Lenin, Gandhi, and Mao has been due mainly to their political success, the authors of the list of "major advances" consider them to be original contributors to social science because they wrote

13. This is quite different from the suggestion of Robert W. Friedrichs that sociologists adopt either the mode of thought of "priests" or that of "prophets"; see his *Sociology of Sociology* (New York, 1970), pp. 57–109. My argument is that neither the priestly nor the prophetic model is compatible with the scientific endeavor and that it is a puzzle why the role of the social scientist has not been clearly differentiated from these other roles.

14. The most detailed investigation of the relationship between science and ideology is that of Everett E. Ladd, Jr., and Seymour Lipset, *The Politics of American Academics* (New York: McGraw-Hill, 1975). They show that there exists a clear-cut split between those who introduced their ideology into university affairs and those who do not (see pp. 3:14–16, 6:22, 8:14–28); that the conflict has always been most pronounced in the social sciences (pp. 4:22–25); and that those who favor the politicization of science actually oppose research (pp. 4:9–14). This supports the interpretation that there are actually two different conceptions of the role, one scientific and the other religious-educational.

15. K. W. Deutsch, J. Platt, and D. Senghaas, "Conditions Favoring Major Advances in Social Science," *Science* (February 5, 1971): 450–59.

16. See letters by R. Collins and G. J. Stigler, *Science* (June 17, 1971): 1191.

extensively about their theories and because they attributed their success to techniques derived from those theories. Freud, Jung, and Adler, of course, regarded themselves primarily as scientists. Ostensibly, therefore, all these names are known for scientific innovations which explain in an original way certain observable events.

However, all the theories most closely associated with these names have characteristics which are scientifically unacceptable. Neither the original innovators nor their followers, with the partial exception of the psychoanalysts (see Section V, below), have been willing to submit the theories to scientifically satisfactory testing. They have considered the successes of their techniques to be evidence of the correctness of the theories, while attributing their failures to mistakes or to unpredictable (often sinister) "external" interferences.

Another irregular feature of these cases has been the obscurity of the relationships between parts of the theory. On the one hand, the theories make specific predictions about human and social behavior. On the other hand, the adherents of the theories refuse to consider those specific predictions as so many hypotheses to be tested separately but consider them all as part of a whole. In consequence the predictions can be tested only under conditions of complete systemic change. The persistence of mental illness in spite of therapy is attributed to difficulties in completing the psychoanalysis, not to shortcomings of the theory; and the imperfections of Communist societies are attributed to the fact that the state of a completely classless society has not yet been attained.

Although there can be no logical objection to hypotheses relating to whole systems, in practice such hypotheses may effectively bar all empirical enquiry. Even if there should be an operational definition of a completely accomplished psychoanalysis or of a perfectly classless society, the theory would still not be testable because of the insurmountable practical difficulty of creating the required conditions in even a single case. But even this remote possibility is blocked by the absence of a satisfactory definition of the ultimate state of the system where the predictions are supposed to prevail. We do not know what a completely analyzed or a healthy personality by psychoanalytic criteria is;[17] nor is there any definition of the classless society of the Communist utopia. Therefore, any state ever attainable can still be interpreted as falling short of the requirements of the theory, so that nothing can ever contradict the theory.

Finally, there is a basic ambiguity in the conceptualization of the hypothesized causal chain. The variables of all these theories are partly objective and

17. See Erik H. Erikson, *Childhood and Society* (New York, 1950), for an attempt to arrive at an empirical definition of the concept of a healthy personality. This attempt has done a great deal to strengthen the scientific in contrast to the metaphysical elements in psychoanalysis and has considerably reduced its mystical transformational character by arguing that the importance of the libido was overstated in the original theory.

partly subjective. In psychoanalysis, pathologies of the personality are attributed to parental repression, and in Marxism, alienation, social pathology, and conflict result from the exploitation of one class by the other. But the removal of repression or exploitation is not a sufficient condition for cure. Both kinds of theory also require a change of subjective consciousness. Although, in principle, this change of consciousness is supposed to follow the removal of repressions or of exploitation spontaneously, in practice neither psychoanalysis nor Marxism will rely on spontaneous change of consciousness. Reeducation and proselytization are integral parts of both techniques. This, of course, finally eliminates any possibility of testing, since it can never be found out whether successful predictions are due to changes in the objective conditions or to self-fulfilling prophecy.

All this is, of course, quite well known to social scientists, and therefore some of them are unwilling to give any consideration to such theories. But the majority find it difficult either to ignore or to study these theories as mere objects, and not as part, of social science. It seems that social science faces in these instances a problem which has precedents in the history of the natural sciences. This was the demarcation of science from magic, alchemy, astrology, Mesmerism, and to some extent also from theories such as Naturphilosophie, or the cosmology of Immanuel Velikovsky.[18] Like the varieties of psychoanalysis and Marxism, these are also theories which try to solve scientific problems but which have been resistant to empirical testing. They all contain ideas about the unity of phenomenologically different variables, such as "animal magnetism" (about as precise an expression as "bourgeois liberalism"), or about hidden variables linking together apparently remote phenomena, such as the neo-Platonic world-soul which was thought to be necessary for the operation of all mechanical laws, as well as for human conduct. (The Freudian concept of libido seems to be a recent parallel to this in the social sciences.) Such ideas may contain scientifically valuable elements, as for example hypnosis was an element of Mesmerism. However, their proponents do not formulate testable hypotheses but metaphysical principles which are supposed to have broad but not clearly specified effects, practical applications, and occasionally also some artistic or moral significance. This tends to create a sectarian following united by a feeling of mystical unity between the believers and by an expectation of utopian or wondrous transformations in people, society, or nature, as the case may be. The common characteristic of all these theories, whether they deal with social or natural phenomena, is a

18. See L. Thorndike, *A History of Magic and Experimental Science* (New York, 1958), vol. 7; Allen G. Debus, *Science and Education in the Seventeenth Century* (London, 1970); P. M. Rattansi, "The Social Interpretation of Science in the Seventeenth Century," in *Science and Society, 1600–1900*, ed. Peter Mathias (Cambridge, 1972), pp. 1–32; Andre M. Weitzenhoffer, "Mesmer, Franz Anton." *International Encyclopedia of the Social Sciences* 10:260–62; Barry Gower, supra n. 9; and Alfred De Grazia, ed., *The Velikovsky Affair—The Warfare of Science and Scientism* (New Hyde Park, N.Y., 1966).

kind of short-circuited conception of causality. They attribute direct transformatory power to unverifiable "metaphysical" principles and try to bridge the logical gap in the explanation by rhetoric and group suggestion. Therefore they will be referred to subsequently as "metaphysical theories of transformation," or briefly as "transformational theories." [19]

It is not easy to decide how to deal with such theories. The fact that they may contain a grain of scientific truth makes it difficult to justify rejecting them outright. And their promise of immediate and far-reaching transformations makes them attractive to laypeople as well as to scientists. Until the end of the seventeenth century such theories were indeed considered to be part of science. [20] The attraction to them is particularly great in the social sciences, in which the idea of the "transformation" of objective conditions into subjective states and vice versa is an intuitively much more plausible idea than in the natural sciences.

However, the main problem in either field was not the difficulty of demarcation but the way they dealt with it. Natural scientists have fought transformational theories with determination since the end of the seventeenth century. In case of doubt they tended to err in the direction of greater exclusiveness, as shown by the case of bacteriology and the overreaction to the innocuous speculations of Velikovsky. [21] Even *Naturphilosophie*, which had many of the characteristics of a transformational theory but never became a sect with extrascientific aims, spread mainly in Germany and some smaller countries peripheral in science at the time. It made little headway in France, which was the scientific center at the end of the eighteenth century and early nineteenth century and which had the most developed scientific institutions.

On the other hand, social scientists have always been willing to give transformational theories at least a hearing. Thus, they found objectionable the behavior of natural scientists in the Velikovsky affair. [22] They were far more open to psychoanalysis than natural scientists and would probably be willing to listen to the claims of parapsychologists much more sympathetically than natural scientists.

All this suggests that demarcation of science from transformational theory

19. Cf. C. C. Gillispie, *The Edge of Objectivity: An Essay in the History of Scientific Ideas* (Princeton, 1960), p. 199, about Romanticism in science, which deals with part of this same problem.

20. See J. M. Keynes, "Newton the Man," in *The World of Mathematics*, ed. J. R. Newman, vol. 1 (New York, 1956), pp. 277–85.

21. The suspicion that the denial of spontaneous generation by the bacterial theory was introducing religious elements into science was extremely farfetched. Neither that theory nor the serious students of parapsychology nor Velikovsky could be accused of attempts to confuse criteria of empirical science with those of other fields. But the possibility of such confusion which has existed in all these cases has been enough to arouse suspicion or even hostility against these theories in the scientific community. In bacteriology there was overwhelming experimental evidence in favor of the new theory, so resistance was rapidly overcome. See René Vallery-Radot, *The Life of Pasteur* (New York, 1948), pp. 111–13, 216–22.

22. See De Grazia, supra n. 18.

was logically possible even at a rudimentary stage of scientific development and that differences in this respect between fields and countries were due to institutional conditions.

At first glance, the approach of the social scientists may appear to be the preferable one, since to deny a hearing even to theories which have questionable characteristics requires a justification. However, it seems that natural scientists have a justification. Their requirement that a theory should fit experimental findings imposes on the scientist a severe restraint. He has to stick to the "art of the soluble" [23] and check his imagination, which may run far beyond it. This deprives him of the freedom of the artist and the philosopher, who can develop their imagination freely and who may obtain recognition and fame for the sheer beauty, logical consistency, or associative richness of their vision. The loss of this right to flights of fancy and the acceptance of the discipline of empirical enquiry are sacrifices which natural scientists have to make in order to maintain their unique enterprise.

This intellectual discipline has been socially approved of and maintained by the conviction that as a result of it there can be produced a kind of knowledge which has greater empirical validity and is therefore more consensual and of greater practical value than any other knowledge produced by man. However, the practical application of discoveries is ordinarily a prolonged and complex process, and there are many discoveries which have never been applied to anything practical. The only thing which can be ascertained within limits in nearly all scientific contributions is their empirical validity, which can be taken also as an indication of the ultimate applicability of the discovery. A relationship the existence of which is proved mathematically or validated experimentally is likely to also be practically useful, given the emergence of a technological problem the solution of which requires knowledge of this relationship. However, because such a technological problem may never emerge or may emerge only a long time after the discovery, scientists cannot rely on recognition given for the practical uses of their work. For a scientific discovery, the only social reward which they can reasonably depend on is the recognition by their peers that it is a true and original contribution to knowledge. This is also confirmation of the belief in its ultimate applicability, and hence in its general usefulness. It is, therefore, of crucial importance for the scientific enterprise that recognition be given according to strictly and purely scientific criteria and that recognition should be awarded only by scientists competent to apply those criteria. [24]

For this reason scientists jealously withhold recognition from innovations

23. See Peter B. Medawar, *The Art of the Soluble: Creativity and Originality in Science* (Hammondsworth, 1969), pp. 95–110.
24. For the importance of the reward system for science, see Robert K. Merton, *The Sociology of Science*, pp. 281–382; and Jonathan R. Cole and Stephen Cole, *Social Stratification in Science* (Chicago, 1973).

which are not direct contributions to knowledge. As has been pointed out, this reserve applies to technological contributions, to metaphysics in general, and, a fortiori, to transformational theories. These latter present a particularly serious threat to the proper functioning of the scientific reward system because they claim to arrive at significant, valid, and directly applicable truth without accepting mathematical-experimental discipline, and to make things worse, they appeal for recognition to the broad public, bypassing the authority of the scientific community and the accepted procedures of scientific verification. Giving transformational theories a hearing would probably destroy the whole scientific enterprise. Because of their far-reaching claims (which can be disproved only with great difficulty or not at all) and their appeal to the general public, they would probably succeed in monopolizing all the resources available for scientific work, leaving research according to the accepted methods of science virtually resourceless. An extreme illustration of what could happen to science once theories which reject the scientific procedure are allowed to compete for scientific recognition is provided by the Lysenko case in the USSR.[25] Although some of the events, such as the incarceration and causing the death of the opponents of that unscientific theory, would probably not have happened under more humane regimes than that of Stalin, the monopolization of resources could happen anywhere where such theories were allowed to compete with science. Once it is admitted that theories can be judged by members of the general public applying other than scientific procedures of verification, scientific criteria have a poor chance of prevailing in the face of transformational theories with some public appeal.[26]

But even without such monopolization of resources by deliberate policy, giving a hearing to transformational theories would impose a crushing burden on science. Because, as has been pointed out, these theories are formulated in a way which makes testing impossible or at least endlessly debatable, attempts to evaluate them according to accepted scientific procedure would be so time-consuming and would generate so much irresoluble antagonism that there would be little time and energy left for other work.[27] This is a justifiable ground for the exclusion of such theories from science and the denial of scientific recognition to their founders.

It is not difficult to understand why social scientists have seen these problems in a different light than natural scientists. With few exceptions, social sciences do not possess a tradition of disciplinary training and research com-

25. See David Joravsky, *The Lysenko Affair* (Cambridge, Mass., 1970).

26. This is, of course, what happened on a large scale in German (and other European) social science in the 1920s and the 1930s; see Bleuel, supra n. 5. About similar tendencies today, see David Armstrong, "Fission at Sydney University," and Seymour Lipset, "Politicization and Economics at Harvard," both in *Newsletter* of the International Council on the Future of the University 2, no. 1 (January 1975): 1, 10–14.

27. This was the argument of Michael Polanyi in "The Growth of Science in Society," *Minerva* 5, no. 4 (Summer 1967): 533–46.

parable to the natural sciences. Not having "invested" heavily in the acquisition of highly specialized techniques or in a habit of self-denial in restricting their inquiries to technically soluble problems, and not being dependent as much as the natural scientists on costly laboratories, they feel less threatened by the competition of metaphysical theories of transformation. They also do not perceive as a net loss the time and effort spent on debates and refutations of all or part of such theories, partly because any theory, even if incorrect, which has a social impact is a matter of interest to social scientists and partly because the refutation of false social theories is considered one of the legitimate educational functions of the profession. Furthermore, metaphysical theories of transformation have greater attraction for social than for natural scientists. Social scientists have made relatively few discoveries which have visible and dramatic practical applications like some of the discoveries in natural science. Therefore, the apparent practical successes of transformational theories make them as attractive for social scientists today as magic and alchemy used to be for natural scientists at the end of the seventeenth century. For example, the possibility that the Soviet type of one-party state is capable of resolving problems of social conflict and economic production which have baffled political and economic theory is an alluring one, even if one suspects that the evidence of success is as deceptive as in the claims of healing sects.

In other words, the difference between the policies of natural and social scientists toward transformational theories is a matter of expediency. Natural scientists, who fear that the inclusion of these theories would disrupt their traditional discipline and deprive them of resources for research, prefer to exclude them from science. Social scientists, who have a tradition of more relaxed discipline and who have less reason to fear that the proponents of transformational theories would deprive them of resources for research and of social rewards, are willing to accept these theories as part of their traditions, at least to the extent of seriously debating and refuting them.

In fact, many social scientists consider the inclusion of transformational theories in their field as an advantage. The traditional "positivistic" demarcation of science from other branches of knowledge has been criticized for many years, and there is a tendency nowadays to view transformational theories, and even the doctrinal disputes aroused by them, as a matrix out of which new insights and original theory emerge. Therefore, it has to be seen what evidence there is on the effect of the acceptance of these theories as legitimate innovations on the development of social science.

V

I shall try to answer this question by considering the effects of the most important instances of the admission of metaphysical theories of transformation into twentieth-century social sciences.

The two most influential theories of this kind during the last hundred years have been Marxism and psychoanalysis. The founders of both were brilliant intellectuals and great writers whose work can still be read with enjoyment and intellectual benefit. In addition to or in the process of creating transformational theories, Marx made substantive contributions to sociology, political science, and economics, as did Freud to psychology and sociology. These would have earned them places in the history of these fields, quite apart from their general theories and the political movement started by Marx and the healing sects which emerged from psychoanalysis.

But the fact that they created such theories and that in different ways their writings have been canonized by sectarian followers has greatly modified the manner in which their contributions were absorbed into the social science tradition. The scientifically doubtful aspects of the theories and their association with politically and morally controversial movements have seriously interfered with the scientific exploration of the substantive contributions contained in the theories. Nevertheless, those contributions were eventually recognized. Marx's main contribution to sociology was the idea that the political and social divisions of society could be understood in terms of conflicts of interests between social groups ("classes") performing different economic functions. This idea was originally formulated by economists in the eighteenth century. Marx's own elaborations on the subject, such as the one of the essentially economic determination of all political, religious, or legal thought, and his ideas about the emergence of class consciousness and solidarity, were first approximations to the problem. Some of them, such as his theory of the determination of political views and "ideology" in general by economic interest and the attribution of alienation to class exploitation, turned out to be extremely crude. Other ideas of Marx (and Engels), such as that of "false consciousness," were fruitful insights which, however, had to be reformulated in terms of reference group theory before they could be used for empirical research.[28] What was useful in his ideas has been gradually incorporated in and superseded by subsequent sociological theory, especially early in this century in the work of Max Weber.[29]

There has been a similar process of gradual exploration of Marx's economic ideas, such as the conditions under which a competitive system may result in a socially less than optimal allocation of goods and services, and the relationship between "values" determined by labor and prices determined by competitive mechanisms.[30]

The time and the place of these explorations were often influenced by political conditions. But the methods of exploration were those accepted in so-

28. See W. G. Runciman, *Relative Deprivation and Social Justice* (London, 1966).
29. See Max Weber, *Wirtschaft und Gesellschaft* (Tübingen, 1921–22), pp. 177–80, 631–40.
30. See Johnson, supra n. 12.

ciological and economic research. Research was concerned with specific ideas which could be operationalized and related to empirical observations. In economics this work was highly mathematical. In fact, Marxist economists since the 1940s saw mathematics as the main tool by means of which they would demonstrate the superiority of Marxist over orthodox economic theory. The work was done by individual scholars who had different political persuasions. Some of them were self-styled Marxists, but none of them questioned the possibility of scientific debate and decision based on the mathematical and empirical methods of their discipline.[30a]

In recent years, since about 1968, there has been a new kind of Marxist revival. In contrast to earlier attempts which considered Marxist theory as just a source of scientific hypotheses or as a scientific support or challenge to the political convictions of the investigator, this recent attempt has tried to use Marxism as an alternative kind of scientific theory and method. Its purpose has been to cast doubt on the scientific validity of disciplinary traditions by exposing them as camouflaged "ideological" justifications of the existing state of affairs and to substitute a new kind of science for them.[31]

This attempt has produced an outpouring of polemical writings and a great deal of acrimonious debate and disturbance at scientific meetings. In some universities it led to political discrimination in the hiring of new faculty and to the institution of courses in Marxist sociology or economics. It has produced little substantive research, certainly nothing comparable to the attempts at the exploration of Marx's ideas which began much before this recent movement.

The most conspicuous example of the intellectual barrenness of sectarian approach is the state of Marxist economics in Japan.[31a] Marxist departments of economics engage in interpretations of Marxist texts on traditional lines, ignoring all the advances in Marxian economic theory made by modern techniques.

30a. For a recent example of this kind of endeavor, see the debate on the "transformation problem"; Paul A. Samuelson, "Understanding the Marxian Notion of Exploitation: A Summary of the So-Called Transformation Problem Between Marxian Values of Competitive Prices," *Journal of Economic Literature* 9 (1971): 399–431; Martin Bronfenbrenner, "Samuelson, Marx, and Their Latest Critics," and "Samuelson's Reply on Marxian Matters," ibid., 11 (1973): 58–68; and Baumol-Samuelson-Morishima, "On Marx, the Transformation Problem and Opacity," ibid., 12 (1974): 51–77.

31. Johnson, supra n. 12; Klima, supra n. 2; Armstrong, supra n. 26; and Lipset, supra n. 26. For a programmatic statement of the new radical Marxist economics, see Raymond S. Franklin and William K. Tabb, "The Challenge of Radical Political Economics," *Journal of Economic Issues* 8 (March 1974): 27–50. For an interpretation of the attractions of Marxism, not inconsistent with the present approach but making no distinction between the scientific and sectarian uses of the theory, see Martin Bronfenbrenner, "The Vicissitudes of Marxian Economics," *History of Political Economy* 2 (1970): 205–24.

31a. This is not to say that the exegesis of Marxian texts in Japan has not made important contributions to scholarship. But sectarian seclusion restricts the benefits even from these contributions. For the description of one such contribution and the dogmatic divisions surrounding it, see Thomas L. Sebine, "Uno-Riron: A Japanese Contribution to Marxian Political Economy," *Journal of Economic Literature* 13 (1975): 847–77. See also George M. Beckman, "Marxism in Japan's History," *Asia* 8 (1967): 32–45.

The effect of this revival has been detrimental also for the work of those who did not submit to its demands. Among them it has led to attempts at presenting the traditional scientific interpretation of Marx. This is, of course, a legitimate historical enterprise, but since it has produced nothing new, it has been largely a waste of effort. Furthermore, in the given context it has often amounted to the attribution to Marx's ideas a historical importance out of all proportion to their intellectual as distinct from their political influence.

These differences between the scientific and the sectarian uses of metaphysical theories of transformation are equally evident in the second case to be considered, psychoanalysis. Freud, much more than Marx, had the intention of creating a truly scientific theory. Furthermore, psychoanalysis has made relatively specific predictions, and the degree of involvement which it requires from its adherents does not quite forestall every possibility of testing the theory. In fact, a large number of fruitful hypotheses were derived from psychoanalysis, so that few people would deny that this theory has benefited social science.

But the way the theory was absorbed into social science was far from optimal. In Austria, Germany, and Continental Europe in general, psychoanalysis remained on the margins of social science, partly because its originators insisted that the ideas concerning the transformation of the libido and of the id should be recognized as scientific and because those who opposed this claim agreed to debate these metaphysical points instead of concentrating on the substantive hypotheses contained in psychoanalysis and leaving the metaphysics to others.[32] The use of psychoanalytic hypotheses in experimental research, in studies of the authoritarian personality, and in comparative studies of child rearing occurred only in the 1930s and the 1940s, mainly in the United States, where the approach to the new theory was pragmatic and empirical from the very beginning.[33]

This impression that the consideration of transformational theories as integral systems (as distinct from the consideration of some of the ideas contained in them) has only retarded the development of social science is also supported by the data on major advances of Deutsch et al.[34] According to them, nineteen Austrians and Germans out of a total of thirty-five contributors participated in five significant advances in social science between 1900 and 1918. All of these were advances in substantive theory which generated a great amount of

32. Those who opposed psychoanalysis were probably as much responsible for this development as the psychoanalysts; see Joseph Ben-David, "Roles and Innovation in Medicine," *American Journal of Sociology* 65, no. 6 (May 1960): 557–68. [This volume, chap. 1.]

33. See Robert R. Sears, *Survey of Objective Studies of Psychoanalytic Concepts.* New York, Social Science Research Council, Bull. 51, 1943; T. W. Adorno, Else Frenkel-Brunswik, Daniel J. Levinson, and R. Nevitt Sanford, in collaboration with Betty Aron, Maria Hertz Levinson, and William Morrow, *The Authoritarian Personality* (New York, 1950); John W. M. Whiting and Irvin L. Child, *Child Training Personality* (New Haven, 1953): and Robert R. Sears, E. E. Maccoby, and H. Levin, *Patterns of Child Rearing* (Evanston, Ill., 1957).

34. Supra n. 15.

empirical research. They were Weber's sociology of bureaucracy, culture, and values; psychoanalysis and depth psychology; the role of innovative enterprises in socioeconomic change; gestalt psychology; and sociometry and sociograms. All the contributors to this work except one were native Austrians and Germans.

The period between 1918 and 1938 was one of great ideological turmoil in Germany and to a somewhat lesser extent also in Austria. The defeat of Germany and Austria in the war gave rise to romantic and existentialist social philosophies and to a variety of political utopias. During this period eleven contributors (out of a total of sixty) participated in five significant advances made in these two countries. But two out of these five advances—namely, logical empiricism and the unity of science (which accounts for six out of the twelve contributors) and game theory (which accounts for one contributor from Germany, John von Neumann) were made in the formal disciplines of philosophy and mathematics. To the extent that they became relevant to research in social science, this was the result of work done subsequently in the United States.

The remaining two advances which appear on the list are sociology of knowledge (mainly the work of Karl Mannheim) and the authoritarian personality and family structure studies initiated by M. Horkheimer, H. Marcuse, and E. Fromm. Both of these contributions were direct manifestations of the rise of ideological thought. Mannheim's purpose was to salvage somehow the objective validity of social-scientific thought after having gone far to accept the argument that all social thought was ideologically tainted. His attempt was not successful, and its influence on subsequent research was slight and indirect.[35] The authoritarian-personality studies were also an attempt to elucidate the roots of ideological authoritarianism. They became important only after a considerable reformulation of the ideas which occurred in the United States in the late 1940s.[36] Even then the value of these studies was impaired by ideological biases.[37] As has been pointed out, psychoanalysis also, which had in its beginnings the potential of developing either in a scientific or a sectarian direction, eventually developed in Germany mainly as a sectarian group. The development of the scientific aspect of the theory occurred in the United States, which was relatively unaffected by the metaphysical and sectarian fashions prevailing in Europe.

Finally it should be mentioned that two of the advances, those of Karl Mannheim and of John von Neumann, were made by foreigners working temporarily in Germany.

35. See Edward Shils, "Ideology and Utopia, by Karl Mannheim," *Daedalus* 103, no. 1 (Winter 1973): 83–96.

36. See Adorno et al., supra n. 33.

37. See Edward Shils, "Authoritarianism: 'Right' and 'Left,'" in *Studies in the Scope and Method of the Authoritarian Personality*, ed. Richard Christie and Marie Jahoda (Glencoe, Ill., 1954), pp. 24–49.

This evidence suggests that the discontinuities and doctrinal fights caused by the inclusion of transformational theories have not served as either the root or the stimulus to important innovations in social science. Some of these theories have indeed benefited the social sciences. But in order to derive this benefit there was no need to consider the theories as integrated wholes or to treat their metaphysical and sectarian aspects as issues in social science. As has been shown, the scientific contributions from Marxism and psychoanalysis to the social sciences were made through the selection of particular insights and hypotheses from the total body of the theories; their confrontation with specific ideas from other traditions; and their exploration by strictly scientific methods. On the other hand, the programmatic acceptance of the theories as a whole by some social scientists and their programmatic rejection by others led only to fruitless debates and sectarian conflicts.

In times of political peace, these debates may be no more than a waste of time. But once metaphysical and ideological debates come to be considered a legitimate part of the social sciences—as they had been in Germany prior to the First World War and practically everywhere during the 1950s and the early 1960s[38]—the field becomes defenseless against those who are interested in using it for political purposes.[39] Such attempts have indeed been made as soon as the general political climate changed and relative political consensus gave way to conflict and dissent, following the First World War in Germany and as a result of the revulsion from the war in Vietnam and the inconclusiveness of the Cold War in the late 1960s.

38. For the situation before the First World War, see Marianne Weber, *Max Weber, ein Lebensbild*, 2d ed. (Heidelberg, 1950), pp. 465, 468–69. For the attention paid to metaphysical and ideological issues in the sociology of the 1950s and 1960s, see John Rex, *Key Problems of Sociological Theory* (London, 1961).

39. See supra nn. 5, 11, and 12. One of the few people to foresee these results was Max Weber; see his "The Meaning of 'Ethical Neutrality' in Sociology and Economics," in *Max Weber on Universities: The Power of the State and the Dignity of the Academic Calling in Imperial Germany*, trans. Edward A. Shils (Chicago, 1974), pp. 47–54.

Sociology and Its Uses 18

Sociologists deal with questions of greatest practical importance, such as the conditions of the stability of political systems, the causes and consequences of social inequality, or the prerequisites of modernization. But neither sociologists nor their actual and potential clients have been satisfied with the applicability of the answers provided by sociology.

The main criticism leveled against sociology is that it does not provide hard and fast solutions of a technical kind, such as are popularly attributed to the physical and biological sciences. There is a feeling that sociologists do not really come to grips with practical reality, only talk about it more or less interestingly.

This criticism is widely accepted among sociologists, and they tend to react to it in different ways. Some accept the limited usefulness of sociology for practical purposes as a fact of life and are content to practice sociology for purely intellectual purposes, as a kind of pure science or branch of philosophy. Others try to remedy the situation by following more closely the ways in which research in the natural sciences is used in the solution of technical problems. Finally, there is a third group, which rejects all analogy with the natural sciences, since it does not believe in the possibility of separating facts from value judgments in sociology. They think of sociology as indistinguishable from myth and ideology, which, of course, are very practical endeavors, but not applied science.

The purpose of this paper is to show that the criticism is misplaced, and

I am indebted to Lia Greenfeld for her help with the research and comments on the first draft of this paper.

none of the three alternatives is acceptable. Sociology as practiced today has many potentially useful applications, but because of various misconceptions these are frequently unrecognized, or not made proper use of. In the two subsequent chapters of the paper an attempt will be made to identify these misconceptions and suggest proper uses of sociological inquiry. Following these there will be a discussion of the problem of value neutrality and objectivity in social research under present-day conditions.

What Kind of Science Is Sociology?

Among those who accept sociology as an empirical science, there is much confusion about the question of what kind of science it is. Usually it is regarded as a kind of basic discipline the purpose of which is to generate theories about social phenomena, irrespective of their uses. Therefore, in order to make sociology more useful for society, and more lucrative for its practitioners, they advocate the development of an applied sociology, in order to focus on questions of immediate practical importance, adopt more effective ways of investigation, and concentrate not only on the diagnosis of social problems but also on finding practical means for their solution.

This view is based on a confusion between "basic science," "applied science," and "development." Both basic and applied science are concerned with the discovery of new systematic knowledge and not with immediate applicability. The distinction between them is in the choice of questions. In basic science questions arise from purely intellectual interests, such as investigations on the age of the universe; in applied science, from practical concerns, such as a desire to understand the immune system of the body with the ultimate purpose of preventing and curing illness. Because of this practical starting point, there is an assumption that the results will be eventually of practical value. But only in exceptional, and usually unpredictable cases, are the results immediately usable. Immediate use is expected only from "development," which is a very different process from scientific discovery. It uses available scientific knowledge, conventional wisdom, practical experience, and intuition in order to invent and produce specific products or processes which are economically marketable and politically acceptable.[1] This latter is a very different kind of work from scientific research and is frequently done by people with limited background in research.

According to this classification, sociology is, and has always been, overwhelmingly an applied field. Even historical questions, such as that about the relationship between economic activity and religious beliefs and practices, or

---

1. These definitions of basic and applied science and development are adapted from OECD, 1967, p. 10.

anthropological ones, such as attempts at making sense of the differences in the incest taboo between different societies, are practically motivated. They do not arise out of pure intellectual curiosity but out of an interest in such practical concerns as the differences in the functioning of the economies of different societies or the ways sexual relationships structure and reinforce solidarity between kinship and other kinds of groups.

Answers to such questions are potentially applicable to dealing with practical problems, but the difficulties of creating theories capable of dealing with complex and changing social reality, and the subsequent application of those theories in practice, are very great and poorly understood. An attempt will be made to clarify these difficulties through two examples: the study of the relationship between religious ethos and economic development and racial integration of schools in the United States. The first is the story of a search for theory with potential applications; the second is an attempt at the actual application of an existing theory with obvious practical implications.

The effect of religious ethos on economic development was first studied by Max Weber early in this century (Weber 1952, 1958, 1960, 1968). His problem derived from the widespread practical concern with the characteristics and workings of the capitalist economy. The context of his work was as much political and social as theoretical. To understand the unique characteristics of Western capitalism was important not only for comparative history—to explain the emergence of this unique phenomenon—but also for the practical politician who had to devise economic and social policies in societies in which capitalism was attacked both by representatives of precapitalist groups and world views and by socialists who regarded capitalism as a transitory phase in history approaching its inevitable decline and fall.

In the 1950s, there was a revival of interest in Weber's ideas, again due largely to practical concerns. This time the context was "modernization," namely, the attempt at industrializing and converting to a scientific world view all the primitive and traditional societies of the world within a short span of time. Weber's account of how this happened in the Western societies, where all this development toward "modernity" began, seemed to be an important starting point for a rational approach to this problem.

An attempt to apply Weber's ideas in a technical sense was implied in the work of David McClelland (McClelland 1961, 1966). He tried to break down the Protestant ethos into its motivational and behavioral elements and determine the conditions under which these elements arose. He hypothesized that the most important element in this ethos was the "achievement motive," a general psychological tendency to excel, which can be empirically verified through projective tests (Thematic Apperception Test). He, furthermore, tried to show that this motivation is fostered by certain kinds of child-rearing practices. In order to test his hypothesis, he attempted to relate the prevalence of achievement motivation in different populations to economic growth.

This attempt at straightforward "development" of Weber's ideas into a directly applicable technique failed, partly because McClelland's findings on the positive economic effects of achievement motivation were not accepted (Blaug 1972) and partly because the implementation of his technique—changing child-rearing practices—would have been extremely difficult anyway.

Weber's work has become an important part of present-day thinking on the problems of modernization through another attempt at the application of his theories in a new context, that of Robert N. Bellah (1957). This was one of the first attempts at the systematic explanation of the question of why the Japanese experiment in industrialization succeeded while others failed. According to Bellah, different strands in Tokugawa religiousness were functional equivalents of the Protestant ethos in the creation of a spirit of economic discipline, thus predisposing significant parts of the Japanese people to the successful adoption of modern ways of government and technology. This was no mere application of Weber's theory to a new case but also a modification of that theory in three important respects:

1) Originally the theory was designed to explain the first emergence but not the diffusion of modern capitalism; now it has come to be used in the explanation of its diffusion.

2) Confucian and syncretistic Far Eastern sects, the kinds which Weber found to have been incompatible with the spirit of capitalism, were shown to contain elements positively predisposing people to a certain kind of capitalism.

3) The capitalism implanted to Japan was not identical with the Western model; it was subjected to political controls and assumed organizational forms which had been unforeseen by Weber and perhaps inconsistent with his conception of the phenomenon. This modification of the theory allows one to view modern capitalism as a variety of patterns of industrial and governmental organization, consistent with a variety of social ethoses rooted in different religious-ideological backgrounds (Eisenstadt 1973, pp. 11–115, 231–307). This has not turned Weber's theory into a ready-made technology of modernization but has turned it into a concept of potential practical value which allows for the exploration, and perhaps deliberate engineering, of new types of economic modernization fitted to a variety (but probably still a limited variety) of value systems and ways of life.

This case shows the tortuous and unpredictable ways through which findings of potential practical importance reach the point at which practical application can actually be considered. This is not to say that every case has to be like this one, but it illustrates an important kind of difficulty encountered in the practical application of social theories. In order to understand this difficulty, it will be useful to analyze the case in some detail.

Sociologists want to understand the structure of important phenomena at, or near the point of, their emergence. In the case of "capitalism" and other features of "modernity," this occurred in the nineteenth century, when the "modernization" of Europe took place. As has been pointed out, such understanding was of great practical importance, because the spread of "capitalism" (which is usually a designation for "modernity" as understood in the West, namely, a set of loosely interrelated phenomena, such as private economic enterprise, liberal democracy, and religious tolerance) gave rise to social disorientation which had to be dealt with. The urgency of the need produced instant theories ("ideologies"), such as utilitarianism, positivism, and the different schools of socialism. Because the phenomenon was still new, and the need for orientation acute, the theories were inevitably short on observation and long on speculation and, therefore, of limited practical value. When dogmatically applied, they could be outrightly dangerous. Like the application of clinically untested medical theories, the application of untested social theories usually produces results that are greatly inferior to those of a pragmatic trial and error approach. Weber's work on capitalism was a determined effort at breaking the impasse of ideological dogmatism through looking at the phenomenon with a degree of detachment and moving the discussion from the emotionally charged context of modernity versus traditionalism represented by warring social groups to the context of comparative world history. This made possible the discovery of analytical variables, such as religious and economic ethos, and a nonevaluative interpretation of capitalism and modernity in general. "Capitalism" was no longer an inevitable stage in a predetermined evolutionary sequence—"higher" than the preceding and "lower" than the subsequent ones—encompassing all human societies but a particular concatenation of conditions which occurred at a given place and time. In principle, this opened the way toward constructive practical thinking about the phenomenon. Whereas the evolutionary theories only allowed such "practical" questions as "what side must one take in the political and ideological struggle in order to ensure that one will be on the winning side?"; following Weber, one could ask questions such as "what elements are missing in a situation in order to produce capitalism?" or "how could the capitalist phenomenon be partially modified in order to produce different but still 'modern' social systems?" In practice, these questions were not asked, because modern society was still in its first stages of development, and the phenomenon of modernity was of a single capitalistic type and limited to a small number of societies sharing a common cultural background. Therefore, although the analytical tools for a constructive practical approach to the phenomenon were there, they could not be taken advantage of. It was possible to explain the emergence of capitalism as a peculiar historical phenomenon, but once it emerged it looked as if it had possessed a monolithic structure and an uncontrollable tendency to spread, a view not very different from that of various kinds of evolutionary dialectic. Only with the emergence of successful alternatives to Western capitalism and a great many "failures" in modernization (or one may speak of "successful cases of resistance to modernization") could the theory be modified as done by Bellah and become an element in the practical thinking on, although perhaps still not in practical policies of, modernization.

In this case the difficulty of practical application of the theory was the result of the complex historical nature of the phenomenon: It was virtually impossible to analyze "capitalism" or "modernity" without some time perspective and the emergence of some variation in the broadly defined phenomenon. Theory could not have created either the time perspective or the variation. Only after these emerged in the pragmatic, trial and error world of everyday life could theory use them and arrive at formulations which, in their turn, may conceivably be of use in practice. Thus in this case, arriving at a theory of potential practical applications, one had to go in a roundabout way, forget altogether about applications, and be guided only by the cognitive need to break down the complex phenomena of capitalism and modernity in general into logically coherent elements which make possible a rational understanding and eventually also a degree of practical mastery of the phenomenon. This abandonment of immediate applicability did not eliminate the applied nature of this inquiry. In fact, it was a precondition of eventual applicability, since attempts at producing immediately applicable theories produced only intellectual bias and political propaganda.

The second case, that of school integration, illustrates—as has been pointed out—the difficulties involved in the actual application of a potentially applicable theory. Since the 1950s the courts in the United States faced the question whether de facto segregation of black and white children constituted an infringement of the right to equal educational opportunity. They decided, partly on the basis of sociological evidence, that it did and ordered the elimination of such segregation through busing children from district to district, so as to create racially desegregated schools.

The sociological evidence that next to the pupil's own family background, the strongest influence on his achievement is the family background of his school peers, is convincing and supports the idea of social and racial integration of schools.[2] Yet desegregation through busing has been a highly controversial arrangement and is being considered as causing more harm than good even by many people who identify with the cause of racial equality. In any event, follow-up studies have failed to show any improvement in the educational performance of black children as a result of desegregation (John 1975; Gerald and Miller 1975; Rist 1979).

There is no inconsistency in these attitudes and findings; the theory that racially mixed classes improve education may be right, but its application may

2. That the norms of the white middle-class majority may have important beneficial influence on the black minority in a classroom was suggested by the analysis of survey data; see U.S. Commission on Civil Rights, 1969. These findings were well grounded in theories on the way social influence occurs in groups.

be wrong. Effective application would have required the taking of steps similar to those taken by clinicians before the adoption of a new procedure or medicine. One ought to have found out what kinds and ratios of mixture have the desired effect. For example, a white majority and a black minority might have an entirely different effect than a combination of black majority with a white minority. The attitudes of teachers and pupils toward integration, and their ability to handle misunderstandings and conflicts which arise in interracial contact, are another important condition of success.

One would also have had to consider conditions, such as the costs and benefits of alternative educational inputs, like additional tuition, or better textbooks, and even such details as traffic conditions and weather. Such careful exploration of the conditions of applicability of a new discovery in the natural sciences are undertaken as a matter of course, prior to large-scale application. This was not done in the present case, partly because the matter was treated as a political rather than educational issue but partly because there is no clear understanding of the problems involved in the practical application of sociological knowledge. Thus instead of exploring the conditions of application in advance as necessary development work, the exploration has been done after the adoption of desegregation policies as "evaluation research" (Rist 1979). The resulting damage has been considerable.

This case shows that "development" is an unavoidable step in the application of sociological knowledge. Research, which produces such knowledge, always deals with a limited number of controlled variables, while practice takes place in an environment of uncontrolled variables the number and characters of which are difficult to predict. Science always has to apply to an entire category of cases, while practical solutions have to take into consideration the peculiarities of every single instance. These can be ascertained only through "development."

While these two cases probably do not exhaust the problem, they clarify two important aspects of the relationship between social research and its application:

1) Applied research deals with problems of practical importance, but its aim is not to produce actual solutions, only to contribute toward them by the discovery of the logical structure of the phenomena of practical interest. In order to do so, applied research has to be systematic and guided by criteria of cognitive validity, which during many parts of the research, may temporarily lead it away from the practical issues.

2) The discovery of the logical structure of phenomena and events which one wants to influence in a practical way does not provide a prescription of how to proceed in practice. This will always depend on the particulars of the situation which are usually not (and do not have to be) disclosed by research and professional research workers. Research findings may be crucially important for this "development" work, but research (including applied research)

and "development" are conceptually, and as a rule also socially, two distinct processes, not to be confused with each other.

What Kind of Ends Can Sociology Be Applied to?

Having dealt with the question of how sociological knowledge applicable to practical ends is produced, a few words have to be said about the kinds of practical ends which this knowledge can serve.

The popular expectation from sociology is to produce techniques for the manipulation of people, such as how to increase the effectiveness of advertisement and propaganda, how to "treat" delinquents, or how to "modernize" people who have no desire to become modern.

The assumption behind this kind of use is that people are part of "nature" and sociology is part of "science" and that the task of science is to create "transitive" theories, which make possible the mastery and manipulation of nature, implying also society, by man. Carried to its logical conclusion, this would mean that those who know and are able to manipulate belong to a different moral and metaphysical plane than those who do not know and can be manipulated—a horrifying conception of society and social science.

This conception, rarely verbalized but all too frequently implied in the practice of, and attitudes toward, social research, is not only morally unacceptable but also inconsistent with the logic of sociological inquiry. Social research, like all research, tries to shed light on puzzling phenomena or obscure events and situations. Its purpose is to provide a new cognitive map, which, like a geographic map, enables its user to orient himself or which, like a blueprint, shows how things are constructed and how they work. This knowledge can be used to manipulate things and people. But there is a basic difference between things and people: Things can never know, but people can. In order to use sociological knowledge for the manipulation of people, they have to be kept ignorant.

To be used for manipulation, sociology would have to be turned into the secret love of privileged groups and not public knowledge available to everyone who cares and is capable to study it. Under such conditions of secrecy it would soon turn into some kind of nonscience, since secrecy would deprive it from the ongoing reexamination and correction by a succession of researchers and critics with changing interests and points of view, which give science its progressive and universalistic character.

Therefore, social research as a public scientific pursuit has limited use as a tool for the manipulation of people. Its proper and effective use is to serve as a cognitive map, which reveals to people hidden connections and unintended consequences of their actions and helps them to make better and more responsible choices and resist manipulation by others. In other words, it is a tool of limited usefulness for oppression but one of considerable significance for the intelligent and responsible exercise of freedom.[3]

The Value Neutrality of Social Research

The final question to be discussed is that of value neutrality. One of the principal arguments against social sciences is that it is impossible to keep in them value judgments apart from investigation of facts. According to this criticism, results of social research are subjective and have no claim for scientific validity or technical effectiveness.

The classic rebuttal of this view is that of Max Weber. He distinguished between the choice of problems for research and the process of investigation. Problem choice, according to Weber, is always influenced by the values of the investigator. This cannot be otherwise in a field that investigates social phenomena, because the meaning and significance of these are culturally determined.[4]

But the research process which tries to provide the answers to the problems can and has to be conducted and judged according to strictly universalistic and value-free methods and criteria. Therefore, good research will reduce or eliminate the bias implied in the choice of problems. This view had been widely, although not universally, accepted by sociologists, until the late sixties. Since then there has opened a rift between those who still accept and those who reject it. The rejectionists' point of view rests on a mixture of philosophical and political-moral arguments. They argue that there is nothing in an answer that is not included already in the question. Therefore, if there is bias in the question, there can be no value neutrality either in the process of investigation or the answer. The logical conclusion of this sort of criticism is that indeed sociology is not distinguishable from ideology, or, perhaps, even from religion, and that this fact has to be consciously and programmatically accepted. As a matter of fact, some would argue that natural science is not distinguishable either from ideology or religion and that the whole endeavor of setting up science as a category of enquiry sharply separated from religious thought is itself just another prejudice, the prejudice of a scientistic "religion." Those influenced by Marxism would add that this "religion"—like the more traditionalistic ones—only serves to protect entrenched interests of ruling classes and imperialist nations (Becker 1966; Dolby 1971; Marcuse 1968,

3. This is similar to the practical function attributed to sociology by Edward Shils (1961) and Morris Janowitz (1972).
4. It is evident that Weber's conception of social science is that of an "applied science" in the sense defined in this paper.

144–70; Stammer 1971, 57–78). This latter kind of criticism implied that the idea of value neutrality is not only mistaken but also a morally reprehensible and sinister distortion of reality.

The rationale of this criticism is that because there are points of overlap between social science (or science in general), on the one hand, and magical, religious and ideological thought, on the other, therefore it cannot be asserted that science as objective knowledge is clearly distinguishable from these other kinds of knowledge, which are subjective. This reasoning is based on the fallacious premise, that objectivity and bias are dichotomous phenomena, whereas in fact, they are continuous ones. All systems of belief, including science, are a mixture of bias and objectivity. But the majority of them are institutionalized in a way which is bias preserving, while science is institutionalized in a bias-reducing way.

Paradoxically, the best evidence for this is provided by some instances usually considered as evidence against the value neutrality of science. There has been lately a growing literature, partly stimulated by the views critical of the value neutrality idea, showing that, indeed, in many cases scientists made judgments and decisions out of prejudice, rather than on the intrinsic merits of the case; or that magical and religious belief systems contain important elements of scientific knowledge.[5] Superficially, these findings cast doubt on the value neutrality of science and its demarcability from magic and ideology. However, this is only the case when the distinction between objective and biased is perceived as a dichotomy. Then of course any single instance is enough to contradict the value neutrality view. When the same instances are looked at from a point of view of value neutrality as a continuum, then these very cases become the best evidence of neutrality. They show that bias, even if deeply ingrained and of old standing, is always open to correction in science, as one expects from its bias-reducing mechanisms and methods. Far from providing a ground for doubts in the clear demarcability of science from magic, religion, and ideology, these discoveries of bias in science through scientific investigation are a striking evidence of such demarcability. Religious, magical, and ideological thought would never have led to or tolerated such self-critical disclosures. Thus, far from being contradicted, the distinction of Weber between problem choice, which is always biased, and the research process, which is objective, or—as suggested here—bias reducing, is actually reinforced by the very evidence brought up against it.

Arguments of allegedly systematic bias based on sociological rather than philosophical grounds can be similarly refuted. Much of the attempt at the exposure of bias in sociology is based on the belief that class and ethnic conflict are systematic and ubiquitous sources of sociological prejudice. However, this belief is contradicted by evidence.

5. For cases in which the scientific community did not observe the norm of value neutrality, see Stephen G. Brush (1974) and I. Mitroff (1974). For the scientific characteristics of magical thought, see R. Horton (1967).

A well-known example of alleged class bias is Talcott Parsons's structural-functional theory. It has been frequently argued that this theory was but a camouflage for the justification and celebration of the American system of production and government of his times (Dahrendorf 1958; Lockwood 1950; Mills 1959, 44–49; Gouldner 1979, 167–338). One of the most criticized points in this theory was the postulate of value integration, namely, that there were universally shared values cutting across class lines in modern societies, which maintain allegiance to the system. This postulate flatly contradicted the Marxist postulate, according to which all ideologies were rooted in class conflict. Since class and ideological conflict were in Marxist theory the roots of social change, Parsons's idea about value integration was interpreted as ruling class ideology disguising upper class interest in the status quo as shared social values and preventing thereby the emergence of conflicting class ideologies and social change. However, all this criticism overlooks the fact that the logic of value integration could lead to an interpretation of the class situation in a manner which is in principle no less revolutionary than Marxism. Merton's reformulation of anomie theory was in fact such an interpretation, showing how and why certain classes may become alienated from society, because the shared system of values leads to the adoption of the same goals by all people but does not provide all of them with the means to achieve those goals (Merton 1957). This shows that whatever the motivation behind the formulation of a question for research (it is conceivable, although impossible to ascertain, that Parsons's questions were influenced by his attachment to the status quo in the United States), once a theory is formulated, it becomes subject to confrontation with empirical evidence and logical analysis which are independent of the original bias. Thus when Merton tried to apply the idea of value integration to the attitudes and behavior of different classes in the United States, he perceived in it logical implications, which could not conceivably have served the interest of maintaining the status quo and could actually have been used as a justification of subversion (irrespective of any intention of Merton).

A recent paper of James Coleman goes even further and makes a plausible argument supported by evidence from his own involvement in government-sponsored policy research: that research results can *legitimate a challenge* to policy and thus the authority system that makes the policy (Coleman 1979). His research was not used by the Office of Education, which actually sponsored it, because its conclusions were mainly negative from the point of view of current government policies. Instead, it came to be widely used by protagonists in a conflict involving educational policy. In fact, he concludes, the very uncertainty of research results makes policy research a very disconcerting tool for policymakers.

A second area of allegedly systematic prejudice is that of ethnic conflict. The argument is that in multiracial situations dominant ethnic groups usually have a negative prejudice about the low status groups, partly as a legitimation of the oppression and exploitation of the latter. This prejudice is said to be shared by investigators stemming from the high status groups and to influence their research on the low status group. These investigations are, therefore, deeply imbued with insidious prejudice and, hence, become a source of prejudice themselves and legitimation of oppression.[6]

Although one has to reject the postulate that all members of a group in which there is a negative stereotype about another group have to share this prejudice, it is true that they frequently do and that their questions may be influenced by it. But it is not true that the investigations so instigated necessarily or even usually lead to a reinforcement of the stereotype. There can be little doubt that the work of anthropologists has on the whole reduced the bias against so-called primitive and savage people.

The main thrust of this work has been to translate into Western concepts the ideas of primitive thought and interpret in a universally accessible manner the logic of primitive institutions. Thus, Ruth Benedict's *Patterns of Culture* and Margaret Mead's *Coming of Age in New Guinea* and *Growing Up in Samoa* brought home to a wide reading public the meaning and integrity of primitive cultures and compared institutions of primitive peoples with Western ones in a manner which was usually favorable to the former. And the work of Evans Pritchard and Robin Horton has changed the view which regarded African religion and magic as the childish constructs of inferior minds to one which regards them as a sophisticated and in many ways self-sufficient system of thought (Mead 1928, 1931; Benedict 1934; Evans-Pritchard 1934; Horton 1967).[7]

In all these cases the investigators were, probably, favorably disposed toward the subjects of their investigations. But the bias-reducing effect of investigation also holds true in cases in which the investigator is motivated by negative prejudice. An extreme example of this is the work on Jews produced in institutes for the study of Judaism established by the Nazi regime in Germany during the 1930s. Spreading prejudice about Jews was the purpose of these institutions, and their very constitution was incompatible with the elementary norms of science. Still, those working in these institutions were, at least in some cases, professionally trained historians, with high standards of scholarship. Even if they were Nazis, they tried to produce work acceptable by those standards. As a result, apart from some invectives and obviously distorted interpretations, their work, in several cases, also contains a great deal of good

---

6. For the allegation that there was a correspondence of interests between the colonial rulers and the presentation of the Africans by Western anthropologists, see Gutorm Gjessing (1968); D. Lewis (1973); J. Maquet (1964); B. Magubane (1971). A most extreme statement of the view attributing intended and unintended malice to research done by outsiders in a field related to anthropology is Edward Said (1978). In sociology the argument against outsiders was raised mainly by some black and women sociologists in the United States. These latter have been described, placed in perspective, and discussed by Robert K. Merton (1973, pp. 99–136).

7. For a detailed description of the actual relationships that prevailed between colonial administrators and anthropologists, see Adam Kuper (1973, pp. 123–49).

objective scholarship, which can be used by all scholars, including Jews, to this very day.[8]

Of course, there is no justification for invectives in scientific work, and to undertake so-called scientific work with the expressed purpose of causing harm to the subjects of the research is an insult to science. But, if we consider the results, it is obvious that even limited acceptance of scientific standards produced work which was incomparably more objective and intellectually honest than any work produced by Nazi intellectuals who did not care about scholarly standards. This is not to deny the existence of conscious and unconscious group prejudice in many kinds of social research or to justify those who do not do their best to control their prejudices. It is only to show that even if the attempt at controlling prejudice is less than completely successful, or even in the deplorable cases of an absence of such effort, disciplined scholarly investigation will usually lead to a reduction of prejudice.

Therefore, the recent fashion of exposing the prejudices of present and past investigators of foreign cultures and societies, and using this as a ground for denying their scientific value, is completely misleading. The critics begin with the disclosure of bias in scientific publications and proceed to attribute the negative stereotypes prevailing in society to the bias in these publications. Actually, of course, the negative stereotype in society is preexistent to the scientific investigation and is the source of the prejudice of the investigator.[9] Negative prejudice does not stem from scientific research but either arises spontaneously from conflicts between two groups or is deliberately created by priests or ideologists. The bias reflected in scholarly writings is usually a reduced and qualified remnant of the popular, dogmatic, and ideological stereotype.

Attributing such remnants of prejudice to research is, therefore, erroneous as well as dangerous. The condemnation and suppression of research by outsiders, because of suspected bias, would not be a safeguard against the creation of negative ethnic stereotypes but would eliminate the probably most effective means for reducing them.[10]

In view of all this it seems that Weber's idea about the possibility of disjunction between bias in problem choice and (relative) objectivity in the re-

8. Some examples of publications of considerable historical value by Nazi authors are W. Frank (1939) and W. Grau (1934).

9. However, it has to be emphasized, there is no evidence that outsider bias is unavoidable (except in the trivial sense that every hypothesis is a bias) and—more important—that such bias is systematic, so that it has the same character and direction among all members of a given outgroup.

10. This question is related to, but not identical with, the one discussed in Robert K. Merton (1973). Merton deals with the antecedents which give rise to suspicion of outsider bias and analyzes the cognitive contributions of insider and outsider perspectives. My purpose is to show that irrespective of kinds and degrees of bias, as long as there is a scientific community capable of enforcing scholarly standards in a field, there will be a trend toward reduction of bias in the professional literature.

search process stands up well against criticism in all the contexts in which such criticism has been raised. The question is whether there are other contexts unperceived, or unidentified by the critics, which require modification or complementation of the Weber approach. In the next section an attempt will be made to identify such a context.

The Cartelization of Research Specialties as a Source of Systematic Bias

Weber's disjunction between problem choice and research process was based on the assumption that research workers are by and large engaged in and rewarded for the discovery of truth. He was perfectly aware that there were deviants among research workers but seemed to have thought that this could be dealt with by the usual mechanisms of moral control, namely, exposure and exhortation.[11] The possibility that the entire community of scholars in a given field might develop a systematic bias, without ostensibly deviating from methodological norms, did not occur to him. However, such possibilities may arise, and—it seems—have arisen today.

I shall try to illustrate this point through the case of research on the social and economic correlates of advanced education and research since the 1950s. In sociology, much of this research was closely related to the study of social mobility, namely, the investigation of the question as to what extent was the social status of people determined by the status of their parents. The hypothesis guiding these studies was that there was a great deal of social injustice and inefficiency due to unequal opportunity for members of different classes and that the measurement and public exposure of these inequalities would contribute to their correction. It was hypothesized that in this process of status allocation, the educational system played a critically important role, since depending on how education was organized and distributed, it could serve either as a mechanism of perpetuation of existing status differences or as a mechanism of redistribution of statuses according to purely universalistic standards.[12]

These ideas provided a framework for the comparative study of educational mobility. Rates of mobility were internationally compared, and differences were related to differences in the organization of education as a cause and dif-

11. Weber's views on value neutrality are based on philosophical and methodological arguments. However, these are consistent with and perhaps to some extent imply a sociological view of the scientific community of a kind described many years later by Michael Polanyi (1951, pp. 3–90).

12. D. Glass (1959) and Natalie Rogoff (1953) were the first major publications on the subject. They served as starting points and models for a still continuing literature on mobility. For a recent publication reflecting the present state of the art, see John H. Goldthorpe (1980).

ferences in occupational and manpower structure as an effect. School systems, such as the American, with a high compulsory school-leaving age and a stress on electives in both secondary and higher education, were more equitable and produced an occupational system with a higher fraction of people in professional and technical occupations than countries with more selective and prescriptive systems.

These sociological investigations were logically and politically related to studies in the economics of education. Relative openness of the educational system did not only benefit the individual by providing him with easier access to better occupations but also benefited the economy as a whole. A famous study by E. F. Denison found that a large part of the economic growth in the United States between 1910 and 1960 (23 percent of the annual growth rate) was attributable to the diffusion of education. And there was a great deal of other evidence suggesting a positive relationship between growth of education and knowledge (research, inventions), on the one hand, and personal income and economic growth, on the other. It seemed that exploration of the growth and structure of education and scientific research would be of central importance in understanding and eventually providing a key to influencing the mechanisms of economic growth and class formation. From this background emerged a worldwide research effort consisting of comparative studies of educational mobility, educational and research systems, and in economics, of returns to education and the growth of knowledge (Denison 1962; Vaizey 1964).

Until the sixties this was a typical case of systematic applied research as the term is used in this paper. The starting point of the investigators was the highly practical concern with social justice and efficiency, but they had no clear idea of how and when their work will actually contribute toward these ends. They did not work for governments or in cooperation with civil servants. The original work of Glass and associates which initiated this line of research was funded by the Nuffield and Rockefeller foundations, which probably welcomed its implications for policy but were not themselves implementing any policies.

The circumstances changed in the early sixties. The theoretical framework provided by the studies on educational mobility and related problems seemed to provide a consistent answer to the worldwide search for accelerated economic growth and in particular to the worldwide desire of catching up with, or at least not to fall far behind, the United States.

This gave rise to an unprecedented situation. Much of the research in the field came to be supported by governments, or intergovernmental agencies, such as OECD or UNESCO, and there developed close personal and institutional ties between civil servants and social scientists. Social scientists provided a doctrine that made sense and gave greater coherence and clearer direction to policies devised by the civil service and on many occasions actually participated in the formulation of policies, such as the extension of educational opportunity; structural changes in education, like comprehensive schools; elimination of early streaming in schools; or the substitution of departments for "chairs" in the continental European and Japanese universities.[13]

Intellectually, this coordinated effort in the exploration of the relationship between mobility, education, scientific research, and economic growth has been one of the most successful research undertakings in the history of social science. Much of the work was of high quality, and original. It involved sociology and economics, was sustained, and was coherent. In addition, it had a significant political and social impact. The findings were widely diffused and deeply affected the perception of the educational system and educational policies. Opportunities for entry into secondary and higher education were rapidly expanded.[14] Schools opened up for much greater fractions of the population than ever before. This was accompanied by school reforms on all levels. Curricula were broadened and diversified so as to cater to the abilities and interests of masses of relatively unselected students.

So far, this story may appear as an ideal case of interaction between research and practice. However, about the mid-sixties there began to appear signs which suggested that there was also an insidious negative side to these developments. There was an accumulation of evidence that the possibility of reducing educational and social inequalities through educational expansion was much more limited than generally assumed. The well-known paper of C. Arnold Anderson, "A Skeptical Note on Education and Mobility," casting serious doubt on the effect of education on mobility, appeared as early as 1961 (Halsey et al. 1964, pp. 164–79). The Coleman Report of 1966 showed the limitations of formal education in overcoming educational deficiencies due to poor cultural background, and the fact that the relatively high rates of mobility, attributed partly to the educational system, could occur without a significant reduction of the dependence of the status of sons on that of their fathers was noted by Blau and Duncan in 1967 (Coleman, Campbell et al. 1966; Blau and Duncan 1967).

The limitations of education and of the growth of knowledge as economic assets also became clear during the mid-sixties. Derek de Solla Price showed in 1963 that the expansion of science training at the then current rate was impossible to sustain. Denison himself provided evidence in 1967 that his findings

---

13. Much of the relevant research on the subject during the sixties is summarized in R. H. Halsey et al. (1961); J. Ben-David (1963–64); R. Poignant (1969). For the state of research in economics, see M. Blaug (1972).

14. Perhaps the best known and most effective example of research in preparation of policy in the field of higher education was the "Robbins Report"; see United Kingdom, Committee on Higher Education (1963, Cmnd 2154 and Appendices I–IV, Cmnd 2154 I–IV).

about the importance of investment in education in American economic growth were not paralleled in European economic growth rates since the 1950s.

However, while research thus provided growing evidence about the need for a reappraisal of the views about education, science, mobility, and economic growth, and the policies ensuing from such views, there was in actual fact no such reappraisal. Sociologists and economists did not treat the new findings as requiring a systematic revision of the accepted view on education and mobility, such as was done later by Raymond Boudon, Christopher Jencks, and others (Jencks 1972; Boudon 1973). Mark Blaug's survey of the economics of education shows that in spite of the inconclusiveness of the evidence, there was a great reluctance to the revision of the hypothesis about the positive effect of education on income as well as economic growth throughout the 1960s.[15]

This reluctance was even more marked in policies. The importance attached to educational (and scientific) expansion for the furtherance of mobility and economic growth remained the guiding principle of governmental and intergovernmental policy during the sixties. Only in the seventies, when economic difficulties made the continuation of expansionist policies impossible, was there a reappraisal of these policies.

It is difficult to assert with any certainty that this 5 to 10 years of lag between the discovery of evidence for the need for reappraisal of educational thinking and policies, and the actual reappraisal, was the result of systematic bias among research workers and administrators. It may be argued that it always takes time to conceptualize negative evidence and shape it into a new theory. But my impression from reading the literature and as a participant in this research effort at that time is that there was a kind of bias. The negative evidence was not difficult to conceptualize, and there was considerable awareness of its conceptual implications. But research workers had simply no time to engage in research, the practical implication of which would have been to disclose the limitations of current educational policies. They were deeply involved in "policy research" on such issues as: the planning and establishment of new universities and "centers of excellence"; identifying areas of research in which scientific and technological breakthroughs could be expected and exploring through research the optimal structures for the support and organization of research in these fields; or describing and devising policies for stemming the "brain drain" (migration of scientists and technologists from all over the world to the United States).

Focusing on the systematic implications of the negative findings would

15. M. Blaug (1972, pp. 61–100); however, the change of emphasis became evident in the seventies, manifesting itself in the renewed salience given to the question of demand and supply for educated manpower; see R. B. Freeman (1971).

have required a disengagement of the social scientists from these ongoing policy concerns, which they themselves partly initiated and which they still found important and legitimate. After all, the new evidence did not show that there was anything amiss with the promotion of education and research but only that such promotion would not have all the effects originally expected from it. Therefore, postponement of the systematic elaboration of the new findings seemed as quite a justifiable strategy.

This case by no means constitutes a negative evidence for Weber. As assumed by him, research was bias reducing in this case, too, and produced evidence which went against the initial prejudices of the researchers and their supporters. Still the disjunction between the questions rooted in evaluative attitudes and the answers provided by research performed according to universalistic standards was not complete. The negative evidence was only registered but not followed up to its logical conclusions, not because the research community in the field could not overcome its bias but because it was involved in research supporting practical policies and accorded higher priority to these latter than to the intellectual challenge presented by the new evidence.

This suggests that the logical disjunction between formulating questions and obtaining answers, posited by Weber, has some institutional prerequisites.

The fact that research may lead to results which suggest unanticipated new problems or actually contradict the initial beliefs and prejudices of the investigators is not enough. The results have to be conceptualized, confronted with existing views, and elaborated into new conceptual frameworks. Weber took it for granted that this would be done "automatically," since he assumed that taking advantage of new results was part of the raison d'être of the scientific community. The present case suggests that under circumstances when an entire community active in a field becomes involved with policy research, this process of reconceptualization may be delayed by considerations of policy.

This conclusion reinforces the one reached above on the utility of separating systematic applied research from "development" or "policy research" in sociology. There the argument in favor of such separation rested on the recognition that practical applications involve consideration of particular circumstances and may require intuitive judgments alien to the systematic approach of the scientific investigator. The present case shows that such separation is also necessary to ensure the relative value neutrality of science. This value neutrality is nothing else but the existence of a set of motivations among communities of investigators to evaluate and use research results according to immanently cognitive criteria. If the barriers between scientists and administrators or other practical people are eliminated, these motivations may be considerably weakened. Paradoxically, this would impair not only the intrinsic scientific quality of research, but also its practical utility.

The practical utility of social research consists not only of finding means to achieve stated social ends, but also of discovering unanticipated consequences and ramifications of policies and other social actions. Systematic social research guided by relatively independent scientific considerations is more likely to disclose these latter, than research directly linked to the execution of programs and policies.

References

Anderson, C. A. 1961. "A Skeptical Note on Education and Mobility," *Education, Economy and Society: A Reader in the Sociology of Education* (A. H. Halsey, J. Floud, and C. A. Anderson, eds.) (Free Press, Glencoe), 164–79.

Becker, H. S. 1966. "Whose Side are We On?" *Social Problems* 14 (1966): 239–47.

Bellah, R. N. 1957. *Tokugawa Religion* (Free Press, Glencoe).

Ben-David, J. 1963–64. "Professions in the Class System of Present-Day Societies," *Current Sociology* 12, 3 (1963–64): 247–330.

Benedict, R. 1934. *Patterns of Culture* (Houghton Mifflin, Boston).

Blau, P. M., and Duncan, O. D. (1967), *The American Occupational Structure* (Wiley, New York).

Blaug, M. 1972. *An Introduction to the Economics of Education* (Penguin, Harmondsworth).

Boudon, R. 1973. *Education, Opportunity and Social Inequality: Changing Prospects in Western Society* (Wiley, New York).

Brush, S. G. 1974. "Should the History of Science be Rated 'X'?" *Science* 183 (22 March 1974): 1164–72.

Coleman, J. S. 1979. "The Use of Social Science in the Development of Public Policy," *Conference on Scientific Expertise and the Public* (Oslo, June 1979) (mimeographed). [Published as "Conflicts Between Policy Research and Decision Making," in Hans Skoie (ed.), *Scientific Expertise and the Public: Conference Proceedings* (Oslo: Studies in Research and Higher Education, 1979), pp. 14–21.]

Coleman, J., E. A. Campbell, et al. 1966. *Equality of Educational Opportunity* (U.S. Dept. of Health, Education and Welfare, Office of Education, Washington D.C., U.S. Government Printing Office).

Dahrendorf, R. 1958. "Out of Utopia: Toward a Reorientation of Sociological Analysis," *American Journal of Sociology* 64 (1958): 115–27.

Denison, E. F. 1962. *Sources of Economic Growth in the United States and the Alternatives Before Us* (Committee for Economic Development, New York).

———. 1967. *Why Growth Rates Differ: Post-War Experience in Nine Western Countries* (Brookings Institution, Washington, D.C.).

Dolby, R. G. A. 1971. "The Sociology of Knowledge in Natural Science," *Science Studies* 1:1 (1971): 3–21.

Eisenstadt, S. N. 1973. *Tradition, Change and Modernity* (Wiley, New York).

Evans-Pritchard, E. E. 1934. *Witchcraft, Oracles and Magic Among the Azande* (Clarendon Press, Oxford).

Frank, W. 1939. *Höre Israel! Harden, Lathenau und die moderne Judenfrage* (Hanseatischer Verlag, Hamburg).

Freeman, R. B. 1971. *The Market for College-Trained Manpower: A Study in the Economics of Career Choice* (Harvard University Press, Cambridge).

Gerald, H. B., and Miller, N. 1975. *School Desegregation: A Long-Term Study* (Plenum Press, New York/London).

Gjessing, G. 1968. "The Social Responsibility of the Social Scientist," *Current Anthropology* 9, 5 (1968): 397–403.

Glass, D., ed. 1959. *Social Mobility in Britain* (Routledge & Kegan, London).

Goldthorpe, J. H., et al. 1980. *Social Mobility and Class Structure in Modern Britain* (Clarendon Press, Oxford).

Gouldner, A. 1970. *The Coming Crisis of Western Sociology* (Basic Books, New York).

Grau, W. 1934. *Antisemitismus im späten Mittelalter: Das Ende der Regensburger Judengemeinde* (Duncker & Humblot, Berlin).

Halsey, R. H., J. Floud, and C. A. Anderson, eds., 1961. *Education, Economy and Society: A Reader in the Sociology of Education* (Free Press, Glencoe).

Horton, R. 1967. "African Traditional Thought and Western Science," *Africa* 37: 1–2 (January/April, 1967): 50–71 and 155–87.

Janowitz, M. 1972. "Professionalization of Sociology," *American Journal of Sociology*, 78, 1 (1972): 105–35.

Jencks, C. 1972. *Inequality* (Basic Books, New York).

John, N. H. St. 1975. *School Desegregation; Outcomes for Children* (Wiley, New York).

Kuper, A. 1973. *Anthropologists and Anthropology: The British School 1922–1972* (Allen Lane, London).

Lewis, D. 1973. "Anthropology and Colonialism," *Current Anthropology* 14, 5 (1973): 581–90.

Lockwood, D. (1950), "Some Remarks on 'The Social System,'" *British Journal of Sociology* 7 (1950): 134–46.

Magubane, B. 1971. "A Critical Look at Indices Used in the Study of Social Change in Colonial Africa," *Current Anthropology* 12, 4–5 (October/December 1971): 419–30.

Maquet, J. 1964. "Objectivity in Anthropology," *Current Anthropology* 5, 1 (February 1964): 47–55.

Marcuse, H. 1968. *One Dimensional Man* (Beacon Press, Boston).

McClelland, D. C. 1961. *The Achieving Society* (Van Nostrand, Princeton).

———. 1966. "Does Education Accelerate Economic Growth?" *Economic Development and Cultural Change* (April 1966): 257–78.

Mead, M. 1928. *Coming of Age in Samoa* (Blue Ribbon Books, New York).

———. 1931. *Growing up in New Guinea* (G. Routledge, London).

Merton, R. K. 1957. "Social Structure and *Anomie*," in his *Social Theory and Social Structure* (revised edition) (Free Press, Glencoe), 131–60.

———. 1973. "The Perspectives of Insiders and Outsiders," in his *Sociology of Science: Theoretical and Empirical Investigations* (University of Chicago Press, Chicago), 99–136.

Mills, C. W. 1959. *The Sociological Imagination* (Oxford University Press, New York).

Mitroff, I. 1974. *The Subjective Side of Science, a Philosophical Inquiry in the Psychology of the Apollo Moon Scientists* (Elsevier, Amsterdam).

OECD 1967. *The Overall Level and Structure of R & D Efforts in OECD Countries* (OECD, Paris).

Poignant, R. 1969. *Education and Development in Western Europe, the United States, and the U.S.S.R.—A Comparative Study* (Columbia University, Teachers College Press, originally published in French by Institut Pédagogique National, Paris, 1965).

Polanyi, M. 1951. *The Logic of Liberty* (Routledge & Kegan, London).

Price, D. de Solla. 1963. *Little Science, Big Science* (Columbia University Press, New York).

Rist, R. C. 1979. *Desegregated Schools: Appraisals of an American Experiment* (Academic Press, New York).

Rogoff, N. 1953. *Recent Trends in Occupational Mobility* (Free Press, Glencoe).

Said, E. 1978. *Orientalism* (Pantheon Books, New York).

Shils, E. 1961. "The Calling of Sociology," in *Theories of Society* (T. Parsons et al., eds.), (Free Press, New York), 1430–32.

Stammer, O., ed. 1971. *Max Weber and Sociology Today* (Basil Blackwell, Oxford).

United Kingdom, Committee on Higher Education. 1963. *Higher Education; Report of the Committee Appointed by the Prime Minister under the Chairmanship of Lord Robbins, 1961–63* (H.M.S.O., London).

U.S. Commission on Civil Rights. 1969. *Racial Isolation in the Public Schools: A Report* (U.S. Government Printing Office, Washington, D.C.).

Vaizey, J., ed. 1964. *The Residual Factor and Economic Growth* (OECD, Paris).

Weber, M. 1949. "The Meaning of 'Ethical Neutrality' in Sociology and Economics" and "Objectivity in Social Science and Social Policy," in his *The Methodology of the Social Sciences* (trans. and ed. E. A. Shils and H. A. Finch) (Free Press, Glencoe), 1–112.

———. 1952. *Ancient Judaism* (trans. and ed. H. H. Gerth and D. Martindale) (Free Press, Glencoe).

———. 1958. *The Protestant Ethic and the Spirit of Capitalism* (trans. and ed. T. Parsons) (C. Scribner's Sons, New York).

———. 1960. *The Religion of India: The Sociology of Hinduism and Buddhism* (trans. and ed. H. H. Gerth and D. Martindale) (Free Press, Glencoe).

———. 1968. *The Religion of China: Confucianism and Taoism* (trans. and ed. H. H. Gerth) (Free Press, New York).

Part VI

The Ethos of Science in Question

The Sociology of Scientific Knowledge

Introduction

The notions of the scientific ethos and the scientific role (which are mutually dependent) are central to Ben-David's theoretical framework. The assumption of the existence of such an ethos was shared by the Mertonian school in the sociology of science and was not seriously put in question before the 1970s. At that time, however, a new approach to the sociological study of science and of scientific knowledge emerged. This approach, which draws on a certain interpretation of T. S. Kuhn's philosophy of science, construes science as a multitude of local cultures in which the production of knowledge conforms to specific local norms only and is, moreover, subject to influence by social interests. This stance obviously implies a rejection of the notion of a single scientific ethos and role and, with it, an epistemological relativism. To Ben-David, this approach appeared at once as scientifically untenable and as morally and socially dangerous. "The recurrent attacks on rationality and science and the arguments about the relativity and lack of objectivity of all social thought," he wrote, "is, of course, a problem which concerns not only sociologists but everyone for whom the resolution of social conflicts by rational rather than violent means is important." [1] Ben-David therefore devoted a number of papers to a thorough criticism of the sociology of scientific knowledge and, more important, to an attempt to explain its emergence sociologically.

The survey here entitled "Theoretical Perspectives in the Sociology of Science 1920–1970" (originally published as "Introduction" to a special issue on the sociology of science of the *International Social Science Journal* [1970]) is included here because it draws an insightful picture of the develop-

---

1. [45].

ment of the sociology of science up to 1970. It sets the stage for the developments that were to follow.

"Emergence of National Traditions in the Sociology of Science: The United States and Great Britain" (1978) is devoted to an attempt to account sociologically for the differences of approach to the sociology of science in the United States and in Britain. Its principal point is that the classic, Mertonian sociology of science remained limited to the United States because, for institutional reasons, those interested in the subject in Britain were interested in philosophical reflections on science (this interest shaped their reception of Kuhn's work), were generally critical of the structuralist-functionalist approach to sociology, and did not belong institutionally to departments of sociology. Ben-David stresses that the two approaches are not contradictory or mutually exclusive, however. In his view, the two approaches are complementary and will eventually be integrated in a more comprehensive framework that will become the subject of a large consensus. Needless to say, this anticipation of the future evolution of the sociology of science derives from Ben-David's general notion of science as a consensual activity; as has been noted before (introduction to Part V), Ben-David more than once retraced the history of controversies over specific issues in the sociology of science with the aim of showing precisely that even in the social sciences, research eventually clarifies issues and moves toward a consensus.

"Sociology of Scientific Knowledge" (1981) directly comes to grips with the investigations and theses of the British tradition. The sociology of scientific knowledge affirms that scientific criteria and rationality do not suffice to account for the acceptance of scientific theories and that their possible social uses influence, or even determine, their acceptance. On this view, the notion of scientific role is a mere fiction, indeed an ideology: rather than addressing themselves only to their peers in the scientific community, the producers of knowledge seek acceptance also in what from Ben-David's perspective are incidental reference groups that have particular interests. Thus, the sociology of scientific knowledge runs against the most basic tenets of Ben-David's sociology of science, and this paper critically examines its various components and the relevant evidence, assessing its lasting contributions to the sociology of science.

The essay, " 'Norms of Science' and the Sociological Interpretation of Scientific Behavior" (previously unpublished; written about 1982–1983), covers much the same ground but from a new perspective, and it offers important new insights. At its focus is the question of the ethos of science, namely, whether important aspects of the behavior of scientists can be explained with reference to a set of presumably universally valid institutionalized norms. The first part of the paper, is, in fact, a social history of the debate over this question. It shows how Merton's seminal work on the issue was a response to the perceived threats to science from fascism in the late 1930s. It goes on to explain, now with reference to the internal state of sociological theory, mainly in the United States, why this line of research was not pursued until the late 1950s when—under the impact of new work by Merton and favorable external circumstances—a "paradigm" in the sociology of science emerged. This Mertonian paradigm guided research on reward, stratification, and social control in science until the 1970s. For the breakdown of the consensus over the paradigm, mainly in Europe, Ben-David again offers a sociological explanation. In the late 1960s, a deliberate effort was made in Europe to promote the interdisciplinary study of science, which, it was hoped, might contribute to an improvement of science policy. From this interdisciplinary perspective, the significance of the sociologists' work on the reward system was not adequately appreciated and therefore neglected. Moreover, there was a general change in the perception of science (for which Ben-David sought to account elsewhere; see Part VII, below) that went hand in hand with the introduction of phenomenologically inspired ethnomethodological approaches to the study of science, resulting in the attempts to produce a relativist sociology of scientific knowledge. This part of the paper is thus an attempt to account sociologically for the changing fortunes of the sociological study of the norms of science. It is not without irony that we have here an instance of sociology of scientific knowledge at its best—precisely that kind of inquiry that Ben-David has often, and wrongly, been accused of rejecting.

The second part of the paper addresses the substantive issue and reviews various investigations bearing on the norms of science. It argues that these empirical investigations do not support the contention that universal norms play no role in science.

In "The Ethos of Science: The Last Half-Century" (1980), Ben-David describes and tries to account sociologically for the intellectual and social context from which emerged the relativist sociology of scientific knowledge, namely, the variegated criticisms of science and the associated rejection of the notion of a scientific ethos and of scientific autonomy. He suggests a threefold typology of attitudes toward science and argues that until the 1960s, attacks on the autonomy of science were rare because the denial of a value-free scientific investigation was historically associated with nazism. One reason for the attacks on the scientific ethos from the 1960s onward is that this memory has faded; another important reason is that the scientific ethos has been abused by people working in applied research; further, the ethos emerged in the age of small science, but in the fast-expanding scientific enterprise of the 1960s, it appeared as the ideology of an elite. The subject of science criticism in society at large and its influence on the perception of science by scientists and sociologists of science is treated more extensively in Part VII.

"Academic Market, Ideology, and the Growth of Scientific Knowledge: Physiology in Mid-Nineteenth-Century Germany" (1986) provides a fitting close for this Part. In this paper (as also in [81]), Ben-David confronts his own and A. Zloczower's structural-functional studies of the growth of physiology (chap. 5 above and [19]) with its recent interpretation by T. Lenoir in the tradition of the sociology of scientific knowledge. He argues that the two interpretations are, in fact, complementary: the latter concentrates on "local cultures," while the former is concerned with the integration of such local social systems into the comprehensive nonlocal system of science. Understanding the production of scientific knowledge requires both viewpoints. Ben-David takes his analysis to provide concrete illustration and confirmation of his often repeated claim that scientific inquiry, even in the social sciences, is bound to lead to a consensus.

Theoretical Perspectives 19
in the Sociology of
Science 1920–1970

The sociology of science studies the ways in which scientific research and the diffusion of scientific knowledge are influenced by social conditions and, in their turn, influence social behavior. It deals with such questions as the conditions for the emergence of modern science in a small fraction of human societies; differences in its growth in different societies; the effect of economic, political and religious institutions and of the class system on the organization of scientific work; the influence of the definition of the scientist's role, the structure of laboratory groups, disciplinary organizations, scientific institutes, national systems of scientific research and communication networks of scientists on scientific productivity and creativity; and vice versa, the effect of different types of scientific work (such as basic versus applied; disciplinary versus interdisciplinary, etc.) on these social structures; and finally, the influence of science on the organization of the economy (its influence on productivity is a subject matter for economics), on politics, religion and ideology.

This is a vast array of subjects, many of which have hardly been investigated so far. While originally sociological interest in science was aroused by the social effects attributed to it, the bulk of the work has actually been concerned with the social conditions of scientific work. In the following survey an attempt will be made to trace the development of the field since the early twenties and to explain it in terms of changing social needs which drew attention to the different aspects of the problem, on the one hand, and the development of sociological theory which determined the limits of sociological contributions to the understanding of these problems, on the other.

Originally published as "Introduction" to a special issue, "Sociology of Science," *International Social Science Journal* 22, 1 (1970): 7–27.

The Period of the 1920s and 1930s

The growth of the field can be divided into two periods, the first extending from the early 1920s to the end of the 1930s and the second starting after the Second World War and lasting to date.

The social atmosphere surrounding science during the first period was one of disillusionment. The First World War and the subsequent dislocations of political and social life shook the belief that science (and rational thought in general) would lead to uninterrupted human progress, and the Depression raised the problem of technological unemployment. Things went so far that there were suggestions to declare a "moratorium on inventions." [1]

This situation led to raising questions about the role of science in social change. It was discovered that science and technology (which in Germany were subsumed under the term "civilization" to distinguish them from humanistic and artistic culture) grew in a cumulative way, whereas in other fields of culture growth was discontinuous, consisting of numerous independent and qualitatively different new starts. [2]

This view about the differences in the rate and shape of development in science and technology, on the one hand, and other types of knowledge, on the other, was used by Ogburn for the formulation of his famous "cultural lag" hypothesis, [3] according to which one of the basic sources of conflict in modern societies has been the unequal rate of growth of different cultural fields. Scientific and technological knowledge are cumulative and grow so rapidly that social knowledge cannot keep pace with the changes thus generated.

These ideas had a great deal of apparent plausibility but were couched in such general and vague terms that it was very difficult to derive any specific hypotheses from them. It was far from obvious what precisely were the effects attributable to science and in what way social knowledge and skills are inadequate in dealing with the social problems caused by science.

As a result, empirical research came to be restricted to a few themes which lent themselves to investigation. First the assumption of cumulative growth postulated a certain possibility of quantification. This led to systematic counts of discoveries and to the recognition of many of the methodological problems involved in the quantification of scientific growth. [4] A theoretically more im-

    1. Cf. Bernard Barber, *Science and the Social Order,* pp. 281–82 (New York: Collier Books, 1962).
    2. Cf. Alfred Weber, "Prinzipielles zur Kultursoziologie: Gesellschaftsprozess, Zivilisationsprozess und Kulturbewegung," *Archiv für Sozialwissenschaft und Sozialpolitik* 47 (1920), 1–49.
    3. Cf. W. F. Ogburn, *Social Change* (New York: B. W. Huebsch, 1922). In principle, Ogburn admitted the possibility that the original causes of cultural lag may be ideological or social. But he believed that in the modern Western world technology and science were the sources of change.
    4. Some of the early work in this field was done in the USSR; cf. T. J. Rainoff, "Wave-like Fluctuations of Creative Productivity in the Development of West-European Physics in the Eigh-

portant attempt was testing the hypothesis that the growth of science is immanently determined, so that what must be discovered at any given point in time
is determined by the state of knowledge at the preceding point. Such an assumption is necessary if scientific growth was to be seen as cumulative. The
hypothesis could be tested by an investigation of discoveries. If correct, then
the same discoveries were bound to be made independently of each other at
about the same time, since what different researchers did was determined by
the state of the art as common to all. Findings concerning the prevalence of
multiple discoveries confirmed the hypothesis.[5]

One of the conclusions drawn from these studies of multiple discoveries
was that the course of science and technology is predictable. If it can be
shown retrospectively that important discoveries were made at about the same
time by different people independently of each other, then knowledge of the
possibility of making the discovery must have been widespread. This was
taken as proof that the prediction of technological inventions could be developed into a useful technique. Of course, this conclusion was questionable,
since even if it could be shown that all discoveries are multiple, there still
remained the questions: (a) what fraction of the total research effort at any
time lead to successful discoveries, and (b) how can it be predicted which
efforts will turn out to be successful? In fact, it is known today that successful
attempts are a very small fraction of total effort, which shows that so far, at
least, there is very little predictability.

In any case, the attempt to predict inventions was taken up, especially
when the Depression gave added stimulus to the search for new economic resources and means of influencing and controlling the economy. This led to
some systematic attempts to explore the conditions for technological inventions based on specific hypotheses and empirical evidence.[6] But these attempts dealt only with conditions such as whether the inventor worked on his
own or in a large industrial laboratory; what is the proper training for inventors; and whether patents are an effective way to encourage inventiveness,
and so on. They did not take up at all the problem of differences in the organization of the economy, of scientific work and training in general, and of the

teenth and Nineteenth Centuries," *Isis* 12, 2 (May 1929): 291–92; and Pitirim A. Sorokin has
apparently played a role in the introduction of this quantitative method in the United States, cf.
Frank R. Cowell, *History, Civilization and Culture: An Introduction to the Historical and Social
Philosophy of Pitirim A. Sorokin,* pp. 90–106 (London: Black, 1952). Cf. also S. C. Gilfillan,
The Sociology of Invention, pp. 29–32 (Chicago: Follet, 1935); Joseph Schneider, "The Cultural
Situation as a Condition for the Achievement of Fame," *American Sociological Review* 2 (August
1937): 480–91; Robert K. Merton, "Fluctuations in the Rate of Industrial Inventions," *The
Quarterly Journal of Economics* 59 (May 1935): 456.

5. Cf. Ogburn, op. cit., pp. 90–122; Bernhard J. Stern, *Social Factors in Medical Progress*
(New York: Columbia University Press, 1927); Robert K. Merton, "Singletons and Multiples
in Scientific Discovery," *Proceedings of the American Philosophical Society* 105, 5 (October
1961): 470–86.

6. Cf. U.S. National Resources Committee, Subcommittee on Technology, *Technological
Trends and National Policy* (Washington, D.C.: U.S. Government Printer's Office, 1937), especially the papers by Gilfillan and Ogburn.

social status of the scientist and inventor. In the absence of such knowledge of institutional conditions (and of statistical sophistication to separate out their effects), investigations remained abstract and inconclusive.

Another line of research inspired by the prevailing interest in discovery and inventions and in the uses of science for social welfare was the problem of resistance and suppression.[7] This was not studied as part of the general process of diffusion and adoption of new knowledge but as a problem specific to science and technology.

A common shortcoming of all these studies was their almost total unawareness of the ecological problem. They correctly viewed science and technology as international phenomena, but partly perhaps as a result of this and partly as a result of the virtual absence of a comparative sociology of modern societies at the time, they also tended to disregard the differences between the social settings of scientific and technological work in different countries. Instead they discussed conditions of discovery, invention and resistance as if they were universal like the substantive aspects of science and technology.

That the absence of a comparative sociology played a role in this neglect of the differences in institutional conditions in various countries is indicated by the fact that other writers interested in the social conditions of scientific work did pay attention to these differences.

Interest in these problems goes back at least as far as the seventeenth century when scientists and supporters of science in France wrote reports about the Royal Society of London, advocating the establishment of a similar body in France to serve the advancement of science. And, of course, Bacon's ideas about the proper strategy for the sciences and their adoption by the groups which founded the Royal Society was itself a case of the deliberate planning of an institution on the basis of cogent sociological reasoning. During the nineteenth century and the early decades of the twentieth, studies of foreign scientific establishments became more systematic, the best known being Abraham Flexner's investigations of universities in general and medical schools in particular. Although the declared purpose of these studies was higher education rather than research, Flexner's view of higher education included research, and his work is an excellent survey of conditions of university research in the United States, Germany, the United Kingdom and France, especially in the medical fields.[8]

These studies were made for practical purposes and had little or no theo-

7. Cf. Bernhard J. Stern, "Technological Trends and National Policy," *Technological Trends and National Policy*, op. cit., pp. 39–66 and his *Historical Sociology*, pp. 47–101 (New York: Citadel Press, 1959), and Sir Daniel Hale, J. G. Crowther, J. D. Bernal, *The Frustration of Science* (London, 1935).

8. Abraham Flexner, *Medical Education in Europe* (New York: The Carnegie Foundation, 1912); *Medical Education: A Comparative Study* (New York: Macmillan, 1925); *Universities: American, English, German* (Oxford: Oxford University Press, 1930).

retical pretensions. They were certainly nòt considered as attempts at a systematic explanation of the effects of social conditions on science. But in the 1930s there emerged in the United Kingdom a group of natural scientists (Bernal, Crowther, Hogben, Needham and others) who called themselves "scientific humanists" and actually attempted to found a systematic sociology of science.[9] They were inspired by Marxism and in particular, by their impression of the way science was planned and organized as a part of the economy in the USSR. This example was particularly attractive to them, as it was to many other scientists during the Depression, since it seemed to offer an answer to accusations about the social uselessness or even harmfulness of science. It may be doubted whether they studied Marx carefully, and their use of the Marxist approach was probably derived from Hessen's attempt to explain Newtonian physics as a response to economic needs.[10] This background made them aware of the importance of the organizational and institutional setting of scientific work.

The most important sociological result of the work of this group was Bernal's *The Social Functions of Science*,[11] which contains an impressive amount of systematically collected information on the organization and uses of science in different countries and an attempt to assess the advantages and disadvantages of different arrangements for the advancement of social welfare. The book has lasting value as a comparative description of the organization of science in the 1930s and foreshadows much of what has been done in this field since. But as an effort at understanding the complex relationship between science and society, it was a failure. Instead of trying to account in systematic fashion for differences in organization and policies and their effects, Bernal only used his observations to support his own views about the necessity of planning science in coordination with a Socialist economy.

The same applies to the rest of the work done by the group in the 1930s. Eager to apply science to the advancement of social welfare, they used historical and comparative evidence to show that the development of science has always been determined by the needs of the economy and that the deliberate harnessing of science to welfare purposes was feasible as well as useful for science and society in general.

The final result of all these attempts at the creation of a sociology of science on both sides of the Atlantic in the 1920s and 1930s was thus disappoint-

9. The program of the group was outlined in the collective volume, *Science at the Crossroads* (London: Kniga, 1931). Other representative publications of members of this group were: J. D. Bernal, *The Social Function of Science* (London: Routledge & Sons, 1939); J. G. Crowther, *The Social Relations of Science* (New York: Macmillan, 1941); Lancelot Hogben, *Science for the Citizen* (London: Allen & Unwin, 1938). Crowther, Farrington and especially Needham also made important contributions to the social history of science.

10. B. Hessen, "The Social and Economic Roots of Newton's *Principia*," in *Science at the Crossroads*, pp. 151–76. Cf. also G. N. Clark, *Science and Social Welfare in the Age of Newton* (London: Oxford University Press, 1937), for a critique of Hessen.

11. Cf. n. 9.

ing. The U.S. group, which consisted of professional social scientists, ended up with empirically sound work on inventions which had very limited theoretical significance. The British group were amateur sociologists who, with the exception of Bernal and the later historical work of Needham, handled their empirical material intuitively and were more interested in the practical politics of science than in the discovery of sociological regularities.

While the main reason for these shortcomings was the inadequacy of sociological theory (and in the case of the British group also inadequate sociological preparation of scholars in the field), the fact that both groups worked in the hopeless atmosphere of the Depression probably contributed to the meager results. Pressed by circumstances, they tried to offer immediate practical solutions, rather than working patiently on unsolved theoretical and methodological problems.

Thus perhaps the most lasting contributions to the problems dealt with by both groups came from their respective critics. Lilley, the historian of science and technology, who criticized attempts at the prediction of invention, also made important positive suggestions about the kinds of forecast which could probably be made.[12] He suggested that, instead of trying to predict specific inventions, existing trends should be projected and problems which could be solved mapped out without trying to show by what means solutions would eventually be found.

The most interesting and important development, however, was the conceptualization of the informal social system of science by Michael Polányi.[13] It appears that it was he who first formulated the term "scientific community" and used it as a description of the way scientists enforced strict discipline, amid a great deal of individual freedom, through training, refereeing of publications and purely informal sanctions of approval and disapproval. He also showed how this informal system was related to the intrinsic characteristics of research.

This was a perfectly adequate sociological formulation and could have given rise immediately to the kind of investigations which became widespread only during the 1960s. But Polányi's insights were buried in an address to the Manchester Literary and Philosophical Society (February 1942), published in a book only in 1951, and were put forward as an argument against scientific planning, rather than as a contribution to the sociology of science. As a result they had little influence on sociology or sociologists and had to be virtually rediscovered in the early 1960s to have any impact.[14]

12. Cf. S. Lilley, "Can Prediction Become a Science?" *Discovery* (November 1946): 336–40.
13. In *The Logic of Liberty* pp. 53–57 (London: Routledge & Kegan Paul, 1951).
14. The debate about scientific planning between the "scientific humanists" and the Society for Freedom in Science (the group represented by Polányi which was opposed to planning) was reported in Barber's standard book published in 1951, but there was no reference in it to the concept of "scientific community." Edward Shils was the only sociologist to use the term consis-

The only bridge between the pre- and postwar sociology of science was Merton's work. His *Science, Technology and Society in Seventeenth-Century England*[15] was a thorough sociological study of the rise of modern science in seventeenth-century England. In intention as well as execution it was a pendant to Max Weber's classic, *The Protestant Ethic and the Spirit of Capitalism*. Like the latter book it aroused much controversy and stimulated a great deal of research. Sociologically its most interesting argument was that the values necessary for the rise of modern science, namely, the belief that understanding the laws of nature is a potential way to God (and thus in effect a value in its own right), arose from certain puritan varieties of Protestantism. In addition, he showed that the Puritan way of life was consistent with, and probably predisposed people to, experimental and exact science.

The controversy which arose in the wake of this publication has continued until the present and has added much to sociological perspectives. It emphasizes the importance of other predisposing conditions, such as religious pluralism and social mobility, and weakened the argument about the existence of a direct connection between puritanism and science.[16] But the essential point—that the emergence of modern science requires a basic change in the general social outlook in which rational understanding and mastery of the environment and human affairs replace tradition as the supreme criterion of conduct—has only been strengthened by recent research.

In addition to the explanation of the particular historical event of the rise of science in seventeenth-century England, this was the first adequate conceptualization of a macro-sociological variable—namely, social values—influencing the growth of science. In order to show how such values bear upon scientific activity, science had to be viewed from a sociological point of view, as an activity with its own institutionalized norms of conduct, a view also developed by Merton in the 1930s and 1940s as part of the theoretical work initiated by Talcott Parsons at Harvard,[17] which began to have an impact in the early 1950s, as we shall see below.

tently throughout the 1950s, until it was rediscovered in the early 1960s by a number of historians of science who developed a sociological approach. Cf. Edward Shils, "Scientific Community: Thoughts after Hamburg," *Bulletin of the Atomic Scientists* 10, 5 (May 1954): 151–55, and his *Torment of Secrecy*, pp. 176–82 (Glencoe: The Free Press, 1956); Thomas S. Kuhn, *The Structure of the Scientific Revolutions* (Chicago: University of Chicago Press, 1962). The first systematic sociological treatment of the subject was by Warren H. Hagstrom, in *The Scientific Community* (New York: Basic Books, 1965). Others who contributed to the exploration of the phenomenon without using the term "community" were Gerald Holton, "Scientific Research and Scholarship," *Daedalus* 91, 2 (Spring 1962): 362–99; Derek J. de Solla Price, *Little Science, Big Science* (New York: Columbia University Press, 1963).

15. *Osiris* 4, pt. 2 (1938): 360–632.

16. Cf. Robert K. Merton, "Bibliographical Postscript" to "Puritanism, Pietism and Science," in his *Social Theory and Social Structure* (rev. ed.), pp. 595–606 (Glencoe: The Free Press, 1957), and Joseph Ben-David, "The Scientific Role: The Conditions of Its Establishment in Europe," *Minerva* 4, 1 (Autumn 1965): 15–54.

17. Cf. Robert K. Merton, "Science and the Social Order" and "Science and Democratic Social Structure," in his *Social Theory and Social Structure*, op. cit., pp. 537–61; Talcott Par-

Postwar Developments

Following the Second World War the social functions of science and the atmosphere surrounding it changed radically. Research became an important tool in military and industrial technology in general. Governments and the larger industries no longer needed to be convinced that science was important for them: the question was only how to support and utilize it for their own purposes. First in the United States and then in other countries new governmental agencies were set up for the support and advancement of science. Scientific expenditure grew by leaps and bounds. The total expenditure on research and development (R & D) in the United States was $340 million in 1940 (of which $70 million came from the federal government). By 1965 the total was $20.5 billion,[18] with federal funds amounting to $14.87 billion. As a percentage of GNP, expenditure on research rose from 0.3 to 3.0 during the same period.[19] Developments in other countries were probably no less striking.

Attitudes toward science changed accordingly. In prestige ratings of occupations in the United States, scientists rose from rank 8 in 1947 to rank 3.5 in 1963 and nuclear physicists from rank 18 to 3.5. In 1947, the six occupations in the United States with the most prestige were United States Supreme Court justice; physician; state governor; cabinet member in the federal government; diplomat in the United States Foreign Service; and member of the board of directors of a large corporation. In 1963 the same ranks were occupied by United States Supreme Court justice; physician; nuclear physicist; scientist; government scientist; state governor.[20] Scientists have become an important part of the social elite. Although these changes did not occur in the way and for the reasons expected by U.S. sociologists of science or the British "scientific humanists" in the 1930s, it has become generally recognized that science has important social functions and that science policy is an important public concern.[21]

This led in practically every country to the rise of governmental and academic units investigating the organization of science, problems of scientific manpower and the finances of science. New international organizations, such as UNESCO and the Organization for Economic Cooperation and Development (OECD), have been working on the comparability of the data. The infor-

sons, *The Structure of Social Action* (New York: McGraw-Hill, 1937), and "The Role of Ideas in Social Action" and "The Professions and Social Structure," in his *Essays in Sociological Theory* (2nd ed.), pp. 19–49 (Glencoe: The Free Press, 1954).

18. One United States billion = 1,000 million; one British billion = one million million.

19. Cf. OECD, *United States*, pp. 30, 33 (Paris: OECD, 1968) (*Reviews of National Science Policy*).

20. Cf. Robert W. Hodge, Paul M. Siegel and Peter H. Rossi, "Occupational Prestige in the United States: 1925–1963," in R. Bendix and S. M. Lipset (eds.), *Class, Status and Power*, 2d ed. (New York: Free Press, 1966), p. 324.

21. One of the first documentations of this changing attitude was Vannevar Bush, *Science, The Endless Frontier* (Washington, D.C.: U.S. Government Printing Office, 1945).

mation which became available on all these subjects is of the same kind as that used in Bernal's pioneering work, although its amount and precision surpass anything available prior to the Second World War.[22]

There has also been a renewal of interest in the possibility of scientific and technological prediction begun during the Depression by W. F. Ogburn and S. C. Gilfillan in the United States. The term now used is "forecasting," and at times even this word is avoided; attempts are much more cautious than in the 1930s, but some efforts to foresee what could happen in science have become inevitable when investment in research grows as rapidly as it has done since the Second World War.[23]

As far as the practical problems of science policy, scientific organization and the support of research are concerned, there has therefore been much continuity between the questions asked and the information collected during the 1930s and since the Second World War. But a change occurred in the groups interested in these problems. Those interested in the 1930s were small, politically and socially motivated groups of scientists and social scientists. They had a few rudimentary ideas on the subject and tried to convince policymakers of their usefulness. Since the Second World War the questions have been asked by science administrators and politicians trying to find solutions to their own problems and seeking advice from social scientists.

This had an apparently paradoxical effect on the development of the field. Finding themselves in a seller's market and in a generally optimistic atmosphere about science, sociologists of science could afford to refrain from making hasty contributions to practical problems. Instead of trying to foist their ideas on policymakers, they started to go about the problem in the way professional scientists do, namely, by trying to do what was intellectually possible, rather than what happened to be demanded by potential clients. Thus the sociology of science became much more closely tied to sociological theory and research in general than it used to be.

The increasingly systematic and professional nature of work has been reflected in the founding of sections and subcommittees in the sociology of science within national and international sociological associations, in the increasing space devoted to it in sociological and general scientific periodicals and in the existence of a journal, *Minerva* (London), which though covering "science, learning and policy" in general, has to a large extent been devoted to the publication of scholarly papers on science policy and scientific organization.

One of the results of professionalization was that the field became increasingly subdivided according to the major concerns of sociological inquiry. This

22. Cf. the OECD series, *Reviews of National Science Policy*, and the UNESCO series, *Science Policy Studies and Documents*.

23. Cf. Erich Jantsch, *Technological Forecasting in Perspective* (Paris: OECD, 1967), and the COSPUP studies, sponsored by the U.S. National Academy of Sciences.

gave rise to entirely new concerns. The whole field dealing with the organization of laboratories, patterns of communication and other forms of interaction between scientists has no antecedents in the earlier period. It derives from the sociological theories and methods of using interactional variables which only started to develop in the late 1930s, mainly due to the work of Kurt Lewin and his students.

In the attempt to survey this newer literature, I shall, therefore, divide it according to sociological criteria: (a) whether a work uses mainly institutional or interactional variables; and (b) whether it attempts to explain by these variables the context of science, as well as the rate and spatial distribution of scientific production and/or creativity, or to explain only rate and spatial distribution.

With the exception of a recent exploratory work which attempts to define science exhaustively as the consensus arising among groups of investigators,[24] there have been no attempts at the creation of an interactional theory of the conceptual and theoretical content of scientific knowledge.

Of the three remaining possibilities, the most systematic and concentrated research effort in the sociology of science today deals with the interactional study of the scientific community, or more concretely, the networks of communication and social relationships between scientists working in given fields, or in all the fields.[25] This approach was first employed in the study of scientific productivity of research groups within large organizations, and its main representative is Donald Pelz.[26] The recent shift of attention from laboratory groups

24. Cf. John Ziman, *Public Knowledge: The Social Dimension of Science* (Cambridge: The University Press, 1968).

25. Cf. Stephen Cole and Jonathan Cole, "Scientific Output and Recognition: A Study in the Operation of the Reward System in Science," *American Sociological Review* 32, 3 (June 1967): 377–90; Warren H. Hagstrom, *The Scientific Community* (New York: Basic Books, 1965); Diana Crane, "Social Structure in a Group of Scientists: A Test of the 'Invisible College' Hypothesis," *American Sociological Review* 34, 3 (June 1969): 335–52; Herbert Menzel, *Review of Studies in the Flow of Information among Scientists* (New York: Columbia University Bureau of Applied Social Research, 1958), 2 vols. (mimeographed); Nicholas C. Mullins, "The Distribution of Social and Cultural Properties in Informal Communication Networks among Biological Scientists," *American Sociological Review* 33, 5 (October 1968): 786–97; Price, op. cit., pp. 62–91; Derek J. de Solla Price, "Networks of Scientific Papers," *Science* 149 (30 July 1965): 510–15; Derek J. de Solla Price and D. de Beaver, "Collaboration in an Invisible College," *American Psychologist* 21 (November 1966): 1011–18; Harriet Zuckerman, "The Sociology of the Nobel Prizes," *Scientific American* 217, 5 (November 1967): 25–33.

26. Louis B. Barnes, *Organizational Systems and Engineering Groups: A Comparative Study of Two Technical Groups in Industry* (Boston: Division of Research, Harvard Business School, 1960); Paula Brown, "Bureaucracy in a Government Laboratory," *Social Forces* 32 (1954), 259–68; Barney G. Glaser, "Differential Association and the Institutional Motivation of Scientists," *Administrative Science Quarterly* 10, 1 (June 1965): 82–97; Barney G. Glaser, *Organizational Scientists: Their Professional Careers* (Indianapolis: Bobbs-Merrill, 1964); Norman Kaplan, "Professional Scientists in Industry: An Essay Review," *Social Problems* 13, 1 (Summer 1965): 88–97; "The Relation of Creativity to Sociological Variables in Research Organization, in C. W. Taylor and F. Barron (eds.), *Scientific Creativity: Its Recognition and Development* (New York: John Wiley & Son, 1963); "The Role of the Research Administrator," *Administrative Science Quarterly* 4 (1959): 20–42; William Kornhauser, *Scientists in Industry* (Berkeley and Los

to networks—encompassing distinct fields of research—was greatly influenced by the emergence of a view of science as the work of a community in the sociological sense.[27]

The concept of the scientific community was revived and elaborated in an original way by Thomas Kuhn.[28] As this view has become rather basic for the sociology of science, I shall discuss it in some detail. According to it, scientists form a closed community. They investigate a well-defined range of problems with methods and tools adapted for the task. The definition of the problems and the methodology of investigation derive from a professional tradition of theories, methods and skills the acquisition of which requires prolonged training and, as a matter of fact if not of principle, a great deal of indoctrination. The rules of the scientific method, as explicated by logicians of science, do not, according to this view, adequately describe what scientists do. They are not busily engaged in the testing and refutation of existing hypotheses so as to establish new and more generally valid ones. Rather, like people engaged in other occupations, they take it for granted that the existing theories and methods are valid, and they use them for their professional purposes. These are usually not the discovery of new theories but the solution of concrete problems, for example, to measure a constant, to analyze or synthesize a compound, or to explain the functioning of a part of a living organism. In quest of a solution the researcher uses as his "paradigm" the existing traditions in his field. He takes it for granted that such a solution exists, and therefore regards research as a "puzzle."

One of the implications is that science is insulated from external social influence, since what scientists do and the way they do it are determined by their own traditions. The "paradigm" is like a language and a culture. It determines which questions can be asked and which are to be excluded; and it defines norms of conduct and criteria of evaluation. The younger scientists are socialized into it, just as the mature scientists uphold and transmit it to the next generation. By adopting it one enters a community which, like all communities, sensitizes its members to each other and desensitizes them to outsiders.

Angeles: University of California Press, 1962); Simon Marcson, *The Scientists in American Industry: Some Organizational Determinants in Manpower Utilization* (Princeton: Industrial Relations Section, Princeton University, 1960); Donald C. Pelz, G. D. Mellinger and R. C. Davis, *Human Relations in a Research Organization* (Ann Arbor: University of Michigan, Institute for Social Research, 1953), 2 vols. (mimeographed); Donald C. Pelz and Frank M. Andrews, *Scientists in Organizations* (New York: John Wiley & Sons, 1966); Herbert A. Shepard, "Basic Research in the Social System of Pure Science," *Philosophy of Science* 23, 1 (January 1956): 48–57.

27. It must be noted, however, that "community" here refers to a group which is held together merely by a common purpose and common culture, like some religious communities. This must be distinguished from the usage of "community" to describe people bound together by propinquity. For a classification of the different social ties, cf. Edward Shils, "Primordial, Personal, Sacred and Civil Ties," *British Journal of Sociology* 8, 2 (June 1956): 132–34.

28. Cf. n. 14.

For example, modern physics has been the same in the USSR as elsewhere despite the totalistic intellectual claims of communism. Even the famous conflict about genetics did not involve a real intrusion of nonscientific criteria into the thinking of the entire scientific community but represented rather the suppression of a particular part of this community.

Thus, although science is conceived here as the activity of a human group ("the scientific community," or rather "communities" specialized by fields), this group is so effectively insulated from the outside world that the characteristics of different societies in which scientists live and work can for many intents and purposes be disregarded.

Since the norms and goals of these communities are defined by the state of science, their sociology is relatively simple, which of course, does not make them less interesting. Scientific communities can serve as examples of an extreme case of effective social control through minimum informal sanctions. Here is an interesting instance of a group of people held together by common purposes and shared norms without the need for reinforcement by familial, ecological or political ties.

This scheme, however, which Kuhn qualifies as "normal science," does not, in his view, explain scientific change, and his main aim is the explanation of the latter. This is conceived of as a series of "revolutions." Every paradigm sooner or later reaches a point of intellectual exhaustion. Some puzzles persist and resist solution, and after a while the conviction gains ground that they cannot be solved within the existing paradigm. There arises a crisis within the scientific community, like that in any other community when the goals which had once inspired it become unattainable by the accepted means. This is the state which sociologists call *anomie* (normlessness) and which has been widely studied as the background of social deviance and change.[29]

In such periods of crisis, according to Kuhn, the barriers between science and the broad intellectual currents of society break down. In their search for a basically new orientation, scientists become interested in a variety of philosophical ideas and theories far removed from their own specialty. There is no longer a consensus concerning the correct approach to outstanding problems, and it is impossible to predict which thought model, however derived, will provide the starting point for the rise of a valid new paradigm.

The main burden of the concept of scientific revolution is philosophical: to show that the development of science is not cumulative but consists of a series of distinct, disconnected beginnings, growths and declines, like the rise and fall of civilizations. Carried to its extreme this view would, for instance, deny

---

29. Cf.: Emile Durkheim, *Suicide*, pp. 241–76 (Glencoe: The Free Press, 1952); Robert K. Merton, "Social Structure and Anomie," in his *Social Theory and Social Structure*, op. cit., pp. 131–94; Talcott Parsons, *The Social System*, pp. 256–67, 321–25 (Glencoe: The Free Press, 1951).

any continuity of purpose and criteria of evidence between classical and present-day physics, a position which is difficult to accept.[30]

From a sociological point of view, the assertion that revolutions regularly follow the exhaustion of paradigms and occur neither before nor after that point and that, furthermore, "revolutions" are completely discontinuous and different from other types of change would make science a social anomaly. This extreme view of revolution is a postulate made necessary by the assumption that "normally" scientists work within existing paradigms. Hence the abandonment of an existing "paradigm" and the creation of a new one can occur only where the paradigm actually breaks down. Empirically, however, there may be (a) differences between individuals and groups in their perceptions of the breakdown (or exhaustion) of the paradigm either due to their different locations in the scientific community or to differences in their individual sensitivity; and (b) differences in the closure of certain scientific communities—some may have nothing to do with other scientific communities while others may have partially overlapping interests and common personnel. It is possible, therefore, to envisage normative variation leading to as fundamental a change as "revolutions" issuing out of the feelings of frustration and the deliberate search for innovation involving a whole scientific community.[31] This, of course, also implies that paradigmatic behavior is a limiting state which groups of scientists tend to approach but which is never actually attained.

The ideal typical description of this limiting state has been very useful in the conceptualization of scientific interaction. The idea of a community working on the solution of a set of interrelated problems could be translated into a model of relatively closed communication networks where people exchange information with each other, presumably in proportion to their contribution to the total fund of knowledge created by all participants. This could be investigated empirically through the analysis of quotations or questionnaire surveys of communication between scientists, thus lending greater theoretical significance to the empirical studies of scientific communication which have been conducted for some time, partly for practical purposes.[32] The results of these

30. Cf. Dudley Shapere, "The Structure of Scientific Revolutions," *Philosophical Review* 73, 3 (July 1965): 383–94.

31. Cf. Joseph Ben-David, "Scientific Growth: A Sociological View," *Minerva* 3 (Summer 1964): 455–76 on pp. 471–75 [this volume, chap. 14]; and Hagstrom, op. cit., pp. 159–243. For the complexities of the actual structures of groups engaged in the same field of research, cf. Crane, op. cit., and Mullins, op. cit.

32. Cf. American Psychological Association, *Reports of the Project on Scientific Information Exchange in Psychology* (Washington, D.C.: American Psychological Association, 1963); E. Garfield, *The Use of Citation Data in Writing the History of Science* (Philadelphia: Institute for Scientific Information, 1964); M. Libbey and G. Zaltman, *The Role and Distribution of Written Informal Communication in Theoretical High Energy Physics* (New York: American Institute of Physics, 1967); W. J. Paisley, *The Flow of (Behavioral) Science Information: A Review of Research Literature* (Palo Alto: Institute for Communication Research, Stanford University, 1965);

investigations show that networks of scientists working in a given field are less closed than assumed in the ideal-typical descriptions of the scientific community and that the structure of the network has been that of a "circle" or several "circles," the members of which relate to each other through a few leaders, rather than of a cooperative egalitarian community.[33]

Another theoretically important use of the interactional approach has been the study of quotations and the recognition of priorities as an index to the institutionalization of the norms of scientific conduct. Priority conflicts are a good way to investigate the problems of adherence to the scientific norm of disinterestedness. And the exploration of the influence of formal rank or past achievement on scientific recognition, acceptance of papers for publication, and so on, shows the difficulty of enforcement of another institutional norm, that of complete objectivity ("universalism") in scientific judgments. These studies provide a potential link between the interactional and institutional study of scientific behavior. Thus, it appears that priority conflicts have become considerably less frequent during the last hundred years than they used to be, indicating that the professionalization of scientific careers which occurred during this period alleviated the invidious aspects of scientific competition. These studies have also proved useful in the explanation of the differences between the attitudes and habits of scientists in different fields and the conditions of work in those fields.[34]

As to the institutional study of science, one of the most conspicuous differences between the literature prior to the Second World War and recent works has been the virtual disappearance of attempts to explain the content and theories of science on the basis of social conditions. As has been pointed out, such attempts proliferated in the 1930s. They were of two kinds.

The first argued that science, like all other mental products, was somehow influenced by class interests, racial origin or political ideology. This type of argument has not been put forward by reputable scientists or students of science since the early 1950s. Historical studies of the development of scientific thought, and sociological investigation of the way scientists work, have unequivocally shown that the problems investigated by scientists are overwhelm-

---

E. B. Parker, W. J. Paisley and R. Garrett, *Bibliographic Citation as Unobtrusive Measures of Scientific Communication* (Palo Alto: Institute for Communication Research, Stanford University, 1967).

33. Cf. Crane, op. cit.; Mullins, op. cit.

34. Cf. Randall Collins, "Competition and Social Control in Science: An Essay in Theory Construction," *Sociology of Education* 41, 2 (Spring 1968): 123–40; Hagstrom, op. cit.; Robert K. Merton, "Priorities in Scientific Discovery," *American Sociological Review* 22, 6 (December 1954): 635–59; "The Ambivalence of Scientists," *Bulletin of the Johns Hopkins Hospital* 112 (1963): 77–97; "Resistance to the Systematic Study of Multiple Discoveries in Science," *European Journal of Sociology* 4, 2 (1963): 237–82.

ingly determined by conditions internal to the scientific community, such as the "state of the art" and the resources for and organization of scientific work. This is not to say that general philosophical ideas or social concerns may not influence science at all but that the growth of scientific knowledge cannot be systematically explained as resulting from such external conditions. Their effect can only be indirect and is always circumscribed by the internal state of science. The investigation of such indirect effects is difficult, but historians of science have made a number of suggestive studies along these lines.[35] They do not so far provide sufficient basis for sociological generalizations about the conditions under which external influences are likely to impinge on science. There exists only Kuhn's hypothesis that they are more likely to occur at periods of crisis, when the possibility of making new discoveries in a scientific field seems to be exhausted.

The second approach to the explanation of the content of scientific knowledge resulting from social conditions is the attempt to link discoveries in science to the solution of technological problems. As the latter are set by the changing forms of production, this would make it possible to view science as an indirect response to socioeconomic needs.

As has already been pointed out, such an approach was fairly widespread among the scientific humanists of the 1930s. It seemed plausible to seek connections between the revolution in astronomy during the sixteenth and seventeenth centuries and the concern with problems of navigation during that period, just as there is an obvious connection between the hot and cold wars of the past decades and the development of high-energy physics and space exploration at the present. While these circumstances might have increased the supply of scientists and thus sped development, there is no evidence whatsoever to show that they significantly influenced the content of scientific ideas or even the patterns of scientific work. There is even some doubt about the simple relationship between the demand for certain types of knowledge for practical purposes and the volume of relevant scientific activity in any given country. The Spanish and Portuguese, who were among the leading seafaring nations during the crucial growth period of the new astronomy, contributed little to its development, while the partially landlocked Poles and Germans played a central role, since the ideas of Copernicus and Kepler set the framework for the scientific revolution.[36]

Similarly, developments in nuclear research were not responses to technological demand. The relative backwardness of nuclear research in Germany during the Second World War was partly due to reasons analogous to the erst-

35. Cf. Yehuda Elkana, *The Discovery of the Conservation of Energy* (London: Hutchinson Educational, 1974); Alexandre Koyré, *From the Closed World to the Infinite Universe* (New York: Harper Torch Books 1958); Kuhn, op. cit.; L. Pearce Williams, *Michael Faraday* (London: Chapman & Hall, 1963).
36. Cf. G. N. Clark, op. cit.; Polányi, op. cit., pp. 78–83.

while decline of Spanish-Portuguese astronomy. In both cases science-based innovations developed in those countries which provided scientists with the conditions necessary for the maintenance of their autonomy, rather than in response to technological demand. Finally, all developments in nuclear physics necessary for the production of the atomic bomb preceded the idea of its actual production. Even the large-scale organization of research in this field was started in the 1930s by Lawrence at Berkeley. It is true that, subsequent to the Second World War, research on subatomic particles was greatly furthered by financing which became available owing to the original practical applications of atomic research. But the results of this most expensive research had no practical application, which shows how little effect practical ends have on concept and theory.

This is not because scientists lack social responsibility, or are unmotivated to produce useful knowledge, but, as has been pointed out, because what they can do is determined by the state of the art and not by the changing needs of society.

Attempts at explaining the growth of scientific knowledge as a response to technological and ultimately socioeconomic needs are, therefore, as untenable as the attempt to link it systematically to philosophical and political views. Yet, here, too, the conclusion is not that the solution of technological problems cannot be an important impetus for the emergence of new scientific knowledge, merely that the relationship is not simple and direct. Whether setting scientists to the solution of such problems will lead to scientific discoveries (or technological solutions) depends on the changing relationship between theories and methods of different scientific fields and given technological problems. Even where technological solutions are found, this will not necessarily lead to new scientific knowledge.

There is no theory about the conditions under which the solution of technological problems leads to scientific discoveries, but it is possible to investigate the institutional conditions which encourage scientists toward awareness of technological problems and facilitate the adoption and development of "hybrid" fields emerging on the margins of science and technology.[37]

While attempts at the explanation of scientific discoveries resulting from technological preoccupations have been abandoned, there has been a steep rise in inquiries concerning the effects of science on technology. In its most simplistic form this link is seen as a straight line which leads from basic discovery to applied research and then to product development. This belief has been strengthened by econometric analyses revealing the existence of a residual

37. Cf. Joseph Ben-David, "Roles and Innovations in Medicine," *American Journal of Sociology* 65, 6 (May 1960): 557–68 [this volume, chap. 1]; and about cross-fertilization in science in general, Derek J. de Solla Price, *Science Since Babylon*, pp. 1–22 (New Haven and London: Yale University Press, 1961).

factor (probably the increase in knowledge) in economic growth.[38] There have also been a few case studies which show the economic importance of research, especially in some of the most rapidly growing new industries.[39] It was overlooked that the residual factor was not necessarily attributable to scientific research, and certainly not to scientific research performed in all countries where economic growth has occurred.[40]

More specific investigations of the way science influenced technology have so far shown that it is difficult to link technological inventions to scientific discoveries in a systematic way. Schmookler's study of patents in several industries indicates that in most cases inventive activity was the result of economic demand rather than of intellectual opportunity provided by potentially relevant scientific discoveries. Similarly negative results were reached in a more recent study which tries to trace the importance of basic discoveries in the development of modern weapons systems.[41]

This is less surprising than it may appear, since, after all, technological application depends on profitability. The creation of applicable knowledge is, therefore, not a sufficient condition for its technological exploitation. It only creates an opportunity for such use but cannot determine the timing (except its lower limit) or the location of realization.

These studies have not been undertaken by sociologists, yet the problem of how different institutional spheres are empirically linked and how information is diffused from one to the other is a sociological one.

The last approach to be considered here is the institutional study of scientific activity (as distinct from the study of the concepts and theories of science). This means the exploration of conditions which have determined the amount of scientific research and shaped the roles and careers of scientists and the organization of science in different countries at different times.

38. Cf. OECD Study Group in the Economics of Education, *The Residual Factor and Economic Growth* (Paris: OECD, 1964).

39. Cf. C. Freeman and A. Young, *The Research and Development Effort in Western Europe, North America and the Soviet Union: An Experimental International Comparison of Research Expenditure and Manpower in 1962* (Paris: OECD, 1965); W. Gruber, D. Mehte and R. Vernon, "The R and D Factor in International Trade and International Investment of United States Industries," and D. B. Keesing, "The Impact of Research and Development on United States Trade," *Journal of Political Economy* 75, 1 (1967): 20–37 and 38–48, respectively. Particular attention has been paid to economic returns on research of different types in the USSR. For a summary of the views of Soviet experts, cf. E. Zaleski, J. P. Kozlowski, H. Wienert, R. W. Davies, M. J. Berry and R. Amann, *Science Policy in the U.S.S.R.*, pp. 40–7 (Paris: OECD, 1969).

40. Cf. OECD Study Group, op. cit., pp. 47–48, and Marcelo Selowsky, op. cit.

41. Cf. Jacob Schmookler, *Invention and Economic Growth* (Cambridge: Harvard University Press, 1966); C. W. Sherwin and R. S. Isenson, "Project Hindsight," *Science* 156 (1967), 1571–77. C. E. Falk et al., *Technology in Retrospect and Critical Events in Science*, prepared for the National Science Foundation by the Illinois Institute of Technology Research, Chicago, 1968.

This type of study developed under the following circumstances: the idea that the growth of fundamental science—which in contrast to the 1930s now became distinct from technology and applied research in the social science of science—also had an effect on the economy led to public concern with science policy and to attempted measurement of research inputs (manpower and funds). It was a logical next step to try measuring scientific output. This, of course, had been done before, but at the time little importance was attached to the matter: even the small groups of sociologists of science and "scientific humanists" who tried to measure science were mainly interested in its technological applications. As to fundamental science, there was a general reluctance to recognize that, apart from its content and quality, it also had important quantitative aspects represented by more or less research, discovery and diffusion of knowledge. All these resistances have weakened as a result of emerging national and international science policies. Thus, interest in the measurement of scientific output became more continuous and more professional.[42] There have also been important changes in the kind of data used and the types of analyses to which they were subjected. Instead of counting "discoveries" which are difficult to identify, there has been a growing tendency to count publications. And with the advent of the computer and the citation index, it also became possible to perform analyses of quality (measured by numbers of citations).

Another change occurring as a result of the emergence of national science policies was the acceptance of the comparative framework for the sociological study of science. As science is the same everywhere there was in the past a reluctance to study the differences in its institutional context in various countries. Scholars interested in such differences usually considered the advantages and disadvantages of the different systems as judged intuitively by the investigator and his informants. There were no hypotheses about specific relationships between certain aspects and types of research and certain organizational and institutional characteristics of science in different countries.

Only Merton's study dealing with the emergence of modern science and a short paper by him about science in totalitarian countries employed well defined institutional variables and general sociological hypotheses.[43] Both of these were extreme cases concerned with the most general cultural conditions for the existence of science and not with differences between countries where minimal conditions are present.

Recent literature has extended the comparative approach in several directions. Historians of ancient and medieval science have increasingly asked

42. Cf. G. Dobrov, L. Smirnov, V. Klimenuk and A. Savaliev, *Potential Nauki* (Potential of Science) (Kiev: Naukova Dumka, 1969); C. Freeman, "Measurement of Output of Research and Development," UNESCO, 31 January 1969 (mimeographed); D. J. de Solla Price, op. cit., 1963.
43. Cf. nn. 15, 17.

sociological questions, such as "Who were the people taking part in scientific activity in different cultures?" "What were their motives and opportunities?" "What value has been imputed to scientific activity by different social groups and by society at large?"[44]

Sociologists and other social scientists have begun to study the institutional arrangements of science in modern societies. There have been attempts to explain the differences in the structure of scientific institutions as the result of political, economic and class variables.[45] Furthermore, attempts have been made to relate specific features of scientific systems in different countries to specific results. Such characteristics—whether the units of a system are competitive and autonomous, or whether they are arranged as a centralized hierarchy—were found to be important determinants of the quantity of scientific output and the rapidity in diffusion of new scientific fields within the system. Also, the place of professional scientists in the class system was related to the flexibility of systems in the initial adoption of unorthodox lines of research, especially in the applied fields.[46]

44. Good samples of this new sociological concern can be found in A. C. Crombie (ed.), *Scientific Change* (London: Heinemann, 1963).

45. Cf. Joseph Ben-David and Awraham Zloczower, "Universities and Academic Systems in Modern Societies," *European Journal of Sociology* 3, 1 (1962): 45–84 [this volume, chap. 6]; Joseph Ben-David, "Scientific Endeavor in Israel and the United States," *The American Behavioral Scientist* 6, 4 (December 1962): 12–16, and his "The Universities and the Growth of Science in Germany and the United States," *Minerva* 7, 1–2 (Autumn–Winter, 1968–69): 1–35; D. S. L. Cardwell, *The Organization of Science in England* (London: Heinemann, 1957); Renée Fox, "Medical Scientists in a Château," *Science* 136, 3515 (11 May 1962): 476–73; and her "An American Sociologist in the Land of Belgian Medical Research," in Phillip E. Hammond (ed.), *Sociologist at Work*, pp. 345–91 (New York: Basic Books, 1964); Robert Gilpin, *France in the Age of the Scientific State* (Princeton: Princeton University Press, 1968); Robert Gilpin and Christopher Wright (eds.), *Scientists and National Science Policy Making* (New York-London: Columbia University Press, 1964); Daniel Greenberg, *The Politics of American Science* (London: Pelican Books, 1969); Norman Kaplan, "The Western European Scientific Establishment in Transition," *The American Behavioral Scientist* 6, 4 (1962): 17–21; T. Dixon Long, "Policy and Politics in Japanese Science: The Persistence of a Tradition," *Minerva* 7, 3 (Spring 1969): 426–53; Don K. Price, *Government and Science: Their Dynamic Relation in American Democracy* (New York: New York University Press, 1954); *The Scientific Estate* (Cambridge: Harvard University Press, 1965); Hans Skoie, "The Problem of a Small Scientific Community: The Norwegian Case," *Minerva* 7, 3 (Spring 1969): 399–425; Edward Shils, "The Academic Profession in India," *Minerva* 7, 3 (Spring 1969): 345–72; Alvin M. Weinberg, *Reflections on Big Science* (Cambridge: MIT Press, 1967). The historical antecedents of this type of analysis are Max Weber, "Science as a Vocation," in H. H. Gerth and C. W. Mills (eds.), *From Max Weber: Essays in Sociology*, pp. 129–56 (London: Routledge & Kegan Paul, 1947) (originally published in 1922); and Logan Wilson, *The Academic Man* (New York: Oxford University Press, 1942). But both of these were almost exclusively concerned with university teachers.

46. Cf. Joseph Ben-David, "Scientific Productivity and Academic Organization in Nineteenth Century Medicine," *American Sociological Review* 25, 6 (December 1960): 828–43 [this volume, chap. 5]; J. Ben-David and Randall Collins, "Social Factors in the Origins of a New Science: The Case of Psychology," *American Sociological Review* 31, 4 (August 1966): 457–65 [this volume, chap. 2]; Diana Crane, "Scientists at Major and Minor Universities. A Study of Productivity and Recognition," *American Sociological Review* 30, 5 (October 1965): 699–714;

Furthermore, there have been an increasing number of studies dealing with the aspects of science policy and science organization in general or in selected fields in one or several countries, using explicit sociological hypotheses which make results comparable.[47]

These various investigations have not yet crystallized into a consistent sociological view of scientific work. Sociological theorists have concentrated on the description of the value orientations of science in such terms as universalism, rationality, organized skepticism and disinterestedness. These attempts are a logical part of the theoretical scheme represented mainly by Talcott Parsons and introduced to the sociology of science by Merton and Barber[48] of interpreting social structure in terms of certain characteristics of social norms and value orientations prevailing in societies as a whole and in part. The problem of empirical application of this approach is that science seems so central to the normative system of modern societies that only very refined analysis can lead to the discovery of significant and operationally identifiable differences between them in respect of science. On the other hand, if the problem is the place of science in the transition from traditional to modern society, then the differences in norms and values are gross and clearly identifiable. It appears, therefore, that the scheme might prove valuable in helping to understand differences in reactions to the introduction of science in such countries as Japan, China or India, which should constitute promising areas for sociological research.

Another context in which this theoretical scheme might usefully be applied is that of tracing the relationship of science to other social systems. Good examples are investigations of the reward structure of science. Thus the norm of disinterestedness in external rewards—which is essential to safeguarding scientific universalism and creativity—poses problems in the institutionalization of rewards. Scientists are not supposed to be interested in any extrinsic reward except that which is immanent to the discovery of truth, but at the same time

R. Knapp and H. Goodrich, *Origins of American Scientists* (Chicago: University of Chicago Press, 1952); Frank Pfetsch, *Beiträge zur Entwicklung der Wissenschaftspolitik in Deutschland*, Research Report (Heidelberg, 1969); A. Zloczower, *Career Opportunities and the Growth of Scientific Discovery in Nineteenth-Century Germany, with Special Reference to Physiology* (Jerusalem: Hebrew University, 1966 [now published by Arno Press, New York, 1981]).

47. Cf. Bernard Barber, *Drugs and Society* (New York: Russell Sage Foundation, 1967); Terry N. Clark, "Institutionalization and Innovation in Higher Education: Four Conceptual Models," *Administrative Science Quarterly* 13, 1 (June 1968): 1–25; and his *Prophets and Patrons: The French University and the Emergence of the Social Sciences* (Cambridge: Harvard University Press, 1973); Bernard-Pierre Lécuyer, "Histoire et sociologie de la recherche sociale empirique: Problèmes de théorie et de méthode," in Pierre Naville (ed.), *Epistémologie sociologique*, in *Anthropos* (Paris), 6 (December 1968): 119–31; Anthony Oberschall, *Empirical Social Research in Germany, 1848–1914* (Paris-The Hague: Mouton, 1965).

48. Cf. Barber, op. cit., 1962, pp. 122–42; Merton, op. cit., 1957, pp. 550–61; Parsons, op. cit., pp. 335–48.

they participate in formal and informal social relationships where money, power and authority count. The way this conflict is handled in different contexts has been explored in several works. A first systematic attempt to explore the implications of this type of analysis concerning all the norms of science was made by Norman Storer.[49]

The final observation to be made about the present state of the sociology of science is the surprising paucity of studies on the social effects of science.[50] This is all the more strange, since the exploration of these effects appears to be much more important than the investigation of conditions of scientific growth. Indeed Ogburn's "cultural lag" hypothesis, which was perhaps the most important starting point for the sociology of science, dealt precisely with this kind of problem.

This shortcoming is a good illustration of the limited influence social demands can have on the content of science. Sociology of science turned from the explanation of effects to that of the conditions for scientific growth, because the latter was a conceptually soluble, and the former an insoluble, problem. It was possible to identify science and to describe and measure its growth, as it was possible to identify the organizations and institutions which had a direct effect thereon. But the social effects of science are so numerous and diffuse that it is practically impossible to separate them from each other. All the institutions of modern societies have been deeply affected by science and scientific thinking for such a long time that it is extremely difficult to separate that which is from that which is not affected by science. Hence, sociologists tackled what was possible and left what seemed to be impossible alone.

It is conceivable, however, that abstract theoretical work on science as a system of social norms will change the situation in the future. The conceptual framework of viewing science as a set of social norms has proved useful in the past in a few attempted explanations of the sources of hostility toward science in modern societies. It was shown that, under certain conditions, the norms of scientific conduct could neither be insulated from nor made compatible with other institutional norms.[51] Now that there is renewed questioning of the social effects of science, these theoretical developments may serve as a basis for a systematic investigation of the problem.

49. Norman Storer, *The Social System of Science* (New York: Holt, Rinehart & Winston, 1966).

50. Only the technological effects of science are systematically investigated, cf. n. 41, and Daniel Shimshoni, "The Mobile Scientists in the American Instrument Industry," *Minerva* 8 (1970): 59–89. New attempts at the exploration of a broader range of consequences are now being made by the Commission on the Year 2000 of the American Academy of Arts and Sciences and the Harvard University Program on Technology and Society.

51. Cf. Barber, op. cit., 1962, pp. 93–122; Merton, op. cit., 1957, pp. 537–49; and Shils, op. cit., 1956.

Conclusion

Contemporary work in the sociology of science is distinguished from its beginnings prior to the Second World War: (a) by the abandonment of efforts at a sociological explanation of the concepts and theories of science, in favor of concentration on the explanation of scientific activity and its organization; (b) by a growing emphasis on the comparative point of view, instead of the habit of examining science and its institutions in isolation from their social context; and, finally, (c) by the emergence of the interactional study of scientific teams, disciplines and the scientific community in general, in addition to the institutional approach which started in the 1930s.

The composition of groups interested in the social aspects of science has also changed. In the 1930s the majority of groups were natural scientists turned amateur sociologists. Today the majority are social scientists (sociologists, political scientists, and social historians) and only a minority are natural scientists.

The trend toward growing professionalization is bound to become more pronounced in the future, since the subject is now taught at an increasing number of universities in departments of sociology and political science. On the other hand, as is evident from the present survey, it is still impossible to identify the sociology of science with any specific discipline. There are differences of emphasis only between sociologists, political scientists and social historians working in the field, and natural scientists and mathematicians who have taken an interest in it have also made important contributions to all its branches. Owing to the specialized nature of science, the contributions of natural scientists are essential to maintain the vitality of the sociology of science. It is to be hoped, therefore, that the growing professionalization of the field will not lead to the abandonment of its interdisciplinary character.

Emergence of National 20
Traditions in the
Sociology of Science

The United States and Great Britain

This chapter describes the emergence of two different traditions in the sociology of science in the United States and Britain, the differences resulting from the different backgrounds and professional functions of the sociologists of science in the two countries. (For histories and surveys of the development of sociology of science in general, see Cole and Zuckerman 1975; Stehr 1975; Merton and Gaston 1977; Mulkay 1977*a, 1977b*.)

Sociology of Science in the United States

Sociology of science as a distinct specialty emerged in the United States in the 1950s as a result of the work of Robert Merton and his students. Others before him, including several sociologists, had investigated the social aspects of science; but only Merton and his group made a conscious effort to establish a definition of the area, a conceptual framework, and a program of research, and they were the first to make a conscious effort at obtaining recognition for the field as a branch of sociology.

Science and the Social Order (1952), by one of the earliest students of Merton, Bernard Barber, was the first codification of existing knowledge in the field. As is evident from Robert Merton's "Foreword" to the book, which

This research was supported by a grant from the Ford Foundation. A first draft was written while I was a member of the Institute for Advanced Study at Princeton and was read at a joint meeting of the Society for the Social Studies of Science and the Research Committee on Sociology of Science of the International Sociological Association at Cornell University, November 1976.

deals with the reasons for the neglect of sociology of science, the purpose of the book was to show that there was enough knowledge and theoretical importance in the field to warrant its recognition as a sociological specialty. The book had great success and became a standard text and reference for many years. It is still an unparalleled example of a comprehensive and systematic outline of the field and a basic document of the program to make sociology of science a recognized specialty. The theoretical core of this program was the description of science as a social institution with a normative structure and a reward system of its own. This "structural-functional" institutional approach to science developed in comparative and historical macrosociology and was useful in the interpretation of differences between cultures, value change within cultures, and the congruency or incongruency between the norms of different institutions in society. (The classic text of this institutional approach to sociology is Davis 1949.)

Much of the research in the sociology of science before the 1960s dealt with such institutional problems. The best known of these was Merton's discovery of the congruence between Puritanism and science (Merton [1938a] 1970), which contradicted the belief about an inherent conflict between religion and science. This was followed by an investigation of the problem of how science, a universalistic and—in principle—skeptical enterprise, could survive under totalitarian regimes opposed to such norms of behavior (Merton [1938b] 1973c, [1942] 1973a) and by investigations of the effect on industrial research of the contradiction between the scientific norms of altruism and "communism" and the requirements of secrecy and profitability in industry (Marcson 1960; Kornhauser 1962).

Apart from Merton's early study of Puritanism and science, these institutional studies had limited influence. The institutional approach is best suited to the treatment of comparative historical material, but the way sociology developed in the 1950s provided no incentive for the acquisition of historical knowledge. The general expectation was that sociology would follow the example of economics and psychology and adopt quantitative techniques. Few promising graduate students in the 1950s or 1960s in the United States were willing to write a thesis that was not based on quantitative survey research. The alternative of writing theses based on historical-comparative material would have required a kind of erudition that sociology students did not possess; and, in view of the prevailing quantitative trend, they had no compelling reason to acquire such erudition.

If sociology of science was to become a recognized specialty, it had to adopt quantitative techniques (which in the 1950s and early 1960s meant mainly survey research), but the existing (structural-functional) institutional approach was not suited for these. This difficulty was overcome with Merton's discovery of the problematic nature of the reward system in science. Although the crucial paper "Priorities in Scientific Discovery" (1957) was a historical paper written in the tradition of classical qualitative structural-functional analysis, it opened the way to quantitative studies in the sociology of science. Merton's explanation of the apparent incongruency between the selfishly petty behavior of scientists in priority disputes and the scientific norm of "communism" (that is, that scientists might be reluctant to share their results with everyone because they might thereby be deprived of the recognition due to them) suggested that the relationship between the allocation of rewards in science and the behavior expected of scientists was a matter requiring careful study and that the study of competition and stratification could be of central importance in understanding scientific behavior. Competition, allocation of rewards, and stratification could be studied quantitatively, and their quantitative study in science created an opportunity to line up sociology of science alongside general studies of stratification, which constituted one of the central fields of sociological research.

This development of the sociology of science toward articulation with theories of stratification was only a potential in 1957, when Merton's "Priorities" paper was published. The potential was exploited in the 1960s, when Warren Hagstrom, a graduate student at Berkeley, and William Kornhauser, a member of the sociology department, decided to go into the field. In the first result of this collaboration (Kornhauser 1962), the new theoretical possibilities were not fully exploited. They were exploited, however, in Hagstrom's *The Scientific Community* (1965). Although the techniques that Hagstrom employed were rather rudimentary, he made a systematic effort to measure competition, communication, and recognition.

The historical significance of the book was that it was written not by a student of Merton but by a student at an outstanding department where sociology of science had not been previously represented. This was a sign that the specialty was beginning to be recognized as one in which discoveries of theoretical importance for sociology as a whole could be made.

Indeed, the book was a harbinger of a takeoff in the sociology of science. Several of the most promising doctoral students at Columbia in the 1960s— such as Jonathan Cole, Stephen Cole, Diana Crane, and Harriet Zuckerman—chose sociology of science as their main field of research and established a considerable reputation in sociology in general by working on the themes outlined in Merton's "Priorities" paper and Hagstrom's *Scientific Community*. They have since been joined by others.

This success was due not only to the theoretical potentialities of Merton's ideal but also to other influences in the 1960s and the 1970s. One was the work of Derek de Solla Price, which began in the early 1950s and became widely known in the 1960s through two books, *Science Since Babylon* (1961) and *Little Science, Big Science* (1963). Price was interested in measuring the growth of science and discovering its immanent regularities. His interest in social conditions was limited to the restraints imposed on this growth by the facts that only a small fraction of mankind is capable of cultivating science and that there are rather narrow limits to the capability of people to transmit and absorb information. Models of the rise and decline of special fields were developed by Holton (1962) and by Price (1963, pp. 22–23). Both works used publications and citations in order to evaluate contributions and analyze the development of specialties (see Price 1963, pp. 62–91), thereby providing imaginative examples and suggestions for the quantitative treatment of sociological problems in science. *Science Citation Index,* published since 1963, has been an invaluable tool for this work. Scientific recognition and the flow of communication between scientists could now be measured effectively, and on an unprecedented scale, through citations. Thus, by the mid 1960s all the theoretical ingredients and technical tools required for quantitative studies of stratification and reward in science were in existence and recognized by sociologists. Soon thereafter methods for their effective use were developed by Jonathan and Stephen Cole. This availability explains the rapid rise of systematic and coherent work in this field (Cole and Cole 1973; Gaston 1973, 1978).

During the 1960s and the 1970s, numerous studies of scientific growth, particularly the growth of particular fields and specialties, appeared (Ben-David 1960; Ben-David and Collins 1966; Fisher 1966; Clark 1968, 1973; Crane 1969, 1972; Krantz 1971; Crawford 1971; Mullins 1972, 1973; Griffith and Mullins 1972; Griffith and others 1974; Small and Griffith 1974; Cole and Zuckerman 1975; Breiger 1976; Chubin 1976; Mullins et al. 1977). These studies have not had such a homogeneous theoretical focus as those of reward and stratification. Some of them are conceptually related to the latter, since they explain differences in the growth of science in different countries as the result of differences in prestige and standing between institutions; similarly, they explain the rise of certain new fields as the result of mobility of scientists from field to field, motivated by institutionally determined opportunities. The rise of interest in such studies was greatly influenced by Price's suggestions for the quantitative study of specialty networks, called *invisible colleges* (see Crane 1972), by the *Science Citation Index,* and by Thomas Kuhn's *The Structure of Scientific Revolutions* (1962). Kuhn's influence was less specific than that of Merton and Price, because his ideas were not readily translatable into empirical research and their sociological implications were not sufficiently clear (Barber 1963). But no other book has painted such a vivid and sociologically suggestive picture of the scientific community and made such a consistent attempt to describe the rise and decline of scientific traditions ("paradigms") as a combination of intellectual and social processes. His idea that science advances through revolutions aroused great interest in the investigation of scientific discoveries, especially those that could be described as revolutionary. The general influence of Kuhn's ideas and the use of quantitative techniques lent to this line of research a degree of unity, although nothing like the coherence prevailing in the investigations of stratification and rewards.

These two relatively coherent lines of research are not the whole story of American sociology of science. The study of scientific organizations from the point of view of research management has been a much more continuous tradition, which began in the early 1950s and is still continuing (Shepard 1956; Kaplan 1960, 1964; Glaser 1964; Allen 1966; Gordon and Marquis 1966; Pelz and Andrews 1966; Allen and Cohen 1969). In the 1950s and early 1960s, these studies were closely integrated with the rest of the sociology of science. Since then, however, these investigations have become absorbed in the general area of management studies and are now largely confined to departments of business and public administration; consequently, there has been little contact between investigators of these problems and the rest of the sociologists of science.

The more traditional structural-functional analysis (Storer 1966) and comparative-historical investigations of the institutions of science (Shils 1970; Ben-David 1971; Clark 1973) also have continued. But the reward and stratification studies were the gate through which the majority of graduate students who eventually made contributions entered the field. This particular problem area produced one of the most continuous, clearly formulated, consciously pursued, and technically advanced research programs in sociology. The existence of such a program in the field also raised the salience and attractiveness (for graduate students) of the other lines of inquiry in sociology of science. The fact that these other lines of inquiry did not constitute clearly formulated programs, and were only loosely coordinated conceptually or methodologically, did not really matter, since much research in sociology is of this loosely coordinated kind, and the existence of even one program is sufficient to lift a field above many others.

The emergence of quantitative studies of scientific specialties in the late 1960s added a new line of investigation to the field. Although it had no clear theory, it had a core of common ideas on how scientific innovations occur; above all, it used quantitative techniques for network analysis. Network analysis was not directly related to the reward and stratification research tradition and the normative structural-functional assumptions that gave rise to the reward and stratification tradition. There was no inconsistency between the two lines of research, but a researcher could pursue one of them without paying attention to the other. The emergence of this new line of research made it possible for researchers to avoid the controversy that surrounded the structural-functional approach.

Sociology of Science in Britain

In Great Britain, sociology of science is much younger and has had a history very different from that in the United States. No British sociologist was interested in the field before the 1960s. A few British scientists, in particular

J. D. Bernal (1939), Joseph Needham (1931), and Michael Polanyi (1951), made important contributions to the field during the 1930s and 1940s, but they did not identify themselves as sociologists and did not train students or start programs of research (except Joseph Needham in the history of Chinese science). However, this tradition of prestigious scientists paying serious attention to the social aspects of science created a favorable background for the eventual recognition of social studies of science as an academic field. Therefore, the rise of public interest in the development and social uses of science during the 1950s and 1960s led to the establishment of science units (at Sussex and Edinburgh) and programs for developing courses of study and research in this field (at Manchester). The salience of science and its public discussion attracted to the general field economists, sociologists, philosophers, historians, and people trained in science and engineering. They had neither central leadership nor a common program; but they realized that science had become a socially important phenomenon in their lifetime, and they wanted to understand this development. In contrast to the United States, where this interest was channeled into a preexisting tradition cultivated in graduate departments of sociology, British students had no local tradition and—especially those working in interdisciplinary units—were exposed to a variety of disciplinary backgrounds. Thus, although most economists, historians, philosophers, and sociologists of science are as distinguishable from each other in Britain as elsewhere, the interdisciplinary framework enabled, and perhaps even prompted, a small number of people trained in science of other fields outside sociology—such as B. Barnes, D. Bloor, and R. G. A. Dolby—to become sociologists or to participate in the internal debate on sociological theory.[1]

These British sociologists of science came to the scene in the late 1960s, at a point when the American tradition was beginning to change from overwhelming interest in the reward system to increasing interest in the sociology of scientific specialties. Moreover, even in the United States, the professional definition of the field was much looser than before because of the impact of the work of two nonsociologists, Derek de Solla Price and Thomas S. Kuhn, and the increasingly vocal attacks on structural-functional analysis. The difference in the background and organizational and institutional conditions of work between the American and British group was most obvious in the way the two groups reacted to this situation, and particularly in the way they received the ideas of Kuhn. As has been shown, in the United States this influence was filtered through a strong disciplinary background in sociology. Kuhn's ideas about the developmental phases of scientific knowledge aroused

---

1. There have been no comparable cases in the United States. Psychologists like Griffith (Griffith and Mullins 1972; Griffith et al. 1974) and Krantz (1970, 1971), who did sociological work in this field, have maintained their professional identity. And none of the American historians and philosophers—some of whom have as strong an interest in the sociology of science as

the greatest interest, because these had the most obvious sociological contents and promised to be capable of empirical verification. Much less attention was paid to Kuhn's philosophical relativism and its implications for a sociology of knowledge, partly because Kuhn himself was not too clear about his own relativism (the "commensurability" of "paradigms") and partly because professional sociologists were acquainted with Merton's ([1945] 1973b) essay "Paradigm for the Sociology of Knowledge" and were aware of the immense difficulty involved in investigations of the sociology of knowledge. Thus, until about 1970—that is, for about a decade—American sociologists of science did not believe that Kuhn's views competed with those of Merton. They used and quoted both, for different purposes.

In Britain, the reception of Kuhn was very different. Perhaps because of their background in other disciplines, some British sociologists of science could not appreciate the theoretical importance of interpreting science in terms that had systematic sociological meaning. And those who did were usually critical of structural-functional theory. This, of course, was true also of many Americans. But in the United States there was a tendency to avoid purely theoretical debate (at least in the sociology of science), while in Britain—for reasons to be explained below—many sociologists made their careers through debate and criticism. As a result, the implantation of American sociology of science in Britain was accompanied by a reordering of the cognitive structure of the field. Instead of viewing the ideas of Merton, Kuhn, and Price as so many attempts at conceptualizing the complexities of the scientific community, to be used as inputs in an effort to unravel the structure and function of that community by piecemeal empirical research, British sociologists analyzed these ideas philosophically, for their internal consistency and their logical compatibility with one another. Thus, as one of their main innovations, the British sociologists set up two opposing models: the Mertonian "model" of a general scientific community acting according to relatively stable norms and the Kuhnian "model" of scientific communities changing their views and rules through periodic revolutions. Having set up these models as mutually exclusive (which, as has been pointed out, they were not), they criticized the Mertonian model as incongruent with some (not very systematic) observations on how scientists behave and opted for the Kuhnian model (Mulkay 1969; Barnes and Dolby 1970; Dolby 1971; King 1971; Martins 1971). They did so not because Kuhn's model was more congruent with observations (which they did not try to check) but because it dealt with scientific communities as defined by their members' intellectual and scientific concerns, which for everyone except professional sociologists was a much more interesting point of view than the analysis of the norms and the reward system of

---

their British colleagues—published in sociological publications or intervened in sociological controversies.

science. (See the disappointed reaction of Charles Gillispie to Merton's "Priorities" paper, described by Cole and Zuckerman 1975, p. 157.)

The adoption of Kuhn's ideas as a starting point for a program of research was not confined to Britain. As I have pointed out, there was such a trend in the United States as well. But, as long as both Merton's and Kuhn's ideas were treated as hypotheses about different aspects of scientific behavior to be empirically investigated, the possibility of contradictions between some of the implications of these ideas was of little interest. However, when the ideas were approached from a philosophical point of view, then the difference between Kuhn's qualified relativism and Merton's emphasis on relatively stable institutionalized norms of scientific behavior seemed interesting to explore.

This preponderance of philosophical interest among British sociologists is partly a result of the role of sociology in Britain. British academic sociology is primarily undergraduate sociology. The aim of instruction is not to train research workers but to teach people to think, talk, and write about social issues in a clear, coherent, and effective fashion. Theory, or actually a kind of social philosophy, is, therefore, a central rather than a peripheral aspect of sociological study. Sociologists are taught to confront alternative views of society, or aspects of it; to present these views so that they appear internally coherent and mutually exclusive; and to "demolish" some or all of the views by argument. Writing on such subjects—which in the United States would be considered a marginal contribution to scholarship, qualifying one as a college teacher but hardly for appointment in a graduate department—is, apparently, a highly valued activity in Britain. Thus, about half of the sociology of science literature in Britain (an estimate based on classification and count of publications by British authors quoted in Mulkay 1977a) consists of this kind of "theoretical" writing; that is, critical summaries and confrontations of views on the social aspects of science, in particular of Kuhn versus Merton.

Another reason for this interest in Kuhn's relativism is the fact that some of the people in the field, as has been pointed out, are not sociologists by training but scientists and/or philosophers. Several of them do not work in sociology departments but in special interdisciplinary units, charged with giving courses on and generating interest (especially among science and engineering students) in the social aspects of science and, occasionally, with training future (or present) science administrators in the same area. For these types of teachers and/or students, the prospect of learning from science something about the working of a "fair," consensual social reward system—which is one of the most interesting aspects of science for sociologists—is not only uninteresting but actually disturbing. If members of the scientific community act according to the generally accepted norms of science, then sociology adds nothing to what they were taught (explicitly or implicitly) about science. Sociology becomes interesting only if it can show that actually there is no consensus in science and that decisions about what is at any moment accepted as scientific "truth" are arrived at through a process of conflict of interests, power struggle, and "negotiation," as in many other fields of behavior.[2] One can "really" understand science, then, only through disclosure of the social processes that create it. Therefore, it was important to show that the social aspects of science are not confined to the determination of the place and effects of science in society and to social influences on the institutionalization of science and scientific specialties but that the very substance, or cognitive content, of science is also socially determined. The British thus became deeply interested in the sociology of scientific knowledge (Mulkay 1977*a*, p. 245) and impatient with the sociology of science tradition concerned with the institutional aspects of science. Because of their lack of sociological background, some of the British proponents were unaware of the less than glorious history of attempts at a sociology of knowledge and of the extreme difficulties involved in such efforts.[3]

The Two Traditions in the Sociology of Science: Divergence and Convergence

The two national traditions in the sociology of science are not sharply demarcated from each other, and in some areas, such as studies of research management or to some extent studies of the rise and decline of specialties, the traditions overlap considerably. Nevertheless, the two traditions are clearly distinguishable. American research has emphasized the description of general norms of scientific behavior, the exploration of the reward system and stratification in science, and the formation of consensus in the evaluation of scientific work and merit. Studies on these themes have usually been conducted in a framework of structural-functional assumptions, according to which science in general is a well-demarcated, institutionalized activity. Few American sociologists have tackled problems of sociology of knowledge in science. There has been a great preference in American studies for the use of quantitative techniques.

British sociologists of science have been much more concerned with critical evaluation of existing research and with attempts (mainly theoretical) at

2. For a testimony that philosophers and historians of science are particularly interested in what can be learned from social science about the nonconsensual aspects of science, see Kuhn (1970, p. viii). Speaking of his experiences at the Center for Advanced Study in the Behavioral Sciences, he says: "Particularly, I was struck by the number and extent of overt disagreements between social scientists about the nature of legitimate scientific problems and methods. Both history and acquaintance made me doubt that practitioners of the natural sciences possess firmer or more permanent answers to such questions than their colleagues in social science."

3. Thus, neither of the two most comprehensive British works on the sociology of scientific knowledge (Barnes 1974; Bloor 1976) quotes Merton's ([1945] 1973*b*) basic paper on the subject. At the same time, both authors are deeply influenced by Mary Douglas's neo-Durkheimism, which is not widely accepted among sociologists.

creating a sociology of scientific knowledge. On the whole, they have been critical of structural-functional analysis, and their view of science has tended to be much more relativistic than in the United States. According to them, scientific norms and "truths" are changing from field to field and time to time, more under the impact of "negotiations" between opposing interests than of new discoveries. Therefore, they are much more interested in scientific conflicts than in consensus. They have concentrated on the sociology of particular fields rather than on science in general and have only employed quantitative techniques in rare cases.

As has been pointed out, these differences are related to differences in the intellectual background and professional functions of the two groups. The Americans are professionally trained sociologists working at graduate departments. They have intellectual contacts with historians and philosophers of science who have sociological interests, but professionally they are clearly separated from them. In Britain the definition of who is a sociologist is much looser. Many of the British were trained in science and philosophy and became sociologists after the completion of their formal training. British sociologists of science teach mainly undergraduates and are frequently attached to interdisciplinary units.

Historically, the American tradition preceded the British one, and part of the difference between them is probably due to the fact that the British tradition emerged at a time when the American tradition was in a state of transition and when structural functionalism was also being strongly criticized in the United States. Thus some American sociologists from the younger generation (and a number of American historians with a strong interest in sociology) are sympathetic to the British views, but theirs is only a philosophical sympathy. In their research work they follow the local, rather than the British, style. Therefore, the difference between the two traditions is not merely a generational one, and there remains a difference even if one compares scholars of the same generation from the two countries.

The preceding explanation of the differences between the styles of work, preferences in problem choice, and philosophical views of science does not imply any evaluation of the relative merits of the two national traditions. Although they are often presented, especially in Britain, as mutually exclusive, they are actually parallel or even complementary traditions. It is not less interesting to investigate institutional characteristics (norms, rewards, formal and informal social structures) common to all scientific fields than to investigate social characteristics peculiar to certain fields, or events, in science; it is as legitimate to ask questions about consensus as about conflicts in science; and it is difficult to tell whether it is more important to concentrate on how the intellectual characteristics common to all the sciences influence the behavior of scientists or on how the social characteristics of scientists affect the contents of their work.

This chapter illustrates the complementarity rather than mutual exclusiveness of these questions. It deals with scientific conflict and the effects of the social characteristics of scientists on the contents of their work—questions typical to the British tradition. However, what is said here cannot be construed as supporting the philosophical views preferred in Britain, namely, that scientific views are determined by social ("external") conditions, rather than by the internal logic of scientific traditions and inherent characteristics of the phenomenal world, and that permanent conflict, rather than the formation of consensus, is the typical process of science. The chapter only shows that in this particular case the problems and approaches preferred by members of two groups of sociologists were socially determined; it says nothing about the origins of those problems and approaches. If we were to inquire into origins, we would find that they are internally determined.

The problems and approaches from which members of both groups made their choices were derived from ideas available to them in the sociological and philosophical traditions of the 1960s. These were the structural-functional approach as developed by Talcott Parsons and others (including Robert Merton); the attempts at correcting, modifying, or replacing that approach which emerged in the 1950s in the wake of the comprehensive effort to develop structural-functional theory; and survey research and analysis as initiated by Samuel Stouffer and Paul Lazarsfeld. In philosophy, Karl Popper provided a concept of science that aptly characterized what has been common to all scientific fields since the seventeenth century and therefore was excellently suited for the study of science as a social institution. But for the same reason it also presented an obvious challenge to the next generation of philosophers of science—such as P. K. Feyerabend, T. S. Kuhn, Imre Lakatos, and Stephen Toulmin—who found Popper's concept of science insufficient for the analysis of scientific change and of the differences between scientific fields. Their attempts to create a more historicist view of science led to a revival of interest in the sociology of knowledge of Durkheim and Mannheim. Without this background of the internal history of sociological and philosophical ideas, sociological interpretations would make little sense, since they could not explain how the interests of these groups actually led to the creation of the particular ideas characteristic to them. In other words, without the existence of a common background that has an "internal" logical structure and determines the available alternatives, the choices made by the two groups are incomprehensible. A historian concentrating on the emergence of present issues and approaches in the sociology of science (and uninterested in the question of why some people, or groups, chose some rather than other issues and approaches) could easily depict the present state of the field as characterized by internalist doctrine. Such a presentation would also be a consensual one and would assume the existence of common norms, since it would place controversies into a commonly agreed-on framework of problems and would discuss any divergences of view as transitory states to be eliminated by further investigation conducted according to recognized norms.

Of course, both the externalist-conflictual and internalist-consensual presentation would be partial ones. In this field, as in other fields of science, we have two kinds of processes. One is the ongoing emergence of groups devoted to the exploration of a particular issue or of a particular set of hypotheses. The emergence and composition of these groups are likely to be influenced by social conditions, although such groups will usually work on problems derived from existing traditions or combination of traditions (Ben-David 1960; Ben-David and Collins 1966). The relationship to other groups working in the same or related areas will often be determined by competition for scarce resources and rewards (such as recognition, appointments to positions, research grants, or honors). Especially in nonexpanding systems, this competition may lead to conflicts, such as attempts by the well-established groups to suppress new ones, or attempts by the new groups to overthrow well-established ones. Although in the large majority of cases the conflict is over resources and rewards, and not about mutually exclusive explanations of the same phenomena, such groups will often try to present their views as a contradiction and refutation of those of competing groups and thus justify their claims for withholding rewards and resources from the latter.[4] Such conflicts may vary in intensity but are usually of short duration. Typically, they are resolved by recognition of the new field as a new specialty—that is, by growing differentiation in the scientific division of labor rather than by revolutionary takeovers or counterrevolutionary suppression (see, for example, Zloczower 1960). In other words, conflicts are resolved by the formation of a new consensus.

Thus there is in science a second, long-term process that counteracts short-term conflicts. This long-term process determines the selection of ideas, problems, and solutions for incorporation into the traditions of given scientific fields. It involves several groups and generations, some of whom are neutral toward the original conflict of interests. Their attitudes toward the contribution of the competing groups, therefore, will be determined by the utility of those contributions for the rational explanation of the phenomena in question. Of course, neither the norms of selection nor the definition of the phenomena will be quite stable, but, nevertheless, when people act in contexts related to

4. This interpretation of scientific conflict evidently differs from those prevalent in current philosophical literature (Kuhn 1970; Lakatos 1970) and accepted by most sociologists—that literature tends to take the metaphysical reasons given for the conflicts at their face value and to regard them as the basis of the conflict. According to the present interpretation, differences in problem choice and approach are often stated in metaphysical terms to make the differences *appear* reconcilable and thus to justify a conflict that may be useful as a weapon in the fight for resources. Evidence in support of this interpretation is provided by cases in which innovations giving rise to metaphysical conflict in one place are accommodated without a trace of such conflict at another. Thus psychoanalysis was assimilated into American academic psychology without any of the conflicts raised in continental Europe; another example is the difference between the early history of bacteriology in Europe compared to its history in the United States and Japan.

this selection process (such as refereeing papers; reviewing published work; awarding grants, positions, or prizes; or scanning the literature of adjacent fields for information and ideas useful for their own research), they will tend to adopt much more universalistic criteria and will try to act more dispassionately than when competing for resources and recognition with other groups (Ben-David 1977).

The existence of such a process of selection is also observable in the brief history of the two national traditions described in this chapter. Evaluation of individual contributions is often taking place according to criteria common to both traditions, and evaluation eventually influences practice. Thus reviews of literature have been critical of the absence of empirical studies of the relationship between social processes and cognitive development in science (Mulkay 1977a, p. 136). It seems that such criticism is having an effect on research, and current work is increasingly turning away from programmatic statements and toward empirical investigations. These investigations will be judged on the basis of their originality, internal consistency, and cogency of their evidence—an evaluation process that will probably lead to gradual convergence of judgments about the contributions of the two schools.

However, we must keep in mind that the relationship between short-term and long-term processes in science is a purely historical one. There is no law of nature, or of progress, to ensure that the sectarian spirit of conflict that arises in some scientific groups will be inevitably subjected to a selection process according to the traditional norms of science. It took the efforts and inventiveness of many generations to establish an institutional mechanism in natural science that has worked more or less as here outlined since the seventeenth century (without, however, eliminating quack medicine, magic or astrology, or—under appropriate conditions—phenomena such as Lysenkoism). In the social sciences the mechanism works much less smoothly, and attempts at sectarian closure of schools is an everyday occurrence on the social scientific scene, as exemplified by psychoanalytic, Marxist, and similar groups. Competition capable of transcending conflict of interests between particular groups is no more automatically ensured in the realm of scientific ideas than in the realm of politics and economics. There will always be groups that prefer monopoly and some that will only have a chance when granted monopolistic privileges, and such groups will do whatever they can do to obtain it.

References

Allen, T. J. "Communication Channels in the Transfer of Technology." *Industrial Management Review*, 8 (1966): 87–98.

Allen, T. J., and S. I. Cohen. "Information Flow in Research and Development Laboratories." *Administrative Science Quarterly* 14 (1969): 12–19.

Barber, B. *Science and the Social Order.* New York: Free Press, 1952.
————. "Review of T. S. Kuhn. 'The Structure of Scientific Revolutions.'" *American Sociological Review* 28 (1963): 298–299.
Barnes, B. *Scientific Knowledge and Sociological Theory.* London: Routledge & Kegan Paul, 1974.
Barnes, B., and R. G. A. Dolby. "The Scientific Ethos: A Deviant Viewpoint." *European Journal of Sociology* 2 (1970): 3–25.
Ben-David, J. "Roles and Innovations in Medicine." *American Journal of Sociology* 65 (1960): 557–568. [This volume, chap. 1.]
————. *The Scientist's Role in Society: A Comparative Study.* Englewood Cliffs, N.J.: Prentice-Hall, 1971.
————. "Organization, Social Control, and Cognitive Change in Science." In J. Ben-David and T. N. Clark (eds.), *Culture and Its Creators.* Chicago: University of Chicago Press, 1977. [This volume, chap. 15.]
Ben-David, J., and R. Collins. "Social Factors in the Origins of a New Science: The Case of Psychology." *American Sociological Review* 31 (1966): 451–465. [This volume, chap. 2.]
Bernal, J. D. *The Social Function of Science.* London: Routledge & Kegan Paul, 1939.
Bloor, D. *Knowledge and Social Imagery.* London: Routledge & Kegan Paul, 1976.
Blume, S. S., and R. Sinclair. "Chemists in British Universities: A Study of the Reward System in Science." *American Sociological Review* 38 (1973): 126–138.
Breiger, R. L. "Career Attributes and Network Structure: A Block Model Study of a Biomedical Research Speciality." *American Sociological Review* 41 (1976): 117–135.
Chubin, D. "The Conceptualization of Scientific Specialties." *Sociological Quarterly* 17 (1976): 448–476.
Clark, T. N. "Institutionalization of Innovations in Higher Education: Four Models." *Administrative Science Quarterly* 13 (1968): 1–25.
————. *Prophets and Patrons: The French University and the Emergence of the Social Sciences.* Cambridge: Harvard University Press, 1973.
Cole, J. R., and S. Cole. *Social Stratification in Science.* Chicago: University of Chicago Press, 1973.
Cole, J. R., and H. Zuckerman. "The Emergence of a Scientific Specialty: The Self-Exemplifying Case of the Sociology of Science." In L. A. Coser (ed.), *The Idea of Social Structure.* New York: Harcourt Brace Jovanovich, 1975.
Crane, D. "Social Structure in a Group of Scientists: A Test of the 'Invisible College' Hypothesis." *American Sociological Review* 36 (1969): 335–352.
————. *Invisible Colleges: Diffusion of Knowledge in Scientific Communities.* Chicago: University of Chicago Press, 1972.
Crawford, S. "Informal Communication Among Scientists in Sleep Research." *Journal of the American Society for Information Science* 22 (1971): 301–310.
Davis, K. *Human Society.* New York: Macmillan, 1949.
Dolby, R. G. A. "The Sociology of Knowledge in Natural Science." *Science Studies* 1 (1971): 3–21.
Fisher, C. S. "The Death of a Mathematical Theory: A Study in the Sociology of Knowledge." *Archive for History of Exact Science* 3 (1966): 137–59.

Gaston, J. *Originality and Competition in Science.* Chicago: University of Chicago Press, 1973.

——. *The Reward System in British and American Science.* New York: Wiley-Interscience, 1978.

Glaser, B. G. *Organizational Scientists.* Indianapolis: Bobbs-Merrill, 1964.

Gordon, G., and S. Marquis. "Freedom, Visibility of Consequences and Scientific Innovation." *American Journal of Sociology* 72 (1966): 95–202.

Griffith, B. C., and N. C. Mullins. "Coherent Social Groups in Scientific Change." *Science* 177 (1972): 959–64.

Griffith, B. C., et al. "The Structure of Scientific Literatures. II: Toward a Macro- and Microstructure for Science." *Science Studies* 4 (1974): 339–65.

Hagstrom, W. O. *The Scientific Community,* New York: Basic Books, 1965.

Holton, G. "Models for Understanding the Growth and Excellence of Scientific Research." In S. R. Graubard and G. Holton (eds.), *Excellence and Leadership in a Democracy.* New York: Columbia University Press, 1962.

Kaplan, N. "Some Organizational Factors Affecting Creativity." *IRE Transactions on Engineering Management* EM-7 (1960): 24–30.

——. "Organization: Will It Choke or Promote the Growth of Science?" In K. Hill (ed.), *The Management of Scientists.* Boston: Beacon Press, 1964.

King, M. D. "Reason, Tradition and the Progressiveness of Science." *History and Theory* 10 (1971): 3–32.

Kornhauser, W. (with the assistance of W. O. Hagstrom). *Scientists in Industry.* Berkeley and Los Angeles: University of California Press, 1962.

Krantz, D. "Do You Know What Your Neighbors Are Doing? A Study of Scientific Communication in Europe." *International Journal of Psychology* 5 (1970): 221–226.

——. "The Separate Worlds of Operant and Non-operant Psychology." *Journal of Applied Behavior Analysis* 4 (1971): 61–70.

Kuhn, T. S. *The Structure of Scientific Revolutions.* Chicago: University of Chicago Press, 1962.

Lakatos, I. "Falsification and the Methodology of Scientific Research Programmes." In I. Lakatos and A. Musgrave (eds.), *Criticism and the Growth of Knowledge.* Cambridge: Cambridge University Press, 1970.

Marcson, S. *The Scientist in American Industry.* New York: Harper & Row, 1960.

Martins, H. "The Kuhnian 'Revolution' and Its Implications for Sociology." In A. H. Nossiter, T. Hanson, and S. Rokkan (eds.), *Imagination and Precision in Political Analysis.* London: Faber, 1971.

Merton, R. K. "Priorities in Scientific Discovery: A Chapter in the Sociology of Science." *American Sociological Review* 22 (1957): 635–659.

——. *Science, Technology and Society in Seventeenth-Century England* [1938a]. New York: Harper & Row, 1970.

——. "The Normative Structure of Science" [1942]. In *The Sociology of Science.* Chicago: University of Chicago Press, 1973a.

——. "Paradigm for the Sociology of Knowledge" [1945]. In *The Sociology of Science.* Chicago: University of Chicago Press, 1973b.

——. "Science and the Social Order" [1938b]. In *The Sociology of Science.* Chicago: University of Chicago Press, 1973c.

Merton, R. K., and J. Gaston. (eds.). *The Sociology of Science in Europe.* Carbondale: Southern Illinois University Press, 1977.

Mulkay, M. J. "Some Aspects of Growth in the Natural Sciences." *Social Research* 36 (1969): 22–52.

———. "The Sociology of Science in Britain." In R. K. Merton and J. Gaston (eds.), *The Sociology of Science in Europe.* Carbondale: Southern Illinois University Press, 1977*a*.

———. "Sociology of the Scientific Research Community." In I. Spiegel-Rösing and D. de S. Price (eds.), *Science, Technology and Society.* Beverly Hills, Calif.: Sage, 1977*b*.

Mullins, N. C. "The Development of a Scientific Specialty: The Phage Group and the Origin of Molecular Biology." *Minerva* 10 (1972): 51–82.

———. *Theories and Theory Groups in Contemporary American Sociology.* New York: Harper & Row, 1973.

Mullins, N. C., et al. "The Group Structure of Co-Citation Clusters: A Comparative Study." *American Sociological Review* 42 (1977): 552–562.

Needham, J. (ed.). *Science at the Crossroads: Papers Presented to the International Congress of the History of Science and Technology.* London: Cass, 1931.

Pelz, D., and F. Andrews. *Scientists in Organizations.* New York: Wiley, 1966.

Polanyi, M. *The Logic of Liberty: Reflexions and Rejoinders.* London: Routledge & Kegan Paul, 1951.

Price, D. de S. *Science Since Babylon.* New Haven: Yale University Press, 1961.

———. *Little Science, Big Science.* New York: Columbia University Press, 1963.

Shepard, H. A. "Nine Dilemmas in Industrial Research." *Administrative Science Quarterly* 1 (1956): 295–309.

Shils, E. "Tradition, Ecology and Institution in the History of Sociology." *Daedalus* 99 (1970): 760–825.

Small, H. G., and B. C. Griffith "The Structure of Scientific Literatures. I: Identifying and Graphing Specialties." *Science Studies* 4 (1974): 17–40.

Stehr, N. "Zur Soziologie der Wissenschaftssoziologie." In N. Stehr and R. König (eds.), *Wissenschaftssoziologie.* Opladen, West Germany: Westdeutscher Verlag, 1975.

Storer, N. *The Social System of Science.* New York: Holt, Rinehart and Winston, 1966.

Whitley, R. D. "Communication Nets in Science: Status and Citation Patterns in Animal Physiology." *Sociological Review* 17 (1969): 219–34.

Zloczower, A. *Career Opportunities and the Growth of Scientific Discovery in 19th-Century Germany, with Special Reference to Physiology.* Jerusalem: Hebrew University, 1960. [Now published by Arno Press, New York, 1981.]

Sociology of Scientific Knowledge 21

I

Sociology of science began to be recognized as a specialty within sociology in the 1960s. During the decade most of the work was concentrated in the United States and dealt primarily with problems of competition, allocation of rewards, social control, and stratification in science. A second major interest was the exploration of communication networks in science, especially as a reflection of the rise and decline of scientific specialties. The interest in historical-comparative studies of the emergence and growth of modern science and its organization in different societies which characterized the field in its earlier stages became peripheral during the sixties, because the central tendency in sociological research favored themes which could be investigated by quantitative methods.

All this changed drastically during the seventies as a result of changes in the location and uses made of sociology of science and in the characteristics of the practitioners in the field. Throughout the sixties there was much concern with the scientific and technological backwardness of Europe compared with the United States. This was widely reported in the press and debated in the OECD and houses of legislature. Civil servants, politicians, and scientific statesmen were all interested in sociology of science as a field of potential use in the reformation of scientific institutions and the acceleration of scientific and technological growth in Europe.

This practical, "lay" interest had several repercussions on the development of the field. It greatly facilitated the establishment of special institutional arrangements for research and teaching in the sociology, economics, and politics of science, such as the Science Policy Research Unit at the University of Sussex and the Science Studies Unit at the University of Edinburgh, and attracted to the field a number of younger scholars trained in experimental science, philosophy, or history of science. Because of the practical and extra-disciplinary origins of much of the interests in, and of some of the practitioners of, the field, the new institutions were usually conceived as interdisciplinary ventures. They were institutions for the "social study of science" rather than the "sociology of science." Thus, a significant part of sociology of science in Europe—especially in Britain—has been practiced in interdisciplinary units rather than departments of sociology.

From the perspective of this largely interdisciplinary and policy-oriented background, the interests of sociologists of science in the reward system, norms, and stratification in science appeared as narrow and parochial. It was disappointing that much of sociology of science was the sociology of the scientific profession and did not deal with the contents of science and matters of science policy. During the seventies this dissatisfaction with the state of the field assumed a critical tone. This was probably related to the emergence of critical and hostile attitudes toward science and higher education in general, but the contents of the criticism were determined by problems immanent to sociology in general and the sociology of science in particular. The criticism focused on two issues: the alleged deficiencies of the structural-functional approach in sociology of science, particularly of the use of "scientific norms" as a key concept in the description and interpretation of the institutional framework of science (Mulkay 1969; Barnes and Dolby 1970), and the absence of a sociology of scientific knowledge (Barnes 1974; Bloor 1976; Mulkay 1979). It is with the latter issue that this paper is concerned.[1]

II

The sociology of scientific knowledge became a subject of controversy in the 1970s. Prior to this sociology of science was to a large extent the sociology of the scientific profession. This is not to say that sociologists had not dealt previously with problems of scientific knowledge. Traditional themes in the sociology of science have been the conditions of scientific discovery and

1. There are a number of up-to-date surveys and bibliographies of the literature on sociology of science (Merton and Gaston 1977; Lécuyer 1978; Mulkay and Milic 1980; Gaston 1979), and there is no point adding another one to them. Therefore, this paper is not intended to convey an exhaustive and balanced picture of the field but rather to focus on controversial issues concerning the sociology of scientific knowledge, which in my view is of central importance to the field. I have dealt with these issues and with debates about the norms of science in several recent papers (Ben-David 1977, 1978).

I am grateful to Gad Freudenthal for a discussion of the part of the paper dealing with the sociology of knowledge.

invention, namely, what social types are likely to be innovators (Gilfillan 1935), the description and explanation of independent multiple discoveries (Ogburn and Thomas 1922; Merton 1973*b*); the exploration of the causes of resistance to discoveries (Stern 1959; Barber 1961); the importance of scientists moving from field to field (role-hybrids) in the creation of new fields of science (Ben-David 1960; Ben-David and Collins 1966); and the role of technology and technologists in the generation of scientific ideas (Zilsel 1942).

Still, sociologists of science were careful to distinguish their field of interest from the "sociology of knowledge," because the tradition which went under that name was based on epistemological theories and empirical investigations unacceptable to the majority of sociologists. The sociology of knowledge tradition assumed that all ideas, irrespective of their truth, were socially conditioned. According to the Durkheimian version of this theory, the basic categories of thought, such as the conceptions of space, time, and causality, are rooted in language which reflects primarily social relationships. For example, recurrent social activities such as religious festivals create a cyclical conception of time; classifications of natural objects reflect the division of the tribe into clans (Durkheim and Mauss 1903 [1963]; Durkheim 1912 [1954]). In the Mannheimian version of sociology of knowledge, the determining conditions are the perspectives of different groups, such as social classes, generations, or occupational groups. These perspectives are derived from the social location and interests of the groups and determine the way members of different groups conceive of history and politics (Mannheim 1936, 1953). Neither Durkheim nor Mannheim considered that their sociology implied scientific relativism. Social determination of thought does not necessarily imply inadequate or erroneous thought, only a partial perspective on reality, which is correct or at least more or less adequate for the purpose in a given situation. Furthermore, according to both, this limitation can be transcended under social conditions which require such transcendence. Thus, according to Durkheim, advanced division of labor and intercultural and international communication give rise to a situation in which classifications of things and definitions of categories reflecting the social patterns of particular groups become inadequate, since they now have to serve as the basis of communication between many groups. Therefore, thought and language have to be reorganized according to universally valid logical categories, and things have to be classified according to immanent principles transcending the particular circumstances of different societies (Durkheim 1954). Mannheim—who restricts his sociology of knowledge to social and political thought—manages to maintain the possibility of an objectively valid social science by rooting it in the interests and perspective of a particular social group: the intellectuals who, recruited from all classes, ages, religions, and, by descent, occupational groups, have to establish a common universalistic frame of discourse in order to communicate with each other (Mannheim 1936). Thus, in both cases, the emergence of "objective" scientific thought is determined by the emergence of an appropriate social structure or group. Once emerged, however, it develops its own logic of universal, and not only contextual, validity.

The reason for the rejection of these theories by sociologists of science was that the empirical evidence on covariation between social base and the structure of knowledge was never satisfactorily established and because none of the theories of sociology of knowledge contained a satisfactory explanation of how, by means of what mechanisms, knowledge is determined by the social base (Merton 1973a). The rejection of sociology of knowledge seemed also preferable from the point of view of the epistemologies prevailing among sociologists, according to which "rationality" as conceived by scientists is a sufficient basis for the acceptance or rejection of theories, requiring no further social underpinning. This, rather than Marx's and Mannheim's exemption of science from social determination—as asserted in recent literature—was the reason for the rejection of "sociology of knowledge" by most sociologists. However, only the Durkheimian and Mannheimian doctrines, based on a sociologistic epistemology according to which forms of thought are determined by social structure and group, were rejected. Other approaches to sociology of knowledge, including sociology of science, were not.

Thus, sociologists were quite willing to hypothesize about the social conditions of the selection or rejection of problems or themes, or the flow of interdisciplinary influences. They stopped short, however, of attributing to social conditions the determination of the conceptual and logical structure of scientific arguments. The possibility of the derivation of scientific ideas from social conditions in individual cases was admitted, but these were not regarded as sociologically more instructive than the apocryphal story about Newton and the apple (Ben-David 1971).

The original debate on sociology of knowledge took place in the thirties and forties, first mainly in France and Germany (Aron 1950). Its conclusions were summed up in 1945 by Merton in a paper which was considered by most sociologists as definitive (Merton 1973a). After that date and until the late sixties—that is, during the formative period of sociology of science—Durkheimian and Mannheimian sociology of knowledge was of little interest to sociologists. That is why this kind of sociology of knowledge was virtually disregarded throughout this time.

Sociology of knowledge was kept alive mainly outside the mainstream of sociology. The Marxist and Mannheimian traditions were cultivated by Herbert Marcuse in the United States and by Jürgen Habermas in Germany (Marcuse 1964; Habermas 1968, 1972), and Durkheimian sociology of knowledge was maintained in France by historians of non-European and ancient civilizations (Granet 1930; Vernant 1965) and was revived in England by the anthropologist Mary Douglas (1975).

During the seventies, this tradition exerted increasing influence in the sociology of science, particularly in Britain. The confluence of the rise of "anti-positivistic" trends, such as Marxism, phenomenology, and ethnomethodology in sociology, and the rise of relativistic constructivist philosophies of science provided the intellectual background of this turn of interests. This was reinforced by the student revolt and attendant attacks on science and scientism and by the influx into the rapidly extending field of sociology of science in Europe of people initially trained in other fields, such as philosophy, history of science, or natural sciences. These latter were attracted to Durkheimian and Mannheimian sociologies of knowledge because these sociologies seemed to throw new light on science as a cognitive tradition. The fact that they were probably unaware of past disappointments with these sociologies of knowledge perhaps increased their confidence in the prospects of a revival of these theories.

Much of the resulting literature has been programmatic. The argument put forward is that

> sociological understanding must start with an appreciation of actors' normal practice as it is, and of its inadequacies as they themselves define them. He [the sociologist] must make action intelligible through detailed and extensive insight into the nature of actors' perspectives, their categories and typifications, the assumptions which mediate their response, the models which organize their cognition, the rules they normally follow [Barnes, 1974: 43].

There is no difference in this respect between science, myth, or ideology. Arguments and evidence only make sense within these partly verbalized and partly nonverbalized traditions evolved by particular groups.

This is not to say that there are no criteria of judgment. Within each tradition it is quite possible to decide what is right or wrong or good or bad science. (Also, what is good or bad myth or magic?) But one has to beware of accepting at face value the formalities of scientific procedure and judgment as they appear in published scientific papers or reports of referees. The objective and impersonal tone of these and their insistence on the universal validity of evidence and arguments are, according to the new sociologists of knowledge, misleading, since the concepts and methods which are employed in these documents have "meaning only when interpreted by the members of actual social groupings. The way in which these interpretations are realised depends on the outcome of contingent negotiations among those members" (Mulkay 1979: 91).

These arguments are explicitly based on philosophies of science which deny the existence of pure observational language and assert that "facts" are determined by theory; further, that there is no perfect overlap between a theoretical system and any given set of empirical observations. This means that all observations can be explained by more than one theory, and the choice between them depends on contingent preference. However, this philosophy does not imply that the "subjective" elements in this process have to be social ones. The assumption of the new sociology of knowledge that they are, in fact, always social is—as Freudenthal has pointed out—the result of the following confusion: Since the decision of what theory to accept always depends on considerations connected with the particular case in question, there is a process of deliberation which involves debate, examination of evidence from different points of view, voicing of preferences, and the like. This is not unlike court procedure, which frequently involves conflicting interpretations of evidence and law. Some sociologists use the fitting term "negotiation" as a description of this process and assume that, since this is by definition a social process, its outcome must be socially determined. This conclusion is, of course, a non sequitur. The fact that negotiation is a social process does not mean that its outcome is determined by social conditions or considerations. A group of scientists trying to find the best solution to a problem are likely to search for intellectual criteria, such as economy and scope of explanation and consistency with other theories, in choosing among possible theories (Freudenthal 1980). Even errors may be due to faulty cognitive strategies (Nisbett and Ross 1980) rather than socially generated bias.

The claim for the necessity of a sociology of scientific knowledge can be somewhat strengthened by the argument that since there are no rules of logic which are necessarily true and "all criteria of truth are relative to a local culture" (Hesse 1980: 42; see also p. 39), there has to be a contextual sociological interpretation of every case of scientific judgment. The "rationality" of the judgment is not sufficient, since the very choice of rational criteria and the kind of rationality chosen only make sense in a given context. What is rational to a physicist may not be rational to a clergyman, and the behavior of both can be understood only in their social contexts. This led to the proposal of a so-called strong program of sociology of scientific knowledge. The essence of this is that causal explanation of the same sociological kind is required of the emergence and acceptance of any belief irrespective of "truth or falsity, rationality or irrationality, success or failure" (Bloor 1976: 4–5).

Closer examination of this argument shows that it is sociologically irrelevant. There may be good reasons for the rejection of extraempirical or extrasocial grounds of rationality, but this alters very little the practical need for some kind of rationality in judgments. Indeed, this is admitted by the proponents of the strong program. Thus, according to Barnes, not

> any collection of utterances at all may be treated as sociologically equivalent. Institutionalized belief systems are a special set: they are all capable of being readily transmitted in socialization. Actors are not of limitless plasticity; they cannot be socialized into operating with any collection of beliefs or utterances. [The] . . . very general point, that there are limits to the possibility of human thought, is doubtless correct [Barnes 1974: 43].

Thus, the insistence that scientific knowledge is as much influenced by social circumstances as any other kind of knowledge goes hand in hand with the qualification that these circumstances do not determine the validity of the knowledge in question. And although the rules to judge validity are said to be highly context-dependent, it is admitted that there are "limits to the possibility of human thought," which implies the admission of some standards which are not socially determined.

The point is made even clearer by Mary Hesse.

> The strong thesis does not imply . . . that there is no distinction between the various kinds of rational rules adopted in a society on the one hand and their conventions on the other. There may be hierarchies of rules and conventions, in which some conventions may be justified by argument in terms of some rational rules, and some subsets of those rules in terms of others [Hesse 1980: 56].

This means that for practical purposes the strong thesis has to be considerably weakened, and the principle that the same causal explanation has to be given to all beliefs, irrespective of rationality or irrationality, cannot be consistently maintained. Within a scientific culture—which today includes practically all societies—the acceptance of one scientific theory in preference to another for such rational reasons as greater economy or wider applicability does not require further explanation, since these are relatively fixed criteria applicable to all cases. Beyond these, there are a great variety of models prevailing at different times in different fields, which are being drawn upon for the solution of scientific problems. The choice between these and the combination and manipulation of them is, so to speak, the art of science. Although this process may involve give-and-take and controversy, it does not involve the negotiation of new rules in every case. This is a process of interpretation and search for good fit within boundaries laid down by available models, somewhat like finding the proper precedents and interpretations in case law (Gilbert 1976).

The sociological analysis of particular cases will rarely reveal anything about the causes of the adoption of the criteria of judgment, since those causes lie back in the past, at the point when science in general, or a specialty in particular, was first institutionalized. Therefore, the explanation of each particular case has to be based primarily on the rationale of the traditions of a given field, and science in general.

On the other hand, cases in which the accepted logic of science, or of a given field, is overridden in favor of outside and, from a scientific point of view, irrational considerations (such as political ideology, opportunism, or bias, as in the Lysenko case), require specific explanations based on a variety of circumstances. Thus, the symmetry between the explanation of rational and nonrational behavior in science, as required by the "strong program," cannot be maintained, and the argument that the new philosophical positions logically imply the need for a "strong program" of sociology of knowledge cannot be accepted.[2]

III

This review of the sociological implications of the new philosophies provides some criteria for the classification and evaluation of the research carried out under the auspices of the new sociology of knowledge or used by the school as fitting into its program.

Three lines of research can be distinguished: case studies of scientific discoveries and controversies about them, the purpose of which is to show the role of extraneous nonscientific influences on the generation of scientific theories and the instability and context-dependence of the cognitive criteria employed in scientific theories; studies purporting to establish a systematic relationship between the social location of the scientist and the type of theory adopted by him; and attempts to find common features between science and other systems of belief, such as myth or magic.

The first type of investigation has been partly discussed above in connection with the debate on scientific norms. Some of these studies focus on marginal phenomena, such as the Velikovsky affair, parapsychology, or the identification of UFOs (Mulkay 1969; Collins and Pinch 1979; Westrum 1977). Others deal with segments of the developments of certain fields, showing how people try to orient themselves in a still-developing area such as the early stages of the exploration of gravitational waves or moon exploration (H. Collins 1975; Mitroff 1974). They illustrate processes of negotiation but not how negotiations are eventually concluded. Here I shall discuss some case studies of a third type, which include also the conclusion of controversies and the emergence of a new consensus.

These are the studies of Forman on quantum mechanics in Germany in the twenties, Frankel's study on the reception of wave mechanics in the early decades of the nineteenth century in France and England, and Wynne's study of the rejection of the J Phenomenon in physics in the 1920s (Forman 1971; Frankel 1976; Wynne 1976). The first two studies were undertaken as efforts to investigate the Kuhnian model of scientific revolution and were designed to demonstrate the importance of extrascientific, general social and cultural factors in the rise and adoption of fundamentally new ("revolutionary") approaches to the investigation of the phenomena in question. Neither of the cases does, in fact, establish such influence. Although Forman shows that de-

2. Indeed, this is more than implied in Hesse's discussion of the "strong thesis." "The 'strong' thesis has not become so weak as to be indistinguishable from something any rationalist or realist could accept" (1980: 57).

velopments in quantum mechanics leading to the discovery of the uncertainty principle were preceded by Spengler's relativistic views on science, there is only the weakest and most circumstantial evidence of the existence of any specific link between philosophical view and discoveries in quantum mechanics. It is more likely that Spengler's views were influenced by the existence of mathematics based on different axiomatic systems. As to the adoption of the new theories by the community of physicists, the evidence flatly contradicts any explanation of external causation. Although the new theories were found philosophically objectionable by some members of the physics community, they were recognized without any attempt at suppression or distortion. If there was "negotiation" here, it was guided by purely internal intellectual considerations.

The case of wave theory is even more unequivocal. In that case there is no suggestion of any external causation, except the possibility that the discoverer of the new theory, Fresnel, was an outsider (he lived in the provinces and worked as an engineer) among physicists, which might have made him more open-minded toward the unorthodox wave theory (the orthodoxy was corpuscularianism). This is a reasonable and old sociological hypothesis of some value—which, however, does not pretend to explain anything about the contents of the discovery, only the propensity to think in unorthodox ways. As far as the acceptance of the new theory is concerned, recognition was granted without delay on the basis of a crucial experiment, and the progress of the new theory was unimpeded in spite of the attempts of some persons with lifetime commitment to corpuscularianism to preserve what could be preserved of their own theories.

The main point is not that it is erroneous to quote these cases as examples supporting the idea about the importance of contingent factors in the outcome of "negotiations" about the recognition of scientific discoveries. This error is so obvious that it cannot do any harm, and rationalists can easily enlist these studies in their repertoire. The main harm is that by trying to attribute to all kinds of contingent social factors an importance they did not have in order to fit them for the strong program (which proscribes rationality as an explanation), attention is focused on the philosophical question of rationality (which has to be decided anyway without assistance from sociology), and the way is barred to useful and important lines of investigation suggested by these two studies. Thus, it seems that sociologically the most interesting observations are that the two cases show striking parallels. The criteria of rationality adopted in both cases were by and large similar. Personal philosophies and metaphysical views of nature in neither case were allowed to influence the recognition of discoveries, and recognition in both cases was accorded on the basis of purely internal criteria. This means that—at least at the centers of world physics—there had been considerable stability of criteria of rationality by the early nineteenth century, allowing intellectual revolutions to occur without the need, so to speak, of changing the constitution. This raises questions such as when this kind of rationality was institutionalized (Ben-David 1977); to what extent this kind of rationality was institutionalized also on the peripheries of the community of physicists, and in disciplines other than physics. Thus, Frankel suggests that British physicists did not apply the rules as strictly as did the French because science in England was less professionalized than in France (Frankel 1976); and the question of whether metaphysical considerations should influence scientific decisions was actually a subject of debate in the USSR in the twenties (Joravsky 1961; Graham 1974). These questions are interesting only as long as it is admitted that there is a difference between conduct according to principles of some scientific logic[3] and according to other, contingent considerations. If all the cases of conduct are reduced to "negotiations" reflecting a changing variety of considerations, then there is nothing left to compare, and every case becomes just another illustration of what its author or interpreter understands under the loose term of "negotiation" and of the alleged nonrationality of scientific judgment.

The J Phenomenon[4] discussed by Wynne (1976) is of interest because it deals with the rejection, rather than the acceptance, of a new idea. Wynne shows that in this case an idea was rejected, not as a result of any clear-cut evidence against it but on the grounds that its author, C. J. Barkla, adopted a theoretical approach and techniques of investigation, which appeared as unfruitful and unduly complicated by practically all the other physicists. The paper does not show that this decision was not "rational" in terms of the goals and criteria of judgment of the physics community but only that instead of admitting that this was a choice based on experience and intuition, physicists involved in or writing about the case made it appear as if the decision were taken on the basis of specific negative evidence (which, according to Wynne, was not available). This is an interesting observation, which links up with other observations about the ways scientific publications try to reconstruct the conclusions of their authors in a way that tries to eliminate all the traces of guesswork from the process (Medawar 1963) but, somewhat contrary to Wynne's interpretation, does not show that "this was not a scientifically determined standpoint." The considerations against Barkla—namely, that his approach was unduly complex, unpromising in terms of research results, technically clumsy, and not clearly stated or worked out by its author—were of a kind typical to the procedures of science in general and not the outcome of "negotiations" resulting in rules specific to the particular group of physicists involved in the research (Polanyi 1967).

To conclude, these studies of the processes of discovery and controversy

3. Even though the generality and stability of this logic may be open to debate.
4. This was a suggestion put forward by C. G. Barkla, a famous physicist, in the 1920s about the holistic organic nature of X-ray radiation. The suggestion was not developed into a theory by its author and was rejected by other physicists.

have provided increasingly rich and interesting descriptive material of these processes. But the sociological interpretation of this material has been held up by the attempt to use it for the purpose of illustrating the absence of consensual rules based on some kind of logic immanent to the problems investigated.[5]

The second kind of research in the sociology of scientific knowledge is that which tries to establish a systematic relationship between the social location of the researcher and the type of theory adopted by him. This attempt is, of course, directly influenced by the Marxian-Mannheimian tradition.

The original tradition sought to establish a relationship primarily between the interests and perspectives of social classes (peasants, workers, bourgeois, aristocrats) and political ideologies, such as different kinds of socialism, liberalism, and conservatism (Mannheim 1936, 1953). In this form, the theory cannot be applied to science. However, it has been shown quite convincingly that for some scientists there was a close relationship between their scientific interests and their general world view. Thus, it has been argued that the corpuscularian theory of matter composed of inert atoms moved by external force as the only causal principle of motion and rest was seen as lending support to a moderately conservative interpretation of the social order. Society, like nature, was seen to be ruled by laws imposed by God, which—in the case of society—had to be implemented by the church and the state. It is suggested that the need for such a moderately conservative ideology was one of the motives leading to the formulation of the Newtonian mechanical philosophy relying essentially on spiritual forces (M. Jacob 1976; J. Jacob 1977; Jacob and Jacob 1980). A similar kind of argument has been put forward about Karl Pearson's interest in biometrics, as determined by his involvement in the eugenics movement, which in turn is seen as an expression of the bid of the new professional classes for social leadership based on talent in England at around the turn of the century (Norton 1978; MacKenzie 1978).

These studies show that scientific theories can serve a variety of rather specific political and ideological purposes. They also suggest that these latter purposes might have had some influence on the choice of scientific problems (such as, in the case of Pearson, biometrics) and perhaps also on the scientific model preferred or proposed (such as Newton's idea that gravitation operates through immaterial forces). These are important contributions to the social history of science, but in order to evaluate their importance for sociology it must be asked whether the relationship between the social interests of scientists and their scientific ideas exists only in some or in all cases; and whether social interest or perspective initially associated with a theory, such as the association of a low-church Anglican and Whig perspective with corpuscularian

---

5. However, this tendency is not universally characteristic of the literature. For a useful exception, see Böhme (1977).

physics, continues to exist over time, thus perpetuating ideological basis in the guise of scientific tradition.

The answer to these questions is negative. All the case studies show that ideological bias is not a general phenomenon in science. Thus, while Norton and MacKenzie make a fairly convincing case about the ideological significance of Pearson's interest in statistics, MacKenzie's attempt to link Yule's statistical approach to an allegedly conservative temper and downwardly mobile upper-class origins is purely conjectural. And there is clear evidence in both cases that the relationship with ideology does not extend beyond the original stage. Newtonian physics was subsequently adopted by physicists of many religious and political persuasions. And the relationship among elitist socialism, eugenics, and correlational methods of statistics dissolved in the generation following that of Pearson (MacKenzie 1978).

No success can be claimed for the new Marxian-Mannheimian attempts to find a systematic (that is, a permanent and regular, not just occasional) relationship among macrosocial location, ideology, and scientific theory.[6] Indeed, there is little reason to expect that there should be such relationships. Even in the field of political ideology, where the existence of a link between social provenance and ideology is highly plausible, there is no evidence that there are actually such permanent links (beyond such trivialities that workers tend to prefer parties favoring workers and that capitalists usually shy away from anticapitalist parties). Political theories, like other theories, develop a logic and potentialities of their own, which can be used in an unpredictable variety of contexts. Furthermore, they become subject to "internal" elaboration and criticism by people who do not necessarily share the same social perspectives as the originators of the theories. Therefore, the relationship between location of persons and their theories is unstable and variable even in the social field and far more so in the natural sciences (Ben-David 1971; Elias 1971).

If systematic relationships are to be found between social location and scientific theory, they will have to be sought not in such macrosocial circumstances as class, race, or sex but in more microsocial conditions, such as educational background and professional affiliation, place of work, rank, and the way the work of particular scientists, or of entire specialties, is used by and depends for support on different publics. These things will probably have an effect on the selection of topics for research, and perhaps also on theoretical preferences. Of course, there are innumerable ways in which these factors can

6. See Hesse (1980: 55–56). Bloor's recent attempt (1981) to argue the contrary does not rest on new evidence. It only suggests an interesting new explanation of the correspondence between the classification of social and natural objects hypothesized by Durkheim and Mauss. The correspondence derives from the social uses made of images of nature, such as the use of corpuscularian theory for low church propaganda. But he does not show that such correspondence occurs regularly, or is likely to occur regularly, and that particular social uses of scientific theories are being widely shared and continued over generations.

be related to each other, and it is not easy to perceive any regularity in these relationships. But, for example, there is a great deal of plausibility in such ideas that the more mature a field is, the more likely it will be integrated with a variety of extradisciplinary uses and interests, such as practical applications, professional training, or even political interests (this is what German sociologists of science call "Finalisierung"; in English, "goal directedness" [Pfetsch 1979]). There are probably similar differences between fields, which may be integrated with extrascientific factors in different ways and degrees. It stands to reason that such developments and differences may affect the criteria of evaluation and the intellectual character of scientific inquiry. For example, the social sciences, which—as a rule—have a large lay audience interested in these fields for a variety of vaguely defined purposes of ideological and intellectual enjoyment and orientation in the world, tend to adopt a criterion of originality approaching that of literature and are much less exacting in terms of logical consistency and empirical testability than are the natural sciences (Ben-David 1975). Or the involvement of social scientists and psychologists in Project Head Start, which tried to combat educational backwardness through compensatory education, had apparently much to do with opposition to Jensen's hereditary views on intelligence (Harwood 1977).

The articulation of science or particular scientific fields with extrascientific publics and interests has been the subject of a great deal of discussion and inquiry (Blume 1974; Ezrahi 1971; Price 1965; Chubin and Studer 1978; Ravetz 1971; Weingart 1977; Van den Daele et al. 1977; Nelkin 1979). However, most of this literature has been concerned with the political control or political effects of scientific inquiry and has paid relatively little attention to the effects of these involvements with different publics on the style and structure of scientific inquiry.

The least controversial part of the new sociology of scientific knowledge is the attempt to investigate the similarities between science and other belief systems, such as myth, magic, and religion. This tendency links up with a long tradition in the history of science (Thorndike 1958) and in anthropology (Evans-Pritchard 1937), but in recent literature there has been a change of emphasis. Whereas previously the purpose was to detect the ways in which science was or became demarcated from these other areas of belief (Malinowski 1954), recently the purpose has been to show the positive input from these other systems of belief to science (Rattansi 1972), or the functional and structural correspondences among scientific, mythical, and magical thought (Horton 1967; Horton and Finnegan 1973; Holton 1973, 1978; Elkana 1977; O'Flaherty 1980). These raise interesting suggestions about the fluidity of the boundaries between different systems of knowledge and have advanced our understanding of nonscientific systems of knowledge and the transition from those systems to science (Horton 1967; Goody 1977). Like the case studies on the ideological involvement of science, they have also helped to place scientific developments in the context of general cultural and social history (Brush 1967). But so far this work has not been integrated into sociology of science in any systematic way.

Conclusion

The decade of the 1970s was a period of intensive debate and considerable development and change in the sociology of scientific knowledge. The new attention paid to the process of cognitive clarification and decisions has been also an advance in the sociology of scientific knowledge. But perhaps even more fruitful has been the revival of interest in historical and anthropological studies of scientific discoveries, controversies, and comparative systems of thought. While the so-called strong program of eliminating every internalist and rational explanation of scientific choice and judgment has been a failure, these studies have renewed the original historical and comparative interests of sociology of science. The 1960s trend of encapsulating the field into a narrow segment of sociological research thus has been reversed and the perspective reopened to philosophy, history, and anthropology. Paradoxically, utilization of classical sociological theory, which was disregarded by sociological research at the very point when it received one of its most mature formulations, by Talcott Parsons, has also been enhanced.[7]

No paper on recent developments in the sociology of science can ignore the "revolutionary" circumstances which prevailed in the field during the seventies. Those pressing for innovation frequently resorted to programmatic declarations about the need to replace the "old" structural-functional sociology of science with neo-Marxian, phenomenological, and ethnomethodological approaches. The assumption that the gap between old and new sociology of science was unbridgeable and that there had to be a choice between the two was underscored by the assertion that the new sociology of science was logically linked to new antipositivistic philosophies of science, just as the old one was wedded to positivism. This assertion was erroneous, as indeed should have been expected. If the relationship between methodological rules and empirical procedures is bound to be loose and open to different interpretations even in a narrow specialty, one can hardly expect to find a necessary relationship between general epistemological theories and an empirical subject like sociology.[8] In addition to being erroneous, this attempt to link sociological

7. There has been little interest among the new sociologists of science in Parsons. But there has been much interest in Durkheim (Bloor 1981), and the theoretical links between Parsons and such new sociological schools as phenomenology and ethnomethodology have been pointed out by R. Collins (1975).
8. This, of course, does not include philosophies such as those of Kuhn (1970) and Lakatos, which contain explicit sociological hypotheses about the emergence and growth of new fields.

investigations directly to philosophical theories was also frequently harmful, because it reduced many investigations to sheer attempts at demonstrating philosophical points (which did not require such demonstration) and barred the way to the formulation of empirically investigable problems.

The effect of philosophical and ideological commitments on sociology of science during the seventies has by now been largely spent. What has remained is a wealth of new observations which must be sifted out, conceptualized, and classified with the aid of sociological models capable of making sense of them.

References

Aron, R. 1950. *La sociologie allemande contemporaine*. Paris: Presses Universitaires de France.

Barber, B. 1961. "Resistance by scientists to scientific discovery." *Science* 134: 596–602.

Barnes, B. 1974. *Scientific Knowledge and Sociological Theory*. London: Routledge & Kegan Paul.

Barnes, B., and R. G. Dolby. 1970. "The scientific ethos: A deviant viewpoint." *European Journal of Sociology* 2: 3–25.

Ben-David, J. 1978. "Emergence of national traditions in the sociology of science," in J. Gaston (ed.), *The Sociology of Science*. San Francisco: Jossey-Bass. [This volume, chap. 20.]

———. 1977. "Organization, social control and cognitive change in science," in J. Ben-David and T. N. Clark (eds.), *Culture and Its Creators: Essays in Honor of Edward Shils*. Chicago: University of Chicago Press. [This volume, chap. 15.]

———. 1975. "Innovations and their recognition in social science." *History of Political Economy (HOPE)* 7: 434–55. [This volume, chap. 17.]

———. 1971. *The Scientist's Role in Society: A Comparative Study*. Englewood Cliffs, NJ: Prentice-Hall.

———. 1960. "Roles and innovations in Medicine." *American Journal of Sociology* 65: 557–68. [This volume chap. 1.]

Ben-David, J., and R. Collins. 1966. "Social factors in the origins of a new science: The case of psychology." *American Sociological Review* 31: 451–564. [This volume, chap. 2]

Bloor, D. 1976. *Knowledge and Social Imagery*. London: Routledge & Kegan Paul.

———. 1982. "Durkheim and Mauss revisited: Classification and the sociology of knowledge." *Studies in History and Philosophy of Science* 13: 267–97.

Blume, S. S. 1974. *Toward a Political Sociology of Science*. New York: Free Press.

Böhme, G. 1977. "Cognitive norms, knowledge-interests, and the constitution of the scientific object: A case study in the functioning of roles for experimentation," in E. Mendelsohn, R. Weingart, and R. Whitley (eds.), *The Social Production of Scientific Knowledge*. Boston, Dordrecht: Reidel.

Brush, S. G. 1967. "Science and culture in the nineteenth century: Thermodynamics and history." *Graduate Journal* 7: 477–565.

Chubin, D. E., and K. E. Studer. 1978. "The politics of cancer." *Theory and Society* 6: 55–74.

Collins, H. 1975. "The seven sexes: A study in the sociology of a phenomenon, or the replication of experiments in physics." *Sociology* 9: 205–224.

Collins, H., and T. Pinch. 1979. "The construction of the paranormal: Nothing unscientific is happening," in R. Wallis (ed.), *On the Margins of Science: The Social Construction of Rejected Knowledge*. Sociological Review Monograph no. 27. University of Keele.

Collins, R. 1975. *Conflict Sociology*. New York: Academic Press.

Daele, W. van den, W. Krohn, and P. Weingart. 1977. "The political direction of scientific development," in E. Mendelsohn, P. Weingart, and R. Whitley (eds.), *The Social Production of Scientific Knowledge*. Boston, Dordrecht: Reidel.

Dahrendorf, R. (1958). "Out of utopia: Toward a re-orientation of sociological analysis." *American Journal of Sociology* 64: 115–27.

Douglas, M. 1975. *Implicit Meanings: Essays in Anthropology*. London: Routledge & Kegan Paul.

Durkheim, E. 1954 [1912]. *The Elementary Forms of Religious Life*. New York: Free Press.

Durkheim, E., and M. Mauss 1963 [1903]. *Primitive Classifications*. London: Cohen & West.

Elias, N. 1971. "Sociology of knowledge: New perspectives." *Sociology* 5: 149–68, 335–70.

Elkana, Y. 1977. "The distinctiveness and universality of science: Reflections on the work of Professor Robin Horton." *Minerva* 15: 155–73.

Evans-Pritchard, E. E. 1937. *Witchcraft, Oracles and Magic Among the Azande*. Oxford: Clarendon Press.

Ezrahi, Y. 1971. "The political resources of American science." *Science Studies* 1: 117–133.

Forman, P. 1971. "Weimar culture, causality, and quantum theory, 1918–1927." *Historical Studies in the Physical Sciences* 3: 1–116.

Frankel, E. 1976. "Corpuscular optics and the wave theory of light." *Social Studies of Science* 6: 141–84.

Freudenthal, G. 1980. "Wissenssoziologie der Naturwissenschaften: Bedingungen und Grenzen ihrer Möglichkeit." [in N. Stehr and V. Meja (eds.), *Wissenssoziologie (Kölner Zeitschrift für Soziologie und Sozialpsychologie*, Sonderheft 22/1980). Opladen: Westdeutscher Verlag, 1981, pp. 153–62].

Gaston, J. 1979. "Problems and problematics in the sociology of science: The second decade," in P. Durbin (ed.), *A Guide to Historical Philosophical and Social Science Studies of Science*. New York: Free Press.

Gilbert, G. N. 1976. "The transformation of research findings into scientific knowledge." *Social Studies of Science* 6: 281–306.

Gilfillan, S. C. 1935. *The Sociology of Invention*. Chicago: Follett.

Goody, J. 1977. "Literacy, criticism and the growth of knowledge," in J. Ben-David and T. N. Clark (eds.), *Culture and Its Creators: Essays in Honor of Edward Shils*. Chicago: University of Chicago Press.

Gouldner, A. 1970. *The Coming Crisis in Western Sociology*. New York: Basic Books.

Graham, L. 1974. *Science and Philosophy in the Soviet Union*. New York: Vintage.

Granet, M. 1930. *Chinese Civilization*. London: Routledge & Kegan Paul.

Habermas, J. 1972. *Knowledge and Human Interests*. London: Heinemann.

————. 1968. *Technik und Wissenschaft als Ideologie*. Frankfurt: Suhrkamp.

Harwood, J. 1977. "The race-intelligence controversy: A sociological approach, II. 'external' factors." *Social Studies of Science* 7: 1–30.

Hesse, M. 1980. *Revolutions and Reconstructions in the Philosophy of Science*. Brighton: Harvester Press.

Holton, G. 1978. *The Scientific Imagination*. Cambridge: Harvard University Press.

————. 1973. *Thematic Origins of Scientific Thought*. Cambridge: Cambridge University Press.

Horton, R. 1967. "African traditional thought and western science." *Africa* 37: 50–71, 155–185.

Horton, R. and R. Finnegan (eds.). 1973. *Modes of Thought*. London: Faber and Faber.

Jacob, J. R. 1977. *Robert Boyle and the English Revolution*. New York: Burt Franklin.

Horton, R. and M. Jacob. 1980. "The Anglican origins of modern science: The metaphysical foundations of the Whig Constitution." *Isis* 71: 251–276.

Jacob, M. C. 1976. *The Newtonians and the English Revolution 1689–1720*. Ithaca: Cornell University Press.

Joravsky, D. 1961. *Soviet Marxism and Natural Science, 1917–1932*. New York: Columbia University Press.

Kuhn, T. S. 1970. *The Structure of Scientific Revolutions*. Chicago: University of Chicago Press.

Lécuyer, B.-P. 1978. "Bilan et perspectives de la sociologie de la science." *European Journal of Sociology* 19: 257–336.

MacKenzie, D. 1978. "Statistical theory and social interests: A case study." *Social Studies of Science* 8: 34–84.

Malinowski, B. 1954. *Magic, Science and Religion, and Other Essays*. Garden City, N.Y.: Doubleday.

Mannheim, K. 1953. "Conservative thought," in *Essays on Sociology and Social Psychology*. London: Routledge & Kegan Paul.

————. 1936. *Ideology and Utopia*. London: Routledge & Kegan Paul.

Marcuse, H. (1964). *One-Dimensional Man*. Boston: Beacon.

Medawar, P. B. 1963. "Is the scientific paper a fraud?" *The Listener* 12: 377–378.

Merton, R. K. 1973*a*. "Paradigm for a sociology of knowledge," in *The Sociology of Science: Theoretical and Empirical Investigations*. (ed. and intro. by N. W. Storer). Chicago: University of Chicago Press.

————. 1973*b*. "Singletons and multiples in science," in *The Sociology of Science: Theoretical and Empirical Investigations* (ed. and intro. by N. W. Storer). Chicago: University of Chicago Press.

Merton, R. K. and J. Gaston. 1977. *The Sociology of Science in Europe*. Carbondale: Southern Illinois University Press.

Mitroff, I. 1974. *The Subjective Side of Science*. New York: Elsevier.

Mulkay, M. 1979. *Science and the Sociology of Knowledge*. London: George Allen & Unwin.

————. 1969. "Some aspects of the cultural growth in the natural sciences." *Social Research* 36: 22–52.

Mulkay, M., and V. Milic. 1980. "The sociology of science in East and West." *Current Sociology* 28: 23–42.

Nelkin, D. 1979. "Science as a source of political conflict," in T. Segerstedt (ed.), *Ethics for Science Policy: Proceedings of a Nobel Symposium Held at Sodergarn, Sweden, 10–15 August 1978*. Oxford: Pergamon.

Nisbett, R., and I. Ross. 1980. *Human Inference: Strategies and Shortcomings of Social Judgment*. Englewood Cliffs, N.J.: Prentice-Hall.

Norton, B. 1978. "Karl Pearson and statistics: The social origins of scientific innovation." *Social Studies of Science* 8: 3–34.

O'Flaherty, W. D. 1980. "Inside and outside the mouth of God: The boundary between myth and reality." *Daedalus* 109: 93–126.

Ogburn, W. F., and D. Thomas. 1922. "Are inventions inevitable?" *Political Science Quarterly* 37: 83–98.

Pfetsch, F. 1979. "The finalization debate in Germany: Some comments and explanations." *Social Studies of Science* 9: 115–24.

Polanyi, M. 1967. "The growth of science in society." *Minerva* 5: 533–45.

Price, D. K. 1965. *The Scientific Estate*. Cambridge: Harvard University Press.

Rattansi, P. M. 1972. "The social interpretation of science in the seventeenth century," in P. Mathias (ed.), *Science and Society: 1600–1900*. Cambridge: Cambridge University Press.

Ravetz, J. 1971. *Scientific Knowledge and Its Social Problems*. Oxford: Clarendon Press.

Stern, B. 1959. "Resistance to medical change," in *Historical Sociology: The Selected Papers of Bernhard J. Stern*. New York: Citadel Press.

Thorndike, L. 1958. *A History of Magic and Experimental Science*. 8 vols. New York: Columbia University Press.

Vernant, J.-P. 1965. *Mythe et pensée chez les Grecs: Etudes de psychologie historique*. Paris: Maspero.

Weingart, P. 1977. "Wissenschaft heute und ihr Umfeld." *Wirtschaft und Wissenschaft* 3: 33–40.

Westrum, R. 1977. "Social intelligence about anomalies: The case of UFOs." *Social Studies of Science* 7: 271–302.

Wynne, B. 1976. "C. G. Barkla and the J Phenomenon." *Social Studies of Science* 6: 307–47.

Zilsel, E. 1942. "The sociological roots of science." *American Journal of Sociology* 44: 245–79.

The question of whether institutionalized norms play an important role in the behavior of scientists has been hotly debated in the sociology of science during the seventies.

The debate, which has not yet been concluded, was a reaction to the orthodoxy of the fifties and sixties, which considered institutionalized norms as the central concept in the sociological theory of science. In this paper, I shall try to do two things concerning this debate: first, describe the background and history of this debate as a case study of how sociological theory is created, shaped, and transformed, partly by systematic inquiry and partly in response to new problems arising in society; and second, try to arrive at some conclusions about the theoretical importance of scientific norms in view of the available evidence.

Background and Early History

The essays of Merton dealing with the norms, or rather the ethos, of science appeared originally in 1938 and 1942 (Merton 1973, pp. 254–66, 267–78). They were inspired by the feeling that the survival of science as a systematic, dispassionate, and universally respected pursuit of truth was threatened by a variety of anti-intellectual trends, above all, by Nazi ideology

Previously unpublished; written about 1982–1983. This is obviously a draft that has not undergone stylistic polishing. It is published almost unaltered. The manuscript carried indications for three notes that were not found. Some of the subtitles have been added, as have the references. Ed.

and politics. The first essay, "Science and Social Order" (1938), begins with a quote from Max Weber saying that "belief in the value of scientific truth is not derived from nature but is a product of definite cultures." To which Merton hastens to add, "and this belief is readily transmuted into doubt or disbelief." In the introduction to the 1942 essay, "The Normative Structure of Science," he says, "The revolt from science which [a little while before] appeared so improbable as to concern only the timid academician who would ponder all contingencies, however remote, has now been forced upon the attention of scientist and layman alike. Local contagions of anti-intellectualism threaten to become epidemic" (Merton 1973, pp. 254, 267). In these papers, Merton tried to explore the sources of opposition to science and to intellectualism and rationality in general. He thought that such opposition stemmed either from a certain cultural tradition which considers politics as supreme and is unwilling to respect the autonomy and political neutrality of any endeavor or from popular attitudes which are apprehensive about the skeptical spirit of science, do not believe that there can be disinterested pursuit of the truth, and confound the esoterism of science with that of magic, myth, and mysticism. The norms underlying the ethos of science (namely, universalism, disinterestedness, organized skepticism, and "communism") were made explicit in these papers in order to show what elements in science evoked political or populistic opposition or popular misrepresentations.

Beyond this immediate aim, Merton linked his interpretation of contemporary antiscientism with his interpretation of the institutionalization of science in seventeenth-century England. Science, as institutionalized in Western culture since the seventeenth century, is legitimized by a particular constellation of cultural values. That constellation of values had not been adopted in any society prior to seventeenth-century England; therefore, science as an autonomous cultural activity could not have been institutionalized anywhere before, in spite of rather widespread intellectual and practical interest in it (Merton 1938; King 1971). The attacks on science in the 1930s were seen by Merton as further evidence of the dependence of institutionalized science on cultural values: changing political values threatened science with withdrawal of its legitimation and a destruction of the basis of its public support. Merton's point was that the practical uses of science did not provide a sufficient basis for its continuous support. Without cultural values conferring honor on science and prescribing a set of appropriate norms, the scientific community would lose its autonomy, and pursuit of truth would be replaced by changeable instrumental goals as the purpose of research.

Thus, Merton took up the issue of scientific ethos because as a scientist interested in the social aspects of science, he had both a practical and a theoretical interest in understanding the motive forces behind antiscientism. When defeat of the Nazis seemed to remove the political threat to science, the menace of antiscientism seemed to have disappeared, giving place to a period of rapid scientific expansion and general admiration for science. This is probably the reason there was no significant sequel to Merton's work of the forties. Theoretically, the question of whether science required an underpinning by cultural values, or whether its survival was sufficiently ensured by its practical usefulness, continued to be of interest; but that was not enough to stimulate enquiry.

Postwar Developments

The next stimulus to the field came from an internal development in sociology in the late forties and early fifties, namely, Parsons's comprehensive conceptual scheme for the description and analysis of all, in particular, present-day, societies. Science and rationality in general were considered a central feature of this latter type of society, and it was an urgent task within this Parsonian scheme to establish a systematic sociological view of these phenomena of institutionalized science and rationality. The task was carried out by Bernard Barber's *Science and the Social Order* (Barber 1952). Science was presented here as one of the central institutions of modern society, which had to be studied from a sociological point of view, like politics, economy, education, or family. Barber was not content to put forward the case for sociology of science but also attempted to show that the field already possessed enough substantive material and sufficient theory to be recognized as a specialty. This theory was, to a large extent, built around the Mertonian-Parsonian view of science as a normatively regulated and culturally sanctioned social institution. This conception of science, which related primarily to the professional ethos of its practitioners, rather than to the concepts of science, was useful in the conceptualization both of differences in the development of scientific activity in different societies—which was also the original use of the concept for Merton—and of the differences between the behavior of scientists working in different organizations (academic settings, government, agriculture, manufacturing, industry, etc.) within the same society. With the concept of ethos, one could approach all kinds of comparative questions, such as, Why did science as a distinct cultural endeavor emerge only in Western Europe, from where it was imported to other societies? Why was its implantation in some societies more successful than in others? Why is academic science more prestigious than applied science? And why is it difficult to organize industrial research satisfactorily for the scientists?

There were, however, only very few sociologists to follow this research program, probably because comparative sociology was not very popular in the United States in the 1950s and 1960s. To the extent that a comparative research program was at all followed in the United States, it was limited to intracountry comparisons, namely, studies of industrial research (Marcson 1960, Kornhauser 1962). Some comparative historical work was done by sociologists of foreign origin or living outside the United States (Feuer 1963; Ben-

David 1971; Zloczower 1960). Many historians were stimulated by Merton's work on seventeenth-century science (Merton 1938), but they were concerned with the explanation of the single issue of the role of Protestantism in the rise of seventeenth-century science rather than with the general issue of the conditions of the institutionalization of science.

Around 1950, there was thus a paradoxical situation in sociology. Sociological theory, influenced by the monumental efforts of Talcott Parsons, had just assimilated and reconceptualized the great traditions of historical and comparative sociology embedded in the work of Durkheim, Weber, and the British social and American cultural anthropologists; but there were only few sociologists possessing the historical, ethnographic, and linguistic erudition needed for comparative research of the kind implied in the Parsonian program. These few acquired great reputations (e.g., in addition to Merton, Barber, Bellah, Eisenstadt, Smelser) but had rather limited impact on the training of students. Parsonian theory plus some of Durkheim, Weber, and other classics revitalized through the work of Parsons were studied in a disembodied way, in complete disjunction from the research tradition out of which they emerged, and, as a result, they had relatively little influence on research. The training of students and the empirical research in the graduate departments were based on the assumption that sociology was on its way to becoming "scientific" through the adoption of survey research as its principal method, enabling the sociologists to make quantifiable observations and to design research in a manner allowing the testing of hypotheses by methods adopted from biology and psychology. Temporarily, at least, this eliminated history from the intellectual horizon of the large majority of sociologists. Therefore, neither the classic example of Merton nor Barber's virtuosity in putting together a respectably organized body of knowledge from seemingly incoherent bits and pieces of studies and fitting them into a structural-functional framework were sufficient to inspire even a small group large enough for a specialty.

The Mertonian "Paradigm": Norms as Criteria of Allocative Justice and Means of Social Control

The conditions for launching a research program based on the normative conception of science and, incidentally, for the recognition of sociology of science as a specialty emerged only in 1957, as a result of a fortuitous combination of an external and an internal event. The external event was the launching of Sputnik, which generated interest in everything potentially relevant to understanding and facilitating the advancement of science and technology, thus directing attention to the sociology of science. The internal event was a paper by Merton based on research on independent multiple discoveries:

"Priorities in Scientific Discovery" (1957, 1973, pp. 286–324). Multiple discovery was a classic theme in sociology of science (Ogburn 1922; Gilfillan 1935) because it was considered by sociologists as evidence of the collective, "social," nature of scientific research. This was a reasonable interpretation of the phenomenon, but the observation was sociologically trivial. Merton's work gave this old theme new meaning by focusing not on the fact of multiple discovery but on a phenomenon frequently accompanying it, namely, clashes about claims to priority between discoverers. In other words, he shifted the context, and instead of looking at the phenomenon from the point of view of scientific discovery, he now looked at it from the point of view of scientific ethos. This derived from his conceptual framework, for clashes about priority suggested a potential deviance from scientific norms, which prescribed disinterestedness and communism (i.e., considering one's discoveries as a contribution to the common effort of the entire scientific community). Observance of these norms, as of all social norms, was bound to conflict occasionally with individual interests, and multiple discoveries were one of those occasions. Therefore, Merton considered priority disputes as of strategic importance for the study of social control and deviance in science. His analysis showed that the conceptual framework of the normative structure, or the ethos, of science was useful not only for large-scale comparative and historical studies, or for comparing the attitudes of scientists working in different types of organizations, but also for the study of the recognition and rewarding of scientific discoveries. Furthermore, such studies of competition, reward allocation, deviance, and social control in science could be subsumed under the study of social stratification and control in general. Thus, sociology of science became linked to a theoretically and methodologically central issue in sociology.

Under these conditions, sociology of science began to grow during the sixties. At the meetings of the international and national sociological associations, well-attended sessions were devoted to the subject; in 1966, the Research Committee on the Sociology of Science was launched at the International Congress of Sociology at Evian and was officially recognized in 1970 at the Varna meetings of the association. This was followed by the establishment of the Society for the Social Study of Science (4S) in the seventies. In 1962, Edward Shils already began publishing *Minerva* (in London), a journal devoted to "science, learning and policy." This was followed in the 1970s by *Science Studies, Science Policy* (subsequently, *Science and Public Policy*), *Pandore*, and *4S Newsletter*. Papers with a sociological approach were increasingly welcomed in periodicals devoted to the history of science, such as *Isis* or the *British Journal of the History of Science*, as well as in sociology journals.

Sociology of science was as diffuse and pluralistic an enterprise as sociology in general. Besides the inquiries about the norms underlying competition, the allocation of rewards and stratification, and the functioning of social control in science, sociologists investigated the social conditions of scientific productivity and innovation, the effects of organization and management in science, the institutionalization of applied research, and the life cycles of scientific specialties. But at the core of this variegated enterprise were the quantitative studies of the scientific reward system, stratification, and social control. The reason for this was that this was the only part of sociology of science which possessed a theoretical underpinning clearly linked to general sociological theory. The assumptions behind the studies of reward allocation in science were the same as those of the Davis-Moore theory of social stratification, namely, that differential allocation of rewards ("stratification") was a necessary means of maintaining motivation and control over a socially important activity and that it could be investigated by the same techniques of multivariate analysis as used in general studies of stratification. This was of crucial importance since as a result, and only as a result of this, graduate students could choose to write a thesis in this field without the risk of cutting themselves off from the mainstream of the discipline. In addition, such a student was no longer repelled by the prospect of having to invest heavily in the history of science and engage in kinds of research far remote from the mainstream of sociology: he could do research in sociology of science using skills acquired in general sociological training, and, after completion of his work, he could transfer his experience to other fields, without having to retrain himself in research methodology.

A further factor which may have contributed to the salience of the studies of the reward system in science is perhaps—however paradoxical this may appear in view of subsequent developments, to be noted below—the great influence of Thomas Kuhn's *The Structure of Scientific Revolutions* (1962). This book—at the intersection of history, philosophy, and sociology of science—has been widely read and acclaimed by sociologists in general, not only by those specializing in the sociology of science. One of the most important ideas of this book is that of a "scientific community," united by its training in and adherence to a "paradigm," namely, a model of doing research on a well-defined set of problems. This idea had a great influence in sociology. Sociologists have always been concerned with the scientific status of their discipline and have occasionally adopted models of different advanced disciplines (or what they believed to be such models) with a view to shaping sociology accordingly. With Kuhn came the idea that a hallmark of mature science is a paradigm, and the quantitative study of reward, stratification, and social control in science was as close to a Kuhnian paradigm as anything in sociology.

As a result, around 1970, sociology of science seemed to be set for rapid and continuous advance. The existence of what looked like a paradigm; a high degree of consensus about the leadership of Merton; a large consensus also over intellectual matters in general within the small but growing field at that time, all these raised the morale of the community. There was also a feeling that the sociological study of (mainly) natural and exact science, which until the late sixties was the object of broad social consensus, would not be affected by the controversies—of partly ideological origin—between schools in general sociology (structural-functionalists, Marxists, ethnomethodologists, etc.). The Mertonian "paradigm" of science as a normatively regulated and intellectually self-disciplining activity seemed to apply also to the sociology of science.

The Rise of Disagreement and Controversy

About 1970, consensus disappeared and sociology of science became a battlefield of all the schools of sociology. One of the sources of this change was a growing public interest in the field and the subsequent transformation of the research personnel in it. Throughout the sixties, there was much concern in Europe with the scientific and technological backwardness of the Continent as compared to the United States. This concern drew attention to the sociology of science, just as concern with Soviet superiority in space technology had drawn attention to it in the late fifties in the United States. Science policy became one of the most important concerns of the OECD and was widely reported on in the press and debated in various houses of legislature. Civil servants, politicians, and scientific statesmen became interested in sociology of science, as a field potentially useful in the reformation of scientific institutions and the acceleration of scientific and technological growth in Europe. Historians of science, too, recognizing that science was not only a set of abstract ideas but also a factor in economic and social development, began to take interest in social aspects of science.

This extradisciplinary interest had several repercussions on the development of the field. It greatly facilitated the establishment of institutional arrangements for research and teaching in the sociology, economics, history, and politics of science. Such units were established at the universities of Sussex, Edinburgh, Bielefeld, Cornell, MIT, and so forth, and attracted to the field a number of younger scholars trained in experimental science, philosophy, or history of science. Because of the practical and extradisciplinary origins of some of the practitioners of the field and of much of the interests in it, the new institutions were usually conceived as interdisciplinary ventures. They were institutions for the "social study of" rather than "sociology of" science. Thus, a significant part of sociology of science, especially in Europe, where there had been no sociological tradition in the field, came to be located within interdisciplinary units, rather than within departments of sociology.

From the perspective of this largely extradisciplinary and policy-oriented background, the interests of sociologists of science in the reward system, norms, and stratification in science appeared as narrow and parochial. It seemed disappointing that much of sociology of science was about the sociology of the scientific profession and less about the contents of science and problems of science policy. Some historians of science felt so and said so even earlier. They wanted sociology to say something about what scientists were actually engaged in, namely, the internal life of research specialties. They were also interested in the interface of science and politics at which economic support for science and the uses of research for practical purposes were decided, rather than in the reward allocation and stratification within the community of pure scientists. Yet these interests were not opposed to, and did not imply criticism of, the structural-functional studies of reward systems. They only produced a tendency to add to, or change, research priorities in the field, such as placing greater emphasis on the study of the emergence and growth of new specialties and of the political and economic conditions for, and results of, research and the support for it.

The source of explicit criticism was opposition to structural-functionalism, in general, and to considering the study of norms and reward systems as the main concept of social analysis, in particular. One kind of criticism concerned the alleged neglect of conflict and power relationships and the resultant presentation of a false image of science as characterized by consensus and conformity. It clamored for a disclosure of conflict, exploitation, and similar phenomena involving power relations, deriving from the economic and political interests and involvements of scientists, instead of trying to view their conduct as a reflection of values and norms inherent in the dispassionate pursuit of truth. The other kind of criticism objected to the assumption of structural-functionalism, or, indeed, of all "positivistic" approaches, that phenomena investigated by sociologists have some kind of objective structure. Phenomenology and ethnomethodology became influential among sociologists of science, giving rise to skepticism about the very idea of an objective reality. For the proponents of this approach, the exclusive task of sociology is the investigation of processes facilitating subjective orderly social interaction, for all reality is only a construct of human minds and their interactions.

These approaches had important implications for the sociology of science. The idea of reality as a social construct implied that our views and hypotheses about nature can also be understood as the result of social processes. This led to the resuscitation and to the reintroduction of sociology of knowledge of both the Durkheimian and the Mannheimian variety into sociology of science. Further, and this is even more important in the present context, both the conflict and the phenomenological approaches reject the view of society as composed of institutions and regulated by norms. They regard norms either as rationalizations disguising interests or as semblances created to maintain an illusion of order. On this view, norms thus are phenomena arising in the scientific activity and have to be explained as results of certain aspects of that activity; by no means can norms explain the structure and the typical processes of that activity. This criticism was not founded on any empirical shortcomings of the normative-institutional analysis. Rather, there was ample evidence in favor of this analysis and no empirical findings to the contrary. The normative analysis was thus rejected on a priori theoretical grounds. This rejection was justified partly by anecdotal evidence and partly by unsystematic attempts to show that research evidence was also consistent with alternative explanations.

The rejection of the structural-functional analysis of science, it seems, followed from an alternative view of science, which had always been propounded by a small minority (Marcuse 1964) but which became popular and widespread during the student revolt of the late sixties and early seventies. Science, which the previous generation of scholars had perceived as an endeavor to find out the truth about the universe by rational means, appeared to many a member of the new generation as an intellectual device designed for the furtherance of particular purposes and selfish interests of those engaged in or paying for research. It is not known what caused this changed perception of science. My guess is that it was a consequence of the self-inflicted American defeat in Vietnam, which was accompanied among university students all over the world by a sense of dillusionment with Western institutions and culture. Science, which in the fifties and sixties had been promoted to the status of one of the chief gods of Western culture, was now turned into one of its chief villains.

Some evidence that this turnabout in the perception of science was indeed caused by external events is provided by the way Kuhn's theory of scientific change was reinterpreted and used in support of the denial of the existence of scientific norms. This theory, which does not affirm, and for about the first eight years of its circulation had not been interpreted as implying, that science did not have some general norms of conduct and criteria of scientific judgment transcending the different paradigms, was suddenly interpreted as implying just that and was set up as a relativistic alternative to the "Mertonian" sociology of science. In point of fact, Kuhn's account was an attempt at bridging the gap between, on the one hand, the apparent conservatism of scientific training and everyday research practice and, on the other, the revolutionary nature of some discoveries. Kuhn also tried to replace the naive view of scientific growth as consisting of linear accumulation of knowledge with a model taking account of the numerous discontinuities and instances of creative destruction in the process. This was now distorted into an image in which science was pictured as an archipelago of volcanic islands ("paradigms"), each distinct and different from the others, constantly emerging and disintegrating into a stormy, shapeless, and lawless sea ("revolutions"), with both islands and sea subject to outside forces, such as class interests or ideologies. Kuhn was interpreted this way to legitimize a revolution from the "Mertonian" sociology of science which could not be justified on the basis of any existing evidence or accepted theory of science. The way this revolution in sociology of science happened is consistent with the view of science as a construct reflecting social interests rather than grappling with the explanation of objective reality observing cognitive and ethical rules.

Scientific Norms: Empirical Findings and Their Interpretation

Having declared the revolution and produced all possible arguments against the significance attributed to, or even the very existence of, scientific norms, sociologists settled down to doing precisely what they had to do according to the norms they had just rejected, namely, investigate empirically the existence and functions of scientific norms. These investigations have been of three kinds: investigations of the behavior of scientists in matters such as recognition, citation, or awarding of prizes, in order to test its consistency with norms of science, research which is, of course, in direct continuation of the tradition of studies of the scientific reward system (Blume and Sinclair 1973; Cole and Cole 1973; Gaston 1978); attitude surveys of scientists with questions supposedly reflecting conformity or nonconformity with the norms (Blisset 1972; Toren 1980); and detailed studies of scientific controversies in order to discover whether or not the actual behavior of scientists followed these rules (Mulkay 1969; Mitroff 1974; Collins 1974; Wynne 1976).

The results are seemingly contradictory. The studies of scientific judgments and allocation of rewards support the structural-functional view of the existence of considerable conformity with the professional ethos (or norms) of science. These have been summarized, discussed, and complemented by Jerry Gaston (Gaston 1978). By and large, they are consistent with the view that the scientific community controls deviance from its norms effectively and judges merit and allocates rewards according to intrinsic scientific criteria. (In most of the studies, there is a suggestion that the prestige of the department in which a scientist was trained or at which he works may influence judgment, but it is not clear whether this is due to attaching greater weight to honor than to merit or whether attachment to a center of excellence is—correctly or erroneously—used as an indicator of scientific merit.) This evidence from statistical studies of the criteria of allocation of rewards is confirmed by the careful survey of historical and contemporary cases of deviance and reaction to deviance in science by Harriet Zuckerman (Zuckerman 1977). There is little doubt, then, that scientists observe the rules of their professional ethic in the allocation of rewards and punishment of fraud and other kinds of deviance.

Mulkay questions the cogency of this evidence (Mulkay and Milic 1980), but he does not produce any counterevidence or alternative interpretation of the evidence.

A different picture emerges from attitude surveys. The outcome of these is inconclusive: answers to some questions show acceptance of the norms, while others suggest rejection. Thus, asked about the danger of other scientists appropriating one's ideas and results before publication, scientists expressed considerable, if not complete, confidence in the ethicality of their colleagues. They suspect that reputation and formal status may influence judgments of referees, but there is no suggestion that such influence is very significant. Again, although many of them think that research which may have socially undesirable effects should, to some extent, be restricted, it yet seems that they agree to such restrictions as an exception to the rule of scientific autonomy, so that their attitude does not amount to a rejection of the claim to autonomy.

The conclusion of the survey studies is also supported by cases in which scientists can be observed acting as judges over their peers. Thus, the rejection of the very unusual cosmological ideas of Velikovsky without examination of the evidence was widely challenged (although no one believed that Velikovsky was right), and it was felt by representatives of the scientific community that the accusation required an answer (De Grazia 1966, Polanyi 1967). A reverse of this case occurred in the controversy following A. Jensen's paper on the importance of heredity in the explanation of the intelligence quotients of blacks and whites (Jensen 1969). This paper was seen by some as advocacy for racial prejudice and was also severely criticized for empirical and methodological shortcomings. Although some of the critics used scientifically acceptable arguments, it was suspected that in their criticism they went beyond accepted cognitive standards and procedures in the field, that is, they infringed on the norms of universalism and disinterestedness. This question was considered important enough for detailed discussion and censure (Barnes 1974; Cronbach 1975). Barnes used this case to show that it can be analyzed without recourse to norms of science. What he actually shows, however, is that the application of methodological rules is equivocal. But the moral question of universalism which he implicitly raises receives an unequivocal answer.

Evidence which may seem to support the view that ethical norms are unimportant because they are routinely transgressed comes from case studies of research under way which explores how scientists behave in formulating their explanations, in accepting or rejecting the claims of others, or in competing with their colleagues. In these situations, scientists are indeed willing to transgress practically all the norms enumerated by Merton and others: they may withhold findings in order to prevent advantage from competitors, they make judgments on the basis of personal prejudice, interpret results arbitrarily in order to fit their theories, and so forth (Mitroff 1974; Feyerabend 1975).

These studies are consistent with the view that rules and norms are produced, used and observed, or transgressed by scientists according to their temporary interests and that controversies and claims are decided on the basis of negotiation and compromise, rather than dispassionate judgment based on clear-cut criteria.

At first sight, it may thus appear that any view on the norms of science can be supported by some of the evidence. But this is only a superficial impression. Actually, there is no contradiction between the results of these three kinds of studies. Rather, they complement each other, and together they provide a coherent and consistent picture, with each kind of study illuminating a part of it.

The studies of the reward system and of reaction to deviance deal with moral issues: whether scientists act fairly in the allocation of rewards and whether justice is done to those infringing the rules. They relate to situations in which scientists sit in judgment over their peers, or where they have to account for the morality of their own behavior. On the basis of the evidence, there is little doubt that in those situations scientists are aware of Merton's norms and try to act according to them.

The case studies of research in progress and of scientific controversies—which manifest an absence of norms—deal with an entirely different situation. Sticking to the legal metaphor, these case studies relate to the processes preceding judgment: the sifting of evidence, the determination of the issues involved and of the laws which apply, and the presentation of the case to the judge and jury. The scientists at this stage act like litigants concerned more with putting together a convincing case than with ultimate truth. They are not, and are not expected to be, dispassionate. Only when their cases are complete do scientists try to look at conflicting evidence or listen to alternative interpretation. They do not always do this with the open-mindedness they expect from others when judging their own case; indeed, they would be angels if they did. All one can expect from them is to accept the judgment of referees and competent users, which, as a rule, they do. This is how all effective law enforcement operates, and one cannot expect anything more in any field of human endeavor.

To regard this kind of behavior as indicating that there are no norms of scientific ethos is an error. To begin with, since much of what is involved at this stage of the research process is a purely cognitive research for an adequate solution of a problem, and since the solution of nontrivial problems involves guesses, uncertainties, and modifications of accepted rules and so cannot be regulated in advance, it is bound to be a more or less disorderly process. There is no expectation of dispassionate objectivity at this stage of the research, for one cannot try to solve a puzzling phenomenon without taking a personal interest in it and pursuing it passionately and with determination. A brainchild needs love and devotion, like a real one. Thus, much of what appears in these case studies as unscientific bias and prejudice is to be seen as a manifestation of the commitment to and involvement in one's work which accompany the problem solution phase of research, and it has nothing to do with the ethos of scientific judgment. Only at the stage when a work is finished and presented to the scientific public can one apply to it relatively stable, methodological criteria, and only then can one judge whether such criteria have been applied fairly, conscientiously, and in good faith.

This interpretation is consistent also with the inconclusiveness of the findings of attitude surveys. Those often put questions without sufficiently specifying the context. But norms of science are not absolute, and since scientists are also citizens, breadwinners, members of families, and so forth, they may be faced with choices between conflicting values and norms and make decisions which are inconsistent with part of them. A good example is provided by Toren's (1980) finding of weak support—only 51 percent—for the norm of disinterestedness on the basis of agreement or disagreement with the statement, "Scientists need not be motivated solely by the contribution of their work to scientific knowledge; they have a right to choose projects which will enhance their reputation and personal interest." But she found more support for the norm when changing the context: the suggestion that scientific work should be judged mainly on the basis of its practical usefulness was rejected by 68 percent. In fact, this latter item is a much more adequate criterion to gauge the acceptance of "disinterestedness" as an ethical norm, since it relates the question to the context of public judgment, which is the only relevant one for the purpose. The first question, which refers to personal motivation, is really unsuitable for the purpose, allowing as it does a great deal of leniency in consideration of circumstances, such as financial need, difficulty of finding employment, or service to a nonscientific social purpose. It is surprising— and perhaps very impressive—evidence of the norm of disinterestedness that 51 percent still rejected the statement. It is thus false to think, as Mulkay does (1972), that this uncertainty in the application of norms of science indicates that the norms are meaningless and operationally useless.

Conclusion

This paper began with two questions. What can be learned from the history of normative-institutional analysis of science about the way in which sociological theory is created? And where does the theory stand today: should it be accepted, rejected, modified, or what else?

Concerning the first question, the story we have examined reveals many of the conditions and patterns of behavior which characterize sociology as a discipline. Sociologists, more than anyone else, are vitally involved in and affected by social events. Their professional expertise sensitizes them to appreciate the significance of those events, to guess their causes and their potential effects. Furthermore, they are expected to provide running interpretation of social events as those occur and to provide diagnoses and cures for all the ills of society. The attitude toward them is similar to that toward a physician. There is less confidence in the diagnoses and cures of sociologists than in those of physicians, but there is also less understanding of the need of sociologists to conduct patient investigations into basic problems of no immediate interest before attempting to solve any practical ones. In fact, sociologists themselves are not always convinced that this is necessary, for, contrary to what is the case in the natural sciences, in sociology the investigator has a firsthand insight into many of the assumptions and motives which are used in explanation. Yet the most difficult problem facing sociology is that the subject matter under investigation, society, is constantly changing. Although some basic processes presumably do not change, enough changes to make some questions which are very interesting at the time appear quite uninteresting a short while later, before a satisfactory answer is found to them. As a result, few questions are pursued over enough time to arrive at reasonably well-founded conclusions. In principle, this problem can be overcome by formulating questions with a mind to theoretical rather than practical significance. But this may be easier said than done, since to formulate questions at a level of abstraction and generality to make them impregnable to changes of values and other conditions affecting the state of society may presuppose a more advanced and elaborate theory of society than is available to the investigator. And trying to rise to a high level of abstraction and generality in the absence of such theory may turn out to be an escape from real into make-believe problems or into methodological ritualism.

These are the conditions of sociological practice, and they are clearly reflected in this brief history of normative institutional analysis in sociology of science. Both the beginning of this analysis and the attempts to reject it were, apparently, triggered by political or social events which created peaks of interest in science as a social phenomenon. The systematic, orderly exploration of the problem took place in between these periods of peak interest and did not attract the same attention as the debates of the peak periods.

As to the substantive question of the importance of normative analysis, the conclusion consistent with all the empirical evidence is that norms are important and necessary guidelines in the evaluation and judgment of scientific results and their incorporation into the scientific tradition. They are not sources of motivation to engage in scientific research, and at many phases of the research process, they are entirely in the background. This does not mean that they are unimportant or absent in those phases: the scientist, even when apparently interested in nothing more than achieving some result or persuading others about the superiority of his ideas and work, is aware of the norms and strongly attached to them as essential bulwarks of his or her basic professional interests. Evidence of this is the constant awareness of "real" versus apparent achievement, the conscientiousness with which people perform such time-consuming functions as refereeing, and the vehemence of condemnation of deviance. Scientists may frequently appear to behave as if they were interested merely in a game or in politics. But their game and politics are inspired by distinct values, and they are keenly aware of this distinction.

References

Barber, B. 1952. *Science and the Social Order.* New York: Free Press.
———. 1974. *Scientific Knowledge and Sociological Theory.* London: Routledge and Kegan Paul.
Ben-David, J. 1971. *The Scientist's Role in Society: A Comparative Study.* Englewood Cliffs, N.J.: Prentice Hall.
Blisset, M. 1972. *Politics in Science.* Boston: Little, Brown, and Co.
Blume, S. S., and R. Sinclair. 1973. "Chemists in British Universities: A Study of the Reward System of Science," *American Sociological Review* 38 (1): 126–38.
Cole, J. R., and S. Cole. 1973. *Social Stratification in Science.* Chicago: University of Chicago Press.
Collins, H. 1974. "The T.E.A. Set: Tacit Knowledge and Scientific Networks," *Science Studies* 4: 165–86.
Cronbach, L. 1975. "Five Decades of Public Controversy Over Mental Testing," *American Psychologist* 30 (1): 1–14.
Feuer, L. 1963. *The Scientific Intellectual.* New York: Basic Books.
Feyerabend, P. 1975. *Against Method.* London: New Left Books.
Gaston, J. 1978. *The Reward System in British and American Science.* New York: Wiley.
Gilfillan, S. C. 1935. *The Sociology of Invention.* Chicago: Follett.
Grazia, A. de, ed. 1966. *The Velikovsky Affair—The Warfare of Science and Scientism.* New York: University Books.
Jensen, A. R. 1969. "How Much Can We Boost IQ and Scholastic Achievement?" *Harvard Educational Review* 39: 1–123.
King, M. D. 1971. "Reason, Tradition, and the Progressiveness of Science," *History and Theory* 10: 3–32.
Kornhauser, W. 1962. With the assistance of W. O. Hagstrom. *Scientists in Industry: Conflict and Accommodation.* Berkeley and Los Angeles: University of California Press.
Kuhn, T. S. 1962. *The Structure of Scientific Revolutions.* Chicago: University of Chicago Press.
Marcson, S. 1960. *The Scientist in American Industry: Some Organizational Determinants in Manpower Utilization.* New York: Harper.
Marcuse, H. 1964. *One-Dimensional Man.* Boston: Beacon Press.
Merton, R. K. 1938. *Science, Technology and Society in Seventeenth-Century England.* Reprinted with a new Introduction by the author. New York: Harper & Row, 1970.

————. 1973. *The Sociology of Science* (edited by N. W. Storer). Chicago: University of Chicago Press.

Mitroff, I. I. 1974. "Norms and Counter-Norms in a Select Group of the Apollo Moon Scientists: A Case-Study of the Ambivalence of Scientists," *American Sociological Review* 39: 579–95.

Mulkay, M. J. 1969. "Some Aspects of Cultural Growth in the Natural Sciences," *Social Research* 36 (1): 22–52.

————. 1972. *The Social Process of Innovation*. London: Macmillan.

Mulkay, M., and V. Milic. 1980. "The Sociology of Science in East and West," *Current Sociology* 28: 23–42.

Ogburn, W. F. 1922. *Social Change*. New York: Huebsch.

Polanyi, M. 1967. "The Growth of Science in Society," *Minerva* 5: 533–45.

Toren, N. (1980). "The New Code of Scientists," *IEEE Transactions on Engineering and Management* EM-7:78-84.

Wynne, B. 1976. "C. G. Barkla and the J Phenomenon: A Case Study in the Treatment of Deviance in Physics," *Social Studies of Science* 6: 307–47.

Zloczower, A. 1960. *Career Opportunities and Growth of Scientific Discovery in 19th-Century Germany with Special Reference to Physiology*. Jerusalem: Hebrew University. [Now published by Arno Press, New York, 1981.]

Zuckerman, H. 1977. *Scientific Elite: Nobel Laureates in the United States*. New York: The Free Press.

The Ethos of Science: 23
The Last Half-Century

Ethos—an "emotionally toned complex of rules, prescriptions, mores, beliefs, values, and presuppositions which are held to be binding" (Merton 1976, p. 258) upon a category of persons—is something very difficult to describe in terms of its contents. It is felt that any description must be both trivial, since it is a description of something known to everybody, and grossly misleading, because no description is capable of properly rendering the complexity, the nuances of meaning and the emotional overtones of an ethos.

Furthermore, an ethos is a controversial notion. It is relatively easy to determine what is science, or what is, say, Protestantism. One can read textbooks, research reports or the *Institutes of the Christian Religion* of Calvin. But any statement about the ethos (or the spirit) of these things will raise objections, such as: What about scientists who do not act in the so-called spirit of science? Were Nazi scientists, like Johannes Stark, not scientists? And if they were, does it make sense to speak about the ethos of science? Because of these difficulties and ambiguities the concept of ethos will tend to be avoided both by the scientific as well as by the practical mind as something too elusive to be dealt with rationally. Some will deny its practical importance and regard it as mere rhetoric which is nice and proper for some occasions but is not to be taken seriously. Those who take it seriously still prefer to invoke it only ritually on proper occasions as befitting things which possess an element of elusive and ineffable sacredness. There are important things, such as to do good, which can only be trivialized by being talked about, and the scientific ethos may be one of them.

It is the professional predicament of sociologists—an intellectual species engaged in exploring the relationship between human intentions and conduct—to study such difficult and elusive phenomena. The purpose of this paper is to explore the fate of a particular ethos, that of the scientists, during the last half century. In the early thirties there were controversies about science similar to those prevailing today. As an upshot of these, attempts were made in the late thirties and early forties to describe explicitly the ethos (or "morality," "code of conduct," "ethics") of science. The sociologist Robert Merton attempted to do so in order to interpret the situation of science under democracy and totalitarianism in 1938 (Merton 1973, pp. 254–78). He characterized this ethos in terms of intellectual honesty, universalism, organized skepticism, disinterestedness, "communism" (the view that scientific knowledge should be public and accessible to everyone capable of using it), and involving the demand that "theories or generalizations be evaluated in terms of their logical consistency and consonance with facts" (Merton 1973, pp. 258–59). This description was later supplemented by Michael Polanyi, a physical chemist turned into a philosopher of science (Polanyi 1951) who stressed the importance of the autonomy of the individual scientist and of the informal sanctions and rewards of the scientific community as means of controlling the conduct of scientists. Although Polanyi's statement was made as part of a polemic with other scientists, his description of the scientific community and Merton's characterization of its norms of conduct were accepted as correct by the large majority of scientists and observers of science. This consensus about the scientific ethos abruptly changed in the late sixties, and the questions whether an ethos was really characteristic of the conduct of scientists, or, if so, whether that ethos was socially and morally worthwhile, became the subject of passionate controversy (Stehr 1978).

The question which I propose to explore is why Merton's and Polanyi's description of the scientific ethos was acceptable until the late sixties, and why it has become so controversial since then, in the hope that this exploration will also cast some light on the nature and significance of this ethos.

Historical Context

The answer to the question of why attitudes toward the scientific ethos changed so radically lies in the changing historical context. Merton's original formulations related to a three-cornered debate on science which has gone on since the thirties between those who stress the importance of the intellectual and institutional demarcation of science from politics, religion, ideology, and economic interest (to be called "demarcationists"); those who think that science could and had to provide a blueprint for the rational (scientific) planning and management of society as a whole, including scientific research itself ("scientific supremacists"); and those who want to subordinate science to politics and ideology ("subordinationists"). This is a practical debate about the social role of scientists, which in the thirties, was directly related to the three competing forms of government—democracy, communism, and fascism.

Theoretically, it is possible to link each two of these views in a coalition against the third: the supremacist and subordinationist views which deny the demarcation of science against the demarcationist view; the demarcationist and the supremacist views, both of which are consistent with recognition of the intellectual and moral autonomy of science, versus the position which demands subordination of science to politics and ideology; and finally it is also possible to align the demarcationist with the subordinationist view, as two positions consistent with low involvement of science in politics, against the supremacist view requiring a high degree of political involvement.

It is evident that these different possibilities of coalition formation are the result of ambiguities inherent in all the three positions. The demarcationist and the subordinationist position are consistent with both high or low political involvement; while the supremacist position is consistent with low and high degrees of autonomy of science, since once demarcation between science and other things is abolished, supremacy of science can mean anything, including the supremacy of the latest thoughts of a dictator declared as science. On the other hand, each position represents an unequivocal stand on some issue. Thus the demarcationist position is unequivocally committed to the autonomy of science, the supremacist position is unequivocal on requiring a high degree of political and ideological involvement, and the subordinationist position is unequivocal on the absence of autonomy.

During the thirties there had been an increasing convergence between the demarcationist and the supremacist positions in the Western countries. The reason for this was that the third view, that of the subordination of science to politics and ideology, was adopted by National Socialist Germany. Subordination of science to politics and ideology under that regime was particularly reprehensible, because of the irrational and cruelly oppressive character of nazism. Furthermore, one of the first acts of the regime was the removal of Jews and Marxists from all public office, including universities. Since many Jews, Socialists, and Communists were prominent in science, this created a sharp confrontation between the National Socialist regime and the scientific community right from the beginning. As a result, by the end of the nineteen thirties, there emerged a kind of a popular front in science, uniting democrats with radical Socialists and Communists in a common front of believers in science and rationality, against National Socialists and Fascists who placed irrational belief in charismatic leaders and myths of race and nationality above science. As has been shown, this coalition was not logically determined. Marxism was, in principle, also consistent with denial of scientific autonomy, and Stalinist attitudes and practices toward science were not different from those of the Nazis (for example, Lysenkoism was officially supported already in 1935; Joravsky 1970). But Russian reality was not sufficiently known to scientists in the West, and among Western scientists the cleavage between Democrats and Communists did not appear as irreconcilable. They got along with each other reasonably well but not with the Nazis.

This is not to say that there were no cleavages between Marxists and non-Marxist scientists. However, these cleavages did not affect their fundamental views of science, only their strategies of how to advance the cause of science to the best advantage of both science and society (both groups also believed in a basic identity of interests between science and society). During the thirties and the forties there was much debate, especially in England, between the Marxist-inspired so-called scientific humanists who advocated planning by science of science as well as of society in general and opponents of planning organized in the Society for Freedom in Science (Barber 1962, pp. 303–10; Bernal 1939; Polanyi 1951). But favorable or hostile to planning, they all agreed what science was about and who was a respectable scientist. There is no doubt that the characterization of the scientific ethos described above fitted this consensus. Due to this consensus, planning of science was not conceived of as a contradiction to the autonomy of science. Those in favor of planning conceived of it as something done by scientists with a deep understanding of science. Thus even views, such as those of Michael Polanyi, recommending reliance on the self-regulation of the scientific community, rather than the planning of research, were not totally unacceptable to those in favor of planning. They did not reject the idea of a relatively autonomous scientific community but only argued that this community had to participate actively in the planning and management of the applications of science for social purposes.

The Cold War of the late forties and the fifties did not disrupt the consensus on the ethos of science. Stalinist terror, on the one hand, and McCarthyite oppression, on the other, only reinforced the feeling of scientists that they were a community of like-minded people reaching out to each other across the boundaries of nations and ideologies and that they possessed an ethos which could make a valuable contribution toward saving mankind from tyrannies of the right and the left and the prevention of war. UNESCO, in its early days, the Pugwash conferences, and the movement toward establishing international unions and associations in every field of science were all manifestations of the potency of the belief in the scientific ethos and the existence of a self-regulating scientific community.

Thus the consensus about, and adherence to, the scientific ethos between the thirties and the fifties was the result of the common interest of the majority of practicing scientists in the West, and—although they had few opportunities to say so—probably also in the East, in the autonomy of the scientific community as a protection against persecutors of scientists.

The Beginning of the
Science Debate in the Late Sixties

What brought this consensus to an abrupt end in the late sixties, giving rise to widespread opposition to those ideas during the last decade? There has been a spate of publications criticizing the concept of the scientific ethos on factual as well as moral grounds. The factual critics have tried to show that scientists do not act according to the ethos of science; that the norms included in that ethos, such as universalism and disinterestedness, are not peculiar to science; that scientists use those norms only as a professional ideology to advertise or justify their interests and not as a guide to their own conduct; and that the norms actually observed by scientists are not derived from an ethos common to most scientists but are changing technical norms implicit in the state of specific fields at given periods of time (Barnes and Dolby 1970; Brush 1974; King 1971; Mitroff 1974a, 1974b; Mulkay 1969, 1972; Spiegel-Rösing 1973). The moral critics cast doubt on the validity of the traditional scientific ethos under present, or perhaps all, conditions. The autonomy of science appears to them as a blueprint for social irresponsibility, if not actual complicity with morally reprehensible uses of science (Ravetz 1971, pp. 307–13).

Logically, the two kinds of criticisms are independent of each other. The factual question of whether there is a scientific ethos or not could be decided, in principle, by empirical inquiry. And irrespective of the outcome of such investigation, one may consider such an ethos as desirable, superfluous, or harmful.

However, although the bulk of empirical evidence shows that scientists are aware of and observe such norms as universalism or intellectual honesty (Ben-David 1977a; Gaston 1978; Stehr 1978), there are enough exceptions and ambiguities in this evidence to allow interpretation of the findings as negative by those who wish to do so.

Therefore, the factual and the moral criticisms are frequently presented as mutually supporting each other in a coherent argument against the institutional autonomy of science. They are interpreted as evidence that science is not and cannot be demarcated from political, social, and other intellectual concerns but is a historically and socially conditioned phenomenon. Consequently, according to the critics, there cannot be a specific scientific ethos, except as a means to impress and mystify the public. The implicit or explicit message of these critical writings is that the idea that science is an intellectually distinct activity with a morality of its own should be rejected and that scientific inquiry should be subject to more stringent social and political control than at present. Views on the nature of this control vary, but it is not the kind of control by rational scientific planning which was advocated by Bernal, Waddington, and other left-wing scientists in the thirties and forties. Then science was to be in control; now it is to be controlled.

The reason for this change of attitudes toward science in intellectual circles can be explained partly as a result of the disappearance of the conditions which gave rise to the coalition between the usually liberal demarcationists and left-wing scientific supremacists from the late thirties to the fifties and partly to conditions which changed the composition and the social and political functions of the scientific community since the last World War.

The demise of McCarthyism in the United States and of Stalinism in the Soviet Union, on the one hand, and the fact that the association between nazism and the suppression of the autonomy of science was increasingly forgotten, on the other, created an opportunity for the realignment of the positions toward science.

The first signs of this were the reemergence of philosophies such as that of H. Marcuse and J. Habermas (Marcuse 1964; Habermas 1970) which were critical of science as a one-sided and in various ways "oppressive" endeavor. These philosophies have their roots in romantic and existentialist philosophies of the nineteenth century (Aliotta 1914, pp. xv–xvi; Forman 1971; Spengler 1939, vol. 1, pp. 58–60, 391–98; Toulmin 1972), but since the fifties these philosophical critics were frequently identified with some neo-Marxist positions.

These views which stress the determination of scientific thought by external conditions, such as class interests, cultural values, and religious beliefs, were current among Marxist theoreticians in the twenties (Joravsky 1961, pp. 62–75, 152–53, 184–97). This is a very different kind of Marxism from that of the radical scientists in the thirties and the forties. In principle, of course, they all identified Marxism with science. However, for the Marxist philosophers of the sixties, "science" meant primarily Marxism, while for the practicing scientists of the radical movements of the thirties and the forties "science" meant primarily experimental science. Therefore, for the former Marxists, the identification of science and ideological politics meant a subordination of science to politics, while for the latter it meant subordination of politics to science (Bernal 1939, p. 231; Waddington 1948). Once the principle of demarcation is discarded, the position of scientific supremacism can easily shift into a position which is actually subordinationist. As has been pointed out, it only depends on what you decide to call "science."

The fact that the Marxist position in this debate is represented today mainly by philosophically, and not scientifically, trained people, has probably had considerable part in shifting the Marxist position from a view in which science determines politics to one favoring the subordination of science to politics. This realignment of Western neo-Marxism with romantic and ideological attitudes toward science was, of course, very difficult as long as the latter were associated with national socialism, but as has been pointed out, it became possible eventually as memory of that association lapsed.

However, philosophers had little influence outside their own circles before the mid-sixties, and their direct influence has been very limited even since then. Therefore their influence alone cannot explain the adoption of critical and hostile attitudes toward the autonomy of science and the ethics of science (such as universalism, disinterestedness) among such large parts of the intellectual public, especially the young.

Changes in Science
Since The Second World War

This more widespread change in the attitudes toward science can be explained by the changing composition of the scientific community and the uses made of science, or rather of scientific autonomy, since the last World War. The groups engaged in the debate on the social aspects of science in Britain and the United States in the thirties and the forties were small groups of outstanding natural scientists and a few social scientists. The times in which they formulated their ideas were full of great discoveries and advances in their respective fields. The scientific ethos, which is an ethos of research workers in pure science who contribute to the advancement of knowledge, fitted these people and fitted the times.

During the sixties there was a tremendous expansion of universities and research establishments. However, the opportunities to make discoveries did not increase proportionately (Price 1963, pp. 92–94), perhaps because the larger numbers reduced the average ability of scientists, and perhaps for reasons intrinsic to the growth of knowledge. In any event, for many of the new recruits to research, and some of the older ones, research was boring and without intellectual prospects. And toward the late sixties, the economic prospects also deteriorated. Many of the new recruits to science worked actually as science teachers, textbook writers, research assistants, and technicians (often in applied work). The scientific ethos which is concerned with the conduct of original research and its evaluation did not fit this kind of work. It was not "disinterested," nor was it meant as a contribution to universally shared knowledge but to a variety of much more immediate and practical purposes. However, because of the rapid expansion of higher education, many of the scientific workers who were not researchers in the traditional sense, found employment in universities, which adopted—in the sixties, more than ever before—a definition of the academic teacher as an active and original contributor to research (Ben-David 1977b, pp. 116–23). As a result, the norms of evaluating scientific work as original contributions to knowledge were ostensibly applied to work which was not original and was not meant to be. It is no surprise that for many scientific workers and observers of the scientific scene, the scientific ethos appeared as hypocritical and oppressively "elitist."

The problems caused by the uses, or more precisely, misuses, of scientific autonomy go back to the World War when the scientific community in the West actively recruited itself to contribute to the war effort. This event was turned into a kind of myth to symbolize the crucial significance of autonomous science for society. To the extent that scientists considered their warfare as a defense against the threat to scientific integrity presented by nazism, this myth may have had some substance. But the myth has also been used for other purposes. It has presented the scientific community, setting its own goals for research and enforcing compliance with its standards through criticism and other informal means, not merely as a social framework particularly suited to the advancement of knowledge but also as an infallible source of political and—by implication—economic, or other social wisdom. An organized effort in military research and development undertaken for political purposes, which was not different from other parts of the war effort, was presented as something initiated and accomplished by the scientific community for its own purposes and under its own direction, as if the ethos of science were capable of defining political goals and the autonomous scientific community could carry out organized warfare.

This misrepresentation of science continued after the war. In the scientific euphoria of the postwar period, science was seen in the United States, and subsequently everywhere else, as an "endless frontier," providing improvements in "national health, the creation of new enterprises, bringing new jobs, and the betterment of the national standard of living" (Bush 1945, p. vii).

There was a confusion about the role of science in the determination of social goals. Some scientists came very near to thinking that what was good for scientists was always good for society. They were willing to undertake any research irrespective of its intended uses or justify any research by empty promises of application, if such promise was likely to facilitate the granting of funds. In fact, some of them believed that there was a kind of preordained identity between the interests of democratically elected governments and science. This was a completely illegitimate extension of the scientific ethos to matters of political or economic morality. Questions such as whether one should undertake research for military purposes, or to find new sources of energy, or to solve a social or health problem, are not more scientific than the question whether one should work on the development of a certain kind of merchandise. There is nothing in the scientific code of ethics to answer such questions. A scientist has to make up his mind on such questions on the basis of the same kind of considerations as a worker, an engineer, a businessman, or anyone else. If he refuses to work on socially desirable projects, because they are not scientifically interesting for him, he may be accused of selfishness, not of any breach of the scientific ethos. If he agrees to work on them because of scientific interest, in spite of his knowledge that the results, say, of military research, will be used for undesirable purposes, the accusation will still be only selfishness. In both cases the moral dilemma of the scientist will not be different from that of the entrepreneur, or worker, or anyone else, namely, whether this is or is not a situation in which one's legitimate professional preferences have to be set aside in face of more important considerations.

The background of this confusion of scientific with general morality is the Baconian belief that science leads to socially useful innovations. Scientists have always believed in this and advertised the contributions of science to such things as the suppression of contagious illness or the generation of electricity. The assumption behind this advertisement is that curing of illness and providing light in the dark are uncontroversial human goals, and therefore their pursuit is consistent with the universalism and disinterestedness of science. This is, of course, a fallacy, which disregards that every technological achievement has its costs, which are, in principle, always controversial. It is, therefore, both misleading and, in the long run, imprudent to identify the technological uses of science with science. A good example of this has been the atomic power stations, which were regarded as uncontroversial blessings until a few years ago and are now very controversial.

But the most important instance of such a shift from a (relatively) uncontroversial to a highly controversial involvement of scientists in development projects was in the field of military R&D. Defense of one's country was in the past considered as an uncontroversial virtue, whether one's country was right or wrong. This moral norm has changed gradually and since the last World War people no longer accepted patriotism as a virtue when it was exercised in defense of morally objectionable regimes. This change of attitude did not discriminate between scientists, generals, industrialists, or others, only between degrees of involvement. Nevertheless, as has been pointed out, scientists acting in the Baconian tradition did everything to identify science as such with the service to the war effort of the Allied nations. This paid off very well in terms of publicity and public support for science until the Vietnam war, but then the confusion between the responsibilities of the scientific community in safeguarding the integrity of the scientific enterprise, and the political responsibilities of scientists as citizens, led to a crisis. Those who opposed the war on political grounds thought that opposition to it was also required by the scientific ethos as opposition to nazism used to be justified by that ethos. They certainly believed that the war required the severance of all the links established between the military and the scientific community in the United States since the last World War. Those favoring the war against the Communists considered the opponents of the war as enemies of freedom, including freedom of science. They could also justify their position by analogies between nazism and communism. Thus the scientific ethos could provide no guidance for conduct in this situation of great stress and conflict. Although this was primarily an internal American conflict, it engulfed many scientists around the world. The disarray in which the scientific community found itself in face of this war contrasted sharply with the unity with which it faced the war against the Axis.

This disarray was deepened by further controversies about the cost of science-based technologies—previously held as entirely beneficial—such as water pollution caused by fertilizers, or the just mentioned real or imagined dangers of nuclear power plants. All this weakened the belief in the efficacy of the scientific ethos and the self-regulation of the scientific community. It is not surprising that many observers felt that there was no relationship between that ethos and what scientists were actually engaged in. The habit of using the rhetorics of the scientific ethos in connection with policies or actions that served no scientific purpose led to widespread distrust of the methods. These developments explain why there has been such widespread disillusionment with the ethos of science since the sixties. To recapitulate, the causes of this development were:

1. The lapse of memory which severed the link between nazism and philosophies subordinating science to politics and made those philosophies now acceptable to radicals of the left. This undermined the consensus that had existed between scientists of the broad political center and the left about the value of the scientific ethos.

2. The emergence of a new coalition led by people opposed to the intellectual and moral autonomy of science on philosophical or political grounds and supported by philosophically and politically noncommitted circles. This occurred partly because the fast-growing scientific enterprise—like all fast-growing things—created also a lot of frustration and partly because scientists involved in politically and economically motivated development projects tried to interpret their involvement in terms of the scientific ethos, although in many of the cases in question the norms of scientific detachment and disinterestedness were inapplicable and patently transgressed.

The Ethos of Science Today

If this analysis is correct then the problem with the scientific ethos is that the rapid expansion of research and its applications led to the emergence of new roles and functions related to science, which were different from those performed by scientists in the past. This does not mean that the traditional norms of scientific conduct are now irrelevant but only that there may have to be additional norms and that the application of the accepted norms to new situations requires careful thought. But this is not the way people perceive the situation today. Thinking on public affairs is dominated by political interests, and the terms of the debate on science, public morality, and politics are determined by the antiscientific leaders of the new coalition critical toward science. Their interpretation of the situation, that the events reviewed before show that science has entered a new era which makes the traditional ethos of science obsolete, is accepted without much questioning. Therefore, it is easy today to criticize such precepts as adherence to logic and evidence and insistence on the autonomy of the scientist to pursue his personal vision and follow his own imagination. Those who believe in these values in their hearts are on the defensive. Since it is much more fashionable to find fault with the conduct of scientists than to praise it, they find it more prudent to talk about what needs to be revised in the ethos of science than about what of it needs to be safeguarded.

The consequences of this situation were clearly in evidence in the famous debate over mental testing during 1969–1971 in the United States and to some extent also in England. The debate was set off by a paper published by a psychologist, Arthur Jensen, in the *Harvard Educational Review* in 1969. The paper contained evidence about differences between the performance of whites and blacks on intelligence tests and attributed part of the differences to inheritance. Although the article was scholarly and far from racist, it could have been misused for antiblack propaganda. This potential misuse of the paper had to be noticed and reacted to if scientists were to take seriously their responsibilities for the social consequences of research. However, the way the debate was actually conducted did little toward making research workers more sensitive to their responsibilities. The three kinds of questions implied in the problem, namely, whether Jensen's conclusions were supported by his and other evidence, whether the research contributed to the scientific understanding of intelligence and/or to educational technology (as it claimed to have done), and whether the publication of the results did actually increase racial prejudice and discrimination, were deliberately treated as inseparable from each other by the leftist critics of Jensen.

Some of the critics refused to treat any part of the problem as amenable to decision by scientific inquiry. And there was a widespread tendency to judge all evidence (at least in fact, if not in principle) strictly on the basis of whether it supported the "right" view, namely, the absence of any inherited components in intelligence. Thus a later paper by another psychologist, Richard Herrnstein (1971), which contained nothing that could have been used in racist agitation was condemned as much as Jensen's paper, and both Herrnstein and Jensen were subject to threats of violence and humiliation.

At about the same time, a book based on rather flimsy and misleadingly presented evidence, claiming to show that differences in educational attainments were the result of the attitudes of teachers (Rosenthal and Jacobsen 1968), was hailed as a breakthrough in the field.

The importance of this case is not the inexcusable behavior of campus radicals, and the utter irresponsibility of some of the press (not that these should be overlooked) but the extent to which the debate took place in terms laid down by those denying the autonomy of science. Thus many scholars condemned Jensen not for any actual effects his work might have had but for making any statement at all about race and intelligence. And Herrnstein was rebuked by a serious philosopher for not having raised philosophical questions about the rewards allotted to people with high mental ability (Cronbach 1975, p. 6). There were very few people who defended those attacked or even the importance of investigations on the components of intelligence, and there were many who, while not actually joining in the attack, found it necessary to let it be known that they were on the "right" side. They voiced only a sort of ritual disapproval of the attackers and went out of their way to find fault with those who were attacked. It took six years after the events began until a leading psychologist, Lee Cronbach, finally published a paper which placed the controversy into perspective (showing that the same issues were raised in the past) and sorted out the different questions involved in the debate in a manner which makes possible their dispassionate appraisal (Cronbach 1975).

It seems that the recent controversy about recombinant DNA research was also conducted on similar lines. The issue was deliberately politicized, and subsequently any attempt at separating the scientific from the political controversy was met with open hostility and resistance on the part of scientists and intellectuals favoring political control of research.

The moral of these episodes as well as of the preceding analysis of the debate on the scientific ethos is that a clear distinction has to be made between the need to regulate new technologies and the clamor to curtail the freedom of scientific inquiry by subjecting it to political control and direction. The regulation of technologies is not a new thing. The manufacture of potentially dangerous substances, the generation and distribution of electricity, and practically every modern technology (railways, cars, etc.) have been regulated by laws for a long time. It goes without saying that by the same token there has to be regulation also of the new technologies, such as nuclear power plants, the use of radioactive material for medical or industrial purposes, or of data banks for the collection of information on individuals.

In addition, it is very important that scientists participating in economically and politically motivated development projects should not be allowed to hide behind the smokescreen of scientific disinterestedness but requested to accept straightforward economic accountability and political responsibility for what they do. This has always been necessary but was frequently forgotten in the past. It is also likely that monitoring the consequences of scientific research and technology will become a standard function of science.

But all this has nothing to do with a denial of the scientific ethos and politically detached inquiry. On the contrary the evidence shows that the greater the social impact of science, and hence the importance of monitoring its effects, the more important it is to safeguard its autonomy. On issues such as the inheritance of intelligence or recombinant DNA, the public will be little helped by scientists acting as spokesmen for political views. This function can be performed by others as well or better than by scientists. What is needed are precisely the traditional scientific virtues of dispassionate, hard-headed, and independent inquiry and judgment.

Subjection of scientific research to controls on the assumption that the social impact of science has been so overwhelming that one can no longer speak of politically neutral science, and that therefore, society cannot afford to leave the responsibility for research in the hands of scientists is a proposition which goes far beyond what is practically required. In order to understand its implications it should be realized that although the argument is presented as a new one—we are warned of the dangers of radiation, genetic engineering, and new, insidious, and all-pervasive effects of science—there is actually nothing new in the demand for the social control of science. The view that science should be subordinated to politics and ideology is an age-old one which can be defended on many philosophical grounds (Toulmin 1972). But while the argument for the subjection of science, or everything else, to political controls or the so-called interests of society may sound plausible, the attempts at putting this view into practice have been less than glorious. The historical instances of adoption of this position as official policy were the Inquisition, the Jacobine terror in the French Revolution, and as has been pointed out above, more recently, nazism. Those who so easily dismiss the political neutrality of science as an untenable position may find reason to think about the matter again if they will realize that in its contemporary form, this view was formulated by Nazi philosophers of science, as can be seen from the following quotation:

> In the future, one will no more adopt the fiction of enfeebled neutrality in science than in law, economy, the State or public life generally. The method of science, is indeed only a reflection of the method of government (Ernst Krieck, quoted by Merton [1973] p. 259, n. 17).

These instances of the endeavor to subject science to political control did not come about by chance. Those who advocate the subjection of science to political controls are not concerned primarily with the improvement of the social uses made of scientific discoveries since that can be taken care of by the regulation of technology. What they really want is to control the development of society. Science as it exists today is as disturbing to them as it was for Bellarmin, since free inquiry is a potential source of unpredictable criticism, discovery, and innovation. They believe in the existence of a supreme wisdom, such as a religion (like Islam or Judaism); an ideology (such as Marxism); or some manifestation of the "popular will" (frequently represented by self-appointed spokesmen), and that these sources contain the "true" answers to all the important problems of mankind or, at least, their own nation. Therefore, they have no use for science as a source of truth and are willing to accept it only as a source of potentially harmful or useful technologies. Of course, if science is nothing but a source of technology, then there is every justification to regulate and guide research according to politically determined goals.

From this point of view, which is essentially the point of view of the large majority of the subordinationists, the most disturbing things about science are the political and moral implications of the scientific approach: the idea that one has to try and define problems in a way amenable to rational, empirically testable solutions, which can be accepted by any person irrespective of religious creeds or politics; and that the "truths" so arrived at, however well tested, are always only tentative truths subject to change by new unsuspected evidence. In other words, they can accept science as some kind of specialized knowledge but not as a philosophical method to establish what is false and what is (under specified conditions) true. That method is, of course, implied by the scientific ethos. From all this stem the attempts to show that there is no connection between scientific research and scientific ethos and the insistence that there is no such thing as science in general but only a multitude of discrete historically determined scientific traditions.

This is the explanation of the historical connection between totalistic politics and the subordinationist view of science. The vigilante tactics employed by those favoring politically controlled science, such as personal terror and victimization, and the resistance to attempts at the breaking down of controversial issues into elements which can be scientifically investigated, and the insistence of defining all aspects of controversial decisions about research and its uses as political, suggests that the historical connection between the subordinationist position and totalistic politics has not been severed. Therefore, the attacks on the scientific ethos today may be no more a sign of its loss of importance than it was in the thirties. On the contrary, it may be a sign of increased importance.

Quite apart from the political and ideological implications of opposition to the scientific ethos, there are practical reasons to doubt the utility of the subordinationist position. The idea that anyone, including scientists, can decide what knowledge should be forbidden or acquired is naive and dangerous. Scientists (not to mention others) have neither the knowledge to foretell the uses to be made of discoveries nor even what discoveries will be made. Even if they had such knowledge, they would not have the power to enforce their decisions, and the real control would be in the hands of bureaucrats and politicians.

This would mean that those who have scientific imagination and vision would have to work on problems laid down by people lacking such imagination and vision (although they might have some other kind of vision). This could seriously damage the vitality and originality of research but would provide no safeguard from issues of discoveries for socially undesirable purposes. In fact it would increase the danger of misuse, since the monitoring of the implications and effects of discoveries would be controlled by the same bureaucratic and political authorities who would also control, and decide about, research. The likelihood that such authorities would suppress informed and independent assessment of potential dangers resulting from their research decisions would be infinitely greater than under a system which respects freedom of scientific inquiry and upholds standards of universalism, detachment, and critical skepticism in scientific judgments as required by the ethos of science.

References

Aliotta, A. 1914. *The Idealistic Reaction Against Science,* translated by Agnes Mc-Caskill. London: Macmillan.

Barber, B. 1962. *Science and the Social Order.* New York: Collier. 2d ed.

Barnes, S. B., and R. G. A. Dolby. 1970. "The Scientific Ethos: A Deviant Viewpoint," *European Journal of Sociology* 11: 3–25.

Ben-David, J. 1977*a*. "Organization, Social Control and Cognitive Change in Science," in J. Ben-David and T. N. Clark (eds.), *Culture and its Creators.* Chicago: University of Chicago Press. [This volume, chap. 15.]

———. 1977*b*. *Centers of Learning: Britain, France, Germany, United States.* New York, McGraw-Hill. 1977.

Bernal, J. D. 1939. *The Social Function of Science.* London: Routledge & Kegan Paul.

Brush, S. G. 1974. "Should History of Science be Rated X?" *Science* 183, 4130: 1164–83.

Bush, V. 1945. *Science, The Endless Frontier.* Washington, D.C.: U.S. Government Printing Office.

Cronbach, L. 1975. "Five Decades of Public Controversy Over Mental Testing," *American Psychologist* 30, 1: 1–14.

Forman, P. 1971. "Weimar Culture, Causality and Quantum Theory, 1918–1927," *Historical Studies in Physical Sciences* 3:1–116.

Gaston, J. 1978. *The Reward System in British and American Science.* New York: Wiley.

Habermas, J. 1970. "Technology and Science as 'Ideology,'" in his *Toward a Rational Society,* pp. 81–122. Boston: Beacon Press.

Herrnstein, R. 1971. "I.Q." *Atlantic Monthly* 228, 3:43–64.

Jensen, A. R. 1969. "How Much Can We Boost IQ and Scholastic Achievement?" *Harvard Educational Review* 39:1–123.

Joravsky, D. 1961. *Soviet Marxism and Natural Science 1917–1932.* New York: Columbia University Press.

———. 1970. *The Lysenko Affair.* Cambridge: Harvard University Press.

King, M. D. 1971. "Reason Tradition and Progressiveness of Science," *History and Theory* 10:3–32.

Marcuse, H. 1964. *One-Dimensional Man.* London: Routledge and Kegan Paul, Boston: Beacon Press.

Merton, R. K. 1938. "Science and the Social Order," *Philosophy of Science* 5: 321–37.

―――. 1942. "Science and Technology in a Democratic Order," *Journal of Legal and Political Science* 1:115–26.

―――. 1945. "Sociology of Knowledge," in G. Gurvitch and W. E. Moore (eds). *Twentieth Century Sociology.* New York: Philosophical Library.

(These three items are reprinted as chapters 12, 13 and 1 of Merton, R. K. (1973), *The Sociology of Science* (edited by N. W. Storer). Chicago: University of Chicago Press. Page numbers refer to this publication.)

Mitroff, I. I. 1974*a.* "Norms and Counter-Norms in a Select Group of the Apollo Moon Scientists: A Case Study of the Ambivalence of Scientists," *American Sociological Review* 39:579–595.

―――. 1974*b. The Subjective Side of Science.* Amsterdam: Elsevier.

Mulkay, M. J. 1969. "Some Aspects of Cultural Growth in the Natural Sciences," *Social Research* 36, 1:22–52.

―――. 1972. *The Social Process of Innovation.* London: Macmillan.

Polanyi, M. 1951. *The Logic of Liberty.* Chicago: University of Chicago Press.

Popper, K. R. 1957. *The Poverty of Historicism.* London: Routledge and Kegan Paul.

Price, D. de S. 1963. *Little Science, Big Science.* New York: Columbia University Press.

Ravetz, J. R. 1971. *Scientific Knowledge and Its Social Problems.* Oxford: Clarendon Press.

Rosenthal, R., and L. Jacobsen. 1968. *Pygmalion in the Classroom.* New York: Holt, Rinehart and Winston.

Spengler, O. 1939. *The Decline of the West.* New York: Alfred A. Knopf.

Spiegel-Rösing, I. 1973. *Wissenschaftsentwicklung und Wissenschaftssteuerung: Einführung und Material zur Wissenschaftsforschung* Frankfurt am Main: Athenaeum.

Stehr, N. 1978. "The Ethos of Science Revisited: Social Norms and Cognitive Norms," *Sociological Inquiry* 48, 3–4:172–96.

Toulmin, S. 1972. "The Historical Background of the Anti-Science Movement," in Ciba Foundation Symposium: *Civilisation and Science in Conflict or Collaboration.* New York: Elsevier.

Waddington, C. H. 1948. *The Scientific Attitude.* West Drayton: Penguin Books. (2d rev. ed.).

Academic Market, 24
Ideology, and the Growth
of Scientific Knowledge:
Physiology in Mid-
Nineteenth-Century
Germany

The Background and the Problem

Sociology of knowledge was very popular in continental European sociology during the 1920s and 1930s, went into almost complete oblivion during and after World War II, to reappear again with added force about 1970 (Curtis and Petras 1970; Fuhrman 1980; Hamilton 1974; Merton 1973*a*; Remmling 1967; Stark 1958). This recent interest in the sociology of knowledge has been distinguished from prewar sociology of knowledge by three characteristics: (1) the field is now as popular in Britain as on the continent of Europe and has many adherents also in the United States; (2) it also claims as its domain science, a branch of knowledge which was not considered amenable to sociological interpretation by the central Mannheimian school of the prewar period (although there were even then attempts to include science); and (3) sociology of science has strong support among philosophers and historians of science (Barnes 1977; Bloor 1976; Hesse 1980; Mulkay 1979; Mulkay and Milič 1980). What has remained unchanged is that the field claims to replace universalistic methodologies and epistemologies of science and cognition in general with relativistic criteria of truth varying from social context to social context. Therefore, the research program has also remained similar and consists of attempts to reinterpret important cultural events, such as scientific discoveries, as the outcomes of the social motivations and interests of the discoverers acting in particular historical and/or organizational situations rather than as events in a coherent chain of attempts to find logically satisfactory explanations of puzzling phenomena of nature.

This research was supported by the Spencer Foundation.

501

This approach has not been universally accepted. There is an ongoing debate among sociologists of science, paralleled by one among philosophers, between those in favor of and those against the attempts at a reduction of scientific knowledge to the interplay of social forces.[1]

The purpose of this paper is to examine whether the terms in which these debates are conducted in sociology are adequate to the present state of research. It will be suggested that they are not and that the issues have to be reconceptualized in order to bring them in line with the results of empirical studies.

To begin, I shall state some propositions formulated in the early 1970s, shortly after the recent debate had started (Ben-David 1971). First, scientists, as well as other thinkers, go about finding answers to their problems through examining the relevant information and by analyzing the problems with the aid of whatever conceptual tools are available to them in the disciplinary and/or professional traditions they have inherited.

In addition, every scientist may, and probably will, be influenced by a variety of other conditions, such as personal or collective interests, political currents, religious beliefs, and knowledge derived from other intellectual traditions than those of his field of research. These may help or hinder the finding of satisfactory solutions to the problems under investigation by drawing his attention to, or distracting it from, data and ideas important for the solution or by creating emotional attachments helpful or harmful in finding a solution. Therefore, such influences may be important in the explanation of the work of any particular individual or group or the explanation of any particular discovery.

When, however, the purpose is not the explanation of one-time events but the development of a disciplinary or subdisciplinary tradition, the importance of these changing historical conditions will tend to be eliminated. All subsequent users of a contribution to a tradition will approach it from the point of view of its usefulness for the solution of the substantive problems of the field. Like the original contributors, they will also be influenced by a variety of conditions not related to the tradition in question. Since, however, the considerations internal to the field are constant, while the unrelated "external" influences vary from person to person, the effects of these external influences on the development of the field will probably be eliminated in the long run. This process of selection need not be very prolonged, since it is speeded up by the

1. There were emotional elements in this difference of opinion. But many also found the very concern with the demarcation of science constricting. This reaction was, however, not entirely undesirable. No one was deterred from asking exciting new questions about the demarcationists' no-man's-land, namely, the relationship between science and other fields; and the fact that there was no empirical evidence to show that scientific knowledge was indeed shaped by social conditions was eventually taken as a challenge, leading to an increasing flow of empirical research from about the mid-1970s on.

decentralization of the scientific effort which ensures some instant randomization of external influences and by the socialization and reward system in science which tends to select for success researchers who have the intellectual perspicacity and emotional discipline to keep out of their work influences not contributing to the solution of scientific problems they are working on.

Therefore, it was concluded that these external influences will not be "systematic," that is, "regular and predictable. Occasional influences may provide the theme for historical investigations but not for a sociology of science" (Ben-David 1971, p. 8). Furthermore, it was argued that this was true not only of natural scientists but also of social scientists and political and moral philosophers. These, of course, will ask questions relating to the current state of society, which is the subject matter of their inquiries, but will still deal with those problems with conceptual tools acquired in the course of their training in intellectual traditions which are the creation of people from many ages and societies. These traditions are and can only be held together by an internal logic and interest in long-lasting specific problems, not by the changing variety of social conditions, beliefs, and other influences impinging on the people who created, and contributed to, them in different ages and societies.

These views were supported by empirical evidence, such as a comparison of the success of field theories, probably influenced by romantic *Naturphilosophie*, in physics, and the rejection of these ideas in biology—in which they had originally much greater influence—because in biology they did not prove useful for empirical research.

Two Views of Physiology in Mid-Nineteenth-Century Germany

With a single exception (Mulkay and Milić 1980) these arguments were not paid attention to by the protagonists of a sociology of scientific knowledge. Nevertheless, I still believe them as essentially correct, although in need of some change of emphasis. In the following I shall try to show their usefulness through the analysis of a historical case, that of physiology in mid-nineteenth-century Germany.

Timothy Lenoir, a historian of science interested in the relationship between philosophical and political ideas and biological theory, and well versed in sociology of science, has recently investigated the rise of the "organic physics" school, comprising Brücke, Helmholtz, C. Ludwig, and, in particular, the career of E. Dubois-Reymond, who was the main ideologist of this group (Lenoir 1983). The subject matter of his work partially overlapped the work that Awraham Zloczower and I did about twenty years ago and can usefully serve as an illustration of the change in the sociological perspective during the intervening period (Ben-David 1960; Ben-David and Zloczower 1961; Zloczower 1981).

When Zloczower and I looked at the steep rise of German scientific research in the middle of the nineteenth century, we addressed the following questions: (1) What were the conditions in the German states which motivated so many people of outstanding ability to take up research as a vocation and those in power to encourage and support their endeavor? (2) How did it happen that in spite of the initial predominance of idealistic and romantic views on science, and an explicit prejudice against experimental research at universities, experimental fields, namely, chemistry and physiology first, followed later by physics, gained within a short time so much the upper hand, that eventually—beginning in the 1850s—German scholars attempted to turn even philosophy into an experimental science (an effort which eventually gave rise to experimental psychology)? (See Ben-David and Collins 1966.)

We found the answer to these questions in the existence of a—by the standards of those times—large (about twenty-four universities), decentralized academic system, in which the universities (or rather the Ministries of the various Länder financing the universities—Turner 1970) fiercely competed with each other for academic fame. This created a sellers' market for able and successful researchers working at the forefront of science. The opportunities were particularly favorable in the experimental sciences, in which success was judged by relatively objective standards, academic recognition was worldwide, and the opportunity to start a new specialty—and thus to realize the dream of every competitor in a market for obtaining at least a temporary monopoly—was greater than in the humanities. These conditions attracted talented people and gave them the bargaining power needed to obtain new academic positions and good laboratories and to overcome the prejudice against experimental fields.

Physiology was a particularly good illustration of the way the system worked. Originally a subsidiary branch of anatomy, it became a separate and autonomous field due to the successful bargaining of Carl Ludwig with the University of Zurich when offered a chair at that university. The precedent of Zurich was followed by all other universities. The extremely productive and inspiring Ludwig went on eventually to Leipzig to establish at that wealthy university a center for research and training of unprecedented size and importance.

The view of science implied in this model is that of a scientific community doing its best when provided with sufficient funds, able to work in an institution which safeguards its autonomy and to apply purely intellectual criteria in the selection of research problems and evaluation of results (Merton 1973b, 1973c; Polanyi 1951). To this model should be added competition, to keep both scientists and university administrators on their toes.

Therefore, the research strategy followed by us was as follows: first to examine the structure of the university system and then to concentrate on the way this structure affected careers and research, in particular the growth of new specialties and disciplines.

Lenoir accepts this account as part of the story and adds important new information to it, but his view of science and his basic theoretical model are different. If I may characterize the approach that Zloczower and I take as looking primarily at the internal social structure of science and considering the interface with the environment only from the point of view of the conditions needed to secure the boundaries and sustenance of the internal structure, then one can characterize Lenoir's approach as concentrating primarily on the interface and regarding the internal system as much more unstable and punctured by many more interpenetrations of people and ideas than we assumed. Even more important is that Zloczower and I were interested only in the growth of research and academic recognition of new fields of inquiry, while Lenoir wants to give a sociological explanation of how and why certain scientific ideas arose and/or became adopted by scientists in a given field.

His different perspective suggests to him questions not asked by us. He asks: Who were those attracted to physiology? What were their purposes prior to entering this field? What extrascientific resources did they bring with them in order to forge ahead in the field? How did they manipulate the internal environment in order to realize their preconceived goals? How did they balance, at various times, their scientific work with their political and status interests? How did they find a way to relate their research interests to their social ambitions?

Thus, we obtain a new, different picture: At its center is a group of very able young men, from upwardly mobile middle-class backgrounds, fired with ambition to "occupy a respected position in society," who chose science as a vocation in which one could do something important for society and as an avenue of upward mobility. All but one of them (Carl Ludwig) were students of Johannes Müller, whose laboratory was the foremost in physiology during the 1830s (Cranefield 1957).

The most interesting question addressed by Lenoir is: Why did this group of people choose a radical biophysical program, "organic physics," for their research which, as Cranefield had shown, was not quite practicable at that time? Lenoir stresses that there was in this an element of revolt against Müller and an attempt at establishing themselves as a distinct group (a kind of "product differentiation"). Above all, he shows that the serious study of physics which all the members of this group undertook (Helmholtz eventually became a physicist, and Dubois-Reymond was also suggested for a chair in physics at one time) was related to their participation in a scientific-political movement in Berlin headed by Gustav Magnus.

Magnus was an experimental physicist of bourgeois background who fought against the monopoly of the theoretical physicists at the University of Berlin. He succeeded in obtaining a full professorship, which meant official recognition of experimental physics, in 1845. The discrimination against experimental physics—a field which he believed was of greatest importance for industry—was for him part of the same system of aristocratic prejudice and absolutist authoritarianism which also discriminated against the "working bourgeoisie" and kept Germany dismembered into a number of small states, the existence of which was in the interest only of the members of the royal or princely families ruling those states. Cultivating and teaching physics, in particular experimental physics, was for him a mission of spreading enlightenment and knowledge useful for economic growth.

The organic physicists, alongside a number of junior officers from the army engineering corps, inventors (like Siemens, Halske, and Leonhardt), and several university students joined Magnus in the Berlin Physical Association established in 1845. This was done partly out of their wish to perfect themselves in their different professional endeavors through the application of physics and partly because they shared with Magnus the prevailing liberal views on political, economic, and academic reform. Thus, organic physics was not simply an endeavor to advance physiological knowledge but was also part of a world view, related to sociopolitical ideology.

To consider their scientific views as part of the liberal world view must have been an encouraging and exhilarating feeling during the pre-1848 period when liberalism was on the rise and seemed to be on the verge of political success. Identification with the liberal movement and advocacy of academic reform could also appear, at that time, as useful for the advancement of the views and careers of the organic physicists. It is quite likely that these circumstances were instrumental in welding these young physiologists into a cohesive group, with a boldly declared purpose and program of reconstituting physiology on purely physical-chemical foundations.

Following the failure of the Revolution, their mood changed, and for a while they felt that their hopes for scientific and professional advancement would have to be given up together with their hopes for political reform. Fortunately, their fate did not depend on support from the political friends or on ideological climate. They could still resort to the internal system of science and get ahead according to the politically neutral criterion of scientific success and recognition concentrating on research and publication. Eventually, all of them attained central positions in world science and in the German academic system. They could and did wait within the safe precincts of the university for the turning of the political tide. When this came about, and the semiliberal political mood of the 1860s and 1870s, shared now by the highest circles, officially favored experimental science, the ambitious physiologists were not averse to returning to the public arena, adding intellectual luster to the economic and military successes of the new German empire and benefiting from favors granted to them on the assumption that research was useful for industry, the military, and the country as a whole.

An Attempt at Sociological Interpretation

Several remarks can be made on this comparison of these two studies of German physiology: (1) They do not contradict each other; (2) nevertheless, they convey significantly different views of physiology and physiologists; (3) it would be a pity to relegate the kind of study done by Lenoir to some place outside sociology (as I suggested twelve years ago; see Ben-David 1971); but (4) it is far from obvious how to incorporate it into sociology.

I shall attempt to deal with this last problem (which is the core of this paper) by making some more detailed comparisons. First, I shall discuss the question apparently asked in both the earlier and later studies: Why was experimental physiology—at that time a field having no practical application—so attractive to many able young people and thus destined to develop rapidly?

For Zloczower and me this question was inseparable from the parallel question about chemistry, which was the other experimental field that underwent a spectacular process of growth at about the same time. The explanation we suggested was that these two fields were particularly favored by the conditions then prevailing in the competitive academic system. In Germany both fields came under the sway of speculative *Naturphilosophie* and other philosophical systems during the first three decades of the nineteenth century. These theories proved to be relatively sterile for experimental research (although theoretically some of the ideas proved valuable—Lenoir 1982), and as a result German physiology and chemistry were backward in comparison with their development in France or in the school of Berzelius in Sweden, which rejected speculation and adopted an experimental-quantitative approach. While in Germany research was stagnating, in France and Sweden it advanced impressively. What happened as a consequence was predictable by the market model: Sooner or later someone was bound to import the new approach from abroad and, once imported and having proved successful in one place—philosophical opposition notwithstanding—it would spread rapidly throughout the system. And this is precisely what happened. The work of Stephen Turner (1971) and now the present paper by Lenoir have added important details to the picture, such as who made the decisions about appointments and how and under what conditions those decisions were made, but these have only confirmed the usefulness of the academic market model.[2]

2. By the way, this model also fits the fact that the development of experimental physics lagged considerably behind that of chemistry and physiology (a point not sufficiently considered

Lenoir, who looks at physiology from the viewpoint of its place in the context of German society as a whole, pays no attention to its parallel with chemistry. What he sees, and to which we did not pay attention, is the link of this field with experimental physics, and beyond this with technology and industry in general. Physiology, perceived as "organic physics," had a particular attraction to young people like Dubois-Reymond, Helmholtz, Ludwig, and Brücke, because this approach based physiology on a general principle of reducing the mysteries of life to measurable and experimentally testable physical and chemical processes which, they believed, was a world view bound to emerge victorious not only in science but also in society as a whole. Their youthful scientific aspirations were reinforced by a vision of playing a leading role in the liberal reform of their society.

At first blush it may appear that the same question revealed two different stories and resulted in two different answers. However, there are, in fact, two different questions here. One question is: Why were so many able and energetic people attracted to physiology? The second question is: Why did they, or at least some of them, commit themselves in the early and mid-1840s to a dogmatically conceived and aggressively declared research program of "organic physics"? The first question is common to both investigations, and the answers are not mutually exclusive. One can be attracted to a field for several reasons, and several people can be attracted for different reasons. The opportunities for success in research offered by experimental fields could attract people to either chemistry or physiology; some people might have been attracted to them also by ideology and social ambition. This latter kind of motivation might have played a part in the case of Dubois-Reymond and perhaps two or three others. But, I maintain, this was not a necessary or even important cause for the young people's interest in the field; the important and sufficient cause was the existence of favorable conditions in the academic market in chemistry and physiology and the intellectual opportunities available in both fields.

On the other hand, the adoption of the organic physics research program in a demonstrative and somewhat dogmatic manner can be explained only as a result of the ideological attractiveness of the particular approach and cannot be dealt with by the academic market model. This is consistent with the fact that after 1848, when they had to rely for success exclusively on the academic market, all but one (Dubois-Reymond) of the organic physicists either abandoned physiology or disregarded the program in their actual research (Cranefield 1957).

---

before). German physicists, unlike biologists and chemists, had never accepted *Naturphilosophie* (although their disdain for experimental physics was sometimes, probably wrongly, attributed to the influence of this philosophy). Theoretical physics was, and continued to be, an internationally respected and successful field, and there was nothing ostensibly better that could be offered by experimentalists such as Gustav Magnus. Unlike chemistry and physiology, in physics the experimentalists did not have a competitive advantage.

Another issue which illustrates the relationship between the approaches of these two sets of investigations is the importance attributed in Lenoir's paper to the class background and affiliation of the physiologists—an issue which was quite disregarded by Zloczower and me. It appears paradoxical that this should have proved a variable of importance to a historian, while it was found to be of no significance by a pair of sociologists (especially in view of the fact that one of the pair was a Marxian scholar).

This discrepancy is, again, the result of a difference between two points of view. Lenoir is interested in the place of science in the class system and politics of the German states, especially Prussia, in the 1840s. From this point of view, experimental science, like industry, appears as a new avenue for the middle classes toward improving their status in society. Exploring the social background and the career choices of those who entered a scientific profession because, or partly because, they regarded it as an avenue to success suited to their circumstances and tastes is an excellent way of viewing physiology in the broadest social context, as well as coming to grips with the individual biographies of some key scientific figures of the day. Placing science in this context can show how politics can be linked to the furthering of the interest of scientific fields and the advancement of some scientists.

As against this, the earlier work that Zloczower and I did derived from a different interest: How did the phenomenon called science arise, spread, and grow in what can be loosely referred to as the Western world and later also in the entire world? We were well aware that politics, religion, and ideology had at times favored and at other times opposed science; that science had been very frequently used for political, ideological, and, of course, economic purposes; that quite a few scientists had welcomed, or even initiated, these uses; and that some (many fewer) scientists had bent their scientific views to political and other nonscientific uses. But the phenomenon we were interested in was how, despite all this, scientific research on an ever-broadening range of problems retained a coherence, continuity, and constancy of purpose to produce improved knowledge through rational inquiry and systematic observation and experimentation.

If one could view science as a ship trying to keep on course amidst storms and dangerous reefs, requiring many detours, then one could say that Lenoir is interested in the winds, currents, and reefs without which one could not explain the actual course taken by the ship, while we were interested in the steering mechanism of the ship which determines its long-term direction. Of course, there are also favorable winds, currents, and sealanes which propel and guide the ship on its intended course, and then the two viewpoints converge. The adoption of the physicalist program described in this paper was such a case of temporary convergence.

For us, the fascinating aspect of German physiology, and German science in general, during the nineteenth century was that, whereas previously the support and flourishing of science had depended almost entirely on favorable political and ideological conditions (on favorable "winds and currents"), in the nineteenth century there emerged a relatively autonomous and competitive academic system, capable of advancing research rapidly, with no need for justifying claims for the support of science by specific nonscientific purposes and values. Sticking to the nautical simile, it was something like the transition from sailing vessels to steamships.

Therefore, the decisive issue was that looking at the development of German academic science, or at specific fields of science, from the foundation of the University of Berlin in 1809 to about the time of World War I, one could see a logic that was reasonably consistent with the academic market model and was relatively independent from the numerous changes of the political and class systems. From this point of view, the class-consciousness and liberal involvement of the most important group of physiologists in the 1840s was an insignificant phenomenon; the most important thing was that the system led to rapid growth and innovation between about the 1830s and the 1870s (when growth was deflected to new specialties), irrespective of the revolution and its suppression in the 1840s.

What these comparisons show is that the same social events and phenomena could be viewed as parts of two different social systems: The group of young "organic physicists" in the 1840s could be located in the social system of prerevolutionary Berlin; at the same time they could also be located in the nineteenth-century German academic system. Furthermore, within each of these systems the group in question can be at the center of the picture, as in the study done by Lenoir, or part of a panoramic view of a larger scene, as in the investigations done by Zloczower and me. Or, it is possible to try to do both, to focus first on the group picture and then to look at the panoramic picture, locating in it the group by, so to speak, magnifying the spot where they are.

All of these ways of looking at the events are sociological. Whether the question is about a one-time event, such as the emergence of the organic physics program, or about a class and chain of events, such as the growth of experimental sciences in Germany during a period of time, makes the analysis neither more nor less sociological, as long as the answer to the question locates the event in an appropriate social system.

This is not to say that one should be content with case studies of one-time events. It is important to search for parallels and precedents. The confluence between a social movement, its political ideology and scientific world view, which served as an explanation of the emergence of the organic physics program, may have similarities with the confluence between the Puritan ethos and Baconian research strategy; or with the congruence between latitudinarian Anglicanism and a corpuscularian view of physical nature in seventeenth-century England (Jacob and Jacob 1980; Merton 1973b; Webster 1975).

Another category of events into which the sociology of organic physics could be fitted may be a seemingly recurring relationship between reductionist approaches in science and moderately reformist ideologies in politics, such as have been witnessed in England beginning in the 1650s and ending at the turn of the century; in pre-Revolutionary and post-Thermidor France in the eighteenth century; or in the Western democracies from the end of World War II to the late 1960s (Ben-David 1983).

Conclusions for the Sociology of Scientific Knowledge

One clear conclusion from the present discussion is that the sociology of scientific knowledge represented by interpretations such as those of Lenoir, J. R. Jacob, and M. C. Jacob have no implications for epistemology. The scientific world views and programs discussed in these interpretations might have been embraced with enthusiasm because of ideological reasons. But the scientific success of those adopting them as manifested in the incorporation of their discoveries in the disciplinary tradition was determined by their usefulness for the solution of specific substantive problems. The relationship between science, ideology, and social structure established in these studies is functional and does not postulate a commitment to any relativistic or other epistemology. This substantiates the assertion made in the beginning of the paper that the continuing debate about the alleged relativistic epistemological implications of the sociology of scientific knowledge has no relationship to the findings of empirical research.

However, there may be another issue arising from recent research which ought to be formulated and addressed. Placing the concerns in the local and temporary framework, such as the prerevolutionary social system of Berlin or Paris, or the social system of a "school," makes it possible to reconstruct a kind of local and temporary knowledge state in science—namely, a picture of this state as it looks from the point of view of people deeply involved not only in their research but perhaps also in politics, personal conflicts, religious commitments, career concerns, and so forth.

The integration of these local and temporary knowledge states in a history showing the long-term development of scientific traditions is a task still to be accomplished. This paper is an attempt to make such an integration.

It seems, however, that there is a tendency among some sociologists and philosophers of science to deny the legitimacy of such attempts on the ground that they are based on an erroneous reconstruction of social and intellectual history in which developments are viewed from their end point backward, rather than in the sequence in which they actually occurred, when the outcome, at each point, was still unpredictable.

This is an argument which needs to be heeded. But while one has to be aware of the pitfalls of reconstructing the past from the point of view of the present, one must equally be aware of the pitfalls of trying to view it as a kind of biological evolution, which is completely blind as far as the future is concerned, and the outcome of which is determined by some kind of natural selection and survival of the fittest.[3]

The point is that what is being selected out in the social world are social and cultural systems, such as human roles, intellectual contributions, institutions, and cultural traditions, which are not analogous to the biological species, the object of evolutionary selection. Social systems have an ability to modify themselves as well as their environment in quite fundamental ways and are designed to act for the attainment of long-range purposes. Taking into account these long-range purposes of social systems, and paying attention to the social devices—usually norms—by which the longtime (relative) stability of these systems is secured, is not a falsification of the past but the only way of its realistic reconstruction.

Concentrating exclusively on the local and temporary social systems in which scientific activity takes place to the exclusion of the longer-term, normatively regulated academic or other systems, will not disclose a "naturalistic" unbiased view of the social conditions of science, or any other tradition, but a mutilated one. The temporary-local and the long-term normative systems are equally needed in making sense of any social or cultural development.

References

Barnes, Barry. *Interests and Growth of Knowledge*. London: Routledge & Kegan Paul, 1977.

Ben-David, Joseph. "Scientific Productivity and Academic Organization in 19th-Century Medicine." *American Sociological Review* 25 (1960):828–43. [This volume, chap. 5.]

———. *The Scientist's Role in Society: A Comparative Study*. Englewood Cliffs, N.J.: Prentice-Hall, 1971.

———. "Science, Scientism and Anti-Scientism." [In Tord Ganelius (ed.), *Progress in Science and Its Social Conditions. Nobel Symposium 58 held at Lidingö, Sweden, 15–19 August 1983*. (Oxford: Pergamon Press, 1986), pp. 61–68; this volume, chap. 25.]

3. For an example of such—probably unintentional—evolutionary imagery, see Bourdieu (1981): "The structure of the scientific field at any given moment is defined by the state of power distribution between the protagonists in the struggle (agents or institutions), i.e., by the structure of the distribution of the specific capital, the result of previous struggles which is objectified in institutions and disposition and commands the strategies and objective chances of the different agents or institutions in the present struggles" (p. 267). Elsewhere in the same paper he speaks about science not being "an exception to the fundamental laws of all fields—in particular the law of interest, which is capable of introducing ruthless violence into the most 'disinterested' scientific struggles" (p. 273).

Ben-David, Joseph, and Randall Collins. "Social Factors in the Origins of a New Science: The Case of Psychology." *American Sociological Review* 31 (1966): 451–565. [This volume, chap. 2.]

Ben-David, Joseph, and A. Zloczower. "The Idea of the University and the Academic Market Place." *European Journal of Sociology* 2 (1961): 303–14.

Bloor, David. *Knowledge and Social Imagery.* London: Routledge & Kegan Paul, 1976.

Bourdieu, Pierre. "The Specificity of the Scientific Field." In *French Sociology: Rupture and Renewal Since 1968,* edited by C. Lemert. New York: Columbia University Press, 1981 [1975].

Cranefield, Paul F. "The Organic Physics of 1847 and the Biophysics of Today." *Journal of the History of Medicine and Allied Sciences* 12 (1957): 407–23.

Curtis, James, and John W. Petras (eds.). *The Sociology of Knowledge: A Reader.* New York: Praeger, 1970.

Fuhrman, Ellsworth. *The Sociology of Knowledge in America, 1883–1915.* Charlottesville: University of Virginia Press, 1980.

Hamilton, Peter. *Knowledge and Social Structure: An Introduction to the Classical Argument in the Sociology of Knowledge.* London: Routledge & Kegan Paul, 1974.

Hesse, Mary. *Revolutions and Reconstructions in the Philosophy of Science.* Bloomington: Indiana University Press, 1980.

Jacob, J. R. *Robert Boyle and the English Revolution.* New York: Burt Franklin, 1977.

Jacob, J. R., and M. C. Jacob. "The Anglican Origins of Modern Science: The Metaphysical Foundation of the Whig Constitution." *Isis* 71 (1980): 251–67.

Jacob, M. C. *The Newtonians and the English Revolution.* Ithaca: Cornell University Press, 1976.

Kuhn, Thomas S. *The Structure of Scientific Revolutions.* Chicago: University of Chicago Press, 1970.

Lenoir, Timothy. *The Strategy of Life: Teleology and Mechanics in Nineteenth-Century German Biology.* Dordrecht: Reidel, 1982.

———. "Social Interests and the Organic Physics of 1847." [In Edna Ullmann-Margalit (ed.), *Science in Reflection* (= *The Israel Colloquium: Studies in History, Philosophy, and Sociology of Science,* vol. 3. = *Boston Studies in the Philosophy of Science,* vol. 110) (Dordrecht: Kluwer, 1988), pp. 169–91.]

Merton, Robert K. "Paradigm for a Sociology of Knowledge." In *The Sociology of Science: Theoretical and Empirical Investigations,* edited and introduced by N. W. Storer. Chicago: University of Chicago Press, 1973a[1945].

———. "Science and the Social Order." In *The Sociology of Science.* 1973b[1938].

———. "Normative Structure of Science." In *The Sociology of Science.* 1973c [1942].

Mulkay, Michael. *Science and the Sociology of Knowledge.* London: George Allen & Unwin, 1979.

Mulkay, Michael, and V. Milič. "The Sociology of Science in East and West." *Current Sociology* 28 (1980): 23–42.

Polanyi, Michael. *The Logic of Liberty.* London: Routledge & Kegan Paul, 1951.

Remmling, Gunter. *Road to Suspicion.* Chicago: University of Chicago Press, 1967.

Stark, Werner. *The Sociology of Knowledge.* London: Routledge & Kegan Paul, 1958.

Turner, R. Stephen. "The Growth of Professional Research in Prussia, 1818–1848, Causes and Contexts." *Historical Studies in the Physical Sciences* 3 (1971): 137–82.

Webster, Charles. *The Great Instauration: Science, Medicine and Reform, 1626–1660.* London: Duckworth, 1975.

Zloczower, A. *Career Opportunities and the Growth of Scientific Discovery in Nineteenth-Century Germany, with Special Reference to the Development of Physiology.* New York: Arno Press, 1981.

Part VII

The Changing Fortunes
of the Ethos of Science

A Historical and Sociological Perspective

Introduction

Ben-David, we have repeatedly noted, was committed to the scientific ethos as a method of conducting the search for truth and, consequently, directing human affairs. In this context, "scientific ethos" must be understood broadly, as characterizing a rational, nonauthoritarian approach to knowledge, an approach that is free from any a priori commitments, is liberal and democratic in its attitude toward the freedom of thought, and, specifically, upholds the autonomy of science. Moreover, the scientific ethos, by its very essence, implies universalism, whereas any system of thought not following it (religion, ideology) is necessarily particularistic (of class, nation, etc.).

When, in the late 1960s, in conjunction with and in sequel to the 1968 students' movement, a rising tide of science criticism clearly became perceptible in the United States and in Western Europe, Ben-David felt both existentially and intellectually concerned. Since he shared Max Weber's and R. K. Merton's conviction that science and, more generally, the scientific ethos need special social conditions to thrive, he endeavored to determine what changes in social conditions caused that sudden and unexpected rise of what he labeled "anti-scientism": an attitude of hostility to the very ethos of science. This was the main subject of Ben-David's work during the last three or four years of his life. He first exposed his explanation of the phenomenon in his lecture at the 1983 Nobel Symposium, entitled "Science, Scientism, and Anti-Scientism" (chap. 25, below). Essentially, he argued that antiscientism is a reaction not to the state of science but of society: science has become an integral part of the scientistic utopia of modern society, and when, as a result of economic or political developments, expectations people placed in that utopia are disappointed, then the attitude toward science and all it stands for changes; science

517

then comes to be regarded as a "god that failed" and people become receptive to antiscientism.

Although Ben-David believed that in the 1983 lecture he already gave the clue to the understanding of the alternating waves of scientism and antiscientism, he decided to pursue further a systematic historical investigation of the changing attitudes toward science and rationality. On his death, he left two related texts bearing on this subject (in addition to the only indirectly related " 'Norms of Science' and the Sociological Interpretation of Scientific Behavior," chap. 22, above): (i) a typescript with the title "Changing Perceptions of Science"; and (ii) a handwritten manuscript of what was destined to become a monograph, with the working title, "The Ethos of Science, Social Perceptions of Science, and Political Ideologies." Ben-David outlined the "theoretical framework" of the planned monograph as follows:

1. To explain changes in the scientific ethos as a function of changing political ideologies and social perceptions of science, specifically, explaining the changes in the scientific ethos from 1930 to the present, placing the emergence of the ethos and its contents within the social situation of scientists in this period. (Scientific ethos is the dependent variable.)

2. To explore the effects of these changes on science itself, on scientific work (specifically, which scientific disciplines were affected?), on the ethics, norms, and values of scientists themselves, and on politics. (Scientific ethos is the independent variable.)

3. To reconsider the question of the value neutrality of science and to develop new formulations(?).

4. To explore the formulations of the scientific ethos in reaction to (a) antiscientism; (b) Communist scientism turning into antiscientism; (c) the new intense involvement with governments; (d) the bankruptcy of ideologies and religions.

Actually, the handwritten manuscript turns out to be a rough draft of (1) only.

A comparison of *i* and *ii* showed that great parts of the former were incorporated into the latter. Since the remaining parts of *i* also usefully complement *ii* and since *ii* anyway needed a measure of editing, it was decided to integrate *i* and *ii* into a single comprehensive text. It is the outcome of this fusion which is printed below (chap. 26), under the more general title of *ii*.

Editing a text whose author did not live to revise it is a probing task. I have limited my emendations to occasional changes of the order of sentences or paragraphs, elimination of redundancy, stylistic improvements, and so forth, with a view to improving the readability. In this task, the help of Bonnie Lindstrom (Chicago) has been most valuable. It goes without saying that I have done my best to remain faithful to Ben-David's intentions. The text deliberately preserves its unfinished character.

The subjects and theses of chapters 25 and 26 obviously overlap in part, and some formulations occur in both of them. The focus of the arguments developed in the two works is different, however. Since the overlap is fairly limited, it was decided to leave both texts as they are.

"The Ethos of Science" exposes a very general vision of the role of scientific and rational thinking in Western society since the seventeenth century, in its changing relations to other, nonrational, forms of thought, namely, religion and ideology. Ben-David writes from the vantage point of the commitment to the universalistic world view centered around science, a world view that reached an apotheosis in the two decades following 1945; he views with great concern what seemed to him a falling back on particularistic forms of thought and conduct, forms that necessarily sow the seeds of violent conflicts. The style is swift and hurried: Ben-David knew he was severely ill and palpably wrote under great pressure to complete his intellectual testament.

Science, Scientism and Anti-Scientism 25

The phenomenon to be discussed here is the swings of attitudes centering around science, namely, the transition from extremes of utopian belief in the potentialities of science for the augmentation of welfare and solution of all kinds of problems to the opposite extreme of viewing science—at least science as it exists today—as a source of sinister dangers to humanity, such as a lopsided development of the human intellect; the stunting of moral and religious sensibilities; the destruction of environment; and the threat to the survival of mankind resulting from the invention of superweapons and ways of manipulating heredity and behavior. In this paper an attempt will be made to answer the questions of what causes these swings and how they affect the growth of science. The attempt will be based on the exploration of the changing perceptions of, and attitudes toward, science as reflected in debates and writings on science policy and the social functions of science since the last World War. These debates took place among social scientists and administrators interested in the relations between science and society. The majority of practicing scientists and the general public have been only vaguely aware of these debates and have not been very much interested in them. They are part of what is frequently dismissed as "ideology," namely, a set of ideas of allegedly no interest or consequence to anyone except a few intellectuals. However, as will be suggested later, they serve as a framework of public discourse and may eventually influence policy and social action.[1]

Research for this paper was supported by the Spencer Foundation.
1. This was clearly recognized by J. M. Keynes and stated in the well-known passage at the end of his *The General Theory of Employment, Interest and Money* (Keynes 1942, p. 383).

The Emergence and Growing Pains of Science Policy

The period between the last World War and the 1970s witnessed such a swing of opinions. Scientists emerged from the War—at least in the United States, Britain, and Canada—with enhanced prestige, as a kind of estate which has a public mission and a legitimate claim to political influence and support from public funds (Price, 1965).

Of course, governments had supported scientific research before, but nowhere outside the USSR was science as a comprehensive endeavor treated as a public responsibility and an essential part of the economy before the last World War. The idea existed also in other countries. Many British scientists believed in the need for increased public support of science for politically sanctioned purposes (Wersky 1978, pp. 28–37). And the Popular Front government in France made a first step toward establishing science in this way in the 1930s (Weart 1979, pp. 33–86). This public use and support of science was conceived as part of a more comprehensive Socialist planning of society. The classic case for such planning with science as a central part of the scheme was put forward by J. D. Bernal in his *The Social Function of Science* (1939). Few people would have predicted at that time that many of the suggestions of Bernal would become actual policy first in the United States and subsequently in Europe and elsewhere within a few years.

This radical change in the public standing of science occurred during the war. In Britain and the United States there was an almost total mobilization of scientists (including, this time, social scientists) for the war effort. War economy was socialized economy, and scientists, like manufacturers, were used for specific missions useful for the war effort. These missions were usually initiated or suggested by scientists. Once adopted by the governments, work on them was organized on a large scale, reminiscent of the Soviet research system. There were large bureaucratized hierarchical units with scientific directors, military supervisors, and strict rules (not always enforced) of secrecy. Directors and military supervisors had access to the political leadership and were a marginal part of it. The rank-and-file researchers had no such access, no detailed political information and chafed under the authoritative hierarchical order, so different from the customs and traditions of peacetime research. But they put up with these conditions, partly because they saw them as transitory, meant only for the duration of the war, and partly because war-socialism created full employment for all trained scientists and placed at their disposal funds on an unprecedented scale. The problem facing the scientists at the end of the war was how to preserve the benefits of lavish support of research for themselves and society (they believed that there was no contradiction between their interests and those of society), without having to submit continually to an organization and discipline, which they found stifling, oppressive, and inconsistent with the requirements of free communication and autonomy of the individual researcher.

This dilemma gave rise to an outburst of organizational and ideological activity among scientists which resulted in the United States in the establishment of federally funded agencies, such as the NSF, for the systematic support of basic research performed mainly at the universities; the retention and conversion to nonmilitary or partly nonmilitary research of some very large-scale research facilities (such as Lawrence Radiation Laboratory or Oak Ridge); and a continuation of contracted research, by various branches of the military and government departments. Thus wartime government responsibility for science was continued in peacetime without a significant reduction in scale but with the removal of restrictions on scientific freedom. The level of support and activity which was attained during the war through total mobilization became a floor from which peacetime developments were to start.

This conception and organization of science still prevails in the United States and has been adopted with few modifications in the other industrially advanced countries outside the Soviet bloc. In this conception the existence of an effectively functioning system of research in all the major branches of science is considered as a national interest of great importance, and governments accept responsibility for the maintenance and updating of these systems. These research systems consist of central (and a few other) funding agencies; the universities; a number of research institutes in the applied, and in some countries also in basic, fields; and industrial research and development, frequently subsidized by the state. What is regarded as sufficient support is always the outcome of negotiations, but it is believed that there are internationally recognized standards in all fields of science below which no advanced country can afford to sink. As a result, references to attainments and practices of other countries are used as more or less commonly accepted standards in these negotiations.

This requisite of keeping abreast of new developments provided a benchmark for the public support of science in all the countries, except the United States, which set the standards. However, no one knew how to establish those standards. It was generally taken for granted that the growth of science was good for society, but no one knew how to determine what was an adequate investment in science. Therefore, in order to ensure support sufficient for further advance, American scientists adopted a strategy which was an extension of their wartime experience. This consisted of proposing large research and development projects, which could be adopted by the government as serving important national interests. In the beginning scientists could use the credit earned through such wartime successes as the development of radar, nuclear bombs, penicillin, and DDT. Then there came the electronics revolution and the long-term promise of developing atomic energy for peaceful uses. In 1957, after the launching of the first Sputnik, the leaders of

American science resorted themselves to the argument of the need to keep abreast. They painted a (largely imaginary) picture of Soviet superiority in science and demanded increased support in order to close this alleged gap.

By the sixties there emerged a new rationale for investment in science. This was based on a variety of evidence and theory. Econometric studies showed that a large part of the growth of the American economy over a certain period of time was attributable to the increase of knowledge. This tied in with other theories and practical experience about the worthwhileness of investing in research and extended into an argument that investment in research deserved highest priority on purely utilitarian grounds. According to this argument adequate investment in science was that which made possible the funding of every competent research proposal.[2] The result of all this was that R & D expenditure, scientific manpower, and publications in the United States and several other countries grew at a rate higher than that of the growth of the economy and the population.

Thoughtful scientists and other observers knew very well that such force-feeding of science leading to accelerated growth was a feasible public policy only when there was a reasonable expectation that massive research and development effort would lead to the solution of some well-defined social or national needs and that it could not be maintained beyond a rather limited time (Price 1963, pp. 92–115). But statesmen of science preferred to disregard this problem and to take advantage of the opportunities as long as they lasted (Orlans 1968, p. 155). In the later sixties it became evident that the policy would have to be given up. It was increasingly difficult to produce further sensational scientific feats, or even inspiring research goals which could be held out as worthy of concentrated national effort. The space program received tremendous publicity, and "putting a man on the moon" became an officially endorsed slogan, but probably very few people were really enthusiastic about it. And there were also spectacular failures, such as "Project Mohole." The arguments for further increasing the scientific effort sounded increasingly hollow, and there began a serious questioning of the belief in the benefits of scientific growth and the oracular status of the leaders of the scientific community.[3]

In Europe disillusionment came a bit later, because the Continent had still a long way to go in order to catch up with the United States and Britain. Universities and research facilities on the continent of Europe were still suffering from the aftermath of nazism and the devastations of the war. But by the early seventies the syndrome of searching for new collective goals and spectacular

2. The principle of trying to fund every competent proposal was actually adopted by some American funding agencies.

3. This point was aptly put by William Carey: "Some of the cohorts of science appear to have wanted all the prerogatives of a state religion without any of the embarrassments" (Orlans 1968, p. 266). See also Price (1965, pp. 11–20).

results began to appear even there. There were attempts at the creation of so-called centers of excellence and of fostering promising specialties in which "breakthroughs" could be expected (such as material science, or brain research).

The idea of a comprehensive science policy was gradually abandoned. It was realized that science was not one but many enterprises and that there could be no single policy for the support of all of them.[4] Furthermore, there are such great differences between the conditions prevailing in the different branches and specialties of science, as well as the general economic and political circumstances of different countries at different times, that the only feasible policy is to make pragmatic case by case decisions, which is actually the practice in most countries today.

The Rise of Anti-Scientism

Returning to the situation around 1970, the disillusionment at that time with the policies of accelerated scientific growth and the involvement of some scientists in morally controversial decisions during the war and after (including the war in Vietnam) is usually interpreted as the cause of anti-scientism, which became popular among some intellectual circles about 1968 (Toulmin 1972). However, I doubt that this was the case. The basis of this doubt is that very few, perhaps none at all, of the critics of accelerated growth joined any of the groups, or made any statements, which could identify them as opposed to science itself or to the kind of science practiced at the time. They were people involved in science policy in various capacities, as senior scientists (mainly in natural sciences), statesmen, administrators, or ideologists of science: the same types of people and sometimes the very same people, only wiser with experience, as those who had previously recommended accelerated growth.[5] The purpose of these critics was not to reduce the status or change the nature of science but to find new rationales, criteria, and objectives for the continued regular support of science.

In contrast, those who were critical of science itself were not concerned with the scale and kinds of support for research (although many of them were probably in favor of the reduction of support); their main concern was with science itself. Instead of asking what went wrong with science policy, they asked what was wrong with science, assuming in advance that something was wrong. They took little interest in projections of need for scientific manpower,

---

4. This is not to say that there is no common cognitive and moral purpose to the scientific endeavor as a whole. But that does not have to be budgeted for.

5. Alvin Weinberg wrote in 1965, "I expect this competition [between demands of medical practice and the demands of medical research—J.B-D], which presently favors research to shift toward. . . ." (Weinberg 1967, p. 103).

or in economic returns to investment in research. Instead, they concerned themselves with the alleged harms done by modern science to society, such as the invention of the "bomb" or contribution to air and water pollution and the association of research with races, classes, or groups whom they considered as exploitative or oppressive. These science critics were also concerned with the allegedly distorting and restrictive effects of science on the quality of present-day culture. In other words, this was not a criticism of science policies but of present-day Western society in general, and the role of science in it in particular. The aim of the criticism was not to change science policies but to change society and science within it fundamentally, perhaps even by revolutionary means. There was an assumption that science was replaceable by some other system of thought, or by another kind of science, and that the emergence of such a more desirable alternative would be furthered by a cultural revolution. This assumption was vaguely rooted in antipositivistic philosophies of science and theories of cultural relativity.[6]

The social characteristics of the participants in this movement were different from those of the critics of science policy. The anti-scientists were mainly students, many of them from the humanities and social sciences, philosophers, historians of science, and social scientists, but relatively few natural scientists.

Neither the contents of anti-scientistic ideology nor the interests and purposes of their proponents related to the specific situation of scientific practice in the 1960s. To the extent that they made use of empirical evidence, this consisted primarily of case studies illustrating the alleged complicity of scientists in morally objectionable research. These were used as bases for conclusions requiring more political control over research and ideological commitment on the part of scientists (Rose and Rose 1969).

However, their views and arguments did not derive from these illustrative cases but were rooted in a long-standing critique of modern science going back to the eighteenth century and perhaps even earlier. This critique, as summarized by Stephen Toulmin, asserts that science disregards the primacy of

---

6. This is not to say that these philosophies and theories are necessarily anti-scientistic. Such theories, as well as other elements of science criticism, can be adopted and shared by people who value science highly. Anti-scientism is not distinguished from other attitudes to science by specific contents but by a reification of science as a sinister force, an emotionally negative attitude to it, and a wish to replace it by some other cognitive system capable of providing equally (or more) valid knowledge without the dehumanizing and ruthless effects attributed to science. This is an inversion of "scientism," which also reifies science but as a benevolent force.

This is a different phenomenon from what is usually described as "anti-science" movement, which includes all kinds of science criticism (Toulmin 1972; Richter 1983). However, at times when anti-scientism is in fashion, it is not always easy to tell rational critics of selected aspects of scientific behavior from anti-scientists, since the latter try to convey the impression that all those with views partially overlapping theirs actually belong to their camp, while those so "recruited" to the anti-scientist camp are not always very prompt to dissociate themselves from it. Rather they prefer to remain silent, let ambiguity about their position prevail, and enjoy the popularity conferred on them by the fashionable movement.

human issues; suppresses individuality and imagination; disregards quality and tries to reduce everything to quantity; is too abstract and unable to relate to the complex nature of real situations; and is altogether mechanical, cold-blooded, and creates a spur for the adoption of policies and practices solely for their technical efficiency without regard for their effect on people and society (Toulmin 1972, pp. 25–27). Another evidence that this anti-scientism was not a reaction to the failures of science policy is that one of the most influential sources of the movement was Herbert Marcuse's *One Dimensional Man*, which had appeared in 1964, much before the policy failures were noticed, and had no reference to these policies.

While this makes it clear that the contents of anti-scientistic ideology had not been formulated in reaction to contemporary events but were a revival of periodically reoccurring themes in Western culture, one could still attribute their reappearance around 1968 to the difficulties encountered by science policies at that time.

It is quite possible that these difficulties contributed in some cases to the adoption of anti-scientistic views, and, of course, they were used by anti-scientists as grist to their mill. However, this was not the source of the widespread adoption and popularity of anti-scientistic ideas, because a very important part of the anti-scientistic movement, the students (most of them from the humanities and social sciences), did probably not have the vaguest idea that science policy was in serious difficulties. They thought they were attacking a vigorous, self-confident, and "dominant" scientific "establishment," which had no awareness of its own shortcomings and had to be made aware of them by attack from the outside.

Therefore, the hypothesis I should like to put forward is that this was not a reaction to the state of science but to the state of society. Students and intellectuals who turned against science were reacting to the disintegration of a world view which emerged in the thirties and forties as a reaction to nazism and was reinforced by victory in the war. In that world view nazism was presented as the embodiment of irrational prejudice, violence, and persecution in general and of violation of the freedom of science in particular. Those opposing nazism were seen as in favor of reason, freedom of science, and rational solution of conflicts.[7] In the late thirties the ideology had a popular front flavor, and communism was seen as belonging to the front of reason and science. However, the wave of Stalinistic oppression following the war, of which the Lysenko affair was one of the most widely known instances, changed this view, and Soviet communism came to be viewed by many people as an ideology incompatible with the freedom of inquiry, and reason and freedom in general.

7. Thus, Merton, discussing the problems of science under totalitarianism in 1937, discusses only nazism. He was not worried about the state of science in the USSR (Merton 1973 [1938, 1942]). See also Ben-David (1980).

This recategorization of the Soviet Union altered the world view which emerged in the thirties in opposition to nazism, since now only the Western world continued to be viewed as a haven of freedom, reason, and science, with institutions capable of mediating political conflicts, and providing unprecedented scope for enterprise and creativity. This world view was reinforced by the political and economic successes of the Western world, such as the relatively peaceful liberation of the colonies and the successful economic reconstruction of Europe and Japan. Science was seen as a central part, actually as a paradigm of, a social order capable of combining individual freedom with responsibility and order. The classic exposition of this view of science as a paradigm of free society was Michael Polanyi's *The Logic of Liberty* (1951). Polanyi's term "the scientific community" became a household word all over the Western world, and although few people read Polanyi, the term had the connotation of a spontaneously coordinated community thriving mainly in liberal societies.

Thus in the fifties and sixties there emerged a new kind of scientistic world view, which differed significantly from earlier forms of scientism. Effective pursuit of science was now linked to a decentralized liberal form of government and economy, whereas previously—as far back as the seventeenth century—scientistic world views favored centralized planning and authoritative government (Weart 1979; Hunter 1981, pp. 122–27). As a result the neo-Baconian utopia of "science as an endless frontier" also became linked to liberal democracy. There was widespread belief in the imminent solubility of all social, political, and economic problems through research and an expectation of the emergence of the "great society" promised by the president of the United States, Lyndon B. Johnson, in which a democratic government would provide the leadership and safeguard the freedom required by enterprise and research to create the means for ever-improving social welfare. Among scientists and spokesmen for science there was tremendous confidence (verging on many occasions on overconfidence and arrogance) about their importance and ability in helping to bring about the realization of this utopia.

It seems that the anti-scientism of many Western intellectuals in the late sixties and early seventies was a reaction to the crisis of this world view in the wake of American defeat in Vietnam, the subsequent political crisis in the United States, and the economic difficulties all over the Western World. Vietnam and the American political crisis were not perceived as merely American problems. The new scientistic world view emerged in the United States (Polanyi had probably more influence there than in Britain), and the successes of the internal and external policies of that country were taken as the criteria by which this world view was to be judged. The failure of American policies was seen as an evidence that this world view was false. Students—who did not raise a finger against acts of political oppression nearer home—demonstrated against the United States and in favor of North Vietnam (about which they had only the vaguest notions) in their tens of thousands in all the major cities of

Europe. The same students at the same time also adopted Marcuse, attacked the existing traditions of science and scholarship, and attempted to replace them with a vague program of endless political and ideological discussions committed to a utopian vision of a participatory society in which all people would be perfectly equal and would equally and spontaneously participate in political and cultural life (including some kind of people's science). This was not a reaction to specific problems created by scientific policies but to a poignant sense of disappointment with a world view in which science was identified with liberal democracy and the promise of wealth and mastery over human fate.

This is not to say that anti-scientism was the central feature of the 1968 and subsequent student revolts. Anti-Americanism and support of North Vietnam were major themes, as was a kind of generalized antinomianism. Science and anti-scientism were of interest only to a minority. But anti-scientism fitted in very well with the general antinomian character of the student movement and was accepted by the latter willingly as an integral component of its world view (which was widely shared by leftist intellectuals).

As suggested previously, this kind of reaction to scientism has had several predecessors in history, such as the attacks on science in reaction to the foundation of the Royal Society, romanticism, and *fin-du-siècle*. All of these were complex cases which it would be difficult to survey here. However, a few words are in place about the latest and closest parallel to the present case, namely, the disillusionment with science in 1918 Germany. Although imperial Germany was a very different kind of society than the United States, Germany until World War I was the undisputed leader in science and higher education and was also looked upon as a country which, due to its cultural superiority, created an efficient industry, good government, and excellent military. Germans were convinced that their science, technology, and military and political leadership made them invincible. Many outstanding scientists shared and fostered this view and participated enthusiastically and successfully in the war effort.

Defeat created a tremendous disillusionment, which was accompanied, among other things, by the emergence of romantic anti-scientistic world views. Oswald Spengler's *Decline of the West* became a most popular book in intellectual circles, and one of the themes of the book, the alleged cultural relativity of Western science (Forman 1971), has been also one of the most popular themes of the science criticism of the late sixties and seventies.

Conclusion

The main argument of this paper has been that a distinction has to be made between the ups and downs of science policies pursued in different countries during the last forty years or so and the wide swing from scientism to anti-scientism, which occurred around 1970. The vicissitudes of science policy reflect objective difficulties in understanding the economic and organizational implications of the new level of scientific activity attained during the war and of the extension of the uses of science far beyond anything experienced before. There was a conviction that the growth of science could be, and should be, fostered by the state, but there was little experience in how this should be done and no criteria of what was adequate investment in science. During the fifties and until about the mid-sixties the accepted view was that practically every investment which could be used by competent researchers was worthwhile. Later, when this policy could no longer be pursued, there began a period of trial and error, which produced ad hoc solutions but no general principles. However, the need for such principles had diminished, since governments, industry, and foundations acquired practical experience in supporting and using research of different kinds in a variety of contexts. As a result, case by case pragmatic administration replaced the search for general principles and comprehensive science policies.

The swing from scientism to anti-scientism around 1970 (and now back to a temporary resting point in the middle?) was not a reflection of the difficulties of finding new rationale for the support of science but was the result of the role of science in the utopias of modern society. In these utopias science is attributed powers to benefit or harm society far beyond those it actually has. Above all, it is attributed godlike or demonic qualities of self-direction. These utopias emerge and swing from one extreme to another as a result of political events, which have little to do with what actually happens in scientific research. It seems that scientism gains the upper hand when there is a period of economic and cultural growth. The experience of such growth creates among people a feeling of mastery over their fate and confidence in dealing with problems rationally. This mastery is—in modern society—attributed to science and faith in science grows, usually beyond reasonable limits. When these periods of growth end, expectations are disappointed, and people begin seeing in science a "god that failed." At this point, they become receptive to anti-scientism.

As pointed out, scientific research and the policies connected with its uses and support are essentially independent from the swings of scientistic utopias. But there has been an interaction between the two processes. Scientists have tended to react to the swings pragmatically: exploiting as much as possible the favorable atmosphere of periods of scientism and protecting themselves from the unfavorable attitudes and accusations during periods of anti-scientism, by claiming immunity on the grounds of the value neutrality of science (of course, some scientists do accept these utopias, but so far they have failed to have a lasting impact because research is in an important sense value-neutral). This was the policy also pursued in recent decades, and from the point of view of the support of scientific research, it has worked well. Scientists and science have probably benefited more from periods of scientism than they were made to repay under periods of anti-scientism. As a result, it seems that the growth of science has not been adversely affected by these recurrent waves of scientism and anti-scientism.

However, there is no ground for extrapolating the pattern of past occurrences into the future. Although swings from scientism to anti-scientism go far back in history, the importance of these utopias may be greater today than in the past, since science is probably much more central to the present-day world view than it has ever been before (for many people it has replaced the idea of God). Under these circumstances the fact that the terms of public discourse on science are to a large extent laid down by scientistic and anti-scientistic utopias and ideologies may have far-reaching consequences. Recent precedents of German racial science and Lysenkoism should not be taken lightly and dismissed as temporary phenomena with little long-term influence on science.[8] They were attempts at subjecting science to ideological-political considerations, the likes of which had not occurred since the seventeenth century. It also has to be remembered that for several years in the seventies, the terms in which science was publicly discussed were almost entirely determined by the anti-scientistic movement. There were accusations against science, and science policy became concerned more with the appeasement of radical critics of science than with the advancement of knowledge. Institutional changes made under those conditions, such as participatory management of university departments and research units, or greatly increased bureaucratic controls over the allocation and spending of research funds, are perceived by many research workers as burdensome and harmful. Therefore, the tactics of the scientific community followed so far may no longer succeed in the future.

References

Ben-David, J. 1980. "The Ethos of Science: The Last Half-Century." In *Science and the Polity*, edited by J. R. Philips and T. J. Conlon. Canberra: Australian Academy of Science, pp. 13–28. [This volume, chap. 23.]

Bernal, J. D. 1939. *The Social Function of Science*. London: Routledge.

Beyerchen, A. D. 1977. *Scientists under Hitler: Politics and the Physics Community in the Third Reich*. New Haven: Yale University Press.

Bush, Vannevar. 1945. *Science the Endless Frontier: A Report to the President*. Washington D.C.: U.S. Government Printing Office.

Forman, Paul. 1971. "Weimar Culture, Causality and Quantum Theory, 1918–1927:

8. Pragmatic economic and military considerations, and perhaps also its intrinsically exact nature, provided physics with relative immunity to such coercion (Joravsky 1961; Graham 1972; Beyerchen 1977). But biology proved to be extremely vulnerable.

Adaptation by German Physicists and Mathematicians to a Hostile Intellectual Environment." In *Historical Studies in the Physical Sciences* 3:1–115.

Graham, Loren R. 1972. *Science and Philosophy in the Soviet Union.* New York: Knopf.

Hunter, Michael. 1981. *Science and Society in Restoration England.* Cambridge: Cambridge University Press.

Joravsky, David. 1961. *Soviet Marxism and Natural Science.* New York: Columbia University Press.

Keynes, Lord John Maynard. 1942. *The General Theory of Employment, Interest and Money.* London: Macmillan.

Marcuse, Herbert. 1964. *One-Dimensional Man.* Boston: Beacon Press.

Merton, Robert. 1973. "Science and the Social Order" (1938); "The Normative Structure of Science" (1942). In his *The Sociology of Science.* Chicago: University of Chicago Press, pp. 254–66, 267–78.

Needham, Joseph. 1979. "History and Human Values: A Chinese Perspective for World Science and Technology." In *Ideology of/in the Natural Sciences,* edited by H. Rose and S. Rose. Cambridge: Schenkman, pp. 231–88.

Orlans, Harold (ed.). 1968. *Science Policy and the University.* Washington, D.C.: Brookings Institution.

Price, Derek de Solla. 1963. *Little Science, Big Science.* New York: Columbia University Press.

Price, Don K. 1965. *The Scientific Estate.* Cambridge: Belknap Press.

Polanyi, Michael. 1951. *The Logic of Liberty.* Chicago: University of Chicago Press.

Richter, Maurice N. 1983. "Anti-Science: Its Features and Forms." Department of Sociology, State University of New York, Albany (unpublished paper).

Rose, H., and S. Rose. 1969. *Science and Society.* London: Allen Lane, The Penguin Press.

Toulmin, Stephen. 1972. "The Historical Background to the Anti-Science Movement." CIBA Foundation Symposium. *Civilization and Science in Conflict or Collaboration.* New York: Elsevier. Pp. 23–32.

Weart, Spencer R. 1979. *Scientists in Power.* Cambridge: Harvard University Press.

Weinberg, Alvin. 1967. *Reflections on Big Science.* Cambridge: MIT Press.

Wersky, Gary. 1978. *The Visible College: The Collective Biography of British Scientific Socialists of the 1930s.* New York: Holt, Rinehart and Winston.

The Ethos of Science in 26
the Context of Different
Political Ideologies and
Changing Perceptions
of Science

I. Scientific Thought in
Western Culture during the
Seventeenth and Eighteenth Centuries

Science has been a central part of Western culture since the seventeenth century. Although inquiry into natural phenomena had been widespread before, during the second half of the seventeenth century this inquiry gained a new self-assurance and social significance which it had never before possessed (Webster 1974; Ben-David 1984 [1971]). For many people, experimental and empirical inquiry became a source of incontrovertible truth whose validity equaled or surpassed that of the Bible. In fact, the discoveries of natural inquiry were no longer regarded as disconnected pieces of knowledge but rather as part of natural philosophy concerned with a coherent explanation of how the universe is constituted and works.

In England, this new conception of science and the mechanistic world view were seen by some of the most significant scientists as being in perfect harmony with, and mutually supportive of, their nonconformist and/or latitudinarian religious world views (Merton 1970 [1938a]; Manuel 1974, 1983). The outstanding scientific creativity which produced unprecedented discoveries, coupled with this deeply felt religion, encouraged the conviction that scientific inquiry would provide a common purpose and vision to all intellec-

This research was supported by the Spencer Foundation. I am indebted to Bonnie Lindstrom for her help with the research.

Previously unpublished; written 1984–1985. For the editing procedures, see introduction to Part VII. Ed.

tual effort and would possibly lead to a reunion of all Christian denominations or to a union of all monotheistic religions.

However, this conjunction of religious belief and scientific practice was a passing moment in history. In subsequent centuries the relationship between science and religion was usually perceived as conflictual rather than harmonious. Indeed, for most people, the unique science *cum* religion was not an acceptable substitute for traditional religion. Religion was perceived as stable and dogmatic, embedded in a written tradition and ritual practices. The source of religious authority and truth was revelation through extraordinary people who served as intermediaries between God and ordinary human beings. Scientific truth, on the other hand, was accessible to anyone capable of mastering the methods and techniques of critical inquiry. Moreover, this truth was changeable: new ideas and methods reveal new layers of truth, placing old beliefs in broader and deeper perspective or discarding them altogether. Traditional religion thus provided a stability of belief and a sense of security that science could not match.

Another major drawback of science as a political substitute for religious belief was that its contributions were overwhelmingly confined to an examination of the physical world. Science had little to contribute on the issues of morality, mercy, love, justice, law, and politics which were of great concern to most people.

Finally, science did not offer sacred rituals and holidays which symbolize belongingness to, and participation in, a community of believers and thereby generate a collective transcendental experience. Scientific discovery may generate a sense of revelation among scientists, but this experience cannot be shared with the layman. In point of fact, although science is in principle open to all, only a few individuals are capable of mastering scientific inquiry; even the few who do achieve mastery of science are still left with most of their religious needs unsatisfied.

The integration of science within the world views of the people who accepted it has therefore been problematic. The claim that science was the best way to discover truth has, as a rule, been accepted. But although in principle the new way to authoritative truth was applicable to all fields of human concern, in practice science revealed little about moral and sacred concerns. From the seventeenth century onward, therefore, the Western world view integrated a new extremely forceful message of truth that progressed piecemeal, unpredictably and was of only limited applicability. Consequently, moral and religious truths continued to be supplied from a variety of traditional sources (religion, philosophy) which were more likely to divide than to unify mankind.

Western (and subsequently other) societies succeeded in maintaining a continuous scientific activity while avoiding clashes with other systems of belief by *institutionalizing science* in a manner which both recognized its intellectual authority and provided incentives and rewards for scientific research. At the same time, scientific institutions tended to restrict the scope of scientific inquiry to fields in which it was possible to define concepts operationally and to test relationships through observation and experiment. The natural and exact sciences possessed these methodological characteristics and dealt with issues unlikely to arouse passion and controversy.

This delimitation of scientific inquiry to universally accepted methods, thereby defusing the potential of political and religious passion, is today described as the "value neutrality" of science. This is an unfortunate term in that it implies that scientists are indifferent to ideologies, religions and regimes (which may be hostile to science). This, of course, is not the case. Moreover, for scientists (and many others) scientific research is a value in itself. Yet, in spite of these qualifications, the term adequately describes the belief and the practice prevailing in science that the significance of a scientific contribution is independent of the personal and social characteristics and motivations of its author.

On the basis of the belief in the superiority of the scientific ways to truth and in the value neutrality of science, scientists claimed and obtained the privilege of "academic freedom": a far-reaching autonomy accorded to the individual scientist and to scientific institutions. Scientists are free to choose research topics and methods, and although their research is often financed by public means, they are accountable only to the informal controls of the scientific community for their results.

Academic freedom has been a constant feature of the life of science in its variegated organizational schemes. It characterizes equally well the Royal Society of London in the second half of the seventeenth century, the modern university established in Germany in the early nineteenth century, and the funding and research institutes which emerged in postwar United States (Ben-David and Collins 1966).

To be sure, safeguarding the autonomy of science was sometimes problematic. But by and large, the institutionalization and autonomy of science was accepted in countries with different traditions and regimes and formed the basis for the emergence of a worldwide scientific profession constituting an informally organized scientific community. Members of this community share the same conception of the scientist's role and of his professional obligations. Each discipline also shares a common conception of the state of the art in its field. As a result, scientists are capable of communicating and cooperating with each other and of recognizing achievement. Similarly, institutional forms which proved useful in one country are relatively easily transferrable elsewhere.

The institutionalization of the value neutrality of science and of academic freedom did not have the same implications for each society. In England, institutionalization facilitated consensus formation in fields in which this was feasible, releasing science from endless and inconclusive philosophical and theological debates; in fact, this freedom of inquiry included also all other spheres of interest. In contrast, in France, the institutionalization of science restricted scientific authority and freedom to professional natural scientists, excluding the *philosophes* who reflected on human and social problems (Hahn 1971).

No matter how or to what purpose academic freedom was instituted, nowhere did the scientific endeavor remain confined within its institutionalized academic boundaries. The belief in the intellectual superiority of scientific inquiry over other cognitive traditions and methods made it inevitable that the "scientific method" would also be extended to an exploration of society. These scientific inquiries into social problems varied in self-confidence but were universally attempted.

From our point of view, the interesting question is how the attempts to scientifically think about man and society were related to religion and traditional ways of thinking. Until the end of the eighteenth century, people believed in religion and did not attribute too much importance to inquiries which barely scratched the surface of issues to which religion and tradition provided comprehensive guidance. In fact, for the large majority of people, religion continued to supply a satisfactory view of the moral and social world. Science was absent from or very peripheral to this world view; its existence and importance were recognized, yet (with the exception of France) science was not seen as a serious challenge to the traditional views. Even philosophers sought to support the older religious beliefs with new and better arguments based on science. "Reconciliation of science with religion" was seen, especially among the Protestant sects, as far from impossible. Christianity could therefore remain a unifying system of belief (excluding, of course, the non-Christian minorities).

However, whereas Christianity provided a unifying view of the moral world, there was no similar unity in the political world. In the eastern and southern reaches of the Christian world, the unity between the Church and royal (and aristocratic) power was rarely questioned. Here political order appeared as preordained; any questions about its legitimacy were tantamount to heresy. In this context, science had no influence. In northwestern Europe, the situation was very different, however. There, the Reformation and subsequently the new philosophies irreversibly destroyed the belief in a preordained harmony between the religious and the political order. Where (as in France) an absolutist monarch claimed that such a harmony existed, the educated classes rejected the claim. This allowed the spirit of rational inquiry increasingly to penetrate the political world. Concomitantly, there appeared political groups whose arguments were borrowed from the new political philosophers and who demanded a say in matters of public interest.

In northern and western Europe, then, the tendency to apply rational inquiry to matters political and economic spread rapidly. However, the concrete form which these inquiries took varied with the political practices of the corresponding societies. Some countries (e.g., England) had a fairly democratic social order with widespread political participation; others, like France, had absolutist regimes. Consequently, political inquiry in England tended to be much more empirical, tentative and practically oriented than in France. In England, it was taken for granted that the political world consisted of a plurality of competing groups; the problem of political philosophy was how to reconcile their interests and make them work toward a common purpose. In contrast, in France, the philosophers were concerned with the basis of political authority; the problem for them was to alter the political world in accordance with an ideal political organization.

This difference is particularly striking in the treatment of religion. In England, some political thinkers, realizing that it was an important source of belief and sentiment for the people to whom scientific inquiry remained irrelevant, left religion alone. Other English political philosophers speculated about religion in a fairly objective manner, as either a social institution or a way of thinking. The French political philosophers, on the other hand, saw organized religion (Catholicism) as one of the mainstays of the absolutist regime; indeed, the chief source of prejudice and obscurantism. They therefore believed that religion had to be stripped of all political power and relegated entirely to the private realm.

Thus, while political thinkers in England and later in the United States were concerned with how the political and economic order was constituted or could be changed, their French counterparts were primarily engaged in undermining the very bases of religious belief and political authority. Through education and propaganda, they wished to create a new man, free of inherited prejudice and capable of thinking correctly (i.e., scientifically) about social and moral issues. With their largely destructive inquiries they ventured far into the social-moral realm, disregarding the needs of the broad mass of the population for a moral orientation.

By the end of the eighteenth century, then, there were two distinct strands in the tradition of scientific social thought. One studied social behavior and institutions as understandable and manipulable phenomena, rooted in the basic needs of social order and survival and possessing a rationale of their own. This strand is comparable to the social sciences of today. The other strand viewed traditional political and religious institutions as means of establishing the rule of a minority social group over the rest of society. For these thinkers, the purpose of social science was consequently to understand, expose and eliminate those means of domination in order that the human mind and human society could be completely reorganized and drastically reformed in a scientific mold.

Both strands belong to what is called the "Enlightenment tradition," and both were seen as scientific. Indeed, both used (or believed they were using) canons of scientific inquiry, and both felt free from traditional authority and responsible only to the authority of scientific procedure and method.

A third eighteenth-century tradition, romanticism, was initially considered scientific because its core was neither religious nor political. However, in point of fact, romanticism was alien to science: in fact, it rejected the central—namely, Newtonian—tradition of science. The romantics rejected Newtonianism on two grounds. First, they claimed that Newtonian science dealt essentially with a dead nature. The Newtonians, they argued, construe nature as composed of inert particles, thereby making it into the suitable subject of mathematical physics. In their own view, philosophy of nature should integrate the intuitive holistic visions of the poets and the lovers of nature and those of the practical arts as cultivated by craftsmen. Specifically, the Newtonian analytical approach may be applicable in physics (although this too was occasionally denied, as in Goethe's *Farbenlehre*) but not in chemistry or in biology where, they maintained, only holistic and intuitive approaches are appropriate. Second, the romantics criticized the value neutrality of the Newtonian tradition for its denial of a universal search for moral significance in life or in the universe. An intuitive, holistic science, the romantics believed, would invest the physical reality with a moral dimension.

Ostensibly, romantic philosophy was not opposed to science, for no one declared himself an opponent of science in this century. And yet, in retrospect and from a sociological point of view, we can see that this philosophy constituted a threat to science. For in romanticism the physical and the moral universes were linked together in a way that conferred a central role to arbitrary intuition. This crucial tenet, together with the absence of any requirement for technical discipline and competence, opened the way to the subordination of would-be scientific knowledge claims to nonscientific considerations. In the romantic perspective, the task of determining what is good science (or science at all) did not belong solely to the community of competent scientists but was the business of all those who claimed for themselves competence on the basis of personal intuition or practical experience. Romanticism, in other words, denied the autonomy of science. Therefore, this view of science could have undone the entire development of institutionalized science during the eighteenth century.

II. The Nineteenth Century:
The Rise of Ideologies

During the nineteenth century the diffusion and use of these alternative concepts of the scientific approach were determined by the political conditions prevalent in each country. The French Revolution provided an opportunity for a comprehensive, drastic transformation of society according to the ideas of the political philosophers. To a large extent the experiments initiated by the revolutionaries proved to be failures, but some of the ideas on how to build a society led to the establishment of up-to-date and exemplary institutions, such as the *grandes écoles*. The philosophical ideas of the revolution, however, were incapable of solving the central problem of democratic politics: how to ensure common solidarity and public responsibility for law and order while safeguarding individual freedom. France, viewed by all of Continental Europe as *the* experiment in democracy, floundered until the advent of the Third Republic. The failure of this experiment explains the predicament of the scientistic movement in the nineteenth century.

The problems of nineteenth-century French politics were analyzed by Alexis de Tocqueville (1969) who asked why, although France and the United States shared a common core of ideas, democracy worked in the United States and not in France. He found two main differences. The first was the near universal participation of Americans in practical politics through direct participation in town meetings and other structures of local politics. The autonomy of local government from state and federal control encouraged participation. In France, by contrast, local autonomy, already eroded under the Old Regime, had been completely abolished during the revolution. The revolutionary principle that all arrangements intervening between the citizen and the central state must be abolished disregarded an obvious and practical question: how could a diverse and dispersed citizenry understand political problems of the nation and participate in their solution without an opportunity to learn first in their local governments?

The other difference which de Tocqueville found important was that in France, the Church was seen as a threat to secular politics, a threat which could be counteracted only by the creation of agnostic philosphies. For French political thinkers, religion meant the Catholic church and its alliance with the ancien régime. Organized religion was seen as a threat to democracy because Catholicism insisted on doctrinal monopoly and did not respect freedom of thought and speech. American politicians, by contrast, saw religious life as a plurality of competing denominations, each seeking to control the moral and socially responsible behavior of their members and thus helping create a citizenry which could be relied upon to fulfill its civic duties. Therefore, American politicians and intellectuals respected religion in general, irrespective of denomination, whereas their French counterparts engaged in antireligious propaganda, undermined the moral control of the Catholic church (the only organization to exercise such control), and created a citizenry concerned only with their private interests rather than responsibility for the public good.

De Tocqueville's hypotheses were quite valuable in explaining the differences between France and the United States. They did not have any practical influence, however, for the centralism and anticlericalism were too deeply ingrained in the French political tradition to be modified by the impact of a scholarly treatise. Nevertheless, after 1870, France (and the rest of Europe) found its way to stable democratic and, to some extent, liberal politics.

Joseph Schumpeter's theory, explaining why democracy and liberalism eventually developed on the Continent, stressed that liberalism, especially in the economic arena, worked too well to be ignored (1950 [1942]). The Continental ruling classes, which still legitimated their inherited power and privileges by religion and tradition, allowed the entrepreneurial middle classes to rise in power and influence and protected them from Socialists and other groups opposed to capitalism. Toward the end of the nineteenth century, this symbiosis between aristocrats and capitalists was the most widespread form of government in Europe.

The very success of the tacit alliance between capitalism and aristocracy created the social forces which accelerated the process of decline in social stability. This is the context in which the development of critical social thought has to be understood. The welfare produced by the success of the capitalist economy gave rise to a numerous and frequently unemployed intellectual class which was extremely fertile in producing subversive and redeeming ideas of freedom and equality, undermining the status quo and promising a utopian future. Nor was liberalism acceptable to the national minorities whose upper and middle classes were only allowed to play a secondary role, or to the cruelly oppressed peasant classes in Eastern Europe, totally excluded from politics.

Originally, social criticism and utopian visions were part of the scientistic tradition of the Enlightenment, but by the nineteenth century, there had emerged a new tradition opposed to liberalism and capitalism: nationalism. This new tradition of conservative ideology had two strands (Mannheim 1986 [1925]).

One strand was moderate and rational, in principle quite compatible with a scientific approach to politics. Edmund Burke's ideas can serve as an example: Burke's only criticism of scientific ideologies pertained to their refusal to rely on the accumulated political wisdom of ages and the inherited political skills of aristocratic ruling classes.

But there was also another strand of conservative ideology: A radical nationalism steeped in romanticism. The romantics perceived the nation as animated by a national spirit, *Volksgeist,* reflecting a deep tie between a people and its territory, expressed through language, literature, history, and political traditions and known intuitively by political and cultural leaders. The romantics ascribed this national spirit with a lawfulness and regularity of its own and a utopian redeeming quality: social and political problems would simply disappear if one's national collectivity could express itself freely without political or spiritual submission to foreign powers.

These ideas were unscientific in the sense accepted by institutionalized science in that their criteria for truth were intuition and empathy. In fact, it was (and is) very difficult to understand these conservative ideologies: there were no commonly accepted standards for identifying a "national spirit," what constituted its genuine manifestations, or how and under what circumstances these manifestations can become operative. Nevertheless, these ideologies acquired intellectual respectability through scholarly work, a language and an interpretive rationale of their own. Moreover, because the themes they addressed aroused collective solidarity and enthusiasm, they were successful in attracting people to their cause.

One such theme, liberation, aroused fervent emotions. In a sense, nineteenth-century European history is a history of wars of liberation. The Germans fought first against French conquest and then against French supremacy. Other national groups fought the Austrians, Hungarians, Turks, and Russians, culminating by the end of the First World War in the adoption of the ideal of national self-determination and the dismemberment of Europe into chauvinistic nation-states with changing alliances and enmities. This state of affairs is linked to the emergence, throughout the nineteenth century, of national heroes—from Napoleon to Bismarck. The life and work of each of these leaders was interpreted as an expression of the national spirit successfully guiding the nation. The fact that in the long run most of these heroes brought disaster rather than success to their nations was not a circumstance to dampen the belief of true believers.

A related emotionally laden theme was anti-Semitism. Jews were ready-made scapegoats, depicted as parasitic foreigners who—considering their small numbers—played a disproportionately important role in the economic and cultural life of the nation. Romantic nationalists claimed that the Jews, being alien to the "true" spirit of the nation, were harmful.

Thus, by the end of the nineteenth century, a radical ideology had developed, one in which free national and ethnic self-expression was regarded as the condition for the release of regenerative and redemptive forces inherent in the national collectivity. The fact that regeneration and redemption failed to occur was attributed to foreign enemies and increasingly to the alleged internal foe, the Jews. The hatred of and the fight against real or alleged enemies were capable of arousing solidarity and enthusiasm within the nation. In parallel, the creation, rediscovery, and cultivation of literary and other cultural traditions gained an increasing intellectual appeal. All this made the rational tradition of the Enlightenment appear to many people as shallow and superficial. For it could be felt that a holistic world view, emphasizing the uniqueness of the national collectivity within which the individual selves can merge, was capable of creating collective solidarity and devotion to common goals that liberalism or aristocracy (separately or combined) were unable to achieve. To be sure, there was no evidence to support this belief which remained a minority view. However, the enthusiasm of this minority of believers created among them a feeling of confidence with respect to future success.

So strong was the impression created by these national movements that their influence reached politicians and thinkers of the Left, too. Charismatic leaders of the Left were no longer content to create and propagate rational theories of society capable of showing ways to improve the life of mankind; they went on to create mass movements—with themselves as absolute leaders—whose goal was to carry out the mission of social improvement.

Yet, under the influence of the legacy of the Enlightenment, this new left-wing version of collectivism differed from that of the Right. First, the collectivity to which one owed allegiance was one which was to be created in order to replace the primordial ties to the nation into which one was born and in which one was raised. Second, the community was conceived of as universalistic, comprehending (at least in principle) all mankind. But both of these characteristics were liabilities. It is easy to feel devoted to one's nation, but only intellectuals have the power of abstraction to feel part of such artificial entities as the working class, or this or that movement. And universalism greatly limited the extent to which the Left could resort to the politics of hatred of the foreigner and the outsider, which is such an effective means of forging internal solidarity. This was the price to be paid for the continued adherence to the universalistic-scientific tradition of the Enlightenment.

Thus, by the end of the nineteenth century, there had emerged a new approach to the place of science in the political world view of Western societies. Before then, the distinction was between, on the one hand, those who did not expect science to contribute to the creation of a better understanding and better manipulation of social and political life and who therefore continued to rely on tradition for guidance and, on the other hand, those who believed in the utility of the scientific model for the study of—and action within—social and political life. By the end of the nineteenth century, there emerged a group who rejected the model of institutionalized natural science but still accepted a (quasi) scientific model of collectivity, namely, one which was holistic and could be intuitively understood. This group took the understanding and participation in the social collectivity to be the key to effective and up-to-date politics and policies. The upholders of this collectivistic social inquiry and politics differed according to whether their conception of the collectivity was particularistic (namely, mainly nationalistic) or universalistic (predicting the emergence of universalistic collectivities open to all mankind). Hand in hand with this last distinction, the groups differed between those using policies of hatred and scapegoating and those refraining from such policies.

Until the First World War, the significance of these collectivistic "ideological" models and politics was still quite limited. After 1918, their importance increased by leaps and bounds, however, and for a short period of about ten to fifteen years (from about 1930 to 1945), they dominated the public scene in Europe with disastrous consequences.

III. Ideology between the Two World Wars

The First World War changed drastically the delicate balance which existed on the European continent between aristocratic rulers and liberal capitalists. The Russian Revolution, the dismemberment of the Austro-Hungarian monarchy, the deposition of the German emperor, and the rise of fascism in Italy destroyed old-time traditionalism as an important element of the Western world view and politics. This is not to say that suddenly everyone ceased to believe in the mixture of old regime and economic liberalism. For a large, conservative fraction that regime still represented an ideal state of stability, gentility, and prosperity which had been destroyed by radicals, nationalists, and others. These conservatives regarded the new rulers as incompetent and viewed the new situation of the world as unstable. In Austria, Germany, and Hungary, the prewar period was referred to as "peacetime" even as late as the thirties, implying that the present was still a continuation of the unstable wartime and that the prewar balance would be restored. In point of fact, however, European reality and political thinking were moving away from liberalism toward fascism and communism.

The new map of Europe, engineered to an overwhelming extent by liberals, nationalists, and socialists, reflected the attempt to put into practice the idea of national self-determination. Within these old and new nation-states, attempts were made to deal with the problems of poverty, class discrimination, and (where they existed) ethnic problems through social legislation and services. These attempts were not all too successful. Consequently, some groups of people came to believe that only such radical methods as those employed by the Communists and the Fascists could resolve the political stalemate on the European continent. The number of those who believed in a radical solution increased considerably after the economic collapse in 1929 and the rise of the Nazis in Germany in 1933. The idea of a return to "peacetime" regimes seemed no longer feasible. In fact, some of the integrating features of the prewar regimes (e.g., loyalty to the charismatic monarch or leader, militaristic patriotism, adoration of the symbols of national tradition in the style and culture) were incorporated into the new fascism with considerable success, and some of them were adopted also by the Communists. Thus, by the mid-thirties, the competing world views—at least in Europe—were those of fascism and communism. The remnants of other world views, including liberalism, were seen as ineffective and decadent.

Hence, in the nineteen thirties, an ideological polarization emerged in

Europe. Conservatism, rightism, and similar creeds tended to succumb to nazism and fascism, while the Left tended to accept Communist influence within "popular fronts." On both sides, tradition was discarded and replaced by a supposedly more modern "ideology."

Within this context, rational social inquiry could have little influence on politics. True, science played a central role in communism, which, based on Marxism, claimed the status of science. But Communists believed that Marx and Lenin had already found all the answers and therefore studied their writings in an almost scholastic manner. Fascists, on the other hand, were generally suspicious of science, at least in its institutionalized form. Fascists believed that they had a better, more direct way to knowledge than cautious, empirical, and rational inquiry, preferring to dictate what science ought to be rather than trying to learn from scientific research.

Moreover, both communism and fascism were drawing on collectivistic-holistic models of society (albeit of opposite kinds): the Communists advocated a universalistic collectivistic view of society, while the Fascists' outlook was particularistic-nationalist. Both of these collectivistic holistic doctrines were, however, difficult to reconcile with the individualistic models of traditional social scientific inquiry.

The polarization into Left and Right did not occur in the English-speaking and in some of the smaller European countries. There tradition, especially in law and moral and religious matters, was respected, and moderation prevailed on both sides of the political spectrum. Ideologies were distrusted so that social inquiry was widely practiced and cautiously used. Had these English traditions been better known in Europe, they could have suggested a different dichotomization than the prevailing one between Left and Right: instead, it would have been possible to classify societies and social theories according to whether their supreme value is the individual or the collectivity and whether they advocate the supremacy of law or the supremacy of personal leadership (Talmon 1967; Shils 1972).

The Left-Right dichotomy was fostered by the scientific community which generally believed that the attitudes of the Right and the Left toward science were radically different. The Nazis and even the Italian fascists made it clear that although they were not against science per se, politics had to come first; in case of a conflict of interest, science had to be subordinated to politics. In Germany, such conflict of interests indeed existed. Many German scientists were Jews or Socialists, groups whose intellectual influence was incompatible with Nazi racism. Nazis, thus, attacked the traditional ethos of science that prohibited the persecution of scientists on the grounds of race or political views and unequivocally denied the autonomy of science from politics. Some Nazis even elaborated a doctrine of a "German" (or "Aryan") science, claiming that race had a decisive influence on the ability to practice and recognize scientific truth.

The essential point about the Nazi stance to science is that it rejected the concept of a universalistic criterion of truth. For the Nazis, the supreme source and touchstone of truth was the spirit of the national community as expressed by its leader. They did not deny the achievements of science but rather believed that many of those achievements were the result of inspiration from the spirit of German national collectivity. Therefore, they saw no harm in persecuting individual scientists or in infringing on the traditional autonomy of science by subjecting scientists to the control of the party. They believed that these changes would give rise to a new, better science, one catering to humanity not through its universalism but through the leadership of the most superior human group.

In contrast, the Soviet Union appeared as the main protagonist of universalistic science. In the thirties, few people recognized that the authoritarianism of the Left was little different from that of the Right. Left-wing authoritarianism retained, in principle, a measure of universalism; Marxism claimed to be based on scientific principles acceptable to any reasonable person and unaffected by the arbitrary tastes and whims of individuals. Moreover, the Soviet Union supported research on a larger scale and more systematic basis than any Western government.[1] The careful observer could have detected that there was a great deal of ambiguity behind this lavish support and public adherence to the supreme value of science. The attacks on modern physics as insufficiently materialistic, the official support given to Lysenko, and the attacks on Mendelism were clear indicators that there was little respect for the autonomy of science in the Soviet Union. These facts, however, were insufficiently known in the West. The issue was also obfuscated by those who argued that Marxism was itself a science and that therefore the interference of Marxist philosophers with physical or genetic research was not really an external political intrusion into science but rather a legitimate philosophical-scientific debate (Bernal 1939; Wersky 1978). By 1947, however, this defense became untenable when Lysenkoism as an official doctrine was adopted and Mendelian geneticists were openly persecuted (Joravsky 1961).

IV. The Rise of the Science-Centered World View after World War II and the Debate over the Central Planning of Science

In 1945, the Allied victory over Nazi Germany could be interpreted by those who advocated the value of rational inquiry and the autonomy and universality of science as a triumph of the values of the Enlightenment.

1. Even Robert K. Merton, writing in 1938, in his discussion of science under totalitarianism, demarcated science from fascism, not from communism. His underlying assumption was that there was no incompatibility between science and communism (Merton 1938b, 1942; Ben-David 1980).

In fact, at least in the United States, Britain, and Canada, scientists emerged from the war with enhanced prestige. They came to be regarded as a fifth estate, with a public mission and a legitimate claim to political influence and support from public funds (Price 1965). The vision for this new relationship of science and government was outlined in Vannevar Bush's report to the president of the United States. The title of this report, "Science: The Endless Frontier," concisely expresses the spirit of the coming new era (Bush 1945).

The obligation governments felt to ensure a "healthy" level of scientific research in their respective countries can be directly linked to the successes of scientific research during the World War, particularly to the development of the atomic bomb. It was not only the technological achievements as such which gave rise to this new attitude toward research but also the social circumstances under which they were attained. For the initiative for the development of the atomic bomb came from within science, from scientists the most outstanding of whom were European refugees from nazism. Indeed, the technological successes were probably due in part to the spontaneous and enthusiastic support of the war effort by the "scientific community." Although the term "scientific community" (on which more below) was not widely used at the time (Gowing 1977), it was a highly fitting description of the world of science, indeed more fitting than either before or after the war. Scientists felt that they had a collective goal—as scientists—to combat nazism, creating among them an intense sense of collective solidarity and social mission. National, institutional, and disciplinary boundaries, usually quite strong in science, weakened and almost disappeared. Scientists from all disciplines, like members of a social movement, rallied around a few *charismatic* leaders and spontaneously cooperated with each other in order to bring about a better world.

After 1945, the scientific war effort became a potent myth which probably was decisive in the decisions of postwar governments to assume responsibility for the continued support of research in peacetime. It was assumed that the miracles wrought by science in the war would be repeated in peacetime. The sword of science would turn into a ploughshare to provide economic bounty on an unprecedented scale. Science was seen as an inexhaustible resource, an "endless frontier."

The fact that wartime research became such a positive myth was also connected with the emergence of a world view which lent science a meaning of deep moral significance. During the thirties and the war years, a world view developed in which science served as a central symbol. In that world view, nazism was presented as the embodiment of irrational prejudice, violence, and persecution in general and as an enemy of the freedom of science in particular. Those opposing nazism were viewed as favoring reason, the freedom of science, and the rational solution of conflict.

Until the late nineteen forties, the Soviet Union was seen as sharing this science-centered world view: Soviet communism was then considered part and parcel of the scientistic tradition stretching back to the Enlightenment. Marxism was regarded as scientific; many intellectuals and scientists held it to be the only consistent, determined attempt at the creation of a just and rational society, open to all humanity.

This postwar science-centered world view dominated intellectual circles and contributed to the growing involvement of Western governments with science, specifically, to the establishment of a new network of national and international scientific institutions created immediately after the war. The American government decided that it would be a waste to dismantle all the scientific organizations built up during the war and instead purposively set up new national organizations (NSF, NIH, etc.) in order to further science. By adopting this program, the United States seemed to join the countries like the USSR and France (the latter inherited such a program from the Popular Front government of the late thirties) in which the systematic support of science was viewed as a prime government responsibility. This explains how the United States could become the model of how to organize science on a national scale. Indeed, the prevailing view was that in this respect there was no difference between liberal-democratic, Socialist, and Communist countries. All scientists, irrespective of political conviction, accepted the need for systematic, planned support of research by governments. The international organizations for scientific and intellectual cooperation, such as UNESCO and the endless lists of international disciplinary associations, were all predicated on the assumption that there was a consensus among scientists of all countries about the nature of science and its importance in building a new world society.

This general agreement over the necessity to plan scientific research did not prevail for long. Dissenting voices were raised in Britain, where a discussion of this issue had been going on since before the war. In fact, the best-known and most systematic exposition of the case for centrally planned and supported research was J. D. Bernal's *The Social Function of Science* (1939). Bernal was an English Communist, one of a number of brilliant scientists who joined the Party; his book impressed wide circles and triggered the debate. Thus, whereas the practice of government-planned science was initiated in the USSR and to some extent in France during the thirties, the rationale of planning was nowhere so widely and so clearly discussed as in Britain. Not only Communists and fellow travelers but also many scientists opposed to Socialist economy accepted the idea that science was somehow different from the economy and therefore could and should be planned. Only a small group of liberal scientists rejected the idea of the central planning of science. They did so not only on political grounds but also on the grounds that, far from safeguarding rationality, central planning was a source of irrationality and inefficiency in science as in the economy. This view was brilliantly formulated by Michael Polanyi (Polanyi 1951).

Polanyi argued that since the outcomes of fundamental research were unpredictable, research could neither be centrally organized nor planned to attain specific purposes. The way to safeguard continued scientific innovation and advancement is to give the individual researcher freedom as complete as possible. The result will not be intellectual anarchy and incoherence, however, for the claims advanced by any individual researcher are evaluated and sanctioned after the event by the members of the scientific community in the relevant fields. Like a competitive market which establishes consensual prices, free competititon between research workers establishes a consensus about the value of the research contributed.

The significance of Polanyi's work was that it proposed a new and to some extent revolutionary conception of the rationality of science. From the very beginning of organized and institutionalized research, scientists believed in a scientific rationality that provided calculable and manipulable knowledge. They also believed that any society seriously utilizing the scientific approach and effectively cultivating the advancement of knowledge would be a planned society guided by experts. In other words, scientists construed their job to be one of providing enlightened governments with knowledge to enable them to devise rational policies, of which the rational planning of science is but an instance. This is also why scientists thought they could ignore whether or not the governments they advised were authoritarian: as long as governments acted on scientific principles, scientists believed, they could not do much wrong. In this view, science, rationality, and planning were seen as inseparable.

In contrast, Polanyi advanced a concept of a spontaneously collaborating scientific community as the most effective means to advance knowledge. He argued that a free market and liberal democracy were the models best fitting the scientific approach to the organization of society in general. This shift signaled an important and momentous change in the conception of a rational, progressive society. Science in this world view was no longer required to provide a definitive scientific theory of society (which could be authoritatively applied by experts) but was seen as a model community capable of advancing and improving knowledge in a manner which combined freedom, spontaneity, and responsibility. It was a flexible and open world view which made no claim to omniscience; it recognized the limitations of existing scientific knowledge and made no promises to find solutions to all problems. Science in this world view was considered a strategy of improvement, not an authoritative doctrine.

Polanyi's model places freedom and originality at the core of the scientific enterprise, implying that the attempt to plan science is basically irrational and doomed to failure. In this model, authoritarianism is suspect not only of being immoral but also of being irrational and inconsistent with the logic of science. Indeed, within this model of rational inquiry, enterprise and experimentation were encouraged, while risks and unpredictable outcomes were recognized as inherent. And yet the system of inquiry was rational because it was constantly learning from the past.

Polanyi's view of the scientific enterprise and his new conception of authority in science and of the organization of research are expressed in the term "scientific community," the group including all qualified scientific workers doing research in a given field. Individual scientists have the freedom to strike out in new directions in their research with the constraint that the results will be evaluated afterwards by other members of the scientific community. Polanyi showed that it is the informal group, or network, rather than a formal, hierarchic organization of science, which is the adequate framework for the analysis of the interaction between scientists and the contents of science.

This new conception of science was incongruent with the way science was organized and practiced in the Soviet Union. Polanyi's concepts supplemented the thesis concerning the "authoritarianism of the Left" which was put forward by a growing number of political scientists after 1945 (Talmon 1984; Shils 1972). This thesis affirmed that left-wing radicalism is closer to the romantic tradition of spontaneous collectivism than to the rational individualism of the Enlightenment. Polanyi, in fact, shows that even those elements which communism adopted from the rational tradition of the Enlightenment were dated and totally unsuitable to a true understanding of the rationality of science.

Polanyi's theoretical work notwithstanding, until the nineteen fifties the prevailing idea was that the actual working of Soviet science, as distinct from its formal organization, was not fundamentally different from that in the West. Gradually, however, it was realized—to some extent, perhaps, due to the Cold War—that this was not the case. The Lysenko affair provided evidence that within Soviet science, the academic freedom of individual researchers was not respected and that the informal scientific community was not allowed to autonomously exercise its function of evaluating the outcomes of research and establishing an authoritative view of the state of the art in a given field. Despite its claims to be scientific, Soviet Marxism rejected the Enlightenment tradition of the autonomy of science, even in its old, pre-Polanyi form. In the West, therefore, Soviet science was recognized as a particularistic deviation from the norms and standards of the worldwide "scientific community."

This recategorization of the Soviet Union altered the world view which had emerged in the thirties in opposition to nazism. Now only the Western world was viewed as a haven of freedom, reason, and science, with institutions capable of mediating political conflicts and providing unprecedented scope for enterprise and creativity. This world view was reinforced by the political and economic successes of the Western world immediately after the war. Science was seen as a central part, actually as a paradigm, of a social order capable of combining individual freedom with responsibility and legal order. It is this view of science as a paradigm of a free society which found its classic exposition in Michael Polanyi's *The Logic of Liberty* (1951).

In the West, science thus became a central element in the world view of post-World War II society. The scientific method was seen as an approach to the exploration of social as well as of physical life which could be adopted universally. Rational, empirical research was seen as a universally applicable and acceptable tool for dealing with economic and social problems, capable of mediating social and political conflicts without resort to force and violence and of advancing humanity to a better future.

In addition to an acceleration in support for research and education, the belief in this world view manifested itself in the establishment of associations for international scientific cooperation, the institution of training and research in social science, the flourishing of comparative social studies, and the rise of theories on the convergent development of modern society, irrespective of divergent cultural and ideological traditions. In practical affairs the effect of this new world view was even more impressive: old prejudices of nationalism and imperialism were put aside in the Western democracies, a European community was created, the colonies were relatively peacefully liberated, and Japan was democratized.

The idea of science as a progressive, rational force in society (especially in mastery of physical nature) capable of promoting collaboration across religious, national, and ideological boundaries was not new. However, in previous times this view was in competitition with other powerful world views—religious, racial, and nationalistic. In the interwar period national solidarity and exclusion were the most significant principles for most people. These particularistic and frequently conflicting solidarities left little room for mediation. Organized religion was also an immense political force, but because it was usually allied with conservative and nationalistic ideologies, it exacerbated rather than mitigated international conflict.

Therefore, the virtual monopoly of the science-centered world view in the West for more than two decades after World War II was a cultural change of great significance. It seemed to establish a new conception of national and international politics and a new way to mediate conflict.

This science-centered world view had two crucial weaknesses, however. The first is that it contained neither new symbols of solidarity nor a comprehensive system of ethics. It was assumed that these elements would be provided by the largely depoliticized religious communities and by the nation-states, defined primarily as cultural entities and tamed of their nationalism. This turned out to be insufficient. Religion and nationalism, now deprived of their claims to the exclusive loyalty of their members, did not possess sufficient authority. As a result, a state of considerable anomie in social relations developed, observable in the erosion of private and communal morality, and manifested by libertinism and the dissolution of family life.

Another crucial feature—and weakness—of the science-centered world view of that period was what may be called *dogmatic scientism*. By the term "scientism," I refer to any authoritative world view which claims to be derived from allegedly true scientific principles and which contains utopian promises for a dramatic improvement of the human condition. In point of fact, notwithstanding the openness and moderation of the principles of the science-centered world view during the two decades following the Second World War, elements of dogmatic scientism could be observed in the West. Particularly in the United States, the belief in the power and authority of science was at times dogmatic and similar to the attitudes characterizing nineteenth-century ideologies.

One manifestation of this dogmatism was the popular belief in the omnipotence of science. There was a belief (at times not unlike the belief in magic) that investment in research would necessarily produce wealth. Many scientists, intellectuals, and journalists believed that scientific research was the key to all economic development; science, they believed, held the purse strings of the states (Price 1965). Thus, when the late American President Lyndon B. Johnson promised to create a "Great Society," it was taken for granted that "research and development" would discover ways to eliminate both poverty and educational handicaps.

The prestige of scientists rose. Outstanding scientists were treated as "stars" and "superstars"; some of them even began to feel themselves to be superior beings. Scientists claimed for themselves privileges similar to those claimed by an official clergy and demanded for science "the prerogatives of a state religion without any of the embarrassments" (W. Carey, cited in Orlans 1968, p. 266).

Yet, this irrational, dogmatic scientism was not elaborated into a comprehensive authoritative ideology purportedly based on science. There were some attempts in this direction, for example, Skinner's behavioristic utopia, Teilhard de Chardin's attempt to regard science as a new kind of Christian message, and, more recently, sociobiology, but they had a very limited impact.

The basis for this dogmatic scientism lay in the need for public support for underwriting scientific research. In democratic countries, the public has to be persuaded that scientific research contributes to the attainment of public goods. The attempts to persuade the public led often to exaggerating the contributions made by research; science was presented as a kind of omnipotent magic, almost a deity.

These irrational beliefs and attitudes toward science were of course untenable and would have had to be abandoned in any case. It was an open question, however, whether this irrational view of science would be abandoned in favor of a more realistic view, or whether it would be replaced by something even more irrational.

V. The Rise of Criticism of Science in the Nineteen Sixties

About 1968, the perception of science changed dramatically. This anti-scientistic movement, unnoticeable among people at large, emerged among intellectuals. I am using the term "anti-scientism" to describe a world view in which science—at least as understood and practiced today—is seen as the main source, or part of the main source, of human error and misery. Anti-scientism must be distinguished from rational criticism of certain procedures, claims, or applications of science; it is, so to speak, the mirror image of "scientism" in which science is seen as the source of all truth and welfare.

The rational critics of scientific practices and beliefs were scientists, statesmen of science, and philosophers. These critics were the same types of people (and sometimes the very same people, only wiser) as those who had previously recommended accelerated growth of science (Price 1965; Weinberg 1967). They were not attempting to reduce the status or change the nature of science but to find new rationales, criteria, and objectives for its continued regular support.

In fact, the development of postwar science and technology posed new problems in conceptualizing and legimating science. Polanyi's conception of the "scientific community" helped make explicit the links between science and a free liberal society, but it did not account for the new postwar features of science: the importance of research for the economy, the new types of research organizations, and the growing involvement of government and private industry with research. In fact, by the sixties, much research for the advancement of pure knowledge (such as the exploration of elementary particles) had been done by very large groups of scientists who worked in large bureaucracies and were concerned both with advancing their standing within the organization and with advancing the standing of their organization in competition with other organizations engaged in similar work. Furthermore, a very large part of the goods and services produced by applied science and development are designed to satisfy military, rather than civilian, needs. Therefore, the view of science as a community of individual creative scholars motivated by the pursuit of original discovery no longer fitted the actual circumstances under which much research was conducted. Yet this view, elaborated notably by Michael Polanyi and Robert K. Merton, continued to be held by the majority of sociologists of science until the mid-sixties, encouraging suspicion (even among people devoted to the cause of science) that the continued insistence on the autonomy of science, rather than the result of a disinterested search for truth, served selfish purposes.

Beginning in the mid-fifties, a lively debate over the rationale for the public support of research set in. The principal question discussed was, how should scientific research be organized and controlled? The main points at issue were the classification and control of the applied research occupying the area between fundamental research and product development and the economic returns of research in general and specifically of research in certain fields and in different countries. Studies were mostly initiated or conducted by national and international agencies, such as the American National Science Foundation

(NSF) or the Paris-based Organization for Economic Cooperation and Development (OECD). Similarly, "science policy" also became a regular concern of governments, while concomitantly universities began training students and organizing research in this field.

Scientists themselves also contributed to this rational criticism of science. Acutely aware of the growing powers and effects of the new science-based technologies and susbstances, they wished to limit any harmful effects. The most conspicuous criticism of this kind was that voiced by the movement of atomic scientists after the war (Smith 1965). Similarly, the publication of Rachel Carson's *The Silent Spring* (1965) drew attention to the dramatic damage done to the environment by such widely hailed inventions as DDT and other insect killers.

Finally, philosophers pursued a critical examination of the claim that science produced true knowledge. They proceeded mainly through examining cases in which knowledge claims which ultimately were shown to be false were accepted by the scientific community and through an analysis of the nature of scientific controversies.[2]

Although much of this activity was critical of various aspects of the organization and practice of research, this criticism always shared a fundamental perception of science as the core of the modern world view. In fact, no alternative was within sight: religion ceased to be a source of legitimacy and authority in Western democratic societies, while there was little inclination to follow Fascist or Communist ideologies as a substitute science *cum* religion. Thus, until the sixties, the critical inquiry into science and science policy did not question science as the core of the world view which emerged after the war, and it was merely intended to clarify and correct this world view in order to make science and research more effective and rational.

In the late sixties, however, a very different kind of science criticism emerged, one which can be adequately characterized as anti-scientistic. This new science criticism differed from the rational criticism of science: its aims and its intellectual and social origins are completely different.

These anti-scientistic critics of science were not concerned with improving science. They did not try to study science with a view to find out what was wrong with certain scientific practices, or science policy, or certain science-based technologies. Rather, from the outset they assumed that something was wrong with science *as such*. They criticized science not in order to improve it but rather to indict it. These critics drew on arguments elaborated by the rational criticis of science, but they used these arguments for a different purpose. For instance, the difficulty in establishing epistemological criteria for a clear-cut demarcation of scientific from nonscientific knowledge was used to support the argument that science was not at all different from religion,

2. Cf. Laudan 1983, for a good retrospective overview.

magic, or ideology. Similarly, the real threat to humanity from atomic and thermonuclear weapons, or the grave environmental problems, were attributed to the callousness, indeed, the very nature, of science.

Underlying this new science criticism was the assumption that science as such could be replaced with a new, radically different type of science. Indeed, one of the major and most influential sources of anti-scientism was Herbert Marcuse's *One Dimensional Man* (Marcuse 1964), which condemns science on the basis of a Hegelian-Marxian philosophy. This alternative science was not to emerge from new, pathbreaking scientific discoveries but through political action which would "break down the barrier" between expert and nonexpert, adopt Socialist forms of work within the laboratory, "open the laboratories to the community," "take science to the factory gates," and make "every man his own scientist." The model to be followed was that of the Chinese Cultural Revolution.[3]

This kind of radical anti-scientism is not a new phenomenon; opposition to modern science has been a recurrent theme in Western culture since the attacks on science in reaction to the founding of the Royal Society. In the second half of the eighteenth century, these anti-science views were systematically formulated within romantic philosophy. The beliefs underlying this anti-scientistic tradition have been summarized by Stephen Toulmin: science is dehumanizing; it disregards the primacy of human issues and suppresses individuality and imagination; it is mechanical and cold-blooded, disregarding quality and trying to reduce everything to quantity; it is too abstract and unable to relate to the complex nature of real situations; and it creates a spur for the adoption of policies and practices solely for their technical efficiency without regard for their effect on people and society (Toulmin 1972).

The question now is, why has an anti-scientism emerged in the late sixties, no less irrational than the scientism it set out to attack? More specifically, why did the criticism of science and of scientism not remain limited to the (legitimate) rational examination of scientific organization and policy?

The contents and the intellectual sources of the anti-scientistic movement leave no doubt that its emergence, or rather revival, had little to do with any concrete feature of science or of the scientific community at that time. The hypothesis I suggest is that this movement did not arise as a reaction to the state of science but rather to the state of society: the reaction by intellectuals against science was a result of doubts about the dominant science-centered world view in which science and the scientific community were linked to the liberal-democratic form of government. In other words, in the late nineteen sixties, the growing disillusionment among the intellectuals with the belief in the Western way of life and in liberal values entailed a similar attitude toward science as a central component of the Western world view.

3. Several of the papers in Rose and Rose 1980 give a good idea of these views.

Until the mid-sixties, the impression prevailed that—largely with the aid of science—humanity had arrived at a stage of undisturbed economic growth and permanent social welfare. The success of the Marshall Plan, the economic and political reconstruction of Japan, and the relatively peaceful liberation of the colonies served as evidence that liberal-democratic societies had at their disposal rational means to deal with their social and economic problems. By the late sixties, this belief was undermined. The United States, the "paradigmatic" Western society, struggled with the problems of race and poverty at home and suffered unexpected reverses in the war in Vietnam. By the end of the sixties, Western economy also began to falter as inflation and unemployment—which had seemed eliminated forever—reappeared to threaten the achievements of the two previous decades. These difficulties were interpreted as signs that the Western world order was beset by problems that defied scientific social thought and inquiry.

These doubts regarding the Western, rational, world view were exacerbated by the impression that different, nonscientific kinds of social thought and practice might be more effective and successful. For instance, the Vietnamese who defeated the Americans did not possess a scientific tradition. Similarly, the OPEC countries reached their strong position not by drawing on a social or economic theory or through industriousness and technical skills but through sheer luck. Thus, in the late sixties it seemed that the Western world view, founded on scientific rationality and on pragmatic empiricism, did not possess a universal and unfailing validity. At the same time, events gave the impression that the Third World possessed world views which, although not scientific, were no less powerful.

The sudden and unexpected change in the perception of science, following a period of belief in scientific omnipotence, had a particularly strong effect on young people who had been brought up in an atmosphere of belief in science and who were under unrelenting pressure to study and achieve in science. They felt cheated and let down. Science, which previously had been presented in an almost deified form, now appeared to them (and to some of their elders) as a *god that failed*. This was particularly true for those who, after having invested much effort and self-discipline in the study of science, discovered that science excludes from its domain the important questions of religion, morality, and beauty. Moreover, science seemed to treat these questions in an arrogant and superficial manner, as if they could be "solved" through scientific inquiry. Indeed, it was increasingly realized that far from being able to deal with these problems adequately, science—and science-based technology—in fact created new, more complex and threatening problems such as pollution and the risk of thermonuclear war.

Furthermore, for many intellectuals, there was a general tendency toward alienation from science and, beyond this, alienation from the Western rational cultural values deriving from the Enlightenment. These intellectuals adopted a general *antinomian attitude* toward the liberal-democratic political order. Anti-scientism was an integral part of this antinomian attitude. Thus, because science was a visible and central symbol of Western postwar society, it served as a target even for those who had little interest in and knowledge of science. To be sure, in society at large there was no turning against science. The majority of people were not directly concerned with science, nor were they willing to abandon a belief in science as the way to attain technological and social improvements. Among intellectuals, however, the massive rise of anti-scientism was a clearly perceptible phenomenon.

The anti-scientistic movement of the late sixties and early seventies, I thus suggest, was not a reaction to specific problems within science. Rather, it arose from a poignant sense of disappointment, indeed a sense of collapse, in a world view in which science and liberal democracy were linked to a largely utopian promise of wealth and mastery over human fate.

As noted earlier, this kind of hostile reaction to scientism had several historical precedents. The most recent one, the antiscientism which emerged in Germany after World War I, can serve as a useful parallel to the situation in the nineteen sixties.

Before World War I, Germany was the undisputed leader in science and higher education. Germans saw their country as one in which their cultural superiority had created an efficient industry, good government, and an excellent military. Germans were convinced that their science, technology, and military and political leadership made them invincible. Many outstanding scientists, sharing and fostering this view, participated enthusiastically and successfully in the war effort.

Defeat created a tremendous disillusionment. Romantic anti-scientistic world views reemerged, as manifested by the popularity in intellectual circles of Oswald Spengler's *Decline of the West* which appeared in 1918. Some of its themes—the cultural relativity of Western science and the impeding decline of Western culture (Forman 1971)—have also been popular themes in the anti-scientistic criticism of the late nineteen sixties and nineteen seventies. This parallelism supports the interpretation that the rise of anti-scientism is a reaction to the political and military failures of societies in which science is a symbol of central importance, rather than a reaction to internal problems within science.

Before World War II (notably during the interwar period), alienation from the Enlightenment tradition as a rule led to a return to pre-Enlightenment religious and political traditions or to nineteenth-century traditions of collectivistic nationalism and racism. After 1945, however, organized religion, nationalism, and racism, the most powerful anti-Enlightenment forces before the war, had been discredited by their passive acceptance of, if not active association with, nazism. Consequently, they offered no viable alternative to the intellectual, political, and economic traditions of democratic liberalism, nor did they offer principles of legitimation which could compete with science as the core of a consistent world view. Thus, the alienation from Western politics and social thought in the late nineteen sixties emerged as a primarily diffuse antinomian attitude, one that had no specific tradition around which to crystallize. In fact, even where Marxism was ostensibly adopted as an ideology, this was usually in its Maoist version which, with its symbols of solidarity, allowed intellectuals to vent their antinomian impulses through a feeling of belongingness to abstractly construed "masses."

This new, allegedly "ideological" movement was not wedded to a specific political doctrine. Its purpose was to replace capitalism with a better society, but it had only very vague ideas of what such a society would be like, or how and by whom it should be ruled. In brief, it was a purely antinomian movement. Like the medieval heresies, it was opposed to the dominant view but bound by the cognitive limits of that view and therefore only capable of inverting it, turning it upside down, and not of replacing it with a new, positive program. This negative nature of its content explains why the anti-science movement was so ephemeral and its legacy so difficult to trace.

In sum, then, in the postwar Western world view, science—perceived as a strategy rather than as a doctrine—was given unprecedented prominence: it has been the only generally recognized source of legitimation and has provided the only accepted strategy for solving problems. This prominence was challenged, and to some degree undermined, by the antinomian outbursts of the late sixties and early seventies. Those outbursts did not produce widely acceptable alternatives, however. It would seem that since the last World War, the science-centered world view, on the one hand, and the anti-science movement, on the other, exhaust the map of public discourse in Western democracies.

In this respect, the situation in many countries of the Third World is radically different. Until the nineteen sixties, it seemed virtually certain that the Third World would adopt the science-centered world view. It now appears, however, that in several cases development went in the opposite direction: elements of the science-centered world view already adopted were rejected for religious and nationalistic world views in a manner reminiscent of the European scene in the nineteenth and early twentieth centuries. Even when these world views transcend national boundaries, they do so particularistically, appealing to limited religious or ethnic groups, such as Arabs, Moslems, or Latin Americans, in the same manner as the appeals for pan-Slavism or pan-Germanism of pre-1939 Europe. In these countries, therefore, it is religious and nationalistic doctrines which determine and delimit public discourse.

The antagonism between the Western science-centered world view and the particularistic world views emerging in many Third World countries makes communication and cooperation increasingly difficult. The West is characterized essentially by the emphasis put on personal freedom and by its progressive and nonviolent character, features which entail an absence of potent sources of social solidarity and morality. The Third World ideologies, by contrast, offer solidarity and, in their religious versions (e.g., Moslem fundamentalism), also possess a powerful source of morality. Communism, the most significant attempt to mediate between the two world views, combines a scientific world view with monolithic coercive power and strict social control.

World views do not determine policy: they set policies into a framework. If the framework is well defined, policies are likely to be more self-assured and purposeful than when the framework becomes confused. Although the particularistic Third World views cannot be a substitute for the universalistic science-centered world view, they can weaken and undermine it, especially, as in the late sixties and early seventies, when allied with an anti-scientistic movement. This is why, since the late sixties, the framework for Western, science-centered policy has become uncertain.

References

Ben-David, Joseph. 1980. "The Ethos of Science: The Last Half-Century," in *Science and Polity*, ed. J. R. Philips and T. J. Conlon. Canberra: Australian Academy of Science. (This volume, chap. 23.)

———. 1984 (1971). *The Scientist's Role in Society*, 2d ed. Chicago: University of Chicago Press.

———. 1986. "Academic Market, Ideology and the Growth of Scientific Knowledge: Physiology in Mid-Nineteenth-Century Germany," in *Approaches to Social Theory*, ed. Siegwart Lindberg, James S. Coleman, and Stefan Nowak. New York: Russell Sage Foundation. [This volume, chap. 24.]

Ben-David, Joseph, and Randall Collins. 1966. "A Comparative Study of Academic Freedom and Student Politics," *Comparative Education Review* 10 (2):220–49. [This volume, chap. 10.]

Bernal, J. D. 1939. *The Social Function of Science*. London: Routledge.

Beyerchen, A. D. 1977. *Scientists under Hitler: Politics and the Physics Community in the Third Reich*. New Haven: Yale University Press.

Bush, Vannevar. 1945. *Science the Endless Frontier: A Report to the President*. Washington, D.C.: U.S. Government Printing Office.

Carson, Rachel. 1962. *The Silent Spring*. Boston: Houghton Mifflin.

Forman, Paul. 1971. "Weimar Culture, Causality and Quantum Theory, 1918–1927: Adaptation by German Physicists and Mathematicians to a Hostile Intellectual Environment," *Historical Studies in the Physical Sciences* 3:1–115.

Gay, Peter. 1968. *Weimar Culture: The Outsider as Insider*. New York: Harper and Row.

Gowing, Margaret. 1977. *Science and Politics*. London: Birkbeck College.

Hahn, Roger I. 1971. *The Anatomy of a Scientific Institution: The Paris Academy of Sciences, 1666–1803*. Berkeley and Los Angeles: University of California Press.

Joravsky, David. 1961. *Soviet Marxism and Natural Science*. New York: Columbia University Press.

Laudan, Larry. 1977. *Progress and Its Problems: Toward a Theory of Scientific Growth*. Berkeley, Los Angeles, London: University of California Press.

———. 1983. *Science and Values*. Berkeley, Los Angeles, London: University of California Press.

Mannheim, Karl. 1986 (1925). *Conservatism: A Contribution to the Sociology of Knowledge*, ed. David Kettler, Volker Meja, and Nico Stehr. London: Routledge and Kegan Paul.

Manuel, Frank. 1974. *The Religion of Isaac Newton: The Fremantle Lectures 1973*. Oxford: Clarendon Press.

———. 1983. *The Changing of the Gods*. Hanover: Brown University.

Marcuse, Herbert. 1964. *One-Dimensional Man*. Boston: Beacon Press.

Merton, Robert. 1970 (1938a). *Science, Technology, and Society in Seventeenth-Century England*. New York: Fertig.

———. 1973 (1938b). "Science and the Social Order," in *The Sociology of Science*. Chicago: University of Chicago Press.

———. 1973 (1942). "The Normative Structure of Science," in *The Sociology of Science*. Chicago: University of Chicago Press.

Orlans, Harold (ed.). 1968. *Science Policy and the University*. Washington, D.C.: Brookings Institute.

Polanyi, Michael. 1951. *The Logic of Liberty*. Chicago: University of Chicago Press.

Price, Don K. 1965. *The Scientific Estate*. Cambridge: Belknap Press.

Rose, H., and S. Rose. 1969. *Science and Society*. London: Penguin Press.

———. 1980. *Ideology of/in the Natural Sciences*. New York: Schenkman.

Schumpeter, Joseph A. 1950 (1942). *Capitalism, Socialism and Democracy*. New York: Harper and Row.

Shils, Edward. 1972. *The Intellectuals and the Powers, and Other Essays*. Chicago: University of Chicago Press.

Smith, Alice K. 1965. *A Peril and a Hope: The Scientists Movement in America, 1945–47*. Chicago: University of Chicago Press.

Tocqueville, Alexis de. 1969. *Democracy in America*, ed. J. P. Mayer, trans. George Lawrence. Garden City, N.Y.: Doubleday Press.

Talmon, Jacob Leib. 1967. *Romanticism and Revolt: Europe 1815–1848*. New York: W. W. Norton.

———. 1984. *Totalitarian Democracy and After: International Colloquium in Memory of Jacob L. Talmon*. Jerusalem: Israel Academy of Sciences and Humanities, Magnes Press.

Toulmin, Stephen. 1972. "The Historical Background to the Anti-Science Movement," CIBA Symposium. *Civilization and Science in Conflict or Collaboration*. New York: Elsevier.

Weart, Spencer. 1979. *Scientists in Power*. Cambridge: Harvard University Press.

Webster, Charles (ed.). 1974. *The Intellectual Revolution of the Seventeenth Century*. London: Routledge and Kegan Paul.

Weinberg, Alvin. 1967. *Reflections on Big Science*. Cambridge: MIT Press.

Wersky, Gary. 1978. *The Visible College: The Collective Biography of British Scientific Socialists of the 1930s*. New York: Holt, Rinehart and Winston.

Bibliography of
Joseph Ben-David's Writings

Papers marked with * are included in this volume. [*Note:* no. 38 (= chap. 19) has been given a different title; only extracts of nos. 3 and 15 are reproduced (chaps. 11 and 4, respectively) and their titles have been supplied by the editor.] Not included in the Bibliography are book-reviews, and review essays that Professor Ben-David himself had excluded from his list of publications.

A. Monographs

1. "The Social Structure of the Professions in Israel." Ph.D. dissertation, Hebrew University, Jerusalem, 1955. (Typescript, in Hebrew; no. H-3.) [For published parts, see nos. 11, 15, and H-4, below.]
2. (Ed.) *Agricultural Planning and Village Community in Israel.* Paris: UNESCO, (1964). (= Arid Zone Research, 23).
* 3. *Fundamental Research and the Universities. Some Comments on International Differences.* Paris: Organisation for Economic Cooperation and Development, 1968.
    3.1 French translation: *La Recherche fondamentale et les universités : Réflexions sur les disparités internationales.* Paris: Organisation de coopération et de développement économiques, 1968.
    3.2 Partial translation into Japanese.
4. *The Scientist's Role in Society: A Comparative Study.* Englewood Cliffs, N.J.: Prentice-Hall, 1971. [For a new edition, see no. 9 below.]
    4.1 Spanish translation: *El Papel de los Científicos en la Sociedad.* Mexico: Trillas, 1974.
    4.2 Portugese translation: *O Papel do Cientista na Sociedade.* São Paulo: Livraria Pioneira Editora.
    4.3 Italian translation: *Scienze e Societa: Uno Studio comparato del ruolo scienziato.* Bologna: Societa Editrice Il Mulino, 1975.
    4.4 Translation into Japanese.

5. *American Higher Education: Directions Old and New.* New York: McGraw Hill, 1972. [For a paperback edition, see no. 6 below.]

6. *Trends in American Higher Education.* Chicago: University of Chicago Press, Phoenix Book P 617, 1974. [Paperback edition of no. 5 above.]

7. *Centers of Learning: Britain, France, Germany, United States.* New York: McGraw Hill, 1977.

8. With Terry N. Clark, eds., *Culture and Its Creators: Essays in Honor of Edward Shils.* Chicago and London: University of Chicago Press, 1977.

9. *The Scientist's Role in Society: A Comparative Study.* Chicago and London: University of Chicago Press, 1984. [Reprint with a new introduction of no. 4 above.]

B. Articles and Reports in Languages Other than Hebrew

10. "Ethnic Differences or Social Change?" In Carl Frankenstein, ed., *Between Past and Future: Essays and Studies on Immigrant Absorption in Israel.* Jerusalem: Henrietta Szold Foundation for Child and Youth Welfare, 1953. Pp. 33–52.

11. "Professions and Social Structure in Israel," *Scripta Hierosolymitana* (Jerusalem) 3 (1956):126–52. ["A partial summary of the author's Ph.D. dissertation in sociology"; see no. 1 above.]

12. With S. N. Eisenstadt. "Inter-generation Tensions in Israel," *International Social Science Bulletin* 8, 1 (1956):54–75.

13. "The Rise of a Salaried Professional Class in Israel," *Transactions of the Third World Congress of Sociology* (International Sociological Association, 1956) 3:302–10.

14. "La nouvelle classe des pays sous-développés," *Esprit* 26 (2), no. 258 (1958): 201–12.

* 15. "The Professional Role of the Physician in Bureaucratized Medicine: A Study in Role Conflict," *Human Relations* 11 (1958):255–74. ["This paper is a revised and abridged version of Part III of the author's Ph.D. dissertation"; see above no. 1.]

16. "San Nicandro: A Sociological Comment," *The Jewish Journal of Sociology* 2, 2 (1960):250–58.

* 17. "Roles and Innovations in Medicine," *American Journal of Sociology* 65, 6 (1960):557–68.

* 18. "Scientific Productivity and Academic Organization in Nineteenth-Century Medicine," *American Sociological Review* 25, 6 (1960):828–43.

19. With Awraham Zloczower. "The Idea of the University and the Academic Market Place," *European Journal of Sociology* 2 (1961):303–14.

20. "Religion and Capitalism" [review article of Kurt Samuelson, *Religion and Economic Action* (London: Heinemann, 1961)], *The Jewish Journal of Sociology* 4, 2 (1962):299–302.

21. "Scientific Endeavor in Israel and the United States," *The American Behavioral Scientist* 6, 4 (1962):12–16.

* 22. With Awraham Zloczower. "Universities and Academic Systems in Modern Societies," *European Journal of Sociology* 3 (1962):pp. 45–84.

23. "Professions in the Class System of Present-Day Societies: A Trend Report and Bibliography," *Current Sociology* 12, 3 (1963–64):247–330.
   23.1 German translation of Chapter I (pp. 247–55): "Akademische Berufe und die Professionalisierung," *Kölner Zeitschrift für Soziologie und Sozialpsychologie*, Sonderheft 5 (1961):104–21.
*24. "Scientific Growth: A Sociological View," *Minerva* 3, 4 (1964):455–76.
25. "The Kibbutz and the Moshav." In Joseph Ben-David (ed.), *Agricultural Planning and Village Community in Israel*. Paris: UNESCO, 1964. Pp. 45–57.
26. "Conforming and Deviant Images of Youth in a New Society," *Transactions of the Fifth World Congress of Sociology* (International Sociological Association, 1964) 4:405–14.
27. "Report on the Discussion," ibid., 71–73.
28. "Professionals and Unions in Israel," *Industrial Relations* 5, 1 (1965):48–66.
29. "The Scientific Role: The Conditions of Its Establishment in Europe," *Minerva* 4, 1 (1965):15–54. [Included with slight modifications in no. 4 above, pp. 45–74.]
30. "Chronicle" [Obituary of Yonina Talmon], *The Jewish Journal of Sociology* 8, 2 (1966):265–66.
*31. With Randall Collins. "Social Factors in the Origins of a New Science: The Case of Psychology," *American Sociological Review* 31, 4 (1966):451–65.
   31.1 German translation: "Soziale Faktoren im Ursprung einer neuen Wissenschaft: der Fall der Psychologie." In Peter Weingart (ed.), *Wissenschaftssoziologie II: Determinanten wissenschaftlicher Entwicklung*. Frankfurt: Athenäum Fischer, 1974. Pp. 122–52.
*32. With Randall Collins. "A Comparative Study of Academic Freedom and Student Politics," *Comparative Education Review* 10, 2 (1966):220–49.
*33. With Lydia Aran. "Socialization and Career Patterns as Determinants of Productivity of Medical Researchers," *Journal of Health and Social Behavior* 9, 1 (1968):3–15.
34. With Haim Adler. *The Impact of Education on Career Expectations and Mobility*. Washington, D.C.: Division of Higher Education Research, U.S. Department of Health, Education and Welfare, Office of Education, 1968. (Mimeo.) 72pp. + Appendixes.
35. "Universities." In *International Encyclopedia of the Social Sciences*, vol. 16. New York: Macmillan and Free Press, 1968. Pp. 191–99.
36. "The Universities and the Growth of Science in Germany and the United States," *Minerva* 7, 1–2 (1968–69):1–35. [Included with modifications in no. 4 above, pp. 129–68.]
37. "Science and the Universities" [review article of Harold Orlans (ed.), *Science Policy and the University* (Washington D.C.: The Brookings Institute, 1968)], *Nature* 223 (July 12, 1969):137–39.
*38. "Introduction," to a special issue "Sociology of Science," *International Social Science Journal* 22, 1 (1970):7–27.
   38.1 French translation: "Introduction," *Revue internationale des sciences sociales* 22, 1 (1970):7–29.
39. "The Rise and Decline of France as a Scientific Centre," *Minerva* 8, 2 (1970):160–79. [Included with slight modifications in no. 4 above, pp. 88–107.]

40. "Political Formats for Science and Technology" [review article of Hilary Rose and Steven Rose, *Science and Society* (London: Allen Lane, The Penguin Press, 1969)], *Science* 169 (September 25, 1970):1299–1301.

*41. "The Profession of Science and Its Powers," *Minerva* 10, 3 (1972):362–83.

*42. "Science and the University System," *International Review of Education* 18, 1 (1972):44–60.

43. "How to Organize Research in the Social Sciences," *Daedalus* 102, 2 (1973):39–51.

44. "The State of Sociological Theory and the Sociological Community: A Review Article," *Comparative Studies in Society and History* 15, 4 (1973):448–72.

45. "The Sociology of Science" [review article of Robert K. Merton, *The Sociology of Science* (Chicago: The University of Chicago Press, 1973)], *New York Times Book Review,* November 11, 1973, pp. 31–34.

46. *The Arab Jewish Conflict: An Israeli View.* Jerusalem: Israeli Universities Study Group for Middle Eastern Affairs, February 1974. (Mimeo.) 42 pp.

47. With Shaul Katz. "Scientific Research and Agricultural Innovation in Israel," *Minerva* 13, 2 (1975):152–82.

48. "Max Weber on Universities: The Power of the State and the Dignity of the Academic Calling in Imperial Germany" [review article of the book by that name translated, edited, and with an introductory note by Edward Shils (Chicago: The University of Chicago Press, 1974)], *American Journal of Sociology* 80, 6 (1975):1463–68.

49. "Probleme einer soziologischen Theorie der Wissenschaft." In Peter Weingart (ed.), *Wissenschaftsforschung.* Frankfurt/New York: Campus Verlag, 1975. Pp. 133–61. [For an enlarged and considerably modified English version, see no. 55 below.]

50. With Teresa A. Sullivan. "Sociology of Science," *Annual Review of Sociology* 1 (1975):203–22.

*51. "Innovations and Their Recognition in Social Science," *History of Political Economy* 7, 4 (1975):434–55.

52. "On the Traditional Morality of Science," *Harvard University, Program On Public Conceptions of Science, Newsletter* 13 (October 1976):24–36.

53. "Science as a Profession and Scientific Professionalism." In Jan J. Loubser, et al. (eds.), *Explorations in General Theory in Social Science: Essays in Honor of Talcott Parsons.* New York/London: Free Press, 1976. Vol. 2. Pp. 874–88.

54. *Report on Visit to Brazil, July 25–August 8, 1976.* Rio de Janeiro: FINEP— Financiadora de Estudos e Projetos, Grupo de Estudos sobre o Desenvolvimento da Ciencia, 1976. (Mimeo.) 23 pp.

*55. "Organization, Social Control, and Cognitive Change in Science." In Joseph Ben-David and Terry N. Clark (eds.), *Culture and Its Creators: Essays in Honor of Edward Shils.* Chicago/London: University of Chicago Press, 1977. Pp. 244–65. [An enlarged and substantially modified version of no. 49 above.]

56. "History, Purpose, and Organization of Academic Research." In *The International Encyclopedia of Higher Education,* vol. 8. San Francisco/Washington/London: Jossey-Bass, 1977. Pp. 3585–90.

*57. "The Central Planning of Science" [review article of J.-J. Salomon, *The Research System: Comparative Survey of the Organization and Financing of Fun-*

damental Research, 3 vols. (Paris: OECD, 1972–1974)], *Minerva* 15, 3–4 (1977): 539–53. [Republished as no. 67 below.]

58. "The Structure and Function of Nineteenth-Century Social Science." In Eric G. Forbes (ed.), *Human Implications of Scientific Advance: Proceedings of the XVth International Congress of the History of Science, Edinburgh, August 10–15, 1977.* Edinburgh: Edinburgh University Press, 1978. Pp. 70–77.

*59. "Emergence of National Traditions in the Sociology of Science: The United States and Great Britain." In Jerry Gaston (ed.), *Sociology of Science*, special double issue of *Sociological Inquiry* 48, 3–4 (1978): 197–218.

60. "The Ethical Responsibility of Social Scientists: A Historical Survey and Comment." In Torgny Segerstedt (ed.), *Ethics for Science Policy: Proceedings of a Nobel Symposium Held at Södergarn, Sweden, 20–25 August 1978.* Oxford: Pergamon Press, 1979. Pp. 31–48.

*61. "Academy, University and Research Institute in the 19th and 20th Centuries: A Study of Changing Functions and Structures." In Erwin K. Scheuch and Heine V. Alemann (eds.), *Das Forschungsinstitut. Formen der Institutionalisierung von Wissenschaft.* Erlangen: Institut für Gesellschaft und Wissenschaft an der Universität Erlangen-Nürnberg, 1978. Pp. 27–45.

62. "Foreword" to Gunnar Boalt et al. (eds.), *Sociologists in Search of Their Intellectual Domain.* Stockholm: Almquist & Wiksell, 1979. Pp. 7–12.

*63. "The Ethos of Science: The Last Half-Century." In J. R. Philips and T. J. Conlon (eds.), *Science and the Polity: Ideals, Illusions, and Realities* (= *Silver Jubilee Symposium*, vol. 1). Canberra: Australian Academy of Science, 1980. Pp. 13–28.

64. "The Impact of the United States on World Higher Education Since World War II." In Shlomo Slonim (ed.), *The American Experience in Historical Perspective* (Conference in Honor of the Bicentennial of American Independence, sponsored by the Hebrew University Jerusalem). Ramat Gan (Israel): Turtledove Publishing, 1979. Pp. 253–71.

65. "Le rôle des gouvernements dans le soutien et la planification de la science." In André Philippart (ed.), *Ordre et désordre en politique scientifique. Symposium Fondation Francqui 28–31 mai 1979.* Brussels: Comité de recherche Science et politique de l'Association internationale de science politique, 1980. Pp. 89–113.

66. "Universities in Israel: Dilemmas of Growth, Diversification and Administration," *Studies in Higher Education* 11, 2 (1986): 105–30.

　　66.1 German translation: "Universitäten in Israel." In Walter Ackerman, Arie Carmon, and David Zucker (eds.), *Erziehung in Israel II.* Stuttgart: Klett-Cotta, 1982. Pp. 363–92.

*67. "The Central Planning of Science." In János Farkas (ed.), *Sociology of Science and Research.* Budapest: Akadémiai Kiadó, 1979. Pp. 473–89. [Essentially identical with no. 57 above.]

68. "U.S. Science in International Perspective," *Scientometrics* 2, 5–6 (1980): 411–21.

*69. "Sociology and Its Uses," *Schweizerische Zeitschrift für Soziologie* 6, 3 (1980): 335–52.

*70. "Sociology of Scientific Knowledge." In James F. Short (ed.), *The State of Sociology: Problems and Prospects.* Beverly Hills: Sage, 1981. Pp. 40–59.

71. "Research and Teaching in the Universities." In John W. Chapman (ed.), *The Western University on Trial*. Berkeley, Los Angeles, London: University of California Press, 1983. Pp. 81–91.

*72. With Shaul Katz. "Scientific Societies, Professional Organizations and the Creation and Dissemination of Practical Knowledge." In *Proceedings of the Global Seminar on The Role of Scientific & Engineering Societies in Development, New Delhi, December 1–5, 1980*. New Delhi: The Indian National Science Academy, 1982. Pp. 153–61.

73. "Rivalität und Kooperation," *HPI: Hochschulpolitische Informationen* (Köln) 14, no. 17 (9 September 1983): 3–6.

74. "Research on Higher Education in Israel," *Higher Education in Europe* 8, 1 (1983): 76–79.

75. "Introduction," to the 1984 printing of *The Scientist's Role in Society* [see no. 9 above].

76. "Science and Values: Work Still to be Done" (review article), *Minerva* 22, 4 (1984): 451–62.

*77. "Puritanism and Modern Science: A Study in the Continuity and Coherence of Sociological Research." In Erik Cohen, Moshe Lissak, and Uri Almagor (eds.), *Comparative Social Dynamics: Essays in Honor of S. N. Eisenstadt*. Boulder, Colo. and London: Westview Press, 1985. Pp. 207–23.

78. "Universities and Graduate Education, Research Role of." In *International Encyclopedia of Education: Research and Studies*, edited by Torsten Husén and T. Neville Postlethwaite. Oxford: Pergamon Press, 1985. Vol. 9. Pp. 5380–87.

*79. "Science, Scientism and Anti-Scientism." In Tord Ganelius (ed.), *Progress in Science and Its Social Conditions. Nobel Symposium 58 held at Lidingö, Sweden, 15–19 August 1983*. Oxford: Pergamon Press, 1986. Pp. 61–68.

*80. "Academic Market, Ideology and the Growth of Scientific Knowledge: Physiology in Mid-Nineteenth-Century Germany." In Siegwart Lindberg, James S. Coleman, and Stefan Nowak (eds.), *Approaches to Social Theory*. New York: Russell Sage Foundation, 1986. Pp. 63–75.

81. "Social Interests in the Organic Physics of 1847: A Comment." In Edna Ullmann-Margalit (ed.), *Science in Reflection* (= *The Israel Colloquium: Studies in History, Philosophy, and Sociology of Science*, vol. 3; = *Boston Studies in the Philosophy of Science*, vol. 110). Dordrecht: Kluwer, 1988. Pp. 193–200. [Comment on Timothy Lenoir, "Social Interests and the Organic Physics of 1847," in the same volume, pp. 169–91.]

82. "Rationality and Scientific Research in the Social Sciences." In S. J. Doorman (ed.), *Images of Science: Scientific Practice and the Public*. Aldershot and Brookfield: Gower, 1989. Pp. 121–34.

*83. "'Norms of Science' and the Sociological Interpretation of Scientific Behavior." In this volume; previously unpublished.

*84. "The Ethos of Science in the Context of Different Political Ideologies and Changing Perceptions of Science." In this volume; previously unpublished.

C. Publications in Hebrew

H-1   "התחלותיה של חברה יהודית מודרנית בהונגריה בראשית המאה ה-י"ט",
ציון, רבעון לחקר תולדות ישראל, כרך י"ז, תשי"ב, עמ' 128–101.

H-2 "החברות בתנועת-נוער והסטאטוס האישי", מגמות, כרך ה'(3), 1954, עמ' 247–227.

H-3 המבנה החברתי של המקצועות בישראל. חיבור לשם קבלת תואר דוקטור לפילוסופיה. (ירושלים, האוניברסיטה העברית, 1956; במכונת כתיבה.) [זהה למס' 1 למעלה.]

H-4 "הסטאטוס החברתי של המורה בישראל", מגמות, כרך ח'(2), 1957, עמ' 212–201.]"החלק הראשון של המאמר מבוסס על עבודת הדוקטור של המחבר"; ר' למעלה, מס' H-3.[

H-5 "הבחינה הסוציולוגית של הבעיה", העבריין, המטפל והחברה. דברים בכנס שנתקיים בירושלים בימים ז-ח ניסן, תשכ"ג]ירושלים, משרד הסעד, המועצה למניעת עבריינות ולטיפול בעבריין, תשכ"ד), עמ' 219–224.

H-6 (עם ש"נ איזנשטדט) יסודות הסוציולוגיה (תל-אביב, המכון הישראלי להשכלה בכתב על-יד המרכז לתרבות ולחנוך, בלי תאריך). מהדורה שניה פורסמה בשם מבוא לסוציולוגיה, והוצאה לאור כנ"ל, 1964.

H-7 "תולדות החינוך. התקופה החדישה. החנוך היהודי הלאומי: ארץ ישראל", אנציקלופדיה חינוכית, כרך ד' (ירושלים, משרד החינוך ומוסד ביאליק, תשכ"ד 1964), עמ' 718–702.

H-8 "תולדות החינוך. התקופה החדישה. החינוך היהודי בין שתי מלחמות העולם: ארץ ישראל", אנציקלופדיה חינוכית, כרך ד', כנ"ל, עמ' 802–785.

H-9 "מדע בארץ קטנה", האוניברסיטה. כתב-עת של האוניברסיטה העברית בירושלים, כרך 10(ב'), אוגוסט 1964, עמ' 17–12.

H-10 "יונינה", על פרופסור יונינה גרבר-טלמון ז"ל. דברים שנאמרו לזכרה . . . ביום השלושים לפטירה י' בסיון תשכ"ו 29.5.66 (ירושלים, הוצאת ספרים ע"ש י"ל מאגנס, תשכ"ו), עמ' 19–16.

H-11 "תמורות במשמעותה החברתית של עבריינות הנוער", הנוער למניעת עבריינות הנוער. דברים בכנס החמישי שנתקיים בירושלים בימים כ"ד-כ"ה בכסלו תשכ"ז. (ירושלים, משרד הסעד, המועצה למניעת עבריינות ולטיפול בעבריין, תשכ"ז), עמ' 44–37.

H-12 "מורה: הסוציולוגיה של המורה", אנציקלופדיה חינוכית, כרך ג' (ירושלים, משרד החינוך ומוסד ביאליק, 1967), עמ' 786–781.

H-13 "מדע, סוציולוגיה של", אנציקלופדיה למדעי החברה, כרך ג' (מרחביה, ספרית פועלים, הוצאת הקיבוץ הארצי השומר הצעיר, 1967), עמ' 253–250.

H-14 (עם אברהם זלוצ'ובר) "אוניברסיטאות ומערכות אקדמיות בחברות מודרניות", מגמות, כרך ט"ו (2/3), 1967, עמ' 163–137.]תרגום של פריט 22 לעיל.[

H-15 (עם אחרים) "דיון על תכנון ההשכלה הגבוהה]בישראל[", האוניברסיטה. כתב-עת של האוניברסיטה העברית בירושלים, כרך 13 (ב'), אוגוסט 1967, עמ' 57–46.

H-16 "חינוך כמקצוע: הסוציולוגיה של התאגדות מורים", אנציקלופדיה חינוכית, כרך ה', (ירושלים, משרד החינוך ומוסד ביאליק, 1969), עמ' 352–345.

H-17 "מוסדות חינוך כמבנה חברתי: בית הספר הגבוה כמבנה חברתי", אנציקלופדיה חינוכית, כרך ה', כנ"ל, עמ' 549–542.

H-18 (עם ר' קולינס) "החופש האקדמי: מחקר השוואתי", מגמות, כרך י"ז (1), 1970, עמ' 49–15.]תרגום מתוקן של פריט 32 לעיל.[

H-19 "מעמד", האנציקלופדיה העברית, כרך כ"ד (ירושלים/תל-אביב, חברה להוצאת אנציקלופדיות, תשל"ב), עמ' 56–52.

H-20 "סוציולוגיה", האנציקלופדיה העברית, כרך כ"ה, כנ"ל, תשל"ד, עמ' 564–554.

H-21 (עם אחרים) "ציונות: רב-שיח", האוניברסיטה. כתב-עת של האוניברסיטה

העברית בירושלים, כרך 23, קיץ תשל"ז, 1977, עמ' 20–3.

H-22 "מגמות חדשות בחינוך הגבוה. הרצאת פתיחה של הקתדרה בסוציולוגיה
על שם ד"ר ג'ורג' וייז 15 לפברואר, 1978", האוניברסיטה. כתב-עת
של האוניברסיטה העברית בירושלים, גליון מס' 24, קיץ תשל"ח, 1978,
עמ' 45–40.

H-23 (עם יהודית נבו, עורכים) הלימודים לתואר "בוגר" במדעים הבסיסיים
בישראל. יום עיון שנערך בירושלים בכ"ה בכסלו תשל"ט (25.12.1978)
מטעם ועדת ההגוי לחקר ההשכלה הגבוהה בישראל (ירושלים, המועצה להשכלה
גבוהה, הועדה לתכנון ולתקצוב, אדר תש"ם—פברואר 1980).

H-24 "מבוא" לנ"ל, שם, עמ' 14–1.

H-25 "'התואר הראשון' הישראלי בפרספקטיבה השוואתית", שם, עמ' 69–54.

H-26 "שנוי ומסורת. מבוא", האנציקלופדיה העברית, כרך ל"ב (ירושלים/תל-אביב,
חברה להוצאת אנציקלופדיות, תשמ"א), עמ' 187–186.

H-27 "האוניברסיטאות בישראל: דילמות של גידול, גיוון וניהול", חינוך
בחברה מתהווה. המערכת הישראלית, נערך על-ידי וולטר אקרמן, אריק
כרמון, דוד צוקר (תל-אביב וירושלים, הוצאת הקיבוץ המאוחד ומוסד
ון ליר בירושלים, תשמ"ה), כרך א', עמ' 562–527. [תרגום של פריט
מס' 66 לעיל.]

Acknowledgments

The following essays by Joseph Ben-David appear with the permission of their original publishers:

"Roles and Innovations in Medicine." *American Journal of Sociology.* 65:6:557–569. Copyright © 1960 by The University of Chicago. Reprinted by permission of The University of Chicago Press.

"Social Factors in the Origins of a New Science: The Case of Psychology." *American Sociological Review.* 31:4, 1966. Reprinted by permission of the American Sociological Association.

"Socialization and Career Patterns as Determinants of Productivity of Medical Researchers." *Journal of Health and Social Behavior.* 9:1, 1968. Reprinted by permission of the American Sociological Association.

"The Concepts of 'Role,' 'Status,' and 'Reference Group': A Theoretical Statement," from *Human Relations.* 11, 1958. Reprinted by permission of Plenum Publishing Corp.

"Universities and Academic Systems in Modern Societies," reproduced with permission from the *Archives européennes de sociologie.* III: 45–84, 1962. "Science and the University System" appeared in the *International Review of Education,* Vol. 18, No. 1 (1972), and is reproduced by kind permission of the UNESCO Institute for Education, Hamburg, FRG.

"Academy, University, and Research Institute in the Nineteenth and Twentieth Centuries: A Study of Changing Functions and Structures," in Scheuch, E. K. and Alemann, H. V. (eds.), *Das Forschungsinstitut: Formen der Institutionalisierung von Wissenschaft,* 1978. Reprinted by permission of the Institut für Gesellschaft und Wissenschaft, Erlangen.

"The Profession of Science and Its Powers," reproduced with permission from *Minerva.* X/3. July 1972, pp. 302–383.

"A Comparative Study of Academic Freedom and Student Politics," from *Comparative Education Review.* 10:2:220–249. Copyright © 1966 by The University of Chicago. Reprinted by permission of The University of Chicago Press.

"Scientific Research and Economic Growth," reprinted with permission from *Fundamental Research and the Universities: Some Comments on International Differences,* OCDE, Paris, 1968, pp. 55–61.

"The Central Planning of Science," reprinted with permission from *Minerva.* XV/3–4, 1977, pp. 539–553.

"Scientific Societies, Professional Organizations, and the Creation and Dissemination of Practical Knowledge," reprinted with permission from *Proceedings of the Global Seminar on the*

Role of Scientific and Engineering Societies in Development (New Delhi, December 1–5, 1980), pp. 153–161. © 1982, The Indian National Science Academy, New Delhi.

"Scientific Growth: A Sociological View," reprinted with permission from *Minerva.* III/4, 1964, pp. 455–476.

"Organization, Social Control, and Cognitive Change in Science," from Ben-David, J. and Clark, T. N. (eds.), *Culture and Its Creators: Essays in Honor of Edward Shils,* 244–265. Copyright © 1977 by The University of Chicago. Reprinted by permission of The University of Chicago Press.

"Puritanism and Modern Science: A Study in the Continuity and Coherence of Sociological Research," from Cohen, E., Lissak, M., and Almagor, U. (eds.), *Comparative Social Dynamics: Essays in Honor of S. N. Eisenstadt,* 207–223, 1985. Reprinted by permission of Westview Press.

"Innovations and Their Recognition in Social Science." *History of Political Economy,* 7(4), 1975. Reprinted by permission of Duke University Press.

"Sociology and Its Uses." Reprinted by permission from *Schweizerische Zeitschrift fur Soziologie.* 6:3:335–352, 1980.

"Theoretical Perspectives in the Sociology of Science 1920–1970." From the *International Social Science Journal,* Vol. XXII, No. 1, pp. 7–27. © UNESCO 1970. Reproduced by permission of UNESCO.

"Emergence of National Traditions in the Sociology of Science: The United States and Great Britain." *Sociological Inquiry.* 48:3–4:197–218, 1978. Reprinted by permission of the University of Texas Press.

"Sociology of Scientific Knowledge," in Short, J. F. (ed.), *The State of Sociology: Problems and Prospects,* pp. 40–59, copyright © 1981 by Sage Publications, Inc. Reprinted by permission of Sage Publications, Inc.

"The Ethos of Science: The Last Half-Century," in Philips, J. R. and Conlon, T. J. (eds.), *Science and the Polity: Ideals, Illusions, and Realities,* 13–28, 1980. Reprinted by permission of The Australian Academy of Science, Canberra.

"Academic Market, Ideology, and the Growth of Scientific Knowledge: Physiology in Mid-Nineteenth-Century Germany." Taken from *Approaches to Social Theory* by Siegwart Lindenberg, James S. Coleman, and Stefan Nowak, editors, pp. 63–75. © 1986 The Russell Sage Foundation. Used with permission of the Russell Sage Foundation.

"Science, Scientism, and Anti-Scientism," reprinted with permission from Ganelius, T. (ed.), *Progress in Science and Its Social Conditions,* 61–68. Copyright © 1986, Pergamon Press PLC.

Index

Index prepared by UC Press Staff

Designer: U.C. Press Staff
Compositor: G & S Typesetters
Text: 10/12 Times Roman
Display: Helvetica Bold
Printer: Braun-Brumfield
Binder: Braun-Brumfield